MASTER Red Hat® Linux® VISUALLY™

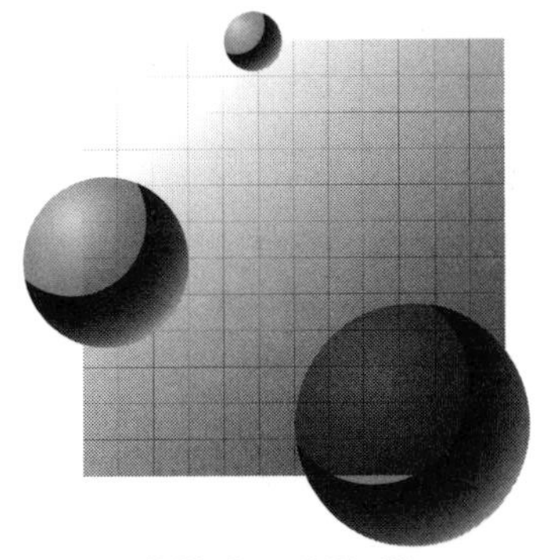

by Michael Bellomo

IDG's 3-D Visual™ Series

From

maranGraphics™

IDG Books Worldwide, Inc.
An International Data Group Company
Foster City, CA • Indianapolis • Chicago • New York

Master Red Hat® Linux® VISUALLY™

Published by
IDG Books Worldwide, Inc.
An International Data Group Company
919 E. Hillsdale Blvd., Suite 400
Foster City, CA 94404
www.idgbooks.com (IDG Books Worldwide Web Site)

Library of Congress Card Number: 00-105128

ISBN: 0-7645-3436-X

Printed in the United States of America

10 9 8 7 6 5 4 3 2 1

1V/RT/QW/QQ/IN

Distributed by CDG Books Canada Inc. for Canada; by Transworld Publishers Limited in the United Kingdom; by IDG Norge Books for Norway; by IDG Sweden Books for Sweden; by IDG Books Australia Publishing Corporation Pty. Ltd. for Australia and New Zealand; by TransQuest Publishers Pte Ltd. for Singapore, Malaysia, Thailand, Indonesia, and Hong Kong; by Gotop Information Inc. for Taiwan; by ICG Muse, Inc. for Japan; by Intersoft for South Africa; by Eyrolles for France; by International Thomson Publishing for Germany, Austria and Switzerland; by Distribuidora Cuspide for Argentina; by LR International for Brazil; by Galileo Libros for Chile; by Ediciones ZETA S.C.R. Ltda. for Peru; by WS Computer Publishing Corporation, Inc., for the Philippines; by Contemporanea de Ediciones for Venezuela; by Express Computer Distributors for the Caribbean and West Indies; by Micronesia Media Distributor, Inc. for Micronesia; by Chips Computadoras S.A. de C.V. for Mexico; by Editorial Norma de Panama S.A. for Panama; by American Bookshops for Finland.

For corporate orders, please call maranGraphics at 800-469-6616.

For general information on IDG Books Worldwide's books in the U.S., please call our Consumer Customer Service department at 800-762-2974. For reseller information, including discounts and premium sales, please call our Reseller Customer Service department at 800-434-3422.

For information on where to purchase IDG Books Worldwide's books outside the U.S., please contact our International Sales department at 317-572-3993 or fax 317-572-4002.

For consumer information on foreign language translations, please contact our Customer Service department at 1-800-434-3422, fax 317-572-4002, or e-mail rights@idgbooks.com.

For information on licensing foreign or domestic rights, please phone +1-650-653-7098.

For sales inquiries and special prices for bulk quantities, please contact our Order Services department at 800-434-3422 or write to the address above.

For information on using IDG Books Worldwide's books in the classroom or for ordering examination copies, please contact our Educational Sales department at 800-434-2086 or fax 317-572-4005.

For press review copies, author interviews, or other publicity information, please contact our Public Relations department at 650-653-7000 or fax 650-653-7500.

For authorization to photocopy items for corporate, personal, or educational use, please contact Copyright Clearance Center, 222 Rosewood Drive, Danvers, MA 01923, or fax 978-750-4470.

Screen shots displayed in this book are based on pre-released software and are subject to change.

Trademark Acknowledgments

U.S. Corporate Sales	U.S. Trade Sales
Contact maranGraphics at (800) 469-6616 or fax (905) 890-9434.	Contact IDG Books at (800) 434-3422 or (650) 653-7000.

ABOUT IDG BOOKS WORLDWIDE

Welcome to the world of IDG Books Worldwide.

IDG Books Worldwide, Inc., is a subsidiary of International Data Group, the world's largest publisher of computer-related information and the leading global provider of information services on information technology. IDG was founded more than 30 years ago by Patrick J. McGovern and now employs more than 9,000 people worldwide. IDG publishes more than 290 computer publications in over 75 countries. More than 90 million people read one or more IDG publications each month.

Launched in 1990, IDG Books Worldwide is today the #1 publisher of best-selling computer books in the United States. We are proud to have received eight awards from the Computer Press Association in recognition of editorial excellence and three from Computer Currents' First Annual Readers' Choice Awards. Our best-selling *...For Dummies®* series has more than 50 million copies in print with translations in 31 languages. IDG Books Worldwide, through a joint venture with IDG's Hi-Tech Beijing, became the first U.S. publisher to publish a computer book in the People's Republic of China. In record time, IDG Books Worldwide has become the first choice for millions of readers around the world who want to learn how to better manage their businesses.

Our mission is simple: Every one of our books is designed to bring extra value and skill-building instructions to the reader. Our books are written by experts who understand and care about our readers. The knowledge base of our editorial staff comes from years of experience in publishing, education, and journalism — experience we use to produce books to carry us into the new millennium. In short, we care about books, so we attract the best people. We devote special attention to details such as audience, interior design, use of icons, and illustrations. And because we use an efficient process of authoring, editing, and desktop publishing our books electronically, we can spend more time ensuring superior content and less time on the technicalities of making books.

You can count on our commitment to deliver high-quality books at competitive prices on topics you want to read about. At IDG Books Worldwide, we continue in the IDG tradition of delivering quality for more than 30 years. You'll find no better book on a subject than one from IDG Books Worldwide.

John Kilcullen
Chairman and CEO
IDG Books Worldwide, Inc.

Eighth Annual Computer Press Awards 1992

Ninth Annual Computer Press Awards 1993

Tenth Annual Computer Press Awards 1994

Eleventh Annual Computer Press Awards 1995

IDG is the world's leading IT media, research and exposition company. Founded in 1964, IDG had 1997 revenues of $2.05 billion and has more than 9,000 employees worldwide. IDG offers the widest range of media options that reach IT buyers in 75 countries representing 95% of worldwide IT spending. IDG's diverse product and services portfolio spans six key areas including print publishing, online publishing, expositions and conferences, market research, education and training, and global marketing services. More than 90 million people read one or more of IDG's 290 magazines and newspapers, including IDG's leading global brands — Computerworld, PC World, Network World, Macworld and the Channel World family of publications. IDG Books Worldwide is one of the fastest-growing computer book publishers in the world, with more than 700 titles in 36 languages. The "...For Dummies®" series alone has more than 50 million copies in print. IDG offers online users the largest network of technology-specific Web sites around the world through IDG.net (http://www.idg.net), which comprises more than 225 targeted Web sites in 55 countries worldwide. International Data Corporation (IDC) is the world's largest provider of information technology data, analysis and consulting, with research centers in over 41 countries and more than 400 research analysts worldwide. IDG World Expo is a leading producer of more than 168 globally branded conferences and expositions in 35 countries including E3 (Electronic Entertainment Expo), Macworld Expo, ComNet, Windows World Expo, ICE (Internet Commerce Expo), Agenda, DEMO, and Spotlight. IDG's training subsidiary, ExecuTrain, is the world's largest computer training company, with more than 230 locations worldwide and 785 training courses. IDG Marketing Services helps industry-leading IT companies build international brand recognition by developing global integrated marketing programs via IDG's print, online and exposition products worldwide. Further information about the company can be found at www.idg.com.

1/26/00

maranGraphics is a family-run business located near Toronto, Canada.

At maranGraphics, we believe in producing great computer books – one book at a time.

maranGraphics has been producing high-technology products for over 25 years, which enables us to offer the computer book community a unique communication process.

Our computer books use an integrated communication process, which is very different from the approach used in other computer books. Each spread is, in essence, a flow chart – the text and screen shots are totally incorporated into the layout of the spread. Introductory text and helpful tips complete the learning experience.

maranGraphics' approach encourages the left and right sides of the brain to work together – resulting in faster orientation and greater memory retention.

Above all, we are very proud of the handcrafted nature of our books. Our carefully-chosen writers are experts in their fields, and spend countless hours researching and organizing the content for each topic. Our artists rebuild every screen shot to provide the best clarity possible, making our screen shots the most precise and easiest to read in the industry. We strive for perfection, and believe that the time spent handcrafting each element results in the best computer books money can buy.

Thank you for purchasing this book. We hope you enjoy it!

Sincerely,

Robert Maran
President
maranGraphics

Please visit us on the Web at:
www.maran.com

CREDITS

Acquisitions, Editorial, and Media Development

Project Editor
Jade Williams

Acquisitions Editor
Martine Edwards

Associate Project Coordinator
Lindsay Sandman

Permissions Editor
Carmen Krikorian

Associate Media Development Specialist
Megan Decraene

Editorial Manager
Kyle Looper

Media Development Manager
Heather Heath Dismore

Editorial Assistant
Candace Nicholson

Production

Book Design
maranGraphics

Project Coordinator
Valery Bourke

Layout
York Graphic Services

Special Art
Craig Dearing, Deborah Naor

Proofreader
York Production Services, Inc.

Indexer
York Production Services, Inc.

Special Help
Angie Hunckler, Clint Lahnen, Jason Luster, Shelley Norris, Mary Jo Richards, Brent Savage, Kathie Schutte

General and Administrative

IDG Books Worldwide, Inc.: John Kilcullen, CEO

IDG Books Technology Publishing Group: Richard Swadley, Senior Vice President and Publisher; Walter R. Bruce III, Vice President and Publisher; Joseph Wikert, Vice President and Publisher; Mary Bednarek, Vice President and Director, Product Development; Andy Cummings, Publishing Director, General User Group; Mary C. Corder, Editorial Director; Barry Pruett, Publishing Director

IDG Books Consumer Publishing Group: Roland Elgey, Senior Vice President and Publisher; Kathleen A. Welton, Vice President and Publisher; Kevin Thornton, Acquisitions Manager; Kristin A. Cocks, Editorial Director

IDG Books Internet Publishing Group: Brenda McLaughlin, Senior Vice President and Publisher; Sofia Marchant, Online Marketing Manager

IDG Books Production for Branded Press: Debbie Stailey, Director of Production; Cindy L. Phipps, Manager of Project Coordination, Production Proofreading, and Indexing; Tony Augsburger, Manager of Prepress, Reprints, and Systems; Laura Carpenter, Production Control Manager; Shelley Lea, Supervisor of Graphics and Design; Debbie J. Gates, Production Systems Specialist; Robert Springer, Supervisor of Proofreading; Trudy Coler, Page Layout Manager; Troy Barnes, Page Layout Supervisor, Kathie Schutte, Senior Page Layout Supervisor; Michael Sullivan, Production Supervisor

Packaging and Book Design: Patty Page, Manager, Promotions Marketing

The publisher would like to give special thanks to Patrick J. McGovern, without whom this book would not have been possible.

About the Author

Michael Bellomo received a degree in law from the University of California, Hastings College of the Law in San Francisco. Despite this awful start, he moved into the technical field and became certified in Unix System Administration from the University of California, Santa Cruz. Currently he has over five and a half years experience as a Unix (Solaris & Linux) and Microsoft Windows NT Network Manager serving with software and financial technology companies in the Silicon Valley.

He is the author of the two latest Linux releases from IDG Books Worldwide, Inc., *Linux Administration For Dummies* and *Debian/GNU Linux For Dummies,* and the Microsoft Windows book *Windows 2000 Administration For Dummies*. He has also contributed several chapters to *Linux For Dummies,* 2nd Edition and *The GIMP (GNU Image Manipulation Program) Bible*, both by IDG Books Worldwide.

Author's Acknowledgments

I'd like to thank Michael 'Mac' McCarthy and the funniest foreign correspondent on this or any other continent, P.J. O'Rourke, for bringing about the conditions that led to the creation of this book.

I am deeply indebted to Jade Williams, Suzanne Thomas, and Tim Borek for their tireless pursuit of excellence in helping me bring this book into a concise and clear kind of order.

RED HAT® LINUX®

I GETTING STARTED

1) Getting Started with Linux Basics
2) Customizing Your Desktop Environment
3) Working with Linux Files
4) Linux Commands in GNOME

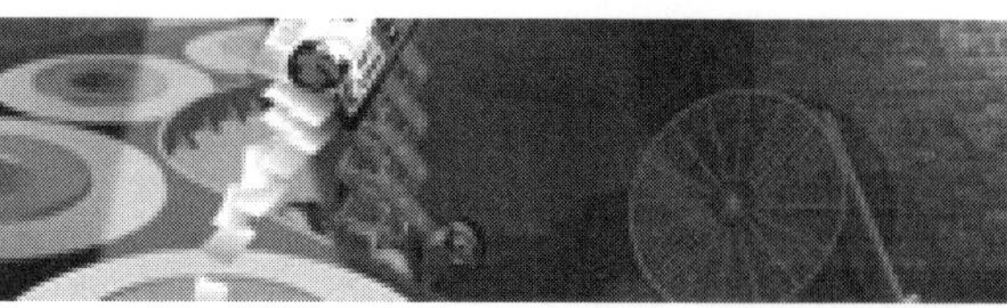

II USING THE LINUX ENVIRONMENT OUTSIDE OF THE GUI

5) Working with Linux Files Outside of GNOME
6) Useful Commands Outside the GNOME
7) The vi Editor
8) Customize the Non-GNOME Environment

III STARTING LINUX ADMINISTRATION

9) The Root User
10) User and Group Account Management
11) File System Management
12) Manage Linux Programs
13) Word Processing in Linux

WHATS INSIDE

IV THE LINUX NETWORK — THE WORLD BEYOND YOUR COMPUTER

14) Networking in the Linux GNOME Environment
15) Remotely Logging onto other Machines
16) Copy Files to and from other Machines

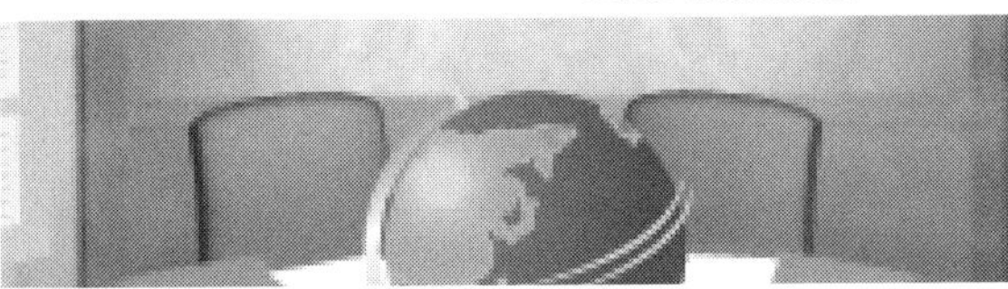

V SHARING FILES AND MACHINES OVER THE NETWORK

17) Set Up Network Printers
18) The Network File System
19) The Network Information System—NIS and Samba NIS Client Configuration
20) Set Up Network Database Users

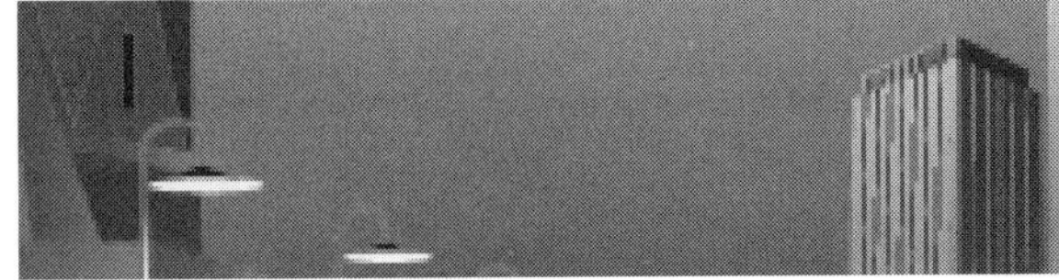

VI THE INTERNET AND ELECTRONIC MAIL

21) Establish Network Connectivity
22) Set Up Your Netscape Browser
23) Install and Configure Apache
24) Send and Receive Mail in the Linux Terminal

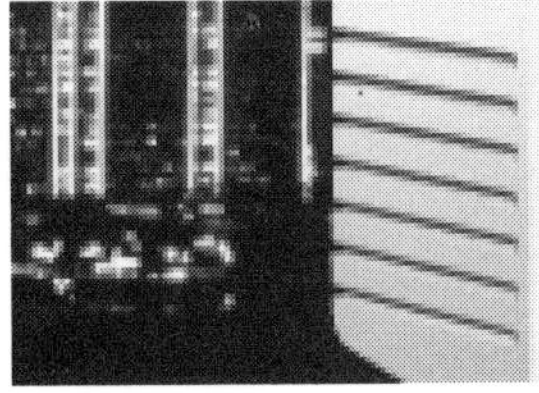

Setting Up E-mail Account...

VII NETWORK SECURITY

25) Your Security Scheme
26) Track Intruders and Users on Your System
27) The Aftermath: What to Do

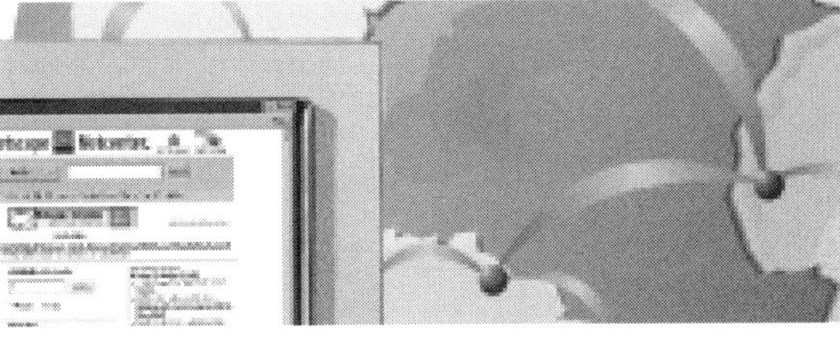

VIII DIASTER PREPARATION AND RECOVERY

28) Back up files
29) The Y2038K Bug
30) Troubleshoot Common Linux Problems

IX APPENDIXES

A) Install Linux
B) Linux Applications You Should Be Aware Of
C) Summary of vi Editor Commands
D) Glossary of Linux Terms and Commands

1 GETTING STARTED

1) GETTING STARTED WITH LINUX BASICS

Introducing the Linux Operating System 4
Tour the GNOME Desktop.....................................8
View the Linux Terminal Window 9
Start Your Linux Machine 10
Log Into Linux 12
Using Buttons and Drop-Down Menus 14
Log Out of Linux 15
Shut Down Linux 16
Shut Down Linux Without Using The GUI 18
Open GNOME Windows
and Linux Terminals 20
Resize Windows 22
Maximize, Minimize, and Close Windows 24
Move and Switch Windows Around 26
Turn Windows into Icons and Bars 28
Move and Copy Files Between Windows 30
Slide Windows When Open 32
Get Help In GNOME 34

2) CUSTOMIZING YOUR DESKTOP ENVIRONMENT

Customize Your GNOME Desktop 40
Select Background Wallpaper 42
Set Keyboard and Mouse Properties 43
Customize Your Screen Saver 44
Select a Desktop Theme 48
Configure GNOME Multimedia and
Peripheral Properties 50
Set Up GNOME Mime Types and
the Default Editor 52

3) WORKING WITH LINUX FILES

Explore The GNOME File Manager 54
Browse the Linux File System in GNOME 58
Change Directories in the Linux GNOME Environment 60
Filter and Find Files 62
Display Hidden Files 64
Create New Files 66
Create New Directories 68
Copy and Move Files or Directories 70
Copy and Move Multiple Files 74
Rename Files and Directories 76
Delete Files and Directories 78

4) LINUX COMMANDS IN GNOME

Launch an Application 80
Close Applications 82
Create Symbolic Links 84
File Permissions 86
File User and Group Ownership 88

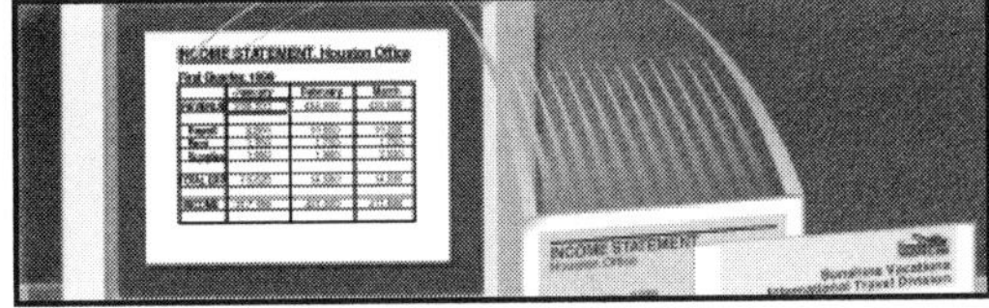

2

USING THE LINUX ENVIRONMENT OUTSIDE OF THE GUI

5) WORKING WITH LINUX FILES OUTSIDE OF GNOME

Open the Linux Terminal Window 92
Change Your Linux Terminal Font 94
Change Linux Terminal Colors 96
List Files 98
Change Directories in the Linux Terminal 104
Create New Files 108
Create New Directories 110
Copy Files in the Linux Terminal 112
Copy Directories in the Linux Terminal 114
Rename Files or Directories 116
Delete Files and Directories 118

6) USEFUL LINUX COMMAND OUTSIDE OF GNOME

Determine Your User Account Identity 122
Determine Who Else Is Logged In 124
Locate Files in the Linux Terminal 126
Create Symbolic Links 130
Move, Name, and Delete Symbolic Links 132
Transfer Output
with the Pipe Command 134
Search with the Grep Command 136
Search for Running Processes 138
Stop Programs with Kill 142
Stop Programs That Do Not Respond to Kill 144
Re-direct Output
with Arrow Keys 146
Make a File Executable 150
Change a File's Ownership 152
Change a File's Group Ownership 152

7) THE VI EDITOR

Start the vi Editor 156
Command and Insert Mode in vi 160
Add Text 162
Delete Text 166
Substitute Text 170
Move Around in vi 172
Search for Words in vi 174
Cut, Copy, and Paste Text 176
Save and Quit vi 180

8) CUSTOMIZING THE NON-GNOME ENVIRONMENT

Determine Your Environment Variables 184
Set the $PATH Variable 188
Source Changes 190
Adding Aliases 192

3 STARTING LINUX ADMINISTRATION

9) THE ROOT USER

Enter the Root User Account 196
Use su Multiple Times 198
Utilize the man Pages 200
Grant and Restrict File Access 202
Use cron to Automate System Tasks 206

10) USER AND GROUP ACCOUNT MANAGEMENT

Use the GNOME LinuxConf Tool 208
List User Accounts 212
Add User Accounts 214
Edit User Accounts 218
Delete User Accounts 222
Disable User Accounts 224
Add User Accounts in the Linux Terminal 226
Edit User Accountsin the Linux Terminal 228
Delete and Disable Accounts
in the Linux Terminal 230
List User Groups 232
Add User Groups 234
Edit User Groups 236
Delete User Groups 238
Add User Groups in the Linux Terminal 240
Edit User Groups in the Linux Terminal 242
Delete User Groups in the Linux Terminal 246

11) MANAGING FILE SYSTEMS

Share Files and Directories 248
List Your File Systems with LinuxConf 250
Determine Allocated and Free Swap Space 252
Create a Linux Floppy Drive 256
Create a DOS Floppy Drive 260
Mount the Floppy Drive from the Linux Terminal 262
Read from the Floppy Disk 264
Copy Files to the Floppy Disk 266
Format Floppy Disks 270
Configure the CD-ROM Drive 272
Mount the CD-ROM Drive 276
Mount the CD-ROM Drive from the Linux Terminal 278
Read and Copy Files from the CD-ROM 280
Eject Floppy Disks and CD-ROMs 284

12) MANAGING LINUX PROGRAMS

Verify Available Disk Space 286
Start the Gnome Red Hat PAckage Manager 290
Verify Packages with RPM 292
Install Software Packageswith RPM 294
Remove Software Packages with RPM 296

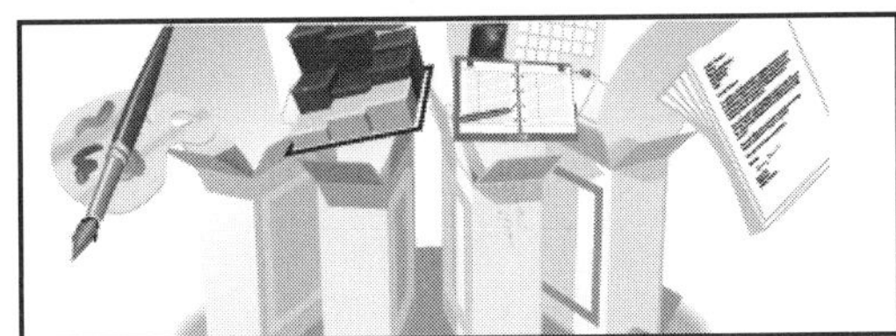

13) WORD PROCESSING IN LINUX

Start and Exit gnotepad+ 298
Create and Save New Documents 300
Open New Documents 302
Insert and Delete Text 304
Move and Copy Text 306
Undo and Redo Changes 308
Search and Replace Text in a Document 310
Print Documents 312
Preferences for gnotepad+ 314
Tear-Off Menus 318

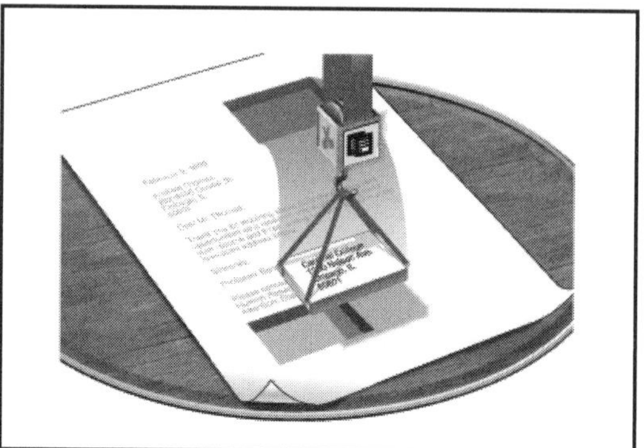

4 THE LINUX NETWORK—THE WORLD BEYOND YOUR COMPUTER

14) NETWORKING IN THE LINUX GNOME ENVIRONMENT

Get Basic Host Information 322
Check Network Connectivity with ping 324
Set Up Default Gateways 326
Set Up the Routed Daemon 328

15) REMOTELY LOGGING INTO OTHER MACHINES

Log In Remotely with rlogin 330
rlogin with the -l Option 332
Use rsh — THE REMOTE SHELL 334
Log In with telnet 336
Give Remote Commands to a Remote Machine 338

16) COPYING FILES TO AND FROM OTHER MACHINES

Copy Files with uucp 340
Copy Files with rcp 342
Copy Files with ftp 344
Transfer Files with Different FTP Options 346
Change Directories while in FTP Mode 350

5 SHARING FILES AND MACHINES OVER THE NETWORK

17) SETTING UP NETWORK PRINTERS

Open the Linux Print System Manager 354
Add a Local Printer 356
Add Remote UNIX Printers 358
Add Windows or NetWare Printers 360
Delete Printers 362
Edit and Test Printers 364

18) THE NETWORK FILE SYSTEM

View NFS Settings in GNOME 368
Add and Delete Exported File Systems 370
Add, Mount, and Remove a Remote NFS File System 374
Add, Mount, and Remove a Remote NFS File System Continued 376

18) THE NETWORK FILE SYSTEM CONTINUED

Select Mounting Options for Exported Systems 380
Select NFS Options for Exported Systems 382

19) THE NETWORK INFORMATION SYSTEM

Configure the NIS Client 384
Set Up a Samba Server 388
Connect Your Machine as a Samba Client 394

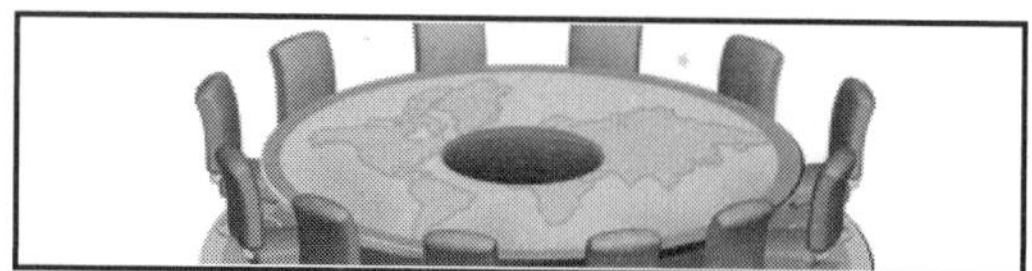

20) SETTING UP NETWORKED DATABASE USERS

Install PostgreSQL, the Linux Database 396
Add the PostgreSQL User 400
Initialize Your PostgreSQL Server 404

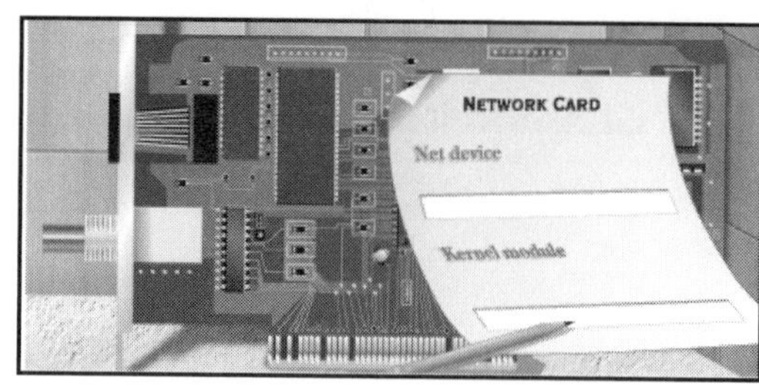

TABLE OF CONTENTS

6 THE INTERNET AND ELECTRONIC MAIL

21) ESTABLISHING NETWORK CONNECTIVITY

Start the Control Panel's Modem & Network Utilities 408
Configure a Modem 410
Enter DNS Information 412
Add and Delete a PPP Interface 414
Configure a Direct Connection 420

22) SETTING UP YOUR NETSCAPE BROWSER

Launch the Netscape Web Browser 424
Browse the Web with Netscape 426
Configure Netscape Appearance and Navigation 428
Configure New Web Page Settings 430
Configure Netscape's Advanced Network Settings 432
Set Up Netscape to Send E-mail 434
Set Up Netscape to Receive E-mail and News ..436
Send and Receive E-mail in Netscape 438

23) INSTALLING AND CONFIGURING APACHE

Install the Apache Web Server 440
Configure Apache 444

24) SENDING AND RECEIVING MAIL IN THE LINUX TERMINAL

Open pine Mail 448
Compose E-mail in Pine 449
Receive E-mail in Pine 450
Delete E-mail in Pine 452
Save E-mail in Pine 453
Navigate and Administer Your Folders 454
Exit the Pine Mail Program 458

7 NETWORK SECURITY

25) YOUR SECURITY SCHEME

Change the User Account Password 460
Set Up Screen Savers to Increase Security 464
Set Password and File Permission Policies 466
Set File Permissions in GNOME 468
Set File Permissions in the Linux Terminal 469

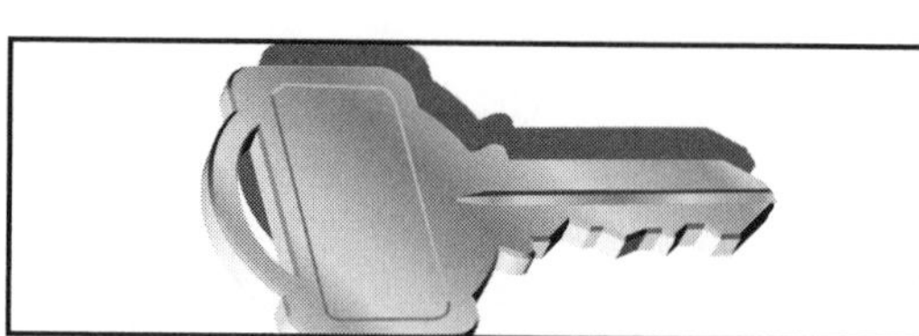

26) TRACKING USERS ON YOUR SYSTEM

Find out Who's on the Machine 470
Retrieve User Information 471
Determine User Activity 472

TABLE OF CONTENTS

27) REPAIRING A SECURITY BREACH

Check System Permissions 474
Check Configuration Logs 478
Shut Down System Daemons 479

8 DISASTER PREPARATION AND RECOVERY

28) BACKING UP FILES

Create a Linux Boot Disk 482
Create a Linux Recovery Disk 484
Back Up Files with tar 486
Restore Files with tar 488
Compress Files with gzip 490

29) THE Y2038K BUG)

Change the System Date 492
Test and Verify with GnomeRPM 496

30) TROUBLESHOOTING COMMON LINUX PROBLEMS

Reassign a Forgotten Root Password 500
Diagnose Device Problems on Reboot 502
Find Disk and CPU Hogs 504
Stop Hung or Spawned Processes 506
Troubleshoot in the GUI 508

9 APPENDIXES

APPENDIX A: INSTALL LINUX

Start the Linux Installation Process 512
Set Up Disk Partitions 516
Set Up Linux Components 518
Set Up Monitor Parameters 520
Set the Base Parameters 524
Set Printers and Root Password 526

APPENDIX B: BEWARE OF LINUX APPLICATIONS

Use the GNOME CD Player 528
Paint with XPaint 530
Organize with GnomeCard 532

APPENDIX C: VI EDITOR COMMANDS

APPENDIX D: LINUX COMMANDS

TABLE OF CONTENTS

SECTION I

1) GETTING STARTED WITH LINUX BASICS

Introducing the Linux Operating System 4
Tour the GNOME Desktop 8
View the Linux Terminal Window 9
Start Your Linux Machine 10
Log Into Linux 12
Using Buttons and Drop-Down Menus 14
Log Out of Linux 15
Shut Down Linux 16
Shut Down Linux Without Using The GUI 18
Open GNOME Windows and Linux Terminals 20
Resize Windows 22
Maximize, Minimize, and Close Windows 24
Move and Switch Windows Around 26
Turn Windows into Icons and Bars 28
Move and Copy Files Between Windows 30
Slide Windows When Open 32
Get Help In GNOME 34

2) CUSTOMIZING YOUR DESKTOP ENVIRONMENT

Customize Your GNOME Desktop 40
Select Background Wallpaper 42
Set Keyboard and Mouse Properties 43
Customize Your Screen Saver 44
Select a Desktop Theme 48
Configure GNOME Multimedia and Peripheral Properties 50
Set Up GNOME Mime Types and the Default Editor 52

3) WORKING WITH LINUX FILES

Explore The GNOME File Manager 54
Browse the Linux File System in GNOME 58
Change Directories in the Linux GNOME Environment 60
Filter and Find Files 62
Display Hidden Files 64
Create New Files 66
Create New Directories 68
Copy and Move Files or Directories 70
Copy and Move Multiple Files 74
Rename Files and Directories 76
Delete Files and Directories 78

4) LINUX COMMANDS IN GNOME

Introduction to DHCP 54
Installing DHCP 56
Authorizing the DHCP Server 60
Creating Scopes 64
Creating Superscopes 70
Creating Multicast Scopes 74
Managing Scopes 78
Configuring Scope Properties 82
Additional Scope Configuration 84
Managing DHCP Servers 88

INTRODUCING THE LINUX OPERATING SYSTEM

Linux is an operating system that Linus Torvalds created at the University of Helsinki in 1991 in response to the high cost and high maintenance of the operating systems then available. Although it's designed to work quickly on even the most primitive computers, Linux is able to handle the networking needs of today's user.

Linux is able to connect multiple users and user groups with e-mail, networked printers, shared file systems, and Web access in a manner similar to the Microsoft operating system.

Linux is an offshoot of UNIX, the basic operating system known for its stability, speed, and lack of a GUI (General User Interface).

In addition, Linux is also an open source code operating system, meaning that any user can modify the code to his specifications.

Linus Torvalds made the decision to make Linux code freely available. This is why Linux is called a "freely distributed" operating system.

Work with GUI in Linux

Linux comes from several different companies, such as Red Hat or Caldera. The CD-ROM set that comes with this book contains Red Hat Linux, so the Red Hat Corporation provides the technical support and online documentation.

The latest development common to all recent versions of Linux is the use of a GUI. In short, the GUI is the desktop that most computer users are used to seeing when turning on their computers. Small images of user programs and files, called icons, sit on the desktop and allow the user to access these files or programs by clicking them with their mouse pointer.

As Linux has become more popular, it has adapted to the use of newer, user friendly GUIs to perform most tasks. The two most popular GUIs that run with the Linux operating system are the K Desktop Environment (KDE) and GNOME. This book focuses on the GNOME (pronounced Guh-NOME) desktop environment because it is supported as the default GUI by one of the most popular releases of Linux, Red Hat 6.1.

Linux versus Windows

Traditionally, the main advantage of Linux is that it is much cheaper than other operating systems. This is still true; for example, you can download the entire Linux operating system free from many places on the Internet. In addition, Linux offers the following advantages:

- Linux can run on outdated machines as ancient as the x386 models.
- When it comes to large-scale server architectures, Linux and its UNIX cousins are more reliable than the Microsoft operating system.
- Linux is more flexible than Windows because the source code is open, which means that users can modify and correct the Linux code.

- Therefore, if you want to develop your own scripts to automate administration tasks, you can. If your script is exceptionally efficient, your creation may become immortalized in future versions of Linux.

Customize Your Linux Environment

Unlike in Windows, there are two areas in Linux that you can customize—the GUI desktop and the Linux environment itself. In the GUI, you have all the flexibility of the Microsoft desktop themes. You can customize your desktop background, edit your screen saver, and set system sounds.

In the Linux environment, you can set properties such as the path that Linux searches to find binaries or programs to execute. If you are logged in as the administrator account, you can alter settings that affect all the users on your network, such as file permissions and account creation.

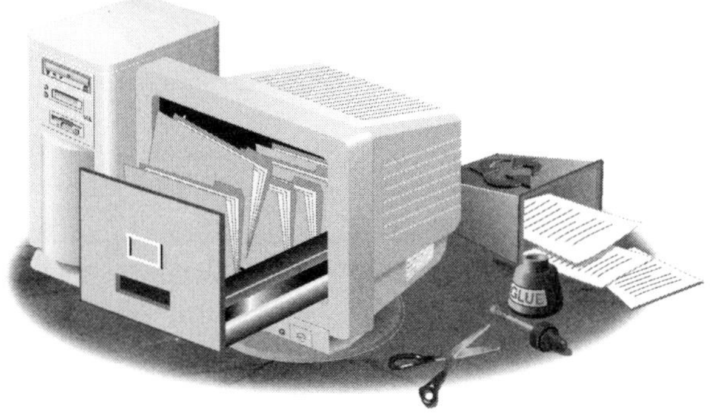

Access Programs on the GNOME

The GNOME Desktop environment is one of the easiest to use in Linux, since it looks a lot like the Windows environment. In addition to opening windows to list icons, folders, and files, you can open Terminal windows.

Terminal windows are direct links to the Linux environment that controls the network, below the desktop and out of sight. If you are from a Windows background, you may think of this as opening a DOS prompt from the Start button or Accessories Panel.

CONTINUED

INTRODUCING THE LINUX OPERATING SYSTEM CONTINUED

Use This Book without a Linux GUI

If you have inherited an older version of Linux that does not use a desktop environment, this book will still be of great value to you. While some tasks in Linux are more accessible with the desktop, some tasks still require knowledge of the Terminal window and the `vi` editor.

You may also be using a version of Linux that has a GUI, but it's not GNOME. For example, the Mandrake release of Linux defaults to the KDE desktop. Again, this book will be of use to you. The basic concepts of a window- and desktop-based environment are universal to all kinds of GUIs. For example, both KDE and GNOME allow you to take snapshots of the screen in the same way, but each uses a differently named program.

User and Group Management

Linux allows you to control the creation and removal of individual user accounts from the administrator's account. In addition, in Linux, you can set up user accounts with defaults so files are created with specific defaults and properties. You can control when and where the user can access the network — a big plus in today's security-conscious environment. You can even temporarily lock a user out of his account if he goes on vacation or leaves the company.

In Linux, you can also create multiple groups for a user account. Whether creating, deleting, or merging groups, Linux allows you to add and remove users from group lists without worrying about redundant entries.

Networking in Linux

Linux is an open operating system because of its ease in connecting to other machines. Entire suites of commands are available to both the administrator and the user for networking, such as coping files with `rcp`, `uucp`, or `ftp`. Linux users also have the option of connecting to other machines and operating them remotely, via the `telnet` or `rlogin` utilities.

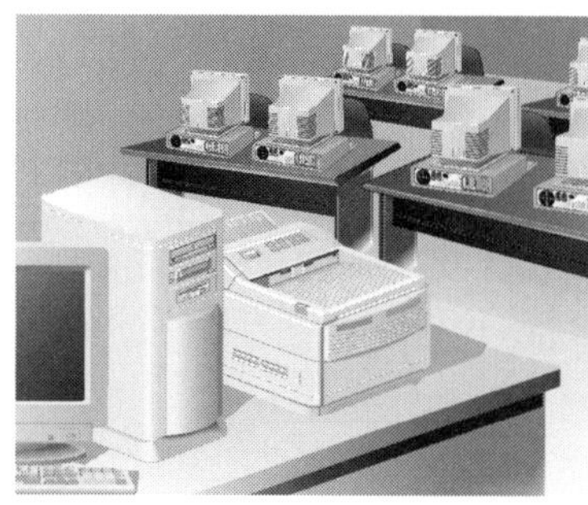

Share Software and Hardware Resources

Linux openness enables the efficient sharing of files and programs between machines by using the Network File System utility. For example, instead of placing a copy of a program on each machine, placing the program in a networked file system allows any machine to mount the system and run the program.

Linux also excels in the ability to share out hardware. If you are on a slow machine, you can run a program remotely, taking advantage of the faster machines on the network. This ability to farm out network tasks also makes Linux a natural when it comes to printing documents on remote network printers

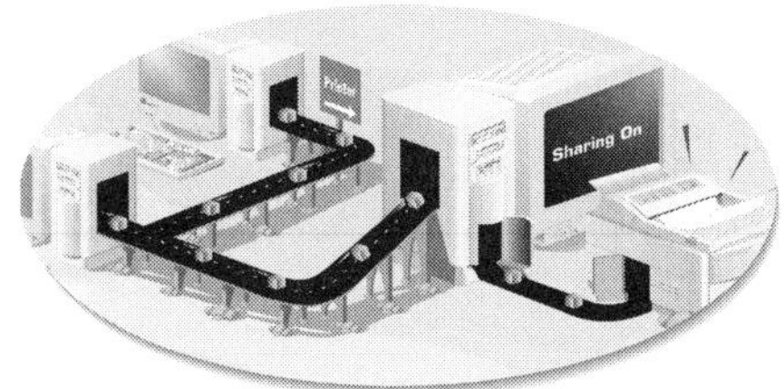

E-Mail and Web Access in Linux

Depending on which version of Linux you are running, you can choose from three or more different e-mail programs. The most popular of the Terminal-based mail programs is pine. Pine works without a GUI, which makes it extremely fast and stable when working with large documents.

The other main player in Linux e-mail is Netscape Mail. Netscape is included as the default Web browser with the latest releases of Linux. Whether you have Netscape Navigator, Messenger, or Communicator, you will find the program that handles both your e-mail and your Web browsing tempting.

Security Issues in Linux

Because Linux is so open for sharing data, security issues may surface. Most security measures in Linux are nothing more than common sense, involving the changing of passwords at regular intervals and the protection of the administrative account.

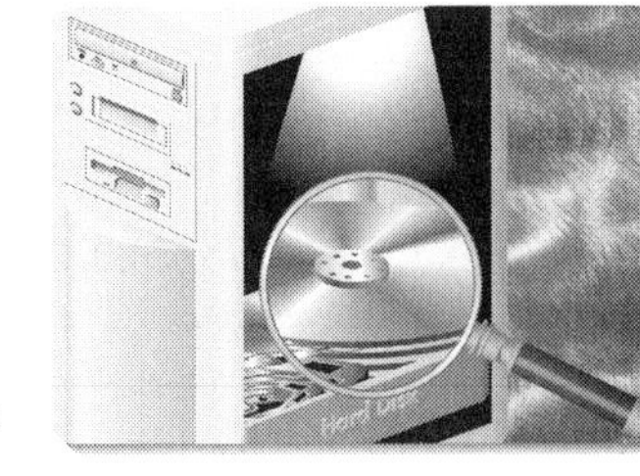

In addition, this book covers how you can protect your most sensitive files, how to select a truly unbreakable password, and how to track an intruder if he does work his way on to your network.

Troubleshooting Linux

After familiarizing yourself with the Terminal environment and how it relates to the GUI desktop, you will find Linux easy to administer. In fact, maintenance in Linux is simpler than in Microsoft because Linux software breaks less often.

This book covers basic troubleshooting and tips on nipping problems in the bud. By using the tools that you learn in this book, you will find yourself troubleshooting problems on your own in no time.

TOUR THE GNOME DESKTOP

Much like Microsoft Windows, the Linux GNOME desktop uses icons and toolbars to display information that allow you to access programs with the click of a mouse. While the exact icons on your screen depend on what utilities you have set up, your desktop should still look similar to the following diagram.

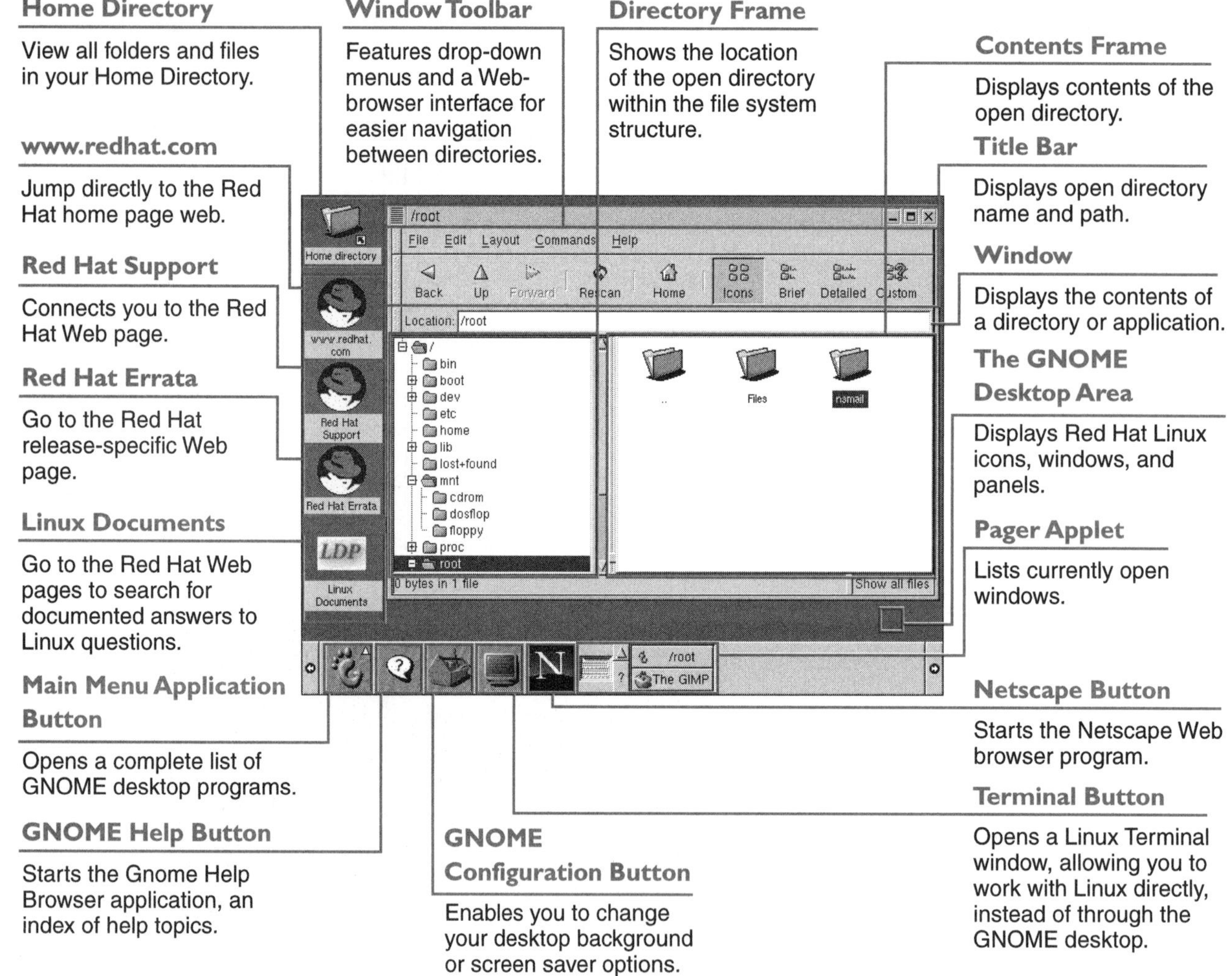

VIEW THE LINUX TERMINAL WINDOW

When you click the Terminal button, you open a Linux Terminal window. A Linux Terminal is a special window that allows you to work with Linux directly, instead of through the GNOME desktop. Because no desktop or icons are inside this window, it normally looks like a blank screen, shaded black or blue. Any commands you type in this window will affect your Linux operating system, but will not change the look or functions of the GNOME desktop.

Terminal Frame

The Terminal frame is the top border of the window. Terminal windows, unlike regular windows, don't have names. Calling up additional Terminals does not allow you to distinguish between each one.

Terminal Window

Allows access directly to the Linux operating system. This window does not contain any icons or toolbars. You can open the window with the Terminal button on the GNOME panel or by right-clicking the desktop and selecting New and Terminal.

Command Prompt

In Linux, the command prompt executes commands that you type at the cursor in the Terminal window. The command prompt often displays the current identity and location of the user. Here, the user is root, and the user is in the /root directory.

Terminal Drop-Down Menus

File, Edit, and Settings are drop-down menus that allow you to edit Terminal properties such as color and size. Help is a drop-down menu that calls up the GNOME User Guide, also accessible by the panel button at the bottom of the desktop.

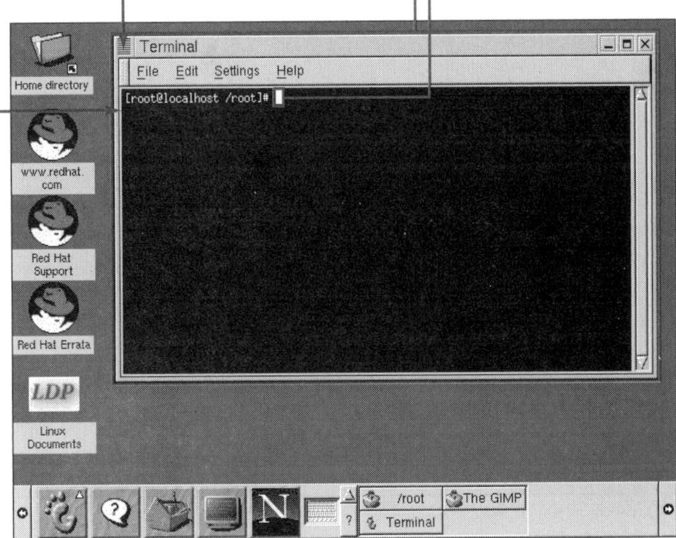

START YOUR LINUX MACHINE

Linux automatically starts when you turn on your computer. Unlike Microsoft Windows, you won't see a splash screen with a pretty picture announcing that you are using Linux. Instead, you will see messages printed to the screen as Linux performs tests on your computer to make sure that everything is running properly from the last time you were logged in. These messages vary depending on the version of Linux that you have on your computer, but all versions of Linux perform similar tasks, such as checking for memory, inserted boot disks, or damaged sectors on your hard drive.

If you are starting Linux for the very first time, you might not see the GNOME desktop when you turn your machine on. Instead, you might come up to a black screen with a login prompt asking you to log in. If your Linux machine does not run GNOME, then you will always use this login procedure.

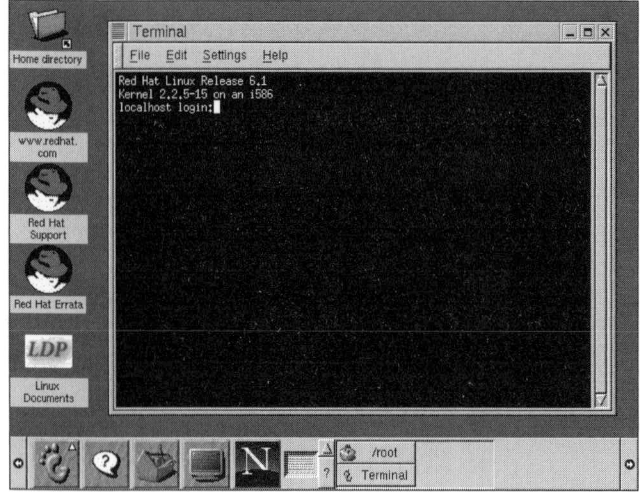

■ Linux login screen lists the Linux release version, the kernel version, type of machine in use, and the system's log in location.

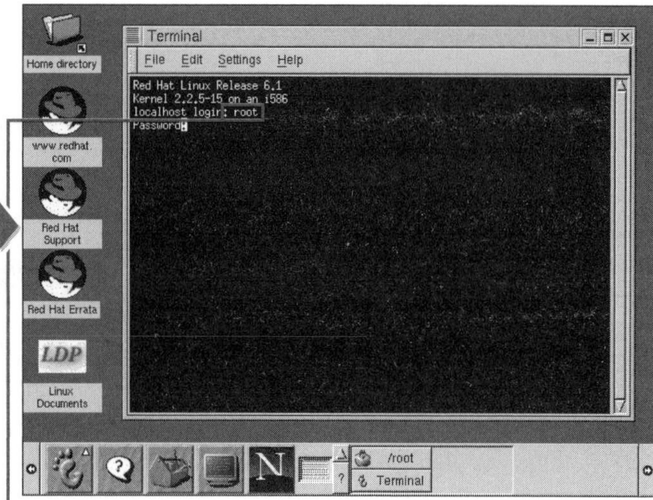

1 Type your user account name at the login prompt.

■ If this is your first time logging in after installing Linux, then you will only have one account to log into — the root account, which is the default administrator account name.

2 Press Enter.

What if Linux reports an error when the machine is rebooted?

- The Linux operating system automatically fixes errors caused by improper shutdown, such as a sudden blackout. If you have a serious error that Linux can't repair, reboot the machine with the Linux rescue disk that came with your installation.

How can I prevent this?

- Always log off your machine properly, as covered in the "Shut Down Linux" section in this chapter.

If I've just installed Linux, how do I know the root account password?

- When you install Linux, it asks you to set the root password before rebooting.

What if I forget the root password?

- You may need to re-install Linux to re-set the password.

I'm typing the password correctly — how come it tells me the password is incorrect?

- Check the Caps Lock key — because Linux is case sensitive, this could interfere with your login attempts.

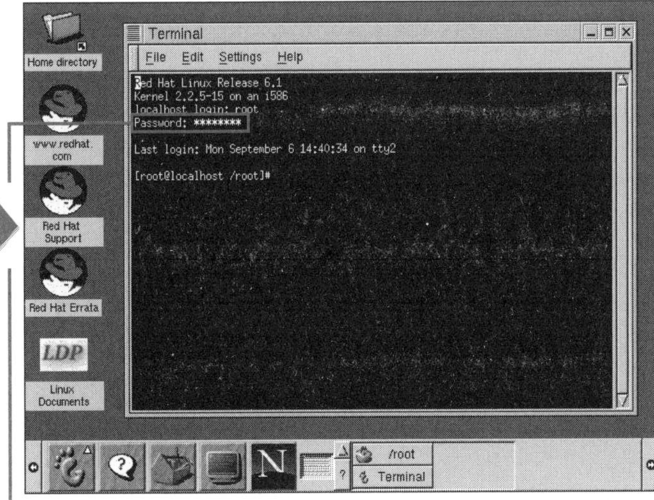

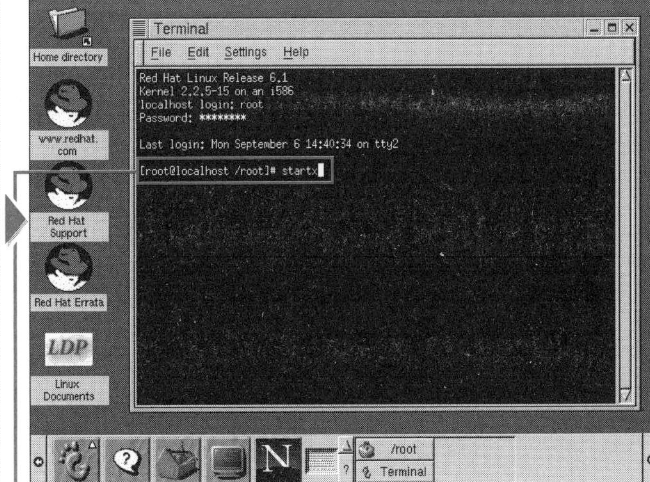

3 Type your password at the prompt.

■ Your password appears as a row of asterisks or as blank characters.

4 Press Enter.

■ The command prompt appears if you typed in your username and password correctly. You are logged in as a user.

5 Type **startx** at the command prompt if you want to work with the GNOME desktop.

6 Press Enter.

■ GNOME starts up and takes you to the desktop.

LOG INTO LINUX

If your version of Linux comes with a Graphic User Interface, such as KDE or GNOME, you will see more than a simple blank screen when asked to log on. Versions of Linux that use GNOME or KDE, such as Red Hat Linux, automatically start up when you switch the machine on.

After performing the standard system checks on the disk drives and software kernel, a version of Linux that uses a GUI brings up a specific login screen. The login screen has a colored background and a dialog box with fields that you enter user account names and passwords into.

When logging in through a GUI login screen, remember to use the Tab key and the mouse instead of pressing the Enter key. On some installations of Linux, pressing Enter will not move the cursor from the field where you type the account name to the field where you type the password.

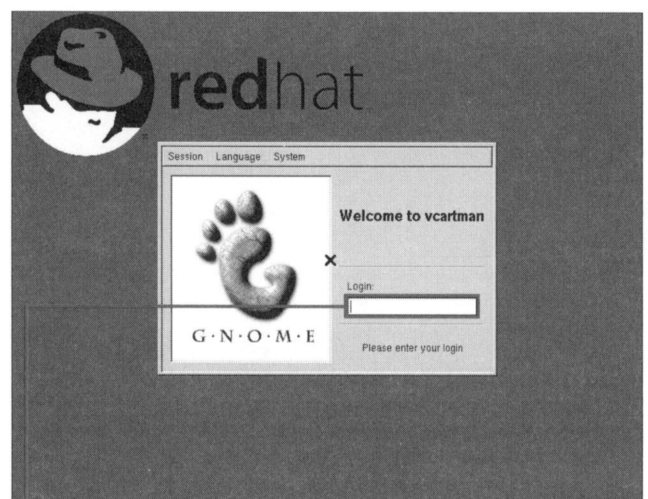

1 In the Login field, type your account name.

2 Press the Tab key to move to the Password field and type your password.

■ The characters may not display on the screen.

3 Press Enter.

■ Once Linux verifies your user account and password, the GNOME desktop environment starts automatically.

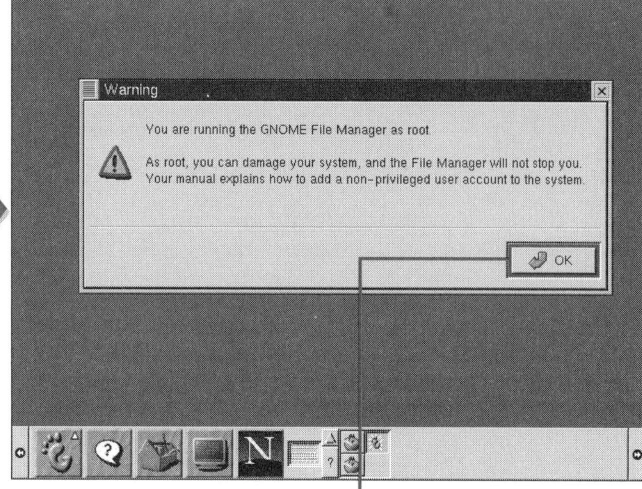

Note: When logging in as root, GNOME displays a warning about logging in as the administrative account.

4 Click the OK button to get past this warning.

What do I do if my version of Linux doesn't display a GUI style login screen?

- If you have a version of Linux such as Red Hat Linux 5.2 or later and you don't get a GUI style login screen, then something may be wrong with your Linux installation. When Linux reboots, watch the system checks that Linux performs for reported errors.

After I type my login name, why can't I move to the next field when I press Enter?

- In a GUI-driven login, you must use the Tab key to move between fields.

When I type my login name and password correctly, Linux still complains that the login name and password are incorrect. How can I solve this?

- Check the Caps Lock key — because Linux is case sensitive, this could interfere with your login attempts.

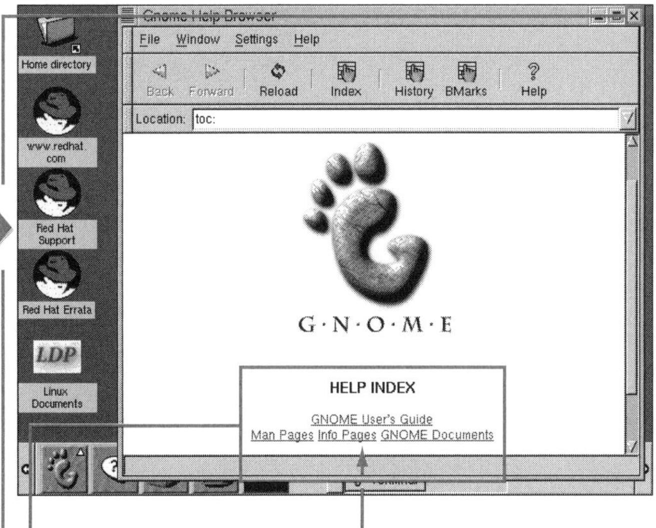

■ By default, GNOME displays the GNOME Help screen.

5 Click the box marked with an X in the upper-right corner to get past this screen.

■ If you want to check out specific topics in GNOME, use your mouse to click any of the text at the bottom of the Help Index screen.

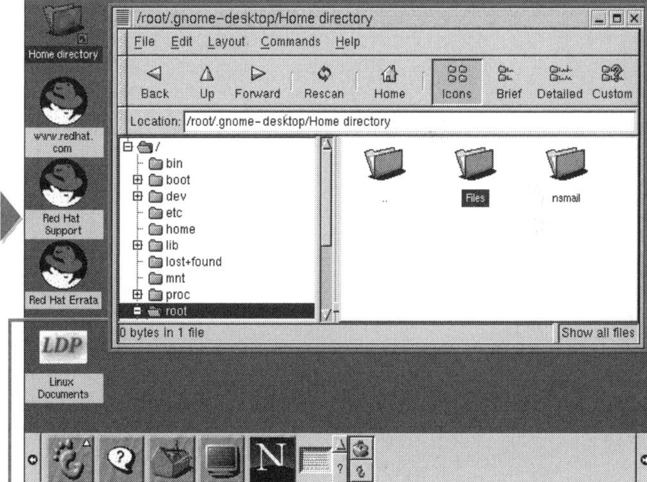

■ The GNOME desktop comes up with an open window that displays the contents of your home directory.

USING BUTTONS AND DROP-DOWN MENUS

In the Linux GNOME environment, you discover that the mouse comes in handy when clicking menu buttons and selecting options from the drop-down menus.

When you click a command on a window's toolbar, GNOME will usually display a menu that drops down beneath the command you originally clicked. Drop-down menus are widely used throughout the GNOME environment for the same reason you see them in Windows 95, 98 or NT: They save crucial desktop space. Displaying 30 commands across a small window toolbar would make for cramped reading; grouping commands under headings like File, Edit, or Settings is more efficient and easier on the eyes.

When you click a menu button, your computer performs the action indicated by the button. When you move your mouse pointer over a button, the button usually highlights, producing a 3-D effect.

When you click a drop-down menu, you see a list of actions that you can select with your mouse. You can find drop-down menus at the top of a window or hidden anywhere on-screen until you click the menu.

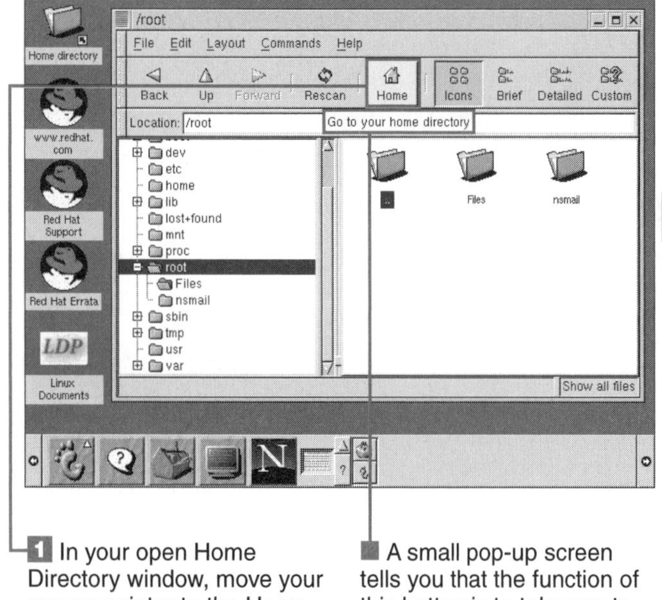

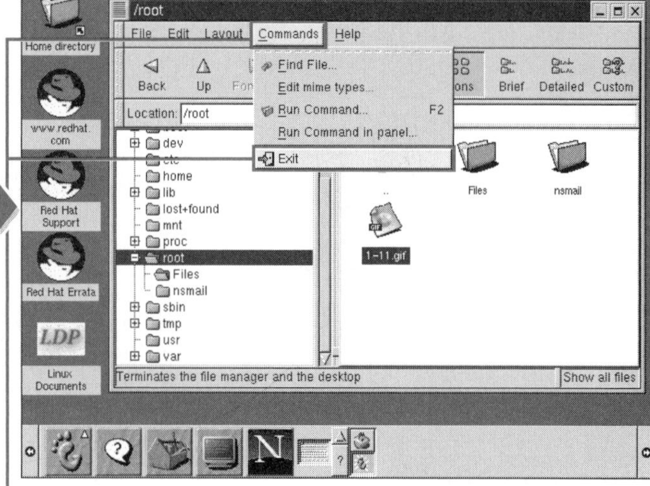

1 In your open Home Directory window, move your mouse pointer to the Home button in the center top section of the window, holding for a few seconds.

■ A small pop-up screen tells you that the function of this button is to take you to your home directory. Not all buttons have this pop-up screen feature, but those that do are very helpful.

2 Click the Home button.

3 Click Commands on the menu toolbar.

■ The drop-down menu appears with several options.

4 Move the mouse pointer over the Exit command.

■ The command highlights, indicating which selection the mouse pointer is over.

5 Click Exit to exit the Home Directory.

LOG OUT OF LINUX

Logging out of Linux serves two purposes. First, logging out of Linux effectively closes all of the sessions where you can do work — preventing others from using your account to change or damage the system. Second, leaving the Linux environment frees up more resources for the remaining users on the system.

Remember, logging out of Linux is not the same as shutting the system down. When you log out of Linux, the operating system is still active — only you are not on the system and able to make edits, change anything, or create files. Shutting the system down has the same effect as turning the power off on your machine.

While this might save some electricity, it also forces you to get back into Linux through the Start Up process.

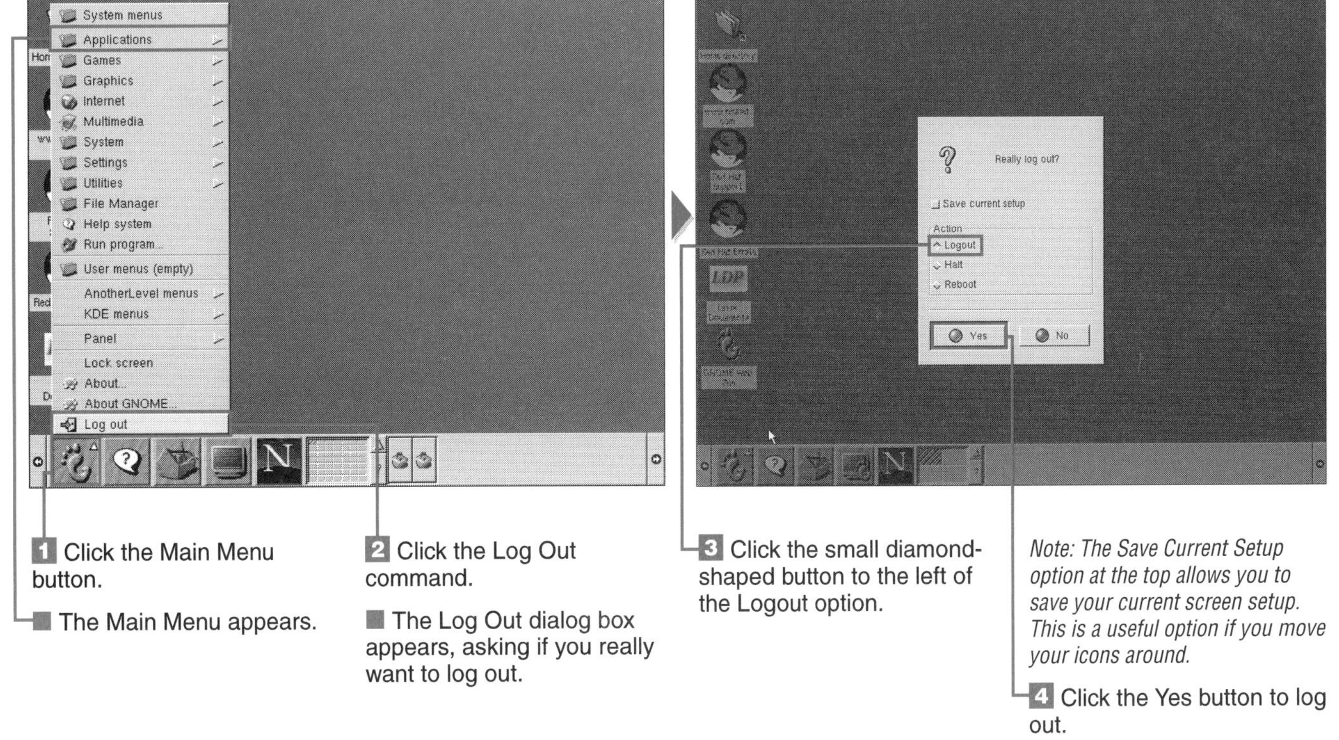

1 Click the Main Menu button.

■ The Main Menu appears.

2 Click the Log Out command.

■ The Log Out dialog box appears, asking if you really want to log out.

3 Click the small diamond-shaped button to the left of the Logout option.

Note: The Save Current Setup option at the top allows you to save your current screen setup. This is a useful option if you move your icons around.

4 Click the Yes button to log out.

SHUT DOWN LINUX

If you run Linux where multiple people access it over a network, you should shut down Linux only when you need to perform system maintenance, prevent an electrical outage, or upgrade hardware. Most upgrades or system maintenance are scheduled outages, meaning that you should plan to shut Linux down ahead of time to do these tasks.

In order to minimize disruption, you should notify your users well in advance that the Linux server will be shutting down and their work may be affected. Ideally, notify people a few days in advance of your shutdown, particularly if the shutdown will last more than an hour or require system testing afterwards. You should also notify them again of the pending shutdown on the same day the shutdown takes place because users are notorious for forgetting about pending shutdowns that could affect their work.

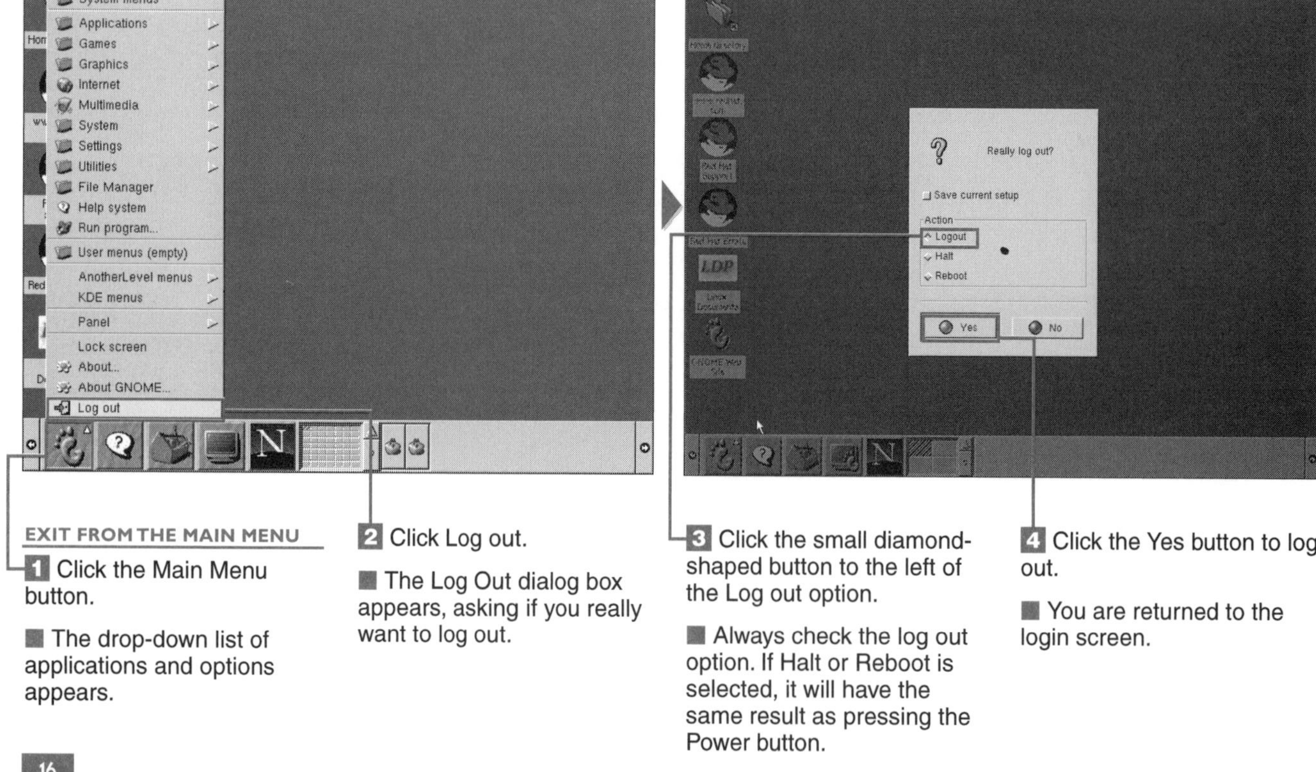

EXIT FROM THE MAIN MENU

1 Click the Main Menu button.

■ The drop-down list of applications and options appears.

2 Click Log out.

■ The Log Out dialog box appears, asking if you really want to log out.

3 Click the small diamond-shaped button to the left of the Log out option.

■ Always check the log out option. If Halt or Reboot is selected, it will have the same result as pressing the Power button.

4 Click the Yes button to log out.

■ You are returned to the login screen.

What's the best way to notify my users of a planned Linux shutdown?

- Send your notices out over e-mail. If you run a computer lab, posting signs on the door or desks is less effective. However, no one ignores personal e-mail.

When should I use halt over reboot?

- Because reboot doesn't turn off the power to the system, use reboot when you want to test changes that you've made to the Linux system. Halt actually powers down your system, so it's best to halt Linux when you plan to touch the hardware inside the machine. Note that to prevent electric shock, you should halt the Linux system *and* physically unplug the machine from the wall socket.

What should I do if the machine is accidentally shut off in a power outage?

- Turn off all the Linux machines on your network. Because you can't perform a standard shutdown with the loss of power, simply press the power switches for each individual machine. This is important because it prevents your blowing a fuse when the electricity is restored, which could blow a fuse. When the power is restored, turn your Linux machines on one at a time to gently bring power usage to what it was before.

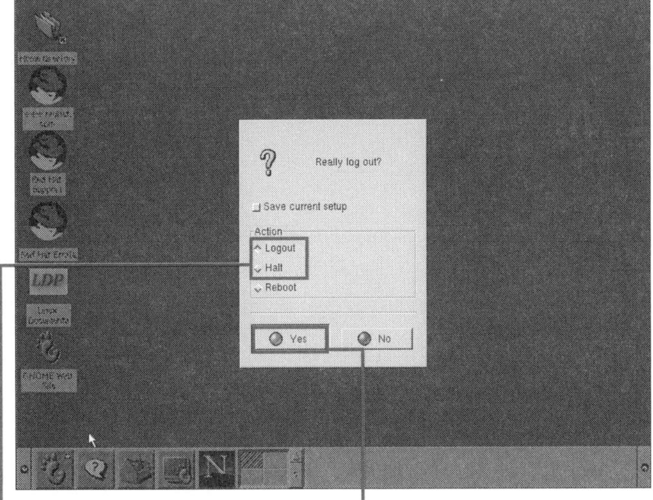

EXIT FROM THE LOG OUT BOX

1 Click the small diamond-shaped button to the left of the Halt or Reboot options to select one of the options.

2 Click the Yes button.

■ You are returned to the login screen.

EXIT FROM THE LOGIN BOX

1 Click System

■ The System drop-down menu appears.

2 Choose an option — Reboot or Halt.

SHUT DOWN LINUX WITHOUT USING THE GUI

If you run Linux where multiple people access it over a network, you should shut down Linux only when you need to perform system maintenance, prevent an electrical outage, or upgrade hardware. Most upgrades or system maintenance are scheduled outages, meaning that you should plan to shut Linux down ahead of time to do these tasks. Upgrades and maintenance that you should schedule include adding new hard drives or peripherals, such as printers or CD-ROM drives.

To minimize disruption, notify your users well in advance that the Linux server will be shutting down and that their work may be affected.

Even if your version of Linux comes with a GUI, consider using this method to shut down your system when performing maintenance on a multi-user network. Unlike the GUI-based Log Out dialog box, the Linux command line offers a couple utilities that come in handy for the final user notification.

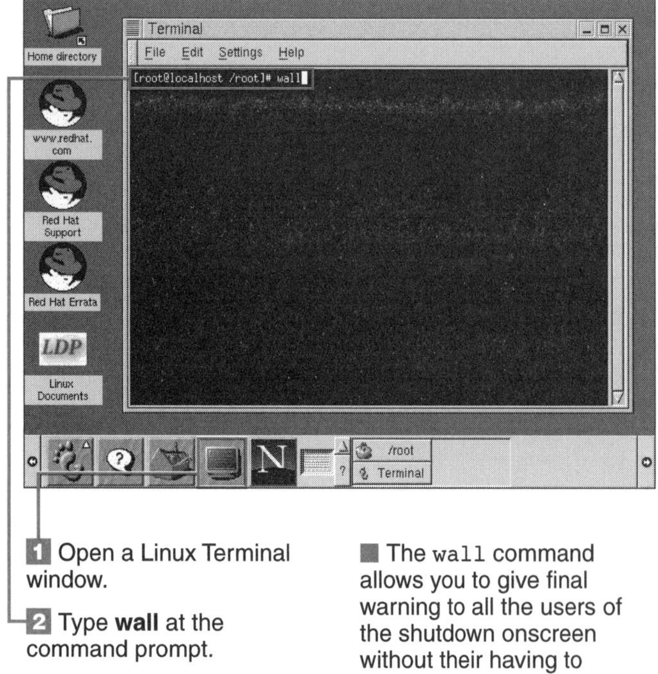

1 Open a Linux Terminal window.

2 Type **wall** at the command prompt.

■ The `wall` command allows you to give final warning to all the users of the shutdown onscreen without their having to check e-mail.

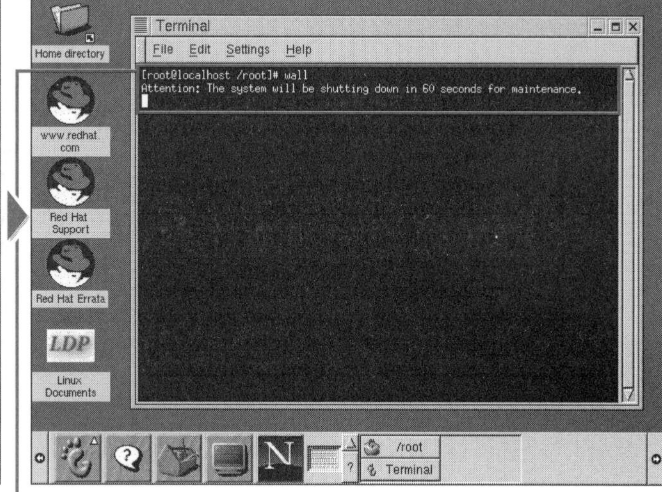

3 Type your message conveying how soon the system is shutting down.

4 Press Ctrl+D to end the message.

When I send the wall command, should I say how long the system maintenance will take?

It's best if you don't include this information. When you send out e-mail to users, you can say that the maintenance will take approximately X number of hours. However, sending out a `wall` command with a statement indicating that the system will be back in five minutes will cause people to wait in front of their machines and get very frustrated if you run into unexpected delays. As a rule, triple the time that you estimate that you can perform the needed work.

How can I set the delay interval in the shutdown command to 2 or 3 minutes instead of 30 or 60 seconds?

By default, the time interval in Linux is seconds. If you want a two-minute delay, simply enter the period in seconds: shutdown -t 120.

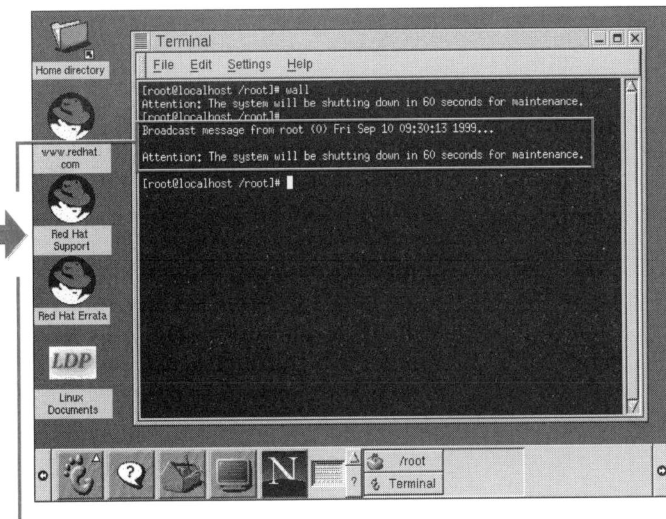

■ Linux displays the broadcast message notification.

5 Press Enter to get the command prompt back.

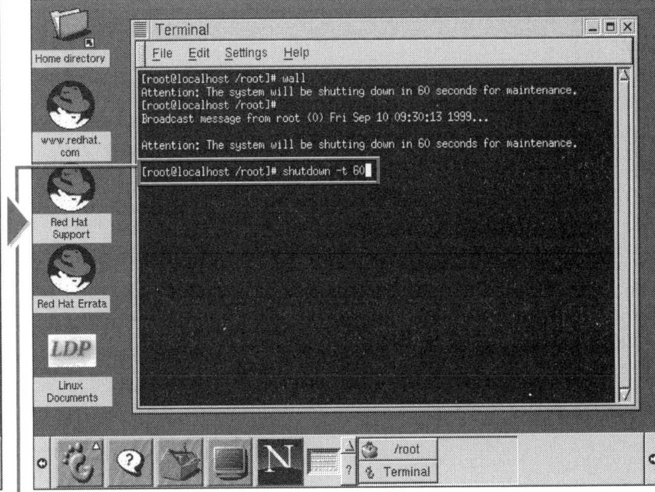

6 Type **shutdown -t 60** at the command prompt.

■ `Shutdown` is another Linux-based utility that allows you to specify how long you want the system to wait before it initiates a halt procedure.

7 Press Enter.

■ Linux waits the specified time period and then automatically initiates the shutdown procedure.

OPEN GNOME WINDOWS AND LINUX TERMINALS

You open windows on the GNOME desktop to either display a program window or to have a different desktop area to view or edit files. Program windows have different drop-down menus and buttons, depending on the program that you open. In contrast, windows that aren't displayed as part of a program, such as windows opened by clicking a folder, have the same Web browser-based interface.

A Linux Terminal is technically considered a window because you can perform certain tasks within its boundaries. However, we stick with the word "Terminal" to avoid confusion because the function of a Terminal is much different than a window. A window displays files or runs programs in the GNOME desktop environment.

In contrast, Terminals allow you to go below the GNOME interface and work with Linux directly. Often, you can only perform certain tasks from the Linux command prompt, accessible through the Linux Terminal. If you are familiar with Windows, think of the Linux Terminal as opening the Windows Registry. The Registry controls system functions that run behind the desktop graphics. Similarly, the Linux Terminal allows you to make changes that affect the system below the level of the desktop.

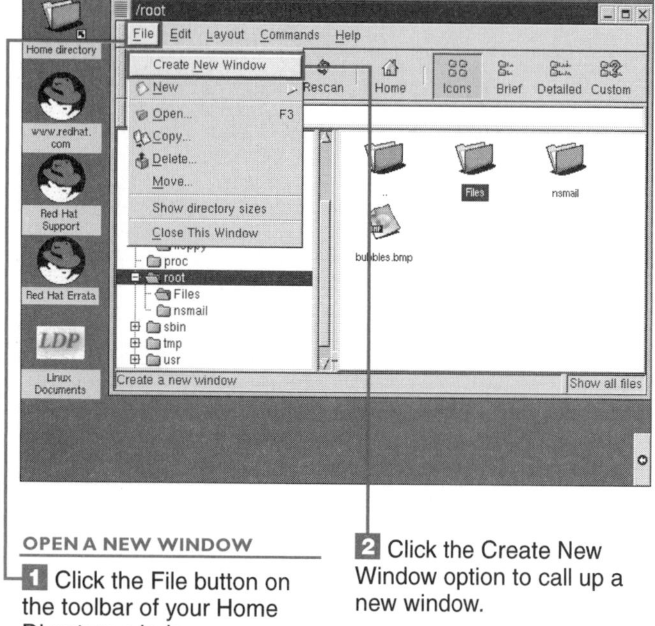

OPEN A NEW WINDOW

1 Click the File button on the toolbar of your Home Directory window.

2 Click the Create New Window option to call up a new window.

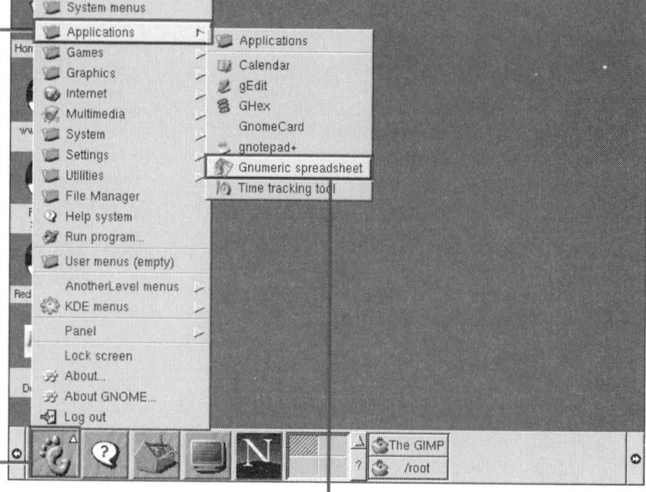

OPEN A LINUX APPLICATION

1 Click the Main Menu button in the lower-left corner of the screen.

2 Move the mouse pointer to Applications.

■ A submenu appears.

3 Select an application.

■ The application window appears.

How can I tell whether one menu will lead to another sub-menu?

- When you call up a menu (such as by clicking the Main Menu Application button), any selection with a sub-menu will have a small right-facing arrow to the right of the menu entry. Moving your mouse pointer over such a menu entry automatically causes the sub-menu to appear.

How can I copy a program's icon from the Application button menu to my desktop?

- Move your mouse pointer to select the icon. Instead of clicking the icon, click and drag the selection to an open area of the desktop. When you release the mouse button, the icon will be copied there.

How can I create a Terminal Emulation button directly on my desktop?

- Click the Terminal Emulation button on the toolbar and drag it to a blank area of desktop.

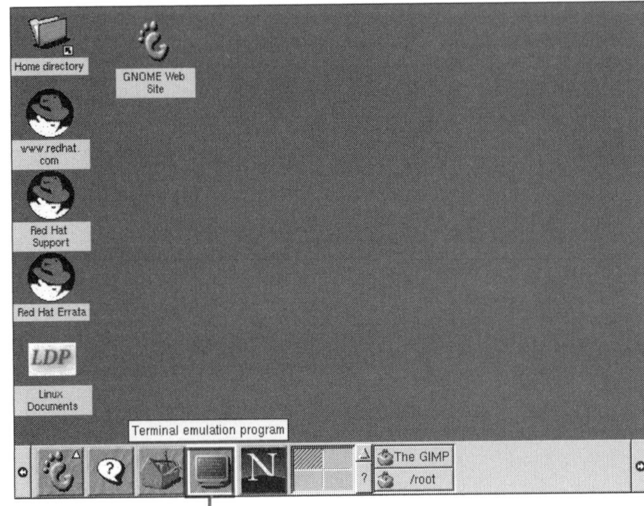

OPEN A LINUX TERMINAL

1 Click the Terminal Emulation button.

■ A Linux Terminal appears.

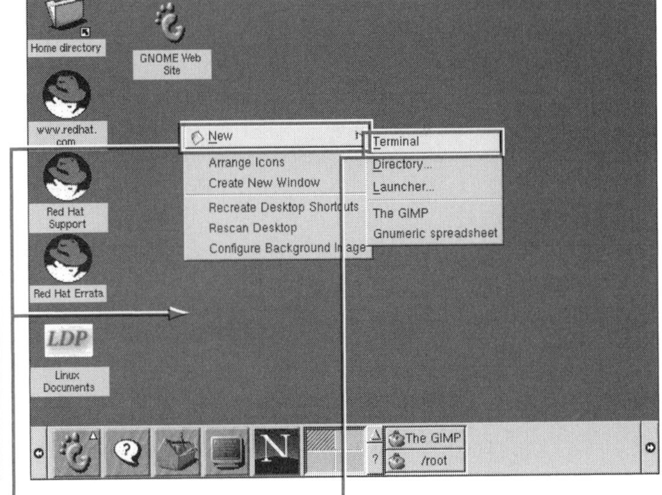

OPEN FROM DESKTOP

1 Right-click any blank area of the desktop.

■ A drop-down menu appears.

2 Move the mouse pointer to the New selection.

■ A submenu appears.

3 Move the pointer to select Terminal and click.

■ This action both brings up the Terminal window and closes the menus.

RESIZE WINDOWS

You may want to resize the windows on your desktop for a number of reasons. If you have multiple windows open on your desktop, you might need to adjust the size of each window so you can work more easily. You might want to shrink a window so you can reach a portion of the desktop. Or you could enlarge a window in order to see more of its contents.

Desktop windows also allow you to resize the frames or the interior divisions of the window to display more space in certain areas. Most commonly, you can split the Home Directory in GNOME into two frames, the left with the file system and the right displaying the files in the current directory. You can enlarge one area at the expense of the other if you want a clearer view of the file contents or the file system.

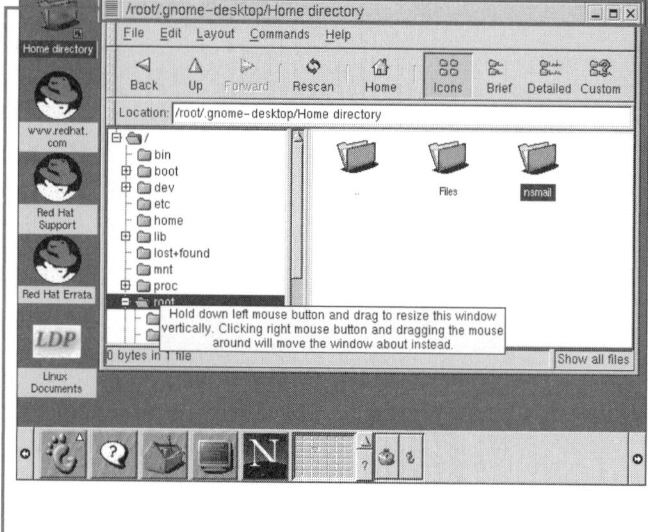

RESIZE THE HEIGHT

1 To resize the window as taller or shorter, click and drag the upper or lower border of the window.

■ When you place the mouse pointer in the right spot, the pointer icon changes from a diagonal pointer to an up-down arrow.

2 Release the mouse button and the window resizes.

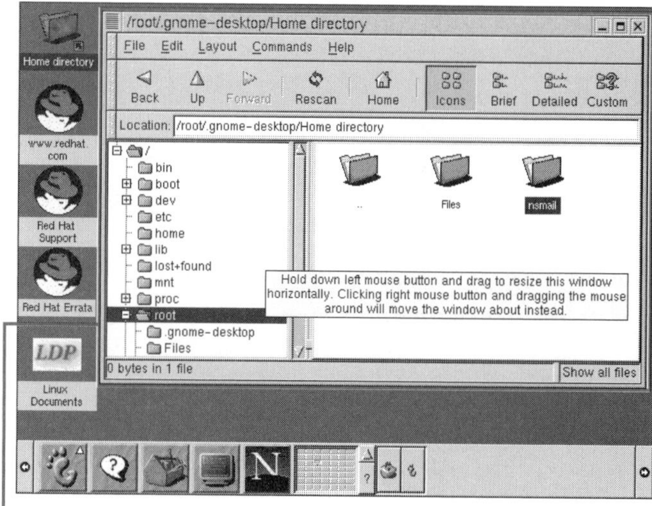

RESIZE THE WIDTH

1 To resize width of the window, click and drag the left or right border of the window.

■ When you place the mouse pointer in the right spot, the pointer icon changes from a diagonal pointer to a left-right arrow.

2 Release the mouse button and the window resizes.

How can I prevent windows from overlapping when I resize them?

- Pay attention to the black outline when dragging the window borders. The outline is there so you can tell exactly where the window is going to fit when you release the mouse button.

What do I do if the edge of the window is off screen so I can't grab it to resize it the way I want?

- Your can move the entire window so you can grab the border you want. This is covered in the "Move and Switch Windows Around" section of this chapter.

How do I view files in a window if I've increased the size of the window but still can't see everything?

- Use the scrollbars inside each window frame. The scrollbars automatically appear if more files or file systems are off screen. Click and drag the scrollbar to move around inside the frame.

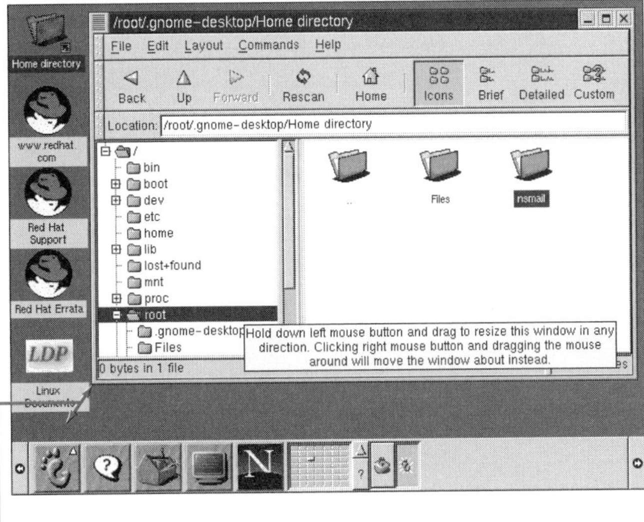

RESIZE THE BORDERS

1 To resize the borders of a window, click and drag the border of the window in any corner.

■ When you place the mouse pointer in the right spot, the pointer icon changes from a diagonal pointer to a wider pointer.

2 Release the mouse button and the window resizes.

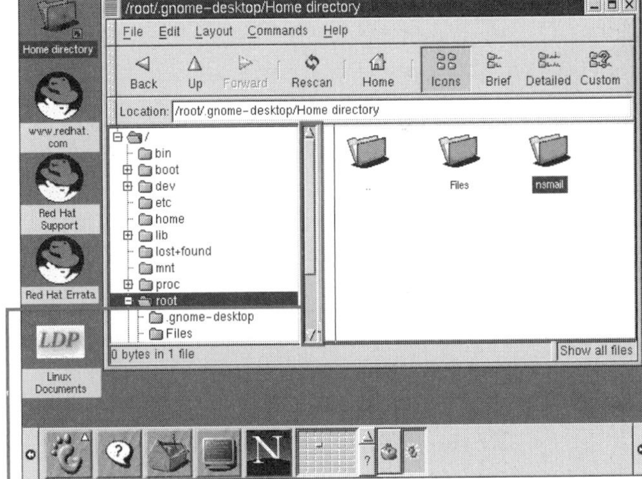

RESIZE INTERNAL DIVIDER

1 To resize the internal dividers of the window (frames), move the mouse pointer over the small gray square located between the frames, to the right of the scrollbar.

■ When you place the mouse pointer in the right spot, the pointer icon changes from a diagonal pointer to a crosshairs icon.

2 Release the mouse button.

MAXIMIZE, MINIMIZE, AND CLOSE WINDOWS

Whether working with a desktop window, a program window, or a Linux Terminal, there are three buttons that will always have identical purposes in each kind of window. These buttons are located at the upper left of each window and will allow you to maximize, minimize, or close the window or Terminal.

You may want to maximize a window to see as much of the window's contents as possible. On the other hand, if you need more space on the desktop, minimizing a window is a convenient method to get the window out of the way without closing the program or Terminal. Closing the window itself is an easy way to terminate the program it was running or to prepare to log out of the Linux desktop environment. However, keep in mind that closing a window can end a program, losing any data that you haven't saved.

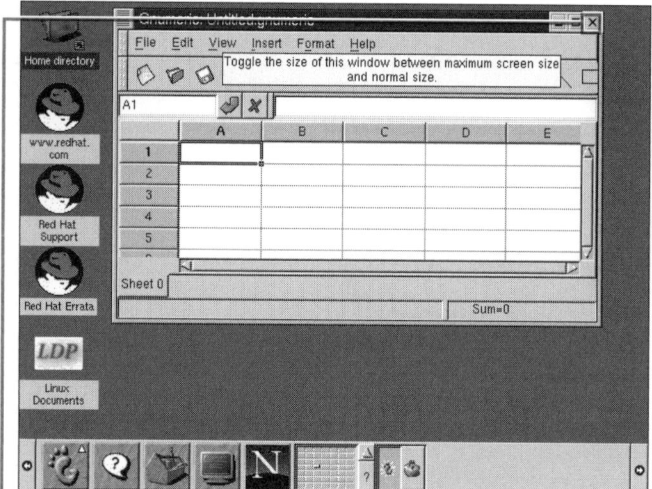

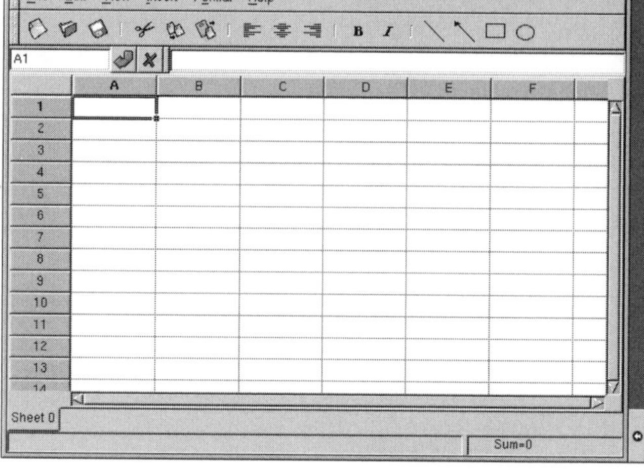

MAXIMIZE A WINDOW

1 To maximize a window, move your mouse pointer over the Maximize button and click.

■ The Maximize button is the second of the three buttons in the upper right corner. The button shows a little square with a dark line across the top.

■ The maximized window takes up the entire screen.

Note: Maximizing windows gives you more window space but doesn't proportionally increase the size of the icons or directories.

How do I restore a window to its former size?

- If you've maximized the window, click the Maximize button again to restore the window to it's original size. But when you minimize a window, it creates an icon of itself on the GNOME toolbar at the bottom of the screen. Click that icon to restore the window. If you the window is close, open a new one.

What if I want to restore a window and then resize it, not minimize or maximize it?

- Once you restore the window, simply resize it using the directions in the "Resize Windows" section of this chapter.

How do I force a window to close?

- Some program windows refuse to close if their programs malfunction. If this happens, right-click the Close button to force the program to quit. For this reason, the Close button is also known as the Kill button.

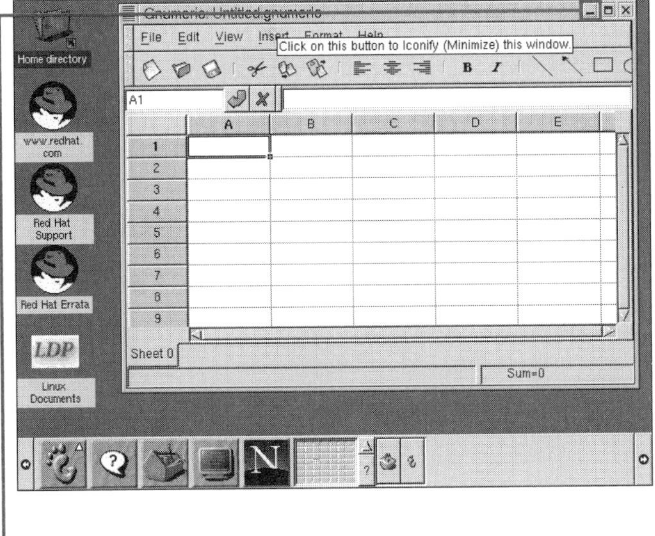

MINIMIZE A WINDOW

1 To minimize a window, move your mouse pointer over the Minimize button and click.

■ On any window, the Minimize button has a dark line drawn across the bottom of the button.

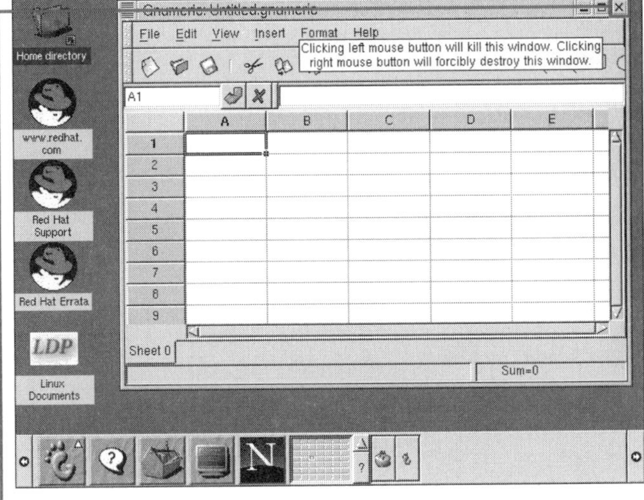

CLOSE A WINDOW

1 To close a window, move your mouse pointer over the Close button and click.

■ The Close button has a dark X icon.

MOVE AND SWITCH WINDOWS AROUND

When working with more than one window open, it is useful to know how to move windows around to prevent overlapping. It's also helpful knowing how to switch between windows so that you can jump between tasks on the desktop. This allows you to work more efficiently.

When you are working with multiple windows, note that only one window is active at any given time. A window that is inactive is not the same as a window that is closed. Windows that aren't active still have their programs running or their command prompts available.

If your goal is to move windows around to can see what you are doing in multiple locations on the desktop, follow this task. Also see the "Resize Windows" section earlier in this chapter.

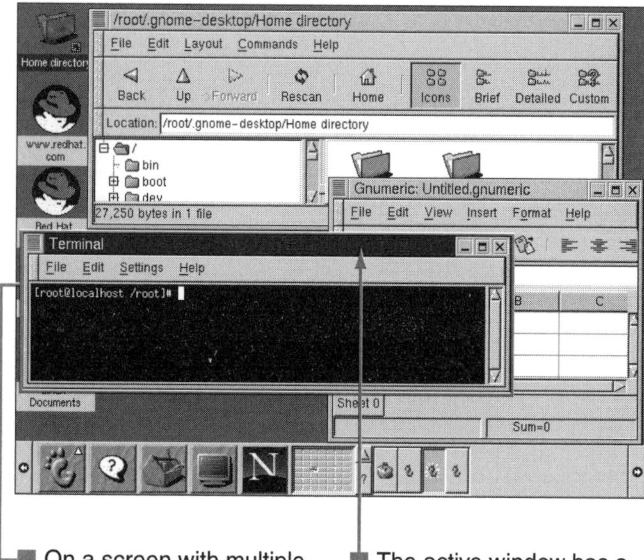

■ On a screen with multiple windows, only one window can be active at any time. Of the three windows here, the Terminal window is active. The active window is always in the foreground.

■ The active window has a darkened drag bar, which is the topmost portion of the window toolbar.

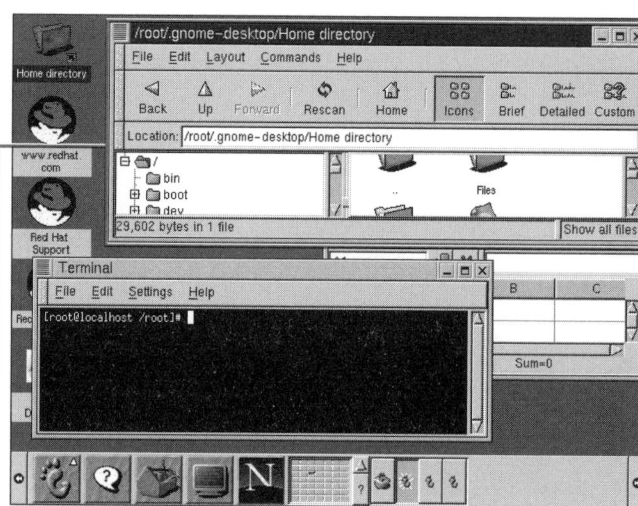

1 Click a window to make it active.

■ Activating a different window brings it to the foreground, but it can end up obscuring other windows. Making the Home Directory window active hides the Gnumeric application.

What are some other ways to prevent overlapping windows on a desktop with limited space?

- The next section on turning windows into icons and bars allows additional methods of preventing overlapping besides resizing and moving windows around on the desktop.

What if I lose a window completely behind another, larger window?

- Make the larger window active and then minimize it. This allows you to click and drag the smaller, previously hidden window to an area of the desktop where it won't be eclipsed by the larger window.

How many windows should I have open on the desktop?

- There is no minimum or maximum to the number of windows you can have open, though having an excessive number open at the same time can cause older machines to slow down slightly. However, unless you are cutting and pasting information between windows, having one window open and leaving other ones closed is simplest.

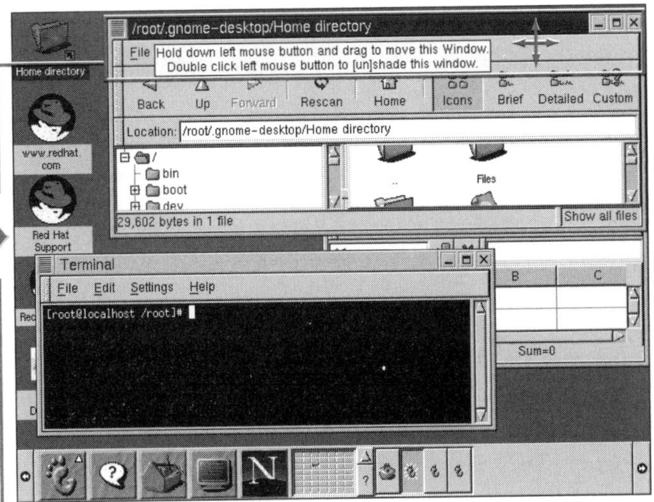

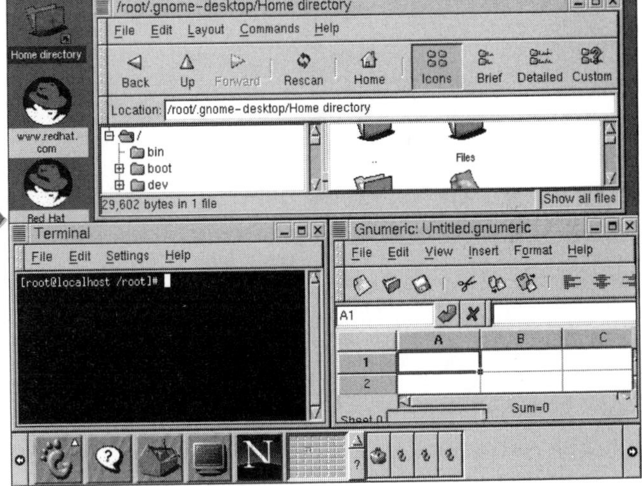

2 Hold the mouse pointer over the drag bar of the window.

■ When you have the pointer in the right location, the diagonal pointer turns into a four-point icon that looks like a compass.

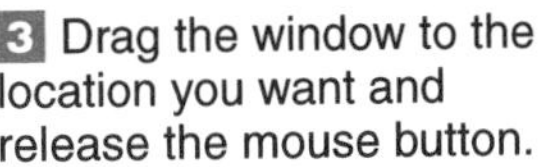

3 Drag the window to the location you want and release the mouse button.

Note: Moving and resizing windows avoids problems with overlapping.

TURN WINDOWS INTO ICONS AND BARS

By turning a window into an icon on the GNOME toolbar or shrinking the window to the size of its drag bar, you can increase the space on your desktop while leaving multiple windows open.

Iconifying the window is simply another process of minimizing it for saving space on the desktop and also for easy retrieval. Shrinking the window to the drag bar is much like rolling up a curtain. When you want to restore the window, it can be rolled back down again.

Shrinking and restoring a window does not affect the information or application in the window. For example, if you are running a word processing application in an iconified window, the program will continue to run unless the window is actually closed. The text will not be altered or re-formatted by the change in the window's shape or status.

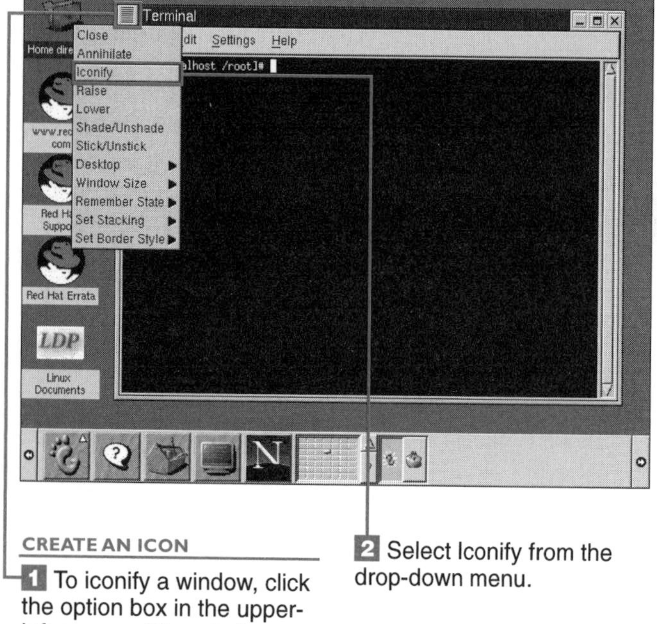

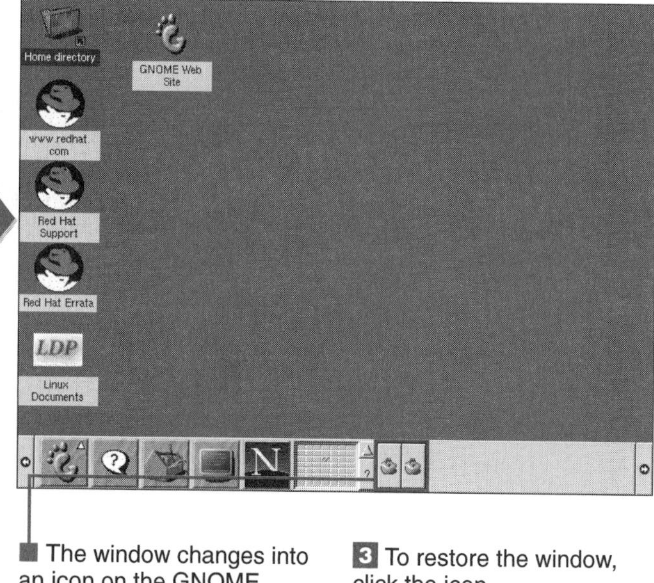

CREATE AN ICON

1 To iconify a window, click the option box in the upper-left corner of the window.

2 Select Iconify from the drop-down menu.

■ The window changes into an icon on the GNOME toolbar at the bottom of the screen.

3 To restore the window, click the icon.

How can I close a window after iconifying it?

- To do this, restore the window by clicking the newly created icon on the GNOME toolbar. Next, select the Close button in the upper right corner of the window to close it.

How can I minimize a window any further after turning it into a drag bar?

- The drag bar still has the Minimize, Maximize, and Close buttons on it as if it were a regular window. After converting the window to a drag bar, click the Minimize button or iconify it to completely take it off the desktop.

How can I close a window after turning it into a drag bar?

- The drag bar still has the Minimize, Maximize, and Close buttons on it as if it were a regular window. Click the Close button on the drag bar and the window closes permanently.

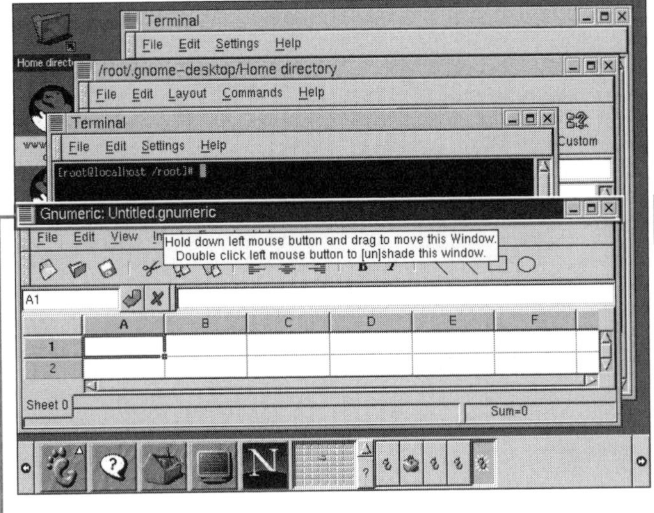

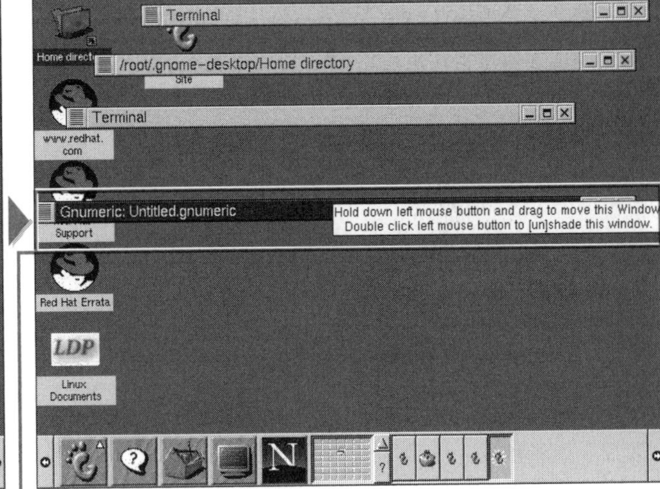

CREATE A DRAG BAR

1 To change a window into a drag bar, click the window to make it active.

2 Place the mouse pointer over the drag bar of the window.

3 Double-click the left mouse button to change the window into a drag bar.

4 To restore the window, double-click the drag bar again.

■ After reducing each window to drag bars, you can easily locate the window you want to open and close. The drag bar remains on-screen in place of the window.

MOVE AND COPY FILES BETWEEN WINDOWS

You may want to use the GNOME desktop environment to move or copy files into different areas. Often, instead of copying a file to multiple locations, you can make use of the Linux network system and place a file in a common directory that all users can access.

While you can do this with one open window, it's usually easier if you have two windows open. This allows you to click and drag a file from one area into another without having to browse through different directories to get to the location where you want to put the file.

In this example, you want to move a file called `testcut` from the `/root` directory to the `/tmp` directory so more people can look at it. Begin with an open window to the root account's Home Directory. Conveniently, this directory usually can be found on the desktop, labeled Home Directory.

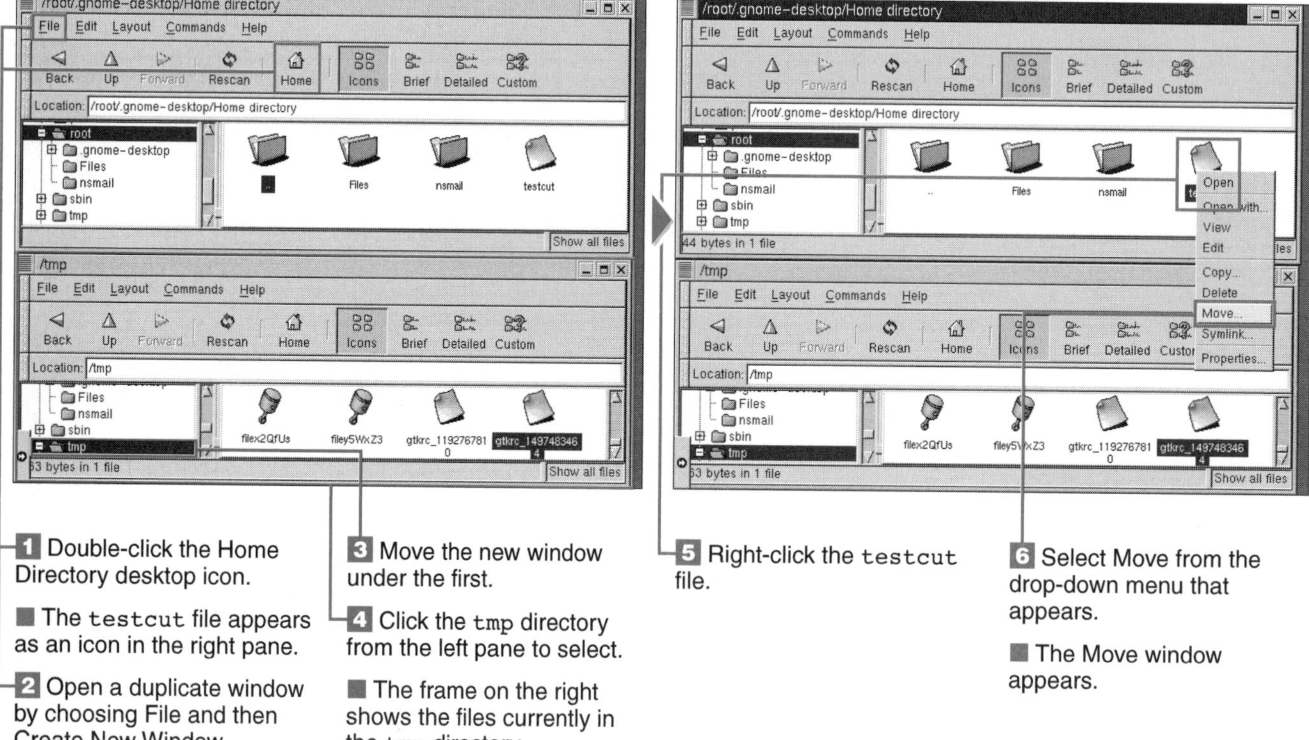

1 Double-click the Home Directory desktop icon.

■ The `testcut` file appears as an icon in the right pane.

2 Open a duplicate window by choosing File and then Create New Window.

3 Move the new window under the first.

4 Click the `tmp` directory from the left pane to select.

■ The frame on the right shows the files currently in the `tmp` directory.

5 Right-click the `testcut` file.

6 Select Move from the drop-down menu that appears.

■ The Move window appears.

Are there any other ways to move files between windows?

- Clicking and dragging the file between the windows works almost as well as using the drop-down menus described above. While clicking and dragging is faster and simpler, it doesn't give you the Advanced options available to you in the Move menu.

What Advanced Options are there?

- If you click the Advanced tab in the Move Option box, your file will preserve its symbolic links. Symbolic links are special files that allow Linux system programs, called binaries, to specify where they want to look for information.

What about copying the file testcut instead of moving it??

- When you right-click `testcut`, one of the options in the menu that appears is Copy instead of Move. This places a copy by default into the second open window on your desktop.

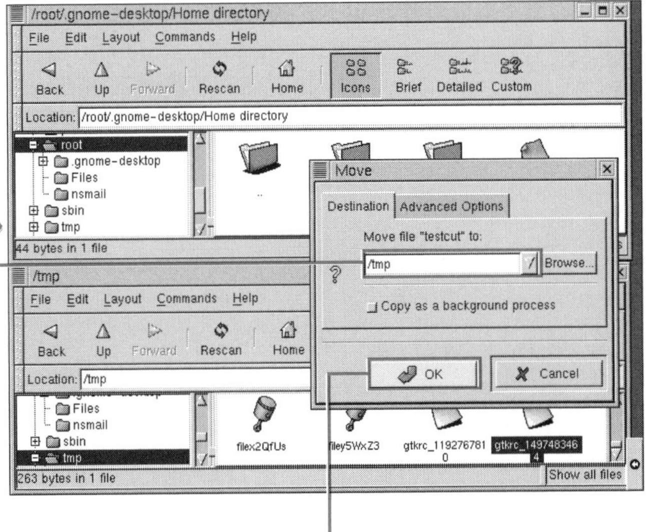

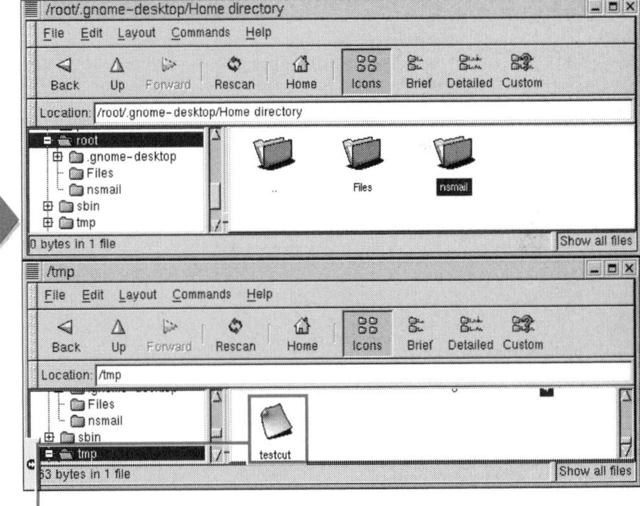

7 In the Move File Testcut To field, type **/tmp** if it is not there.

■ The `/tmp` should already be in the field. This is one of the benefits of opening the two windows. GNOME already assumes that this second window is where you want to copy the file.

8 Click the OK button.

■ The result is instantly visible. `Testcut` is removed from the Home Directory right frame and placed in the `/tmp` directory area.

SLIDE WINDOWS WHEN OPEN

The Enlightenment Window Manager is a window managing utility that has been incorporated into the GNOME desktop environment. Enlightenment works mostly behind the scenes, ensuring that your windows display icons and folders clearly and in proper order. With Enlightenment, you can change the appearance of the windows displayed in GNOME, the desktop environment, and the system keyboard shortcuts.

I explore the Enlightenment Window manager more thoroughly in Chapter 2. However, you can get a feel for what it is right now as you learn to move around and change items in the GNOME environment.

Normally, when you click an icon or the Terminal Emulation button, the created window pops into existence on the desktop. If this is too harsh on your eyes, or you just want to experiment with different effects on your desktop, try setting the Enlightenment Window Manager to make your windows slide.

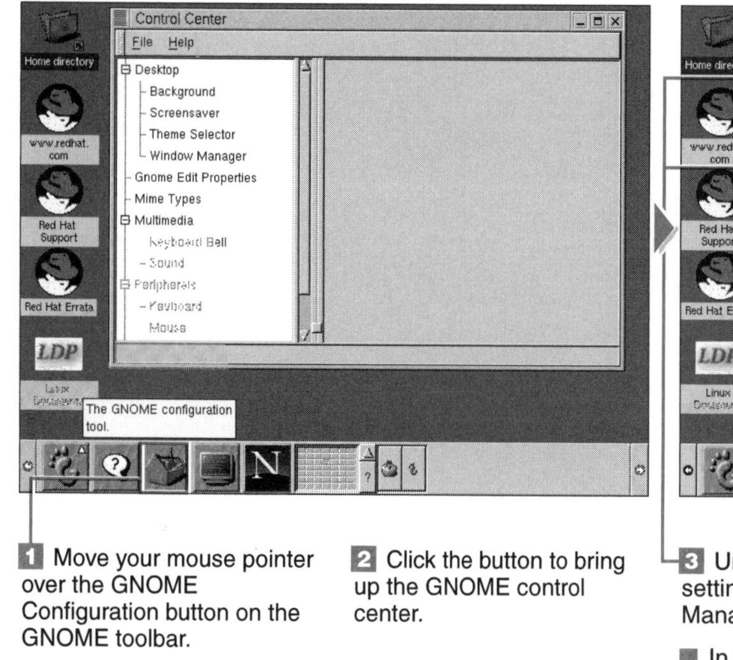

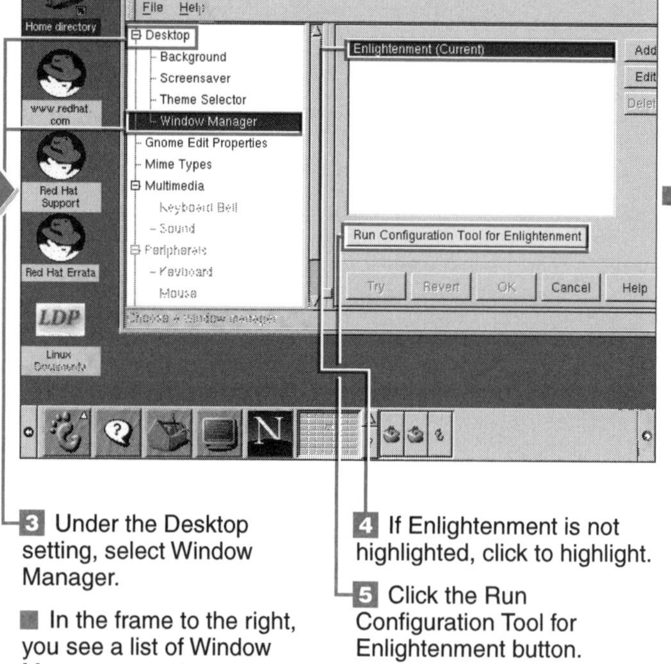

1 Move your mouse pointer over the GNOME Configuration button on the GNOME toolbar.

2 Click the button to bring up the GNOME control center.

3 Under the Desktop setting, select Window Manager.

■ In the frame to the right, you see a list of Window Managers running on GNOME. The default is Enlightenment.

4 If Enlightenment is not highlighted, click to highlight.

5 Click the Run Configuration Tool for Enlightenment button.

How can I preview the effects that I want to try?

- After clicking Apply in the Enlightenment Configuration Editor window, don't close the Editor window. Instead, bring up another window or Terminal to see how the object's appearance or behavior has changed.

Are there recommended settings for different machines?

- There are no real recommendations, but some of the more advanced effects, such as the window sliding behavior, may slow down older, less powerful machines.

What if I have an older machine that slows down significantly when using advanced windowing effects?

- Consider installing more RAM in your computer system. RAM, or random access memory, can be purchased and installed at your local computer store for minimal cost.

How can I restore the original system settings?

- Under Basic Options, click the Reset All Settings to System Defaults and Exit button (in the lower-middle section of the screen) to restore your old settings.

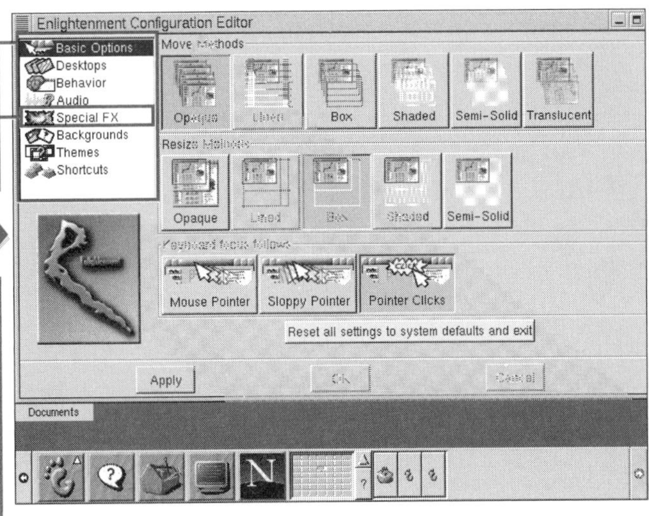

■ The Enlightenment Configuration Editor comes up listing its options in the upper-left frame.

6 Select Special FX.

■ At a later time, come back and explore the other options available to Enlightenment, such as the Shortcuts and Behavior settings.

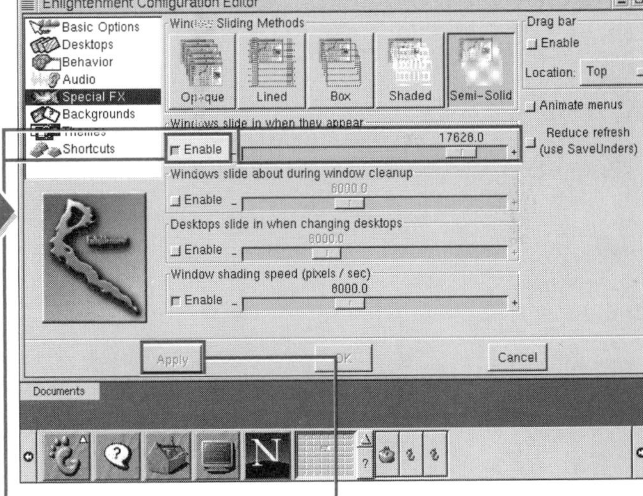

■ In the center of the screen, you see the setting Window slide in when they appear.

7 Click the Enable button.

8 Click and drag the bar.

■ Move the bar to the left to increase the speed and to the right to decrease it.

9 Click Apply to accept this setting.

GET HELP IN GNOME

On the GNOME desktop, you have several ways of finding documentation on Linux or GUI configurations. The desktop icons point to online documentation. When you click these icons, Netscape automatically starts, logging you into the World Wide Web and droping down the Web page with the requested information.

In case you don't want to wait for a connection or you don't have access to the world outside your Linux network, excellent documentation exists local to the machine as well. The GNOME Help Index is a GUI-based documentation system that works with a Web-style interface.

The Help Index is especially useful in that it covers both GNOME-specific and Linux-specific topics. Whether you need to find out how to configure an obscure GNOME utility or find out the syntax for a command in the Linux Terminal, the Help Index likely has what you need.

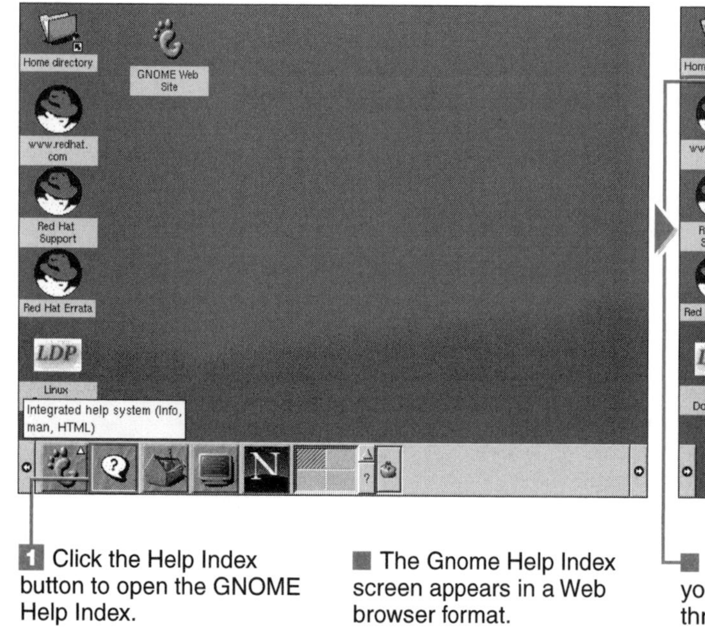

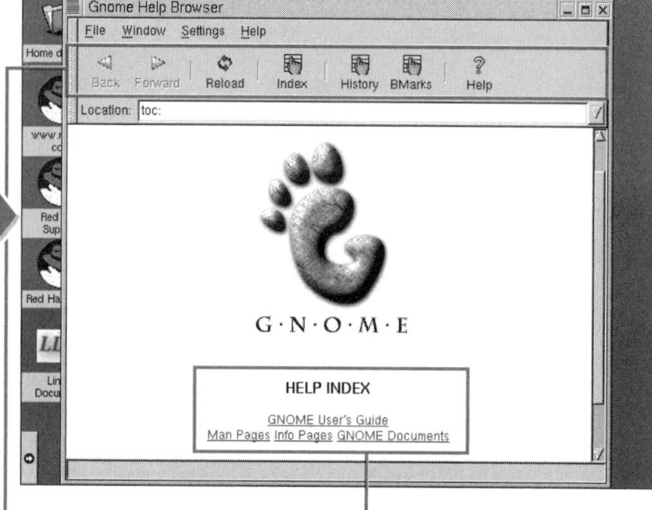

1 Click the Help Index button to open the GNOME Help Index.

■ The Gnome Help Index screen appears in a Web browser format.

■ The upper toolbar allows you to move back and forth through index pages or to specific areas of the Index.

■ Text hyperlinks are toward the bottom of the screen. A hyperlink is a portion text that takes you to the documents described.

On a color monitor, most hyperlinks are colored blue. If I use a monochrome monitor, how can I tell if a piece of text in the GNOME Help Index is a hyperlink?

- On most black and white monitors, a hyperlink will noticeably darken when you move your mouse pointer over it. Also, the pointer will normally turn into a little hand.

Is the GNOME Help Index made by Red Hat?

- The GNOME Help Index is actually made by the programmers who created the GNOME desktop, which gives Linux its Windows-like environment.

Does it have Red Hat Help Index topics?

- The GNOME Help Index doesn't come with any topics specific to Red Hat's flavor of Linux. This is because GNOME is a desktop GUI that is growing rapidly in popularity, so it has been bundled with several different brands of Linux, such as Debian.

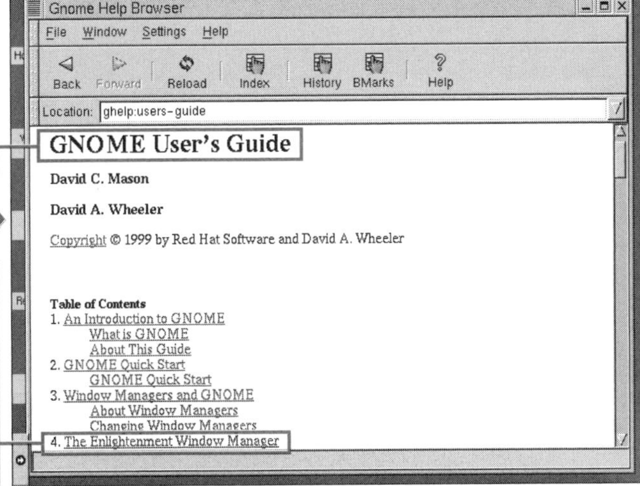

2 Click the GNOME User's Guide hyperlink to get to the User's Guide.

■ The GNOME users guide is the documentation area that is most specific to learning about the GNOME environment.

■ Each part of the text that is underlined is a specific hyperlink to more information on that GNOME subject.

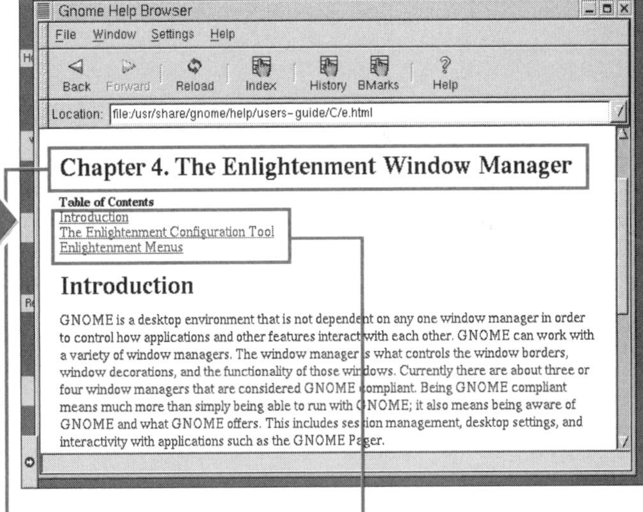

3 Click The Enlightenment Window Manager hyperlink to get more information.

■ More detailed information about Enlightenment displays.

CONTINUED

GET HELP IN GNOME CONTINUED

The GNOME Help Browser controls are laid out in a manner that can make your task of finding the information you need much easier and intuitive. Like many of the windows in the GNOME environment under the Red Hat brand of Linux, the GNOME Help browser is set up in the manner of a Web browser.

A Web browser is a program designed to enable you to move between different pages of information on the World Wide Web. The designers of the GNOME Help browser saw a similar need to jump between pages of information within their program.

Like in the Netscape or Internet Explorer Web browser, you can click buttons to move back and forward while searching for information within the GNOME Help browser application. These buttons are laid out intuitively in the toolbar at the top of the application window.

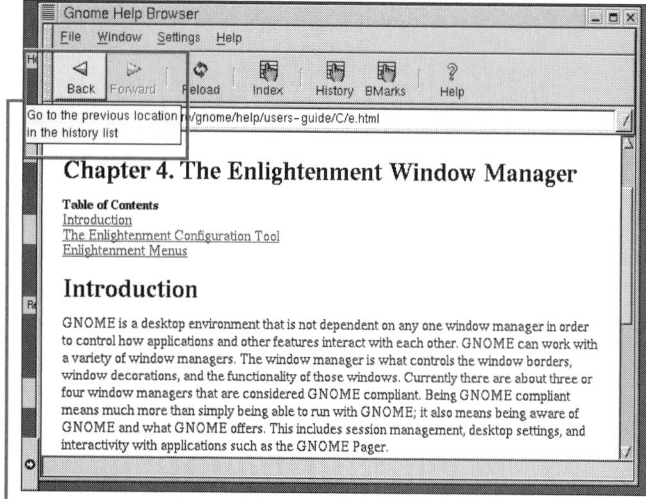

4 Click the Back button on the GNOME Help Browser toolbar to go back a screen in the GNOME Help browser.

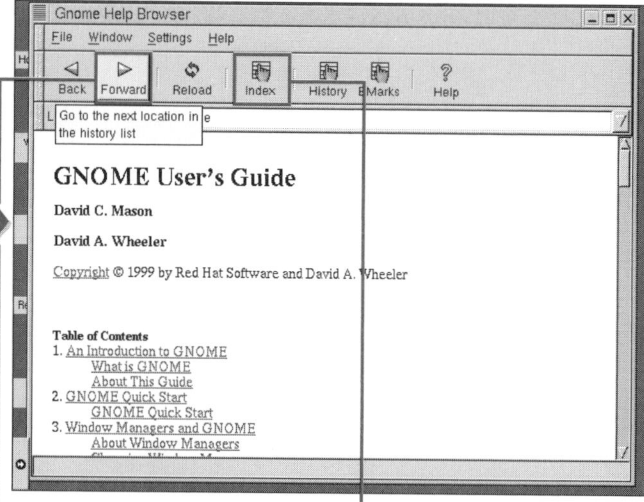

5 Click the Forward button on the GNOME Help browser toolbar to go forward a screen in the GNOME Help browse.

6 Click the Index button to return to the GNOME Help Index screen.

How are the Info Pages Organized?

- The information in the Info Pages is arranged in alphabetical order. If you first look at the Info Pages and the order doesn't make sense, it's because the alphabetically ordered topics are listed left to right, not top to bottom. This is a common spot for confusion because the Info pages appear to be organized into columns at first glance.

What is the Reload button used for?

- The Help Browser duplicates the functions of a Web browser's window. This includes having a Reload button. If the information you need is displayed improperly or cut off on the screen, you can click this button and have the screen re-loaded for proper viewing.

Can I print Help Topics out on my printer?

- You can't print topics directly to a printer. However, you could try to copy and paste the topic into a word processor.

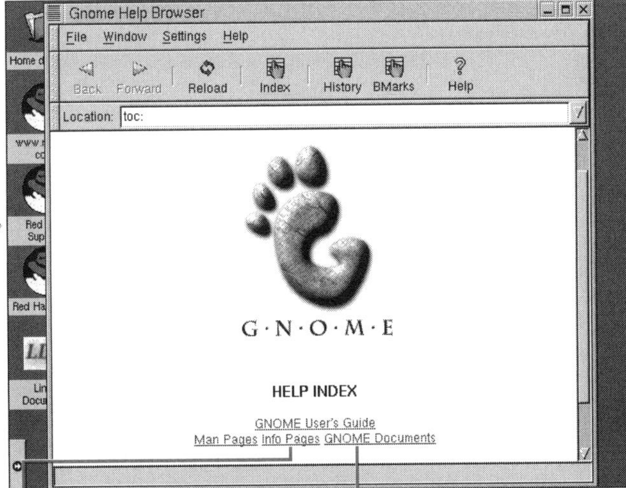

7 Click the Info pages hyperlink for details about specific Linux utilities used with the GNOME environment.

8 Click the GNOME Documents hyperlink.

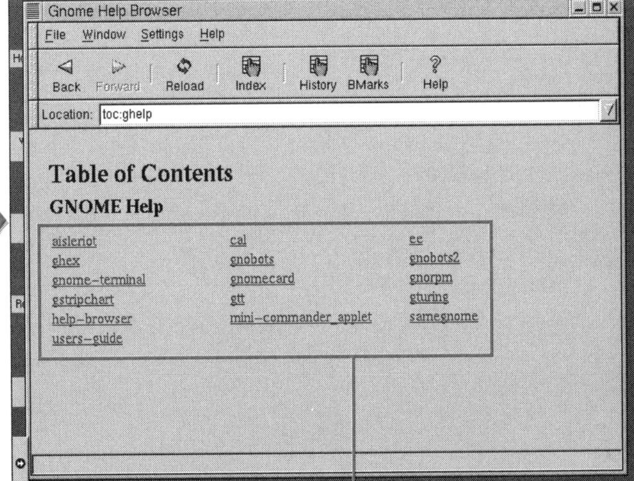

■ The GNOME documentation covers more GNOME environment utilities. Each section is a hyperlink to more information.

CONTINUED

GET HELP IN GNOME CONTINUED

The most extensive and widely available source for Help Topics and general Linux information is the Man pages. Short for Manual, these pages focus on giving you highly technical information. While this may not be as useful to a beginner starting out in Linux, it's very helpful if you want to learn all the possible permutations of a given command or utility.

Man pages also come with another limitation if you are still learning the GNOME environment. Since the man pages pre-date GNOME itself, most of the information in a man page refers to commands or utilities that don't work under GNOME. Instead, you would need to use this information with commands that must be run in the Linux Terminal window.

You can most easily access the man pages from the Help Browser by clicking the Index button and locating the Man Pages hyperlink on the Index page.

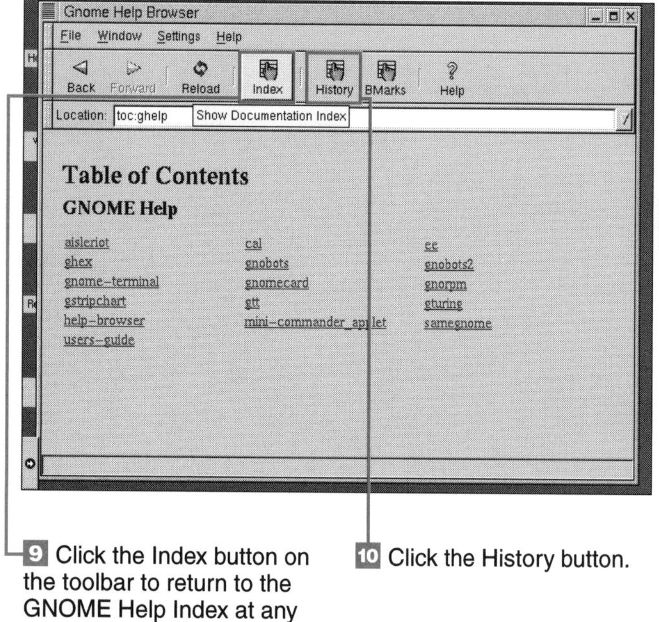

9 Click the Index button on the toolbar to return to the GNOME Help Index at any point.

10 Click the History button.

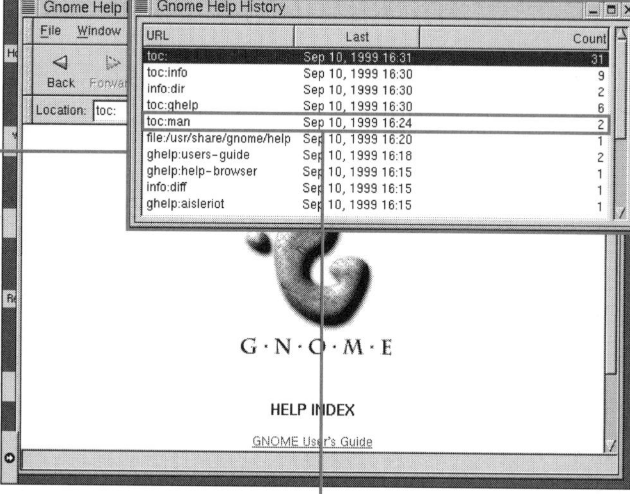

■ The History screen lists the order of each area that you visited in the Help Documentation, along with the date and time of each visit.

■ Double-clicking an entry takes you back to its page of information.

11 Click the Man Pages hyperlink at the bottom of the GNOME Help Index screen.

Where do I go if I need help with the Help Index?

- Click the toolbar button with a question mark on it. This button explains some of the more obscure parts of the GNOME Help Index.

How can I get back to an area of the Help Index I want to visit without going through the History menu?

- If you will revisit an area, choose File and then Add Bookmark. In the future, you can jump back to that bookmarked page by pressing the button on the window toolbar.

Where do I go if I can't find the answer I was looking for?

- Remember that the GNOME Help Index is only part of the help documentation in Linux. The icons on the desktop, such as Linux Documents and Red Hat Support, lead you to the World Wide Web, where you can browse more technical documents.

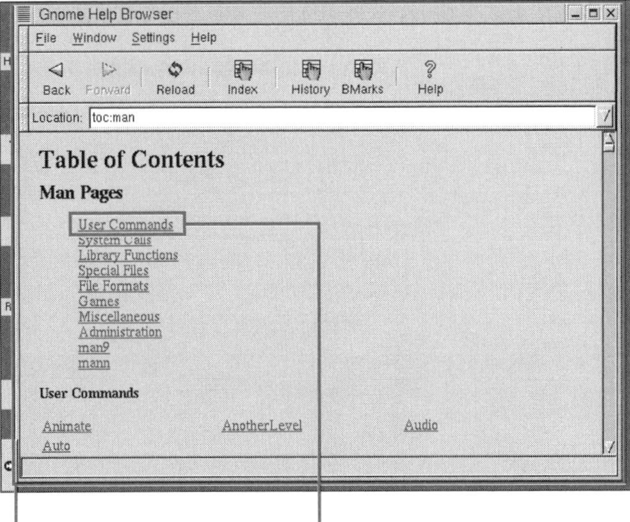

■ The man pages contain information on how to use Linux commands and utilities that work from the command line in a Linux Terminal.

■ The man pages are listed alphabetically within several categories. You will use the User commands most.

12 Click User Commands under the Man Pages listing.

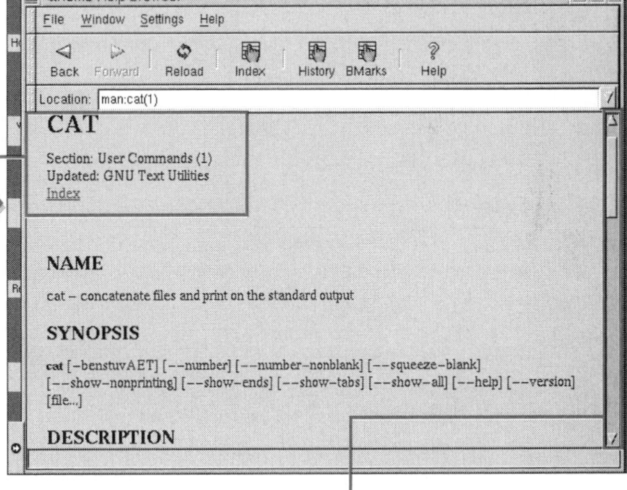

13 Scroll down until you see the `cat` hyperlink and click.

■ Man pages are extensive, so be prepared to use the scroll bar to look for your information.

■ Read the page and all the command options for each command carefully.

CUSTOMIZE YOUR GNOME DESKTOP

You can customize your GNOME desktop to match your own personal style or to set the desktop up with a color scheme that you find pleasing to your eyes. Part of the fun working with a GUI-based system like GNOME is the ability to decorate your work area with color patterns or pictures.

Besides allowing you to express your creative side, being able to manipulate the appearance of your desktop can also help you avoid eyestrain or compensate for a monitor that may not be bright or dark enough.

The most commonly customized feature on the desktop is the desktop background. You can change the color of the desktop background to a completely different one, or you can simply select a different shade of the same color for easier viewing. If you want to try something more complex, you can also grade the color to give your background a three-dimensional effect.

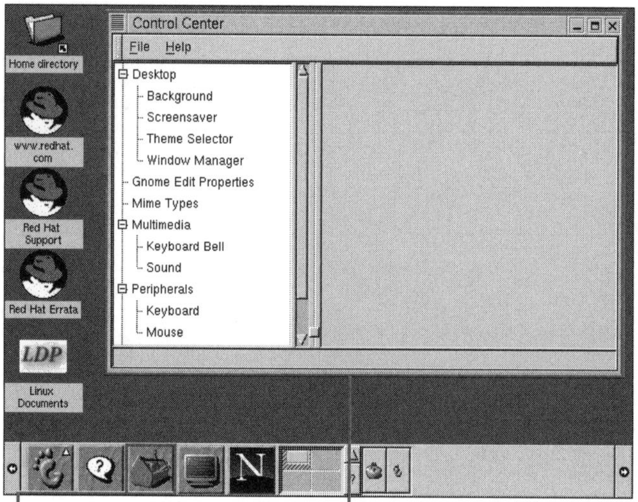

1 Click the GNOME Configuration Tool button.

■ The Control Center window appears.

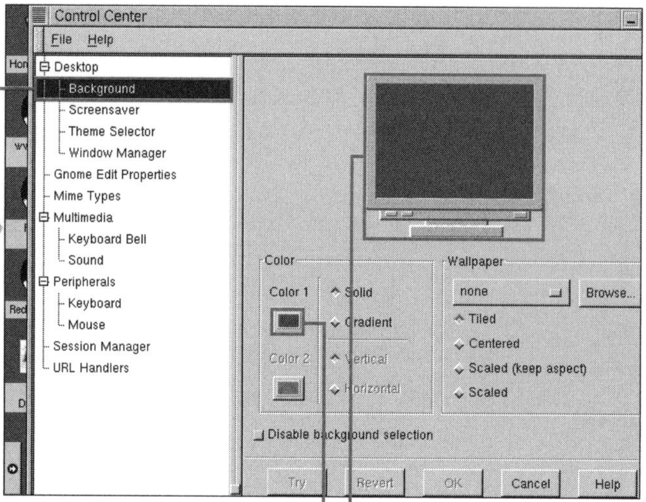

2 Click Background to get the Background options.

■ The graphic of the monitor automatically previews the changes you make before you actually apply them.

3 To change the main color on your desktop, click the small square displaying the color under Color 1.

TIPS

How can I adjust the color on the color wheel if I have a black and white screen?

- While you can't adjust for red versus blue, on a black and white screen you can use the color wheel to adjust the scale and brightness of the gray tones on the screen. The Gradient controls work very well in grayscale.

What do I do if I have no wallpaper in my default wallpaper location?

- You can get patterns from another Linux machine or PC by saving the patterns to a disk. You learn more about using floppies in Linux and GNOME later in Chapter 11.

How can I save pictures off the Internet and use them as wallpaper?

- When you're in Netscape or Internet Explorer, click the File pull-down menu and select Save As. Then, follow the same directions as for placing wallpaper images in the default location.

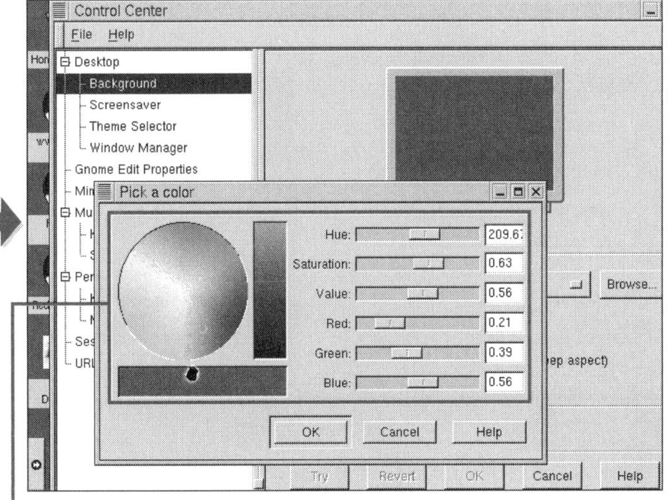

4 On the Pick a Color screen, you can pick a color either by clicking anywhere on the color wheel, or by clicking and dragging the color slide bars to the right of the wheel.

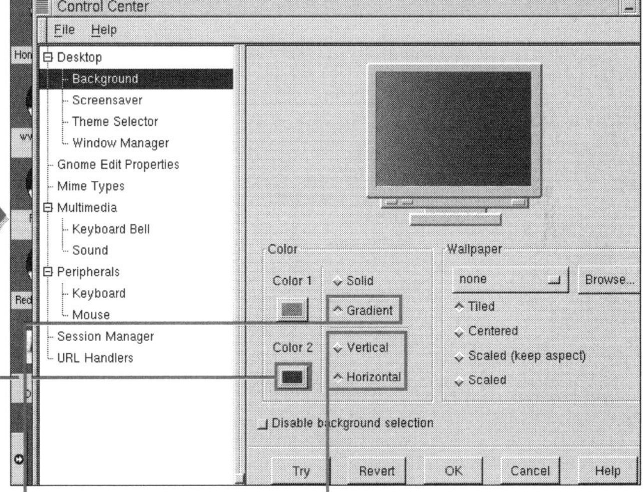

5 Click the Gradient button.

■ Color 1 is blended with the color in the Color 2 square.

6 Click the Color 2 square to select a different color for that square.

7 Use the Pick a Color screen to customize your color.

8 Click the Vertical or Horizontal buttons to determine whether the colors are blended from top to bottom, or right to left.

SELECT BACKGROUND WALLPAPER

You can actually add pictures, shapes, or patterns to your desktop background to provide a more colorful and attractive working environment.

The pictures or shapes you place in the background are called *background wallpaper*, or wallpaper for short. This is because the process of pasting a picture or pattern on your desktop is very similar to hanging up a new pattern of wallpaper in your house or apartment.

Wallpaper, unlike color solids and gradients, does not come standard with most Linux installations because there is such a wide range of monitors with different capabilities on the market. For example, if Red Hat were to include background wallpaper that incorporated a three-dimensional image, older monitors might be unable to draw the figure accurately, leading to desktop distortion, or monitor burnout.

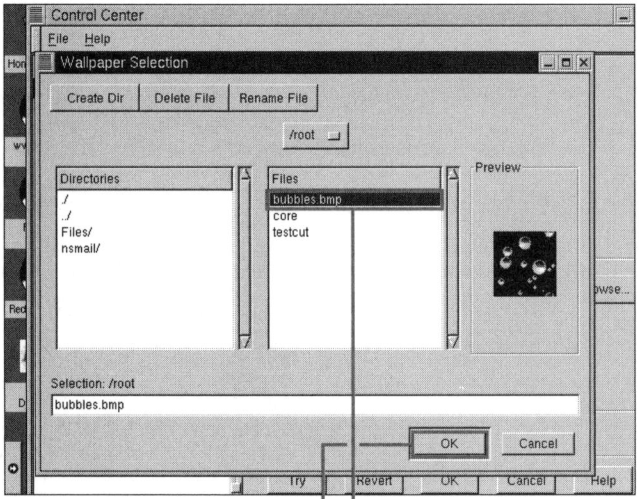

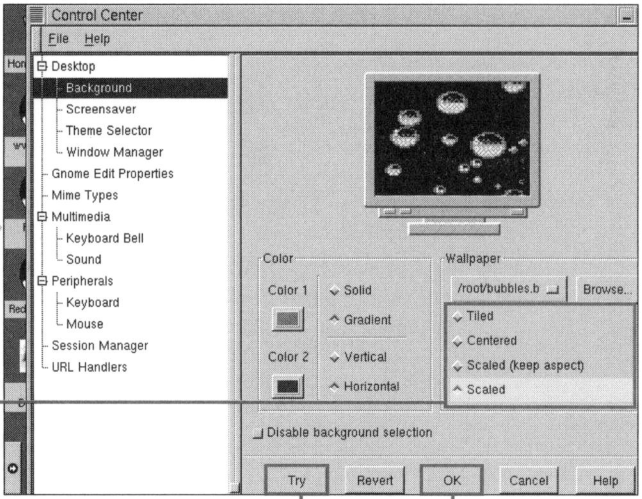

1 Click the Browse button in the Control Center window.

■ The Wallpaper Selection window appears.

2 To import a pattern for wallpaper, click a selection in the Files field.

■ The file name appears in the Selection field.

3 Click the OK button to accept your selection.

4 To select how a pattern displays, click any of the diamond buttons in the Wallpaper area.

■ You can select whether the wallpaper is to be set as tiles, centered on the screen, or scaled.

5 To apply the result to your desktop, click Try.

6 Click OK to accept it.

SET KEYBOARD AND MOUSE PROPERTIES

You can also set your keyboard and mouse properties in the GNOME desktop. This allows you to set up your system's peripherals according to your desires and natural reflexes.

Setting up your keyboard and mouse to repeat strokes or clicks as needed can save you a lot of frustration down the road. Without this ability, you might find yourself hammering repeatedly at the space bar or Enter key to add lines or spaces to a large document, which is fatiguing to you and can prematurely wear out your keyboard.

Luckily, in GNOME the speed that the mouse pointer moves across the screen is highly customizable.

Some people prefer that the mouse pointer move across the entire desktop with a flick of the wrist; others, such as graphic artists, prefer to have much more control and accuracy with each mouse movement. You can even set the all-important mouse to be a left-handed versus right-handed one.

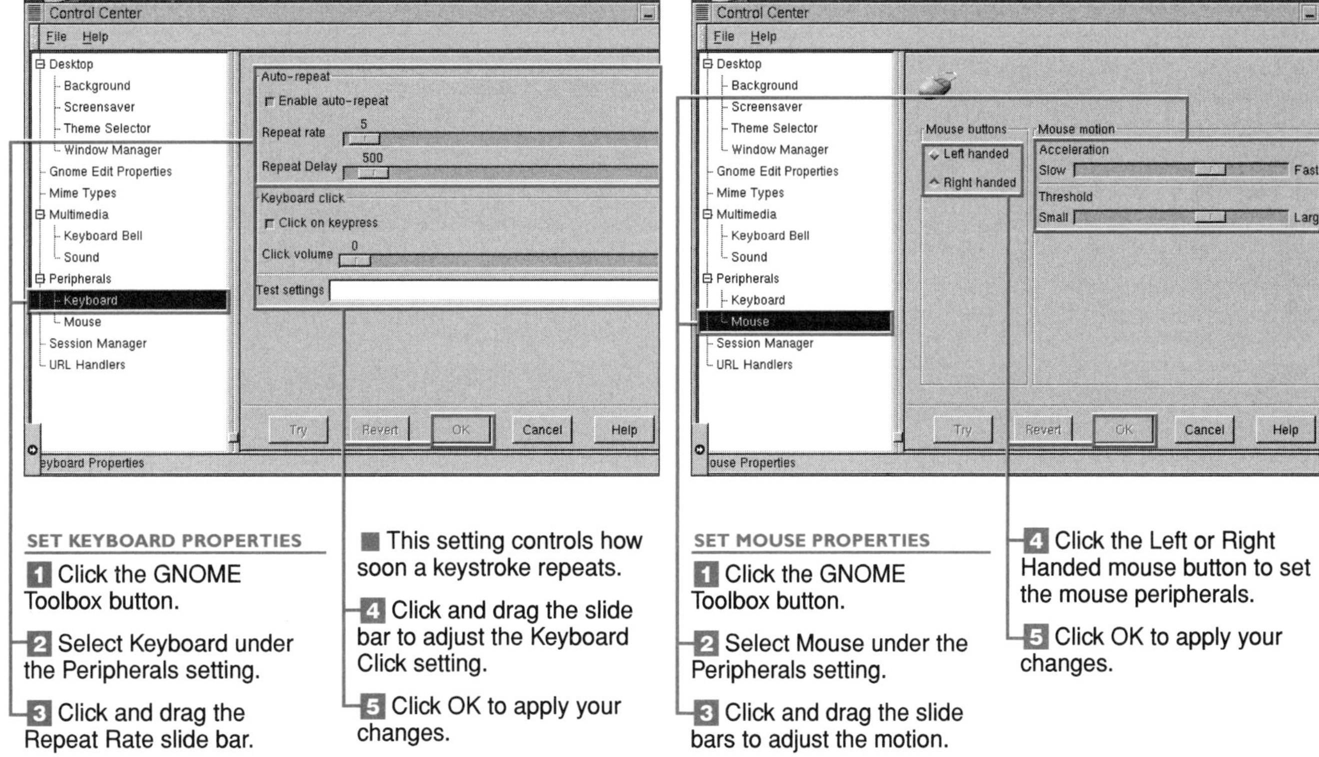

SET KEYBOARD PROPERTIES

1 Click the GNOME Toolbox button.

2 Select Keyboard under the Peripherals setting.

3 Click and drag the Repeat Rate slide bar.

■ This setting controls how soon a keystroke repeats.

4 Click and drag the slide bar to adjust the Keyboard Click setting.

5 Click OK to apply your changes.

SET MOUSE PROPERTIES

1 Click the GNOME Toolbox button.

2 Select Mouse under the Peripherals setting.

3 Click and drag the slide bars to adjust the motion.

4 Click the Left or Right Handed mouse button to set the mouse peripherals.

5 Click OK to apply your changes.

CUSTOMIZE YOUR SCREEN SAVER

Screen savers are programs that automatically start up when your computer is left inactive for a set amount of time. These programs serve several purposes, depending on how you configure them. These programs can prolong the life of your monitor, reduce electricity consumption when you're not using your computer, and even prevent someone from viewing or vandalizing your user account.

The main purpose of a screen saver is to prevent screen *burn-in*. The image on a computer screen is composed of phosphor dots that glow when struck by electrons. If the image doesn't change for a long time, that image can literally get burned into the screen, blurring any new image that is displayed.

A screen saver program is designed to extend the life of your monitor by preventing this burn-in. By displaying a constantly changing pattern, it's impossible for an image to permanently imprint on the screen.

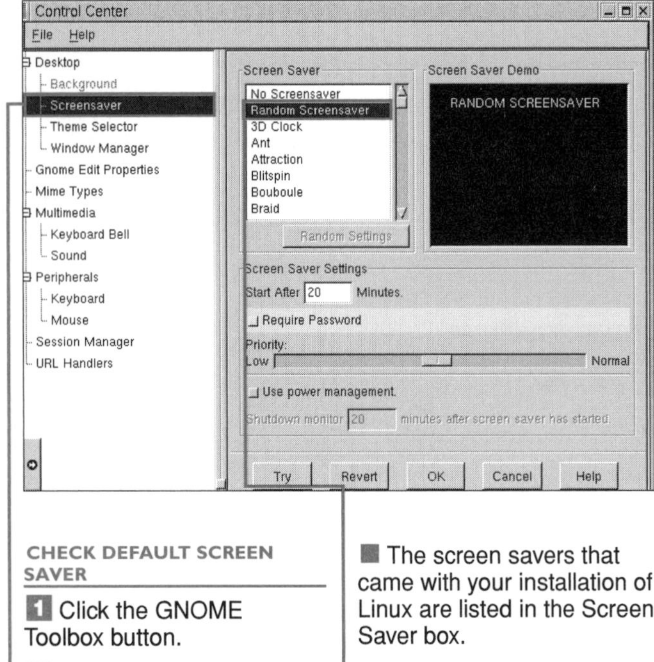

CHECK DEFAULT SCREEN SAVER

1 Click the GNOME Toolbox button.

2 Select Screensaver under Desktop in the Control Center window.

■ The screen savers that came with your installation of Linux are listed in the Screen Saver box.

■ The default setting is usually Random Screensaver.

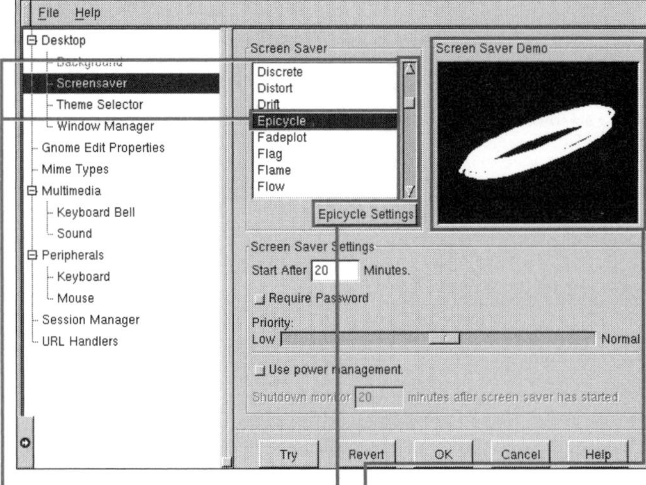

CHANGE SCREEN SAVERS

1 Click and drag the scrollbar to see the entire list of screen savers available.

2 Click the name of a different screen saver from the screen saver list to preview.

■ The Screen Saver Demo area gives you an idea of what the screen saver will look like.

3 Click the Epicycle Settings button to adjust the settings for this particular screen saver.

How can I prevent screen burn-in without the visual distraction of a screen saver?

- If the movement and colors of a screen saver are too distracting for you, then you can select No Screensaver in the Screen Saver selection window. When your computer is left inactive for the given setting time, the screen simply goes blank.

How many screen savers do I have available to use?

- A standard Red Hat Linux installation, such as the one that comes with this book, will generally come with 40–50 different kinds of screen savers. Even the most basic Linux installations come with six or seven generic screen savers.

Who makes Red Hat screen savers?

- Red Hat Linux screen savers are made, like most Linux utilities, by programmers who simply feel the need for a new screen saver utility. Sometimes, a Linux developer will even make his new creation publicly available over the Internet.

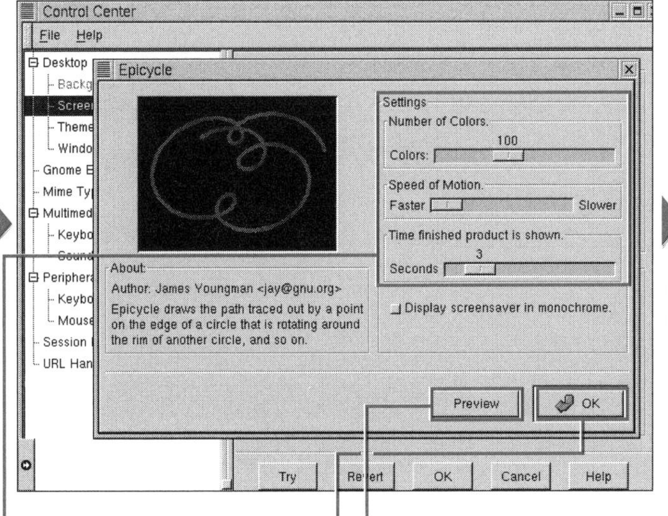

■ The Epicycle window appears.

4 Click and drag the slide bars to change the colors, speed, and duration of the screen image.

5 Click the Preview button to see what the screen saver will look like on your screen.

6 Click OK to return to the Control Center window.

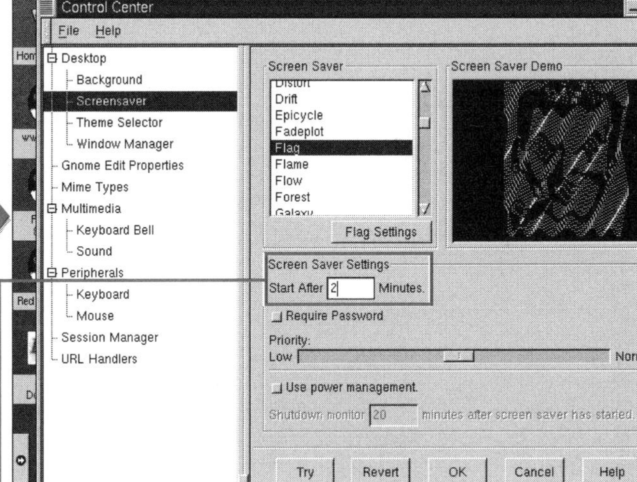

7 To adjust the time it takes to start the Screen Saver, click the Start After Minutes text box.

8 Use the Backspace key to delete the default setting and then type a different setting.

CONTINUED

CUSTOMIZE YOUR SCREEN SAVER
CONTINUED

The additional options that you can specify with your screen saver help you to control access to your computer or to decrease the amount of power that your computer uses.

You can specify that your computer requires a password when you configure your screen saver. Whenever you leave your computer unattended for a given period of time, the screen saver will turn on as usual. The difference now is that whenever you — or anyone else — stop the screen saver by touching the keyboard or the mouse, you have to enter your account name and password. This decreases the chance that someone can view your account information without your permission.

Power Management shuts down the screen saver program and blacks out your screen entirely after a set period of time. This decreases your overall consumption of electricity when you're not using your computer.

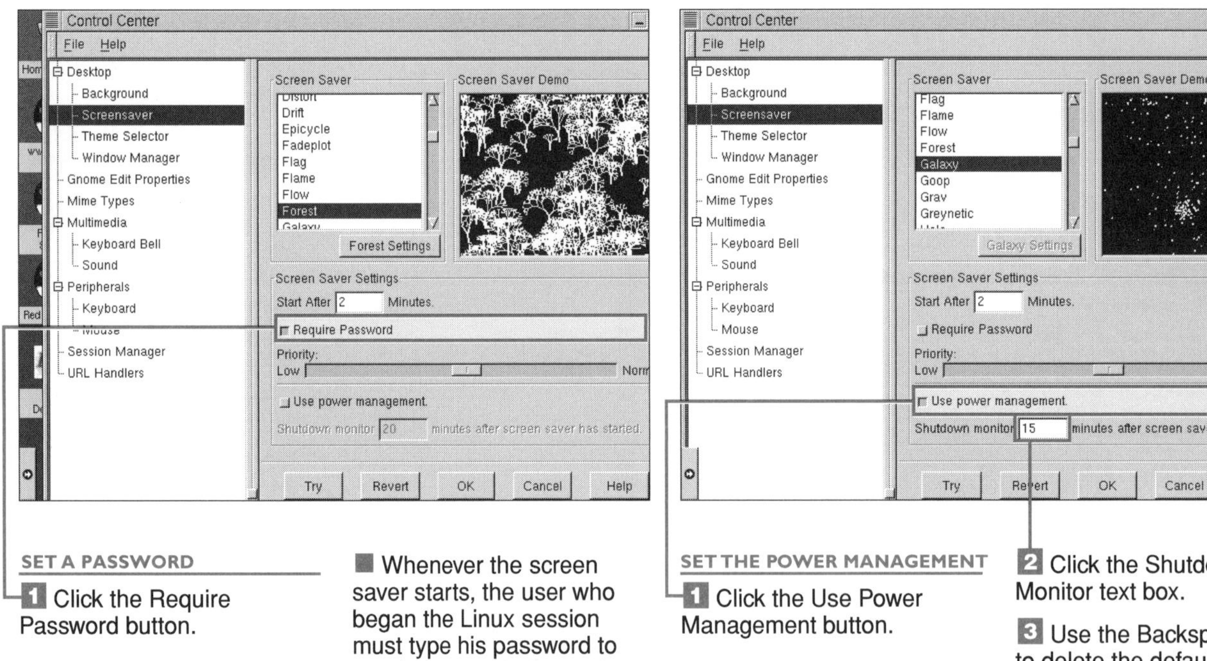

SET A PASSWORD

1 Click the Require Password button.

■ Whenever the screen saver starts, the user who began the Linux session must type his password to regain access to the system.

SET THE POWER MANAGEMENT

1 Click the Use Power Management button.

2 Click the Shutdown Monitor text box.

3 Use the Backspace key to delete the default setting and then type a different number.

Can I select a No Screensaver option?

- Yes, by scrolling down to the No Screensaver setting in the Screen Saver Control Center window.

How can I select No Screensaver and have my computer just power down the monitor?

- Ignoring the screen saver selection and focusing on the Start After and Shutdown Monitor fields can do this. Make sure that the Start After screen saver setting is at least one minute later than the setting for Shutdown Monitor setting. After the monitor is powered down, the screen saver won't start, saving more energy. Note that the hard drive is not shut off, so no data is lost in the Shutdown Monitor mode.

How can I import screen savers from other machines?

- You can import screen savers from other machines the same way you import desktop wallpaper. See the Tips section in the "Customizing Your GNOME Desktop" section.

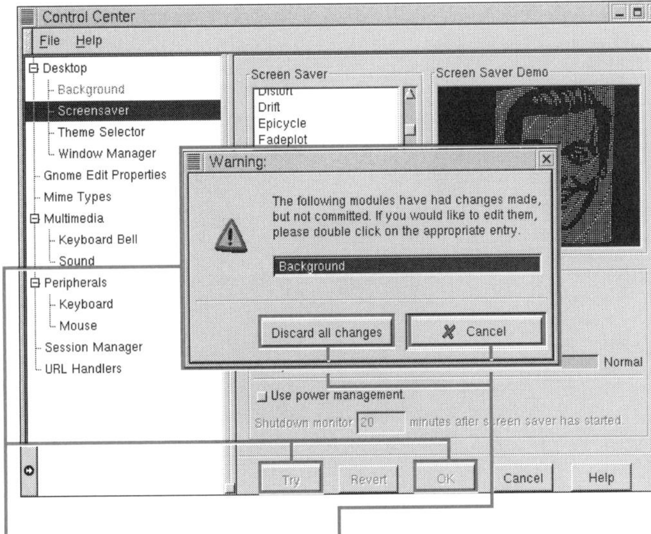

TEST CHANGES

1 Click the Try button.

2 Save the changes by clicking the OK button.

■ If you don't click OK, you get the GNOME Warning screen.

3 Click Discard All Changes to cancel your changes.

4 To keep your changes, click Cancel.

5 Click the OK button before exiting the Control Center.

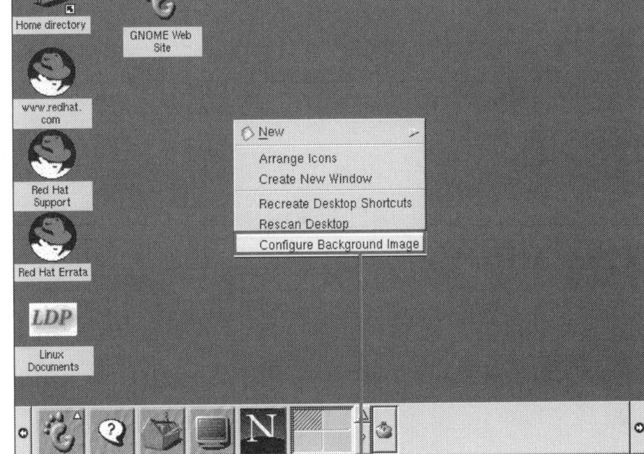

CALL UP BACKGROUND

1 An alternate way to call up background and screen saver settings is to right-click the desktop.

■ A pull-down menu appears.

2 Move the mouse pointer down to the Configure Background Image setting and select it.

■ The GNOME Control Center opens.

SELECT A DESKTOP THEME

A *desktop theme* is a pre-selected configuration of colors and fonts for your desktop environment. Themes offer slightly less control over customizing the GNOME desktop environment, but the colors, window borders, and fonts are coordinated to give the desktop a certain look and feel. Normally, a Red Hat Linux release comes with between 6 and 12 themes that are installed by default with your operating system.

Since desktop themes are so color dependent, you may get limited use out of changing their settings on a monitor with limited color arrangements. Similarly, if you use a black-and-white monitor, you might be limited to schemes that show grayscale well.

Like the wallpaper and screen saver settings, the Control Center allows you to preview what the settings will look like by displaying the result in the lower half of the right Control Center frame.

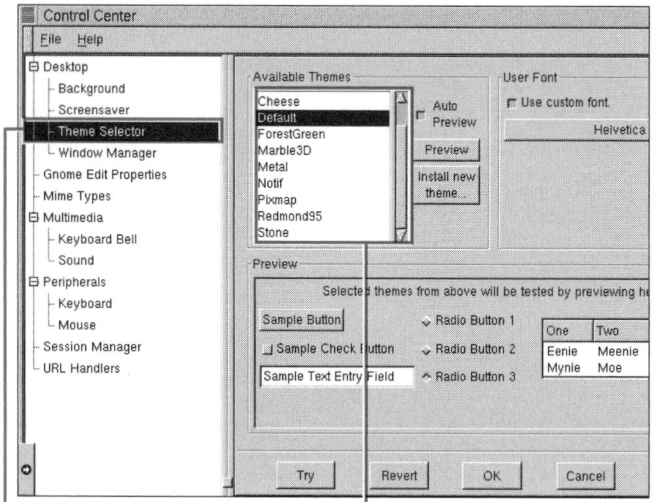

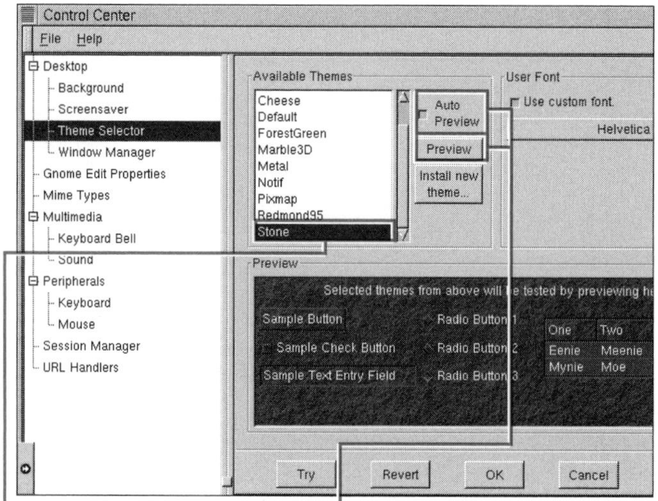

CHECK YOUR THEMES

1 Click the GNOME Toolbox button.

2 Select Theme Selector on the Control Center window.

■ The themes that came with your Linux installation are listed in the Available Themes area. The default setting is listed simply as Default.

CHANGE THEMES

1 Click a different theme, to select it.

2 Click Preview to see what the theme looks like in the Preview window.

3 Click the Auto Preview button if you plan to preview several of the Available Themes.

How can I import a new desktop theme from another computer?

- You can import different themes from other computers by going on the World Wide Web and searching for special themes created by Red Hat Linux users for free distribution.

  Save the theme file on a floppy disk and then import it into the same directory where the other available themes are located. Install the new theme by clicking the Install New Theme button, located directly under the Preview button.

Can I import a new custom font to the Pick a Font window?

- If you load a new font from a floppy disk or off the Internet, make sure that you put the font in the same area that the Pick a Font window pulls the selections from. Bear in mind that computers can be a bit fussy over which fonts they display on the desktop.

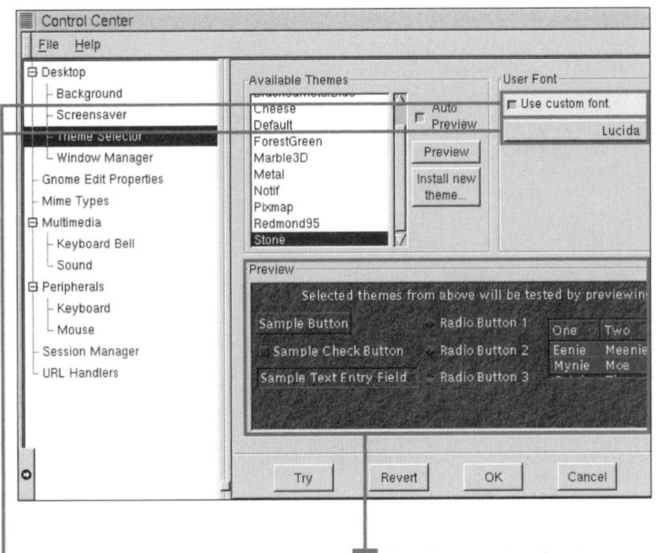

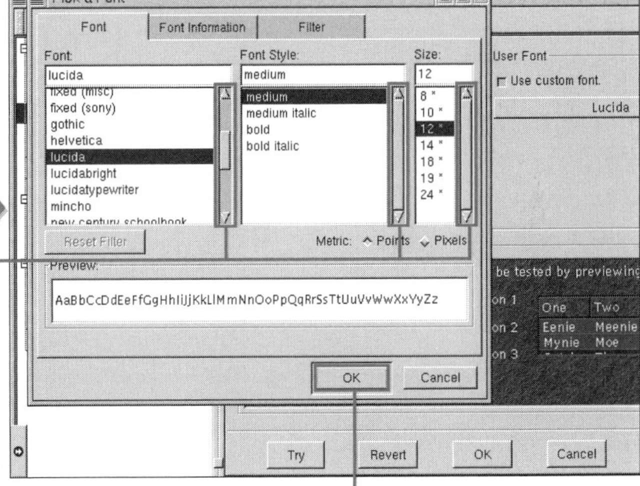

CHANGE FONTS

1 Click the Use Custom Font button in the User Font section.

■ The font in the Preview section changes from the default setting to the font setting.

2 To change the Custom Font, click the Font bar below Use Custom Font to select a new Font.

■ The Pick a Font option box displays.

3 Using the scrollbars in the Font, Font Style, and Size fields, select a new setting.

4 Click OK to accept the new settings.

CONFIGURE GNOME MULTIMEDIA AND PERIPHERAL PROPERTIES

You'll want to get full functionality out of your Linux system, including sound. Although Linux isn't designed as a high-fidelity sound system, it can be easily configured to set up system sounds for alerts and notices. Red Hat Linux, for example, recognizes over 99 percent of all brand-name sound cards. Also, your Linux machine works with any kind of audio speakers you hook up to your computer's audio jack.

Setting up your keyboard bell allows your Linux machine to alert you to a potentially problematic situation if you're typing or composing a document. The keyboard bell is a sound event that will take place if, for example, you accidentally leave something lying on the keyboard that holds down a key for an abnormal length of time. Similarly, sound events are useful to notify you that a given job in Linux is completed — or in error.

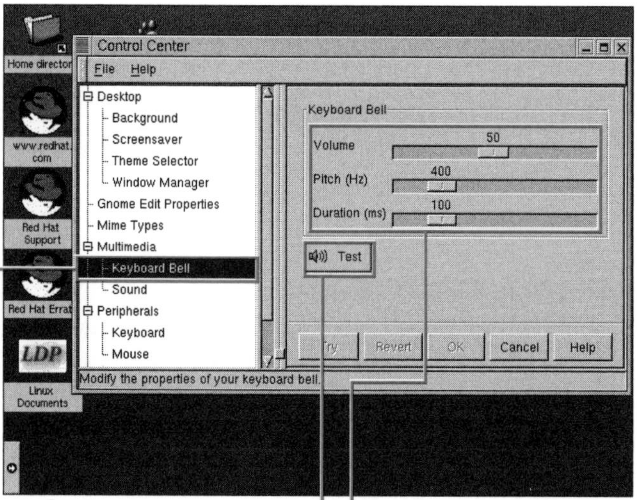

SET KEYBOARD BELL

1 Click the GNOME Toolbox button.

2 Select Keyboard Bell under Multimedia to open the Keyboard Bell screen.

3 Click and drag the Volume, Pitch, and Duration slide bars to set the bell tone.

4 Click the Test button to test your setting.

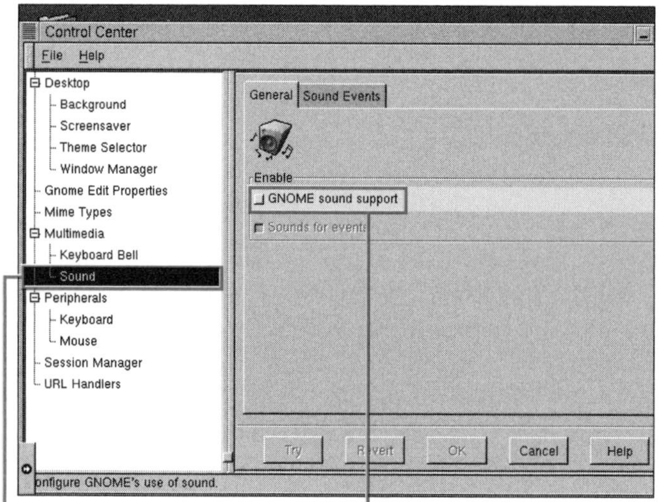

SET THE SOUND

1 Click the GNOME Toolbox button.

2 Select Sound under the Multimedia setting.

3 Click Enable GNOME Sound Support.

■ GNOME automatically selects the proper drivers to work with your sound card.

TIPS

How can I import new sounds to be used on my Linux system?

- You can import different sounds from other computers by saving the theme file on a floppy disk and then importing it into the same directory where the other available themes are located. By default, Linux looks for sounds in `/usr/share/sounds/panel`.

Can I play MP3 files on Linux?

- Not by default. However, you can download free utilities from the Web that will play MP3 files. Check out `www.opensound.com` or any MP3 site that has UNIX programs for running MP3. If it works on UNIX, it will work on Linux.

How can I get sounds on my system to work if Linux doesn't recognize my sound card?

- You might need different drivers for a non-standard sound card. Check out `www.redhat.com` for a list of available solutions and go from there. You can find user-written drivers there for most off-brand cards.

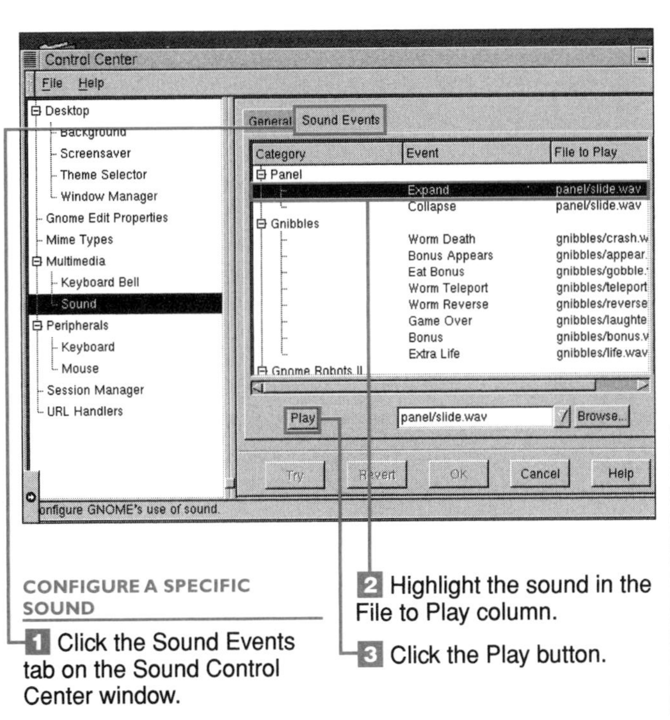

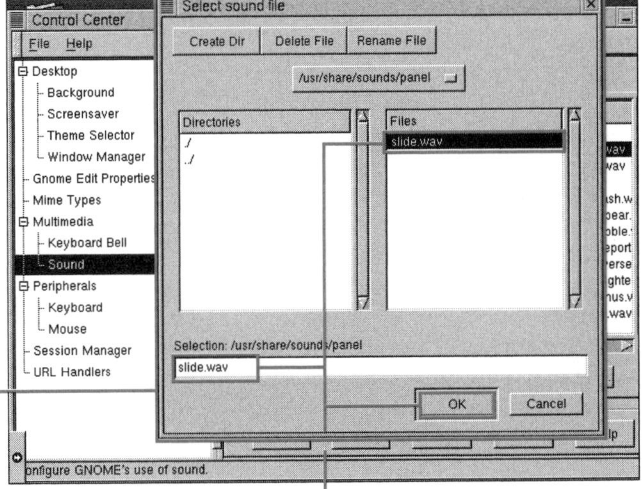

CONFIGURE A SPECIFIC SOUND

1 Click the Sound Events tab on the Sound Control Center window.

■ Sounds are listed by category with events linked to File to Play.

2 Highlight the sound in the File to Play column.

3 Click the Play button.

CHANGE THE SOUND EVENT

1 Click the Browse button in the lower right of the Sound Events screen.

■ The Select Sound File window appears.

2 Select a new sound from the Files list.

■ The selection appears in the field at the bottom of the window.

3 Click OK to apply your selection.

SET UP GNOME MIME TYPES AND THE DEFAULT EDITOR

Mime type refers to how your Linux machine treats files of a certain type. GNOME classifies most files by the type of extension the file has. A file ending in **txt** is treated as a text file, so a word processor is automatically selected to display it. In contrast, a file ending in **bin** will be treated as a binary file and be set to execute itself if selected.

While you won't be configuring the Mime settings too often, you should be familiar with the Settings tool in case you have to add a new file extension for GNOME to handle, such as an MP3 sound file.

You should also familiarize yourself with GNOME's editor choices. When a file is brought up for editing in a Linux terminal, GNOME determines what the default editor will be. It's also helpful to know what other editors you have on tap.

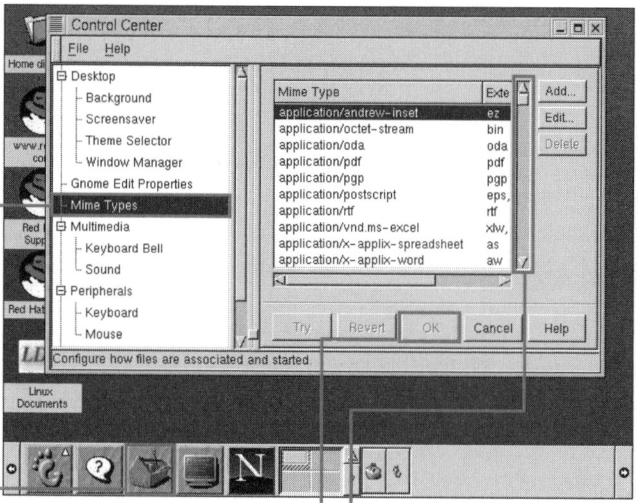

SET MIME PROPERTIES

1. Click the GNOME Toolbox button.
2. Select Mime Types in the Control Center window.
3. Use the scrollbars in the right frame to view the different Mime types.
4. Click OK to apply your changes.

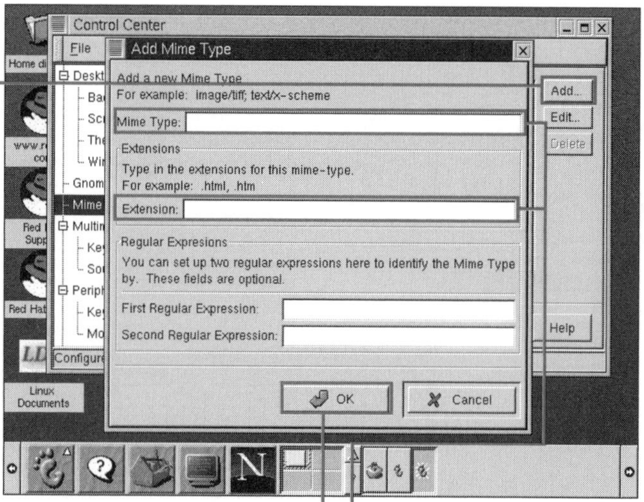

ADD A FILE EXTENSION

1. Click the Add button on the right of the Mime Type screen.

■ The Add MIME Type screen appears.

2. Type the Mime Type and the Extension associated with the file in the first two open fields.
3. Click OK to apply your changes.

How often will I need to add a new Mime type?

- Hardly ever. With the possible exception of the new MP3 files, you shouldn't have to add a bunch of file extensions to work with the vast majority of Linux material. Your GNOME desktop comes with an extensive list of file types it knows how to draw on and use.

Which default editor should I be using?

- Your best bets are to stick with `vi` or emacs, with `vi` being the better of the two.

What are the benefits to running either `vi` or emacs?

- The `vi` editor and the emacs editor are the most widespread of the editors in the Linux/UNIX world. They're used not only to create documents but also to create code and scripts for running your Linux world. Emacs has fallen by the wayside on some new releases, but you'll find `vi` on all Linux systems.

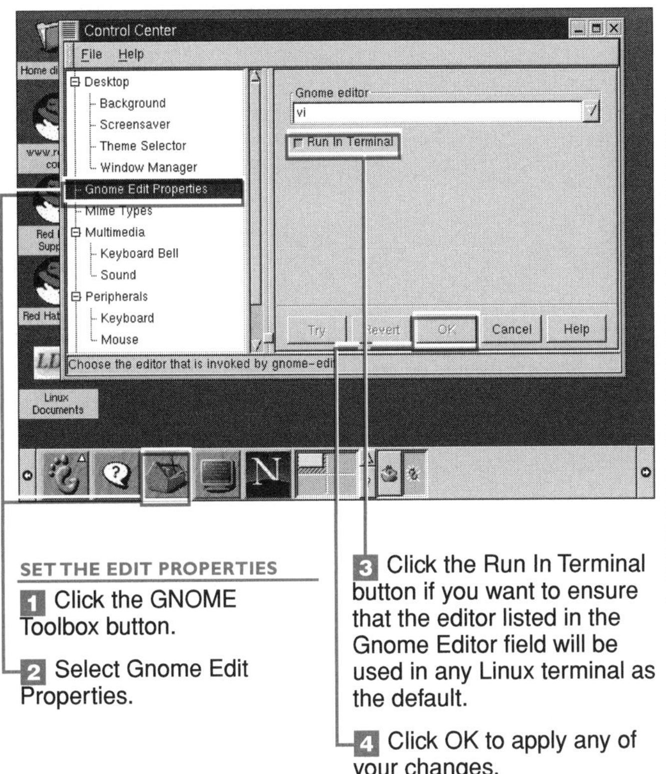

SET THE EDIT PROPERTIES

1 Click the GNOME Toolbox button.

2 Select Gnome Edit Properties.

3 Click the Run In Terminal button if you want to ensure that the editor listed in the Gnome Editor field will be used in any Linux terminal as the default.

4 Click OK to apply any of your changes.

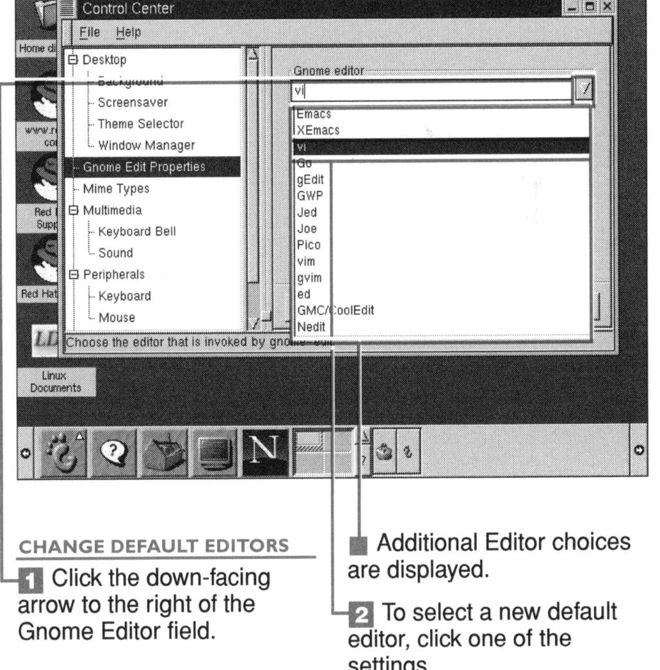

CHANGE DEFAULT EDITORS

1 Click the down-facing arrow to the right of the Gnome Editor field.

■ Additional Editor choices are displayed.

2 To select a new default editor, click one of the settings.

EXPLORE THE GNOME FILE MANAGER

You will spend the vast majority of your time in Linux moving around the file structure. Whether you're in the GNOME desktop environment or in the Linux terminal itself, this process is the same.

GNOME comes with a File Manager, a special window split into two frames. The left frame gives you a tree structure visualization, or tree view, of your directories. If you come from the Microsoft NT world, this should look like the view in Microsoft Explorer.

The right frame is called the directory view or directory frame. This frame displays the contents of the directory you're currently in. By default, the contents are displayed using small icons, much like you would see on a computer running Windows 95, 98, or NT.

You learn about the basic architecture of the Linux file system later in this chapter. But, you should familiarize yourself with the parts of the GUI-based file managing system first.

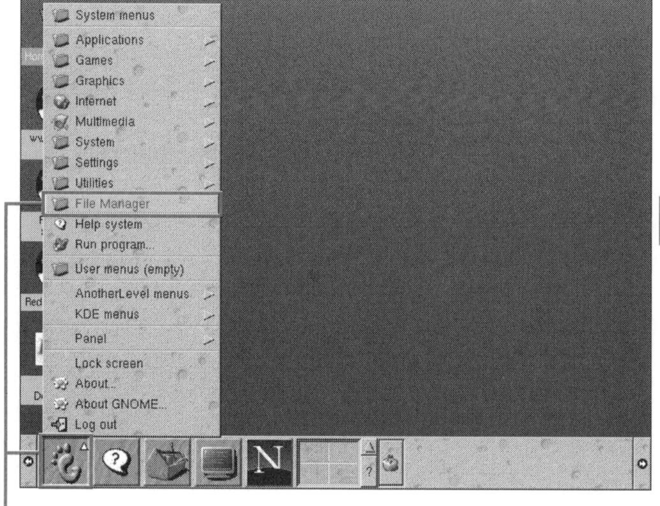

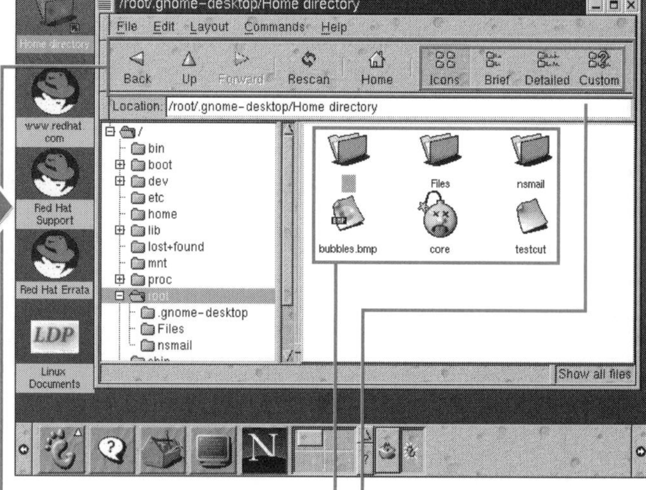

OPEN THE GNOME FILE MANAGER

1 Click the Main Application Menu button.

2 Select File Manager from the drop-down menu.

■ Alternatively, you can just double-click the Home Directory icon in the upper left.

■ Click the Main Application Menu button and then select File Manager.

■ The open File Manager window has arrow buttons on the top toolbar, resembling buttons found in a Web browser.

■ The Icons, Brief, Detailed, and Custom buttons are designed to alter the right-hand, or display frame.

■ In this display view are three directories, which look like half-opened folders, and three individual files.

What other information can I make use of from the File Properties window?

✔ It depends on what your needs are. However, a very useful piece of information in this window is the FileType field. If you're having trouble opening a given file, this field may offer you a clue as to whether you should use a word processing program or a graphics program to open it.

In the File Properties window, there is a field called Last Accessed On. The date the file was last accessed was on a day that I didn't log in. How is this possible?

✔ The Last Accessed On field does not log who last tried to open or edit the file. If someone else uses your machine, or your machine sits on a network, anyone could have opened or edited your file depending on the permissions that you've given it.

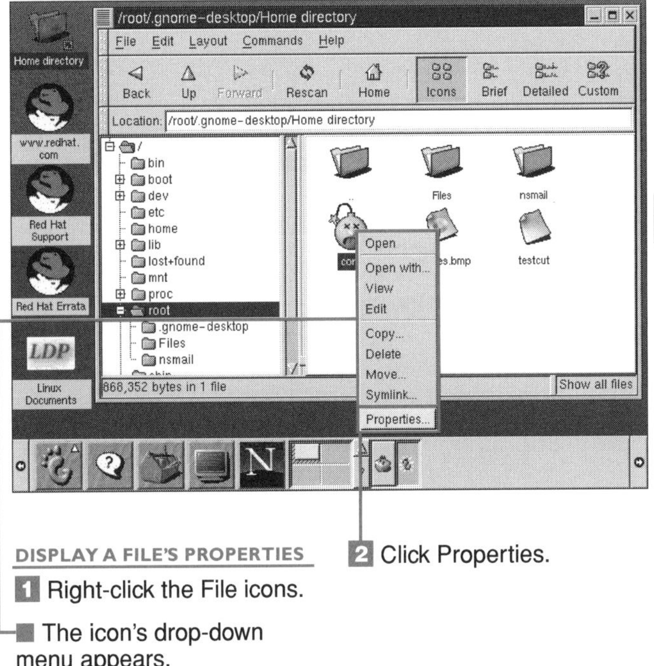

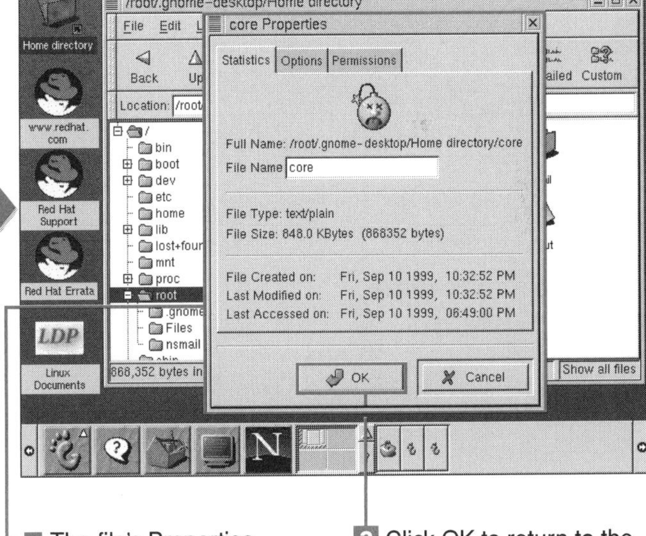

DISPLAY A FILE'S PROPERTIES

1 Right-click the File icons.

■ The icon's drop-down menu appears.

2 Click Properties.

■ The file's Properties window appears with statistics on the file.

3 Click OK to return to the File Manager window.

CONTINUED

EXPLORE THE GNOME FILE MANAGER
CONTINUED

The GNOME File Manager is also able to provide different methods of displaying the files listed in the File Manager window. Similar in function to the display options available in Windows 95, 98, and NT 4.0, the File Manager can display files either by a series of small pictures (icons) or by a text listing.

Displaying files as icons in your File Manager window are the most aesthetically pleasing, but it takes up a lot of space in the window. If you have more than five or six items displayed, you'll have to use the window scroll bars to view all of the files.

In comparison, listing files in a simple text format is more efficient. You can have the File Manager list the items with only their names displayed, or you can require that GNOME list your files with more details, such as file size.

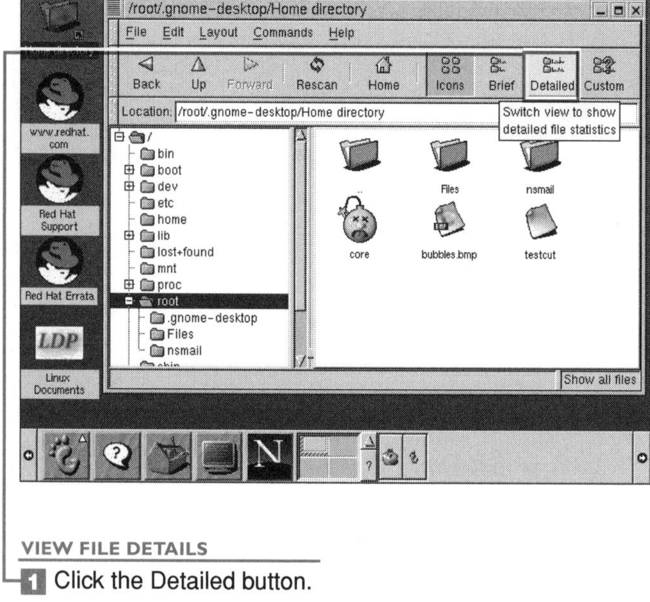

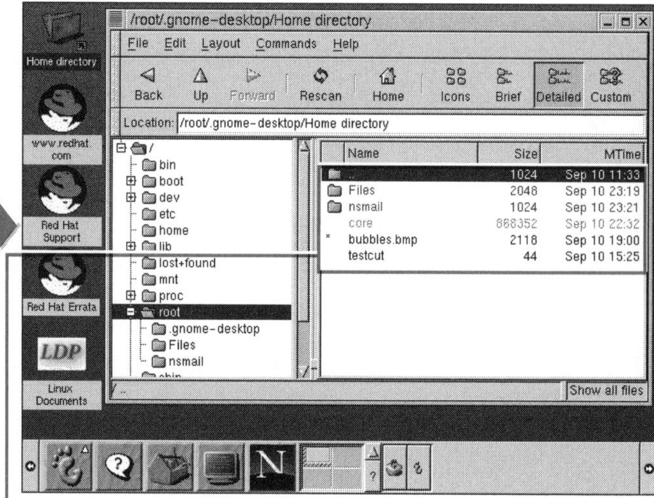

VIEW FILE DETAILS

1. Click the Detailed button.

■ A detailed view of your files appear in the right pane, featuring the filename, file size, and time of creation (MTime).

■ Directories are listed first and then individual files, regardless of the sorting order you select.

Which display style should I use in the File Managers display frame?

✓ That depends on what your needs are. The Icon mode is the friendliest, but when you have a large number of files, the Brief, or Detailed list style is more efficient.

Because no scroll bar is on the right-hand display frame, how can I view any files that don't fit in the frame view?

✓ The GNOME File Manager is intelligent enough to put a scroll bar into place when the number of files in either frame exceeds the amount of viewable space. Scroll bar placement is completely automatic.

What is the significance of the bomb shape of the core file in the File Manager window?

✓ For future reference, you should know that any file called `core` is a mass of gibberish, thrown off when an application dies or is improperly shut down. If you start seeing `core` files on a regular basis, something on your Linux machine may be broken.

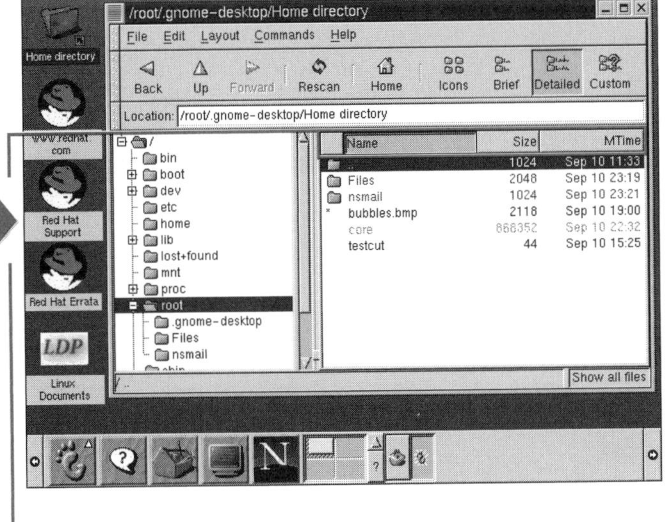

2 Change the sort order of the files in the display frame by clicking the Name, Size, or MTime bar.

■ Name lists files in alphabetical order. Size lists files by size. MTime lists files in the order they were created.

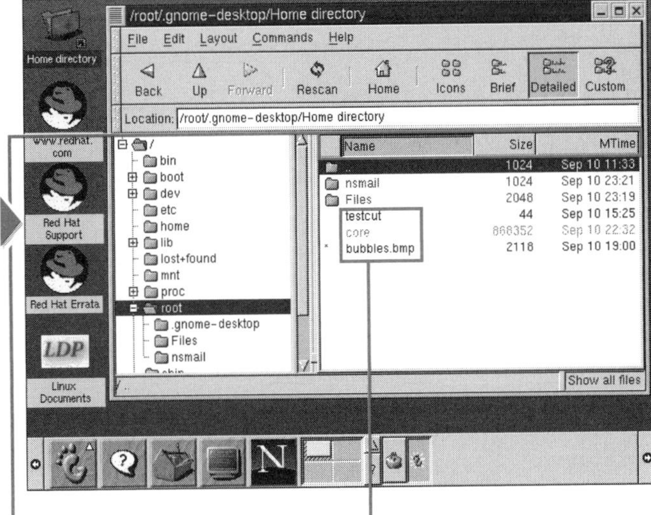

3 Repeat Step 2.

■ The display is now in reverse order.

■ Each of the values on the bar works the same way. Clicking Name once lists the files in alphabetical order. A second click reverses the order.

BROWSE THE LINUX FILE SYSTEM IN GNOME

You can browse through the different directories in the Linux file system once you understand that directories in Linux are organized in a tree structure. When you open a directory, any files or subdirectories inside are displayed as branching out in the GNOME File Manager's left-hand window.

The absolute beginning to the tree-shaped structure of the Linux file system is, appropriately enough, called the `root` directory. The `root` directory is different than the default Home Directory you see when you log in as the root account.

The root file system instead is a couple of levels higher up in the directory structure, symbolized by the slash sign, `/`. After you display the root file system in your File Manager, you see all the rest of the major system directories, such as `/etc`, `/var`, and `/usr` listed as subdirectories to the `root` directory.

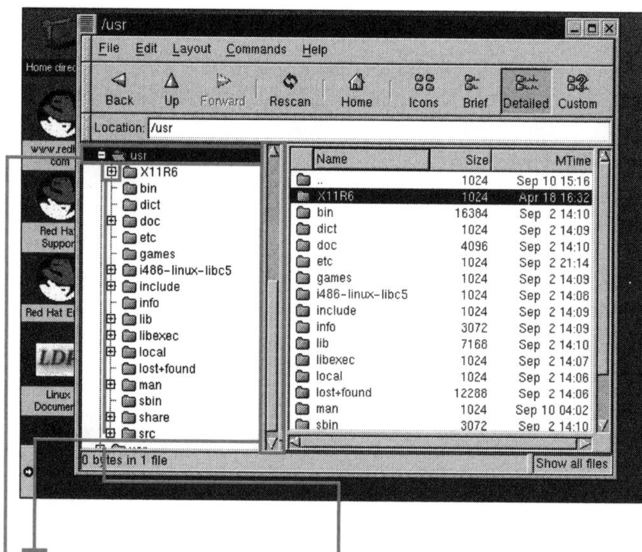

1 To Browse the Linux file system through GNOME, use the scroll bars to scroll through the left pane.

2 Click a directory.

■ While the subdirectories are listed in the right pane, the tree structure does not show the same subdirectories.

■ The tree view of the directory is closed, indicated by the + sign.

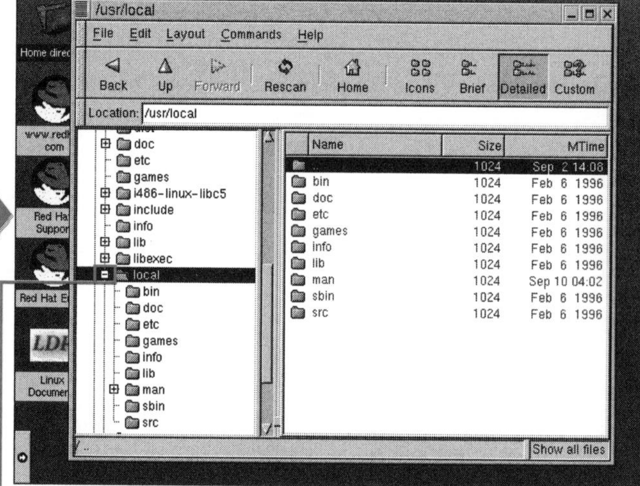

3 Click the + sign next to a directory.

■ The closed setting changes to an open setting (which looks like –).

■ The left frame shows more subdirectories.

TIPS

To which directories will the root account have access?

- The root account is the administrator, so by definition, that account has full access everywhere. Of course, just because you have access doesn't mean you should change everything. In fact, in some areas like `/bin` and `/dev`, you should change things as little as possible to prevent problems with the system.

To which directories will the general user have access?

- This depends on the privileges that you, the root user, grant to everyone else. Usually, user accounts can go anywhere on a Linux system, but they are prevented from making permanent changes to any sensitive areas of the system, such as `/usr` or `/var`.

Which is the best directory in which to store files?

- By default, files are saved to a Home Directory in the `/home` area. You can save files to other locations, but don't store things in the `/tmp` directory. Because that directory is for temporary files, the contents of this directory get dumped and lost every time you reboot the system.

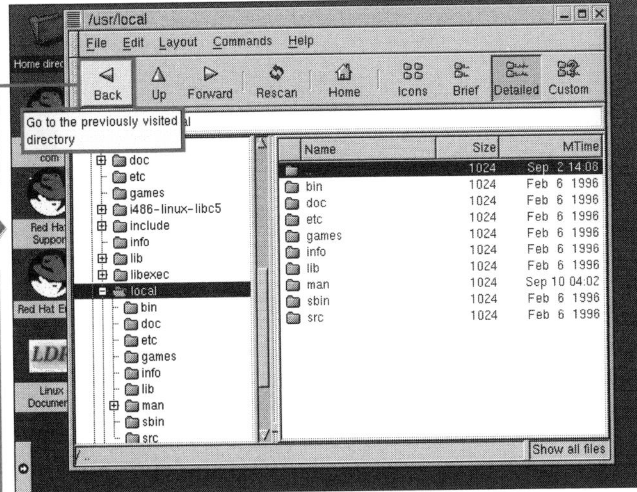

4 Click the Back button in the upper-left corner of the File Manager toolbar.

■ You are returned to the previously selected directory.

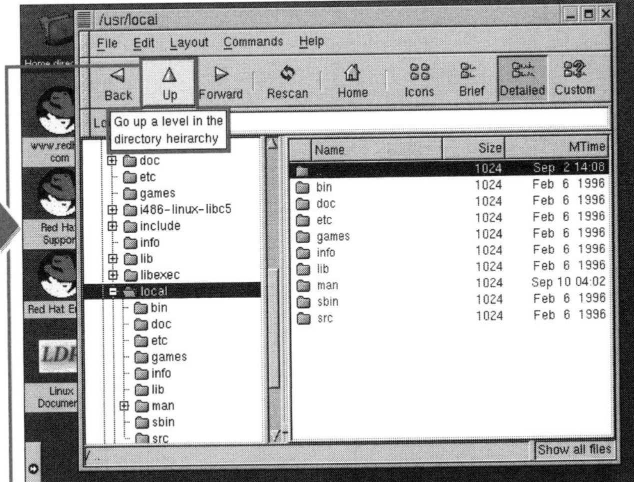

5 Click the Up button on the File Manager toolbar.

■ You go up one directory level.

CHANGE DIRECTORIES IN THE LINUX GNOME ENVIRONMENT

Changing directories to locate and view other directories and files is one of the most common tasks you can perform in Linux. The GNOME desktop environment is similar to Windows 95 or 98 and easy to use. You can use the Web browser style buttons on the toolbar to change directories. However, certain elements, such as the `..` directory icon, are unique to the Linux GNOME desktop environment.

Along the way, you may discover a trick or two on using the GNOME File Manager to keep track of where you are, enabling you to jump back to your starting point at any time without getting lost in the file systems.

For this example, you start off as the root account again, your beginning point is the `/root` directory. Instead of jumping out to the / directory, you can tour some of your personal subdirectories.

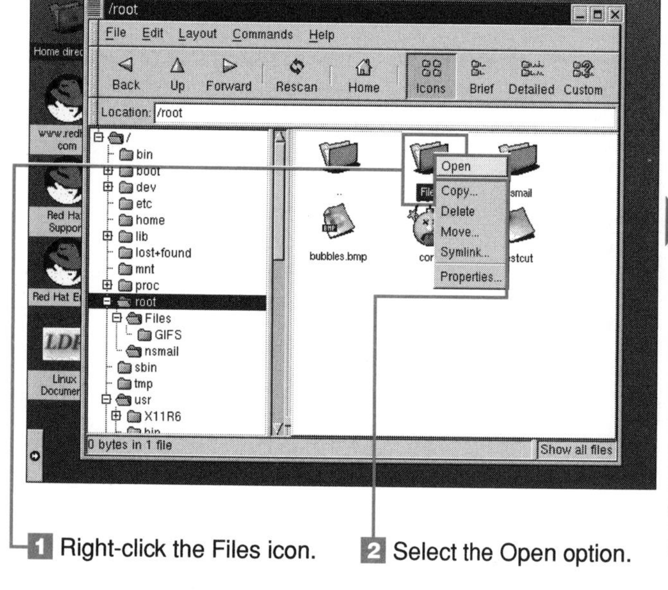

1 Right-click the Files icon.

2 Select the Open option.

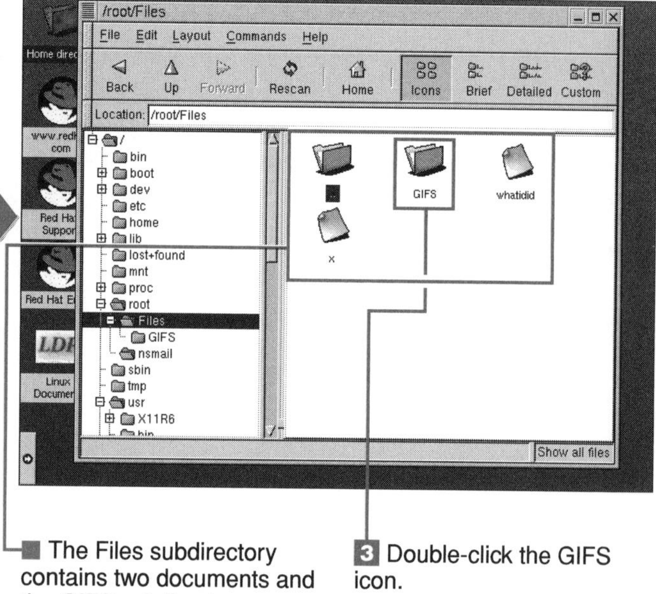

■ The Files subdirectory contains two documents and the GIFS subdirectory.

3 Double-click the GIFS icon.

What can I use the Location text box for?

- Aside from telling you the same information that drag bar does, you can actually change directories in Linux by typing your destination in the text box and pressing Enter. However, this is the way you need to do things in a Linux terminal — so until you need to do this, save yourself some labor and use the mouse.

Why does the .. directory exist when you have the Up button?

- The `..` directory is a holdover from the pre-GUI days of Linux. When you start using the Linux terminal, you see the `..` sign again.

How do I switch all of my directories to a different style of viewing, such as Detailed?

- The GNOME system automatically assumes that, if you're switching the view of your icons to one specific way, you'd like it to be consistent across the board. After you change the viewing method from, say, Icons to Brief, all directory listings you open from that point on will look the same.

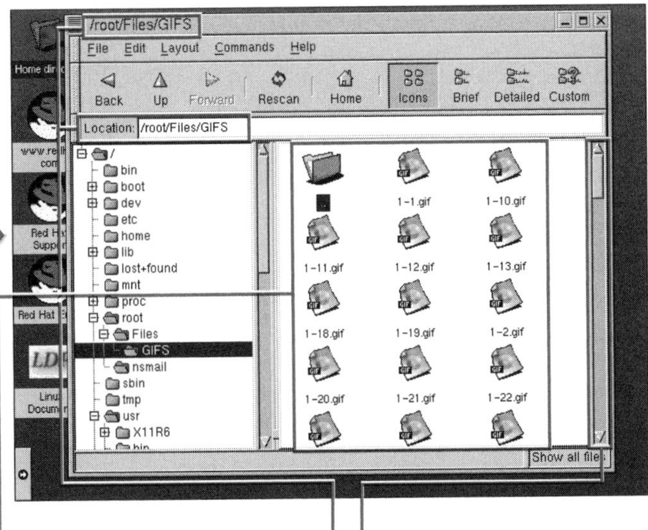

■ The GIFS subdirectory contains a large number of GIF, or graphics files.

4 Use the scroll bars to look at files that are off the screen.

■ Both the drag bar and the Location text box tell you your current location.

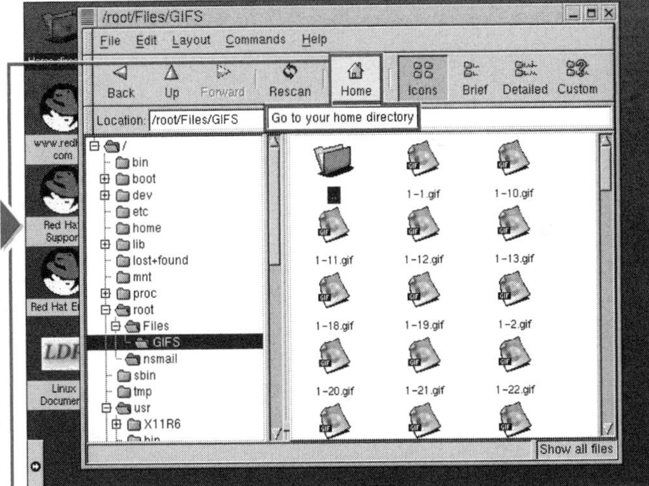

5 Click the Home button.

■ You return to your Home Directory in one step.

FILTER AND FIND FILES

You can list files in Linux in several ways on the desktop. Not only can you list them by name, size, or date of creation, but you can also filter these files in different ways.

Filtering allows you to view files that may otherwise be difficult to find. Filtering is most helpful when you are trying to find a specific type of file, such as a graphics file, when it's buried in a long list of text files.

Also, if you prefer to search for a file by name instead of type, GNOME provides you with the `Find File` command. This command ignores the file type and concentrates on how you've named the file you're searching for.

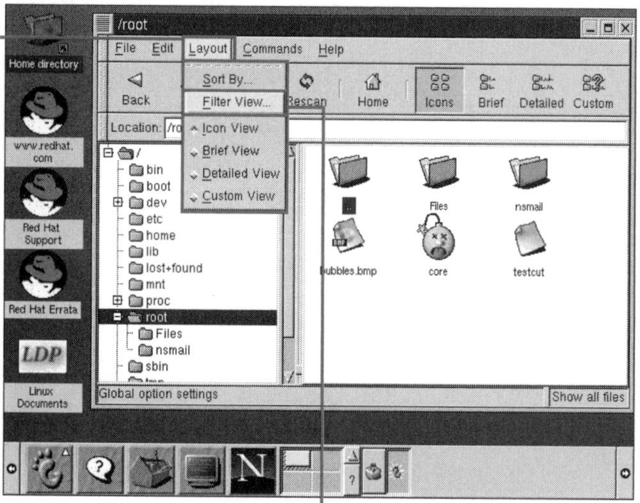

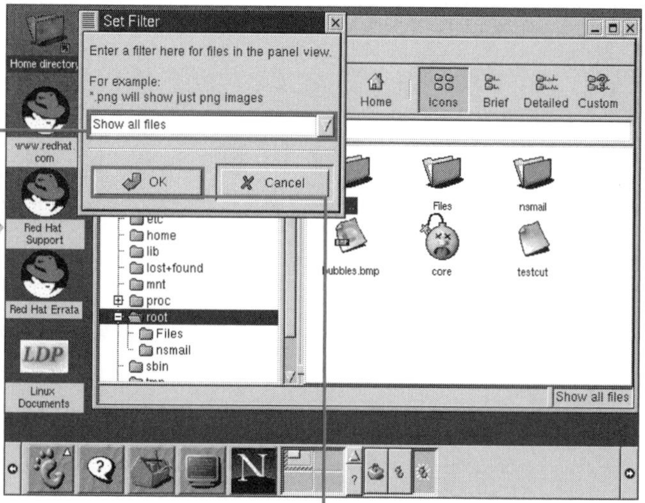

FILTER FILES SEARCH

1 Click Layout.

■ The Layout drop-down menu appears.

2 Click Filter View.

■ The Set Filter screen appears.

3 Click the Show All Files text field.

4 Type a file extension in the field.

5 Click OK to accept your changes.

After I locate the file I was looking for by using the Filtered view, how can I change back to a non-filtered view?

- Click Layout and select Filter View again. Click the downward facing arrow to the right of the text box. A drop-down menu appears, listing the kinds of filters you can use. Select the Show All Files filter by clicking it. The Show All Files filter returns you to the default view, which allows you to see all the files on the system.

How can I do a system-wide search for a file?

- When you open the `Find File` command, type / in the Start At field. Because there is no higher directory than root, you must search the entire file system. However, be warned: This can slow down an older system, so don't perform system-wide searches over the network during peak work periods.

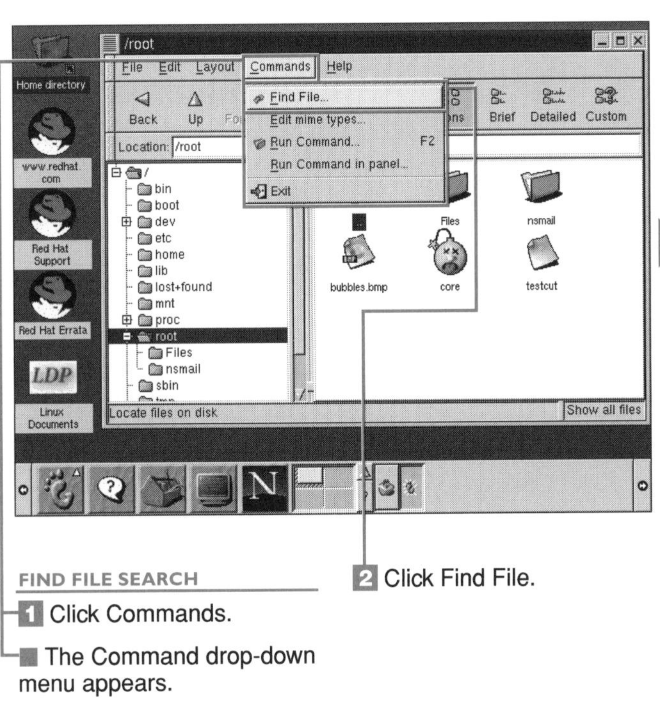

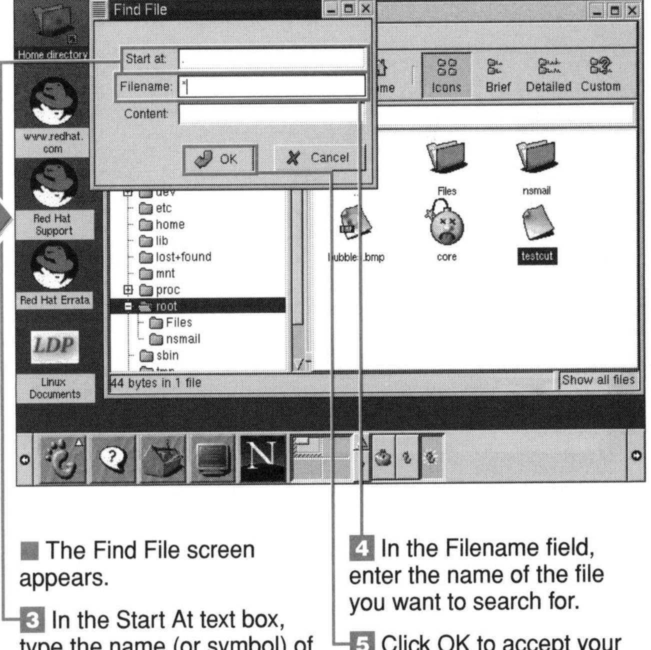

FIND FILE SEARCH

1 Click Commands.

■ The Command drop-down menu appears.

2 Click Find File.

■ The Find File screen appears.

3 In the Start At text box, type the name (or symbol) of the directory where you want to start your search.

4 In the Filename field, enter the name of the file you want to search for.

5 Click OK to accept your information, and Find File is on its way.

DISPLAY HIDDEN FILES

You can specify that your GNOME File Manager displays all the files that are normally kept hidden, or invisible, to the casual observer. The `Preferences` command allows you to display hidden files so that you may view or edit them. However, you should be aware that hidden files are usually made invisible to keep them out of harm's way.

There are several reasons that files are routinely hidden by the Linux system. Often, these files, such as `.cshrc` or `.bashrc`, are control elements of your user environment. Tampering or deleting these files could cause serious damage to your Linux installation.

Files can also be hidden for security purposes; users will sometimes hide files if they contain sensitive information. Finally, many programs that write backup files or log files hide them out of sight to keep the desktop from being too cluttered.

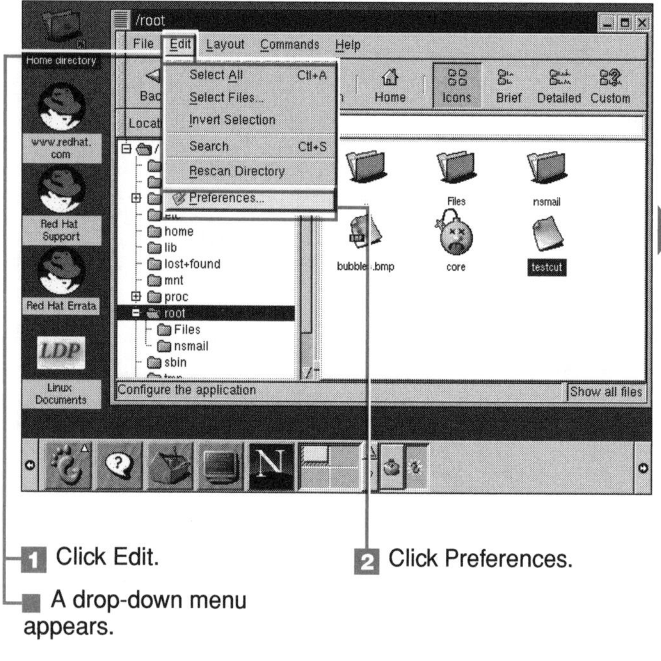

1 Click Edit.

■ A drop-down menu appears.

2 Click Preferences.

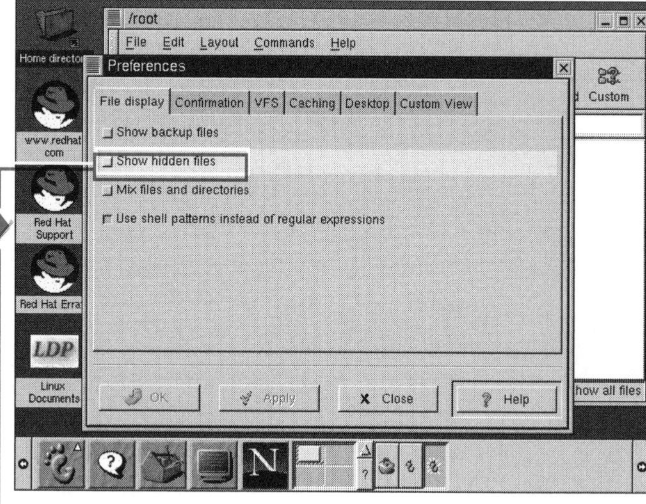

■ The Preferences dialog box appears.

■ By default, the Show Hidden Files button is not depressed, meaning that hidden files are kept hidden.

Note: The OK and Apply buttons are grayed out.

What does the Show Backup Files option in the Preferences screen do?

✔ Selecting this option displays only a certain kind of hidden file; the backup files that are usually created by word processors. Certain word processors such as WordPerfect for Linux have an option to automatically save documents every 15 minutes or so to protect against sudden power failures.

Can I hide a file for simple privacy reasons?

✔ If you add a period to the beginning of the file (changing `mysecret.txt` to `.mysecret.txt`), then the file will be hidden. However, your privacy is better protected if you set the file permissions to allow only *your* account to read the file, rather than trying to just hide the file. You learn about setting file permissions in Chapter 4.

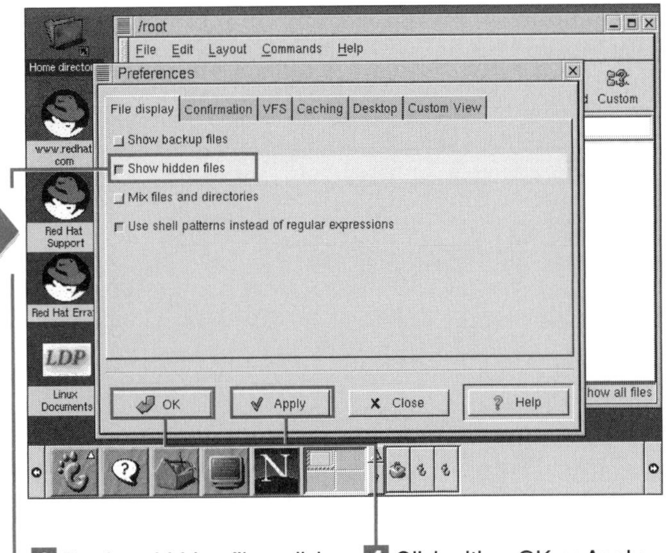

3 To show hidden files, click the Show Hidden Files button.

■ The OK and Apply buttons are now available.

4 Click either OK or Apply for the changes to take place.

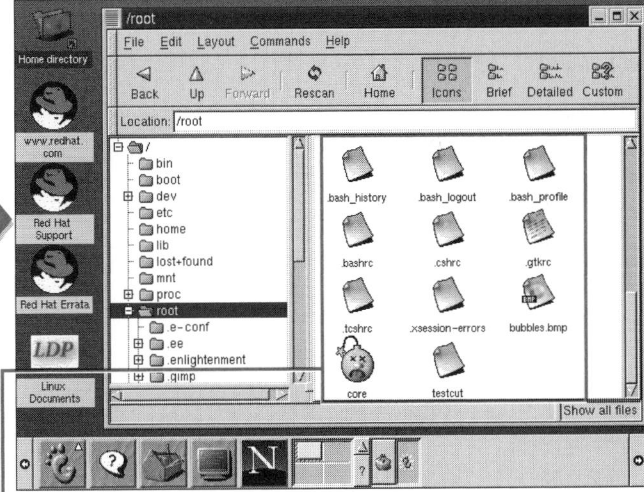

■ The `root` home directory looks considerably different with such a large number of hidden files displayed.

Note: In Linux, all files that start with a period, such as `.cshrc` and `.login`, are automatically hidden from view.

CREATE NEW FILES

Many tasks you perform in Linux allow you — or require you — to create new files or documents. In the GNOME-Linux world, you cannot create new files in the File Manager. The File Manager will allow you to create a new directory to store files by choosing File⇨New and selecting Directory. However, a new file must be the product of a utility or application. You can create new text, graphics, or binary files in Linux depending on the program you're using, though.

For an example of new file creation, open and create a document in the GNOME utility `gnotepad+`. `Gnotepad+` serves a similar purpose to Notepad in the Microsoft World. Just as the vi and emacs editors serve as built-in text editors for the Linux terminals, `gnotepad+` is a standard feature on Linux machines that uses the GNOME desktop environment.

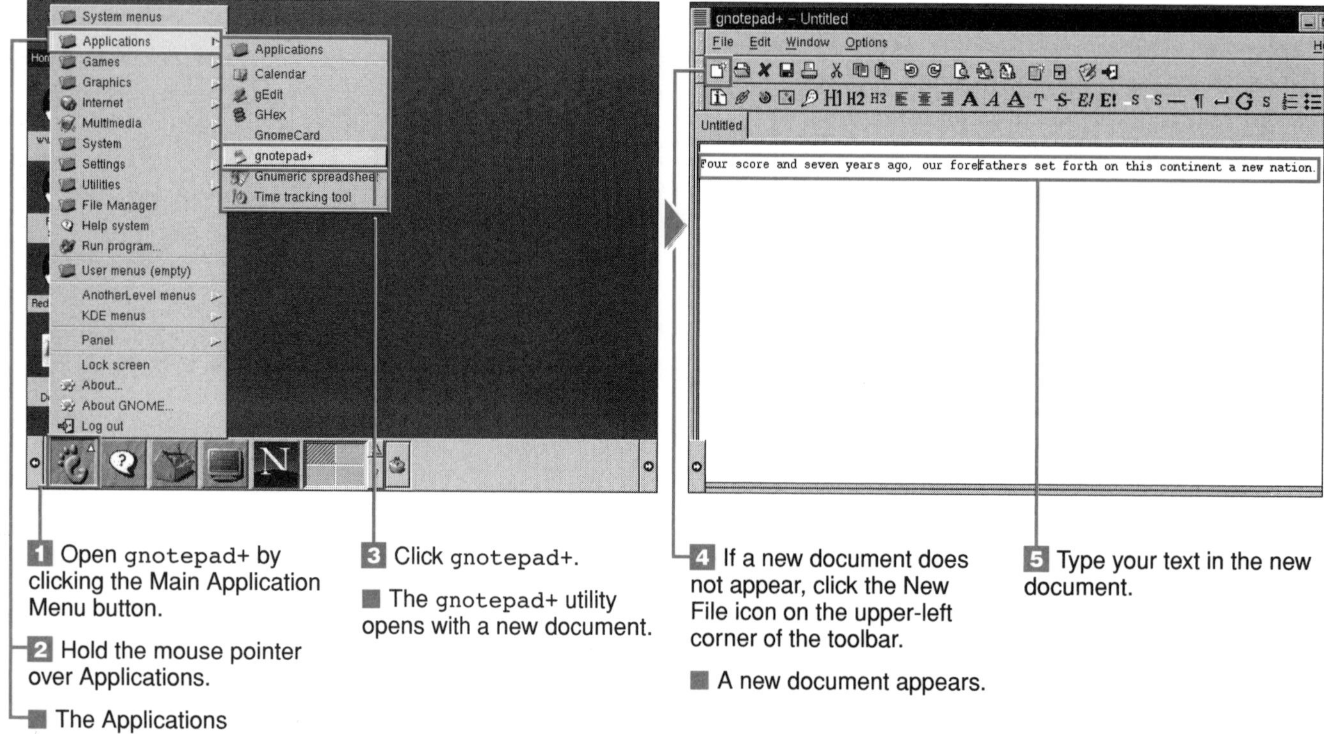

1 Open `gnotepad+` by clicking the Main Application Menu button.

2 Hold the mouse pointer over Applications.

■ The Applications submenu appears.

3 Click `gnotepad+`.

■ The `gnotepad+` utility opens with a new document.

4 If a new document does not appear, click the New File icon on the upper-left corner of the toolbar.

■ A new document appears.

5 Type your text in the new document.

What if I want to save a file to a different location other than my default Home Directory?

- If you want to save your files to a different location, double-click one of the directory options listed in the Directories frame on the left side of the Save As screen. Once you've located the directory you want to save your file in, just click the OK button.

Can I use Save As to save the same document multiple times?

- If you're just saving the file with the same name to preserve changes you've made, you can save yourself some time and simply click the Save icon (which looks like a floppy disk) on the `gnotepad+` toolbar.

How can I save the same document multiple times under a different name?

- In that case, each time you save the file, use Save As to enter a different name — otherwise, you overwrite your original file.

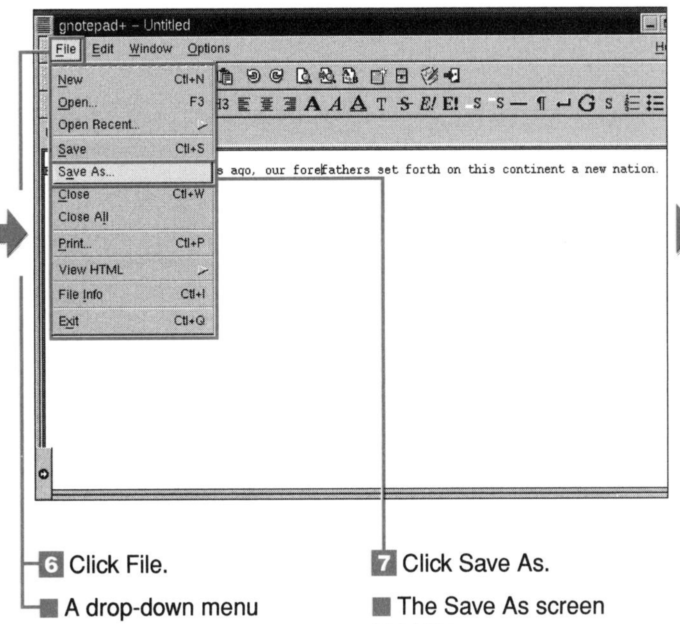

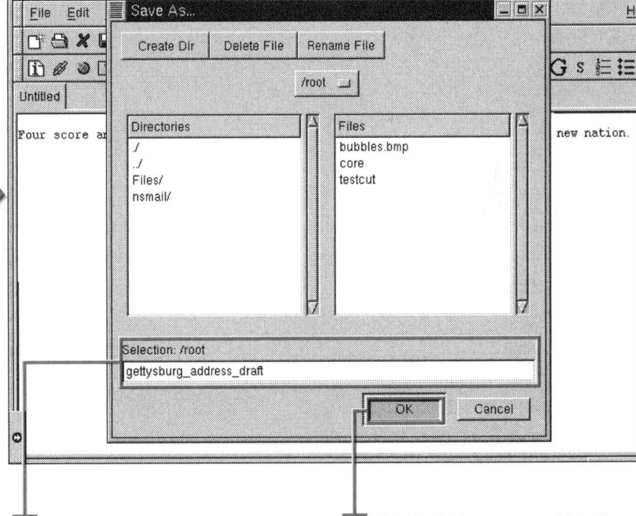

6 Click File.

■ A drop-down menu appears.

7 Click Save As.

■ The Save As screen appears.

8 Type your filename in the open Selection text box.

9 Click OK to save this file.

Note: The default file save location is `/root`, your root account home directory.

CREATE NEW DIRECTORIES

Creating new directories in the Linux GNOME environment is particularly important if you want to keep your desktop and Home Directory organized. Ideally, you should have your directories created and named by category or function. For example, you can label your directories Work, Letters, Games, or Mortgage Stuff.

Directories act as a virtual file cabinet on your desktop. Unlike real-life file cabinets, Linux directories have no limit to the amount of material they can hold (until your hard drive runs out of space), and they can hold more than just sheets of paper. If you wish, you can place sound, graphics, and binary files in your directories.

There are two methods you can use to create a directory in the GNOME desktop environment. First, you can use the New menu command. Alternatively, you can use the Save As menu command. Whichever method you use, the directory created will store files in the same way.

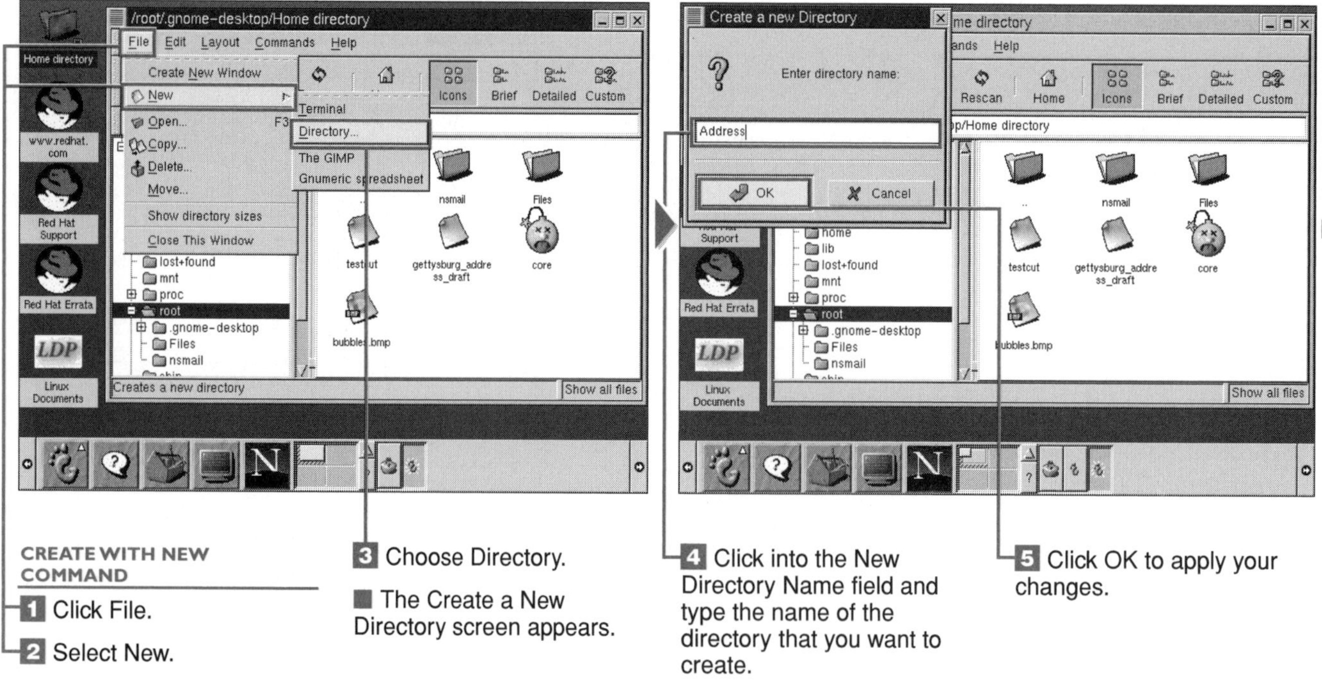

CREATE WITH NEW COMMAND

1 Click File.

2 Select New.

3 Choose Directory.

■ The Create a New Directory screen appears.

4 Click into the New Directory Name field and type the name of the directory that you want to create.

5 Click OK to apply your changes.

What's the difference between a folder and a directory?

- Technically, there is no difference, but traditionally a folder was a directory represented by an icon. In the command-line world of Linux, there are no folders, just directories. To keep with this convention and to avoid confusion, this book calls all directories directories.

What if I want to give my directory a really long filename?

- GNOME doesn't impose character restrictions on directory names, so you can name your directory anything you want—but with the limited space available in the File Manager window, your name will probably be truncated or pushed to another line.

Why can't I see the new directory that I just created?

- If you don't see your new directory, click the Rescan button on the File Manager toolbar, approximately in the center of the window.

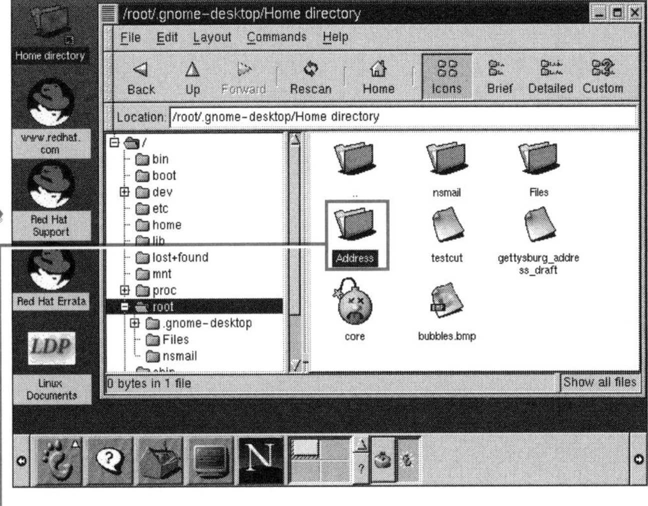

■ A new directory icon appears in the Home Directory.

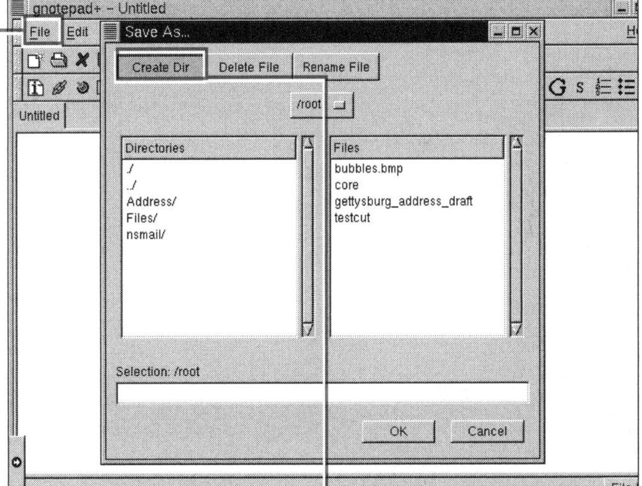

USE THE SAVE AS COMMAND

1 Click File.

■ A drop-down menu appears.

2 Click Save As.

3 In the Save As screen, click the Create Dir button in the upper-left corner.

■ The Create a New Directory screen opens.

Note: You can open this same screen from the File Manager.

COPY AND MOVE FILES OR DIRECTORIES

When you copy a file, you create an exact duplicate of the file in a new location. When you move a file, you effectively create a duplicate of the file in a new location while deleting the original copy in the original location.

Copying and moving files are some of the most important actions in Linux. By learning how to properly move or copy files, you make files more readily available to other users, and make backup copies of important files to prevent a disaster if the system crashes.

An important concept when copying directories is recursiveness. To copy a directory recursively means to copy the directory and all of the files inside of it. When you use the click-and-drag method of copying a directory, the directory is automatically copied recursively.

For this example, you can move a file from the `/root` directory to the Files directory.

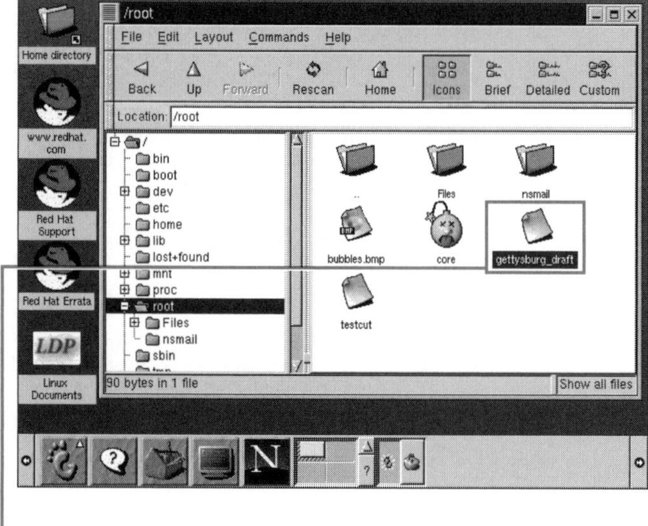

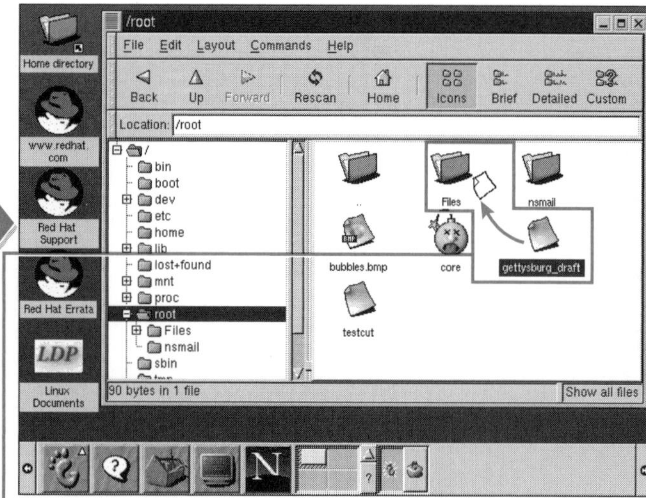

MOVE A DIRECTORY

1 In your Home Directory window, click the file you want to move.

2 Drag the file to the Files directory icon.

Note: When you move a file, the mouse pointer turns into a folded sheet of paper. Make sure you move this folded sheet of paper directly over the new destination directory before releasing the mouse.

How do I copy files using the click-and-drag method?

- If you want to use the click and drag method to copy a file instead of just moving the file from one directory to another, hold the Shift key down while you click and drag. By default, the copying process is recursive.

When I move a file from one directory to another using the click-and-drag method, why does it refuse to stay in its new location?

- There can be several reasons for this. First, the file may not be permissioned to allow you to move or copy it to another location. Second, the location you are copying to may be out of space.

If I try to move a file to a floppy disk and the floppy is full, how can I tell?

- Red Hat Linux displays a dialog box telling you that the disk is full.

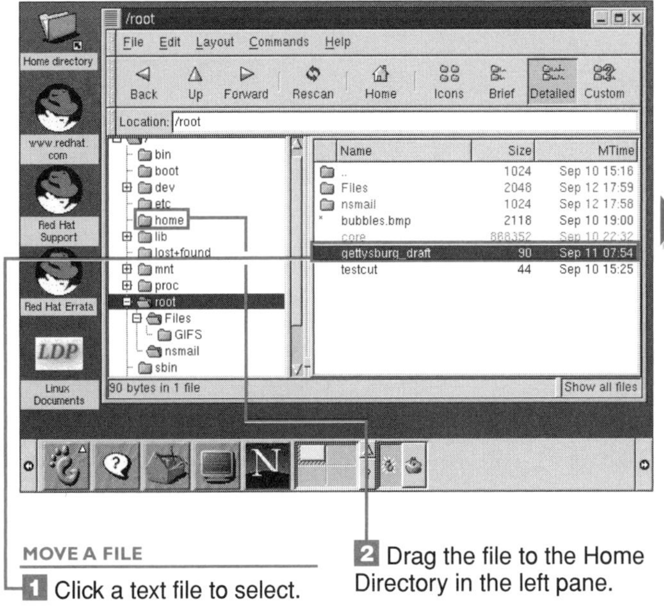

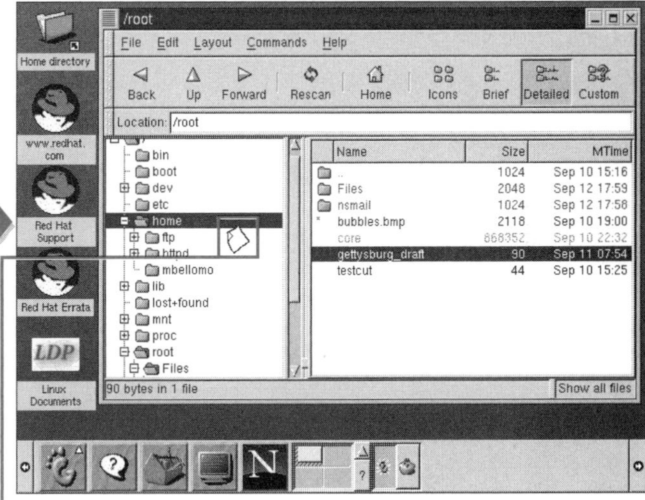

MOVE A FILE

1 Click a text file to select.

2 Drag the file to the Home Directory in the left pane.

■ Your mouse pointer icon turns into a folded sheet of paper.

CONTINUED

COPY AND MOVE FILES OR DIRECTORIES CONTINUED

You can use an alternative method to copy or move files on the Linux GNOME desktop. To use the Menu method, you right-click a file and then select the desired action (Move or Copy) from the menu that appears.

The chief advantage of using the Menu method is that you need a lower level of skill in using the mouse. The Menu method is also easier than using a trackball, since a trackball requires the same level of mouse skills. If you have a cluttered desktop, a small monitor screen, or you just don't have precision mouse skills, the Menu method makes your work in the GNOME desktop much less stressful.

The Menu method of copying or moving files has only one major disadvantage — recursiveness is not automatic. When you use the Menu method, you have to specify that you want to copy all the files within the directory as well.

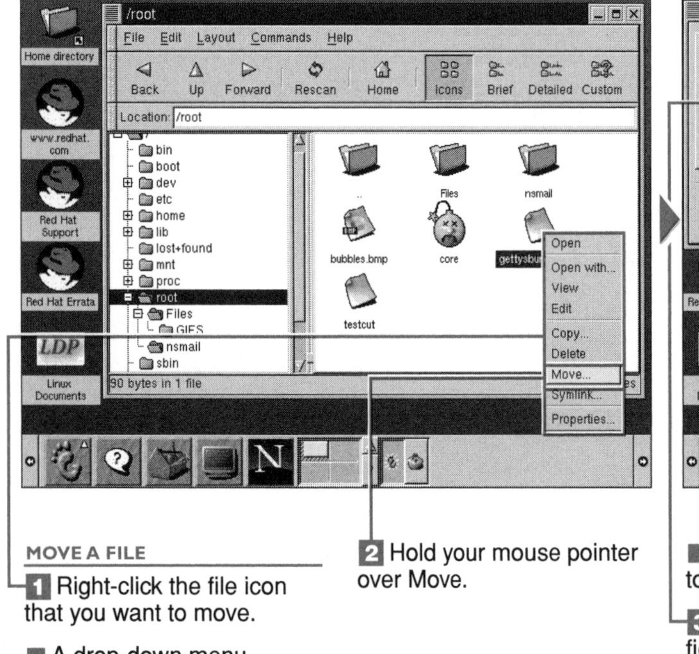

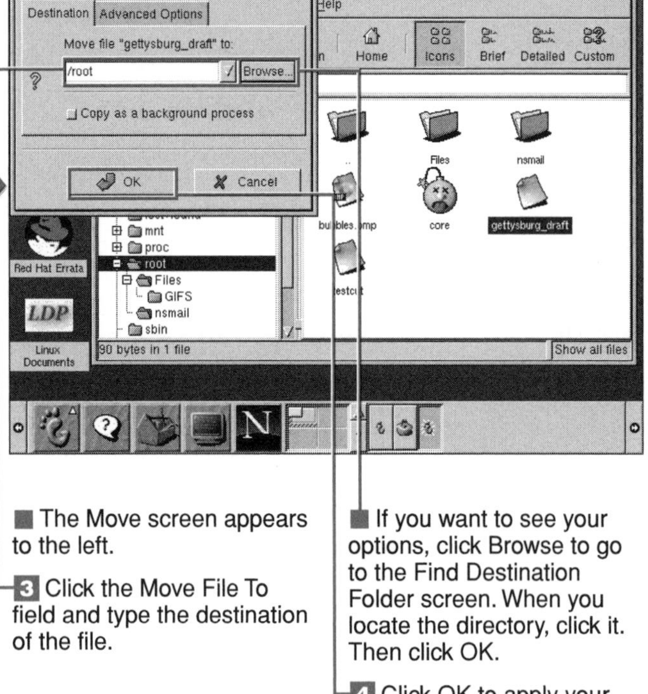

MOVE A FILE

1 Right-click the file icon that you want to move.

■ A drop-down menu appears.

2 Hold your mouse pointer over Move.

■ The Move screen appears to the left.

3 Click the Move File To field and type the destination of the file.

■ If you want to see your options, click Browse to go to the Find Destination Folder screen. When you locate the directory, click it. Then click OK.

4 Click OK to apply your selection.

What does Copy as a Background Process mean?

- You can find the Copy as a Background Process option in the Move screen, beneath the text field where you enter the file's destination. If you are moving a very large file, the copy process could prevent you from working on other tasks while you wait for the copy to finish. This option forces the copy process to run at a slower pace, in the background so that you can finish other tasks.

Do I need to keep typing in the destination of the file I'm copying in the Copy screen's text field when I copy files to one destination repeatedly?

- You don't have to do this. If you plan to copy a number of files to the same location, then you can perform a Multiple Copy. This procedure is described in the task "Copy and Move Multiple Files" later in this chapter.

What if I don't plan to copy all of these files at one time?

- In that case, you don't have to type the same destination in every time as long as you use the downward-facing arrow button to the right of the text field in the Copy screen. Clicking this button provides you with a pop-up list of recently entered copy destinations. Click the listed destination to enter it in the empty text field.

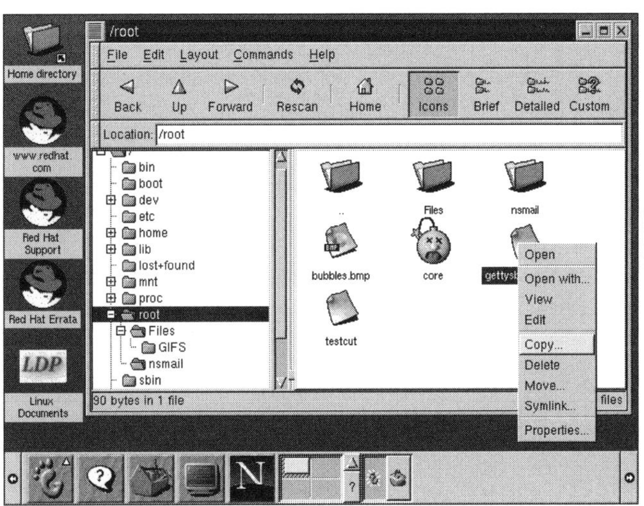

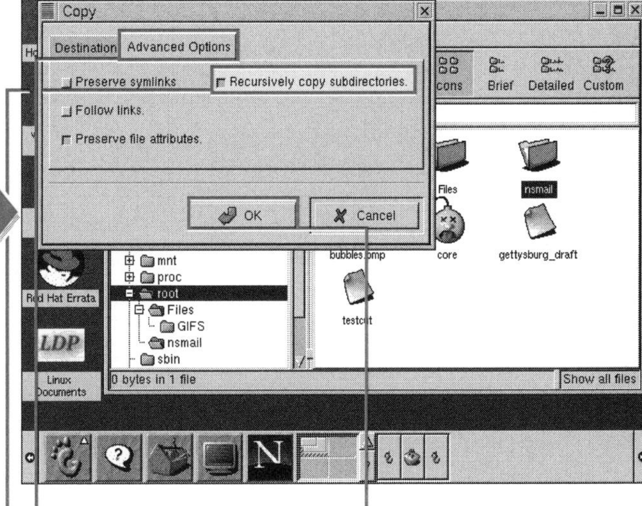

COPY FILES RECURSIVELY

1 Right-click the file icon that you want to copy.

2 Hold your mouse pointer over Copy on the drop-down menu.

■ The Copy dialog box appears to the left.

3 Click the Advanced Options tab in the Copy screen.

4 Click the Recursively Copy Subdirectories button.

5 Click OK to apply your selections.

COPY AND MOVE MULTIPLE FILES

The GNOME environment also allows you to Copy or Move multiple files at one time. Instead of having to go through the Copy or Move screens multiple times, or having to continually move the mouse back and forth as you click and drag one file at a time, you can copy or move an entire block of files.

There is no real limit to the number of files that you can copy or move at the same time. The only risks you take when copying large numbers of files at one time are slowing your machine down, or filling up your copy/move destination before the file transfer is complete. Neither event will cause damage to your machine, but it will prevent you from finishing your task at hand.

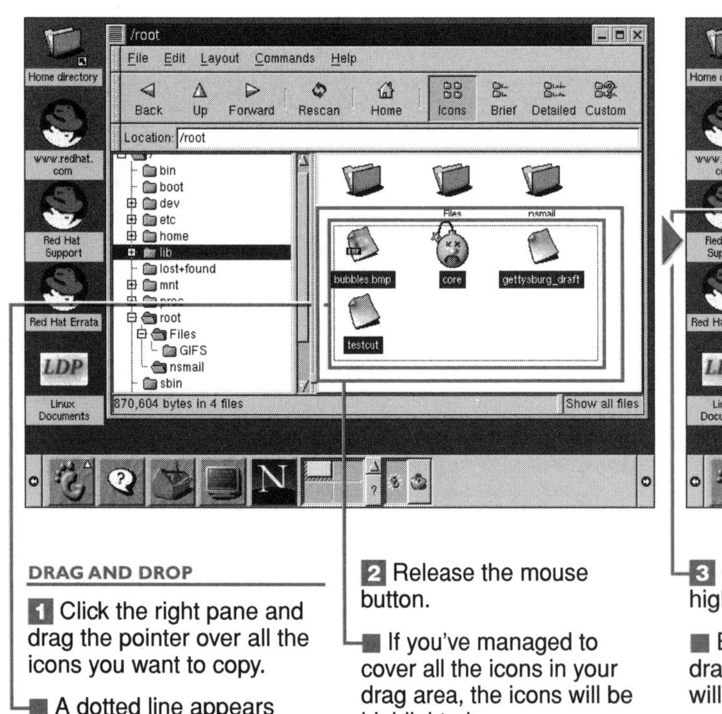

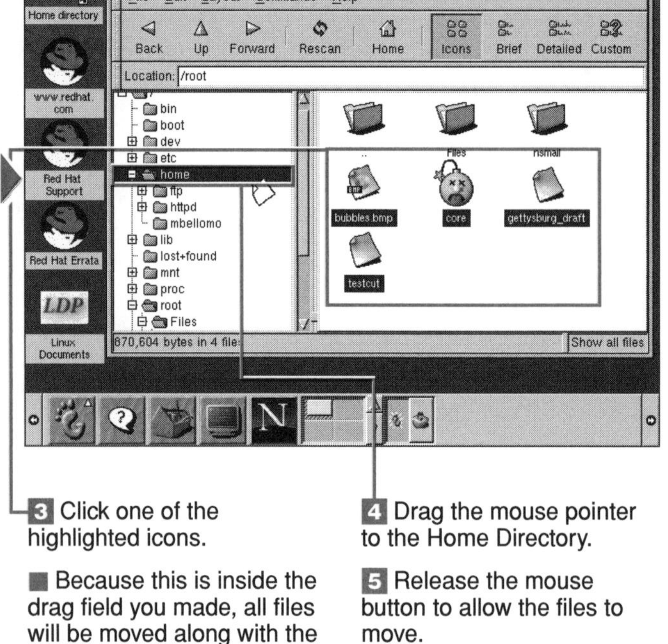

DRAG AND DROP

1 Click the right pane and drag the pointer over all the icons you want to copy.

■ A dotted line appears around the slected area.

2 Release the mouse button.

■ If you've managed to cover all the icons in your drag area, the icons will be highlighted.

3 Click one of the highlighted icons.

■ Because this is inside the drag field you made, all files will be moved along with the one you click.

4 Drag the mouse pointer to the Home Directory.

5 Release the mouse button to allow the files to move.

TIPS

When doing a multiple file copy, do I need to select the recursive option?

- As with single files, you only need to select the recursive option when you are using the right-click Menu method. On the Advanced Options tab, make sure you select the Recursively Copy Subdirectories option.

How do I copy multiple files if my right-hand viewing frame is in Brief or Detailed Mode?

- Click the Icons button in the File Manager window. This way you can use the click-and-drag method to transfer multiple files at one time.

How can I copy a file or directory to a floppy disk?

- As long as you've got a floppy disk in the drive and the floppy is mounted, you can copy files to the `/mnt/dosflop` directory. You learn about setting up your floppy drive and mounting it in Chapter 11.

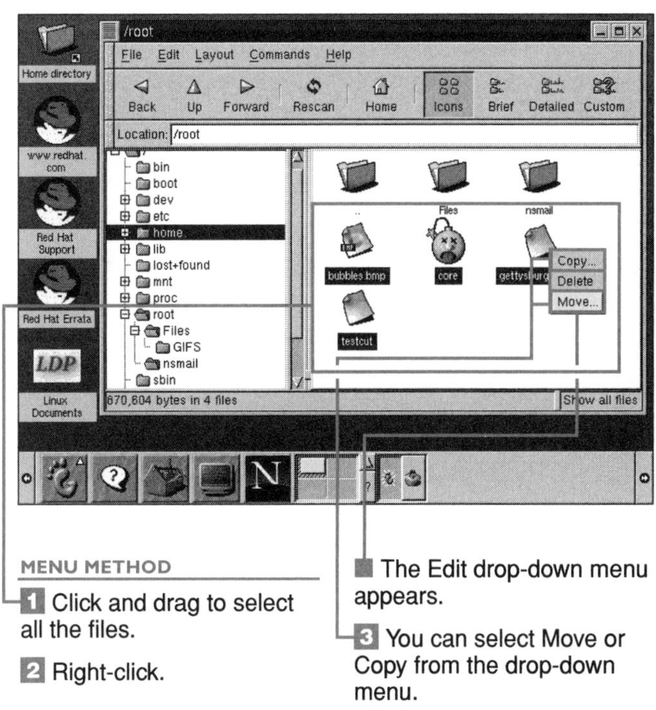

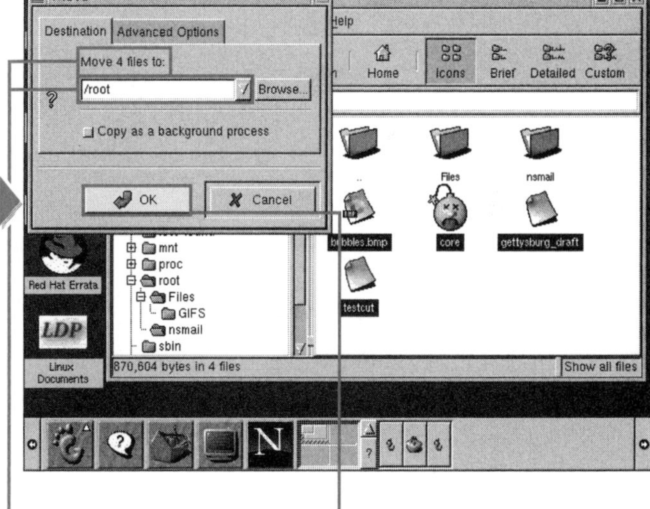

MENU METHOD

1 Click and drag to select all the files.

2 Right-click.

■ The Edit drop-down menu appears.

3 You can select Move or Copy from the drop-down menu.

4 To double-check that you have all the files you want, click the text above the text box.

5 Type the name of the directory where you want to move the files.

6 Click OK to apply your changes.

RENAME FILES AND DIRECTORIES

You can rename any kind of file or directory on the GNOME desktop. By changing the name of a file or directory, you can more effectively organize the contents of your Home Directory by making the icons easier to identify. For example, renaming files like `letter1` and `letter2` to `letter-mom` and `letter-boss` help you recall the file's contents without actually opening it.

In the Linux-GNOME environment, there is no effective limit to the length of the names you can give files. However, GNOME wraps a long filename around in its limited space, effectively cutting it off visually, or obstructing the view of other icons.

Linux automatically warns you if you're naming a file or directory identically to another one. However, the warning will only be issued if the identically named file is in the same directory. To avoid problems, make sure that each file in your environment has a unique identity.

RENAME FILES

1 Right-click the file icon that you want to rename.

■ The Edit drop-down menu appears.

2 Click Properties.

3 In the File Properties dialog box, click the File Name field to highlight.

4 Use the Backspace key to delete the original name of the file.

5 Type the filename that you want to use.

6 Click OK to accept your changes.

Can I use spaces, hyphens, colons, or slashes in filenames?

✔ GNOME doesn't prevent you from using any particular characters in your filenames. However, naming files with slashes or colons can cause confusion when you work with files, especially in the Linux terminal window.

Does renaming directories affect the files stored inside of them?

✔ Renaming directories does not impact files inside the directories. However, be careful about renaming directories that came pre-installed with your Linux machine. Certain programs may look for these directory names so they know how to run or where to store log files.

Can I change the extensions on a file? For example, can I change bubbles.bmp to bubbles.txt?

✔ You can change the file extensions, but the file will most likely become unusable. Because `bubbles` is a graphics file, changing it to a text file will not create a document. Opening it in a word processor will most likely look like a mass of undefined characters.

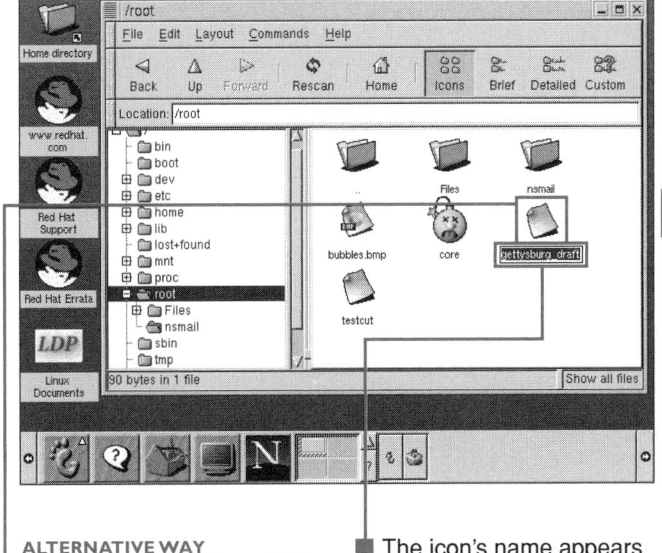

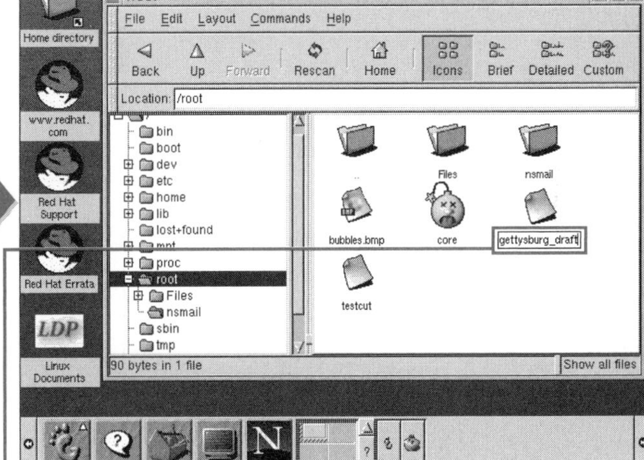

ALTERNATIVE WAY

1 Click the file icon to select it.

■ The file's name highlights.

2 Click the name of the file (Not the icon picture).

■ The icon's name appears highlighted and surrounded by a white border.

3 Use the Backspace key and type in the new name for the file.

4 If you want to change the name of the file slightly, you can click the file's name (not the picture icon) a third time.

■ The icon's name appears with a black border and the text cursor inside the border.

5 Use the Backspace or Arrow keys to move within this text box. Type the name you want to use for this file.

DELETE FILES AND DIRECTORIES

You should make a habit out of deleting files and directories that you no longer need or use, or are produced by system processes. For example, the `core` file is produced when a GNOME or Linux process dies. Ordinarily, these files are very large and don't serve a purpose for the typical user or administrator. You should be familiar with the task of deleting them.

When you delete a file or directory, GNOME asks you if you're sure you want to delete it. GNOME does this because there is no Trash Can or Recycle Bin in Linux: Once a file deletes, it's gone forever.

Linux also offers another safeguard when it comes to deleting directories. If files are inside the directory, GNOME asks if you want to delete all the files inside the directory as well. If you want to keep any files inside the directory, it's best to move or copy them elsewhere.

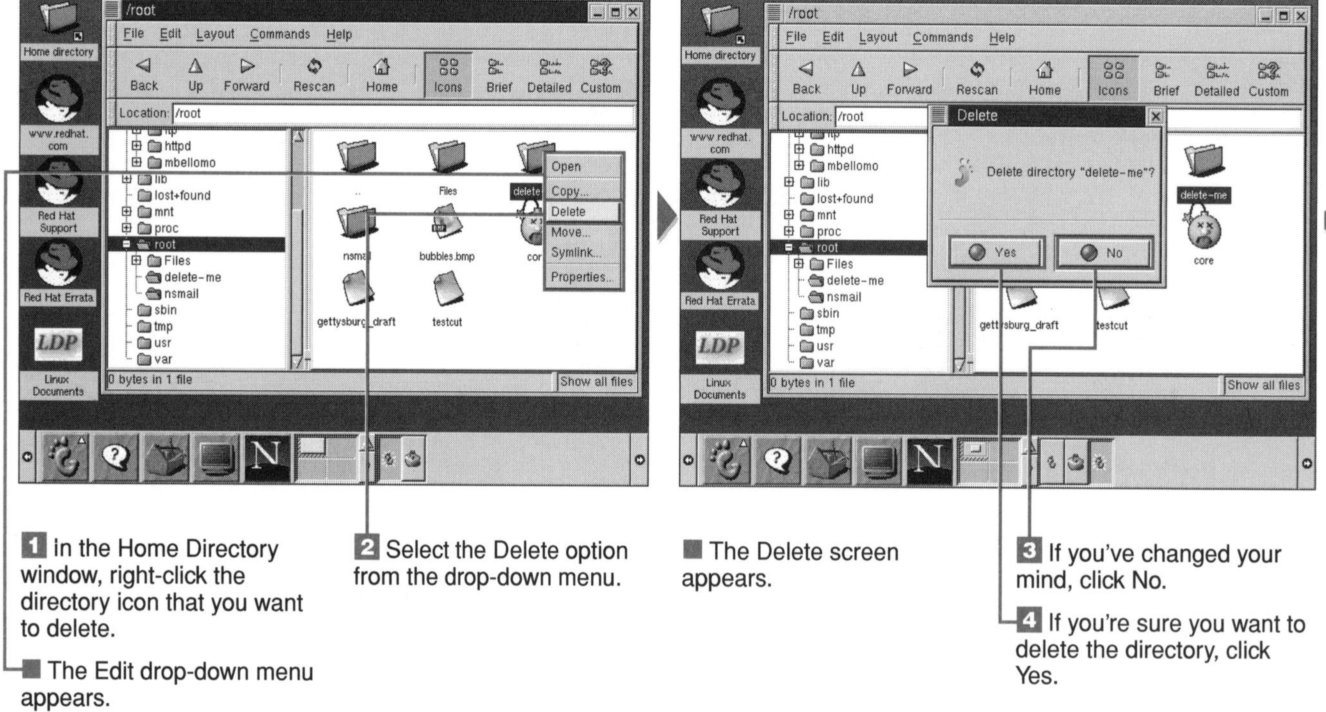

1 In the Home Directory window, right-click the directory icon that you want to delete.

■ The Edit drop-down menu appears.

2 Select the Delete option from the drop-down menu.

■ The Delete screen appears.

3 If you've changed your mind, click No.

4 If you're sure you want to delete the directory, click Yes.

Can I change my mind once a delete is in progress?

- Not if you're deleting a file. If you're deleting a directory and the Delete Progress screen shows that the process is not complete, you can click the Cancel button. This action prevents the remaining files in the directory from being deleted.

How can I delete multiple files at once?

- Use the click-and-drag technique described in "Copy and Move Files or Directories." You still get the warning screens after you actually try to delete the files.

When I'm logged in as a different user, why can't I delete certain files anymore?

- When you're logged in as the root account, you have complete administrative privileges over any file. When you're logged in as a regular user, you can only delete files that you have permission to delete, like your own text or graphics files in your Home directory.

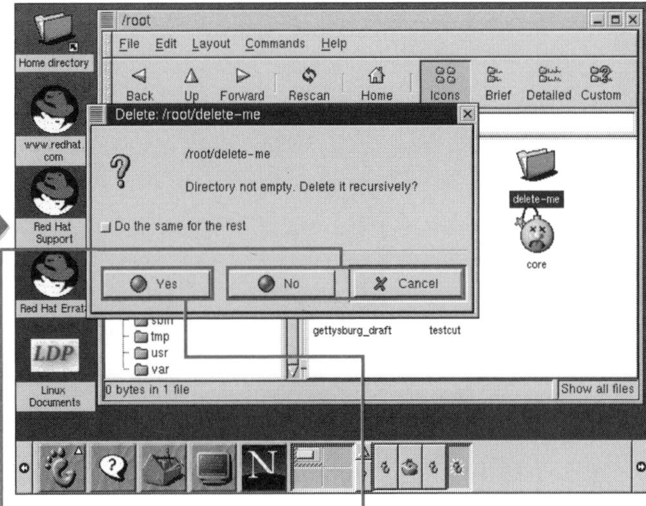

■ A warning screen appears, notifying you that files are inside the directory.

5 If you're not sure that you want to delete this directory and all its contents, click No or Cancel.

6 If you definitely want to delete this directory, click Yes.

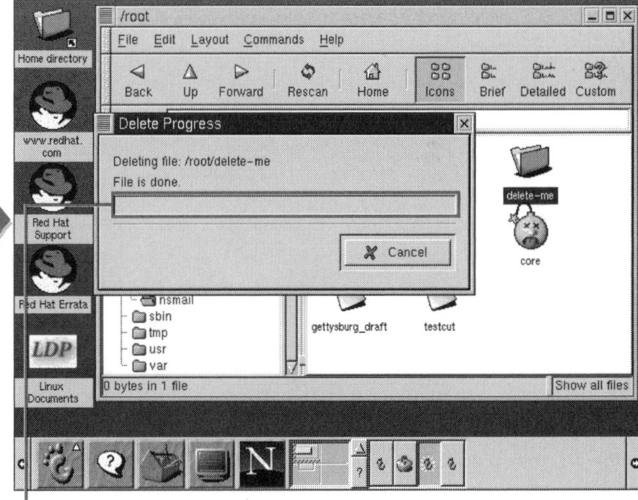

■ After you select Yes, a new screen appears, tracking the delete process. A blue bar scrolls from left to right as the job is completed. If the directory has a lot of material to delete, this process might take anywhere from 2 seconds to 10 minutes.

LAUNCH AN APPLICATION

You can start a program in the GNOME desktop environment several ways. Like Microsoft Windows, the GNOME desktop organizes the majority of its Linux applications in menus that pop up when you press a toolbar button. For example, clicking the Main Application Menu button brings up a large list of programs to choose from, mostly located under the Applications and System submenus. Certain applications, such as the Help documentation or the Netscape Web browser, are also available directly on the GNOME toolbar.

In GNOME, you can double-click an icon on the desktop, in an open user's directory, or in the File Manager view frame — all these actions open the chosen application. If your application doesn't have an icon on the desktop, you can create an icon.

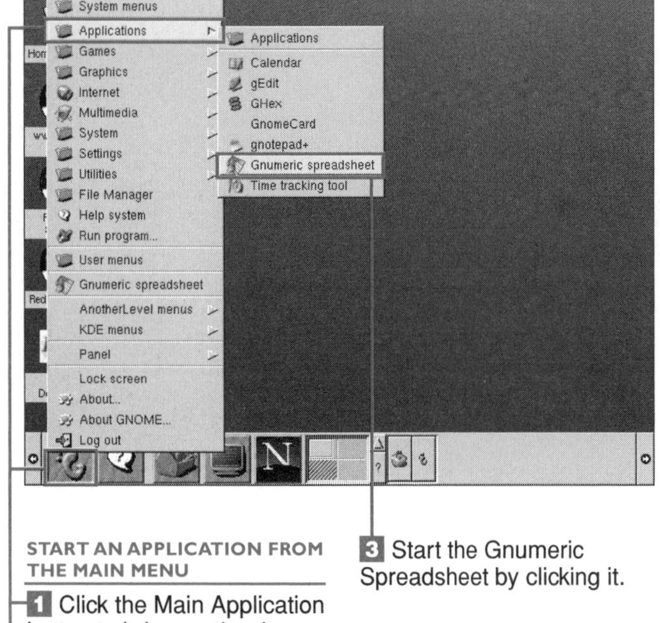

START AN APPLICATION FROM THE MAIN MENU

1 Click the Main Application button to bring up the drop-down menu.

2 Move your mouse pointer to the Applications selection.

3 Start the Gnumeric Spreadsheet by clicking it.

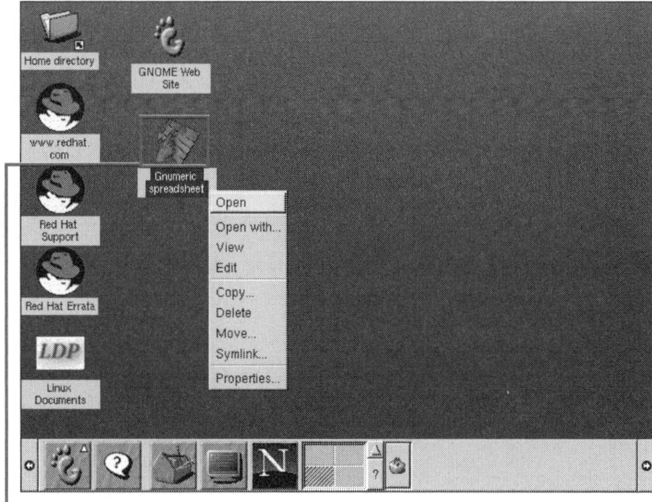

START AN APPLICATION FROM THE DESKTOP

1 If the Gnumeric Spreadsheet icon is on your desktop, double-click it.

Note: Most programs in GNOME, like in Windows, offer visual clues as to their function. The Gnumeric Spreadsheet, for instance, looks like a hand browsing a series of rows and columns

What's the difference between a program and a script?

- A program is a product constructed (or coded) and sold with Linux or GNOME, usually for personal productivity, like word processing. A script is a series of Linux or UNIX commands that are put together in a Linux file and made executable by giving it execute permissions. Unlike programs, scripts are normally used for system maintenance, such as checking for disk problems.

Can I launch one program while I'm running another?

- If you can access the desktop or the GNOME toolbar while one program is running, you can start one or more programs.

How many programs can I run at one time in the Linux environment?

- It depends on how high-powered your Linux machine is. If you're running large programs like WordPerfect for Linux and Netscape, don't run more than two or three at the same time or your system will slow down noticeably.

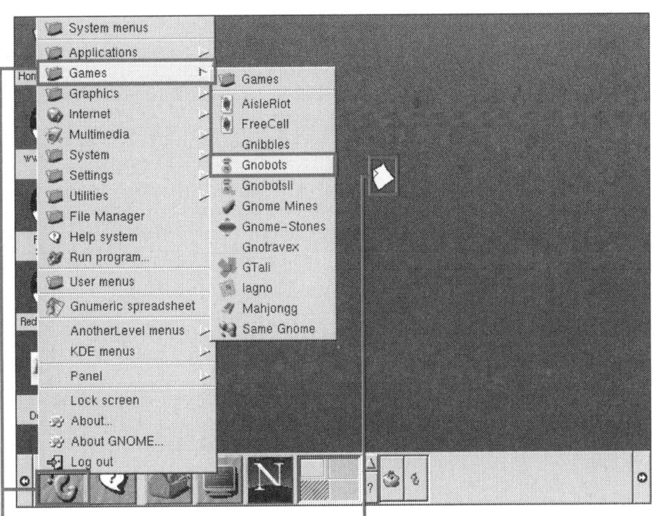

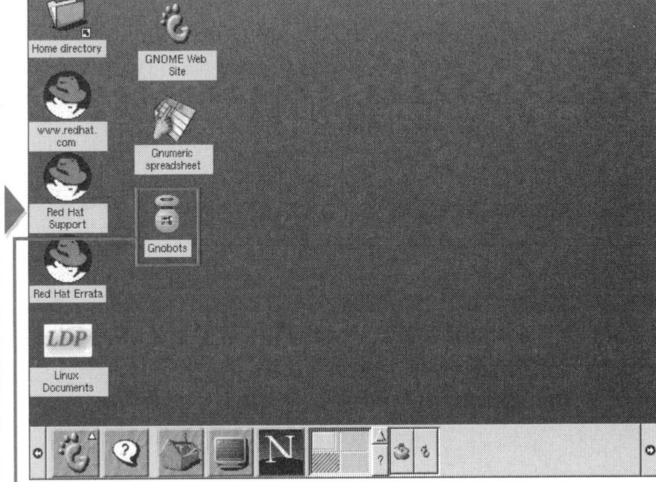

ADD A DESKTOP ICON

1 Click the Main Application Menu button to open the drop-down menu.

2 Move your mouse pointer to Games and then go to Gnobots on the submenu.

3 Click and drag Gnobots to an open area on the desktop.

■ Your mouse pointer turns into a folded sheet of paper.

4 Release the mouse button, and the program appears on your desktop.

■ You can treat the new icon the same way as any other program on the desktop. To start the program, right-click and select Open, or simply double-click it.

CLOSE APPLICATIONS

Closing programs after you're done using them helps free up system resources that other people can put to good use. Closing programs also reduces security risks, both to the system and to your own files. Few temptations are as irresistible to a prankster or a hacker as an open terminal with access to a user's private files.

Starting a program in Linux is known as executing a program; stopping the same program is called killing the program. Killing refers to the sending of a signal to a running program and ordering it to expire, or die in an orderly manner.

In case a program refuses to die, you need to know some techniques to kill it. While `kill` is a literal command that you can use in the Linux terminal, you have different techniques to shut down a program that refuses to die in the GNOME portion of Linux.

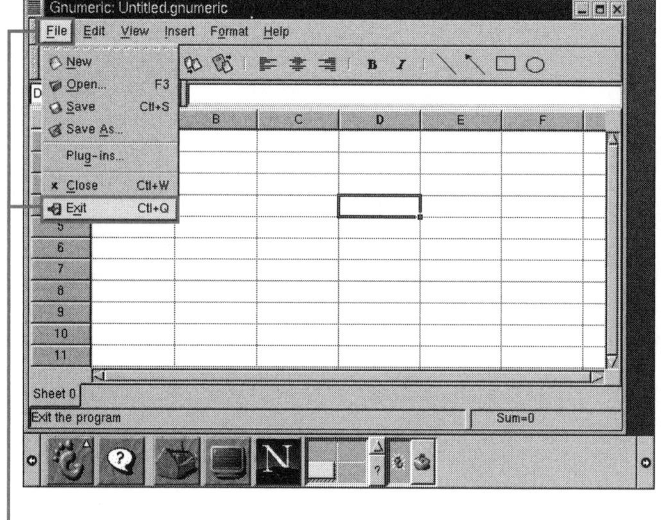

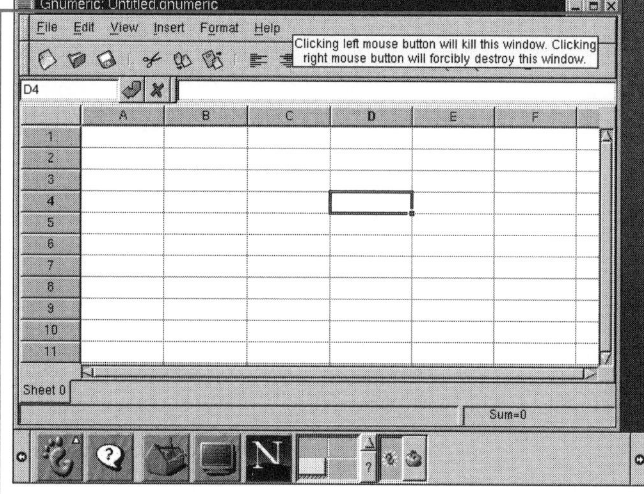

EXIT AN APPLICATION

1 Click File on the toolbar.

■ A drop-down menu appears.

2 Move your mouse pointer to Exit and click.

■ The program shuts down.

Note: Clicking Close doesn't have the same effect as clicking Exit. Close shuts down the spreadsheet you're currently working on, but it leaves the program running and using system resources.

CLOSE AN APPLICATION

1 Move your mouse pointer to the X button and click to close the window and program.

Does deleting a program's icon from the desktop get rid of the program from my File Manager?

- Deleting the icon from the desktop doesn't delete the binary itself in your program files. You may have to perform a Find for the program, as demonstrated in Chapter 3. Once you find the program, you can remove it.

What causes a program to refuse to shut down?

- The most common cause behind a program's constant refusal to shut down is a corrupt program file. Improper shutdowns, power surges, or computer virus programs can corrupt program files.

If corrupt programs freeze or refuse to shut down, how can I prevent my programs from being corrupted?

- You can do two things to keep programs running smoothly. First, never shut down your computer by simply switching off the power. Always follow the proper procedure to log out or shut down. Second, protect your machine against power surges by purchasing a surge protector.

What are my options if a program doesn't shut down after I've logged out and then logged back in?

- You may have to reboot the machine. If so, refer to the Shutdown instructions in Chapter 1 to do this safely.

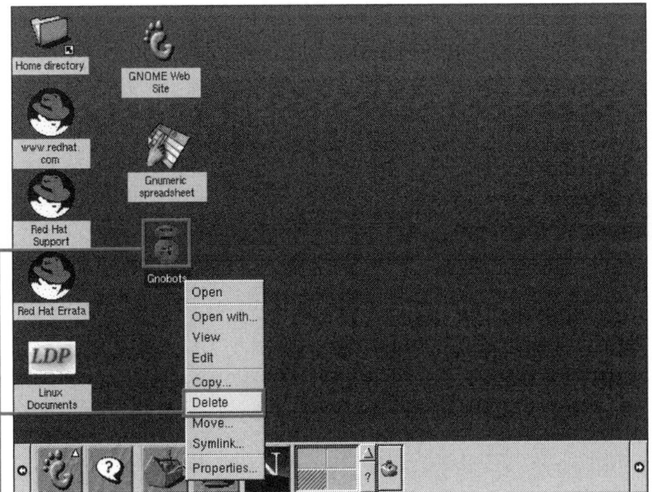

REMOVE AN APPLICATION ICON

1 Right-click the program icon.

2 Select Delete from the drop-down menu.

■ A dialog box appears.

3 Click Yes if you're sure you want to delete the program.

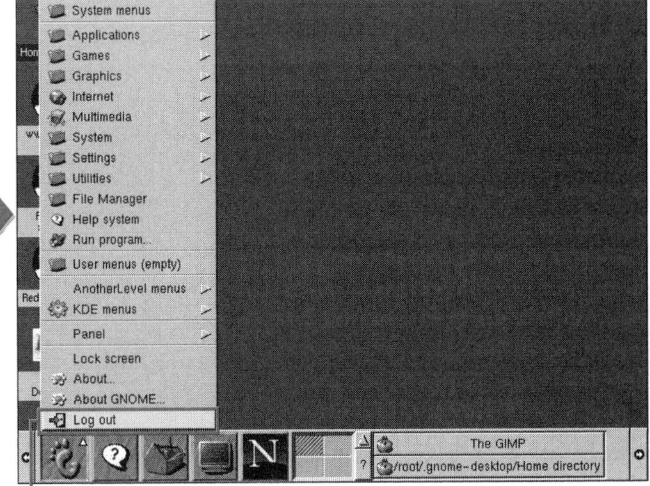

■ If you're unable to shut a program down, log out of the Linux system.

Note: Logging out to shut down a program should only be done if the program refuses to shut down by closing or exiting the program the normal way.

CREATE SYMBOLIC LINKS

If you've gone through the "Launch an Application" section of this chapter, you've already created a type of Symbolic link. A *Symbolic link* is a file that is simply a pointer or symbol leading to the real directory, file, or application.

Symbolic links are useful in linking to a program that you cannot move from a relatively inaccessible location in the Linux file system. More important, a Symbolic link can move a file's access point to an easy to reach area without actually copying the entire file.

These links contain only a small amount of information compared to the size of the file it links to. So compared to physically copying a program to another location, hard drive space and Linux resources are saved. Be sure that the link's location provides easier access, such as the desktop.

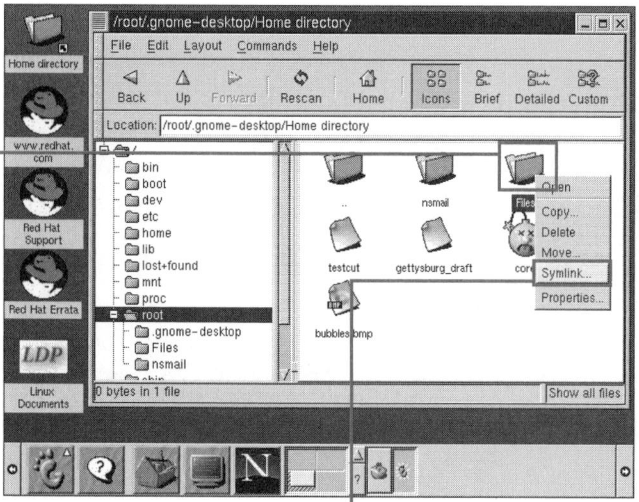

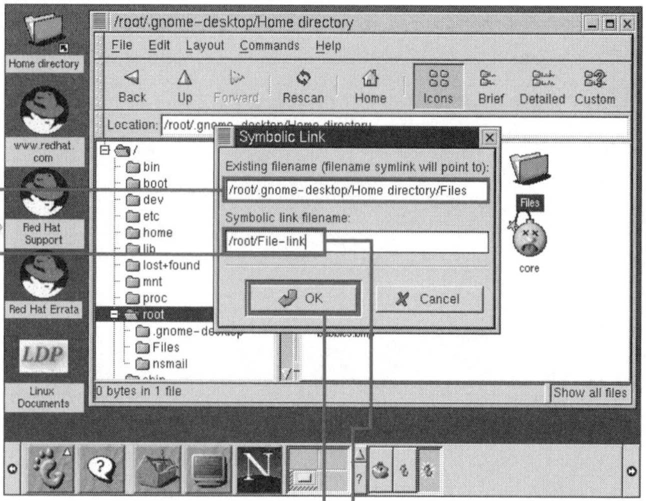

1 Right-click the Files directory icon.

2 Move your mouse pointer over Symlink.

■ GNOME uses the term Symlink for Symbolic link because the term fits better in a drop-down menu.

■ The Symbolic Link option box appears.

■ The top field lists the current location of the directory.

3 Click the bottom field so that the cursor appears in it.

4 Type the location where you want to place the link and the name.

■ For this example, place the link in the same directory and call it File-link.

5 Click OK.

Will deleting the Symbolic link destroy the program?

- Deleting the link is simply removing the extra connection to the program. It doesn't affect the contents of a directory, the text in a file, or the code inside a program.

How can I copy a Symbolic link?

- You can copy a Symbolic link like a program or file. If your link is to a directory, make sure to test the link out and see if you're able to access the subdirectories and files underneath the given directory.

How can I rename a Symbolic link?

- You can rename a link the same way that you change a regular file's name without affecting the link's function. Be sure not to change the link's properties — that is, the location it's pointing to — or the link may end up going nowhere.

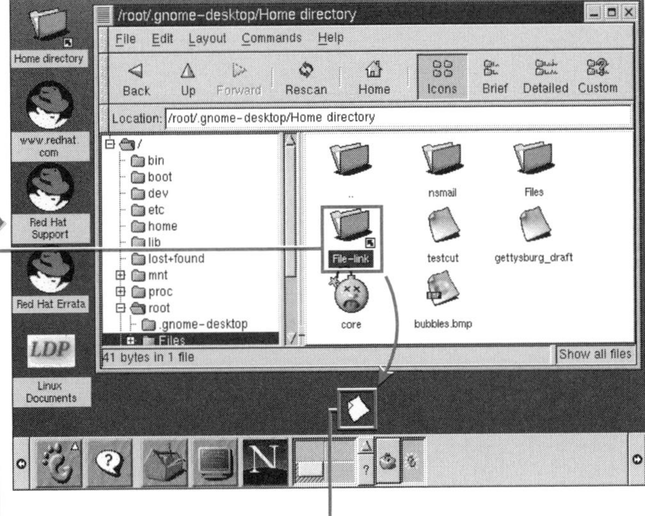

■ The directory link icon looks similar to the original directory, but it has an arrow in the lower-right corner

6 Click the Symbolic link to select it.

7 Drag the link to the desktop

■ Your mouse pointer turns into a folded piece of paper.

8 Release the mouse button and the link appears on the desktop.

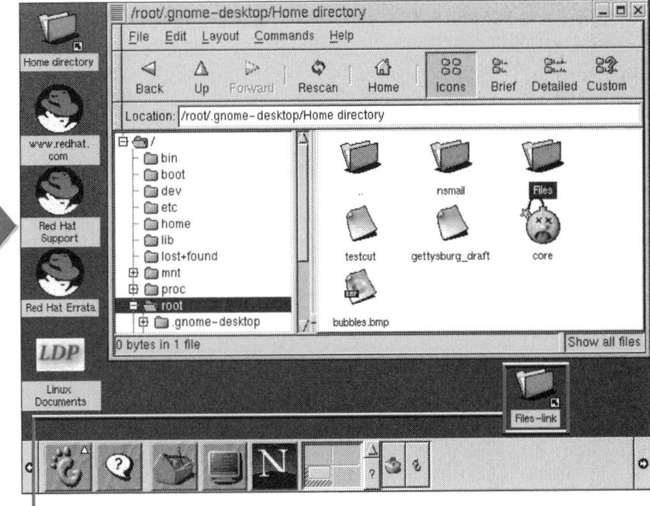

■ The Symbolic link sits on the desktop like any other application or directory. When you double-click the link to open it, you see the same contents as in the original directory in the Linux File Manager window.

FILE PERMISSIONS

In Linux, all files have three kinds of permissioning: readable, writable, and executable. You can open and read a readable file. You can make and save text or code changes to a writable file. Finally, you can start or execute an executable file, like an application or a Linux script.

Setting the permissions on a file is important to both personal privacy and system safety. In Linux system security, the administrator uses the root account to make sure that any network-critical files aren't writable — or even readable — to the general user public.

If you're using the root account, it's important to realize that root is the only account that can ignore permissions. Because of this, take caution in setting permissions on other people's files or you may end up locking them out of their own work!

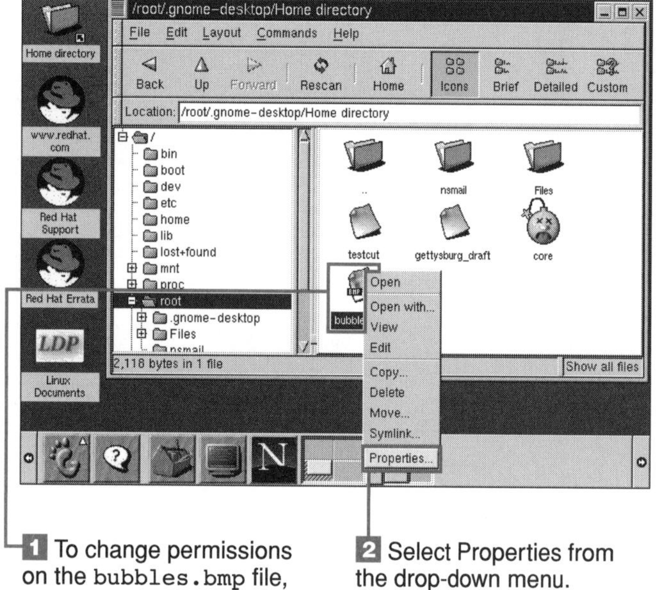

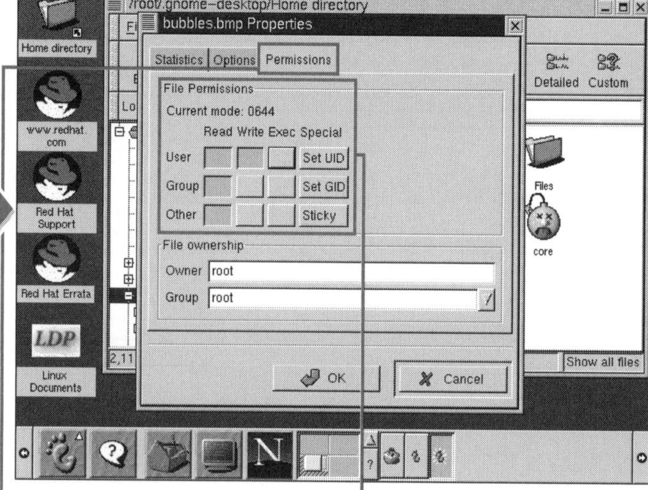

1 To change permissions on the `bubbles.bmp` file, right-click the file icon.

2 Select Properties from the drop-down menu.

3 In the Properties window, click the Permissions tab.

■ In the Permissions window, there are three column titles indicating the types of permissioning: Read, Write, and Execute.

■ The three rows indicate the three user settings: permissions for the file's user or owner; the user's group; and everyone else on the Linux network (indicated by Other).

I have read permissions to a file but I can't save changes to it, what's wrong?

- This is a common permissioning issue. Having read permissions does allow you to make changes to a file, but you can't save the changes! To save changes, you must have write permission to a file.

I have write permissions to the Linux script. I just made some changes and the script won't run, what's wrong?

- Another common permissioning issue with scripts is that the writer forgets to make the script executable. If it's writable but not executable, the editor can change the script all he wants, but Linux cannot run the script.

Can a file be readable, writable, and executable at the same time?

- None of the permissions conflict. So you could indeed make a file readable, writable, and executable all at the same time.

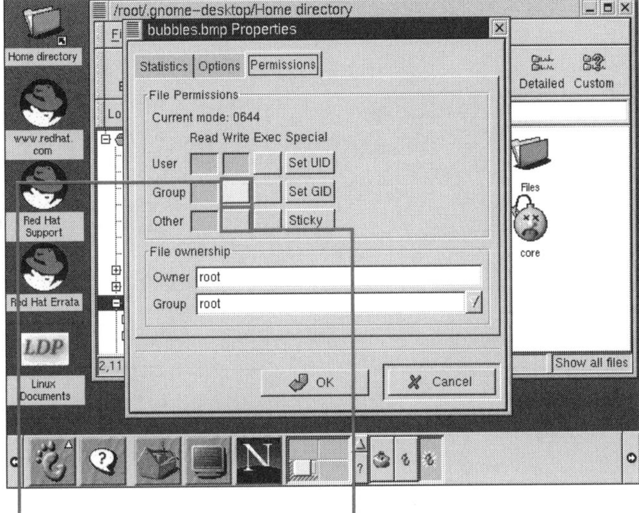

4 To make the file writable for everyone on the network, move the mouse pointer to the second button in the Group row and click to select.

5 Repeat this action for the second button in the Other row.

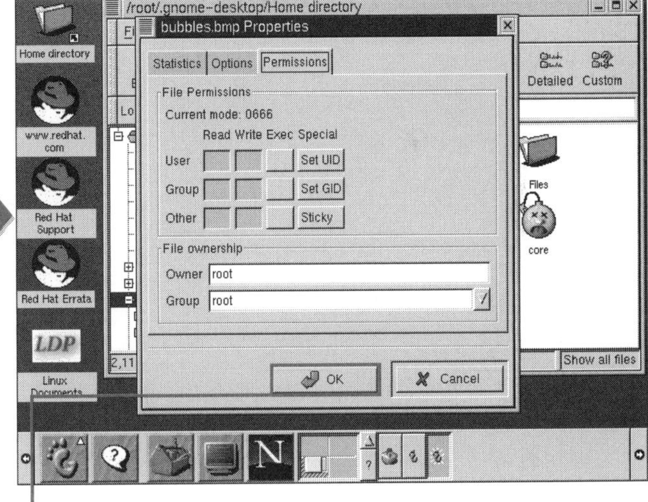

6 Click OK to apply these changes.

FILE USER AND GROUP OWNERSHIP

Unless the file is open to the general public, file permissioning is based on the user account and group membership of the current owner. User accounts are the actual owners of files. User groups are simply combinations of users placed into logical groups for easy administration. For example, an administrator can group users into Engineering, Accounting, or HR groups.

Making a file owned and accessible by a certain group is especially desirable if the file is of common interest to that group but not others. In the case of the Accounting group, having a copy of the latest expense reports is generally available to all.

For HR, fresh, updated copies of personnel or transfer texts is owned and/or edited by all members of that group but not other groups such as Engineering. Members of the Engineering group own all the files related to research and development, but do not have access to sensitive files of other departments, such as Accounting.

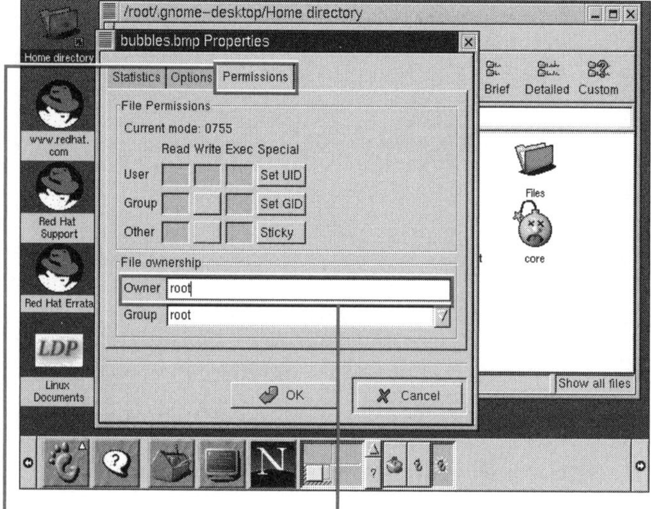

1 To change file ownership, log in as the root account and right-click bubbles.bmp.

2 Click the Properties selection.

3 Click the Permissions tab in the Properties window.

4 Click the Owner field to activate.

5 Use the Backspace key to delete the current user, and type the name of the new owner of the file.

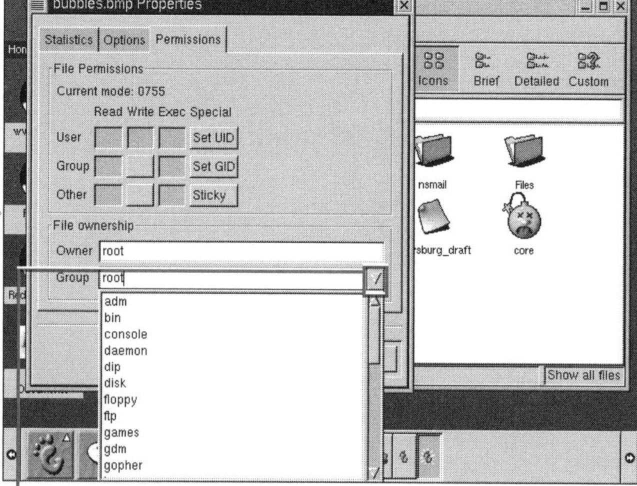

6 To change the user group, click the arrow to the right of the Group field.

■ A drop-down menu appears listing the available user groups.

When should I change group ownership of file but not change the owner of the file?

- Changing the file's group ownership without changing the file's actual owner is useful when people change positions in an organization. A person may move from the accounting to the engineering group, where the new group may need access to the new person's files.

Is there any way I can change file ownership if I'm not logged in as the root account?

- As a security measure, you can only change file ownership to another user as the system administrator. To change file permissions if you're not logged in as root, you'll need to log out and then log back in as the root account.

What happens if set one of my file's permission as readable by everyone, but not readable by anyone in my group?

- Then everyone, including your group, can read that file. The Other setting means everyone on the network. The Groups setting is a subset of the total number of users on the Linux network, so it overrides the Group setting.

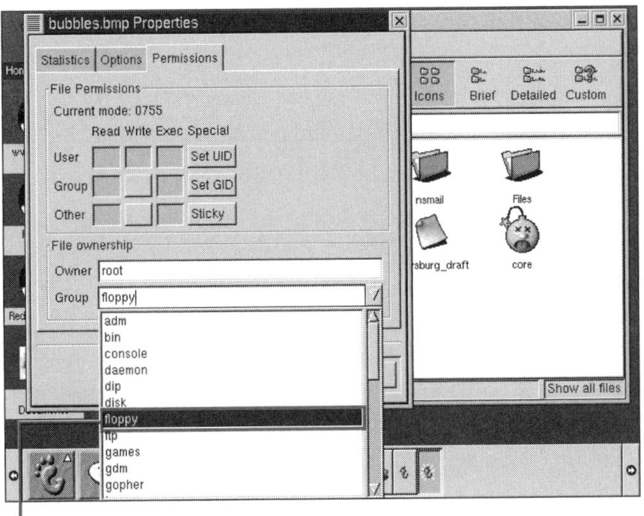

7 Move your pointer over the selection you want to make and click.

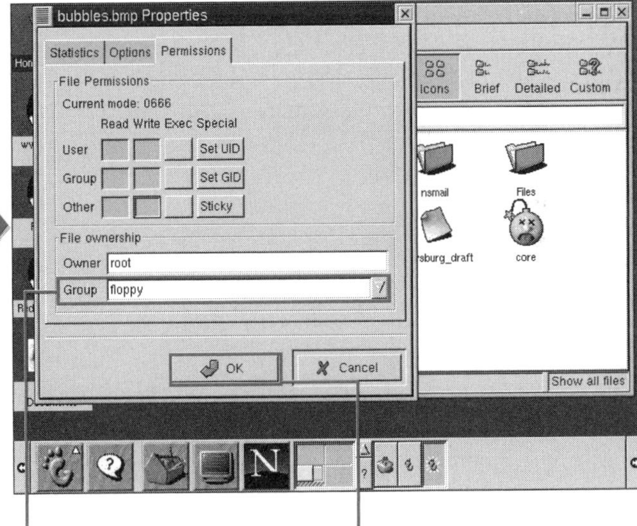

■ The selected group appears in the Group field in the Permissions window.

8 Click OK to accept the changes to the Permissions window.

SECTION II

5) WORKING WITH LINUX FILES OUTSIDE OF GNOME

Open the Linux Terminal Window 92
Change Your Linux Terminal Font 94
Change Linux Terminal Colors 96
List Files 98
Change Directories in the Linux Terminal 104
Create New Files 108
Create New Directories 110
Copy Files in the Linux Terminal 112
Copy Directories in the Linux Terminal 114
Rename Files or Directories 116
Delete Files and Directories 118

6) USEFUL COMMANDS OUTSIDE THE GNOME

Determine Your User Account Identity 122
Determine Who Else Is Logged In 124
Locate Files in the Linux Terminal 126
Create Symbolic Links 130
Move, Name, and Delete Symbolic Links 132
Transfer Output
with the Pipe Command 134
Search with the Grep Command 136
Search for Running Processes 138
Stop Programs with Kill 142
Stop Programs That Do Not Respond
to Kill 144
Re-direct Output
with Arrow Keys 146
Make a File Executable 150
Change a File's Ownership 152
Change a File's Group Ownership 152

USING THE LINUX ENVIRONMENT OUTSIDE OF THE GUI

7) THE VI EDITOR

Start the vi Editor 156
Command and Insert Mode in vi 160
Add Text 162
Delete Text 166
Substitute Text 170
Move Around in vi 172
Search for Words in vi 174
Cut, Copy, and Paste Text 176
Save and Quit vi 180

8) CUSTOMIZING THE NON-GNOME ENVIRONMENT

Determine Your Environment Variables 184
Set the $PATH Variable 188
Source Changes 190
Adding Aliases 192

OPEN THE LINUX TERMINAL WINDOW

You can open a Linux Terminal window in the GNOME desktop to work with programs that will only run outside of the desktop environment. Certain programs and Linux commands can't run in the GNOME desktop environment because they either are older than the GNOME environment or were never designed to work with a graphical user interface.

You have a few different options for opening Linux Terminals in GNOME. First, you can open a Linux Terminal by right-clicking your desktop. Second, you can click the Linux Terminal button on the GNOME toolbar at the base of the screen. Finally, you can open a Linux Terminal from the Main menu.

Whichever way you choose, the results you get — an open Terminal — are identical. Simply select the method that is easiest for you to use.

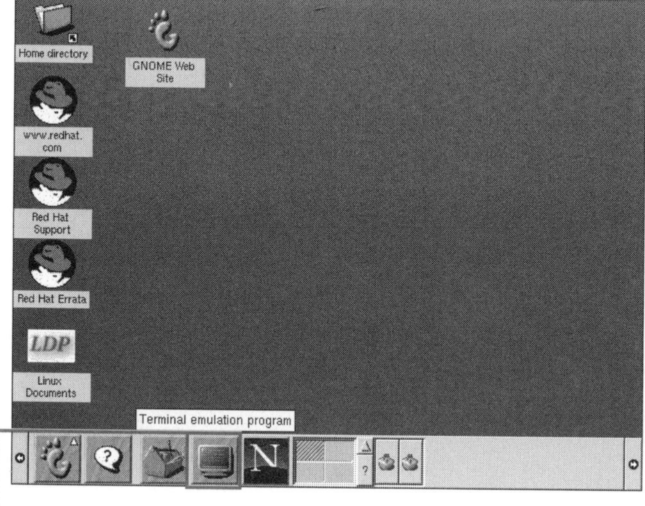

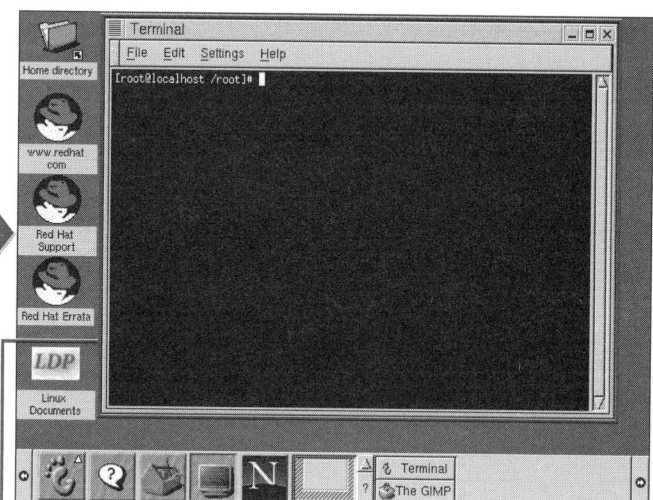

OPEN A TERMINAL FROM THE DESKTOP

1 Place your mouse pointer on the Terminal emulation program button and click.

■ The Terminal window appears. The window border is blue — or dark, if you have a monochrome monitor — indicating that the window is active.

TIPS

How do I create multiple Terminal windows in my GNOME session?

- You can either click the Terminal Emulation Button multiple times or (if you already have a Terminal open) you can left-click the File drop-down menu and select New to bring up a new Terminal.

What happened to my Terminal window — it went gray again!

- When the border of a Terminal window goes gray, it's just in the background. GNOME shuffles its windows in this manner to allow a more organized desktop environment. If you're running something in this window, it's unaffected by being put into the background.

Where can I find more information on working with the Terminal?

- Click Help, listed to the right of File, Edit, and Settings in the Terminal window. Select GNOME Terminal User's Guide from the drop-down menu for more information.

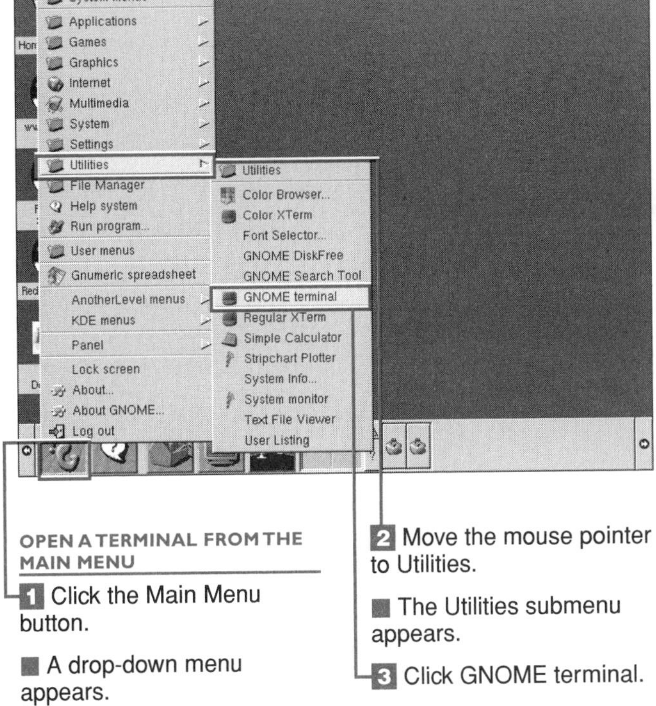

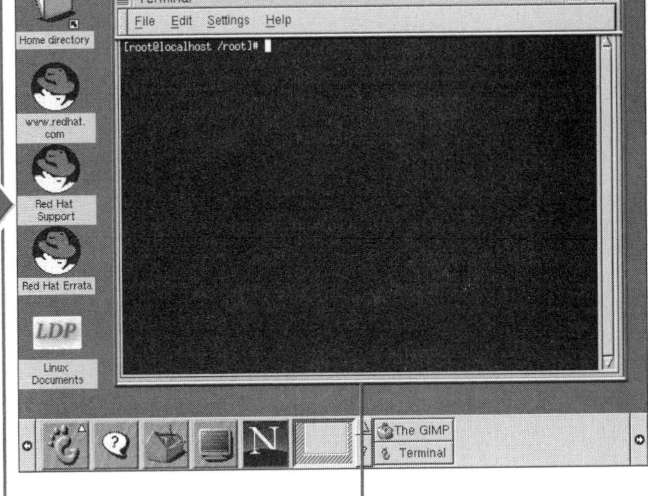

OPEN A TERMINAL FROM THE MAIN MENU

1 Click the Main Menu button.

■ A drop-down menu appears.

2 Move the mouse pointer to Utilities.

■ The Utilities submenu appears.

3 Click GNOME terminal.

■ A new Terminal window appears.

■ The gray border of the Terminal window indicates that the window is not active or in the foreground.

4 Click anywhere in the Terminal window to activate.

■ The border turns blue.

CHANGE YOUR LINUX TERMINAL FONT

You can change the font in your GNOME desktop environment to make your computer screen more stylish or to make your work easier on your eyes. Of course, if your screen is dark, small, or less than crystal clear, you should first consider upgrading your computer's monitor, or buy a newer, larger screen.

If that isn't a realistic option, you can change the font displayed inside your Linux Terminal windows for easier reading. This makes a gigantic difference when you're working at a terminal for longer than 30 minutes, or for smaller periods of time throughout the day.

Reducing eyestrain enables you and your Linux users to work more efficiently and productively. If you're concerned with your health or your user's well being, consider that eyestrain can lead to a host of other problems, including permanent vision loss and migraine headaches.

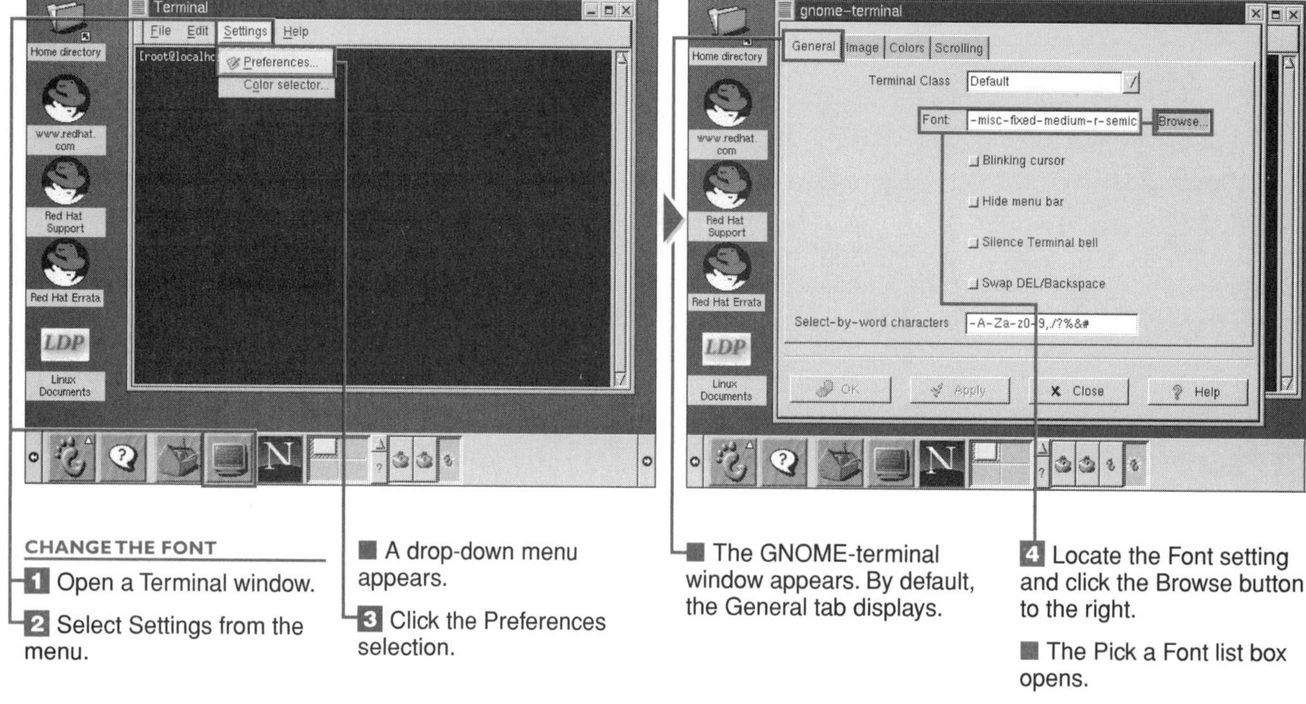

CHANGE THE FONT

1 Open a Terminal window.

2 Select Settings from the menu.

■ A drop-down menu appears.

3 Click the Preferences selection.

■ The GNOME-terminal window appears. By default, the General tab displays.

4 Locate the Font setting and click the Browse button to the right.

■ The Pick a Font list box opens.

Are my new font settings permanent?

- After you change the font setting in the GNOME environment, the Terminal windows you open on your machine reflect your changes until you alter the settings again.

What font style should I use?

- Choosing a font style is mostly a matter of personality. However, if you want to be purely practical about your choice, avoid using a style that is small, cramped, or flowery. These styles of font can cause eyestrain over an extended period of time.

What font size should I use?

- Most of the time, the default settings are adequate. If you have poor lighting or vision, or if your seat is too far from the screen, set your font to size 14. But don't select any larger unless you have a 17-inch monitor, or you may find your Terminals extending past the edge of the screen.

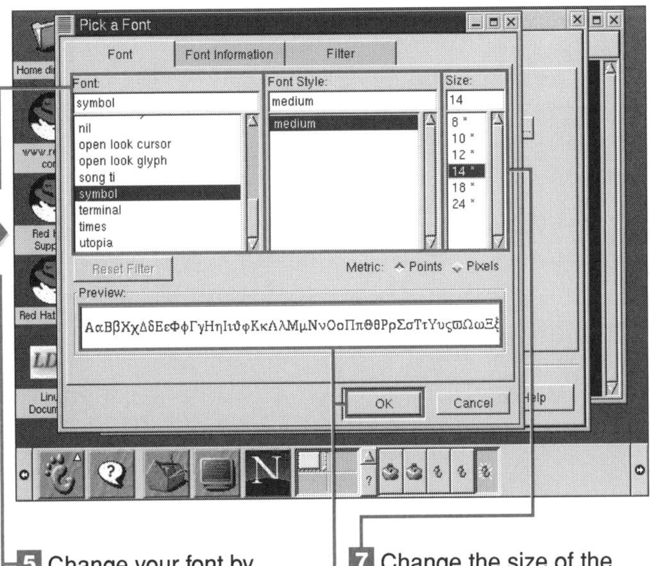

5 Change your font by clicking a selection in the Font list box.

6 Change the font style by clicking a style in the Font Style list box.

7 Change the size of the font by clicking a size number in the Size list box.

8 Click OK.

■ The GNOME-terminal dialog box appears.

9 Click OK.

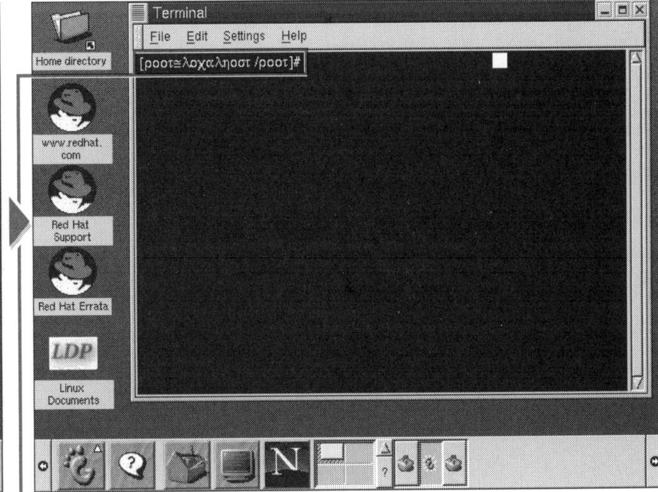

■ Your Terminal window displays the new font.

CHANGE LINUX TERMINAL COLORS

You can change the colors displayed in your Linux Terminal to any shade supported by your monitor. Although the Terminal is not graphics-based like the GNOME desktop, changing the color affects two main areas of the Terminal. First, it affects the color of the font displayed in the Terminal. Second, changing the background color of the Terminal always affects how easy — or difficult — it is to make out the font in the Terminal window.

Color shades are set in the Color Selector screen on a color palette called a *color wheel*. A circular marker in the wheel indicates the currently selected Terminal color.

If you want more red, drag the marker to the top portion of the color wheel, which controls various shades of red. The closer you move toward the center of the circle, the brighter the shade of the color.

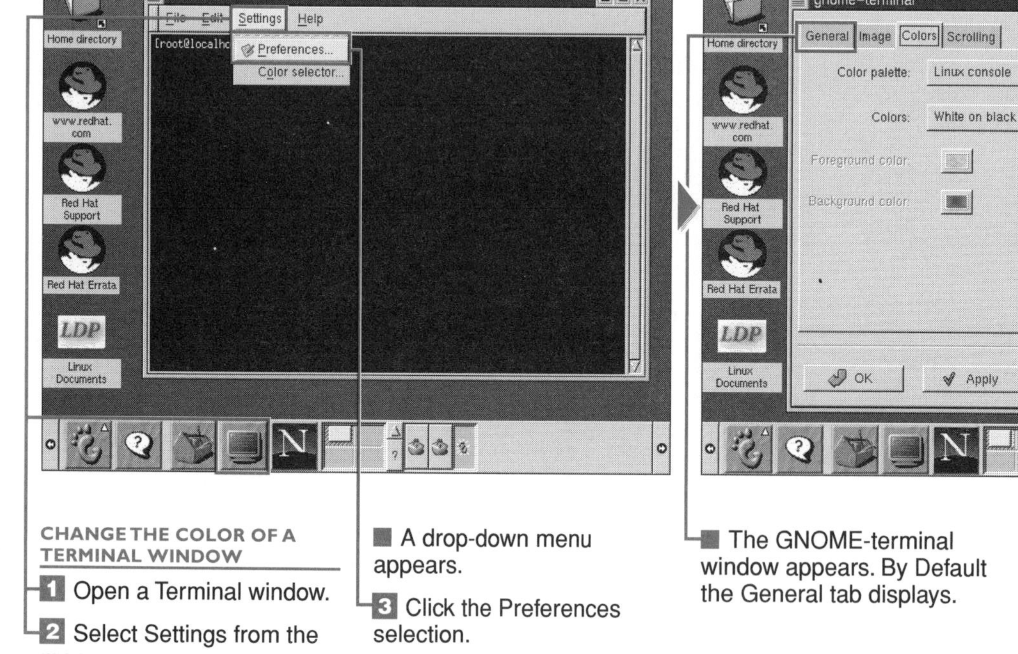

CHANGE THE COLOR OF A TERMINAL WINDOW

1 Open a Terminal window.

2 Select Settings from the menu.

■ A drop-down menu appears.

3 Click the Preferences selection.

■ The GNOME-terminal window appears. By Default the General tab displays.

How can I make my new color settings universal?

- Once you change these settings, all the Terminal windows you open on your machine will look the same (until you change the settings again, of course).

Can I make new color changes to other machines over a network?

- Color selections for Terminals are machine-specific only. If you want to change the default Terminal settings across a network, you have to do it one machine at a time. Luckily, you shouldn't have to do this as the defaults are adequate the vast majority of the time.

Which screen colors should I use?

- Use anything except background colors that match the font color! (Avoid black on black, for instance.) I personally like a soft gold or blue font on black to reduce eyestrain. Other people prefer high contrast so they can get a sharper image.

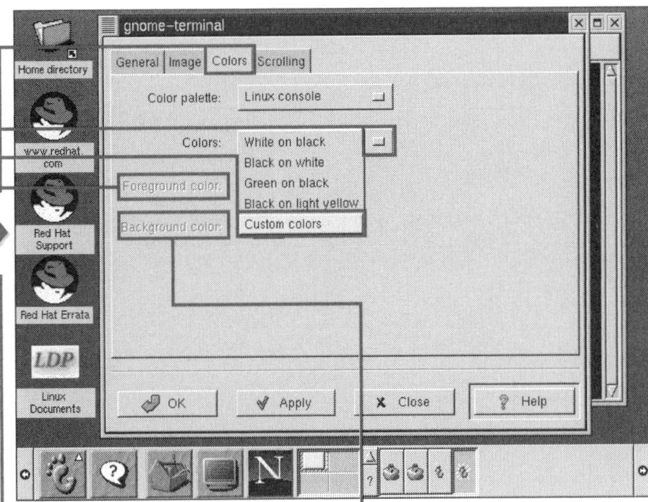

4 Click the Colors tab.

5 Click the Colors pull-down menu button.

6 Select Custom Colors.

7 Click the Foreground color area to set the font color.

8 Click the Background color area.

■ By default, because most text is white, the background is black.

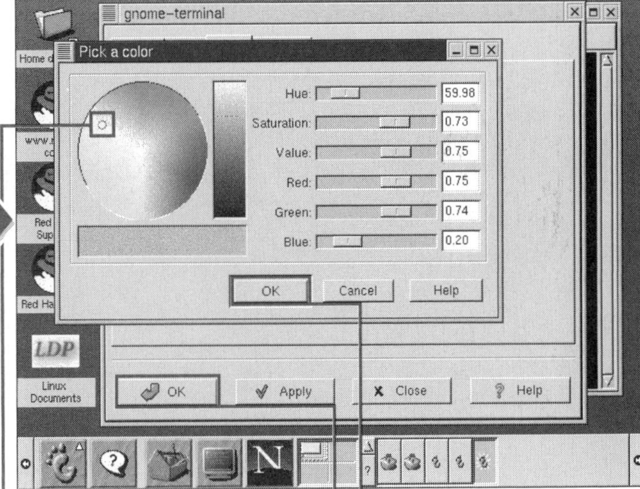

■ The Pick a color window opens.

■ Adjust the color with the color slides to the right.

9 Click and drag the circular mark on the Color Wheel to manipulate the color.

10 To accept your selections, click OK.

■ The GNOME-terminal window appears.

11 Click OK.

■ Your Linux Terminal reflects the changes.

LIST FILES

You can use different command options with the `ls` command (`list`) to find out specific information about files. A *command option*, sometimes just called an option or a flag, is a number or letter that you append to a Linux command, usually separated by a space and a dash. For example, the `ls` command with the appropriate command option to list files in a single column is `ls -1`.

Most Linux command options use letters or numbers. Here, the `1` is used to display information in a certain pattern. Being able to display information on a screen that has been shortened or narrowed to accommodate other windows or Terminals enables you to work in Linux more efficiently, especially if you have a small monitor.

For the following examples, you work as the root account in the root home directory, `/root`.

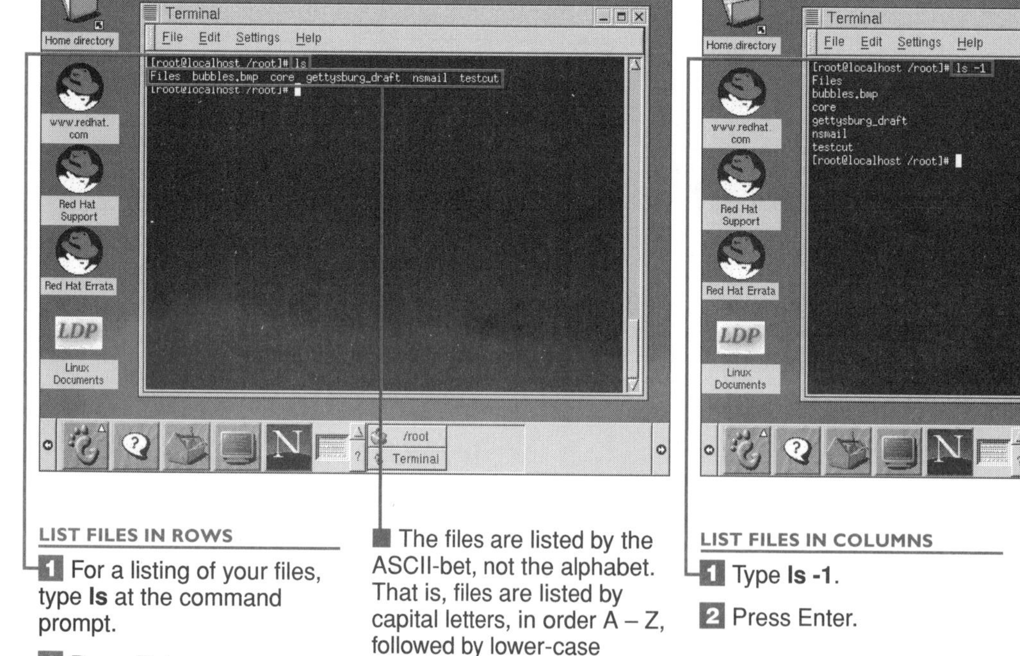

LIST FILES IN ROWS

1 For a listing of your files, type **ls** at the command prompt.

2 Press Enter.

■ The files are listed by the ASCII-bet, not the alphabet. That is, files are listed by capital letters, in order A – Z, followed by lower-case letters, in order a – z.

LIST FILES IN COLUMNS

1 Type **ls -1**.

2 Press Enter.

TIPS

When is listing files by column or row useful?

- Listing files in short rows or columns, such as with the command `ls-1`, is very helpful when you're short on screen space. For example, if you have many windows and Terminals open on the GNOME desktop, you might have to re-adjust the size of your Terminal so that you can see it. If you had to make the Terminal narrower, displaying files in a narrow column would make the list of files easier to read.

If I find a file that takes up a block of disk space, will it fit on a floppy?

- A single block of space takes up 1 kilobyte. A typical disk holds 1,400 kilobytes of information, or 1.4 megabytes (MB). In this way, listing files with size information is helpful in determining if you have enough space to copy or move them.

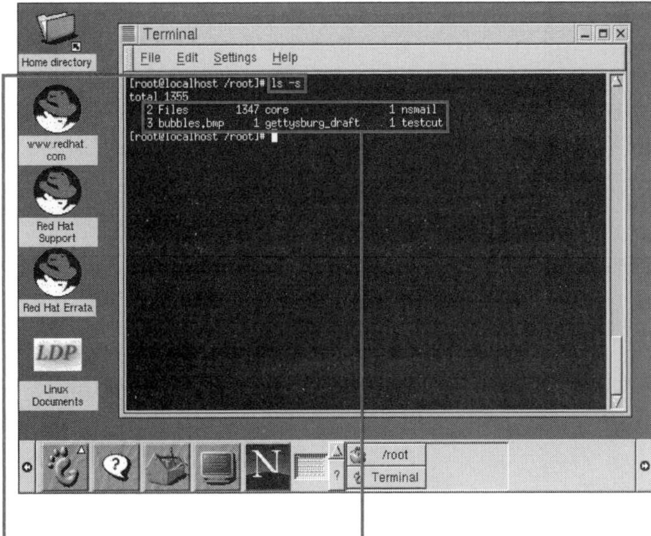

LIST FILES AND SIZE

1 Type **ls -s**.

2 Press Enter.

■ The files appear with their sizes, in *blocks*. A block is equivalent to 1,024 bytes, or 1 kilobyte.

■ Although the files are still listed in the same ASCII order, it's easy to see that the `core` file is by far the largest of the files on display.

LIST FILES BY SIZE

1 Type **ls -S** (be sure to use the capital S).

2 Press Enter.

■ Again, the `core` file is the largest, because it's listed first. The minor disadvantage is that you don't know how big the file is.

CONTINUED

LIST FILES CONTINUED

You can list files in the Linux Terminal along with more information about the file itself. For example, the `ls` command with the appropriate command option to list detailed file information is `ls -l`.

Linux command options use letters that are abbreviations of certain words. In `ls -l`, the `-l` is used because the *l* stands for "long," or detailed, listing.

Knowing specific details about your files can be very helpful if you're trying to find a file that is a certain size or was created on a certain date.

A common command option used with the long listing is `-a`, which displays even hidden files. You are able to stack command options together as long as they don't contradict one another. In the case of `-l` and `-a`, they are very useful together because you get the most information from a list command using them.

LIST DETAILED FILE INFORMATION

1 To get a more detailed listing, use the long form of the ls command by typing **ls –l**.

2 Press Enter.

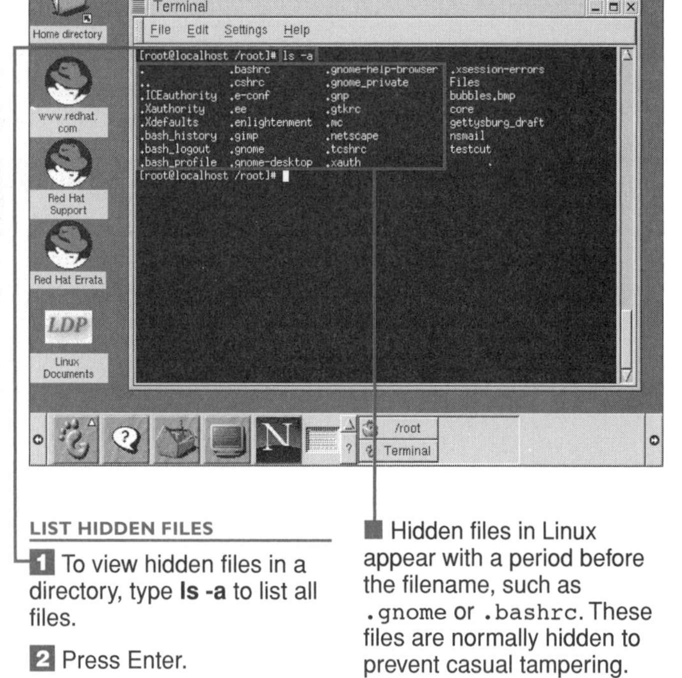

LIST HIDDEN FILES

1 To view hidden files in a directory, type **ls -a** to list all files.

2 Press Enter.

■ Hidden files in Linux appear with a period before the filename, such as `.gnome` or `.bashrc`. These files are normally hidden to prevent casual tampering.

Is there any way that a hidden file won't be seen when using ls with the -a option?

- No, the `-a` option lists everything. Of course, if you're searching for a file that `ls -a` doesn't show, the file could be in a completely different directory.

When you list files by time, does that mean they are listed by the time the file was created?

- The time referred to is not the time that the file was created. Instead, it shows the time that the file was last edited.

When listing files by time, why does Linux display odd times, such as 23:00?

- Linux was built to run for days, weeks, and months without being shut down. Because of this, Linux incorporates the 24-hour clock that is used by the military. If you're not familiar with the system, 23:00 is the equivalent of 11 p.m.

LIST COMPLETE INFORMATION ON ALL FILES

1 To get complete information on all the files in your directory, including the hidden ones, type **ls -la** to do a long listing on all files.

2 Press Enter.

■ Using the `-l` and `-a` options work together in a complimentary manner.

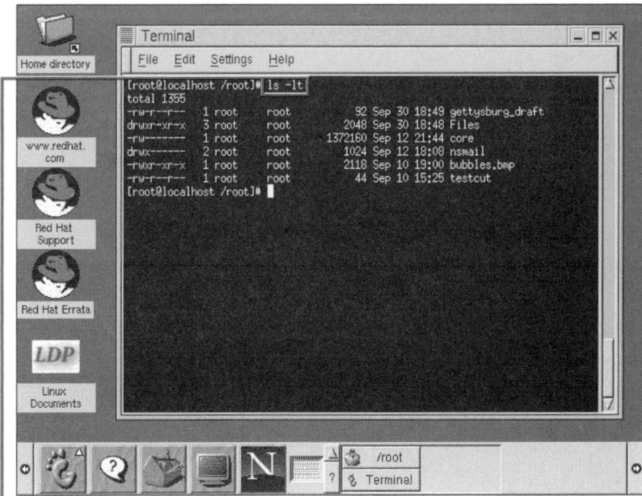

LIST FILES BY TIME

1 Type **ls -lt**.

2 Press Enter to list files by time.

CONTINUED

LIST FILES CONTINUED

You can list files in Linux in more complex ways than simply by size, time, or type of file. Linux enables you to list files in reverse alphabetical order, reverse time-edited order, and even in reverse order by size (smallest to largest, instead of largest to smallest).

If you stack the `r` option with the `list` command, you can list the files in the directory by time edited in reverse order. This enables you to zero in on the most recently edited files.

The most powerful tool that you have at your disposal with the `ls` command is the ability to list files in directories outside of the one in which you are currently. This ability is also called *remote listing*. For example, if you are in the `/root` directory, you don't have to change directories to the `/etc` directory if you want to list the files in `/etc`.

Instead, you can run a single command to list files in any directory on your Linux machine without having to open any new directories or windows on the desktop.

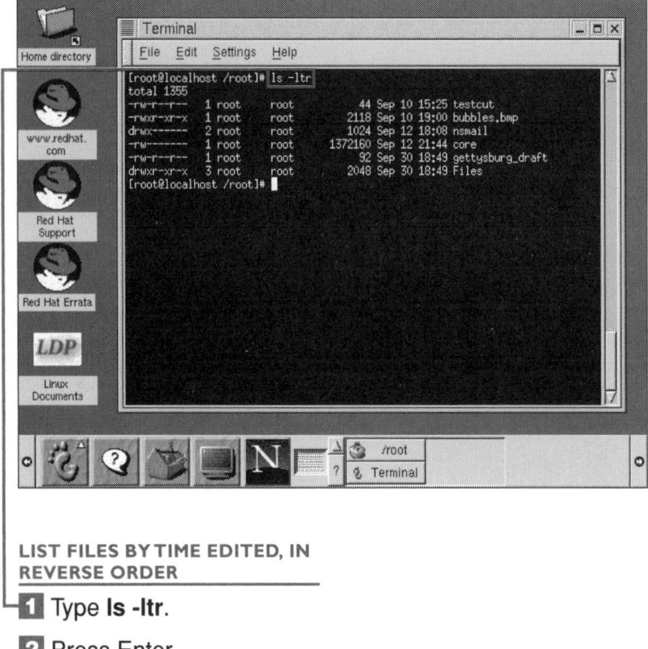

LIST FILES BY TIME EDITED, IN REVERSE ORDER

1 Type **ls -ltr**.

2 Press Enter.

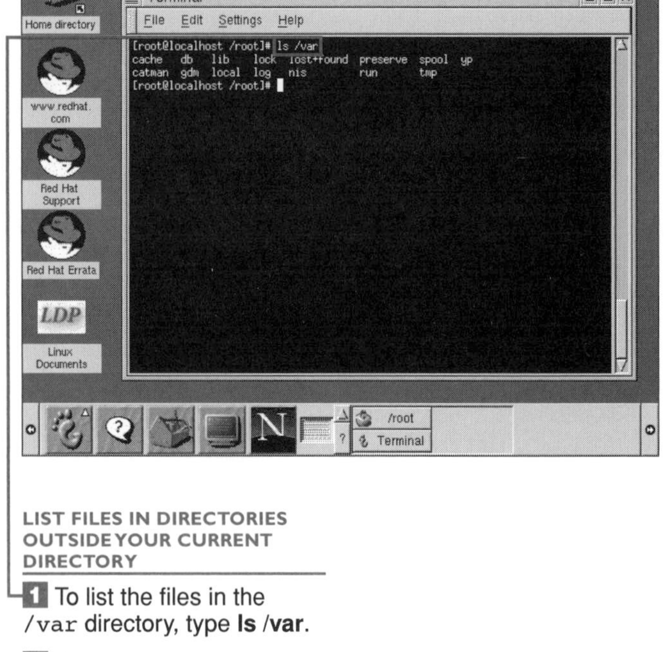

LIST FILES IN DIRECTORIES OUTSIDE YOUR CURRENT DIRECTORY

1 To list the files in the `/var` directory, type **ls /var**.

2 Press Enter.

Are there any limits to the number of options I can stack?

- In theory, no. However, it's very rare that you find more than three useful options stacked together.

How can I list file size in blocks and, at the same time, list the files by block size without the space-wasting result of ls –l?

- Oddly enough, stacking together two almost identical options (`ls –Ss`) will list the files you want, in the order you need.

How is listing a file by Time last altered helpful?

- When I cover Linux security, you learn how helpful this is. Basically, if you can determine when a given file was last edited or touched, you're close to identifying who last did the editing.

STACK OPTIONS IN REMOTE FILE LISTINGS

1. Type **ls -l /var**.

2. Press Enter to do a detailed listing of the `/var` directory.

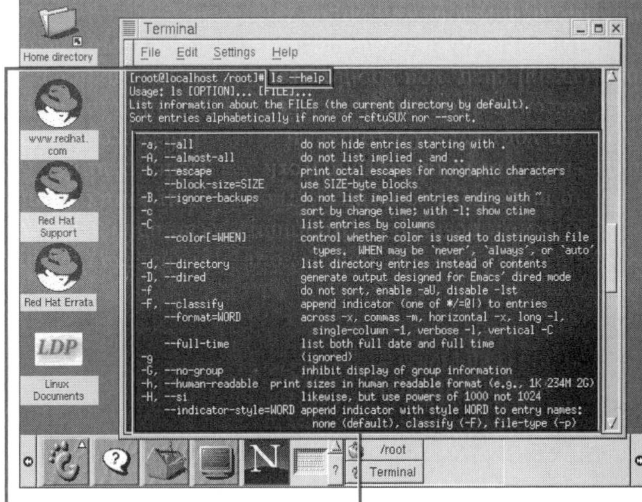

LIST COMMAND OPTIONS

1. Type **ls --help** (note the double-dash).

2. Press Enter.

■ A complete list of the ls command options available to you.

CHANGE DIRECTORIES IN THE LINUX TERMINAL

Getting around the Linux file structure is just as important when you're in the Terminal window as in the GNOME file system. If you're used to a GUI-based lay of the land, you need to practice moving around in the Terminal without the visual cues of an icon or folder. This is worthwhile to learn especially if you're an administrator because you'll be performing this task multiple times on any given day.

To change directories in the Linux Terminal, use the `cd` (change directory) command. Keep in mind that, like the vast majority of Linux commands, the `cd` command is case sensitive. If you try to use `cd` to go to the `Files` directory and you type `files` after the `cd` command at the command prompt, you will not go anywhere or you may end up in the wrong location.

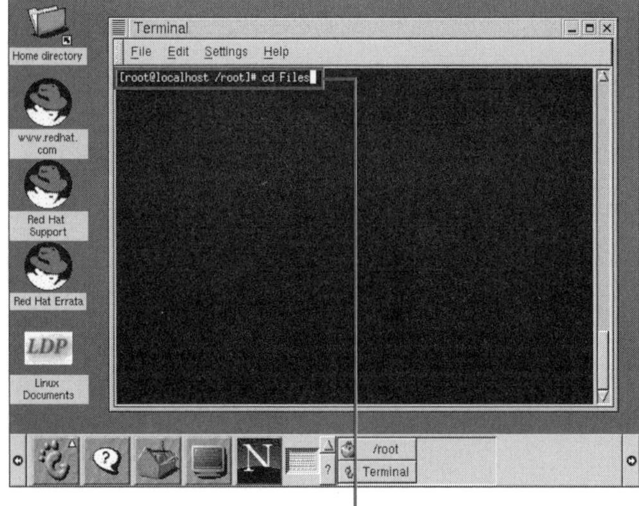

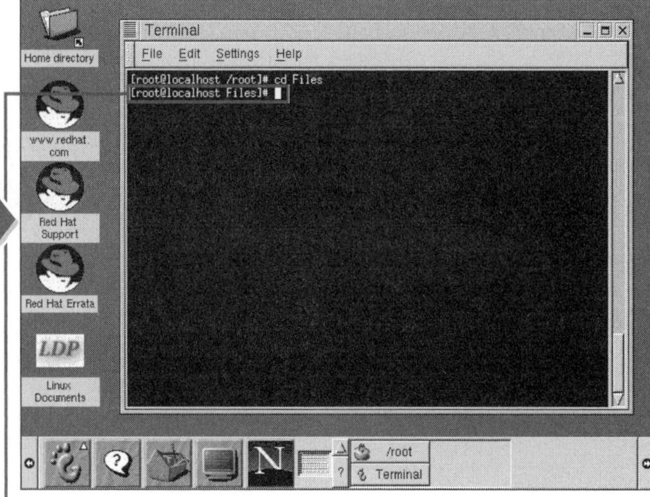

CHANGE DIRECTORIES

1 Click to open a Terminal window.

2 Change to the `Files` directory under your `/root` home directory, by typing **cd Files** at the command prompt.

3 Press Enter.

■ The username is the same (you're still in as `root`), but the location is `Files`. `Files` is the directory you're currently in, but the full path name is `/root/Files`, which is not listed completely.

TIPS

If I don't have execute permissions for a given directory, can I still use the cd command to go to that directory?

- Yes. If you can execute a file, it means that you can start it if it's a Linux program. This won't interfere with you changing directories to that location.

If I don't have write permissions for a given directory, can I still use the cd command to go to that directory?

- This won't be a problem. Lacking write permissions means that you can't edit any of the files in the directory, but you can still `cd` to it.

If I don't have read permissions for a given directory, can I still use the cd command to go to that directory?

- Lacking read permissions will not prevent you from visiting the directory in question. However, you won't be able to view any of the files in the directory.

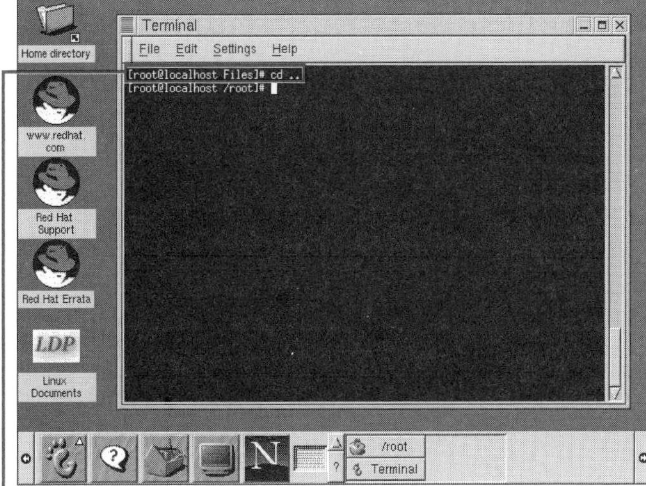

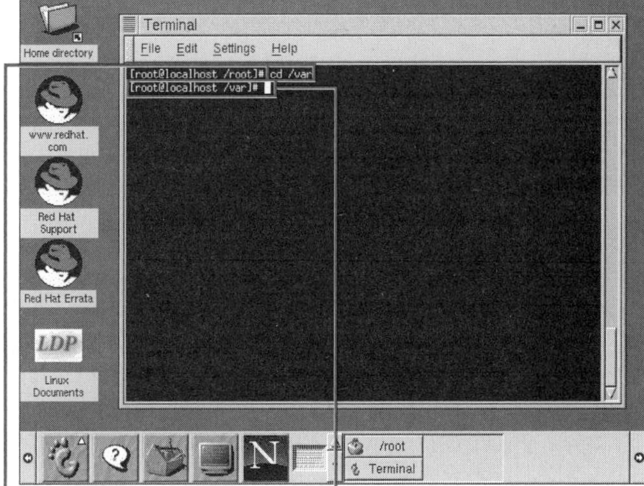

RETURN TO YOUR HOME DIRECTORY

1 Type **cd..** .

■ Using a dash (–) after the `cd` command moves you one directory up from your current location.

2 Press Enter.

■ This takes you one step up from `/root/Files` to `/root`.

MOVE TO A DIFFERENT DIRECTORY

1 To move to the `var` directory, type **cd /var**.

Note: In Linux, moving to a directory outside of your immediate vicinity requires that you use a slash before the name.

2 Press Enter.

■ The directory listing changes to indicate that you're now in the `/var` directory.

CONTINUED

CHANGE DIRECTORIES IN THE LINUX TERMINAL CONTINUED

You can use the change directory command (cd) in the Linux Terminal to move between directories much more quickly than in the GNOME desktop environment.

This ease comes from the ability to specify a jump of several directories in a single command line in the Linux Terminal. By comparison, in the GNOME desktop, you might have to click each directory icon, wait a second or two for the directory window to open, and then repeat the process until you reach your destination. Furthermore, after you reach your destination and complete the task you set out to accomplish, you can easily return to your home directory with a single cd command.

Because you can move so quickly in the Terminal, be sure to make use of the pwd command. pwd tells you your exact location, which is a help when you've been jumping from directory to directory.

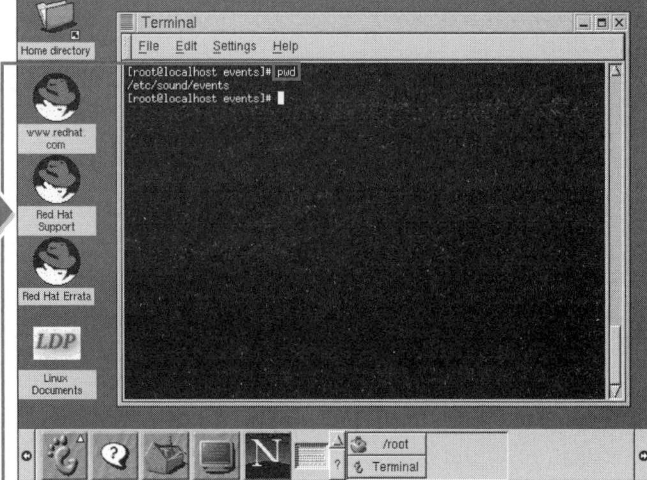

MOVE MULTIPLE DIRECTORIES WITH ONE COMMAND

1 To change directories from /var to /etc/sound/events, type **cd /etc/sound/events**.

2 Press Enter.

- Your location says the events directory, but you're actually deeper into the file system.

- Use the Linux command pwd to see where you are.

3 Type **pwd**.

4 Press Enter.

- You see your actual location, which is /etc/sound/events.

How can I tell what subdirectories are immediately under my location?

- Use the `ls -l` command. Any file with a `d` in the leftmost listing is a directory, not a file.

Is there a way I can tell this at a glance without having to type an ls command?

- Actually, no. This is an advantage of a GUI system — at a glance, you can see what's in a file. In the pure Linex environment of the Terminal, you won't have that luxury and you may have to resort to memory.

Then what's the advantage of using the Terminal?

- You can sometimes move more quickly in the Terminal, as when you type only one command to jump five or six directories away. And finally, in the Terminal, it's easier to get certain kinds of information, such as file permissioning.

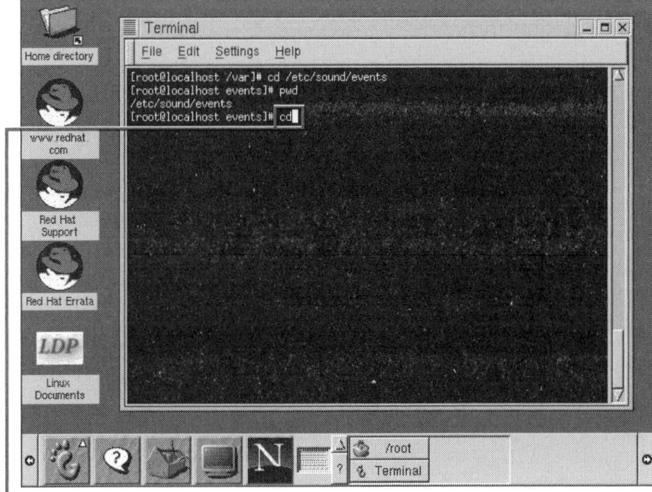

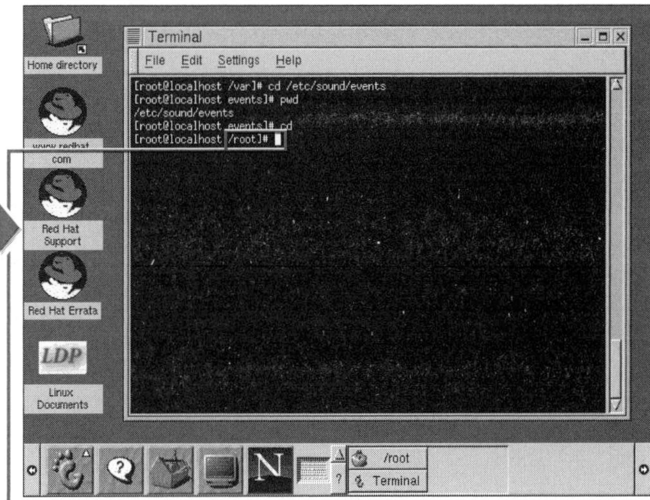

RETURN TO YOUR HOME DIRECTORY

1 To return to your Home Directory, `/root`, type **cd** with no other options.

2 Press Enter.

■ The listing is `/root` again.

CREATE NEW FILES

Creating files in the Linux Terminal is easy. The new file can be the product of a utility, an application, or a regular file you create on the fly. Of course, you have complete flexibility to create new text, graphics, or binary files in Linux, depending on the program you're using.

One of the simplest way to create a new text file is to use the `touch` command. `touch` is not a word-processing program — it's just a simple Linux command.

When you use `touch`, you create a blank text file that can be edited, copied, and moved like any Linux file that actually contains information. You can create blank files with the `touch` command and then use GNOME applications, such as gnotepad or the gnumeric spreadsheet to save information into the file you created with the `touch` command.

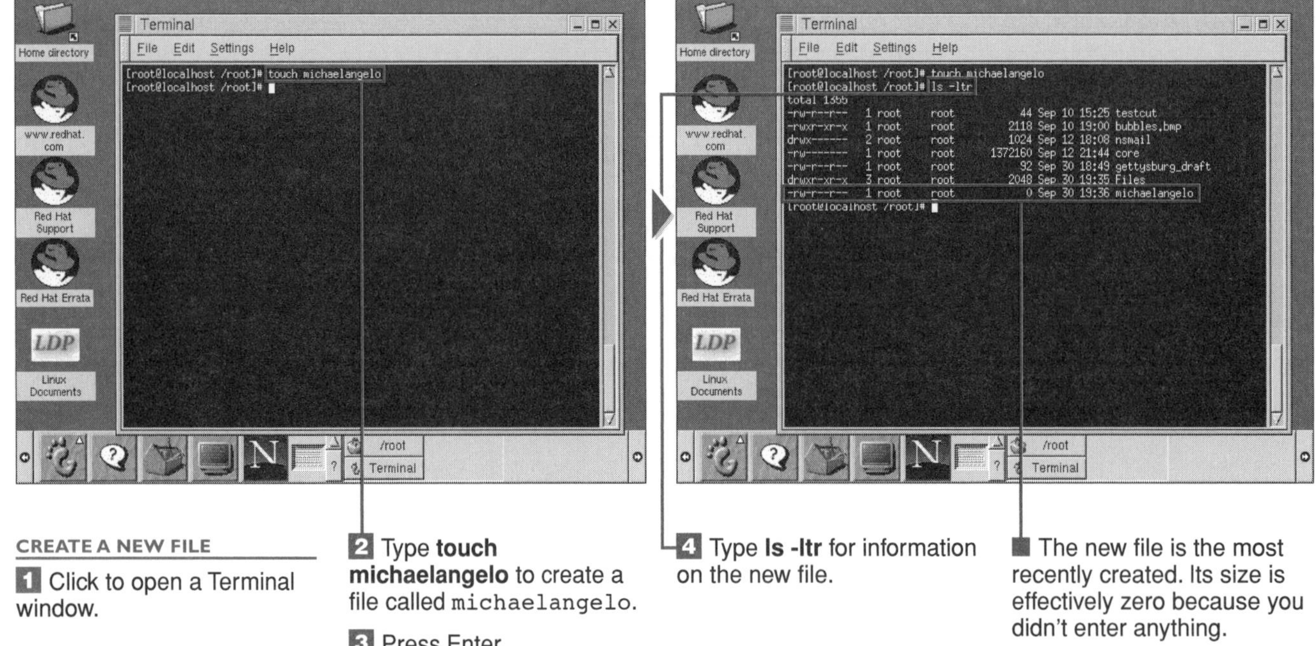

CREATE A NEW FILE

1 Click to open a Terminal window.

2 Type **touch michaelangelo** to create a file called `michaelangelo`.

3 Press Enter.

4 Type **ls -ltr** for information on the new file.

■ The new file is the most recently created. Its size is effectively zero because you didn't enter anything.

Can any user on the system use touch?

- Yes. This is a basic UNIX command that was brought over into the Linux world a long time ago.

Why can't I create files with touch in certain areas?

- Most likely, you're not root and thus you're not permissioned to edit certain directories by adding new files to them. If you are logged in as the root account, you may have permissioned the directory so that nobody can write a new file into it — of course as root you can change this, so it's not 100 percent invulnerable.

What's the use of creating new files if there's nothing inside of them?

- Sometimes, creating a new empty file can serve as a place-holder or a reminder to put data in a certain file. For example, if later in your hectic day you plan to save a certain mail file to a log, you could create the blank file in advance, calling it `mail-log`, and then add to it when you're ready.

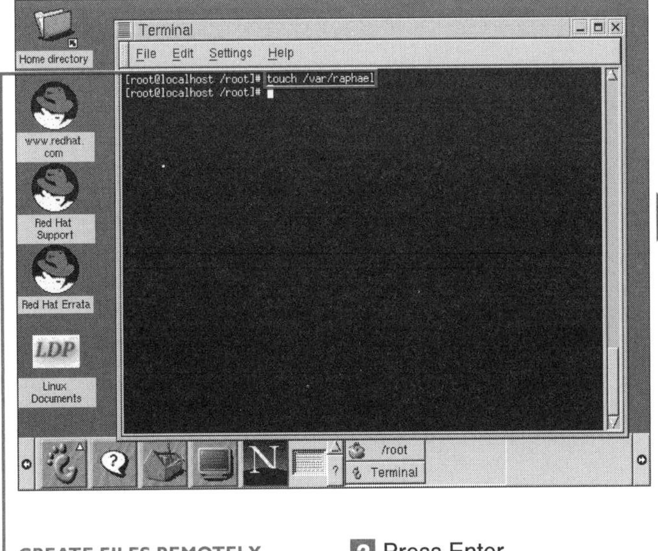

CREATE FILES REMOTELY

1 Type **touch /var/raphael**.

2 Press Enter.

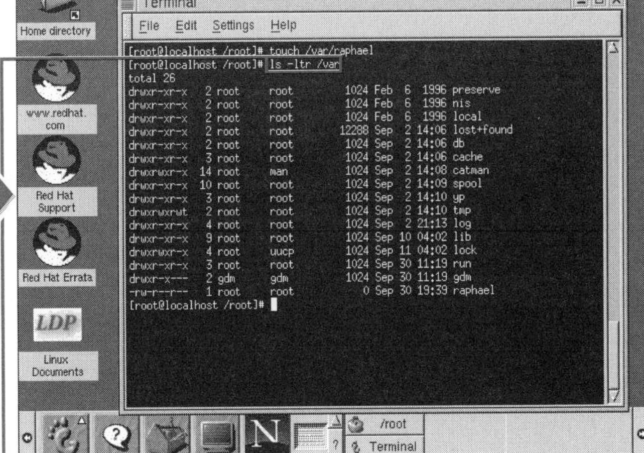

3 To do a remote listing, type **ls –lrt /var**.

4 Press Enter.

CREATE NEW DIRECTORIES

Creating new directories is crucial in the Linux world if you want to keep your environment organized. Use the `mkdir` (make directory) command to create new directories.

In your `home` directory, for example, you might create two separate directories, one called `Work` and one called `Home`. Keeping files organized is easier if you create your directories and name them by some category or function.

When creating directories in the Linux Terminal, do not use the term *folder*. While essentially the same, a folder is a directory represented by an icon. Therefore, to avoid confusion when using icon terms in an environment where no icons exist, you should refer to `/var` and `/etc` as the `var` directory and `etc` directory as opposed to the `var` folder and the `etc` folder.

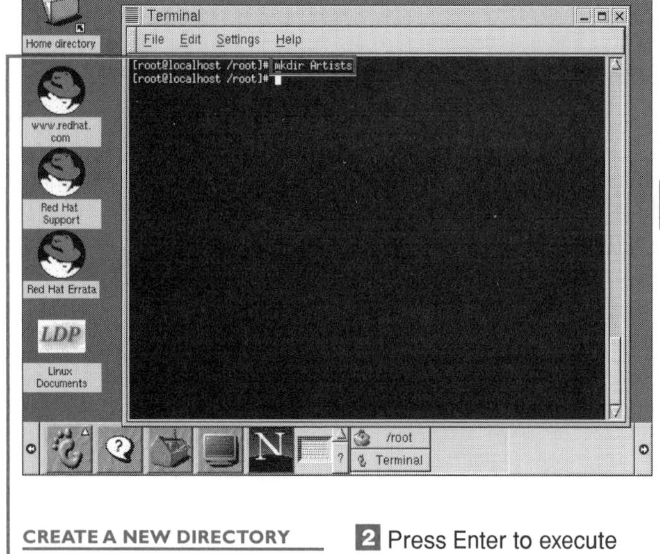

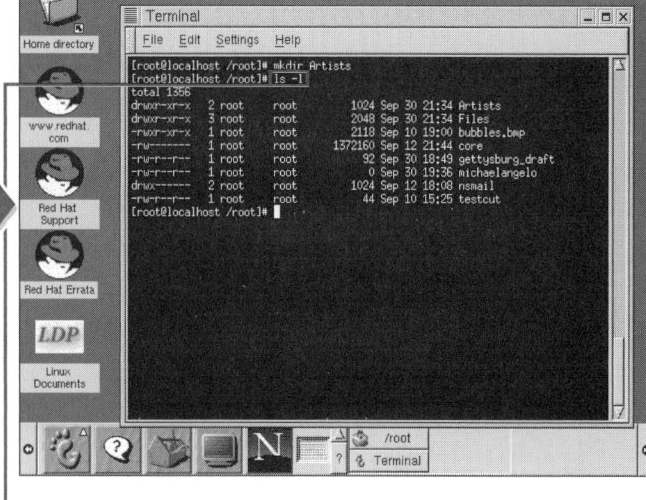

CREATE A NEW DIRECTORY

1 At the command prompt, type **mkdir Artists** to create a new directory called `Artists`.

2 Press Enter to execute the command.

3 Type **ls -l** to see a listing of this directory.

4 Press Enter.

Why does Linux tell you that a file exists when you try to create a directory of the same name? Shouldn't Linux tell you that a directory exists?

- This is an old terminology issue. The short answer is that to the Linux operating system, *everything* — text files, binaries, synbolic links and more — is treated as a file. Therefore, the correct error message is `File exists`.

Are there any restrictions on directory names?

- Linux won't allow you to name directories with slashes in them because it confuses the operating system. You also won't be able to name directories `//`, `/`, or `..` because these symbols already have meaning within the Linux operating system.

Are there names that ideally shouldn't be used?

- Ideally, you never want to use names that already exist, particularly if they're a system directory name. If you're in your `home` directory, you can easily create a directory called `/etc` — but you run the risk of confusing yourself if you're trying to locate programs that rightfully belong in the real `/etc` area.

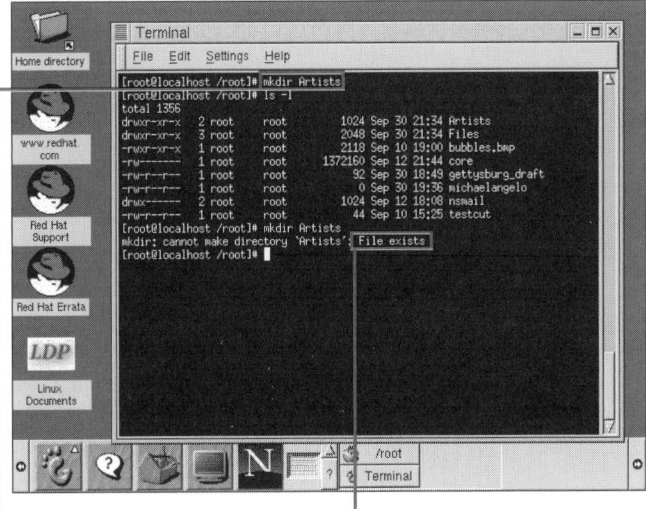

MAKE DIRECTORIES WITH MKDIR

■ `mkdir` safety feature warns before you try to overwrite a directory.

1 Type **mkdir Artists**.

2 Press Enter.

■ You are warned that the file exists.

■ To create a second directory, you must rename or delete the `Artists` directory, or name your directory something else.

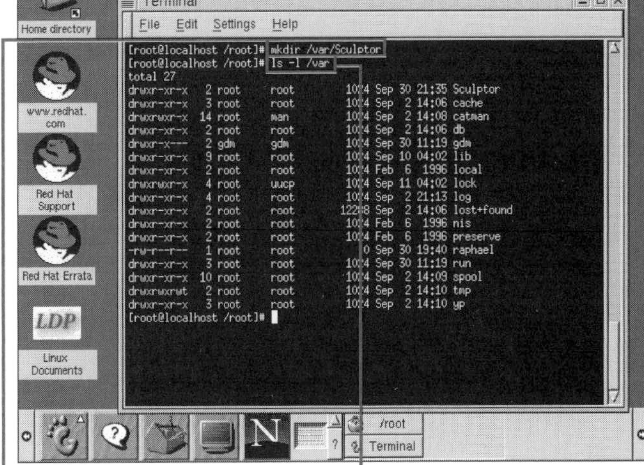

CREATE DIRECTORIES REMOTELY

1 To create the directory Sculptor in the `/var` directory, type **mkdir /var/Sculptor**.

2 Press Enter.

3 Type **ls -l /var**.

4 Press Enter to see the new directory that you created.

COPY FILES IN THE LINUX TERMINAL

You can copy files in the Linux Terminal just as you do in the GNOME file manager. Of course, without a graphic desktop, you won't be relying on menu options to guide you. Also, you won't be able to use the mouse to click and drag files from one location to another. When you make a copy of a file, you're creating an exact duplicate of the file in a new location.

In the Linux Terminal, the copy command is cp. *Recursiveness* is the all-important thing to remember here. When you copy a directory recursively, it means that you're copying the directory and all of the files inside of it. When you rename a directory, recursiveness is automatic. When copying or moving a directory, you have to specify recursiveness. To do so, use the cp command with the command option -R.

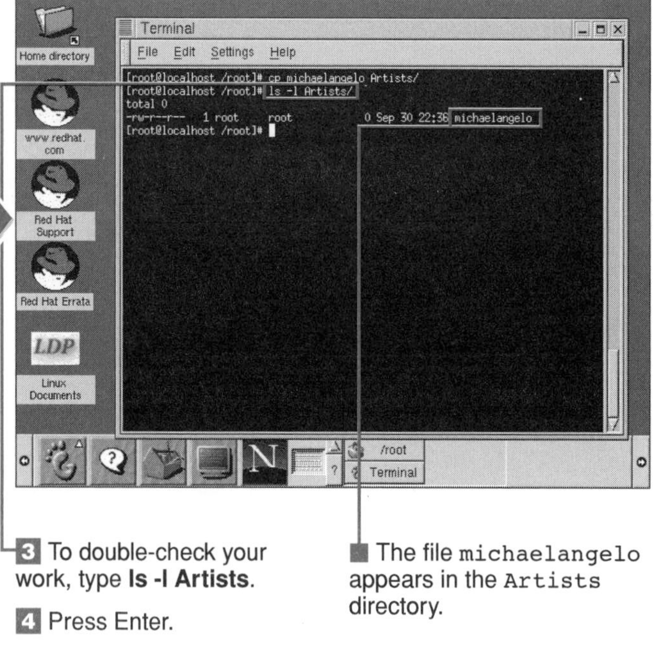

COPY A FILE

1 Type **cp michaelangelo Artists** to copy michaelangelo to Artists.

2 Press Enter.

3 To double-check your work, type **ls -l Artists**.

4 Press Enter.

■ The file michaelangelo appears in the Artists directory.

How can I copy multiple files?

- Copying multiple files is only advisable when all your files start with the same letter (and the same case of letter). For example, if you have three files called `Monalisa`, `Monalisa_2`, and `Monalisa_smile`, you can copy all of them to, for example, the `/var` directory with the command `cp M* /var`.

What if my multiple files all have different names?

- Then it's best to avoid a multiple copy unless you're very diligent. Mistakes and omissions can happen if you have to do the same command again and again. Use your best judgment.

What if I accidentally copy a file over itself?

- You don't have to worry about this in Linux. If you attempt to copy a file to a location where it already exists, you get a message back stating that "this file already exists" or something similar.

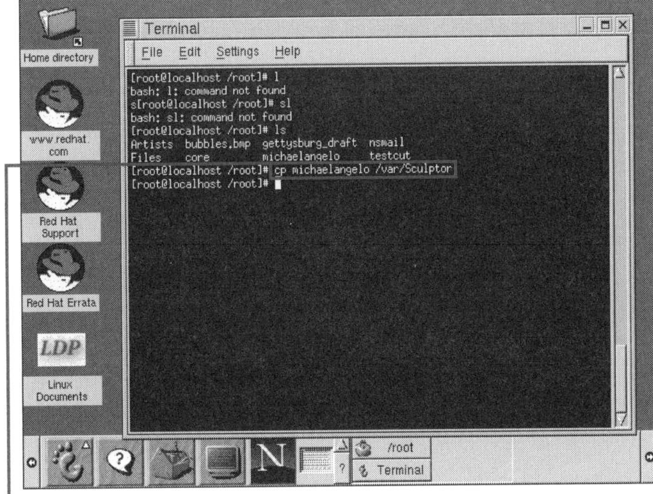

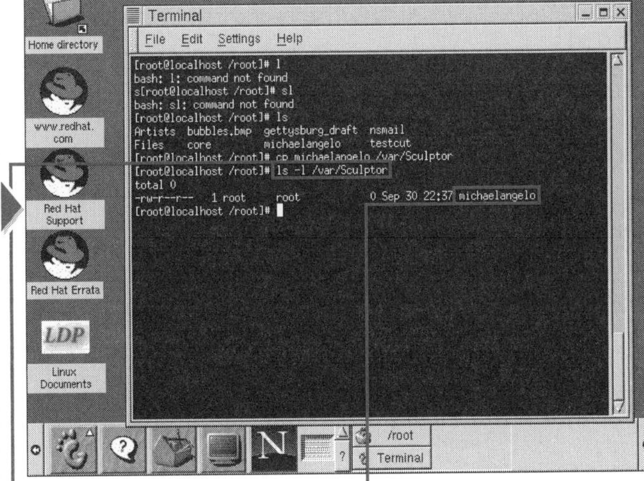

COPY A FILE TO A REMOTE LOCATION

1 Type **cp michaelangelo /var/Sculptor** to copy `michaelangelo` to the `.Sculptor` directory, under `/var`.

■ You must note the entire path for the destination directory.

2 Press Enter.

3 Type **ls -l /var/Sculptor**.

4 Press Enter to get a glimpse of what's inside the `/var/Sculptor` directory.

■ To the right, `michaelangelo` appears.

COPY DIRECTORIES IN THE LINUX TERMINAL

You can copy directories as well as individual files in the Linux Terminal. To copy a directory, you will use the same command that is used for copying files, cp. However, when copying entire directories, you must always use the -R command option for the action to work. -R is short for the "recursive" option that you must also specify to ensure that all the files listed under a given directory are copied along with the directory selected for copying.

Because you must specify the -R option when you copy directories, using the cp command in the Linux Terminal is said to be "automatically recursive." Of course, if it were truly automatic, you wouldn't be required to manually type the option each time, but that is the way that the command was designed in Red Hat's brand of Linux.

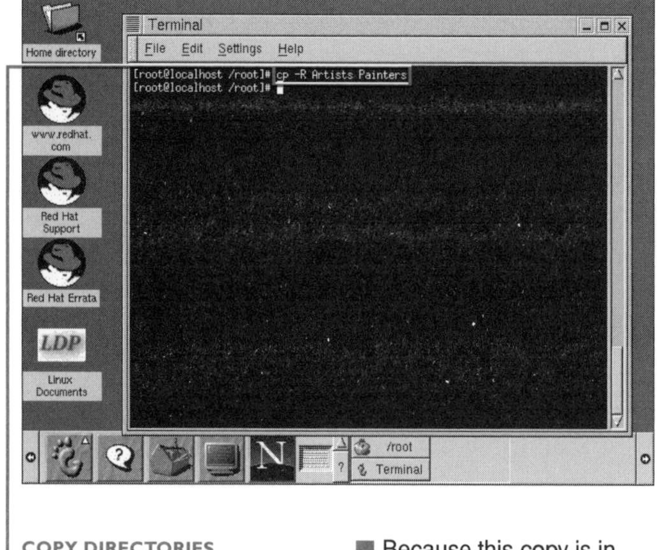

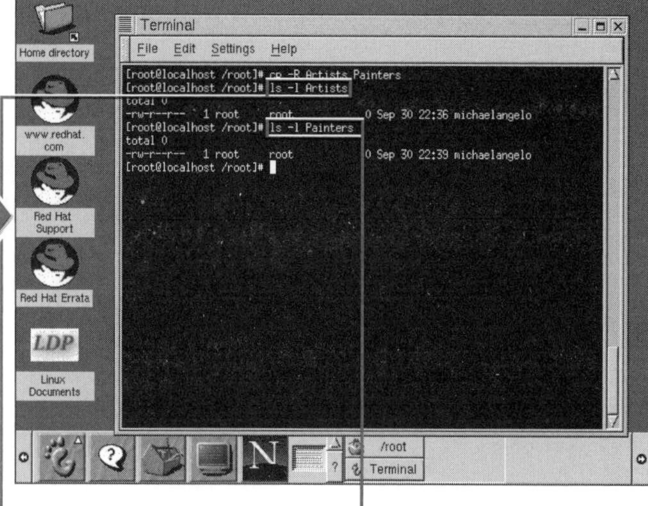

COPY DIRECTORIES

1 Type **cp -R Artists Painters** to make a copy of the Artists directory.

■ Because this copy is in the same /root directory, give it a different name, Painters.

2 Press Enter.

3 To check on this task, type **ls -l Artists** to view the contents of that directory.

■ Michaelangelo is still on the right side.

4 Press Enter.

5 Perform the same command on Painters.

■ The contents should be identical except for the time of creation.

TIPS

What if I don't want to copy a directory with all of its subdirectories and files that it contains?

- Your best bet is to avoid the `cp` command and use the `mkdir` command to just create an empty directory with the name you specify.

What if I accidentally copy a directory over itself?

- The same situation exists with directories as with individual files. If you attempt to copy a directory to a location where it already exists, you get a message back stating that "this directory already exists" or something similar.

How can I copy a file or directory to a floppy disk?

- You can copy files to the `/mnt/floppy` directory. You have to make sure that you've got a floppy disk in the drive and that the floppy is mounted. You learn about setting up your floppy drive and mounting it in Chapter 11.

COPY TO A REMOTE LOCATION

1 Type **cp –R Artists /var/Artists_2** to copy `Artists` to the `/var` directory.

2 Press Enter.

■ You can call the new directory `Artists_2`.

3 Check on the results by typing **ls -l /var**.

4 Press Enter.

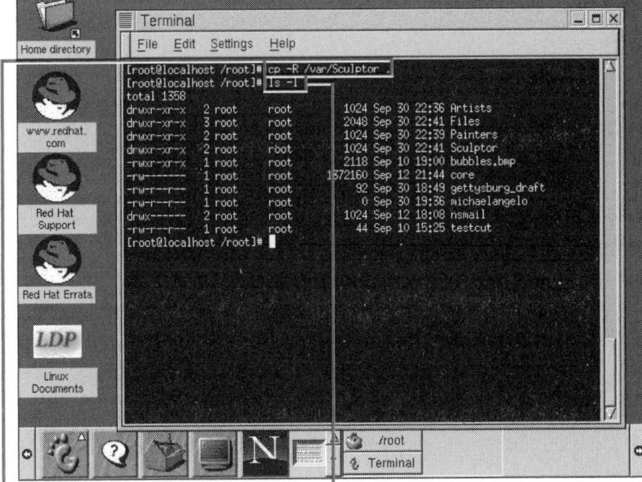

COPY REMOTE TO YOUR HOME DIRECTORY

1 Type **cp -R /var/Sculptor**.

■ You have to put in the full path name of Sculptor's location.

2 Press Enter.

■ This command copies the `/var/Sculptor` directory to your home directory `/root`.

3 Type **ls -l** to see the results.

4 Press Enter.

RENAME FILES OR DIRECTORIES

You can rename any kind of file or directory in the Linux Terminal with the `mv` command. The `mv` command is actually the `move` command in Linux, but it's primarily used for renaming files and directories because it's so convenient.

You can more effectively organize the contents of your `home` directory — any system directory — with a few strategically placed file names.

For example, if you have a complete hodgepodge of reports you've written for school or the office sitting in your home directory, renaming the files in a consistent pattern (also called a *naming scheme*) will help organize your directory.

You could sort out files that were completed for work by renaming them `work1`, `work2`, or `boss_stuff`. Class notes could be organized by naming them after the subject matter (`chem1`, `bio3`). The key to this style of organization is to simply be consistent.

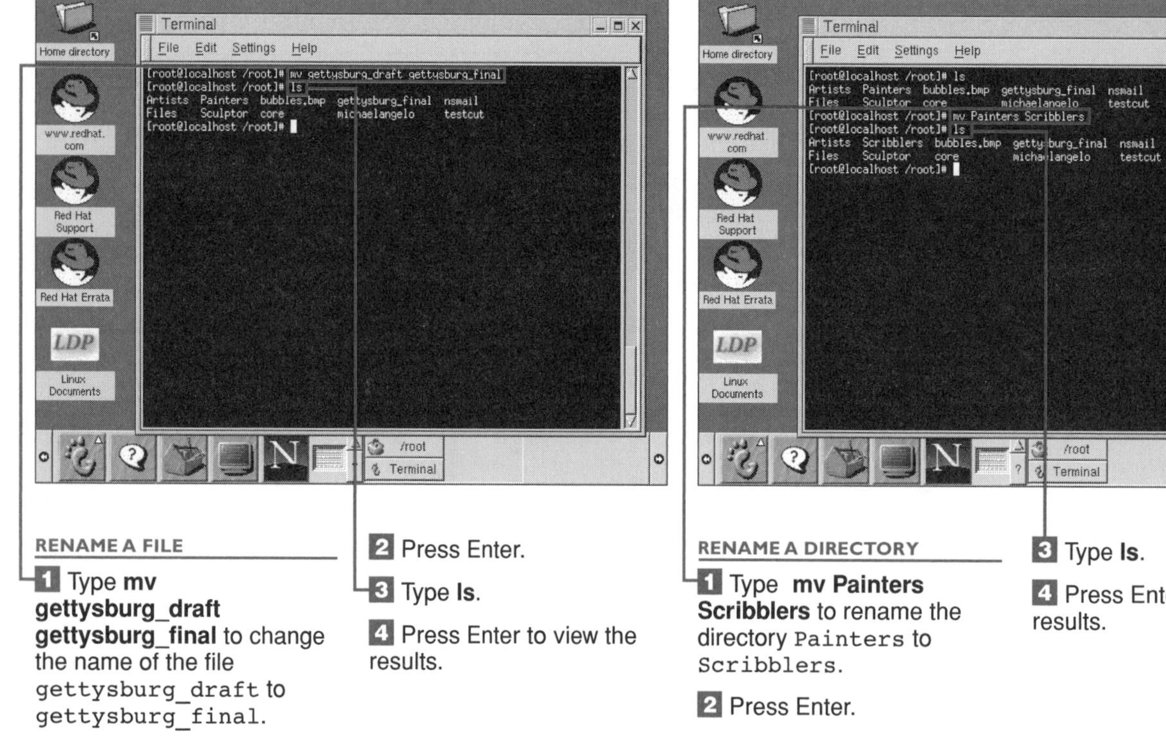

RENAME A FILE

1. Type **mv gettysburg_draft gettysburg_final** to change the name of the file `gettysburg_draft` to `gettysburg_final`.
2. Press Enter.
3. Type **ls**.
4. Press Enter to view the results.

RENAME A DIRECTORY

1. Type **mv Painters Scribblers** to rename the directory `Painters` to `Scribblers`.
2. Press Enter.
3. Type **ls**.
4. Press Enter to view the results.

Can I name files or directories with spaces, hyphens, colons, or slashes?

- Naming files with slashes or colons can cause confusion when you work with files, especially in the Linux Terminal window. You're best off not naming files with any of these symbols.

Does renaming directories affect the files stored inside of them?

- Renaming directories does not affect files inside the directories, so if you wanted to change the name of a directory — and all of its contents — to the name `ditto.txt`, it simply won't work.

Can I change the extensions on a file? For example, can I change bubbles.bmp to bubbles.txt?

- You can change the file extensions with the `mv` command, as follows: `mv bubbles.bmp bubbles.txt`. However, the file will most likely become unusable, so it's best not to do this unless you have no choice in the matter.

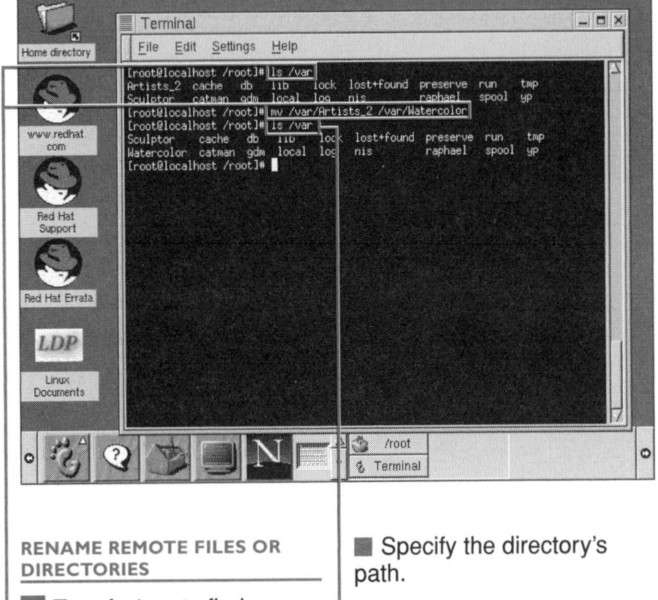

RENAME REMOTE FILES OR DIRECTORIES

1 Type **ls /var** to find `Artists_2`.

2 Type **mv /var/Artists_2 /var/Watercolor** to rename .

■ Specify the directory's path.

3 Press Enter.

4 Type **ls /var** to see the results again.

5 Press Enter.

RENAME A FILE AND MOVE IT AT THE SAME TIME

1 Type **mv Scribblers /var/Oil** to move the directory `Scribblers` out of the `home` directory and into `/var`, while renaming it to `Oil`.

2 Press Enter.

3 Check the result by typing **ls –l /var**.

4 Press Enter.

DELETE FILES AND DIRECTORIES

You delete files and directories in the Linux Terminal with the `rm` command. When you delete a file or directory, Linux asks you if you're sure you want to delete it. Make sure that you pay attention here because once you answer yes, there is no turning back or restoring the file unless you've made a backup copy somewhere else.

You can also delete entire directories in Linux by using the `-R` command option with the `rm` command. Linux offers an additional safeguard when it comes to deleting directories. If there are files inside the directory, GNOME asks if you want to delete all the files inside the directory as well. If you want to keep any files inside the directory, it's best to move or copy them elsewhere.

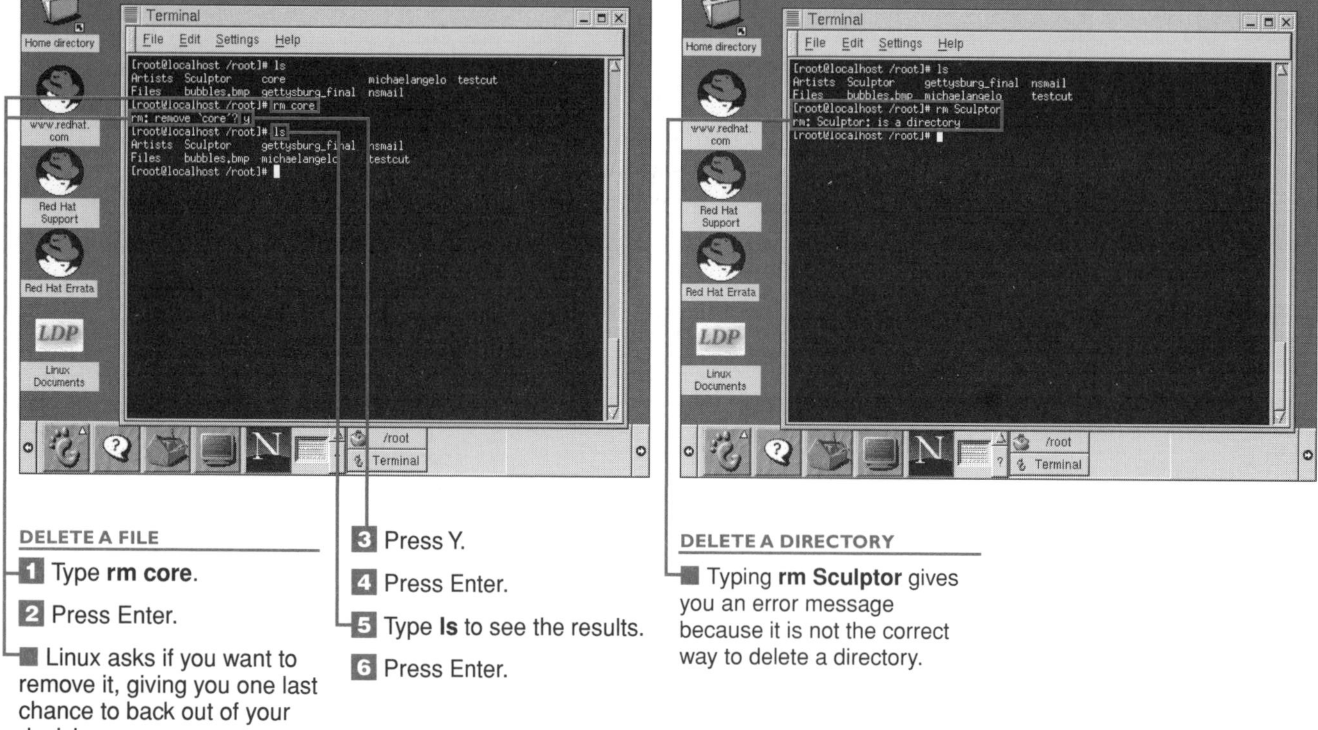

DELETE A FILE

1 Type **rm core**.

2 Press Enter.

■ Linux asks if you want to remove it, giving you one last chance to back out of your decision.

3 Press Y.

4 Press Enter.

5 Type **ls** to see the results.

6 Press Enter.

DELETE A DIRECTORY

■ Typing **rm Sculptor** gives you an error message because it is not the correct way to delete a directory.

Why doesn't Linux delete the file I specify when I press Enter in answer to the "Are you sure you want to delete this message?"

- If you simply press Enter when Linux asks you if you want to delete the file, the file is not deleted. By default, Linux errs on the side of caution. You need to take the affirmative step of typing the lowercase *y* when deleting a file in order for Linux to complete the task.

Are there any files in the Linux environment that you never want to delete?

- Yes. Any files that are hidden unless you uncover them with the `ls -a` command in the Linux Terminal or with the Show Hidden Files preference in GNOME should be left untouched. They are kept hidden for a reason — so that people cannot tamper with them.

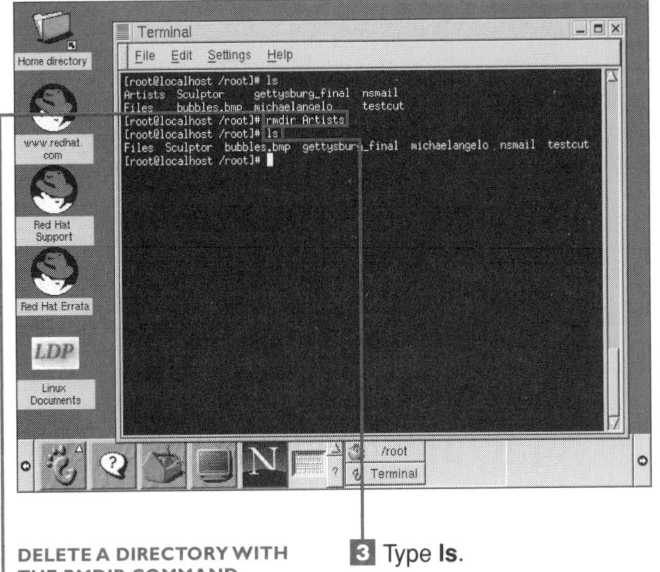

DELETE A DIRECTORY WITH THE RMDIR COMMAND

1 Delete the directory `Artists` by typing **rmdir Artists**.

2 Press Enter.

3 Type **ls**.

4 Press Enter.

Note: This method, while fast, does not give you a warning message, which the `rm –r` method does.

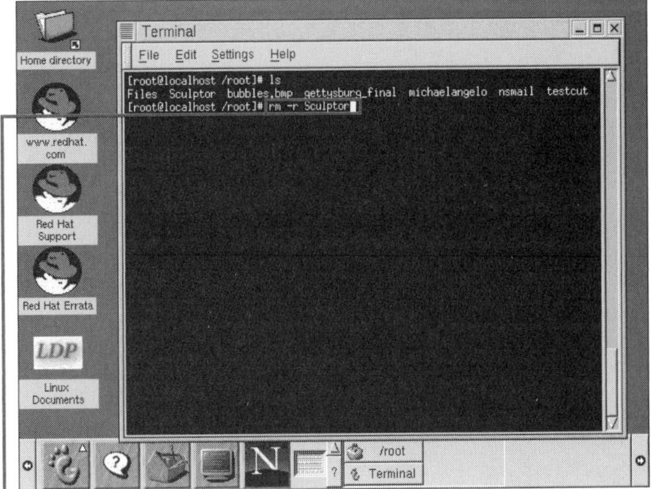

DELETE A DIRECTORY WITH THE RM COMMAND

1 Type **rm –r Sculptor**.

2 Press Enter.

CONTINUED

DELETE FILES AND DIRECTORIES
CONTINUED

You can take advantage of Linux's flexibility with its file system when deleting files or directories. Much like Linux's advantages in allowing you to list files or directories remotely, you can also delete files or directories without having to actually change directories to be in the same location as the object you are removing.

This is an advantage that is specific to working in the Linux Terminal. It's considerably more difficult to delete files remotely in the GNOME desktop environment.

Another advantage to deleting files and directories while in the Terminal is the built-in safeguards that Linux keeps to prevent accidental or spur-of-the-moment deletions. When deleting a file, you get a warning message asking if you want to proceed. When removing an entire directory, Linux actually asks you twice whether you want to go through with erasing the contents of the directory you've selected.

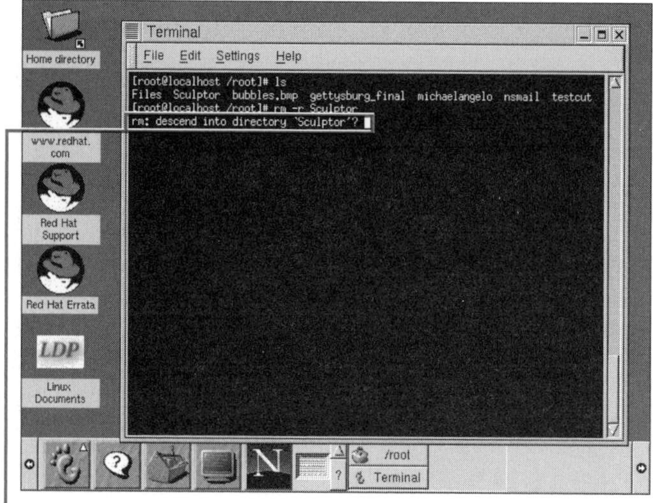

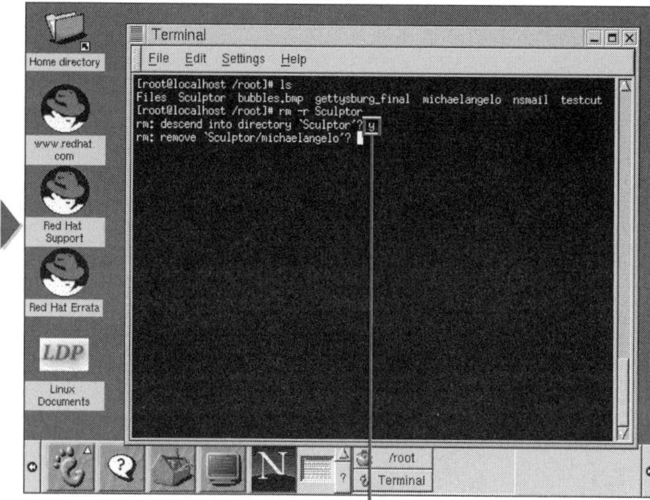

■ You get the first of two warnings. The first asks if you want `rm` to descend into the directory. That's Linux way of asking if there are files inside this directory, are you sure that you want to delete.

3 Press Y if you are sure that you want to delete all the files.

4 Press Enter.

■ The second warning asks you if you want to remove this directory.

Note: Both questions default to No because there is no going back in Linux, no Trash Can or Recycle Bin to empty later.

5 Press Y .

6 Press Enter to execute this.

7 Type **ls** to check the results.

8 Press Enter.

Can I change my mind once a delete is in progress?

- Not really. If you're deleting a truly gigantic file that takes Linux several minutes to get rid of, you can try to kill the delete process; note, however, that you're only able to save whatever the delete function hasn't already deleted.

How can I delete multiple files at once?

- You can use the k as a wildcard (for example, `rm *ing` deletes all files that end in ing). I strongly suggest that you don't do this. The potential for catastrophe by deleting something that is system-critical is too high.

When I'm logged in as a different user, why can't I delete certain files anymore?

- When you're logged in as the `root` account, you have complete administrative privileges over any file. When you're logged in as a regular user, you can only delete files that you're permissioned to, such as your own text or graphics files in your home directory.

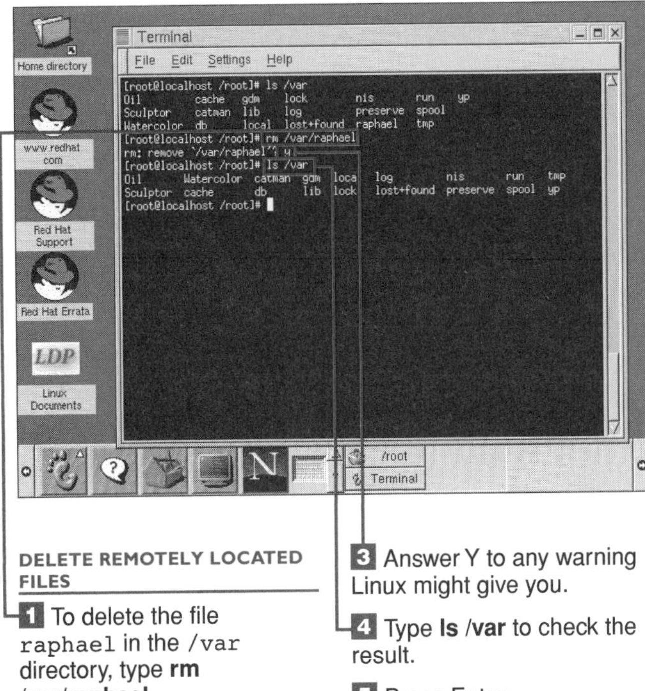

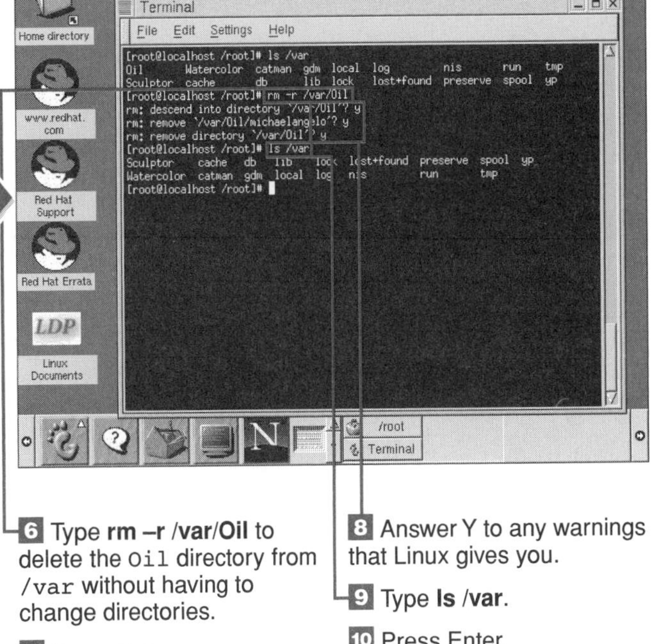

DELETE REMOTELY LOCATED FILES

1. To delete the file `raphael` in the `/var` directory, type **rm /var/raphael**.
2. Press Enter.
3. Answer Y to any warning Linux might give you.
4. Type **ls /var** to check the result.
5. Press Enter.
6. Type **rm –r /var/Oil** to delete the `Oil` directory from `/var` without having to change directories.
7. Press Enter.
8. Answer Y to any warnings that Linux gives you.
9. Type **ls /var**.
10. Press Enter.

DETERMINE YOUR USER ACCOUNT IDENTITY

You need to know who you're logged in as when you edit files or execute commands that could affect the entire Linux system. On the surface, this sounds absurd, but not in Linux. Although you are one person, you can log in several different user accounts. For example, you think you're logged in as an everyday user when you're actually in the `root` administrator account. You can do serious damage to the Linux system and not realize it until it's too late. Better to take advantage of the things you can use to ensure this doesn't happen.

On some Linux systems, the prompt doesn't indicate a person's log in. Many systems have a blank prompt. The prompt, shown as a dollar sign, tells you that the Bourne shell is in use. There are no clues as to the user identity.

To determine a user account's identity, use the `whoami` command. You can also use the `id` utility in place of the `identify` command. `id` gives you more information, including whether the account has `root` privileges.

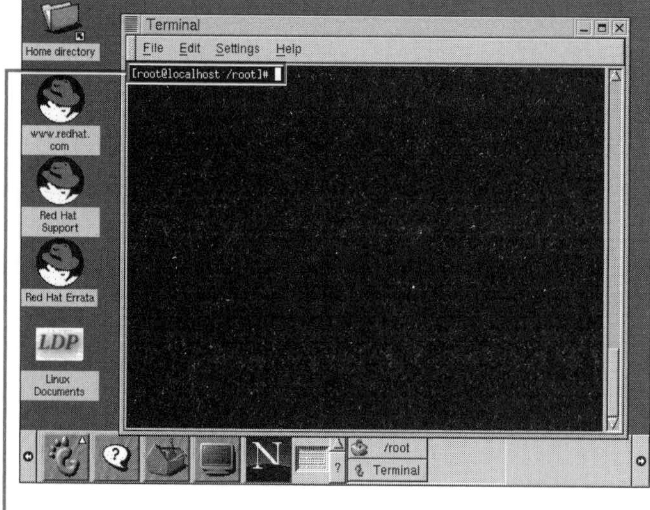

■ By default in most Red Hat installations, the user account identity is listed as the first field left of the prompt.

■ You are logged in as `/root`.

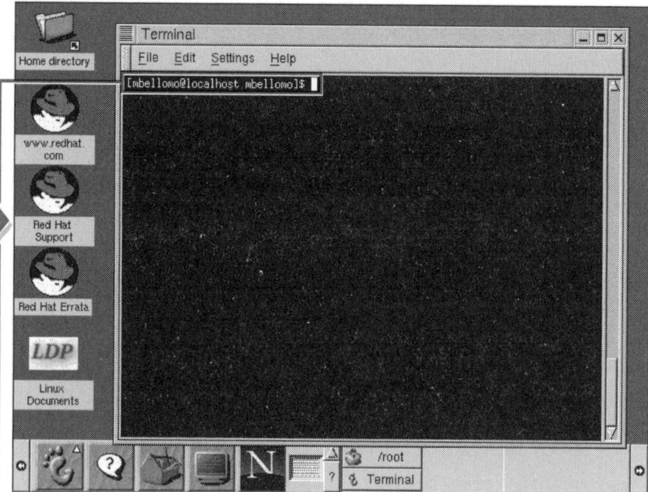

■ You are now logged in to the system as a different user.

What if a user like mbellomo has root privileges?

If the user is not supposed to have `root` access to files, the method shown here is a good way to find out before it becomes a problem. In addition, if you know this account has `root` access, you will likely take more care in the future before leaving this account active when leaving your computer unattended.

Which Linux systems automatically display the user's account name by the prompt?

There doesn't seem to be a perfectly set pattern. By and large, though, the later versions of Linux — which are more advanced and come with more features — tend to have this feature. In fact, most of the Red Hat versions of Linux come with this feature.

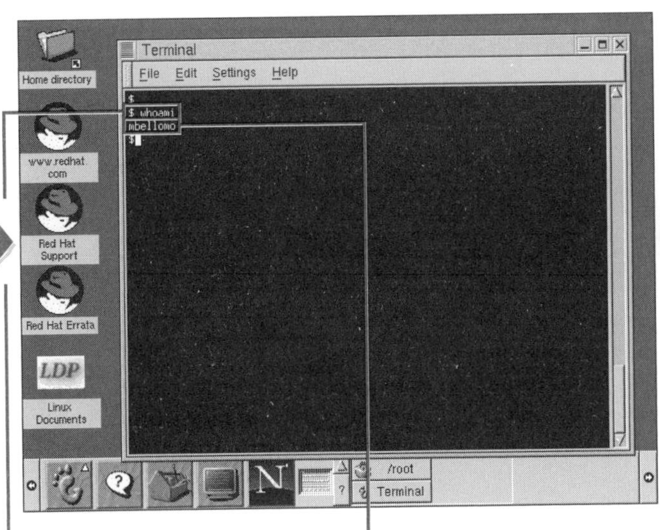

1 Type **whoami** to determine the user identity at the command prompt.

2 Press Enter.

■ The screen displays the user account you're logged in as. This does not tell you whether this user has `root` privileges.

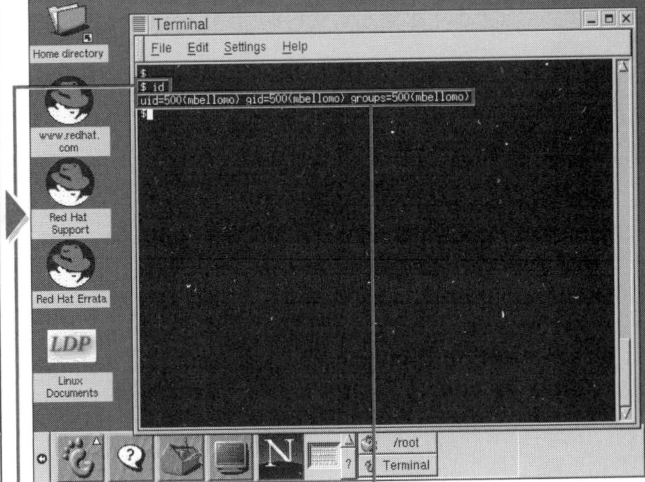

3 Type **id** after the prompt.

4 Press Enter.

■ User `mbellomo` has a user ID (`uid`) and group ID (`gid`) of `500`. If this account had `root` privileges, the number would be `0`.

DETERMINE WHO ELSE IS LOGGED IN

You can determine which user accounts are currently logged in to your Linux system with the who command or the w command. who is especially useful when determining how many users are on the system. The command can give crucial data about when that account user last logged in.

w is not a shortened form of who — it is a separate command. w provides more data than does who, by printing on the top line of its readout the system load averages for the last 1, 5, and 15 minutes. It also shows you not only which users are on your system, but how much CPU time they are taking.

Users who take up large amounts of CPU time place a lot of stress on the system, which can cause problems when the average system load is close to maximum. Use w to check out the load on your system when things run slowly or not at all.

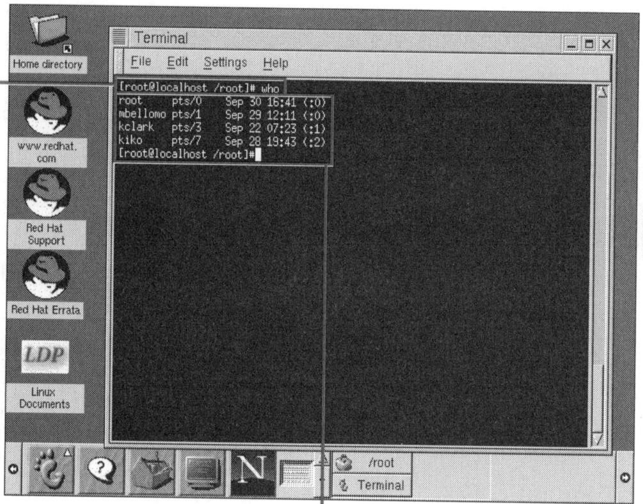

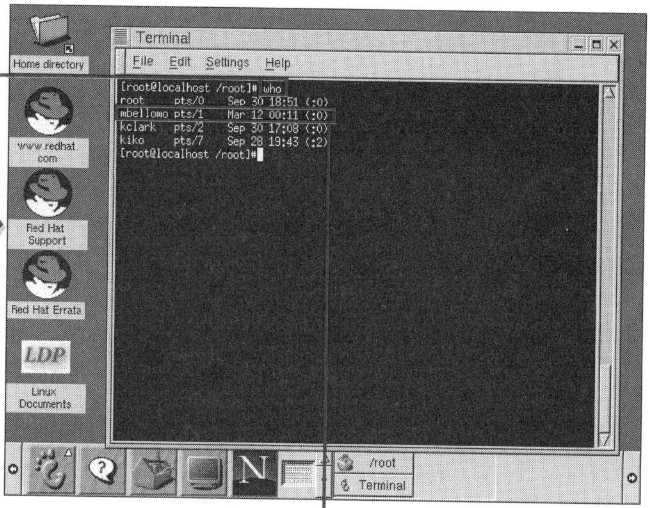

CHECK USER ON SYSTEM

1 To find out who is on your system, type **who** at the command prompt.

2 Press Enter.

■ who displays the users currently on your system.

■ who comes in handy when you are ensuring that your system is secure.

■ The rightmost column lists the time a user logged in.

3 Type **who** at the command prompt.

4 Press Enter.

■ The mbellomo account user logged in several months ago.

Can I use w or who remotely?

✓ You must be on a machine, either as the `root` account or as a more typical user account, to perform `w` or `who`. However, that does not mean that you have to physically be there. You learn more about remotely logging in from other machines in Chapter 16.

What if I see the same person logged in multiple times?

✓ This is a normal occurrence. You will be listed on the `w` or `who` list as many times as you are logged in. Most of the time, those people logged in multiple times run several different processes at once. For example, if you work at a software company, it's not uncommon to find engineers logged in multiple times to test different processes in a program they're writing. You should be concerned only with those accounts that have been active for an excessive period of time.

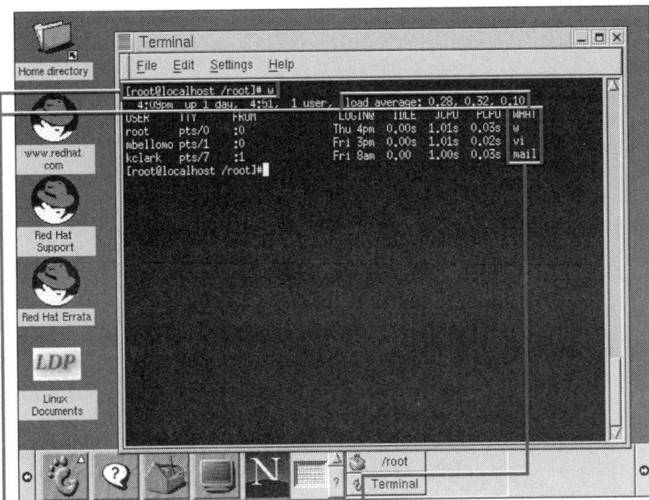

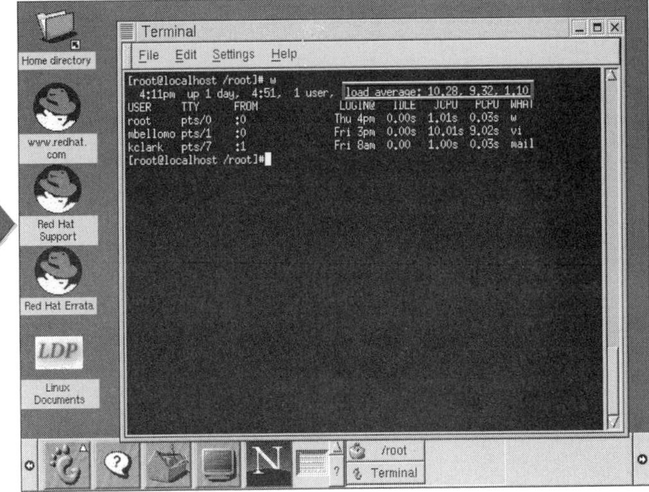

USING THE W COMMAND

1 Press **w** at the command prompt.

2 Press Enter.

■ `w` shows you the system load average in three increments on the top line.

■ The rightmost column, labeled WHAT, tells you what job the user account is performing. The user is using the `vi` editor to edit a file. `kclark` is checking e-mail. `root`, of course, is using `w`.

Note: The average load on the system for 1 and 5 minutes is much higher than the 15-minute reading. Something caused a huge system load in the past 5 to 10 minutes. Look at the user list. User `mbellomo` is causing the problem; his CPU usage is very high.

LOCATE FILES IN THE LINUX TERMINAL

The `find` command, as its name indicates, locates files. Whether you misplaced a file, copied it to an area that you should not have, or it simply seems to have vanished, `find` searches a given area of the system for the missing file.

`find` is automatically recursive, meaning that it searches all the subdirectories under a given search point. For example, if you specify `/var` as the starting point for the search, `find` searches `/var`, `/var/subdirectory`, `/var/sub/subdirectory`, and so on.

It's important to know where to begin your search. You will not find the file under `/var` if the file is in the `/etc` directory tree. If you're not sure of the filename, you can have find search with a wildcard, such as an asterisk.

As an example, use the `find` command in your root home directory to find the file testcut. `find` uses this format:

```
find <search point>
<command option>
<filename>
```

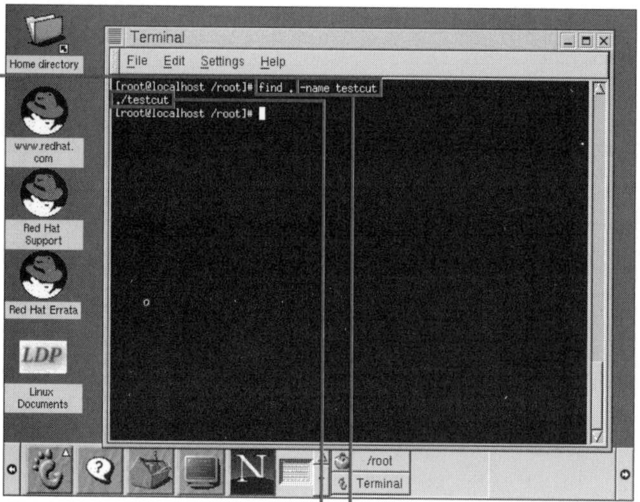

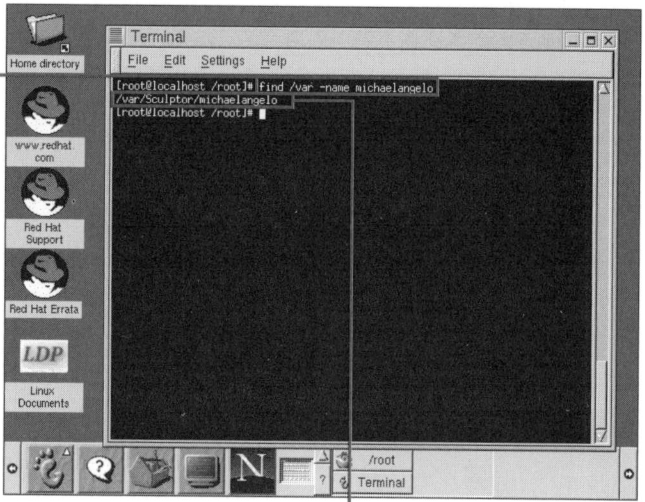

FIND A FILE IN YOUR HOME DIRECTORY

1 Type **find .**.

■ Because you're searching in your current directory, signify this with a single period preceded by a space.

2 Type **–name testcut**.

3 Press Enter.

■ `find` gives you the result: `testcut` exists in the local `./testcut` directory.

FIND A FILE IN A REMOTE DIRECTORY

1 Type **find /var –name michaelangelo** to find the file `michaelangelo` in the `/var` directory (use `/var` as the search point).

2 Press Enter.

■ Linux locates this file under `/var/Sculptor`, because `Sculptor` is a subdirectory of `/var`.

Can Linux search for files in ways other than by name?

- Linux can perform searches for a given file by name, size (in blocks or bytes), creation time, and user identification number, among a number of other methods. However, most of these other methods are very clumsy, which is why searching by filename is the most commonly used option.

What does the asterisk (*) symbol stand for?

- The asterisk literally indicates one or more of any symbol. That is why when you perform a search for a file called `michael*`, you could find `michael`, `michaelb`, or `michaelangelo`.

Can I search for a file named something like michaelangelo by using the wildcard character at the start of the name I search for, such as *ichaelangelo?

- Yes. If you use `*ichaelangelo`, you could find files called `michaelangelo`, `nichaelangelo`, `xichaelangelo` and other oddly named files.

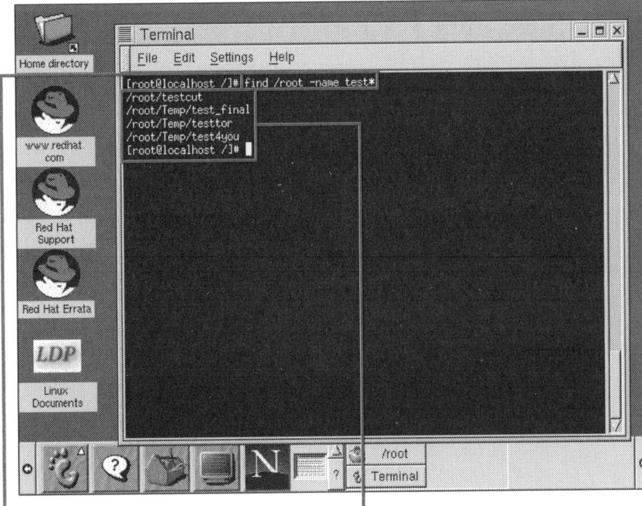

USE FIND WITH A WILDCARD

1. Type **find /root –name test*** to search for any files that start with `test` in your Home Directory.
2. Press Enter.

■ `find` comes back with the files `testcut` in the local directory, and the files `test_final`, `testtor`, and `test4you`, which it found in subdirectory `/root/Temp`.

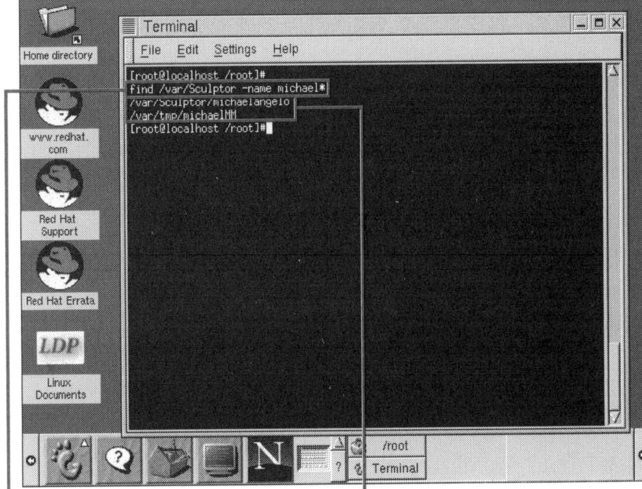

USE FIND WITH WILDCARDS IN REMOTE SEARCHES

1. Type **find /var/Sculptor –name michael***.
2. Press Enter.

■ Linux returns `michaelangelo` under `/var/Sculptor` and `michaelMM` from `/var/tmp`.

CONTINUED

LOCATE FILES IN THE LINUX TERMINAL

CONTINUED

You can use the `find` command in the Linux Terminal to search for files in ways other than by filename.

`uid`, which is short for *user identification number*, is useful when you don't have any idea what the filename is, but you do know the who owns the file. When a user creates a file, that user's identification number is automatically attached to the file.

For example, the files in your root home directory should belong to the `root` account. Because the root account's number is always a `0`, the UID attached to the files in the root home directory should also be `0`. The zero is the User ID for the root user account.

This option gives you the ability to search for files owned by a given user. It's most useful when you're trying to determine whether a user has saved his files to an inappropriate location, such as someone else's home directory.

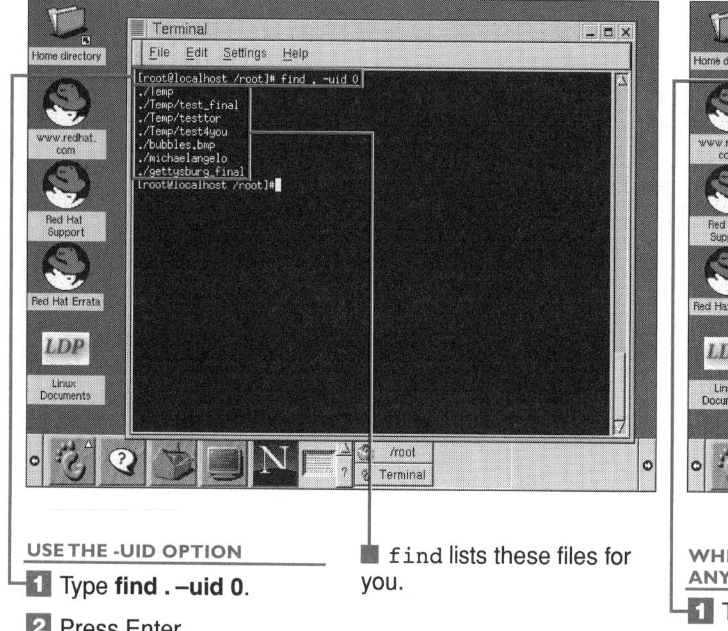

USE THE -UID OPTION

1 Type **find . –uid 0**.

2 Press Enter.

■ `find` lists these files for you.

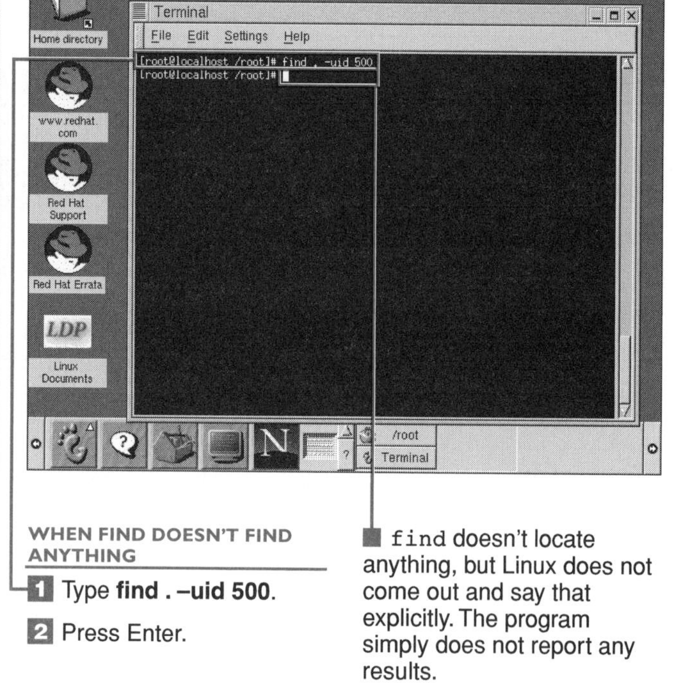

WHEN FIND DOESN'T FIND ANYTHING

1 Type **find . –uid 500**.

2 Press Enter.

■ `find` doesn't locate anything, but Linux does not come out and say that explicitly. The program simply does not report any results.

Can I use find to search a remote machine?

- Yes, but remember that you must be logged in to that remote machine. You do not have to be physically present, which means you can log in remotely. (See Chapter 16 for information on how to log in remotely.)

Are there any limitations to using find?

- `find` is an exceptionally powerful tool. Because it lacks range limits (unless you set them), the command can really slow things down. For example, be careful when using `find` to search under `/`. All directories are subdirectories under this `root`. Searching under `/` at a peak time during the day is a bad idea; it takes a lot of CPU cycles to search every single one of the subdirectories. That can slow things down for everyone.

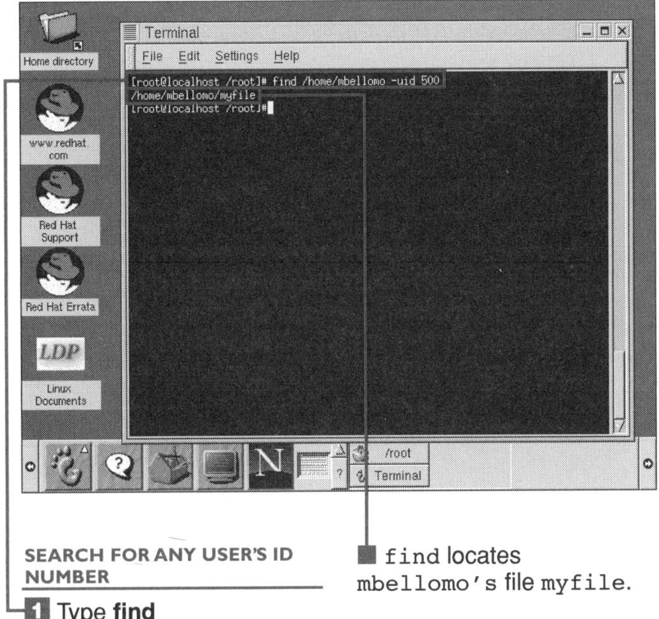

SEARCH FOR ANY USER'S ID NUMBER

1 Type **find /home/mbellomo –uid 500**.

2 Press Enter.

■ `find` locates `mbellomo's` file `myfile`.

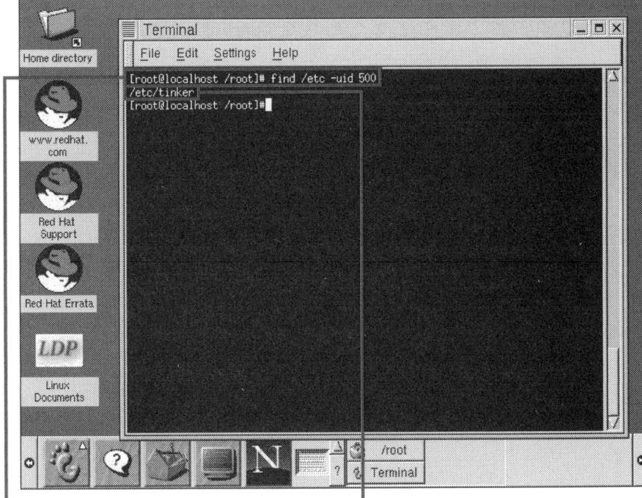

FIND FILES THAT DON'T BELONG

1 Type **find /etc –uid 500** to search for files owned by `mbellomo` (`uid 500`) in the `/etc` directory.

2 Press Enter.

■ Sure enough, the user owns a file called tinker. You can delete this file or speak to him about removing it.

CREATE SYMBOLIC LINKS

You can use symbolic links to create a bridge between files or directories that you use on a frequent basis. Making a link is useful if you need a file that is located in a remote location and it takes some typing to get to reach it (`/etc/sound/events` is a good example).

In Linux, links come in two varieties: soft and hard. The soft kind, which you should use, differs from the hard in the persistence of the link. If your link is broken or somehow damaged, Linux will, after a time, stop trying to use it. A broken hard link can sometimes freeze your entire machine.

You use the `ln` or `link` command to create a link. You use the `-s` option to make the link soft, or `symbolic`.

The format for this command is

```
ln –s <location/name of file> <name of link>
```

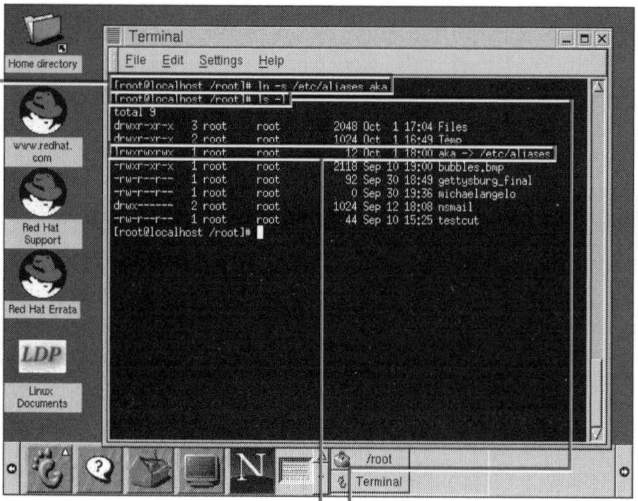

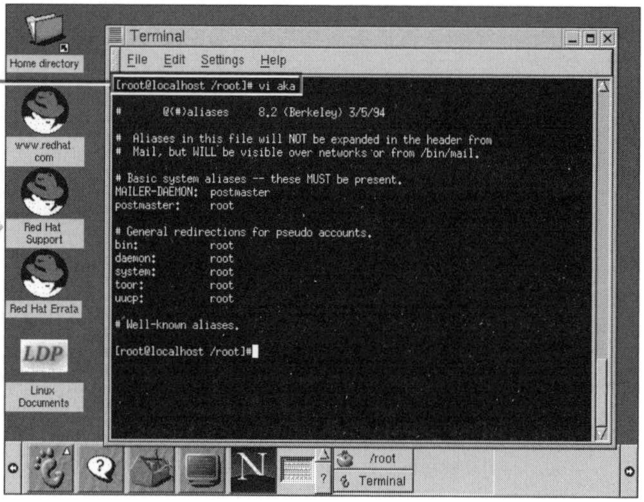

CREATE SYMBOLIC LINKS TO FILES

1 To create a link to the `/etc/aliases` file and then name the link `aka`, type **ln –s /etc/aliases aka**.

2 Press Enter.

3 Type **ls –l**.

4 Press Enter.

■ Notice that the new file `aka` is listed with an `l` in the leftmost column. This identifies it as a link.

5 Type **vi aka**.

6 Press Enter.

■ The link allows you to work on the `/etc/aliases` file without having to go there remotely.

Can I scatter links everywhere so I don't have to leave my home directory?

- You should use links sparingly. If you have too many, you will start forgetting where everything really is!

Can I give my links the same names as the files I link to?

- Yes — but you shouldn't. If your reason for wanting to do this is to make remembering easier, call the link <filename_link> to differentiate it from the original file.

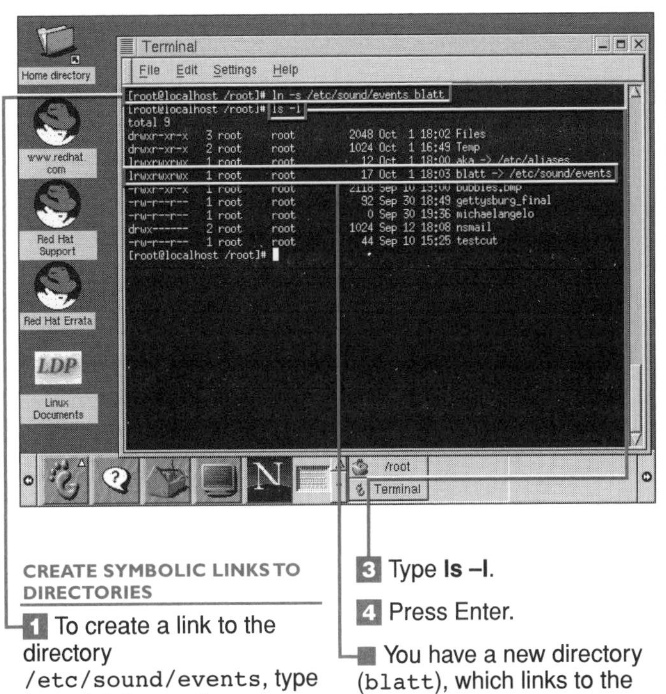

CREATE SYMBOLIC LINKS TO DIRECTORIES

1 To create a link to the directory /etc/sound/events, type **ln –s /etc/sound/events blatt**.

2 Press Enter.

3 Type **ls –l**.

4 Press Enter.

■ You have a new directory (blatt), which links to the /etc/sound/events directory.

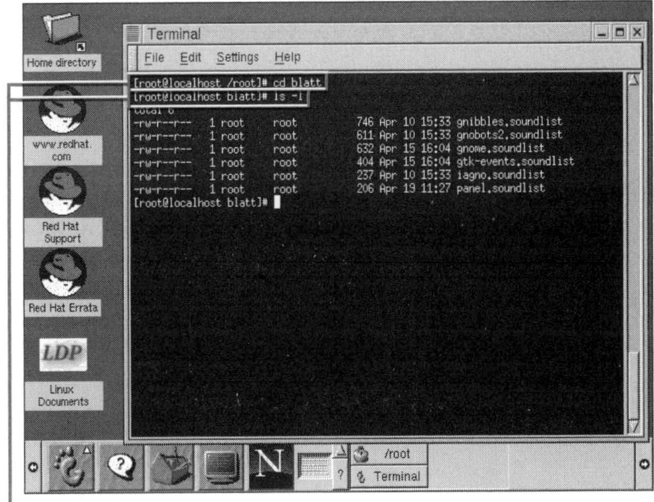

TEST LINK BY CHANGING DIRECTORIES

1 Instead of using cd /etc/sound/events, type **cd blatt**.

2 Press Enter.

3 Type **ls –l**.

4 Press Enter to verify your jump via the link to the directory of your choice.

MOVE, NAME, AND DELETE SYMBOLIC LINKS

You may have trouble remembering your link's name or purpose. There are times when you might need to place the link in a different area, and there may come a time when the link has outlived its usefulness. In these cases you can easily move, rename, or delete the link.

Moving, renaming, and deleting links use basic Linux commands such as `mv` and `rm` — the move and remove commands. If you're not familiar with these commands, see Chapter 5 for a quick refresher course in how to work with them.

Remember that everything in Linux is a file, no matter if it is a directory, text file, or symbolic link. Although links may appear different, Linux treats them exactly like any other file. This blanket approach is helpful because it means that links can be altered with the same commands that are in use everywhere else on the system.

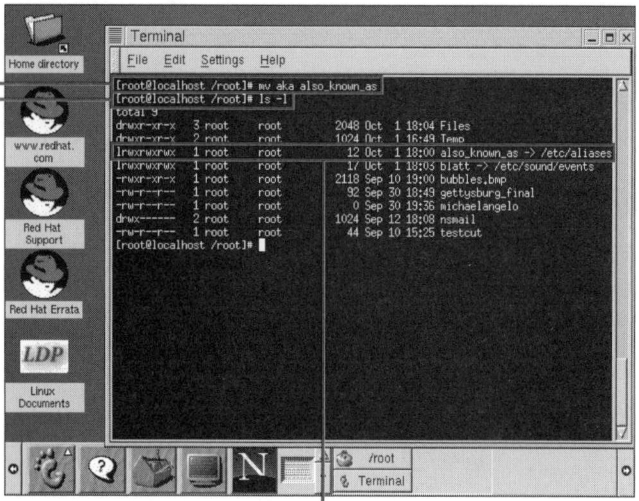

```
[root@localhost /root]# mv aka also_known_as
[root@localhost /root]# ls -l
total 9
drwxr-xr-x   3 root     root         2048 Oct  1 18:04 Files
drwxr-xr-x   2 root     root         1024 Oct  1 16:49 Temp
lrwxrwxrwx   1 root     root           12 Oct  1 18:00 also_known_as -> /etc/aliases
lrwxrwxrwx   1 root     root           17 Oct  1 18:03 blatt -> /etc/sound/events
-rwxr-xr-x   1 root     root         2118 Sep 10 19:00 bubbles.bmp
-rw-r--r--   1 root     root           92 Sep 30 18:49 gettysburg_final
-rw-r--r--   1 root     root            0 Sep 30 19:36 michaelangelo
drwx------   2 root     root         1024 Sep 12 18:08 nsmail
-rw-r--r--   1 root     root           44 Sep 10 15:25 testcut
[root@localhost /root]#
```

RENAME A LINK

1 Rename the link by typing **mv aka also_known_as**.

2 Press Enter.

3 Type **ls –l**.

4 Press Enter to check the result.

■ Although the name of the link is different, the area it points to is the same.

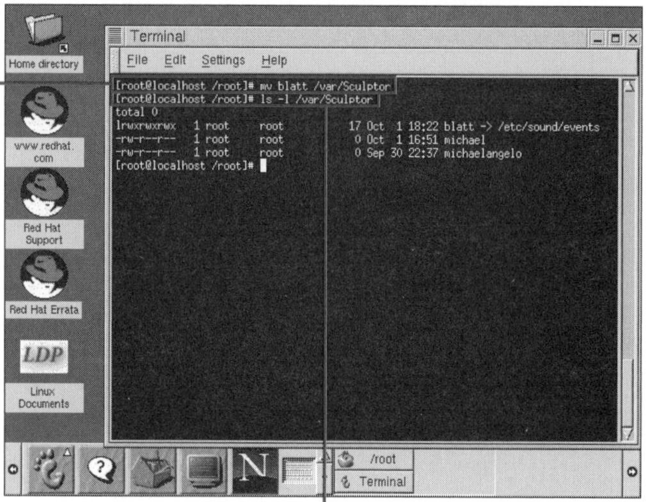

```
[root@localhost /root]# mv blatt /var/Sculptor
[root@localhost /root]# ls -l /var/Sculptor
total 0
lrwxrwxrwx   1 root     root           17 Oct  1 18:22 blatt -> /etc/sound/events
-rw-r--r--   1 root     root            0 Oct  1 16:51 michael
-rw-r--r--   1 root     root            0 Sep 30 22:37 michaelangelo
[root@localhost /root]#
```

MOVE A LINK

1 Type **mv <linkname> </intended directory>**.

2 Press Enter.

3 Type **ls –l </intendeddirectory>**.

4 Press Enter to see the result.

Can I copy links?

- Yes, but you shouldn't as a matter of practice. Making more than one link to a given file or directory increases the chance of confusion and possibility for error.

Can I copy the contents of the link?

- You can do this by using the `cp` command on the files under the link, just as you would copy the files from the original directory.

When should I remove a link?

- You should remove a link whenever its purpose is outdated (for example, to go to an area you don't use anymore). You should also remove a link if it's broken, such as when the original file has been deleted and the link doesn't go anywhere.

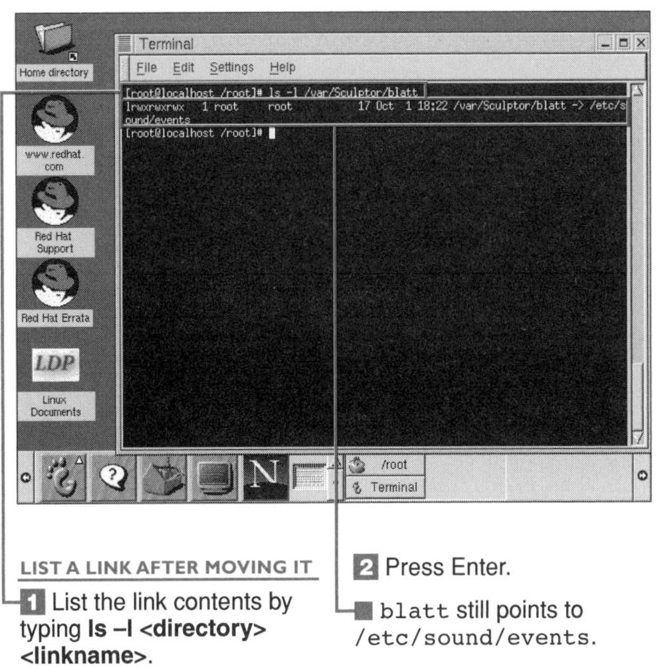

LIST A LINK AFTER MOVING IT

1 List the link contents by typing **ls –l <directory> <linkname>**.

2 Press Enter.

■ `blatt` still points to `/etc/sound/events`.

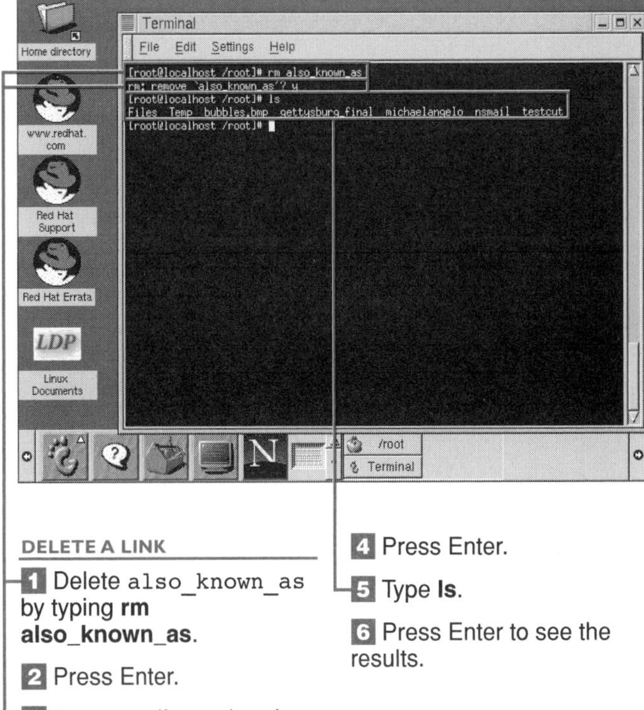

DELETE A LINK

1 Delete `also_known_as` by typing **rm also_known_as**.

2 Press Enter.

3 Answer y (for yes) to the Linux query.

4 Press Enter.

5 Type **ls**.

6 Press Enter to see the results.

TRANSFER OUTPUT WITH THE PIPE COMMAND

You can transfer the output of one Linux command to another with the help of a UNIX shell utility called `pipe`.

You do not type the letters **pipe** to use the utility. The pipe symbol, which looks like |, should be typed from the keyboard. The character normally exists on the keyboard along with the \ key, which is located above the Enter key.

To type this symbol, make sure that you hold the Shift key down when pressing the backslash key. Simply using the Caps Lock function does not allow you to type a pipe — you must create it by pressing Shift+Backslash.

`pipe` is most often used with two commands: `ps` (also known as `process search`) and `cat`. You learn about `ps` later in this chapter. The `cat` command prints out all of the text in a file.

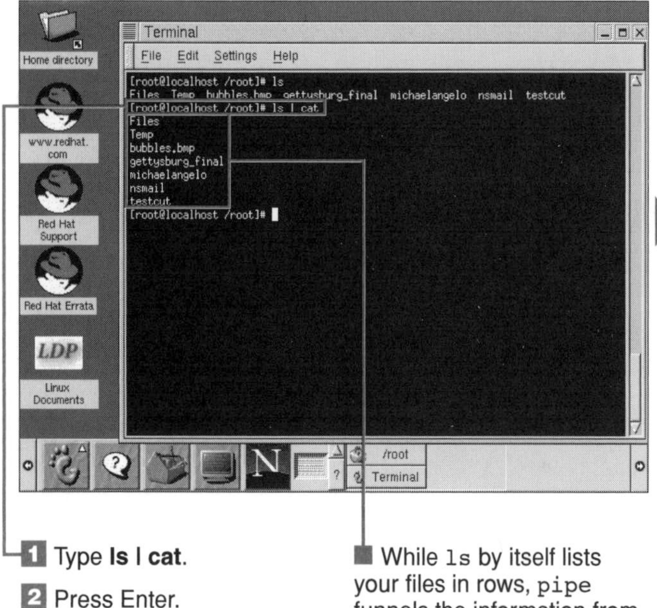

1 Type **ls | cat**.

2 Press Enter.

■ While `ls` by itself lists your files in rows, `pipe` funnels the information from `ls` to `cat`, allowing the information to be printed in column form.

Note: `pipe` can only shuffle data to another command. For example, attempting to `pipe` the contents of the `gettysburg_final` file to `michaelangelo` will not work.

3 Type **cat gettysburg_final | michaelangelo**.

4 Press Enter.

■ Linux says the command is not found. When Linux sees a pipe symbol, it assumes you are linking two different commands, not a command and a file.

How can I fix a broken pipe?

- Make sure that you are not accidentally trying to connect a command and a file. If you are using two commands, make sure that one is not a text-creating command (like `vi`). Barring those difficulties, make sure that one or both commands is functioning properly.

Where does the spilled data from a broken pipe go?

- A broken pipe is a good visual image, but it is slightly misleading. A broken pipe means that data was not sent anywhere. You have not lost any data.

Do I need a space on either side of the pipe symbol?

- No. You can type `ls | cat` or `ls|cat` and both will work. The former style is a lot easier to read than the latter and it is also easier to duplicate if you need to.

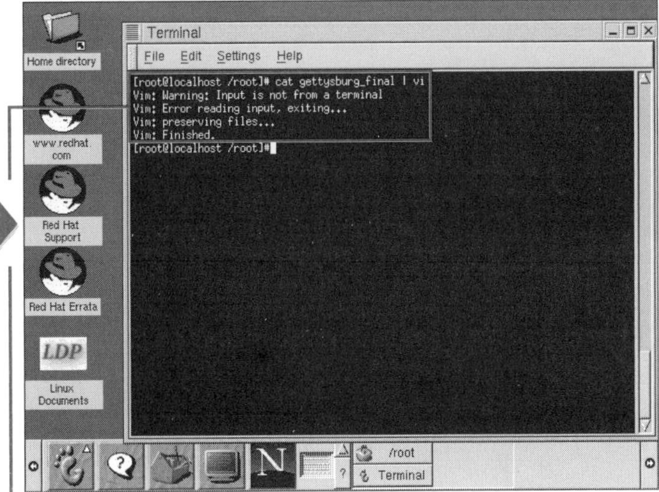

■ Using pipe to input data to the `vi` editor does not work. As shown in this example, piping data to `vi` returns an error message.

■ When you use the `pipe` command, you eventually come across the `Broken pipe` error. Be alert when you see this; your command or program is unable to transmit data between commands.

■ The user incorrectly used `pipe` to transfer data from `cat` to a file.

SEARCH WITH THE GREP COMMAND

You can search for any kind of file or directory with the `find` command. Linux also provides a utility with which you can search for text, numbers, or expressions within a file itself. This utility is the `grep` command and its command options.

`grep` stands for *get regular expression,* which is a sort of a catchall phrase for what it really does. You will find that using `grep` to search for patterns or words is the easiest, most convenient way to locate a phrase or character pattern in a long text file. You will also find that using `grep` with `ps` and the | shell utilities creates one of the most useful combinations in Linux. This is because the | utility allows you to pass large amounts of information to `grep`, which speeds up any search you perform.

The command format for `grep` is

```
grep <searched for
pattern> <file to be
searched>
```

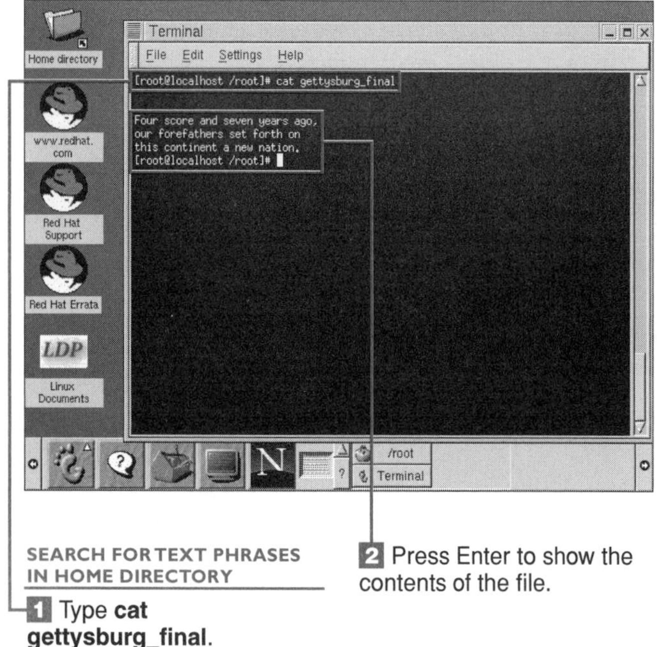

SEARCH FOR TEXT PHRASES IN HOME DIRECTORY

1 Type **cat gettysburg_final**.

2 Press Enter to show the contents of the file.

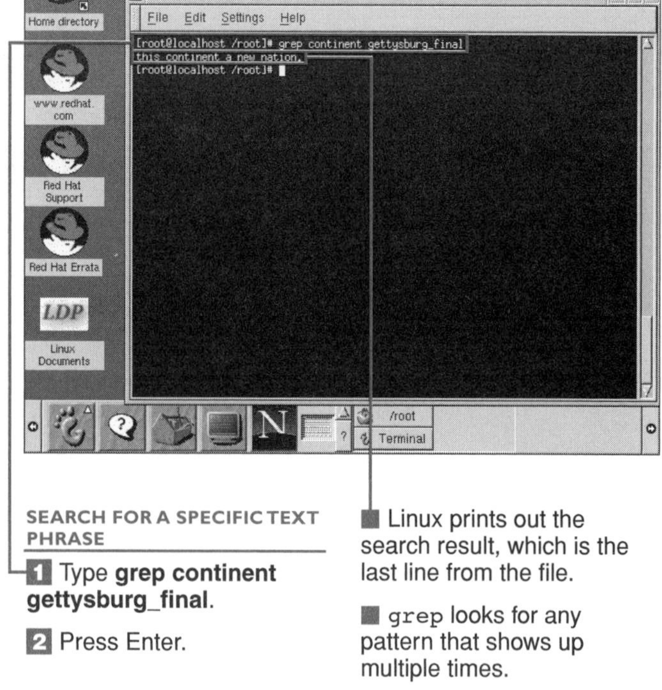

SEARCH FOR A SPECIFIC TEXT PHRASE

1 Type **grep continent gettysburg_final**.

2 Press Enter.

■ Linux prints out the search result, which is the last line from the file.

■ `grep` looks for any pattern that shows up multiple times.

What if I only want a count of how many times a pattern appears in a file?

- You can use the -c option with `grep` If you want to count the lines in the accompanying example that don't start with A, type grep –vc A <filename>. If my file has the word `forefathers` in it but I use `grep` to search for `Forefathers`, will `grep` find the `forefathers` expression? No. `grep` is case sensitive. Using `grep` to search for `Forefathers` will not find the words `forefathers`, `foreFathers`, or any other variation.

Can I have grep search for a term while ignoring whether a letter is upper- or lowercase?

- The `-i` command option allows you to bypass the case sensitivity. If you search for `Forefathers` with `grep` and the `-i` command option, you can find `forefathers`.

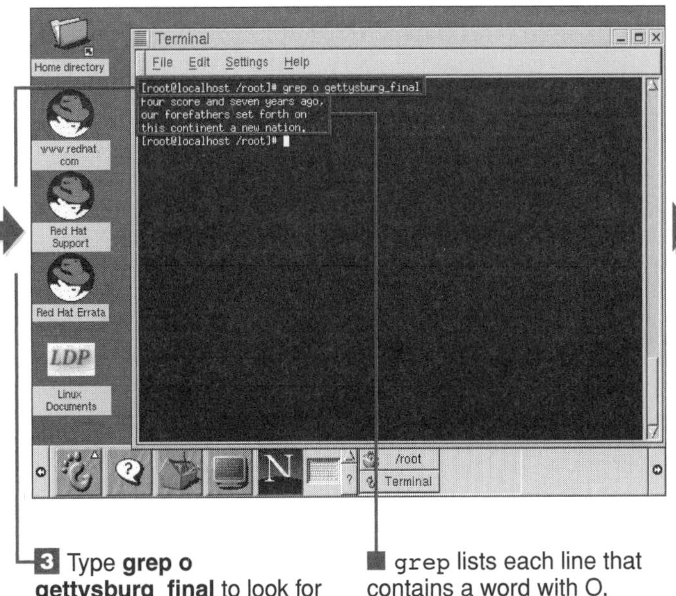

3 Type **grep o gettysburg_final** to look for any word that starts with the letter O.

4 Press Enter.

■ `grep` lists each line that contains a word with O, whether the O is in `of` or `score`.

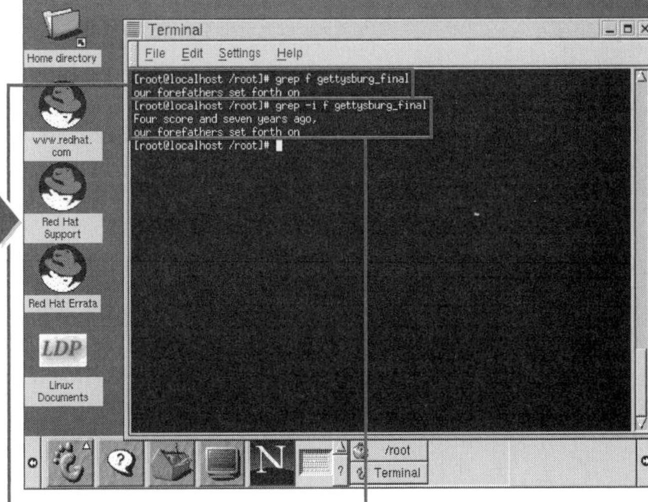

5 Type **grep i gettysburg_final**.

6 Press Enter.

■ The line with `forefathers` and `Four score and seven years ago` displays.

SEARCH FOR RUNNING PROCESSES

You can search for processes that are currently running on your system with ps, the process search command. Process searching is one of the most important functions you can learn on your Linux system. With ps, you can determine if a program is running, who is running it, how long the process has been running, and if it has died. For example, to get a more complete look at what you're running, use the -e (list everything) and -f (full listing) options. You can get even more information, such as the PID (process ID number) by adding the -l (long listing) command option.

The PID is listed in the second column from the left in a `ps -elf` readout. The syntax for process searching is `ps <options>`

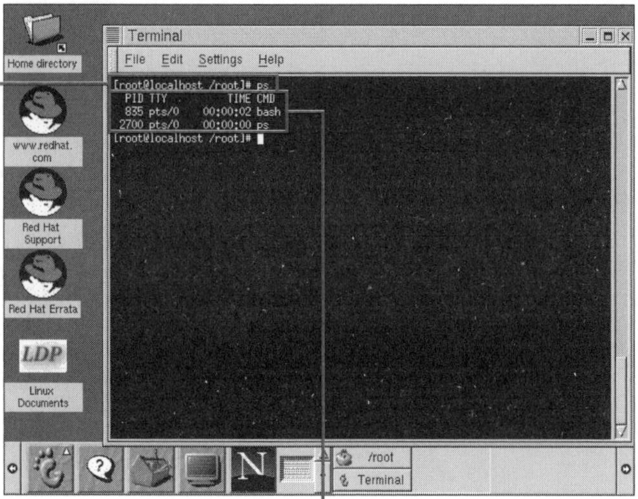
Terminal
File Edit Settings Help
[root@localhost /root]# ps
PID TTY TIME CMD
835 pts/0 00:00:02 bash
2700 pts/0 00:00:00 ps
[root@localhost /root]#
Home directory
www.redhat.com
Red Hat Support
Red Hat Errata
LDP
Linux Documents
/root
Terminal

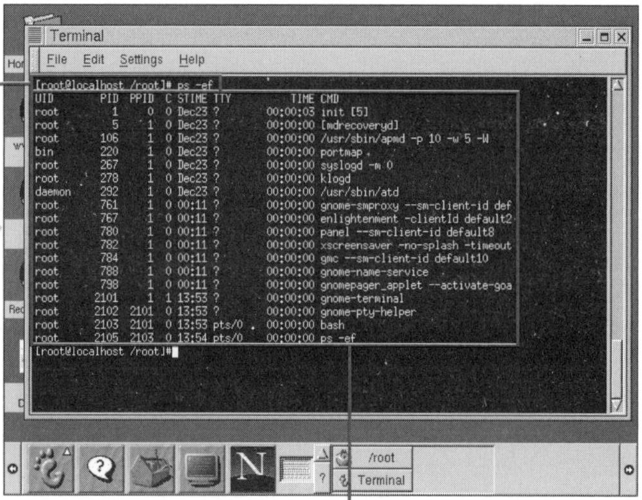
Terminal
File Edit Settings Help
[root@localhost /root]# ps -ef
UID PID PPID C STIME TTY TIME CMD
root 1 0 0 Dec23 ? 00:00:03 init [5]
root 5 1 0 Dec23 ? 00:00:00 [mdrecoveryd]
root 106 1 0 Dec23 ? 00:00:00 /usr/sbin/apmd -p 10 -w 5 -W
bin 220 1 0 Dec23 ? 00:00:00 portmap
root 267 1 0 Dec23 ? 00:00:00 syslogd -m 0
root 278 1 0 Dec23 ? 00:00:00 klogd
daemon 292 1 0 Dec23 ? 00:00:00 /usr/sbin/atd
root 761 1 0 00:11 ? 00:00:00 gnome-smproxy --sm-client-id def
root 767 1 0 00:11 ? 00:00:00 enlightenment -clientId default2
root 780 1 0 00:11 ? 00:00:00 panel --sm-client-id default8
root 782 1 0 00:11 ? 00:00:00 xscreensaver -no-splash -timeout
root 784 1 0 00:11 ? 00:00:00 gmc --sm-client-id default10
root 788 1 0 00:11 ? 00:00:00 gnome-name-service
root 798 1 0 00:11 ? 00:00:00 gnomepager_applet --activate-goa
root 2101 1 1 13:53 ? 00:00:00 gnome-terminal
root 2102 2101 0 13:53 ? 00:00:00 gnome-pty-helper
root 2103 2101 0 13:53 pts/0 00:00:00 bash
root 2105 2103 0 13:54 pts/0 00:00:00 ps -ef
[root@localhost /root]#
/root
Terminal

SEARCH FOR RUNNING SHELLS

1 Type **ps** at the command prompt.

2 Press Enter.

■ `ps` by itself doesn't tell you much; however, it tells you what shell you are running.

■ `bash` stands for the Bourne-again shell.

3 Type **ps –ef** at the command prompt.

4 Press Enter.

■ This lists all the processes running on your machine. Your output will likely scroll off the page.

Will I get different results if I enter the ps command with the options -elf versus efl or fle?

- When using the `process search` command, it doesn't matter in what order the command options are entered. The three combinations return the same results. However, most users who rely on the `ps` command several times a day use `-elf` simply because it is easier to remember and to type.

What other options do I have available with the process search command?

- The `process search` command comes with more command options than do the rest of most Linux commands. `ps` can search for system processes by user identification number (UID), by group, and even by command name. For a full listing of options, type **man ps** at the command prompt and press Enter.

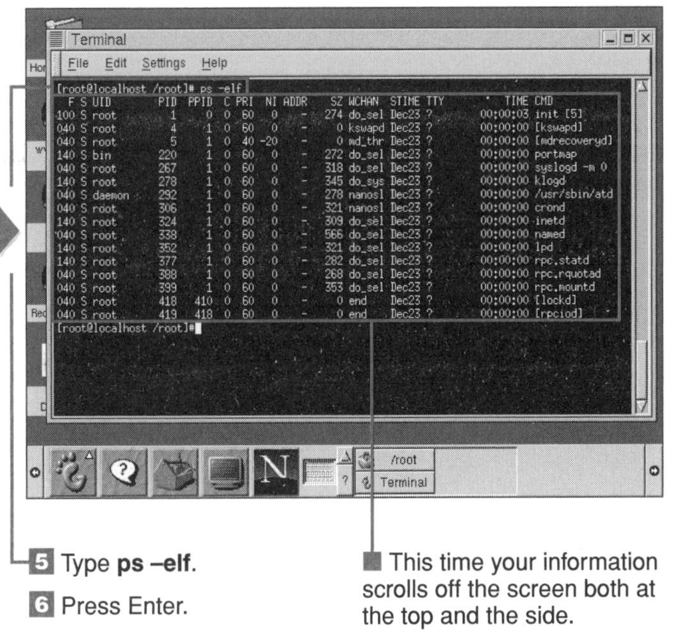

5 Type **ps –elf**.

6 Press Enter.

■ This time your information scrolls off the screen both at the top and the side.

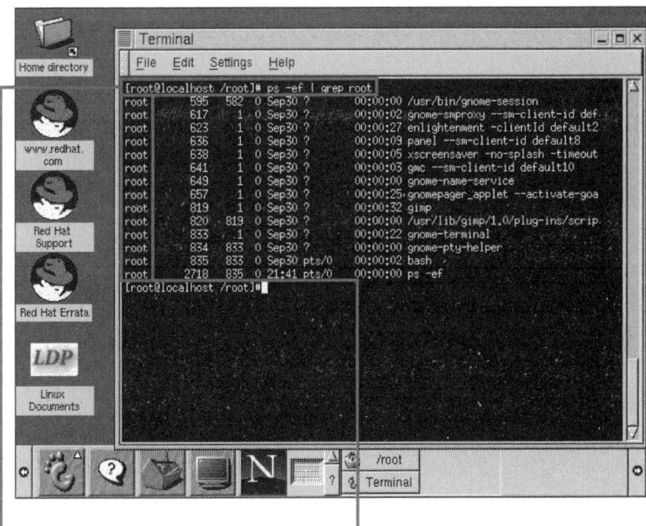

SEARCH FOR ROOT ACCOUNT-OWNED PROCESSES

1 Type **ps –ef | grep root**.

2 Press Enter.

■ The leftmost column listing displays only the root as the user running these processes.

CONTINUED

SEARCH FOR RUNNING PROCESSES
CONTINUED

You can make full use of the `process search` command by using some of its lesser known command options. More importantly, you can take full advantage of the `process search` command's flexibility in the Linux environment by combining it with the | command and the `grep` command.

The | command moves information between commands in Linux. `grep` can search for files or search inside files for text patterns. Both commands are covered earlier in this chapter if you need a quick review.

You can look for a process by using | and `grep` to search by the process ID number. This method works, but it is not recommended. Each process that is started gets a new PID. For this reason, get into the habit of searching for a process by process name or username.

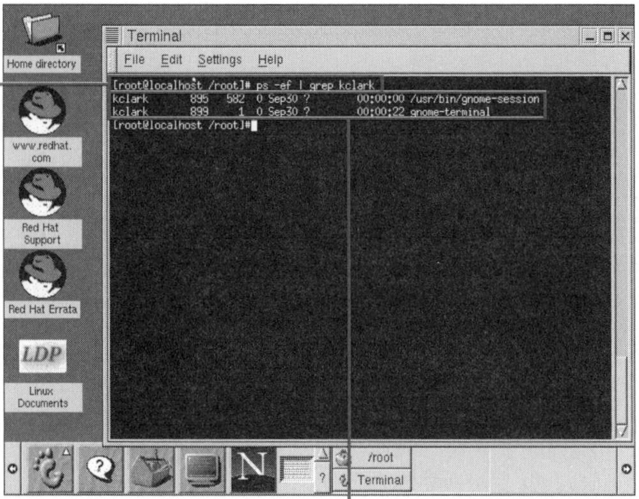
Terminal
File Edit Settings Help
[root@localhost /root]# ps -ef | grep kclark
kclark 895 582 0 Sep30 ? 00:00:00 /usr/bin/gnome-session
kclark 899 1 0 Sep30 ? 00:00:22 gnome-terminal
[root@localhost /root]#
Home directory
www.redhat.com
Red Hat Support
Red Hat Errata
LDP
Linux Documents
/root
Terminal

SEARCH FOR PROCESSES USED BY OTHER USERS

1 Type **ps –ef | grep kclark**.

2 Press Enter.

■ `ps` displays the processes that this user is using.

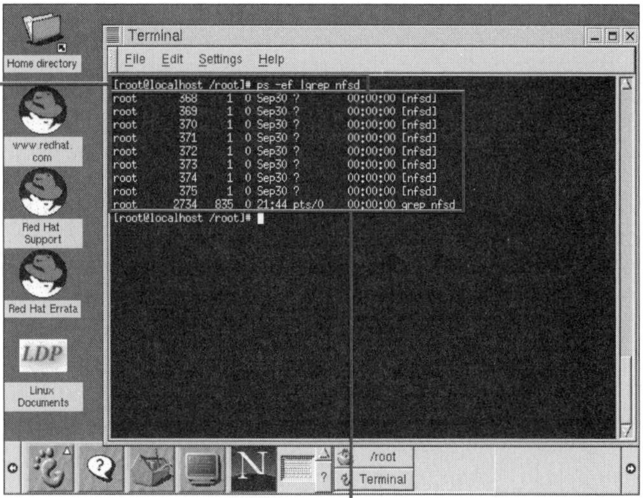
Terminal
File Edit Settings Help
[root@localhost /root]# ps -ef |grep nfsd
root 368 1 0 Sep30 ? 00:00:00 [nfsd]
root 369 1 0 Sep30 ? 00:00:00 [nfsd]
root 370 1 0 Sep30 ? 00:00:00 [nfsd]
root 371 1 0 Sep30 ? 00:00:00 [nfsd]
root 372 1 0 Sep30 ? 00:00:00 [nfsd]
root 373 1 0 Sep30 ? 00:00:00 [nfsd]
root 374 1 0 Sep30 ? 00:00:00 [nfsd]
root 375 1 0 Sep30 ? 00:00:00 [nfsd]
root 2734 835 0 21:44 pts/0 00:00:00 grep nfsd
[root@localhost /root]#
Home directory
www.redhat.com
Red Hat Support
Red Hat Errata
LDP
Linux Documents
/root
Terminal

GREP FOR PROCESSES BY DIFFERENT FIELDS

1 Type **ps –ef | grep nfsd**.

2 Press Enter.

■ `ps` displays multiple `nfsd` (NFS deamon) processes running. They all have different PID numbers.

Can I use ps remotely?

- Yes. You must be on a machine, either as the `root` account or as a more typical user account, to use the process search command. You learn more about remotely logging in later in Chapter 16.

Why do I sometimes see the grep process and at other times I do not?

- Most of the time, you see the `grep` process you ran as part of a `ps` readout. That is because `ps` is taking a snapshot of what you are running as it works. If the `grep` command happens to finish before `ps` finishes, you will not see it in the list. Either way, it will not affect your process search.

I am using ps on a UNIX system and it is acting oddly. Why?

- Depending on the brand of Linux or UNIX you're using, the command options may be different. Some machines use `ps –ef`, while others use `ps –aux` to get results.

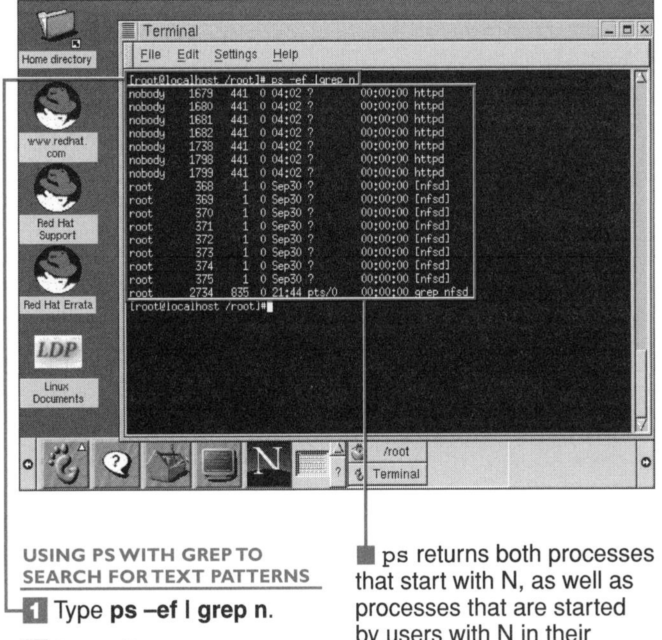

USING PS WITH GREP TO SEARCH FOR TEXT PATTERNS

1. Type **ps –ef | grep n**.
2. Press Enter.

■ `ps` returns both processes that start with N, as well as processes that are started by users with N in their names — or N in any other field.

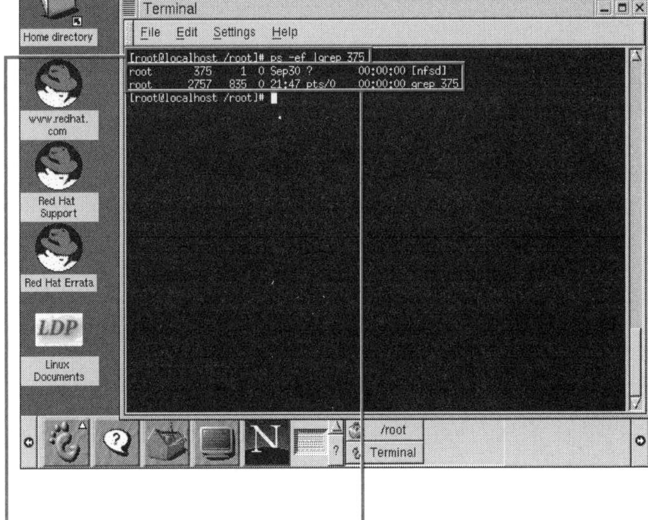

SEARCH FOR PROCESSES BY PID

1. Type **ps –ef | grep 375**.
2. Press Enter.

■ `ps` returns the process with the Process Identification Number (PID) of `375`.

STOP PROGRAMS WITH KILL

You can stop all programs in Linux with the `kill` command. `kill` sends out a signal to terminate a given program if that program is currently running. Although this sounds harsh, by default `kill` actually tells the program to end only after it has completed its exit procedure.

This prevents the program from crashing and leaving behind a `core` file. If you're from the Windows world, having the program complete its exit procedure is the equivalent of having the computer perform its shutdown procedure rather than abruptly switching off the power.

`kill` is used only when a program hangs or refuses to exit. A program hangs in Linux if it malfunctions or is waiting for information to be relayed to it via a pipe or a secondary process. The appropriate format for `kill` is

`kill` *<PIDnumber>*

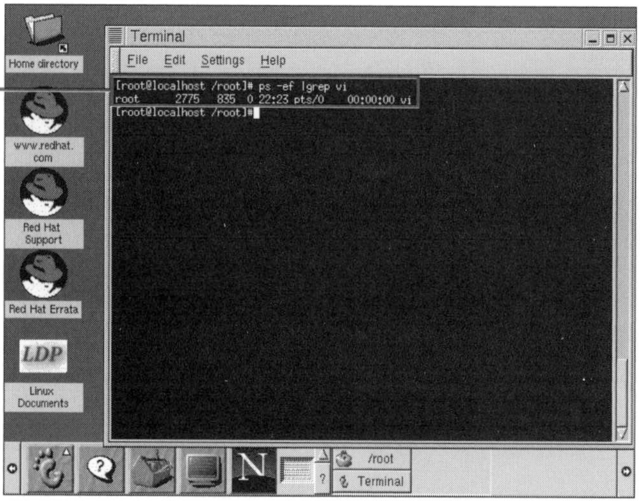

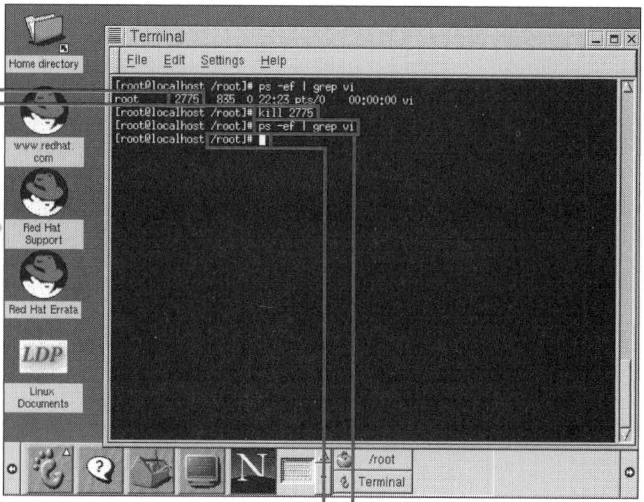

KILL A VI PROCESS

1 Type **ps –ef | grep vi.**

2 Press Enter.

■ The information you need, PID `2775`, is in the second column.

3 Kill the process by typing kill.

4 Press Enter.

5 Double-check the results by typing **ps –ef |grep vi** again.

6 Press Enter.

■ The `vi` processes are gone.

TIPS

Can I kill processes by name instead of by personal identification number?

- You cannot do this because `kill` is written specifically to use only PIDs. If you could kill processes by name, you would also be killing the processes that other people are running.

Can I kill processes by username?

- No. By default, Linux runs several background processes that you need to have work in its operating system, such as GNOME. If you killed everything run by your name, for example, you would also terminate your Linux session.

What if I accidentally send out kill and there is no program running?

- No problem. Your `kill` command is targeted at a specific PID. If the program with that PID is not running, the signal is not received by anyone.

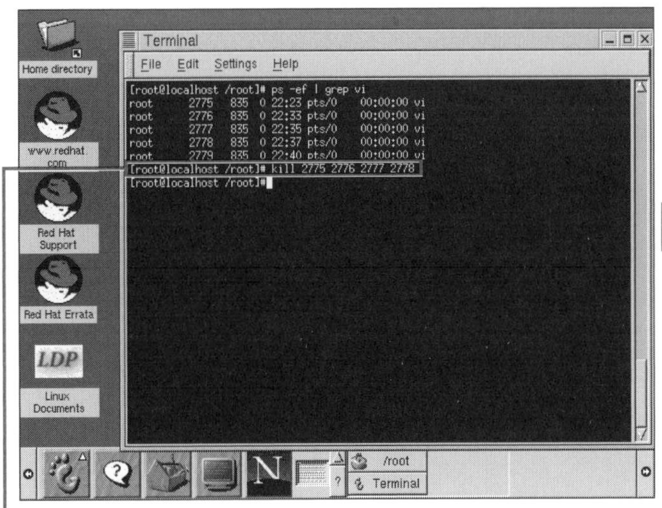

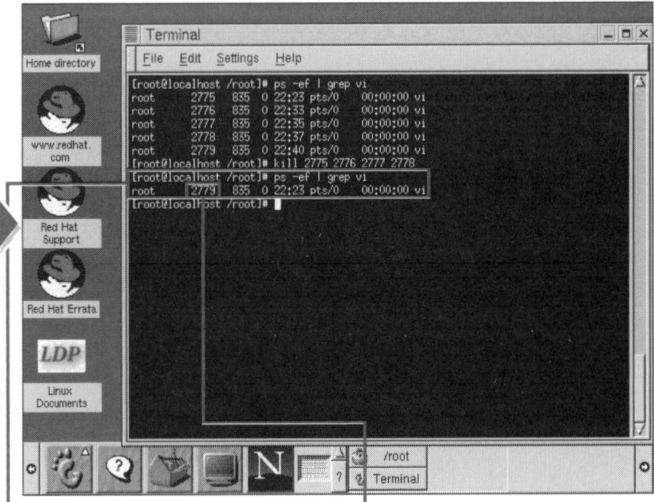

KILL MULTIPLE PROCESSES WITH ONE KILL COMMAND

1 To kill `2775`, `2776`, `2777`, and `2778` but keep `2779`, type **kill 2775 2776 2777 2778**.

2 Press Enter.

3 Check the result by typing **ps -ef | grep vi**.

4 Press Enter.

■ You should see one remaining `vi` process: number `2779`.

STOP PROGRAMS THAT DO NOT RESPOND TO KILL

In a small percentage of cases, a process does not respond to the `kill` command properly. This can happen when a process is hung, meaning that it refuses to die. Refusal to die tends to happen more on a busy machine with dozens of different processes running. It could very well mean that the process is so busy and CPU time is so limited that the process cannot complete its exit cycle.

You still need the `kill` command in this case, but here you pair it with a special command option: `-9`. The `kill –9` command is equal to the `Force Quit` in the Microsoft Windows world. No matter where the program is — in midcommand or nearing completion — the program will terminate immediately. A `core` file may be produced when this occurs. In that case, delete the file.

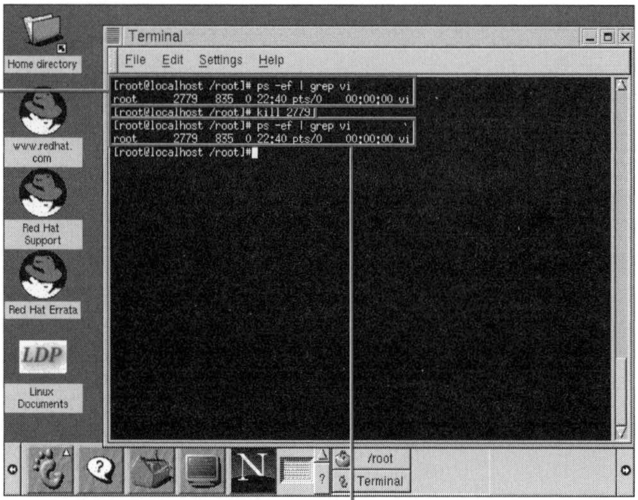

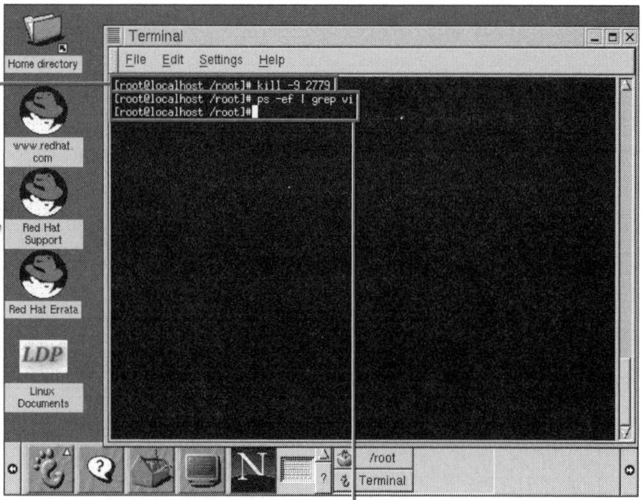

KILL A VI PROCESS

1 Type **ps –ef | grep vi**.

2 Press Enter.

3 Type **kill 2779**.

4 Press Enter.

5 Type ps **–ef | grep vi**.

6 Press Enter.

■ The process is still present.

7 Type kill –9.

8 Press Enter.

9 Type ps **–ef | grep vi**.

10 Press Enter.

■ The process is gone.

How often can I use kill -9?

- Use it sparingly. When you use this command on a program that is vital to your system (such as a print job), other programs (such as the Linux print queue) tend to crash.

What is a core file?

- A `core` file is a dump of all the half-processed data that the killed program was handling when it crashed. `core` files are usually incredibly large, so you must clean up as quickly as possible or you run the risk of running out of space on your disk drive.

Where is a core file produced?

- `core` files are generated in the directory from where you launched a program. For this reason, it is best to consistently start your programs in certain directories, so you can reliably check the presence of `core` files.

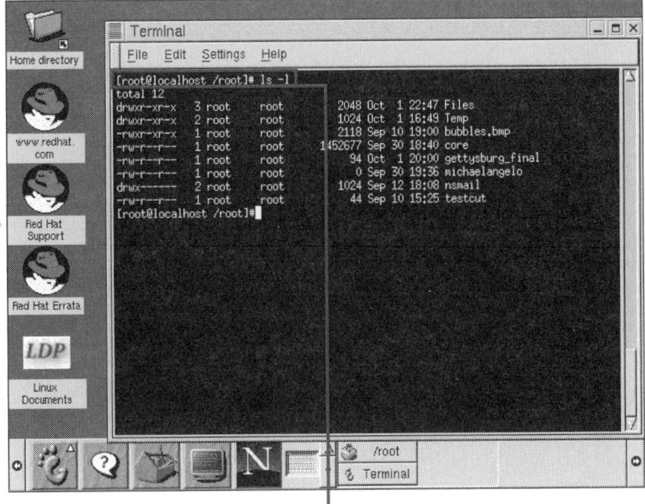

■ After you perform a `kill -9`, check to see whether a core file was produced when the program crashed.

11 Type **ls -l**.

12 Press Enter to see if this file is produced.

REMOVE THE CORE FILE

1 Type **rm core**.

2 Press Enter.

3 Type **ls -l**.

4 Press Enter to make sure the `core` file is gone.

RE-DIRECT OUTPUT WITH ARROW KEYS

You can re-direct the output of a program, binary, or script in the Linux operating system by using the arrow keys, also known as the lesser than and greater than signs.

You will find that the ability to direct output to a file is one of the most useful tools in Linux. This allows you to isolate and read output, such as a log file, from a program at your leisure. If you are short on space in a particular area of your system, you can shunt the data off to a remote location where space is not in high demand.

Note that the re-direction command is a greater than sign (>). The direction of the arrow indicates the direction of the information flow. In this case, the output of the `ls` command was sent to the file `log`. The format for re-direction is normally *<program> <redirection sign> <output file>*

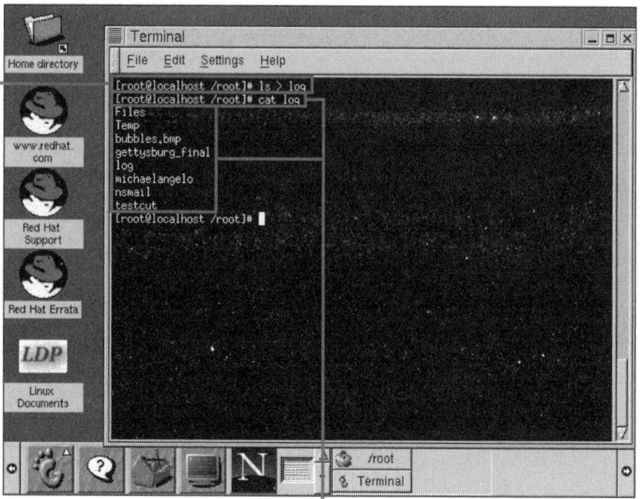

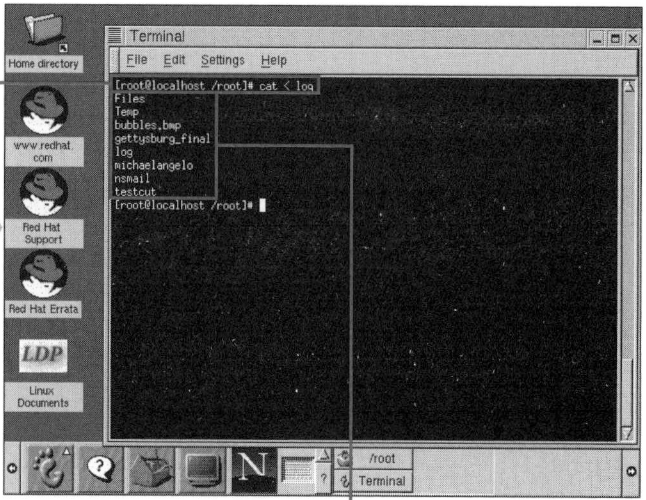

REDIRECT THE OUTPUT OF AN LS COMMAND INTO A FILE

1 Type **ls > log** at the prompt.

2 Press Enter.

■ The file `log` is created.

3 Type **cat log**.

4 Press Enter.

■ The contents of `log` displays — it is the output of the `ls` command.

5 To re-direct the opposite direction, type **cat < log**.

6 Press Enter.

■ The contents of file `log` displays again.

What if I accidentally re-direct information to a file that contains data that I want to save?

- Unfortunately, the new information you sent to your file is rewrites over the data that was already there. The re-direct commands, unlike the removal command `rm`, do not come with any safeguards or warning messages that ask if you want to complete the task. For that reason, never rush through a re-direction task.

Can I re-direct information to a file if I do not have write permissions to the file?

- You cannot do this. Remember that not having write permissions does not mean that you are forbidden from using a text editor on the file. In fact, it means that you cannot edit a file in any way, shape, or form. If you attempt to re-direct information to a file where you lack write permissions, the task will not be completed.

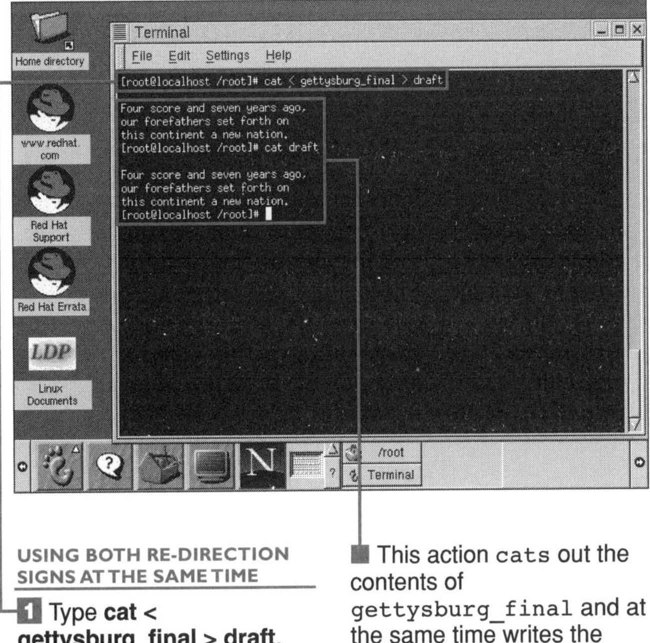


```
[root@localhost /root]# ls > /var/Sculptor/michaelangelo
[root@localhost /root]# cat /var/Sculptor/michaelangelo
651
Files
Temp
bubbles.bmp
draft
gettysburg_final
log
michaelangelo
nsmail
testcut
[root@localhost /root]#
```

USING BOTH RE-DIRECTION SIGNS AT THE SAME TIME

1. Type **cat < gettysburg_final > draft**.
2. Press Enter.

■ This action `cats` out the contents of `gettysburg_final` and at the same time writes the contents to a different file. Information flows from `gettysburg_final` into the `cat` command, printing the output to the screen.

RE-DIRECT FILE OUTPUT TO REMOTE LOCATIONS

1. Type **ls > /var/Sculptor /michaelangelo**.
2. Press Enter.

■ You re-direct the output from the `ls` command.

3. Type **cat /var/Sculptor /michaelangelo**.
4. Press Enter.

■ View your results.

CONTINUED

RE-DIRECT OUTPUT WITH ARROW KEYS CONTINUED

You can use a variation of the re-direct commands where the text or information that you direct to a given file will not overwrite what is already saved inside the file. The >> and << re-direction commands, unlike > and <, re-direct output and append it to a file instead of writing over output.

You will find the append variations on the re-direct commands extremely useful when you want to save the output of multiple re-direct commands in only one file. For example, if you want to re-direct information from the files `chem1`, `chem2`, and `chem3` into a single, large file, you can use the re-direct command to append the contents of these three files into an file appropriately named `chemistry-notes`. Keep in mind that if you are short on disk space, creating large files that hold the output of multiple re-direct commands can quickly fill up your hard disk.

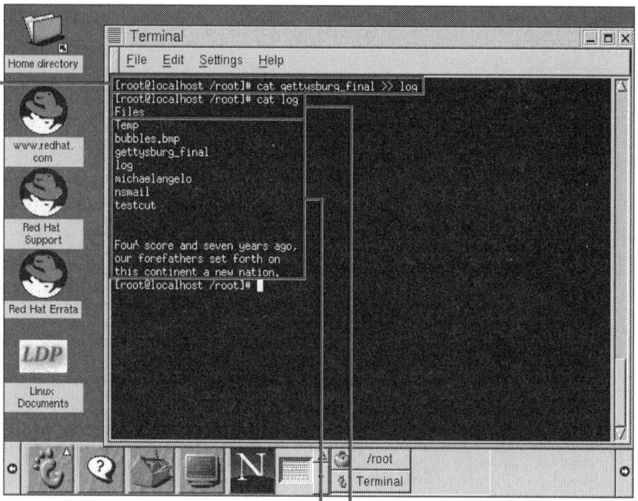

APPEND FILE CONTENTS

1 Type **cat gettysburg_final >> log**.

2 Press Enter.

3 Type **cat log**.

4 Press Enter to view the results.

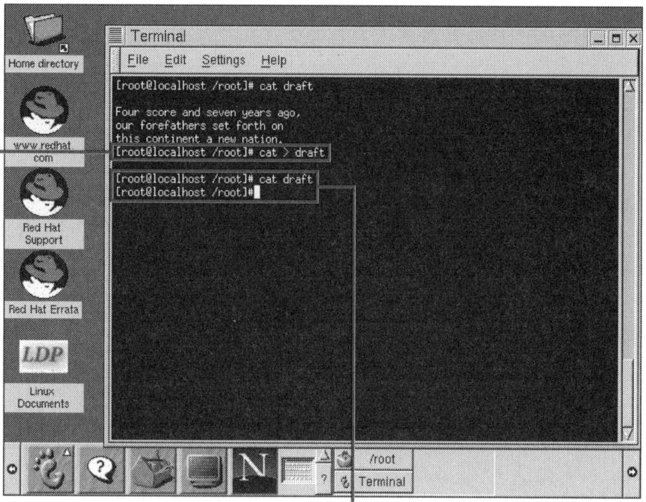

CLEAN OUT A FILE WITHOUT DELETING IT

1 Type **cat > draft**.

2 Press Enter.

3 Nothing is flowing into `draft`, so `cat` the file again.

■ There is no output.

Can I use re-direction instead of a pipe with ps?

✔ Generally speaking, no. In situations when you use a re-direct, you are transferring data from a file to a command, or vice versa. Pipes are designed to move information between separate commands.

What about using re-direction with my ps command instead of a pipe?

✔ This is the reverse of the prior question, so the answer is still no. You can certainly re-direct the output of the `ps` command to a file and then read the file, but that is cumbersome. You will not be able to use re-direct to send the output of `ps` directly through a `grep` command. Instead you would have to use a separate `grep` command on the file you just directed the output to.

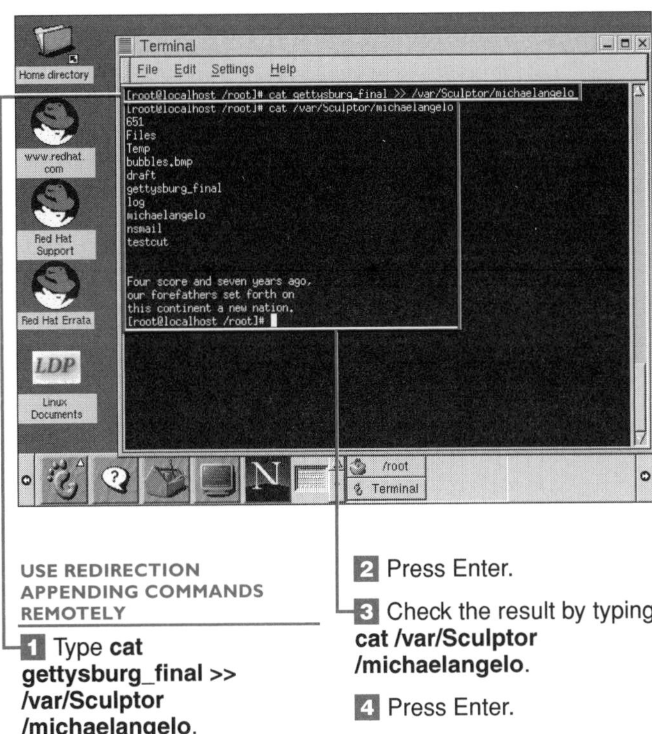

USE REDIRECTION APPENDING COMMANDS REMOTELY

1 Type **cat gettysburg_final >> /var/Sculptor /michaelangelo**.

2 Press Enter.

3 Check the result by typing **cat /var/Sculptor /michaelangelo**.

4 Press Enter.

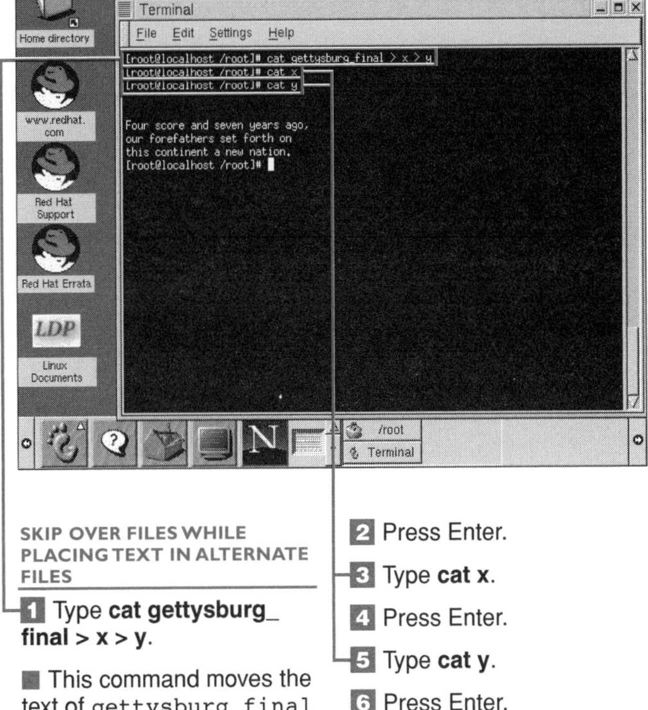

SKIP OVER FILES WHILE PLACING TEXT IN ALTERNATE FILES

1 Type **cat gettysburg_ final > x > y**.

■ This command moves the text of `gettysburg_final` from file x to file y.

2 Press Enter.

3 Type **cat x**.

4 Press Enter.

5 Type **cat y**.

6 Press Enter.

MAKE A FILE EXECUTABLE

You can make a file executable by using the chmod command. Execute, which means that you can execute or start the file as a program, is the third of the three permissions you can give a file. You will find this most handy when you need to convert a file into a script or need to turn off a program so that no one runs it by accident.

Everything in the Linux world is considered a file, whether it is a document or a program. Making a text file executable does not transform it into a program. If you construct your own program with Linux commands (also known as creating a Linux shell script), then making the file executable is the last step you need to ensure that your script runs properly.

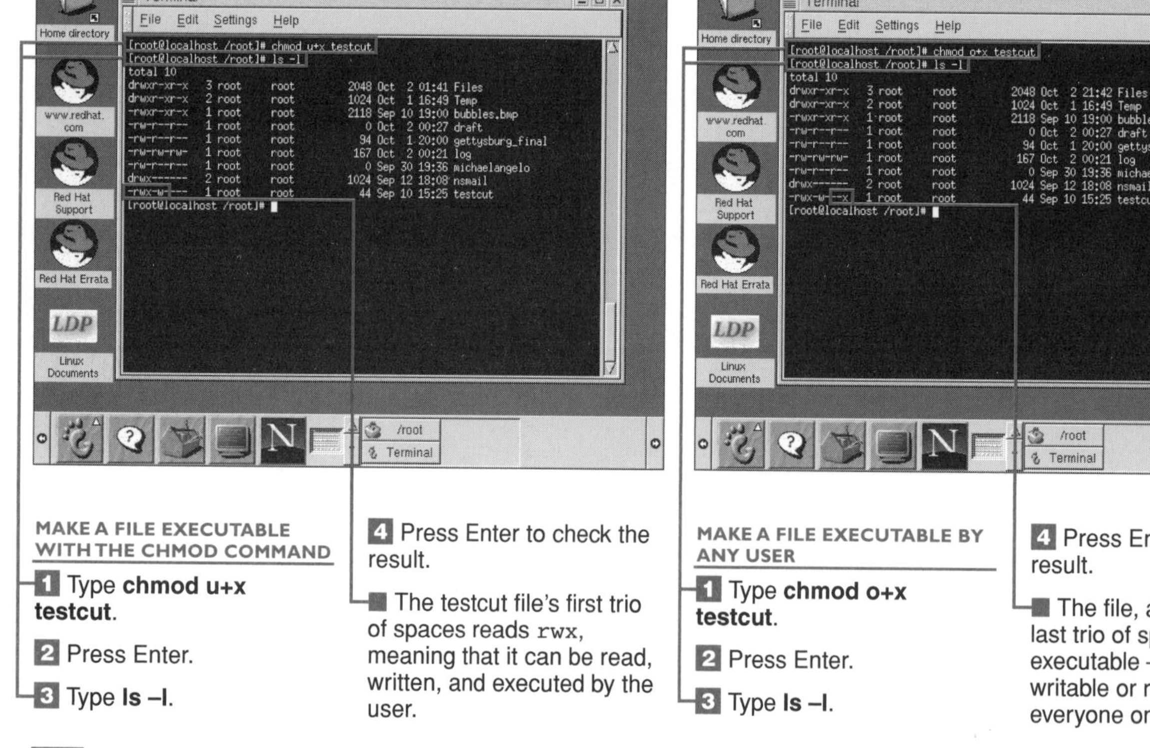

MAKE A FILE EXECUTABLE WITH THE CHMOD COMMAND

1 Type **chmod u+x testcut**.

2 Press Enter.

3 Type **ls –l**.

4 Press Enter to check the result.

■ The testcut file's first trio of spaces reads rwx, meaning that it can be read, written, and executed by the user.

MAKE A FILE EXECUTABLE BY ANY USER

1 Type **chmod o+x testcut**.

2 Press Enter.

3 Type **ls –l**.

4 Press Enter to check the result.

■ The file, according to the last trio of spaces, is now executable — but not writable or readable — by everyone on the system.

How do I execute a program after it is executable?

- Normally, you just need to type the name of the file and press Enter. There are times when you need to do additional tasks, however. You can find more detail in Chapter 8.

What if a file is marked as non-executable to the user group, but is executable by everyone else?

- If a file is marked `-rwxrw-r-x`, everyone — including the user group — can execute that file. The user group is just a subgroup of the total number of Linux users represented by the Other setting in the Linux permissioning scheme.

Why are directories marked executable?

- This is the default setting in Linux. It allows you to enter and exit directories with the `change directories` (`cd`) command.

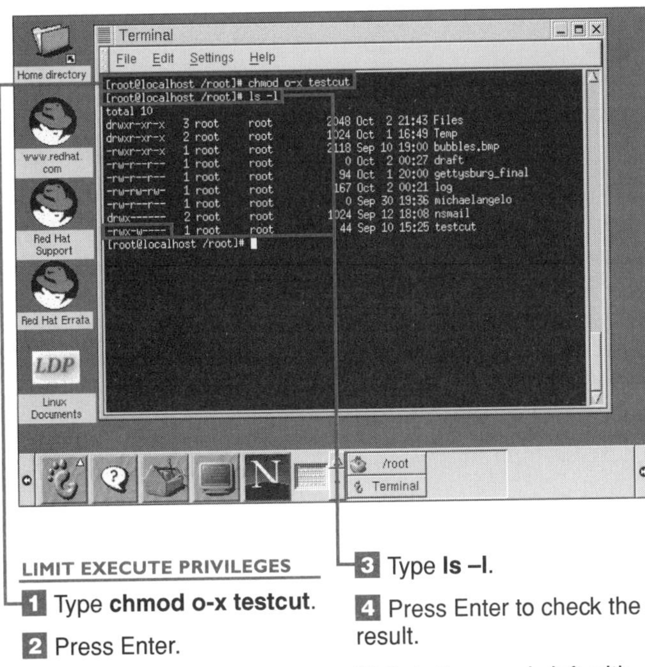

LIMIT EXECUTE PRIVILEGES

1. Type **chmod o-x testcut**.
2. Press Enter.
3. Type **ls –l**.
4. Press Enter to check the result.

■ Only the user is left with execute privileges.

USE COMMAND OPTIONS REMOTELY

1. Type **chmod u+x /var/Sculptor /michaelangelo**.
2. Press Enter.

■ This command grants the user execute permissions to the file `/var/Sculptor/michaelangelo`.

3. Type **ls –l /var/Sculptor**.
4. Press Enter to see the results.

CHANGE A FILE'S OWNERSHIP

You can change the ownership of a file in Linux by using the `chown`, or `change ownership`, command. You want to change the ownership of a file so that it is owned by the `root` account if you want to restrict access without changing the file permissions. Alternatively, you can change the ownership of a file to make it more public and easier to access.

Users can also use this command if they want to transfer ownership of a file to a different user or to the `root` account. Both you and a user who executes this command should know that it is very hard to take back ownership of a file after it is given away. Of course, the `root` account can restore file privileges if `chmod` has been used accidentally. The format for *chown* is `chown` *<new owner> <filename>*.

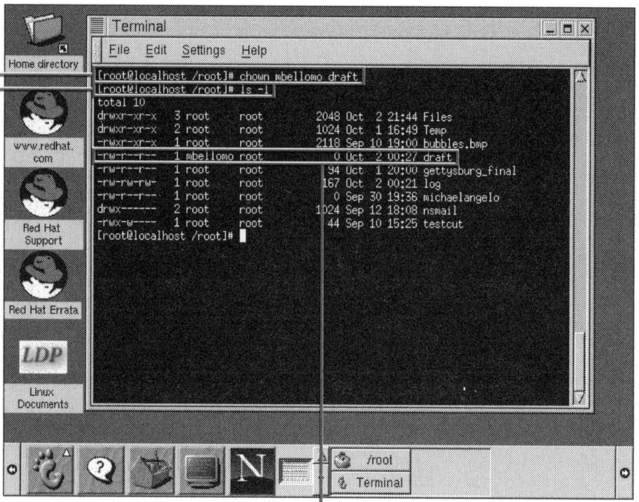

CHANGE OWNERSHIP OF A FILE

1 Type **chown mbellomo draft**.

2 Press Enter.

3 Type **ls –l**.

4 Press Enter to view the results.

■ The ownership of `draft` changes from `root` to `mbellomo`.

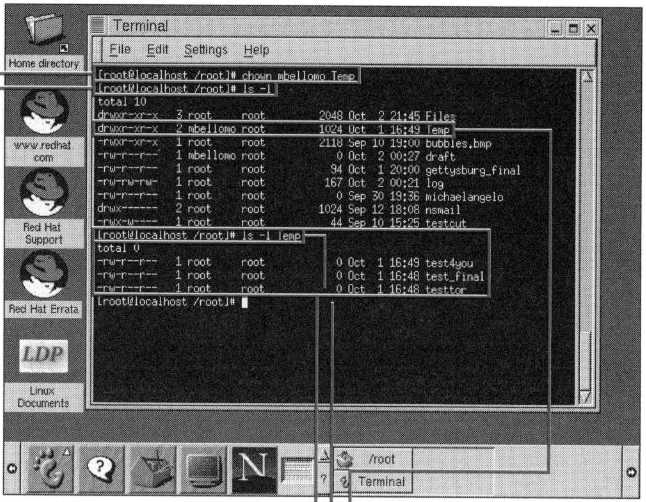

CHANGE OWNERSHIP OF A DIRECTORY

1 Type **chown <user> <directory>**.

2 Press Enter.

3 Type **ls –l**.

4 Press Enter.

■ `mbellomo` now owns `Temp`.

5 Type **ls –l <directory>**.

6 Press Enter.

■ The underlying files are still owned by `root`.

What happens if the directory is owned by one user and the files are owned by another?

- Unless everyone has read and write permissions for the directory and the files underneath, then some odd restrictions take place. The person who owns the files cannot make edits to them because he does not own the directory, and the person who owns the directory will probably be unable to edit the files because he doesn't own them!

Can I change a file's ownership to a nonexistent user account?

- No. Linux checks against the user accounts you have listed in the `/etc/passwd` file (more on this in Chapter 8), and doesn't allow you to change ownership if the user does not exist. Oddly enough, you can change the owner to `nobody` because `nobody` is a Linux default account. Do not take this route if you can help it, though — `nobody` is a dummy account used by the Linux system for maintenance tasks.

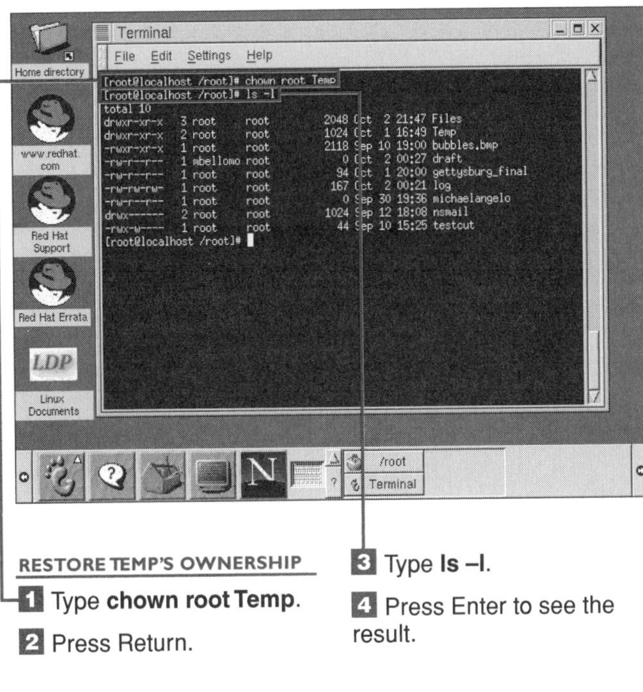

RESTORE TEMP'S OWNERSHIP

1. Type **chown root Temp**.
2. Press Return.
3. Type **ls –l**.
4. Press Enter to see the result.

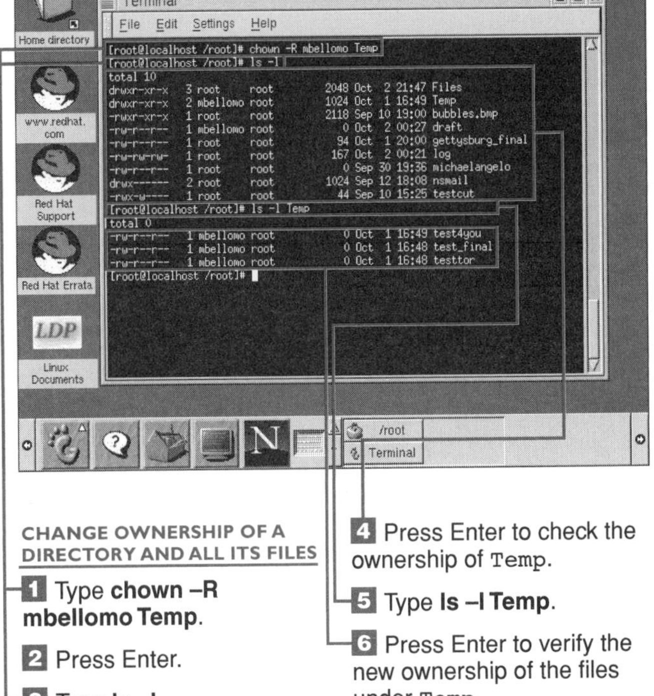

CHANGE OWNERSHIP OF A DIRECTORY AND ALL ITS FILES

1. Type **chown –R mbellomo Temp**.
2. Press Enter.
3. Type **ls –l**.
4. Press Enter to check the ownership of `Temp`.
5. Type **ls –l Temp**.
6. Press Enter to verify the new ownership of the files under `Temp`.

CHANGE THE FILE'S GROUP OWNERSHIP

You can change the group ownership of a file with the `chgrp`, or `change group`, command. Group ownership in the long (`ls –l`) mode is listed in the column to the right of the user ownership. You change the file's group ownership to either restrict access or to make it more publicly available. Group ownership affects the readability, writability, and execution of a file depending on the file's permissioning. If a file is listed as writable by the user and the user's group, then both the user and anyone in the user's group can edit the file. However, no one else outside the user's group has permission to edit the file.

When using the change group command, the format for `chgrp` is

`chgrp` *<new owner> <filename>*

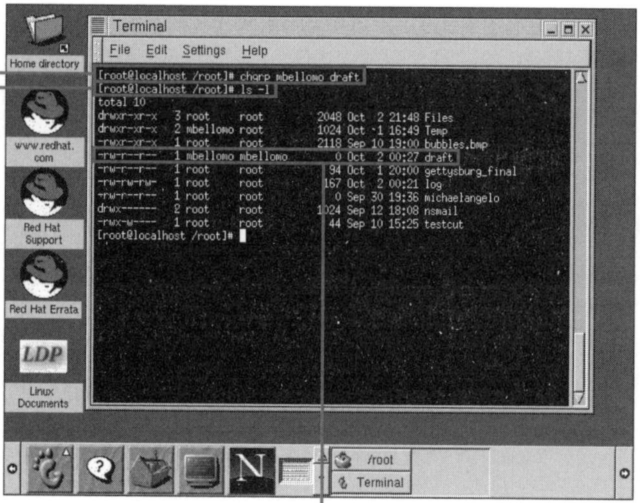

CHANGE THE GROUP OWNERSHIP

1 Type **chgrp <user> <filetoown>**.

2 Press Enter.

3 Type **ls –l**.

4 Press Enter to view the results.

■ `mbellomo` now owns the file draft.

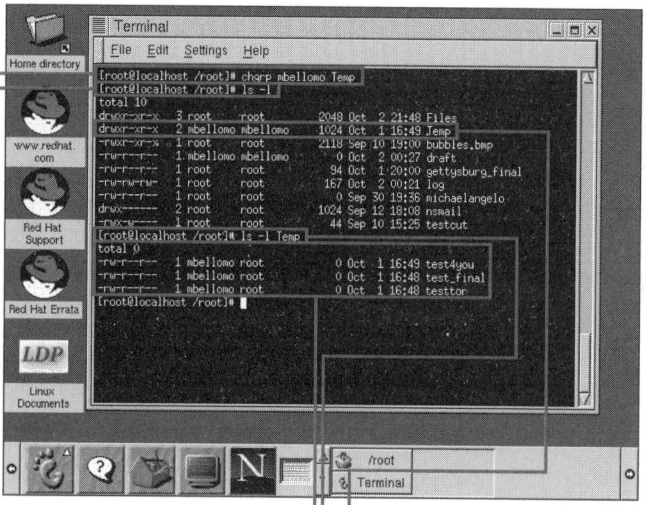

CHANGE THE GROUP OWNERSHIP OF A DIRECTORY

1 Type **chgrp <user> <directory>**.

2 Press Enter.

3 Type **ls –l**.

4 Press Enter.

■ The `mbellomo` group now owns `Temp`.

5 Type **ls –l Temp**.

6 Press Enter.

■ The underlying files are still owned by the `root` group

Can I perform the same kind of permissioning with the chown command?

- Yes, you can use the `chmod g+ or g-` options to grant or restrict permissions as you prefer. However, there are times that Linux programs access files and check the file's ownership and group ownership — not their permissions. `chgrp` is a worthwhile command to learn.

Can I change a file to a nonexistent group?

- Like it is with `chown`, this is not possible. Besides, there are other ways to restrict access to a given file with the `chgrp` command.

How can I make access more restrictive?

- You can do this by changing the group ownership to the `root` account. Because `root` is — by its nature — more restricted, it is the administrator account and can access the file. Of course, this can include yourself, so be selective in using this. You can restrict access by changing the group ownership to the `root` account. Because the `root` account belongs to its own group, only the `root` account will be able to access the file.

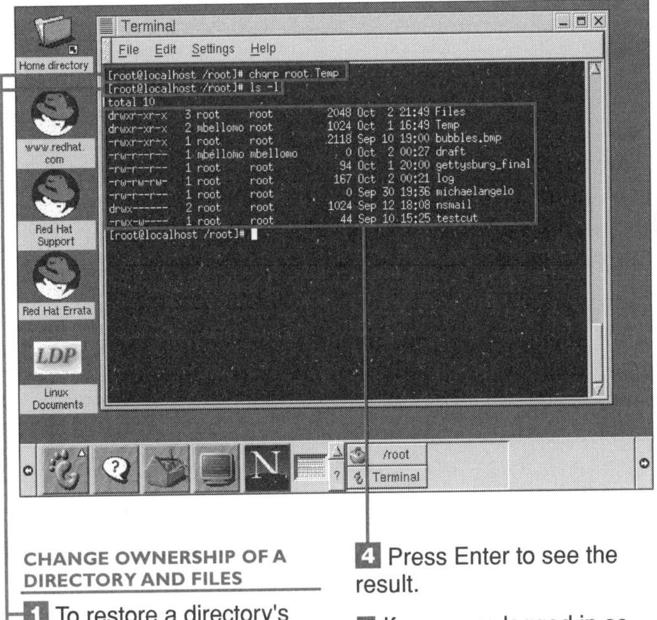

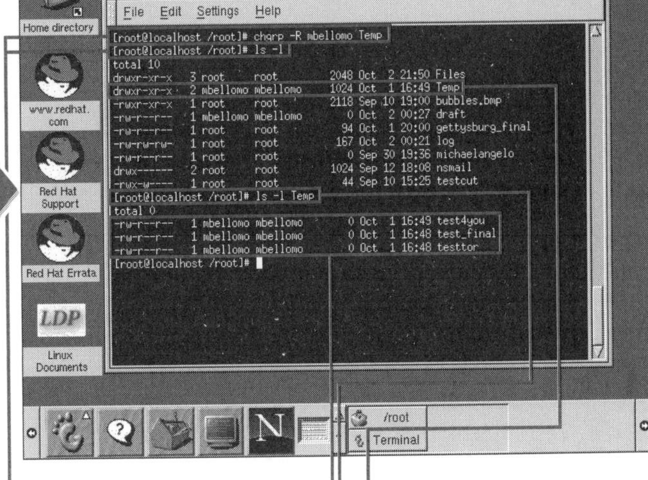

CHANGE OWNERSHIP OF A DIRECTORY AND FILES

1 To restore a directory's group ownership, type **chgrp root <directory>**.

2 Press Enter.

3 Type ls –l.

4 Press Enter to see the result.

■ If you were logged in as any other account besides the `root` administrator, you would be unable to take back this file's group ownership.

5 Type **chgrp –R <user> <directory>**.

6 Press Enter.

7 Type ls –l.

8 Press Enter to check the group ownership of the directory.

9 Type ls **–l <directory>**.

10 Press Enter to verify the new group ownership of the files under the directory.

START THE VI EDITOR

You can use the `vi` editor for everything from creating text documents to writing scripts, editing files, and searching through log files with more detail than the `grep` command. `vi` is to many people the most important utility in the Linux world.

Other text editors exist in Linux, such as emacs, Ex, and the Linux-based WordPerfect or WordStar programs. Only `vi`, however, automatically comes with all Linux installations and is universally popular with users and administrators.

Because `vi` is not graphics based like today's word processors, it can be more challenging and esoteric than most text-processing programs. It's also so incredibly flexible and powerful that whole books are dedicated to its quirks and hidden commands. This book's coverage of `vi` includes showing you the most important and useful commands that you may use on a daily basis.

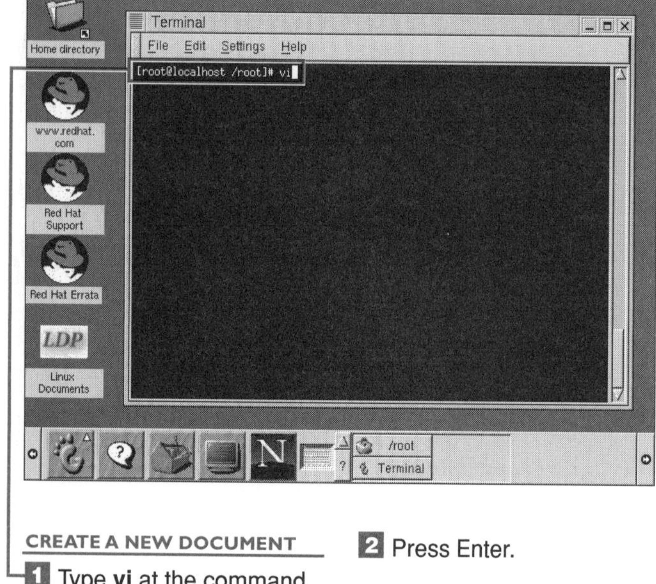

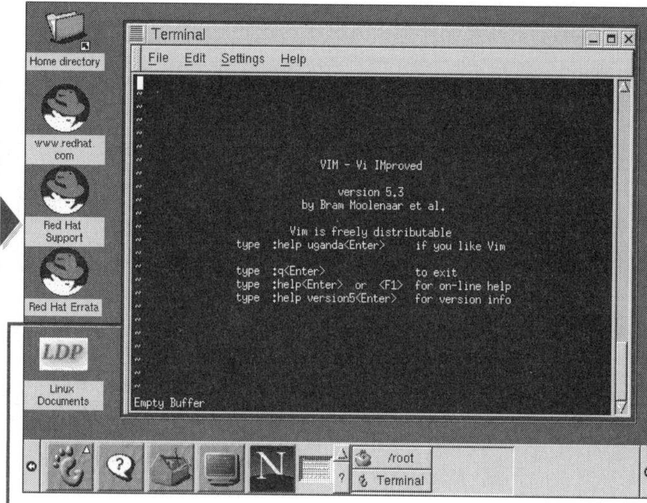

CREATE A NEW DOCUMENT

1 Type **vi** at the command line.

2 Press Enter.

■ The latest version of Red Hat Linux comes with `vim`, a new form of `vi`. When you edit text, this Intro screen disappears.

Is there a way I can bring up the vi editor from the GNOME desktop without going through the Linux Terminal?

- You can't do this, because `vi` is not a graphics-based program that can function in the GNOME environment.

How does creating a file with the vi editor differ from creating a file with the touch command?

- Whether you create a file with the `vi` editor or with the `touch` command, the result is the same — a blank text file. However, when you create a file with `vi`, you automatically start the `vi` text editor. Whatever you type while in `vi` is savable in the new file you just created. `Touch` is simply a command to create a blank file; it is not a complete text editor like `vi`. Of course, when you create a file with `touch`, you can always edit it later with `vi`.

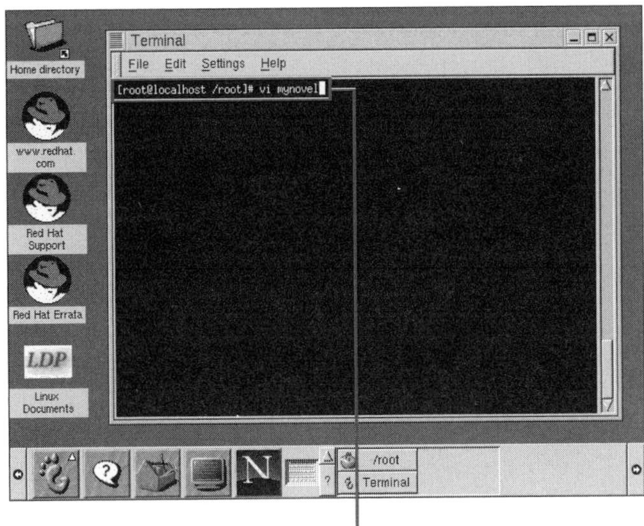

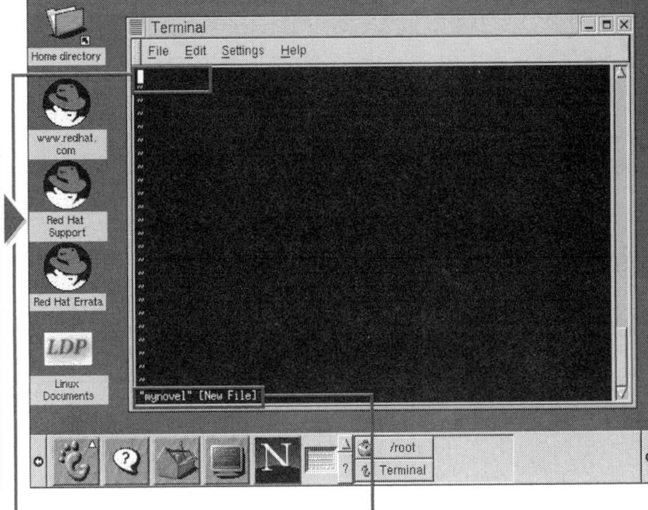

START WITH AN EXISTING FILENAME

Note: You select the name of the file in advance and simply save as you exit the program.

1 To edit the file `mynovel`, type **vi mynovel**.

2 Press Enter.

■ The standard blank `vi` screen appears.

■ The filename appears at the bottom of the screen.

CONTINUED

START THE VI EDITOR CONTINUED

You can edit files that are already in existence with the vi editor. Unlike Microsoft Word, the vi editor has no Open File button. To edit a pre-existing file, you must specify it by name when starting vi.

After you specify the file that you want to edit, you are taken directly to the vi editor screen. Because you open a file at the same time you open the vi editor, this is similar to double-clicking a text file in the Windows environment.

However, vi also comes with an additional advantage that a graphics-based text editor in the Windows or GNOME environment does not have. No matter where you are in the Linux environment, you can open a file to edit in any location. By comparison, in Microsoft Word, you may have to open several different windows to get to the file you want.

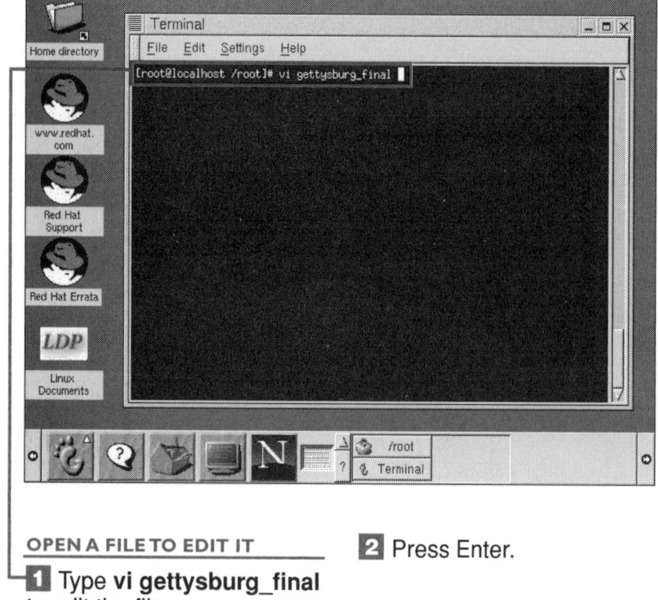

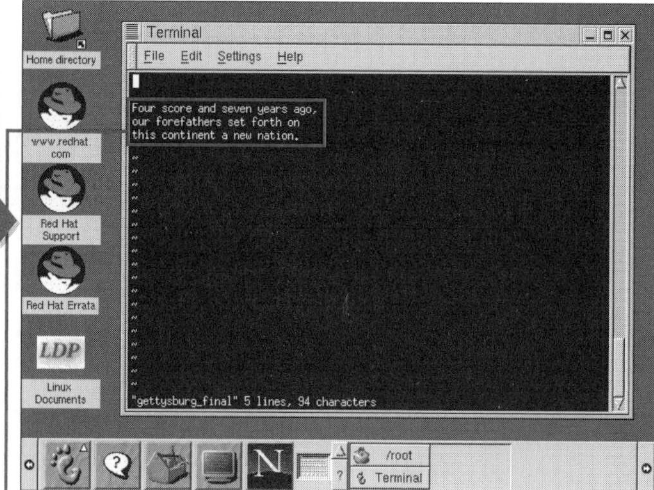

OPEN A FILE TO EDIT IT

1 Type **vi gettysburg_final** to edit the file.

2 Press Enter.

■ The vi screen appears with the contents of the gettysburg_final document, ready for editing.

Why does vi lack toolbars if it's a text processor?

- `vi` is one of the oldest programs, pre-dating Linux itself. It was originally a UNIX utility. It was developed at a time when UNIX machines didn't use monitors — they used teletype machines. To save paper, UNIX — and by extension, Linux and `vi` — are very light on any graphics and long-winded passages.

Are there any limitations to naming a file in vi?

- Do not give your file a name with periods. It's also not a good idea to name your file with any slashes in the name since Linux often lists directories with slashes (`/etc`, `/usr`). Make the name you choose unique.

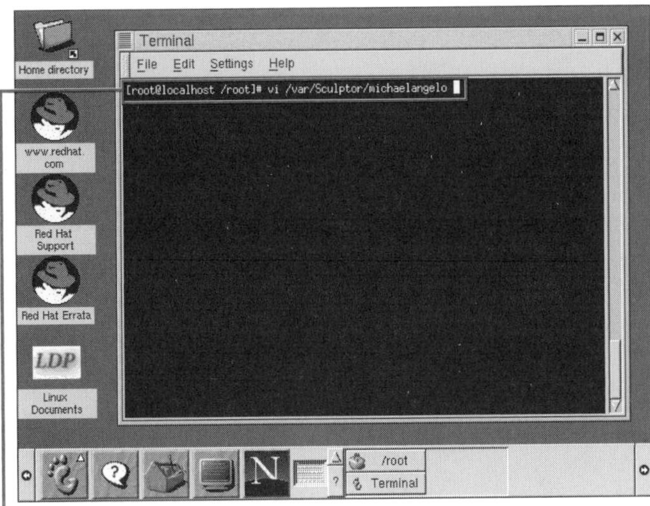

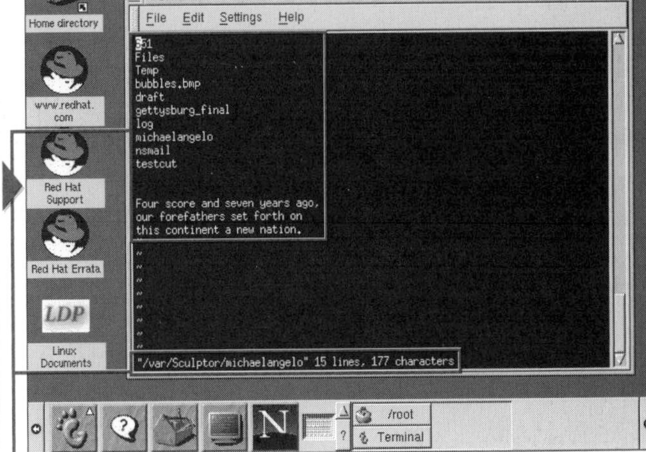

EDIT A FILE IN ANOTHER DIRECTORY

1 Type **vi /var/Sculptor/michaelangelo** to edit the file.

2 Press Enter.

■ You can see the contents, along with the file and the file's full pathname at the bottom of the screen.

COMMAND AND INSERT MODE IN VI

You have two modes that you switch back and forth while you work in the vi editor. One is the Command mode, where you can move around within the document, perform format changes, delete text, quit, or save the document. You may not, however, add text in Command mode.

The INSERT mode works in the opposite manner. When in INSERT mode, you can't perform any of the fancier functions in vi, but you can enter text.

By default, you are always in Command mode in vi. You have several ways to get into INSERT mode. To get back into Command mode, there is only one option — pressing the Esc key, also known as the Escape key. On most keyboards, this key is found set apart from the rest of the key rows in the upper left-hand corner.

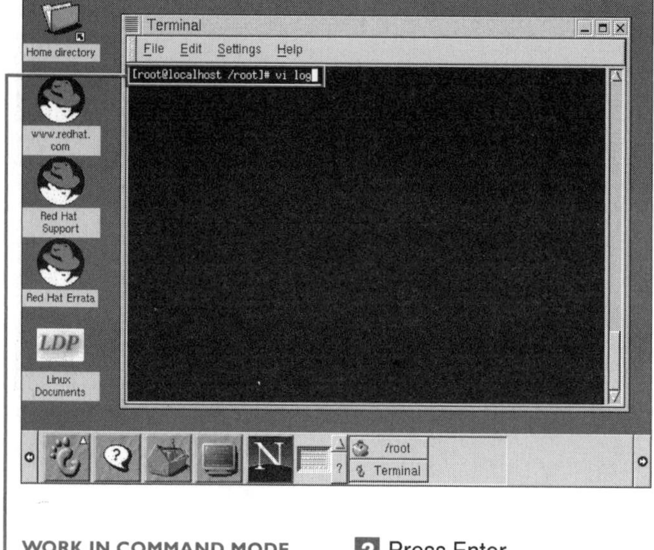

WORK IN COMMAND MODE

1 Type **vi log** to start the vi editor.

2 Press Enter.

■ The vi screen appears with the contents of log in Command mode.

TIPS

Can I use other methods of going from Command mode into INSERT mode?

- Linux offers other ways. The most common is by using the commands to insert a new (blank) line of text or to paste text. (You learn how to do this later in this chapter.)

Are there any other ways of going from INSERT mode to Command mode?

- No. Using the Escape key is the only option available to you when going from INSERT to Command mode.

My version of vi doesn't display Insert when I'm in INSERT mode. How can I tell which mode I'm in?

- Aside from simple experimentation, which can be frustrating, always assume you're in INSERT mode. Press Esc to ensure that you're in Command mode before you try to move the cursor. On most Linux systems, pressing Esc repeatedly rewards you with a little beep.

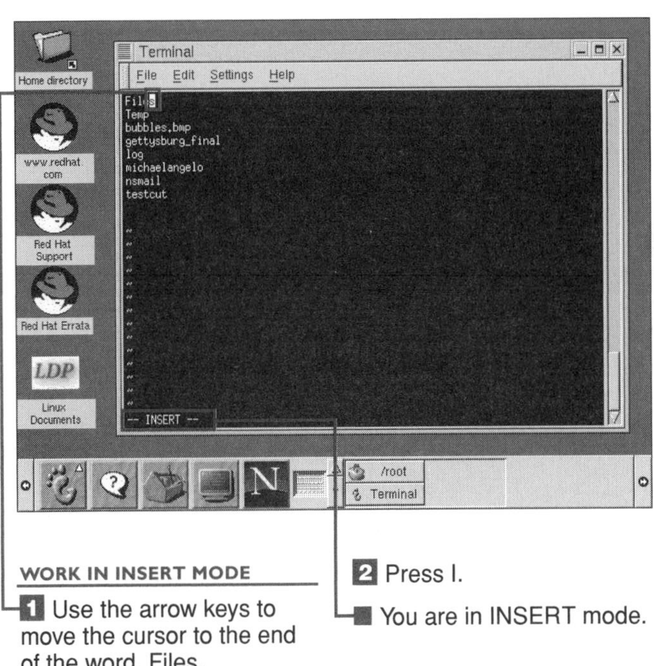

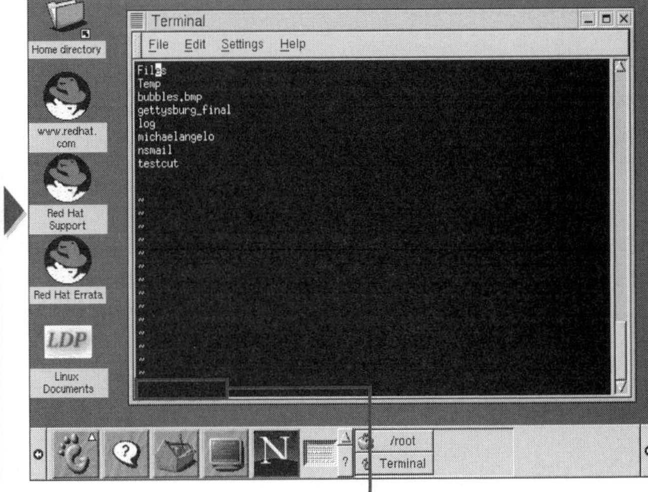

WORK IN INSERT MODE

1 Use the arrow keys to move the cursor to the end of the word, Files.

2 Press I.

- You are in INSERT mode.

3 To exit out of INSERT mode, press the Escape key (Esc).

- The INSERT message disappears.

ADD TEXT

You can add text to documents by using one of the different ways to switch from Command mode into INSERT mode in the `vi` editor. Depending on how you enter INSERT mode, you'll be able to enter text either at the position of the cursor or immediately after it.

Keep in mind that there are separate commands available to insert text in a mass fashion, such as cutting, pasting, or inserting new lines of text. The methods shown here are for adding text at the most basic level, which is simply entering text letter by letter.

You should also note at this point that the `vi` editor is a comparatively simple text editor compared to modern word processors. Because `vi` was designed to also code programs in Linux and the C programming language, it avoids confusing the operating system and C compilers with fancier text-formatting tricks, such as text styling or templates.

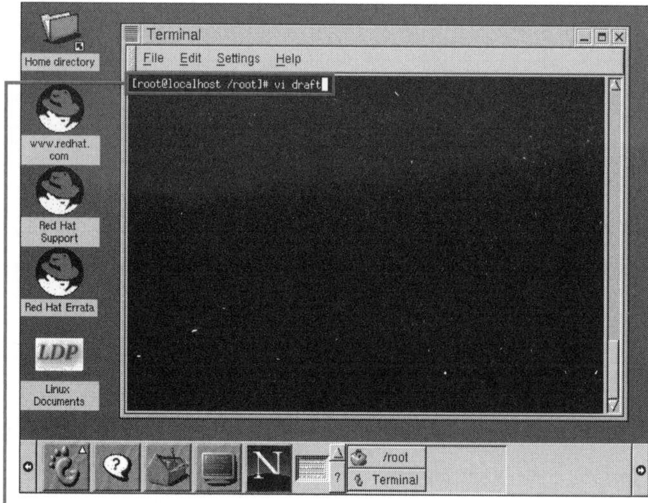

1 Type **vi draft** and press Enter.

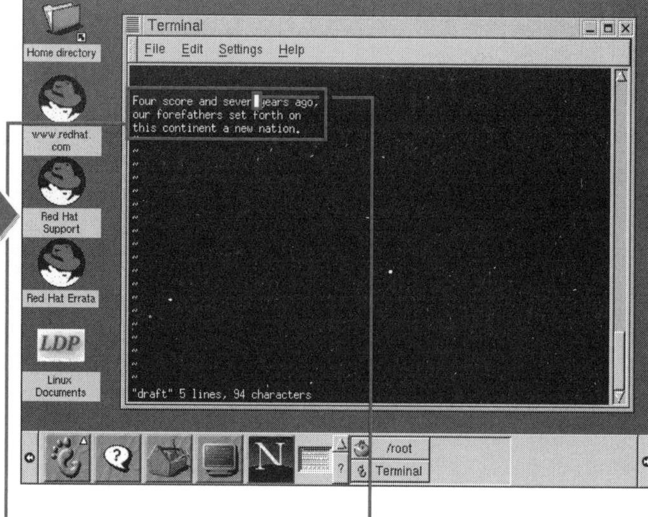

■ The `vi` screen shows the contents (in Command mode).

2 Using your keyboard arrow keys, move the cursor after the word seven.

TIPS

When I want to insert text, what if I type a capital I instead of just entering a lowercase i?

- Entering I will work just as well as an i. This is one of the very few times that Linux isn't being case-sensitive about its commands.

Does the Caps Lock key work in the vi editor when I insert text?

- `vi`, although it doesn't have all the bells and whistles of a graphics-based word processor like Microsoft Word, is still a text processor at heart. The Caps Lock key works the same in `vi` as it would in WordPerfect.

How does the Caps Lock key affect commands I type in the Command mode?

- The Caps Lock key doesn't affect your commands in Command mode at all. If you have to type symbols such as colons, exclamation marks, and dollar signs, use the Shift key.

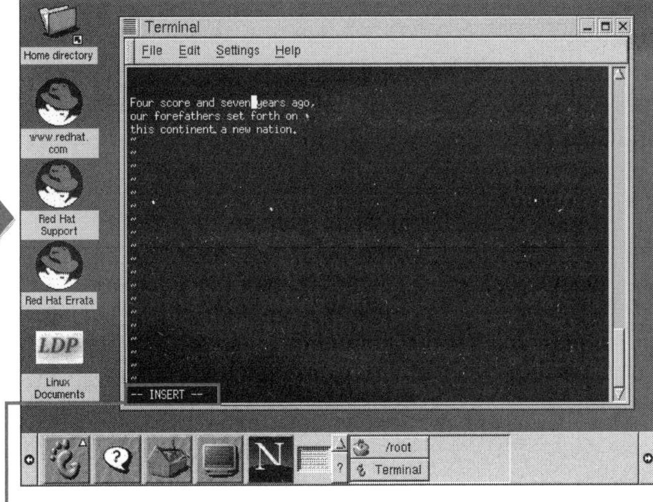

3 Press I to enter INSERT mode. (Do not press Enter.)

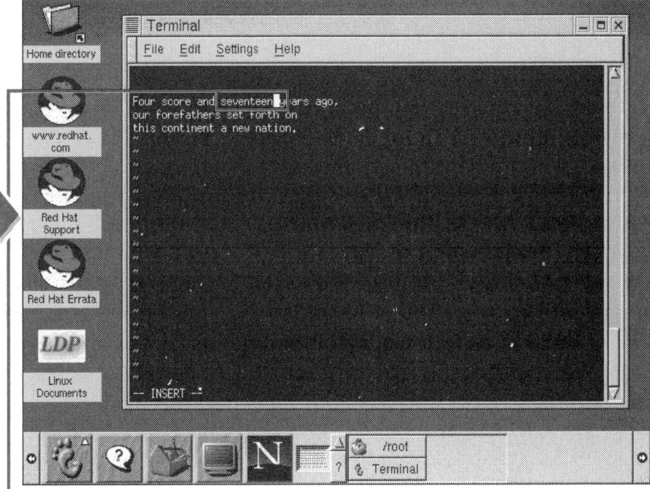

4 Type **teen** to make the word seventeen.

CONTINUED

ADD TEXT CONTINUED

You have another option for inserting text into a document with the `vi` editor. Instead of using the `i` in the Command mode, you can use the `a`.

The `a` command stands for *append*. `append` works exactly like `insert` in that it takes you directly into the `vi` editor's INSERT mode. However, unlike the `insert text` command, using the `append text` command places your new text to the immediate right of the cursor.

As its name suggests, the `append` command is most useful when you work with existing documents. Preexisting documents will normally have a substantial amount of text already inside of them. Moving the cursor to the end of a line at the final paragraph of a document and using the `append` command guarantees that you won't accidentally insert new words inside existing text.

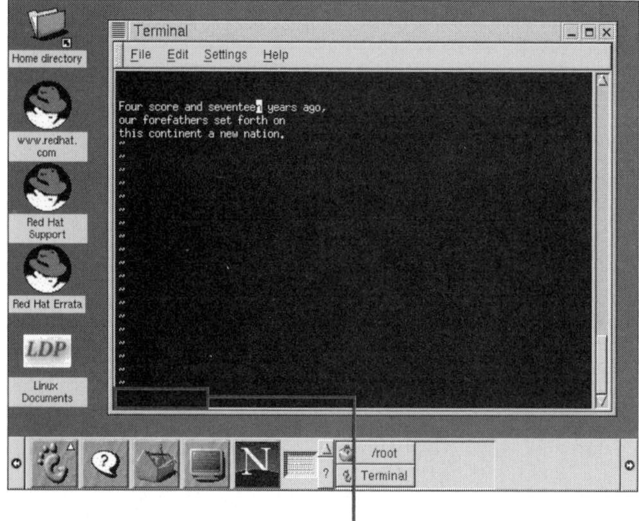

5 Press the Esc key to return to Command mode so you can move to another portion of the document.

■ The Insert message disappears.

6 Use the arrow keys to move the cursor to the e in forefathers.

TIPS

How can I change the font of the text in vi?

- Unfortunately, you can't. Keep in mind that `vi` was designed to code programs in Linux and the C programming language as well as write text.

Can I change the font size of the text, then?

- Not really. Changing the font size or style would be confusing to the operating system and C compilers, so this effect wasn't included. Of course, to help your typing and prevent eyestrain, you can alter the size of the font that displays in your terminal window (see Chapter 5), but this won't print out any larger.

What if I want to write a letter to a friend using fancy fonts?

- You're best off using one of the GUI-based Linux text editors, such as WordPerfect, WordStar, or Gnotepad.

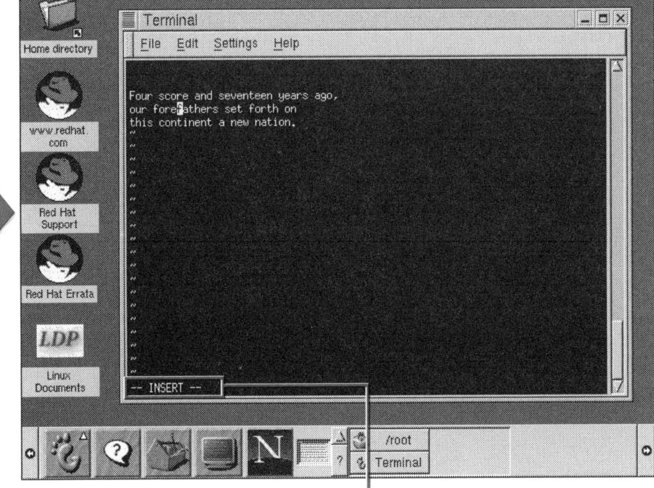

7 Press A.

■ Insert appears at the bottom of the screen.

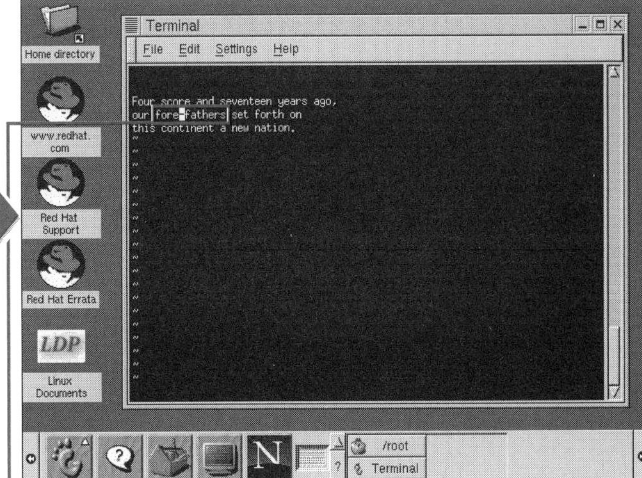

8 Press the hyphen key (–) to make the word forefathers become fore-fathers.

9 Press Esc to return to Command mode.

DELETE TEXT

You can delete text from your vi document in several different ways. You can delete single characters, an entire line of text, or even the entire line in the document itself (in other words, deleting the text and the carriage return). You can even delete characters in the document and simultaneously replace them with different ones.

Knowing which method to use when editing text in the vi editor can save you many extra keystrokes. If you're new to the vi editor, you will find yourself using these commands frequently, as in the beginning it's easy to mistake Command versus INSERT mode when creating new documents.

Note that you can only execute deletion commands in Command mode. As a habit, you can press Esc to ensure that you're in Command mode before trying to delete text.

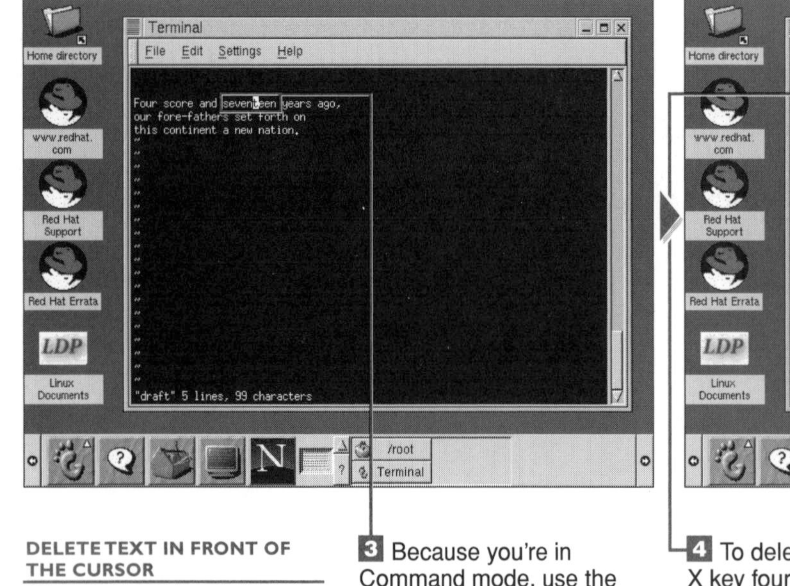

DELETE TEXT IN FRONT OF THE CURSOR

1 Type **vi draft.**

2 Press Enter.

3 Because you're in Command mode, use the arrow keys to move the cursor to the t in seventeen.

4 To delete teen, press the X key four times — once for each letter.

■ Do not press the Shift or Enter key.

What if I want to delete an entire word without having to press X a number of times?

- To delete an entire word, move your cursor over part of the word and press Esc to enter Command mode. Then type **dw** to delete the word at your cursor's location.

Is there a way I can repeat the delete command I just made, without having to type it again?

- If you make sure that you're in Command mode, there is another option. You can enter a colon followed by a period, and then press Enter. `vi` interprets this as a command to repeat the last action you just took.

Does the repeat action work for all commands, or just the delete function?

- Repeat works for all actions. When you specify repeat in `vi`, the editor will repeat the last action you took, whether it involved deleting text or not.

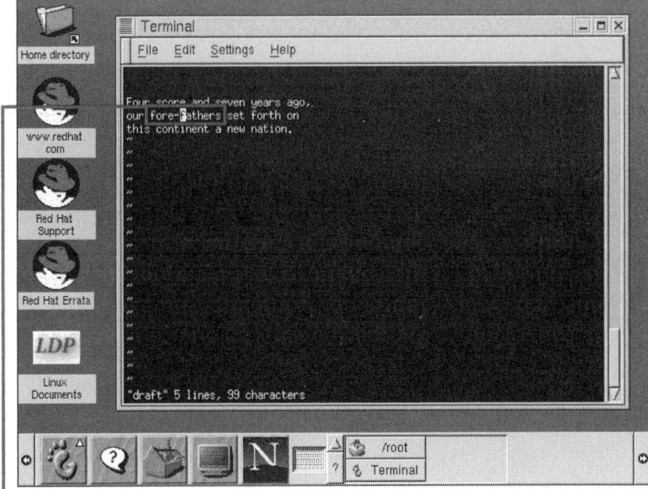

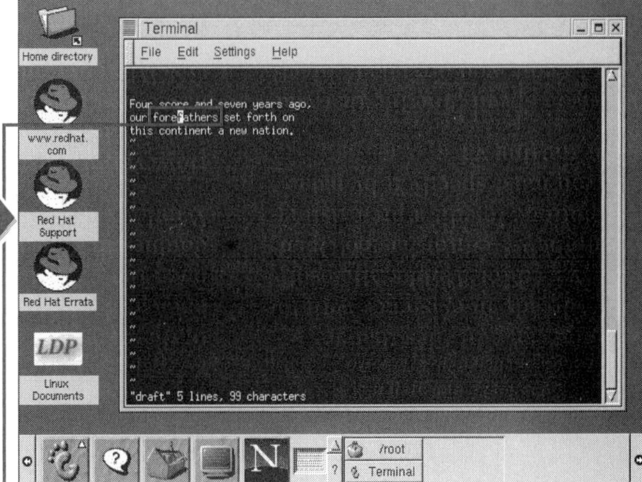

DELETE TEXT BEHIND THE CURSOR

1 In Command mode, use the arrow keys to move to the second f in fore-fathers.

2 Press Shift+X to delete the hyphen.

Note: Using a capital X enables you to delete a character immediately before the cursor.

CONTINUED

DELETE TEXT CONTINUED

You can also delete larger amounts of text in the `vi` editor, up to whole lines at a time. Using only a couple of keystrokes, you can delete lines of text in `vi` much more quickly than with a comparable task in Windows or the GNOME environment. This is because pressing commands on the keyboard is faster than clicking and dragging with the mouse for most editing jobs.

To delete a single line of text, enter the Command mode and use a capital D. A similar command is `dd`, which deletes a line of text and the carriage return accompanying it.

Finally, you can use the letter R in the Command mode to replace old text with new additions.

Note that at the base of the screen, `vi` notifies you that you're performing a REPLACE function. This is another way of telling you that you're in INSERT mode.

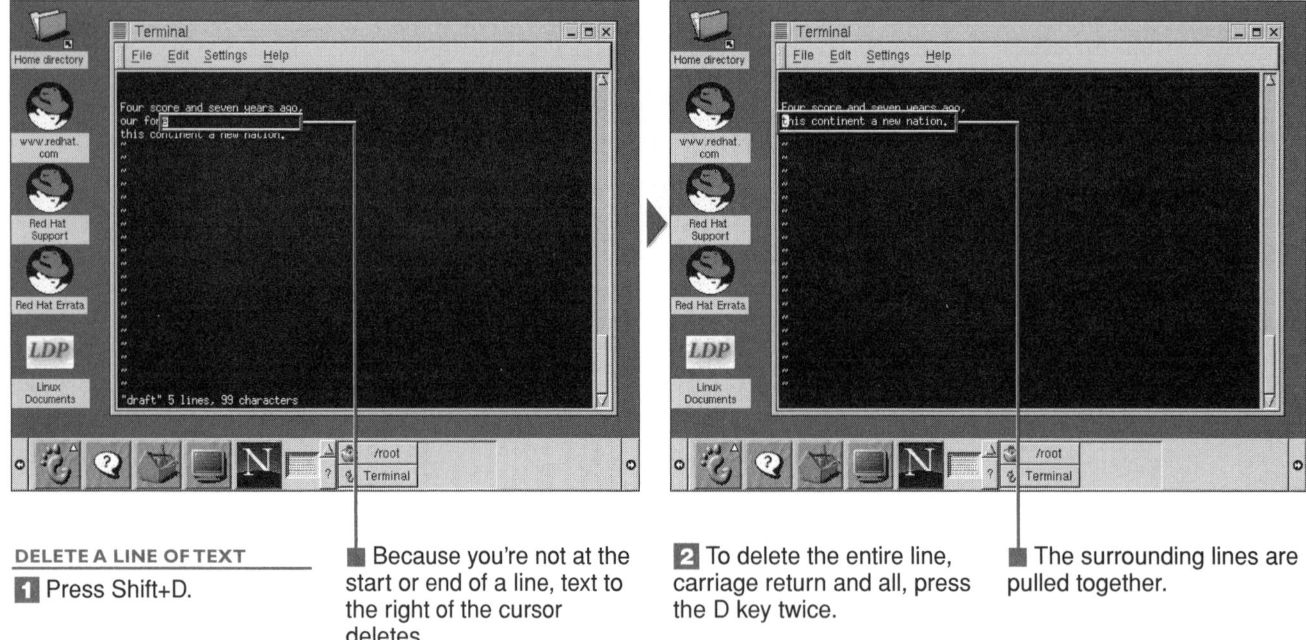

DELETE A LINE OF TEXT

1 Press Shift+D.

■ Because you're not at the start or end of a line, text to the right of the cursor deletes.

2 To delete the entire line, carriage return and all, press the D key twice.

■ The surrounding lines are pulled together.

TIPS

What do I do if I accidentally delete a character?

- You can undo your last command. Press Esc to ensure that you're in Command mode and then press U. If you deleted a character and then performed another action, you wouldn't be able to restore your deletion. Multilevel Undo functions are a recent addition to text editors, and sadly, `vi` lacks this.

What do I do if I delete an entire line?

- You can undo a command to delete an entire line, regardless of whether you used `dd` or `S`. Press Esc to ensure you're in Command mode and press U. Again, if you performed an additional action, you may not be able to restore your line. Use the delete keys cautiously.

REPLACE A WORD

1 Move the cursor to the start of the word nation.

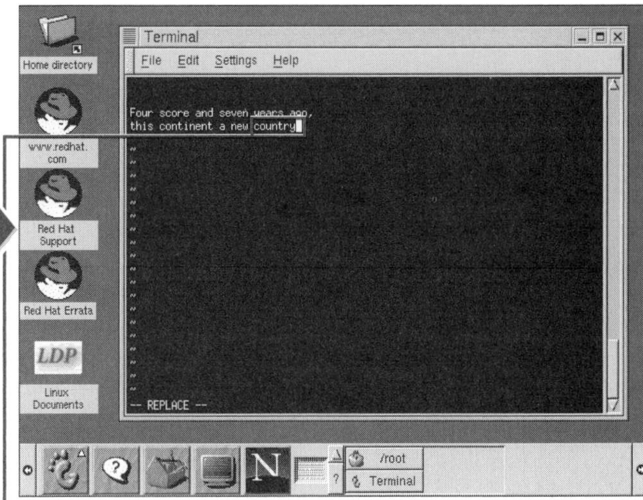

2 Press Shift+R and then type the word country.

■ You replace the word nation with **country**.

■ The period after nation is overwritten.

SUBSTITUTE TEXT

Deleting text and then going back to type in your corrections takes time. Instead, you can use variations on the `replace` command, called *substitution commands*, to save time while editing.

Substituting text enables you to delete and simultaneously replace text with the new characters that you want. This saves you time and keystrokes. Also, it automatically puts you into the all-important INSERT mode. To substitute text and simultaneously replace it character by character, press S.

Because INSERT mode is invoked with these commands, be sure to press Esc when needed to return to Command mode if you need to move the cursor to make further changes to your document. Otherwise, you may unintentionally end up adding letters or characters to your document when you don't need to.

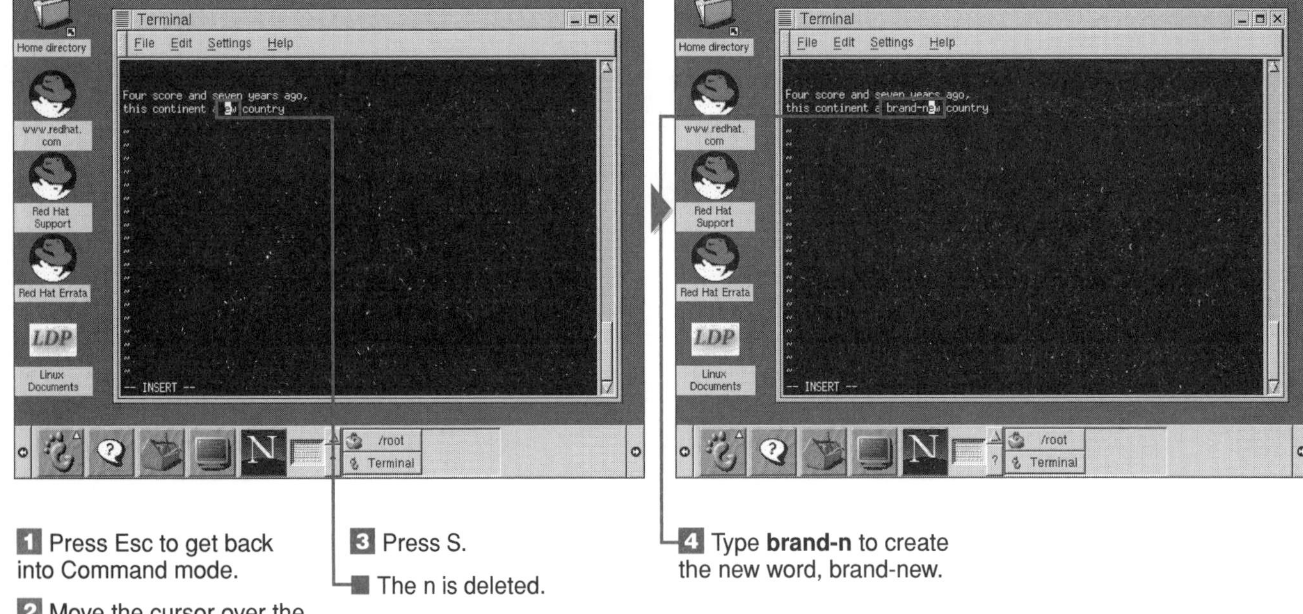

1 Press Esc to get back into Command mode.

2 Move the cursor over the n in new.

3 Press S.

■ The n is deleted.

Note: You're in INSERT mode.

4 Type **brand-n** to create the new word, brand-new.

Is there any way that I can delete text in INSERT mode?

- You can delete characters, but you can't perform deletion functions by the word or line. When you're in INSERT mode, you can use the Delete and Backspace keys like in any other word processor.

What's the difference between Replace, Substitution, and INSERT mode?

- There is no difference. It's a term that `vi` uses to distinguish one form of text manipulation over another.

How can I undo substitution or replacement commands when I make a mistake?

- Press Esc to ensure that you're in Command mode and then press U (*do not* press Shift). The undo command works equally well with any replacement, insertion, deletion, or substitution command.

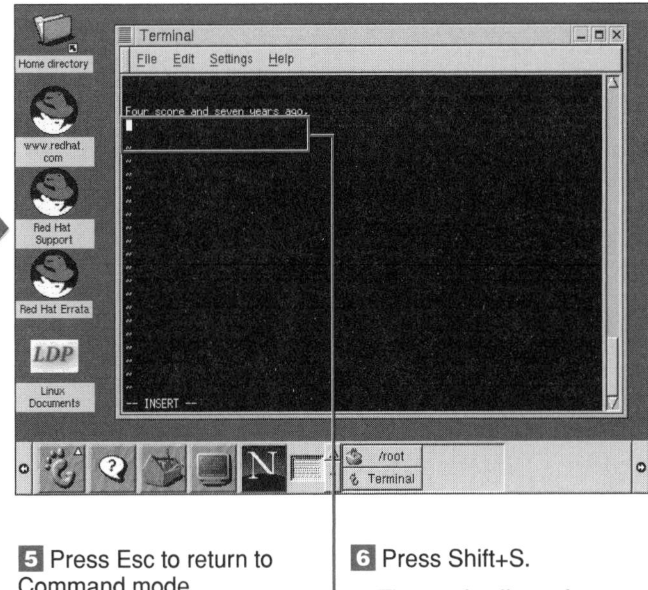

5 Press Esc to return to Command mode.

6 Press Shift+S.

■ The entire line of text disappears.

Note: This does not remove the carriage return.

■ You're placed in Insert mode.

7 Type **I wrote this document** in `vi`.

MOVE AROUND IN VI

You can move around your document with different speeds, depending on the commands you use in vi's Command mode. These are useful commands to know, because vi, with no GUI, has no scroll bar that lets you skip back and forth between sentences or paragraphs.

Although the sample document is small, I use it to demonstrate how you can move around vi more quickly than character by character with the arrow keys. vi is pattern- and line-oriented, rather than scroll bar-oriented, so using vi may actually get you to where you want to be in your document faster than in a GUI-based editor.

Of course, you must perform all of these functions in Command mode. Be sure to press Esc before entering these commands to ensure that you get the result that you want.

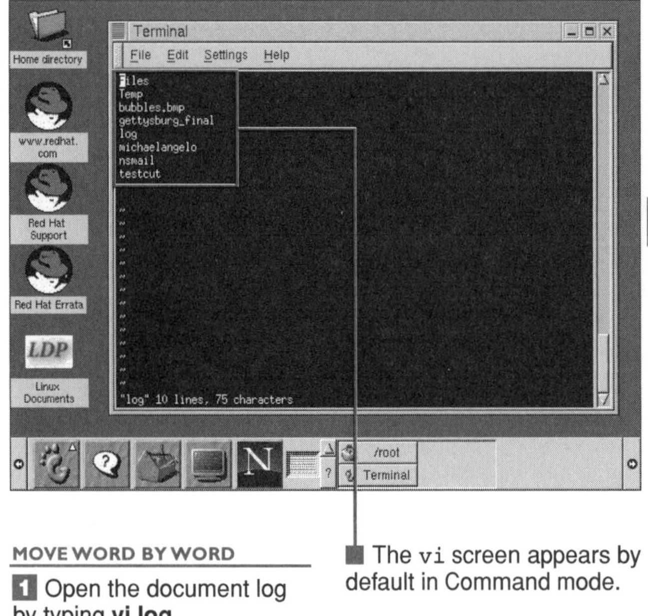

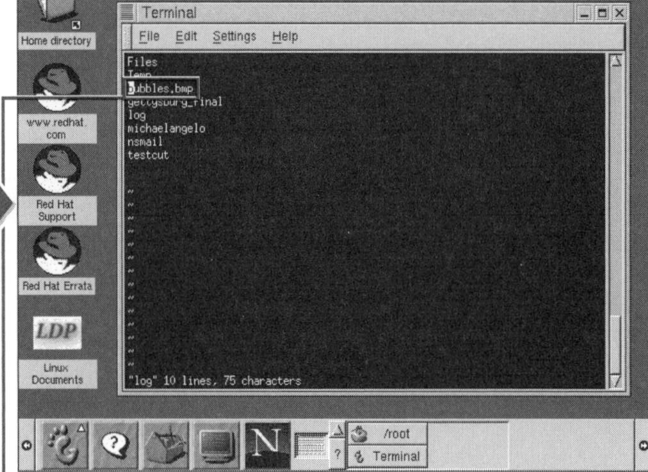

MOVE WORD BY WORD

1 Open the document log by typing **vi log**.

2 Press Enter.

■ The vi screen appears by default in Command mode.

3 To move forward word by word, press W.

4 Press W twice to move to bubbles.bmp.

5 To move back a word, press B.

TIPS

How can I move the cursor to the middle of the screen in one jump?

- Press Shift+M to jump directly to the center of your screen.

What about moving by paragraph?

- You can move to the beginning of the next paragraph by using the French brace, or {. If you want to move to the start of the paragraph before the one your cursor is in, use the opposite French brace, }.

What about moving screen by screen?

- For longer documents, you should move by screen-lengths because you don't have a scrollbar in `vi`. To move forward a screen, press Ctrl+F. To move back a screen, press Ctrl+B.

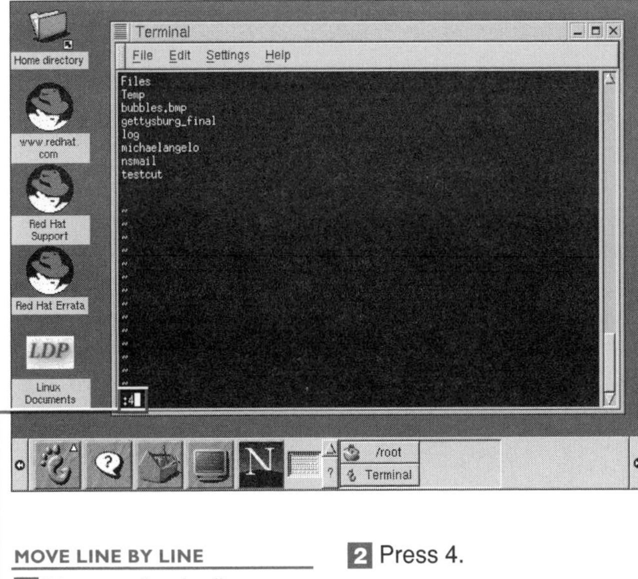

MOVE LINE BY LINE

1 To move line by line, press the colon (:) key.

■ `vi` will not display the colon in the text.

2 Press 4.

3 Press Enter.

■ The cursor moves to the fourth line.

■ The visible colon and line number don't affect anything. You are still in Command mode.

SEARCH FOR WORDS IN VI

You can perform word searches in `vi`. As with all searches in Linux, a search is actually more flexible, because you're really looking for patterns of text in a document. This is particularly useful if you're working with long documents or pages of complex code.

If you're working with a particularly long document, you may also take advantage of the different search directions possible with `vi`. For example, if you're in the middle of a 100-page document and you're sure that the pattern you want is in the first half, you can specify `vi` to search all text above the cursor.

By default, `vi` searches down from the cursor (to the right of the cursor and on to the end of the document).

Again, be sure that you're in Command mode by pressing Esc before using these commands.

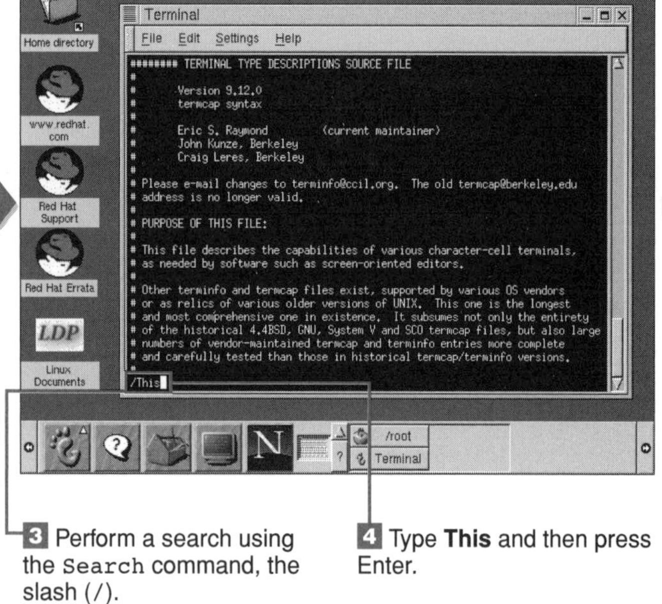

SEARCH FORWARD

1 Type **vi /etc/termcap**.

2 Press Enter.

■ The `vi` screen appears, displaying the contents of `termcap`.

3 Perform a search using the `Search` command, the slash (/).

4 Type **This** and then press Enter.

Are searches in vi case sensitive?

- By default, all searches in `vi` are case sensitive. This is because `vi` is not designed to search for letters; it's designed to search for text patterns. To `vi`, the text patterns *This, this,* and *tHiS* are completely different.

Can you switch the direction of a search while in the middle of a search command?

- Actually, you can. For example, if you're searching for termcap with the slash (searching forward in the document), you can press Shift+N to repeat the search, going in the opposite direction (backward in the document) without having to enter a question mark.

Can I limit my search to one line of the document?

- You can do this by pressing F to search forward of your cursor's position, and Shift+F to search backwards from your cursor position.

■ The cursor jumps to the first word —This.

5 Press N again.

■ Continue until `vi` tells you the search is complete.

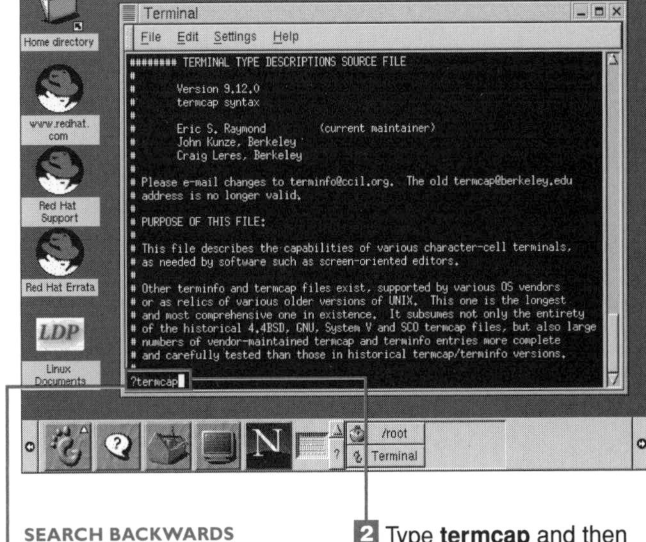

SEARCH BACKWARDS

1 If you want to search backwards, press the question mark (?) key.

2 Type **termcap** and then press Enter to perform a search.

CUT, COPY, AND PASTE TEXT

You can cut lines of text in the vi editor with the Cut command and paste them into a different portion of your document. When you cut text, it disappears similar to a deletion. In fact, the text is stored on a *text buffer,* which is not visible on-screen.

When you paste your cut text back into the document, the location of the paste depends on the location of your cursor. Be sure to move your cursor to exactly where you want the text to be placed. When you paste the text back into the document, the buffer is then free to perform a second cut-and-paste job.

To copy text, use the Paste command to place the text. When you do a copy, you use an oddly named UNIX command called yank.

CUT TEXT

1 Type **vi gettysburg_final**.

2 Press Enter.

■ The vi screen displays in Command mode.

3 Move your cursor to the first line.

What happens if I just hold the D key down when deleting?

- Holding the D key down deletes your entire document, but not all at once. The `vi` editor interprets this as a multiple `dd` commands and starts deleting lines of text very rapidly. A document of a dozen pages of solid text takes half a minute to delete completely.

Is there any way I can delete multiple lines of text at one time in a more controlled manner?

- Yes, there is. When you enter Command mode, enter the number of lines you want to delete from your document (for example, 5) and then type `dd`. Do not include a space between the number and the `dd` command. As soon as you type the `dd` command, the specified five lines of text is removed from the document.

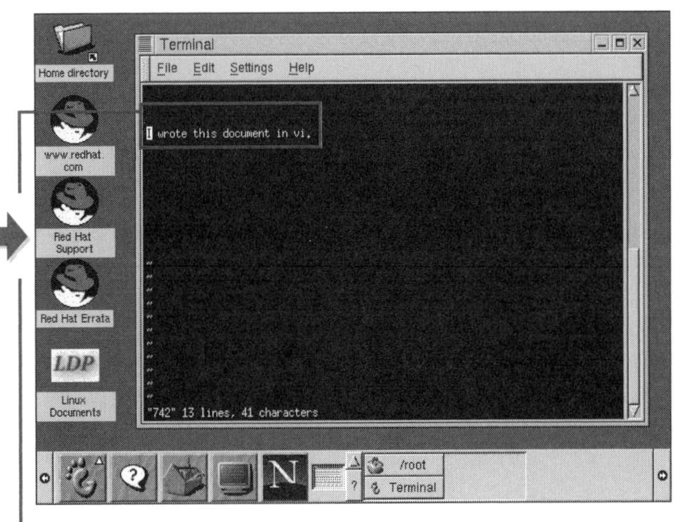

4 Press D twice to delete the line.

PASTE TEXT

1 Move the cursor to the line below the existing line.

CONTINUED

CUT, COPY, AND PASTE TEXT
CONTINUED

You can cut, copy, and paste text with the vi editor just as you would in any graphics based text processor. However, instead of using drop-down menus or clicking on buttons with pictures of scissors, you enter a letter command while in the Command mode.

Make sure you are in Command mode when inserting, copying, or cutting text in the vi editor. To cut or copy text from one spot in the document to another, use the yank command by entering yy in the vi Command mode.

To complete a cut and paste task, use the p, or paste command.

When you cut text, it is stored in a buffer waiting for you to paste it somewhere. When you move the cursor to the spot where you want to insert text, pressing P will place the text after the cursor.

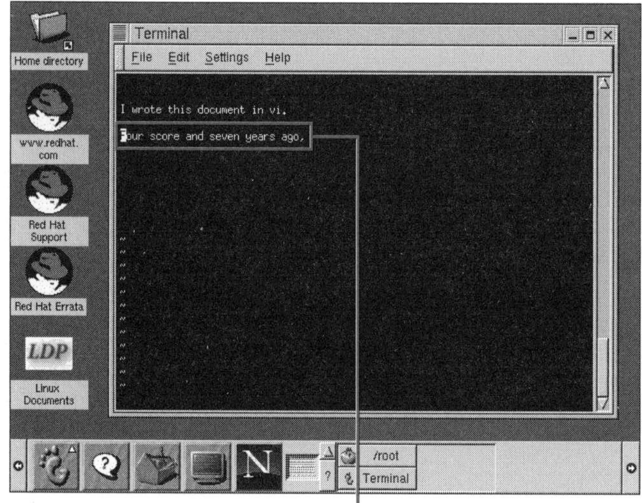

2 Press P to pull this line out of the buffer.

3 Move the cursor to the start of Four score and press Y twice to yank the current line.

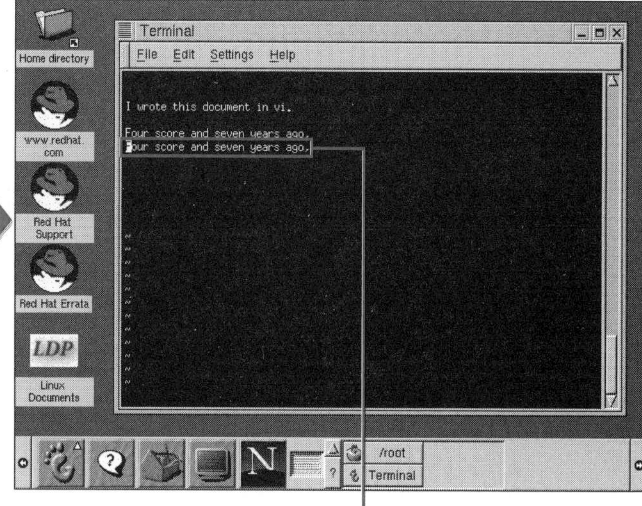

4 Move your cursor to the next line below.

5 Press P to paste in the line.

■ You have two copies of the line.

Are there any other ways to cut and paste in vi?

- If you're using the GNOME, KDE, or any other GUI environment, you can Cut and Paste commands from the drop-down menu at the top of the Linux terminal screen. Select the text by highlighting it with the mouse and then use the drop-down menu commands. Although this is convenient, in many cases Linux will not have this option available.

If my Linux machine doesn't have this available but I want to use it, how can I cut and paste with the mouse?

- Another option is to remotely log into your Linux machine from a Windows machine. Linux will operate in a DOS prompt window on your screen, which has the Edit drop-down menu.

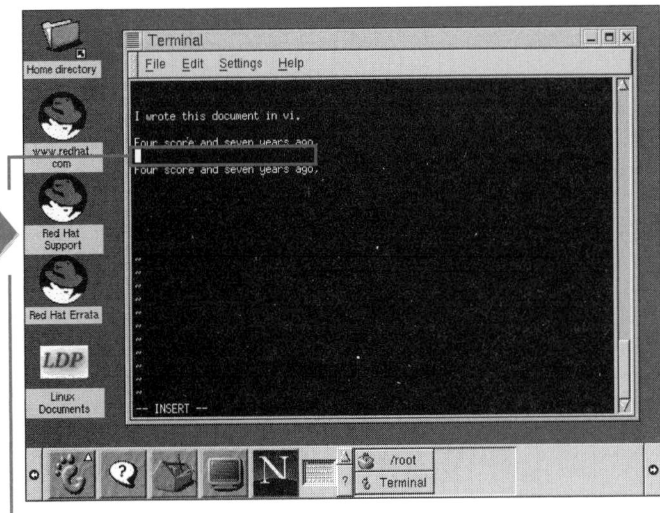

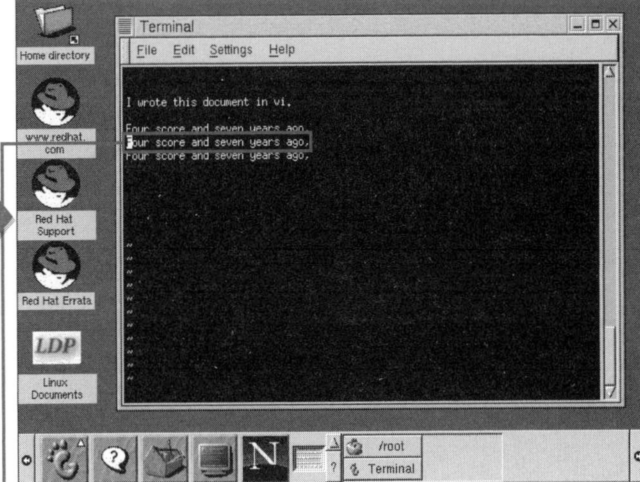

6 Open a new line by pressing Shift+O.

7 Move your cursor into the new line.

8 Press P to paste the line into the space.

SAVE AND QUIT VI

You can save your document and work on it later. You should save documents at regular intervals to prevent data loss if there is a loss of power or other accident. Unlike Microsoft Word, for example, the vi editor does not have a built-in Auto Save feature.

Quitting a document is a combination of Close and Quit if you are familiar with Windows. When you finish in vi, the Quit command exits you from both the document and the vi program. This is unlike Microsoft Word, where you can exit from a document while remaining in the Word program.

Finally, vi doesn't ask you if you want to save changes before you quit. Instead, vi keeps you from quitting at all if you've edited a file in any way. To bypass this, you have to save the file or perform what is called a "forced quit."

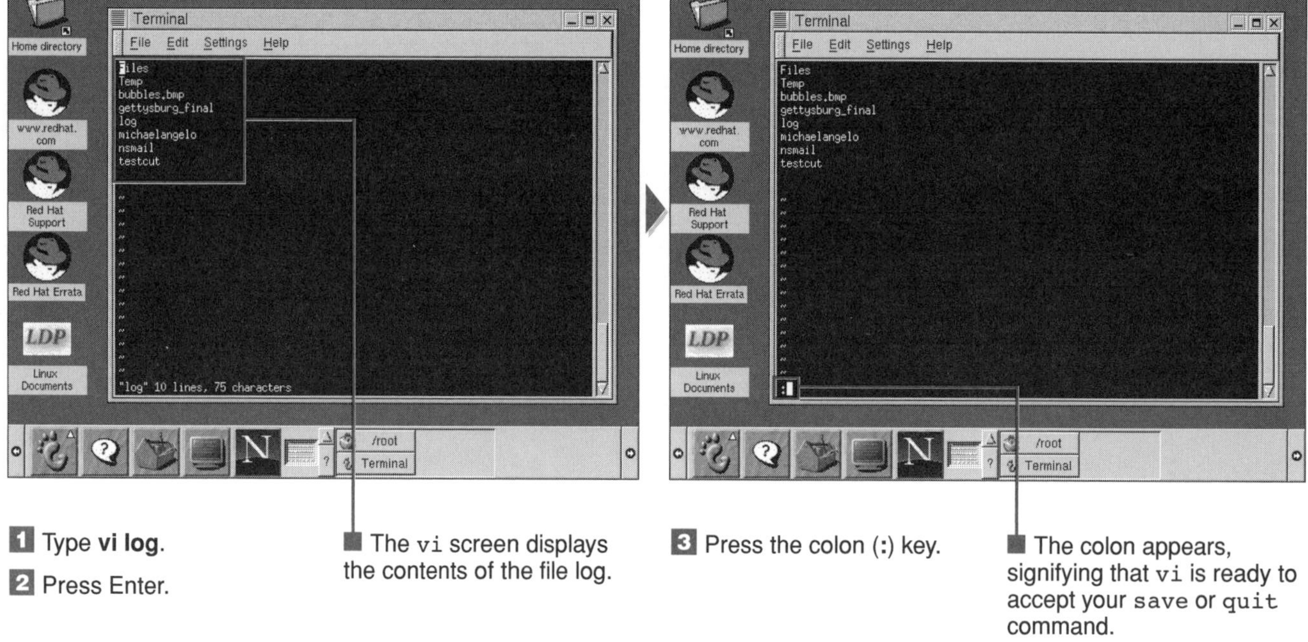

1 Type **vi log**.

2 Press Enter.

■ The vi screen displays the contents of the file log.

3 Press the colon (:) key.

■ The colon appears, signifying that vi is ready to accept your save or quit command.

TIPS

Why doesn't vi ask if I want to save changes made to the document when I exit?

- This was a design decision made by the `vi` editor's initial designers. Instead of asking if you want to save, `vi` notifies you that you made some changes. It leaves the decision of whether to save or not completely in your hands, which follows Linux's philosophy of being as flexible as possible.

When I want to leave the vi editor, I type :we, *w* for write and *e* for exit. Why doesn't vi exit?

- The `vi` editor, like many Linux applications, is very fussy about the commands it accepts. The `e` command normally means to move to the end of a word, which makes no sense when you want to write a file to be saved. The only method that `vi` accepts when you exit is `:wq`.

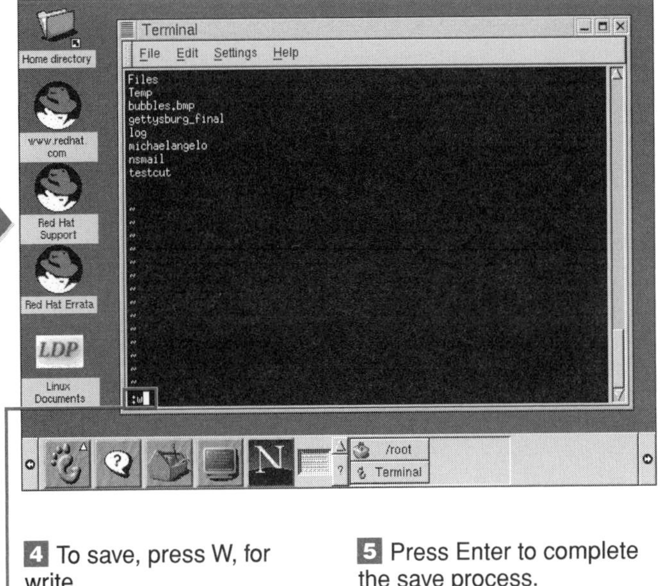

4 To save, press W, for write.

- The w appears next to the colon.

5 Press Enter to complete the save process.

6 To quit `vi` without saving, press the colon (:) key.

7 Press Q.

8 Press Enter to return to the command prompt.

CONTINUED

SAVE AND QUIT VI CONTINUED

You may find on rare occasions that the `vi` editor is not able to save your edits or additions to your Linux system files. This is a built-in security mechanism on some sensitive files such as `/etc/passwd`.

This is different from a set of file permissions preventing you from writing to the file. Instead, it's a special system setting that is used to make sure that you want to save your changes. If you accidentally made a change to the password file and just typed :wq as a force of habit, you could leave users — or yourself — without the ability to get back on the machine.

To save and quit here, you need to use the bang sign (the exclamation mark (!) to force the save command. You can also use this ability to force `vi` to let you leave a file without saving changes that you've made.

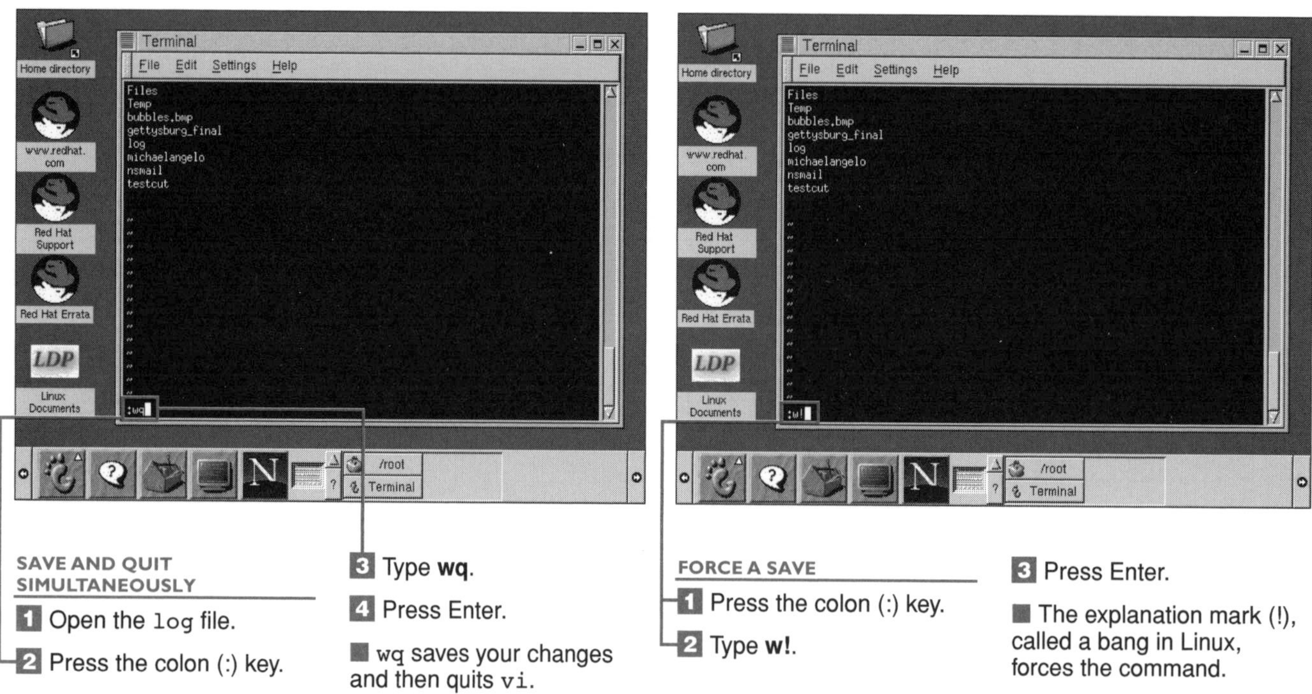

SAVE AND QUIT SIMULTANEOUSLY

1 Open the `log` file.

2 Press the colon (:) key.

3 Type **wq**.

4 Press Enter.

■ `wq` saves your changes and then quits `vi`.

FORCE A SAVE

1 Press the colon (:) key.

2 Type **w!**.

3 Press Enter.

■ The explanation mark (!), called a bang in Linux, forces the command.

TIPS

Why is the exclamation point called a *bang* in Linux?

- The short answer is it's traditional. Also, it's easier to say and avoid confusion. Similarly, in Linux, a pound sign (#) is called a "hash" mark, because you could end up actually using the sign for a British pound in your text, which would cause no end of confusion.

On some documents, even a forced write won't work! Why?

- There are two possibilities. First, even a force write cannot work on a file with no write permissions. Second, you cannot own this file. See Chapter 6 for more information.

What happens if I type :qw instead of :wq?

- Because this would have you quit and then save, it doesn't make any sense. `vi` will complain that this is not a command that it recognizes, forcing you to retype :wq correctly.

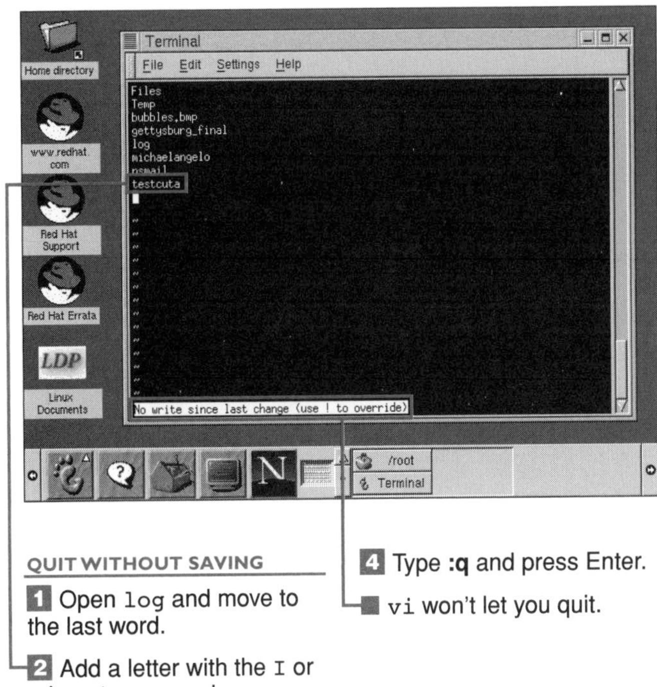

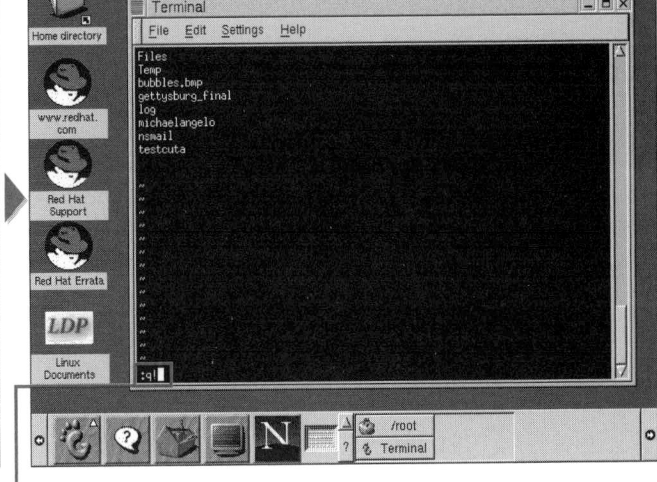

QUIT WITHOUT SAVING

1 Open `log` and move to the last word.

2 Add a letter with the `I` or `A` insert commands.

3 Press Esc.

4 Type **:q** and press Enter.

■ `vi` won't let you quit.

5 Press the colon (:) key.

6 Type **q!** and press Enter.

■ Now `vi` allows you to quit and return to the command prompt.

DETERMINE YOUR ENVIRONMENT VARIABLES

You can change your Linux environment by determining what your Environment Variables are and changing them. Linux Environment Variables are operating parameters or settings that are usually determined by your Linux installation. These variables provide the Linux system with the means to work with you — from your username, user profile, and shell account, to what your command prompt looks like.

Changing your Linux environment through Environment Variables is not the same as changing your GNOME environment with the Preferences pull-down menu. Instead, these variables are set and determined either in the system or in user account files such as `.cshrc` or `.bashrc`.

You can determine settings of individual variables by using the `echo` command. `echo` prints anything written after it back to the screen. If the word after `echo` has a dollar sign, Linux interprets that as a *variable sign* and prints the variable.

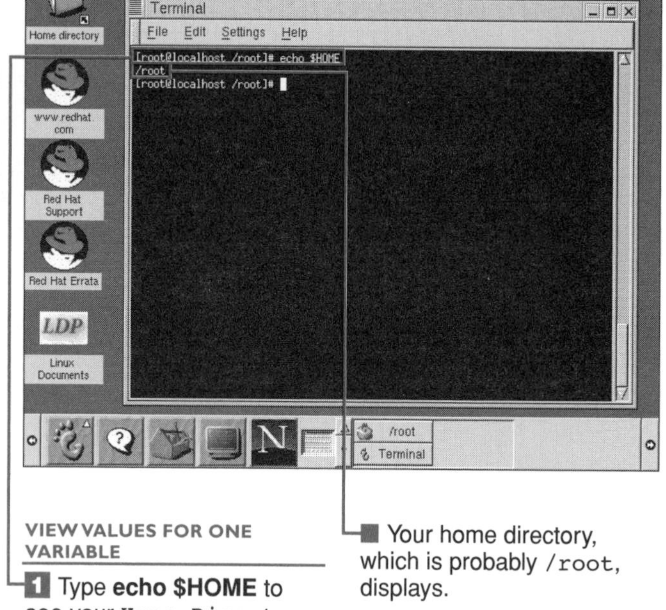

DETERMINE YOUR PRESET ENVIRONMENT VARIABLES

1 Type **env** at the command prompt.

2 Press Enter.

■ Environment Variables appear in all capital letters, and their values are in lowercase letters. For example, the name of your `USER` variable is set to `root`.

VIEW VALUES FOR ONE VARIABLE

1 Type **echo $HOME** to see your `Home Directory` variable.

2 Press Enter.

■ Your home directory, which is probably `/root`, displays.

How can I display two or three variables at one time?

✓ You can use the `echo` command to display more than one variable at a time. However, you need to make sure that you use the dollar sign `($)` in front of each variable that you want to view. For example, if you want to view both your `Home Directory` and `Login Name` variables, type **echo $HOME $LOGNAME** at the command line and press Enter. The variables will display in the order in which you typed them.

Why is it necessary to use the dollar sign ($) in front of the echo command, instead of the the setenv command?

✓ The `setenv` command specifically tells the system that whatever you type following the command becomes a system variable. `Echo`, on the other hand, is a command that just displays data.

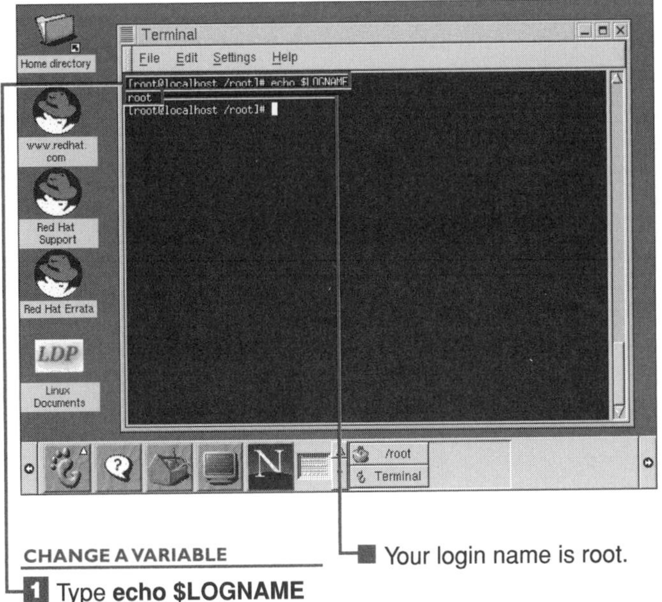

CHANGE A VARIABLE

1 Type **echo $LOGNAME** to find out your login name.

2 Press Enter.

■ Your login name is root.

SET ENVIRONMENT VARIABLES

1 Type **setenv LOGNAME fred**.

2 Press Enter.

Note: When you use `setenv` *as opposed to* `echo`*, you don't need to use the* `$` *sign to indicate that you're setting a variable.*

CONTINUED

DETERMINE YOUR ENVIRONMENT VARIABLES CONTINUED

You can change variables all you want in Linux by using the `setenv` command. However, changing Environment Variables like this is workable, but only temporary. These changes last only for the time you're currently logged in.

For example, if your `LOGNAME` variable is `michael` and you then use `setenv` to change it to `fred`, when you log out, the changes are lost. The next time you log in, the Linux operating system reads the default settings and your old `LOGNAME` variable, `michael`, is reapplied.

To make permanent changes to your variable settings, you should use the `vi` editor to edit the files that actually control the Linux Environment Variables.

These files that actually control your permanent system variable settings are `.cshrc` if you use C-shell, `.login` if you use the Bourne shell, and `.bashrc` if you use the bash, or Bourne-again shell.

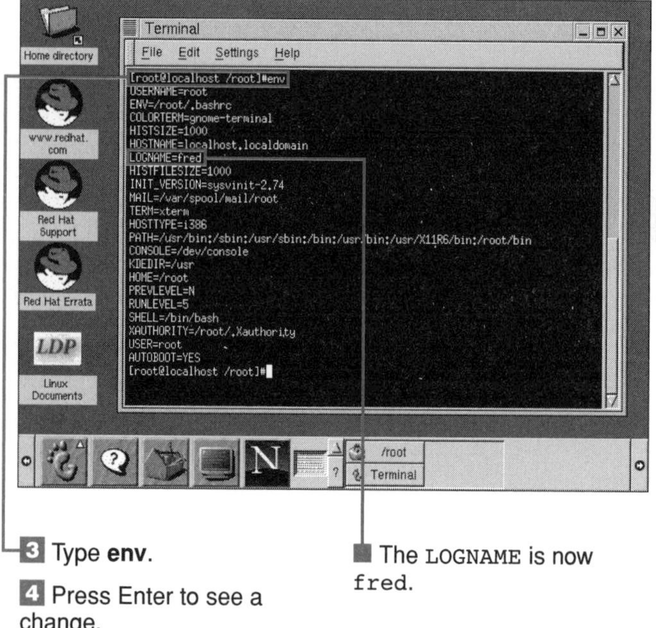

3 Type **env**.

4 Press Enter to see a change.

■ The `LOGNAME` is now `fred`.

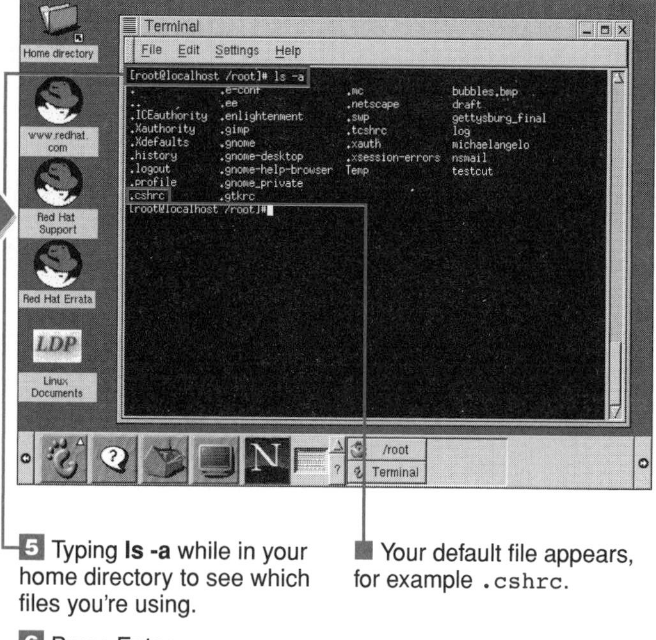

5 Typing **ls -a** while in your home directory to see which files you're using.

6 Press Enter.

■ Your default file appears, for example `.cshrc`.

Why do you have to use ls -a to view the .bashrc or .cshrc files?

- Typing ls a lists all files, including hidden files, in your home directory. All files that control your Environment Variables like `.cshrc` and `.bashrc` have a `.` at the start of their name so that they are hidden unless `ls -a` is used. These files are hidden away so that users are less likely to accidentally alter them.

Why don't you use the $ sign with setenv when you use it with echo?

- `echo` is a more literal command—if you type **echo HOME** and then press return, `HOME` displays on screen. The `setenv` command was designed to work only with Environmental Variables, so you don't need to go out of your way to tell Linux with a $ that this is a variable.

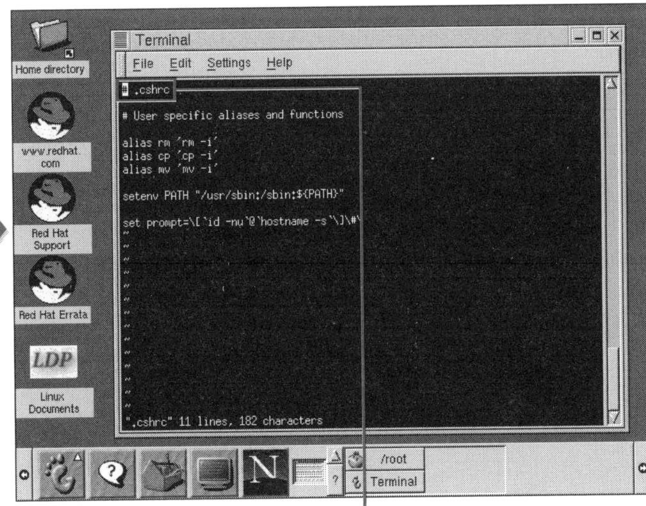

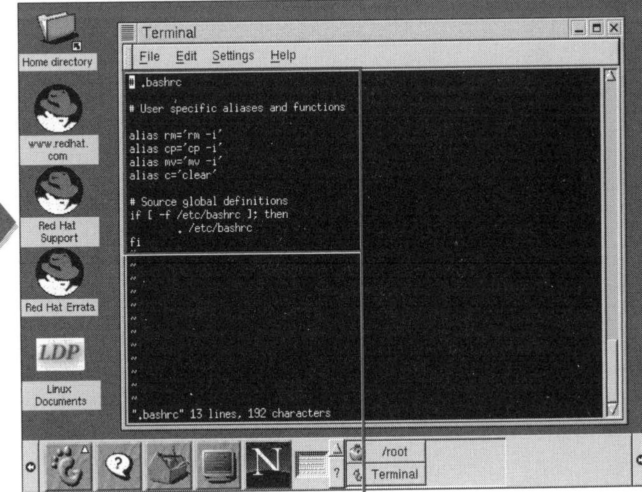

7 To view this file, type **avi .cshrc**

8 Press Enter.

■ The vi screen enables you to browse the `vi .cshrc` file.

■ If you also have a `.bashrc` or `.login` file, use the `vi` editor to read and write to the file.

■ Here's what a `.bashrc` file looks like.

SET THE $PATH VARIABLE

The $PATH variable is one of the most crucial to the operation of your Linux user account. You can set this variable with the setenv command, or you can make a more permanent change with vi in the .cshrc, .bashrc, or .login file. This section looks at how to set this variable on a more permanent basis.

The $PATH variable, or simply the *path* in Linux terms, is the variable that determines where the Linux operating system searches for programs and utilities to run. It also determines the order in which the search is conducted. For example, if your $PATH variable was /usr /usr/bin, then when you start a program, Linux first looks in the /usr directory. If it can't find the program there, it next looks in the /usr/bin directory.

If you frequently use a program that exists outside your path, altering the $PATH variable makes it easier to use.

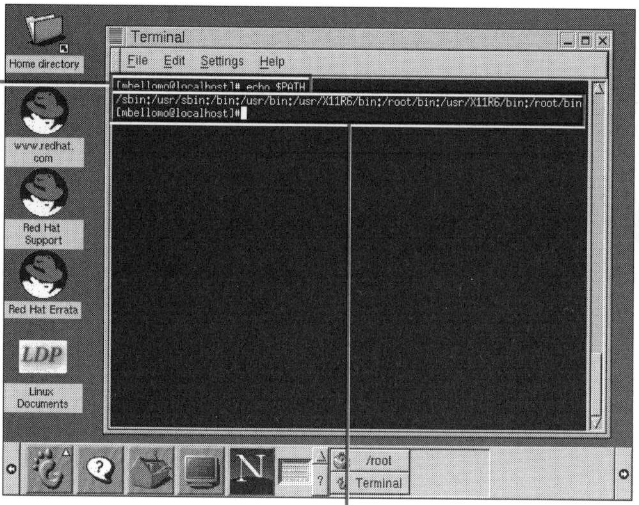

1 To determine the user's path, type **echo $PATH**.

2 Press Enter.

■ When you execute a command, Linux searches for the command in the following directories, in order from left (/sbin) to the right.

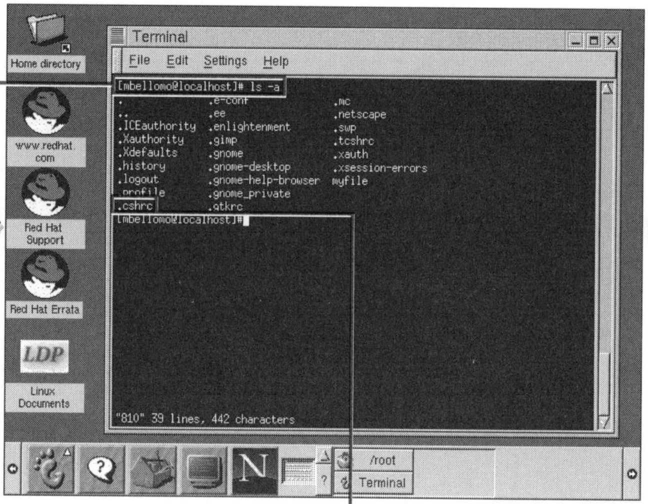

3 Type **ls -a** to list the user's hidden files.

4 Press Enter.

■ User mbellomo has a .cshrc.

To what should I set my path?

- Most of the time, you should keep your path set to the system defaults. However, if you frequently use a utility from a directory that's not in your path, you should edit your path to include that directory.

What's the longest a $PATH should be?

- Path lengths have no limits. However, remember that commands that come from the end of the path line take slightly longer to execute. Of course, this should only be noticeable if you system is running at peak capacity with many users on it at the same time.

How can I run something not in my $PATH?

- The best way to do this is to enter in the entire path of the program or script. For example, if you want to run `/etc/superscript` and `/etc` isn't in your path, you can run this file by typing `/etc/superscript` and pressing Enter.

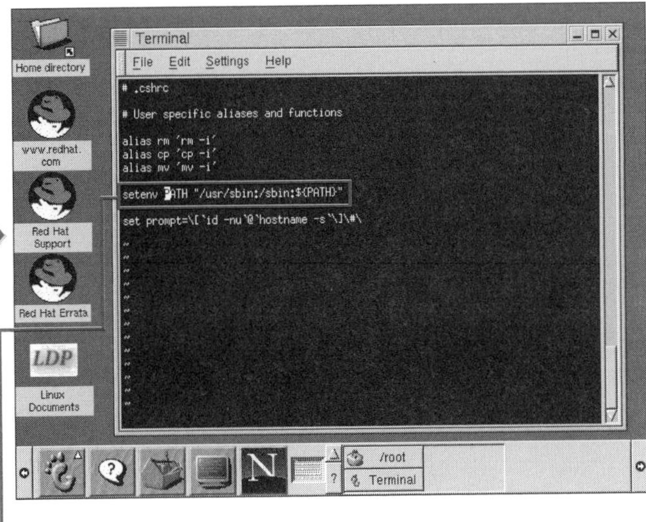

5 Type **vi .cshrc** to work with this file.

6 Press Enter.

■ The file marking `$PATH` appears onscreen.

7 If you don't see the `$PATH` line, type / in `vi` to do a search.

8 Type **PATH** and press Enter.

■ The line that configures path appears.

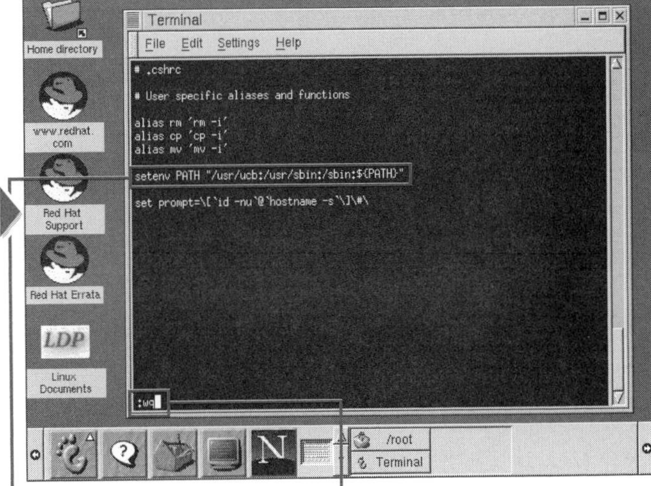

9 Move the cursor with the arrow keys to the first slash in `/usr/sbin`.

10 Type **If/** to get into INSERT mode.

11 Type **/usr/ucb** and a colon to separate the fields.

12 Exit and save by pressing Esc.

13 Type **:wq** and then press Enter.

SOURCE CHANGES

You can apply the changes you make to a `.cshrc`, `.bashrc`, or `.login` file as soon as you make them when you *source* the changes. Rather than waiting for the next time you log out and then back in as the same account to take advantage of your edits, you can immediately have access to the changes.

The `source` command enables you to change your Linux Environment Variables. Sourcing in Linux parallels rebooting in Windows, except that your system state remains unchanged. The Linux system is made to go over your `.cshrc` or other resource files again, ensuring that your changes to the environmental variables are applied.

After the `source` process is complete, you can check the changes with either the `env` or the `echo` command, which I discuss earlier in this chapter.

The following steps use the example of changing `mbellomo`'s path again.

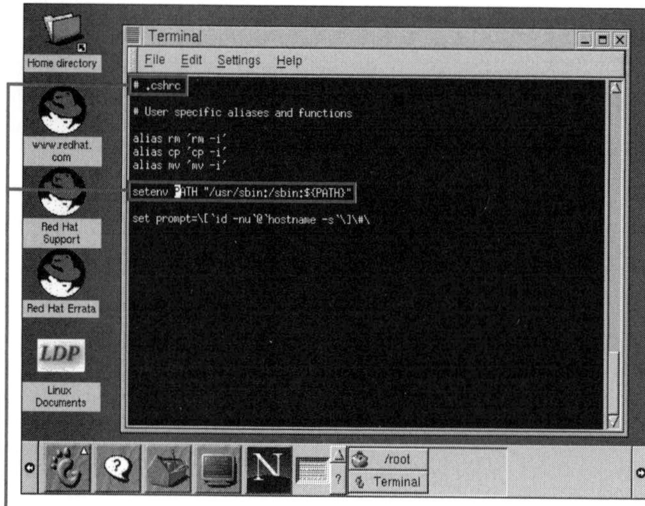

CHANGE A PATH

1 Type **vi .cshrc** and press Enter.

■ The file marking `$PATH` appears on screen.

2 If you don't see the path line, type / in `vi`.

3 Type **PATH** and press Enter.

■ The line that configures the path appears.

SPECIFY A SEARCH

1 Move the cursor with the arrow keys to the first slash in **/usr/sbin**.

2 Type **I** and then type **/usr/ucb**.

3 Press the colon (:) key to separate the fields.

4 Press Esc.

5 Type **:wq** to write and quit, and then press Enter.

What if the variable doesn't change after I type source?

- The variable won't change for a couple of reasons. For example, when you exited your changes, you may have typed `:q!` not `:wq`. Also, you may have changed the wrong system variable. Go back into the system file you're editing to make sure your changes "took."

I heard that you should run source twice. Is this true?

- This isn't a requirement, but the Linux community has felt for a long time that sometimes `source` doesn't work as completely as it should. Because of that, I adopted the habit of using `source` twice when performing changes on my environment. Running it twice doesn't hurt anything.

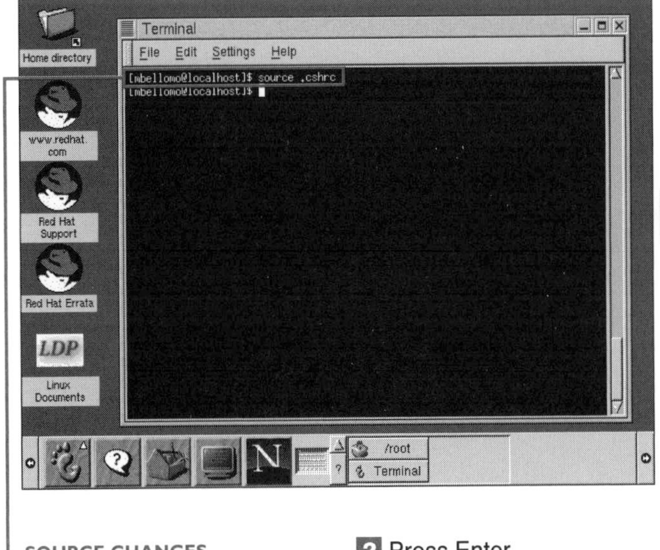

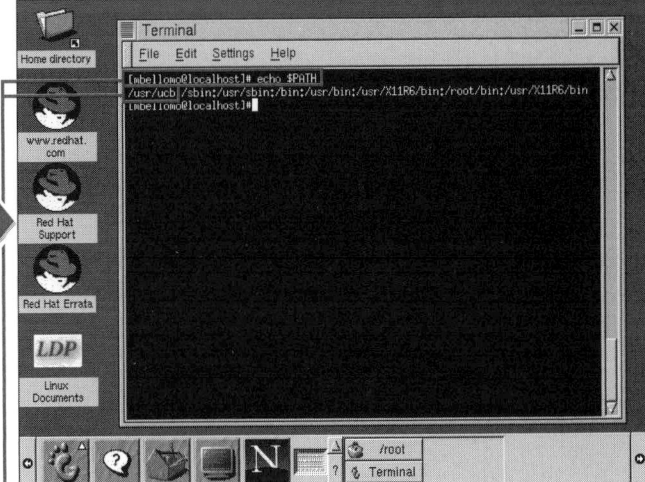

SOURCE CHANGES

1 At the command prompt, type **source .cshrc**.

2 Press Enter.

3 Check the results by typing **echo $PATH**.

■ The new path should begin with `/usr/ucb`.

ADDING ALIASES

You can save yourself a lot of typing in the long run by creating *aliases* for the command strings that you use most frequently. An *alias* in Linux is simply a shorthand expression of a command. You could think of it as a symbolic link not between files, but between commands.

To use an alias that you created, type the alias at the command prompt and press Enter. If you go to a different Linux system with a new account later in life, your aliases are not transferrable. Therefore you must use the regular commands again or create new aliases on the new system.

For example, instead of typing `ls -ltr`, you can create an alias that when you type `l`, you get the `ls -ltr` result.

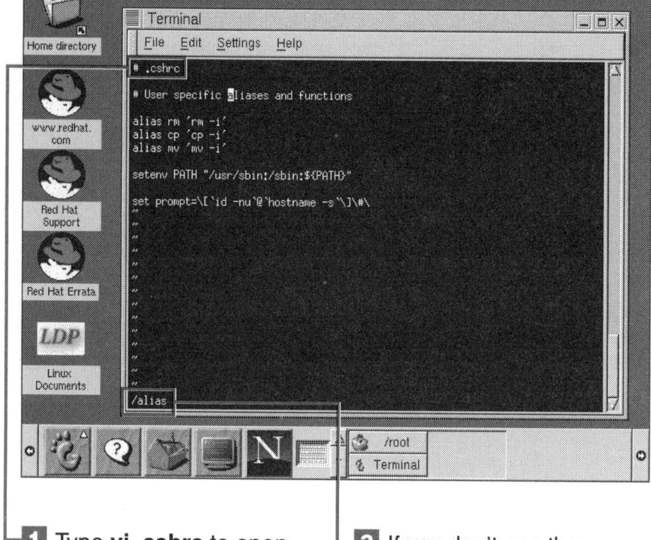

1 Type **vi .cshrc** to open the file.

2 Press Enter.

■ Aliases are kept in a separate stanza in the file.

3 If you don't see the aliases, perform a search by typing **/alias**.

4 Type **alias** and press Enter.

■ Your cursor goes to the first alias in the file.

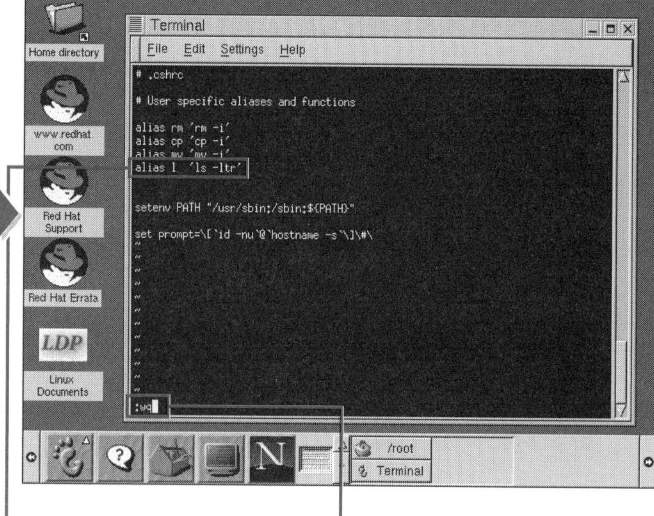

5 Move to an empty line above or below the existing aliases and press I to enter INSERT mode.

6 Type alias **l ls -ltr**.

7 Press Esc to return to Command mode.

8 Type **:wq** to save and exit `vi`.

Are there any aliases you shouldn't make?

- You shouldn't give your aliases certain names. If you name an alias the same as an existing command, you'll cause tremendous confusion to the system. For example, you create an alias `ls -ltr`, naming it `cp`. You may not be able to use the `cp` (copy) command, the alias, or both.

Are these aliases also stored in the /etc/aliases file?

- No. There is a file called `/etc/aliases` on your system, but this is a default system file, listing a number of aliases that come with your version of Linux software.

Can I take my aliases with me to a different account?

- You can do this by `cp`'ing your `.cshrc`, `.login`, or `.bashrc` file to your new account. If you're going to a whole different system, you may have to e-mail the file as an attachment to your new account.

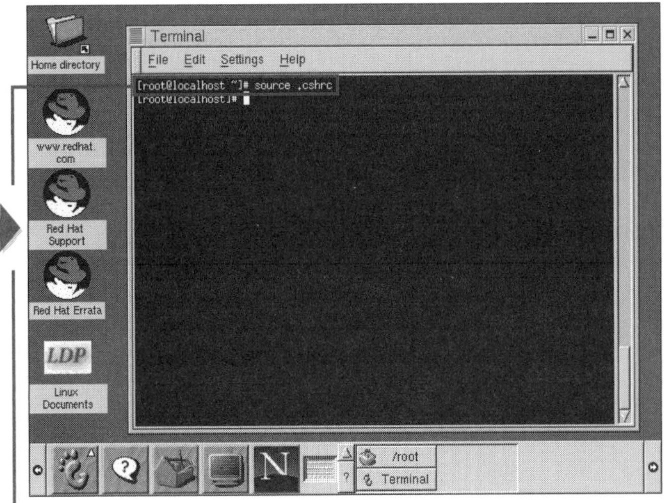

9 Type **source .cshrc**.

10 Press Enter.

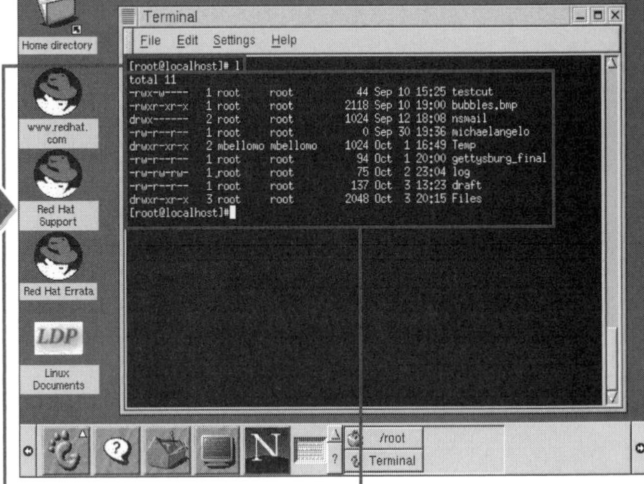

11 To see if the alias works, type the alias **l** and press Enter.

■ Because you're receiving list results in the long form, sorted in reverse order by time. Your alias is now in effect.

SECTION III

9) THE ROOT USER

Enter the Root User Account 196
Use su Multiple Times 198
Utilize the man Pages 200
Grant and Restrict File Access 202
Use cron to Automate System Tasks 206

10) USER AND GROUP ACCOUNT MANAGEMENT

Use the GNOME LinuxConf Tool 208
List User Accounts 212
Add User Accounts 214
Edit User Accounts 218
Delete User Accounts 222
Disable User Accounts 224
Add User Accounts in the Linux Terminal 226
Edit User Accountsin the Linux Terminal 228
Delete and Disable Accounts in the Linux Terminal 230
List User Groups 232
Add User Groups 234
Edit User Groups 236
Delete User Groups 238
Add User Groups in the Linux Terminal 240
Edit User Groups in the Linux Terminal 242
Delete User Groups in the Linux Terminal 246

STARTING LINUX ADMINISTRATION

11) FILE SYSTEM MANAGEMENT

Share Files and Directories 248
List Your File Systems with LinuxConf 250
Determine Allocated and Free Swap Space 252
Create a Linux Floppy Drive 256
Create a DOS Floppy Drive 260
Mount the Floppy Drive from the Linux Terminal 262
Read from the Floppy Disk 264
Copy Files to the Floppy Disk 266
Format Floppy Disks 270
Configure the CD-ROM Drive 272
Mount the CD-ROM Drive 276
Mount the CD-ROM Drive from the Linux Terminal 278
Read and Copy Files from the CD-ROM 280
Eject Floppy Disks and CD-ROMs 284

12) MANAGING LINUX PROGRAMS

Verify Available Disk Space 286
Start the Gnome Red Hat Package Manager..290
Verify Packages with RPM 292
Install Software Packageswith RPM 294
Remove Software Packages with RPM 296

13) WORD PROCESSING IN LINUX

Start and Exit gnotepad+ 298
Create and Save New Documents 300
Open New Documents 302
Insert and Delete Text 304
Move and Copy Text 306
Undo and Redo Changes 308
Search and Replace Text in a Document 310
Print Documents 312
Preferences for gnotepad+ 314
Tear-Off Menus 318

ENTER THE ROOT USER ACCOUNT

The *root user* account is the administrative account that is granted unilateral privileges over all the other accounts and files on the Linux system. For this reason, the root account is also known as the *substitute user* account. As root, you may edit any file, change any permissions you wish.

Any Linux system includes only one root account — but other accounts can be granted the same privileges as root if needed. For security purposes, however, root privileges should be granted out sparingly, if at all.

You can enter the root account in several ways. These range from the typical login to performing the su command. The command su stands for substitute user and is primarily used by the administrator. This becomes the root account when an administrative task is requested or the Linux system needs repair.

Unlike many commands, su can be "nested," or run multiple times during one Linux session.

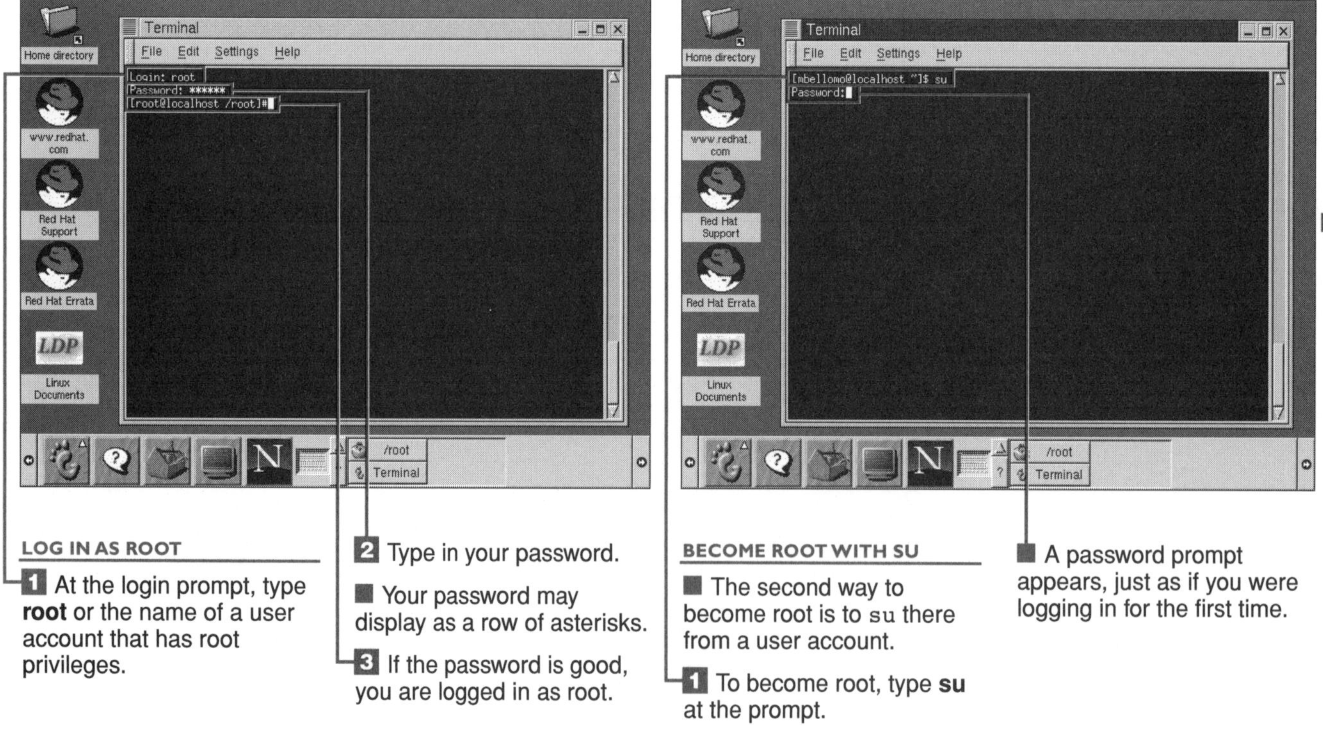

LOG IN AS ROOT

1 At the login prompt, type **root** or the name of a user account that has root privileges.

2 Type in your password.

■ Your password may display as a row of asterisks.

3 If the password is good, you are logged in as root.

BECOME ROOT WITH SU

■ The second way to become root is to su there from a user account.

1 To become root, type **su** at the prompt.

■ A password prompt appears, just as if you were logging in for the first time.

Can root privileges be granted to anyone else?

- Yes. If the existing root account edits a second account to have the same user ID number and group number (zero), Linux interprets that user as equal to root. For more information, see Chapter 9.

How can root access a user's files if the permissions are set strictly to user-only reading and writing?

- Remember that root is the administrative account in Linux. Because this account needs to be able to access any file in order to administer the machine, user-set permissions won't prevent root from viewing or editing the file.

How can root block a user from reading a file that is readable and writeable by everyone?

- Root has the power to delete or terminate entire user accounts. By effectively evicting a user from the system, root can block access. See Chapter 8.

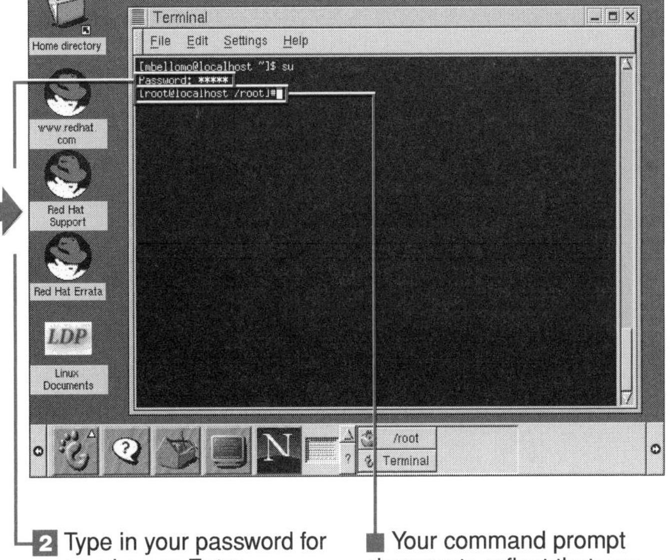

2 Type in your password for root and press Enter.

■ Your command prompt changes to reflect that you are root.

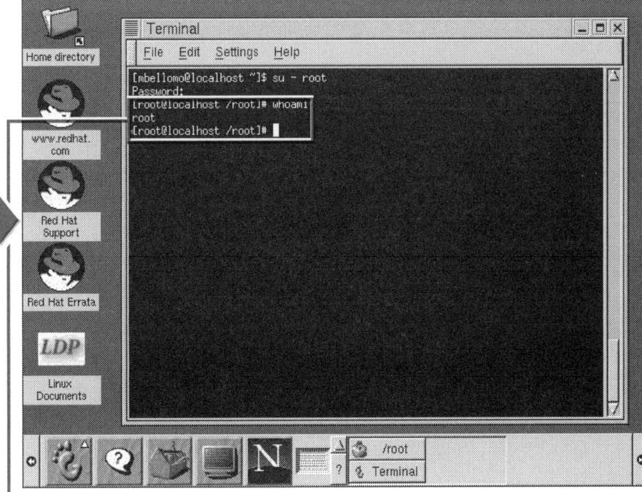

■ If your Linux system doesn't display the account name, use the `whoami` command to check your current log in status. (See Chapter 6.)

USE SU MULTIPLE TIMES

You can use su multiple times in one login session. Unlike many Linux commands, you can can *nest* or run su multiple times during one Linux session. You don't need to become root multiple times when you've already logged in as root — or become root previously.

However, although su stands for *substitute user*, the root account and any other user accounts can also use the su command to morph into another user account. The only restriction on doing this is that anyone seeking to su into another account must know that new account's password.

You'll find this ability most useful as an administrator when you edit programs that affect all users on your system. After editing the file(s) as root, you can switch into a user account to test the output and then return to root if further work is needed.

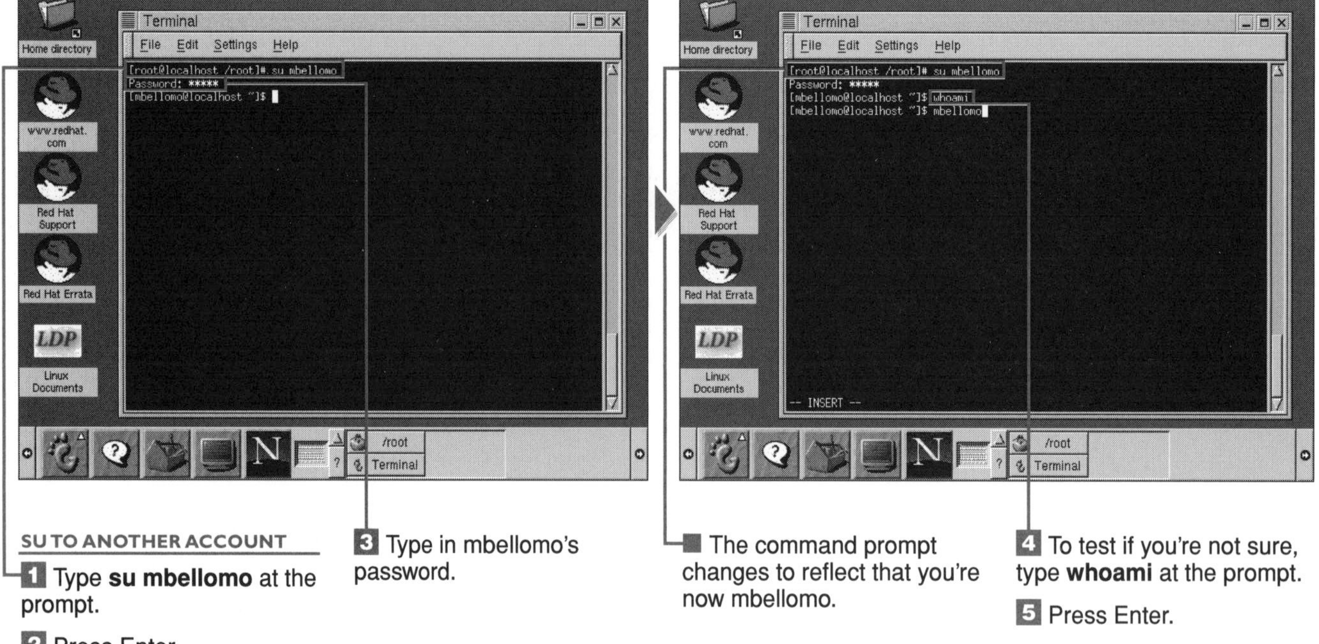

SU TO ANOTHER ACCOUNT

1 Type **su mbellomo** at the prompt.

2 Press Enter.

3 Type in mbellomo's password.

■ The command prompt changes to reflect that you're now mbellomo.

4 To test if you're not sure, type **whoami** at the prompt.

5 Press Enter.

If I su to someone's account, does the person have to be offline?

- In Linux, it doesn't matter whether the person is online. Because Linux is designed to be a completely open system, it accepts multiple logins by the same user account, no matter if they are from logins or `su`.

What if you're root, but you don't know the password for an account you want to enter?

- Either ask the person or, if it's an emergency, edit the `/etc/password` file. See Chapter 9 for more details on how to do this.

Is there any limit to the times you can run su in a session?

- There is no limit, but you run the risk of slowing down the machine if you have multiple `su`'s from one login.

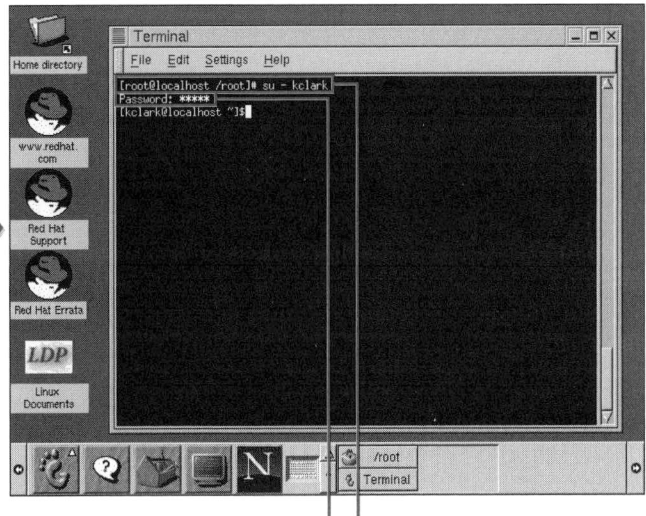

6 To ensure that you're the new user with all the settings of the former user's environment, add a dash (-) after the `su` command.

7 To ensure that you become the account kclark, type **su - kclark**.

8 Press Enter.

9 Type **kclark's** password and press Enter.

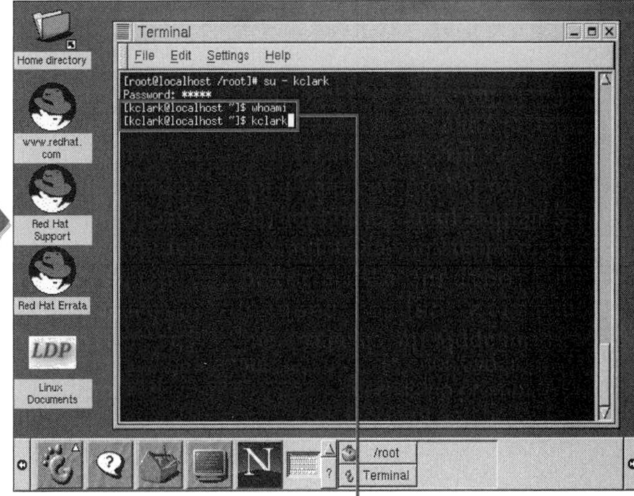

■ This should guarantee your entry into kclark's account and account environment.

10 To check your identity if there is no prompt, type **whoami** and press Enter.

UTILIZE THE MAN PAGES

You can get most of your Linux system administration questions answered, or at least get more information on topics you need to know about, from the `man` pages that come with every Linux machine. The `man` (short for manual) pages are a listing of all the Linux commands that have been passed down from earlier versions of the Linux and UNIX operating system. The `man` pages also list the command's function on your system, as well as provide all the available options that you can run with a given command.

Although at times they're written in very technical terms, the `man` pages are an invaluable source of information if you're trying to determine what command option to use with a particular utility.

Although the `man` pages cover 90 percent of what you'll be using in the Linux terminal window, they don't cover the later, GUI-based utilities, such as GNOME. For information on GNOME options and commands, see Chapters 2 and 3.

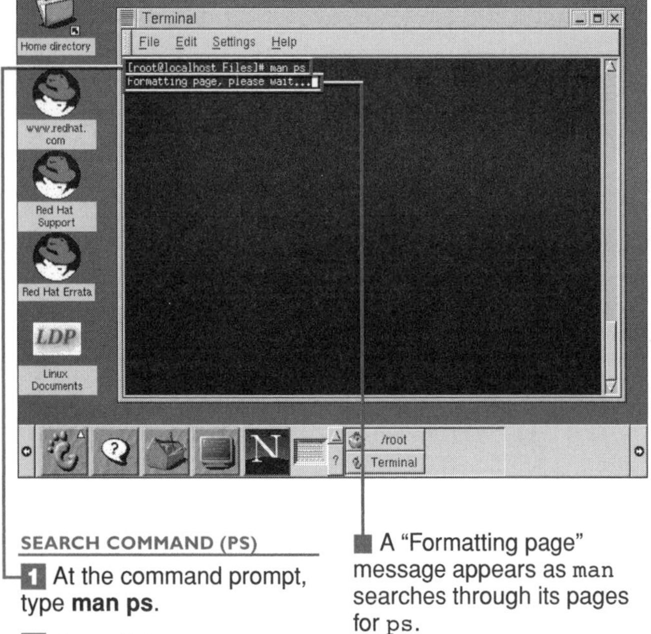

SEARCH COMMAND (PS)

1 At the command prompt, type **man ps**.

2 Press Enter.

■ A "Formatting page" message appears as `man` searches through its pages for `ps`.

■ The `man` page comes up in the `vi` editor window.

■ Although you can't edit the `man` pages, you can scroll and search through the entry.

How do I get man pages?

- man comes automatically with all versions of UNIX and Linux. However, your version of man may be slightly more out of date than others if your system is six or seven years old. An older man page may not include some of the newer commands.

Is root the only user account that can access man?

- man is available for all users, root and otherwise. Only the root account, however, really finds man helpful because most users don't delve into Linux as deeply as root. As an administrator, you'll rely on information in man from time to time.

What if the man page is too technical for me to understand?

- Most man pages are not so technical, just wordy. Take your time and print out a man page if you're not sure what it says.

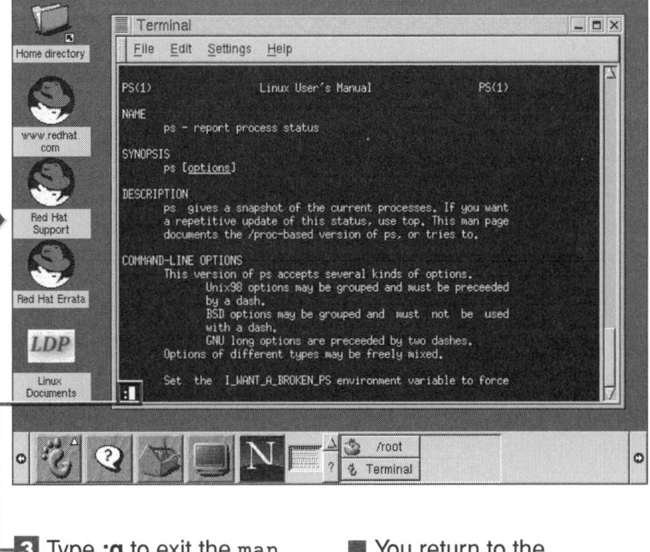

3 Type **:q** to exit the man pages.

4 Press Enter.

■ You return to the command prompt.

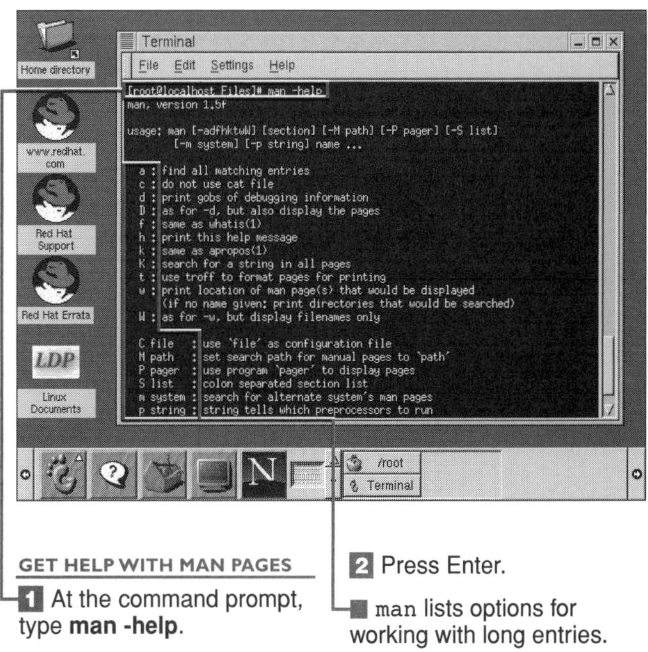

GET HELP WITH MAN PAGES

1 At the command prompt, type **man -help**.

2 Press Enter.

■ man lists options for working with long entries.

GRANT AND RESTRICT FILE ACCESS

As root, you can grant or restrict access to files all over the Linux system for the rest of the users. Determining which files to curtail access to and which to open up for the other users on the system is one of the Linux administrator's more important jobs. For example, a file that contains a company-wide announcement is one that is usually accessible to all employees of the company. On the other hand, files that list accounting or research data has limited access outside of their respective departments.

As a general rule, make files containing information that multiple people or departments need as open as possible. On the other hand, keep system-critical files that control Linux functions like passwords, print files, and basic commands under the equivalent of a lock and key.

To grant maximum access to a file, check the permissions, user, and group ownership. Do this with the `gettysburg_final` file. Chapter 4 explains the commands for changing file permissions.

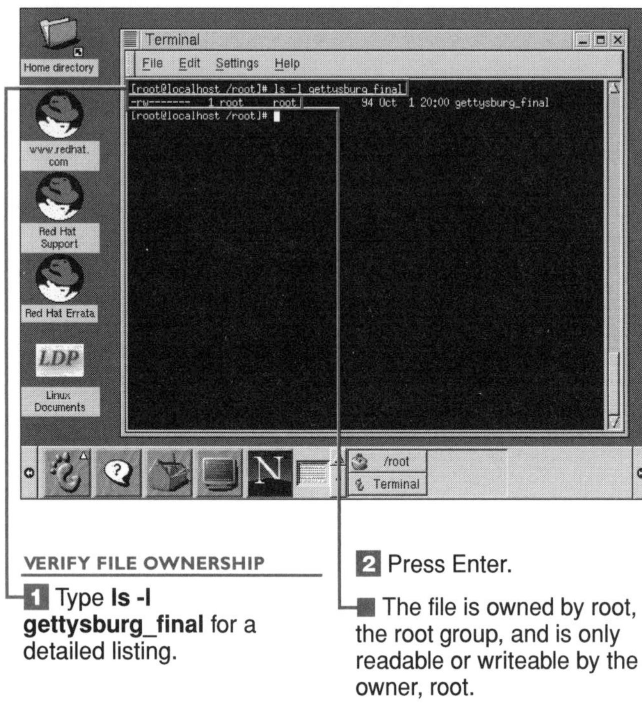

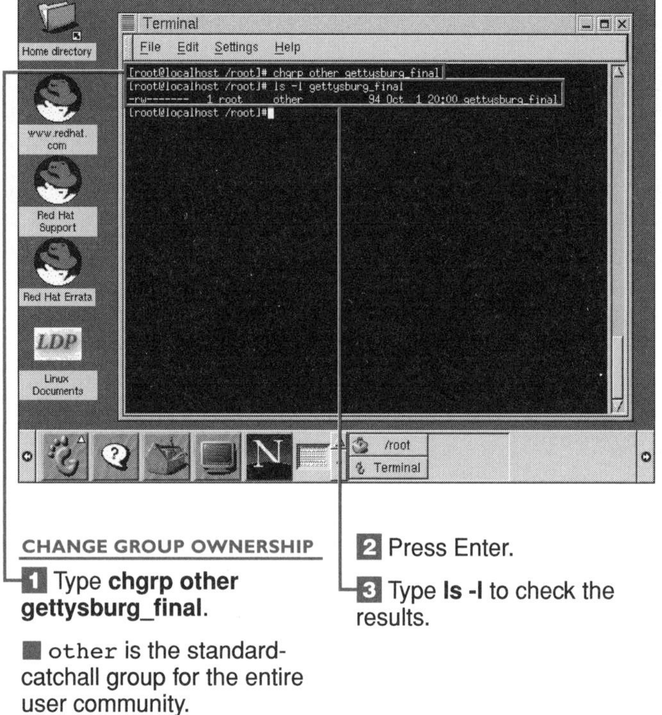

VERIFY FILE OWNERSHIP

1 Type **ls -l gettysburg_final** for a detailed listing.

2 Press Enter.

■ The file is owned by root, the root group, and is only readable or writeable by the owner, root.

CHANGE GROUP OWNERSHIP

1 Type **chgrp other gettysburg_final**.

■ `other` is the standard-catchall group for the entire user community.

2 Press Enter.

3 Type **ls -l** to check the results.

What kinds of files should I change to restrict reading and writing permissions?

- As a rule of thumb, your best bet is to make sure that files critical to the way your system operates are as heavily restricted as possible. Some of these files include, but are not limited to: the printer control file, `/etc/printcap`; the file system table `/etc/fstab`; and most importantly, the password file, `/etc/passwd`. Luckily, the majority of these files are created with limited permissions by default. It never hurts, however, to double-check them.

Which files are best left with the most open, or accessible, permissions?

- Files that you leave as open for everyone to look at or even edit are usually more site specific in nature. For example, if your Linux machine stores data at a major science lab or at a university campus, all of the files containing research should be completely accessible to everyone.

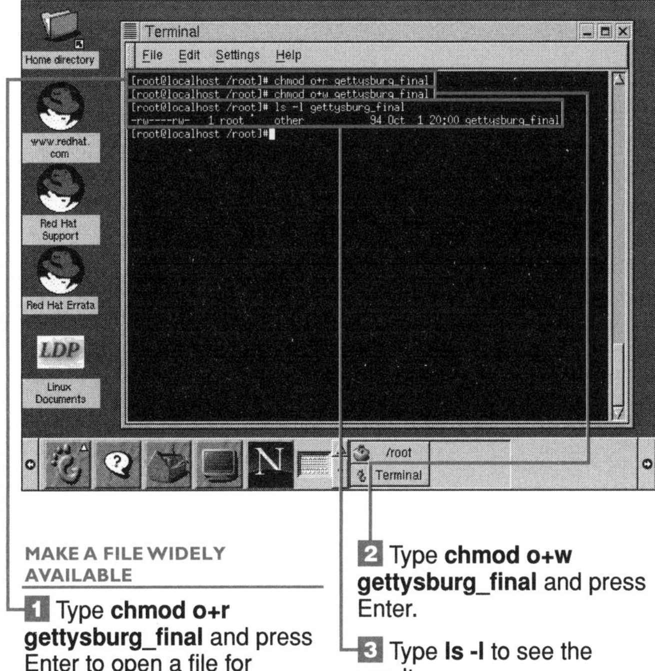

MAKE A FILE WIDELY AVAILABLE

1 Type **chmod o+r gettysburg_final** and press Enter to open a file for everyone.

2 Type **chmod o+w gettysburg_final** and press Enter.

3 Type **ls -l** to see the result.

■ Anyone can read or write to the file.

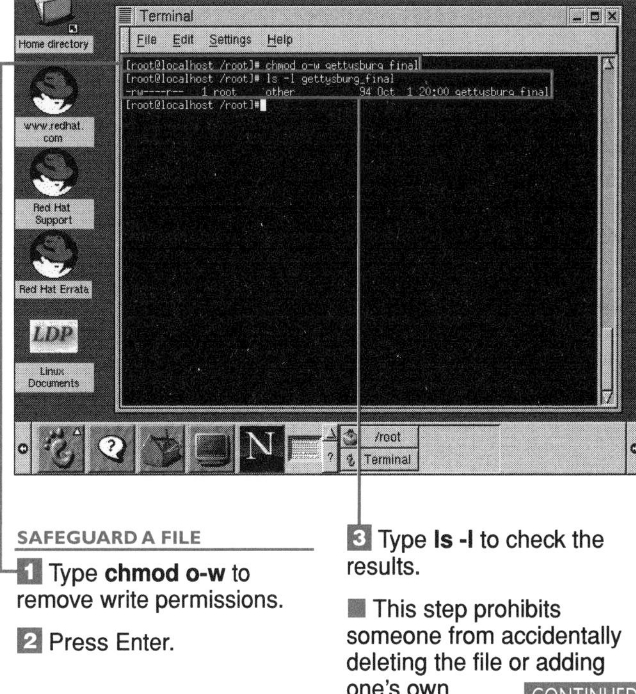

SAFEGUARD A FILE

1 Type **chmod o-w** to remove write permissions.

2 Press Enter.

3 Type **ls -l** to check the results.

■ This step prohibits someone from accidentally deleting the file or adding one's own comments.

CONTINUED

GRANT AND RESTRICT FILE ACCESS

CONTINUED

You can use Linux's ability to restrict access to a specific file by increasing security on your system. Restricting access is an effective way of preventing problems resulting from accidental editing. For example, if you have a file that is critical to the smooth operation of your Linux system (such as `/etc/password`) left accessible to any user, serious problems could result.

A user could decide to edit the file himself to save time in changing his password. A more malicious user could actively seek to wreck your system by deleting or changing other user account passwords. Worst of all, an experienced Linux user could change the root account password, leaving you unable to restore the system.

Because this is such an important issue, I give an example of how to decrease access to a sensitive system file, such as the `/etc/passwd` file.

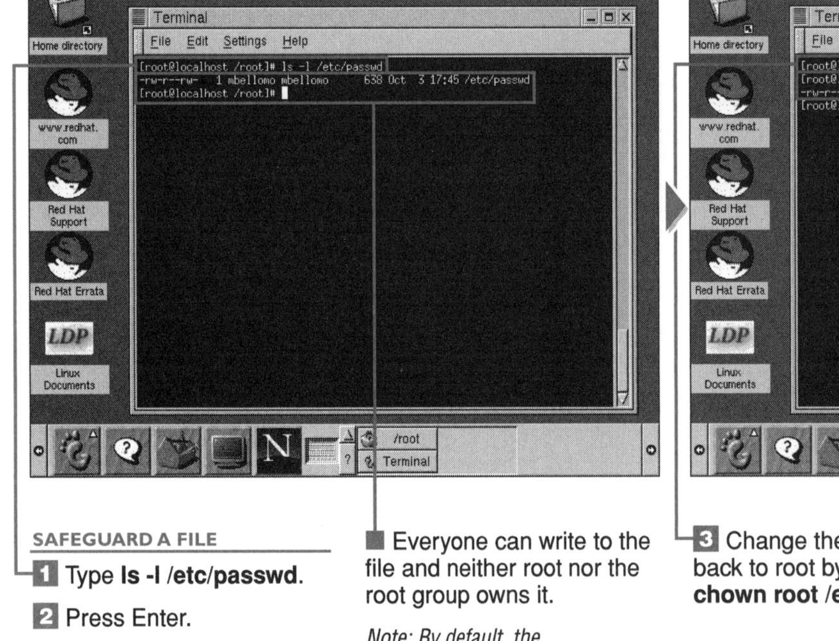

SAFEGUARD A FILE

1 Type **ls -l /etc/passwd**.

2 Press Enter.

■ Everyone can write to the file and neither root nor the root group owns it.

Note: By default, the `/etc/passwd` file is never this open and unrestricted on a Linux system.

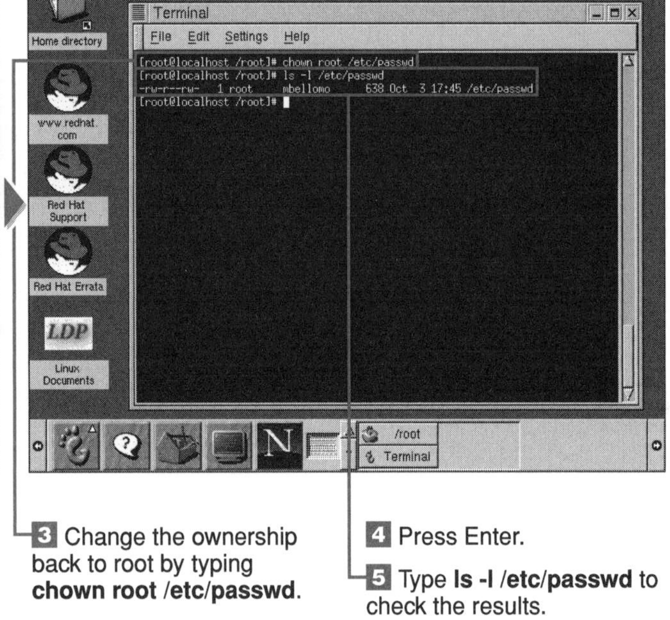

3 Change the ownership back to root by typing **chown root /etc/passwd**.

4 Press Enter.

5 Type **ls -l /etc/passwd** to check the results.

What other ways can file access be restricted?

- In Linux, files starting with a single period (.) don't appear in a `list` command unless the `a` option is used. An extra level of "out-of-sight, out-of-mind" security can be obtained by renaming a file from `myprivatenotes` to `.myprivatenotes`.

How can I restrict access to a program or script?

- The easiest way to do this is to use the `chmod` command with the `x` option. By revoking the file as an executable, no one can run the program.

Instead of restricting permissions to a sensitive file such as /etc/passwd, can I just save a copy of the file in case someone edits or damages it?

- You could do this, but restricting permission to a file like `/etc/passwd` is better because it's a measure to prevent problems before they begin.

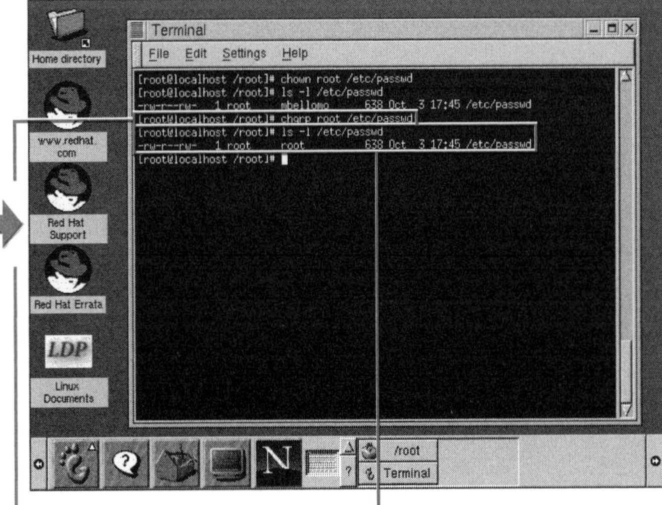

6 Change the group to root by typing **chgrp root /etc/passwd**.

7 Press Enter.

8 Type **ls –l /etc/passwd** to check the results.

9 Remove the write permissions by typing **chmod o-w /etc/passwd**.

10 Press Enter.

11 Type **ls –l /etc/passwd** to check the results.

■ The file is readable and writeable by root only.

USE CRON TO AUTOMATE SYSTEM TASKS

A final program you should be familiar with when it comes to the most basic Linux administration is cron. cron, a reference to Chronos (for time), is the program you can use to automate simple administrative tasks. cron does this by tracking time as kept on your Linux machine. At a prearranged time, cron runs the program you specified as if you'd typed it in on the command line.

cron is always active, but it only follows the instructions given to it in cron table, also known as the crontab. Each user has a crontab that can be read and written to. In the crontab, you must specify the exact time you want a program to run. The time and tasks are written in the crontab in six fields, left to right: Minute, Hour, Day of Month, Month, Day of Week, and the Command you want to run.

In the following example, run the w command every Friday at 4 p.m. and redirect the output to a file called whatchadoing.

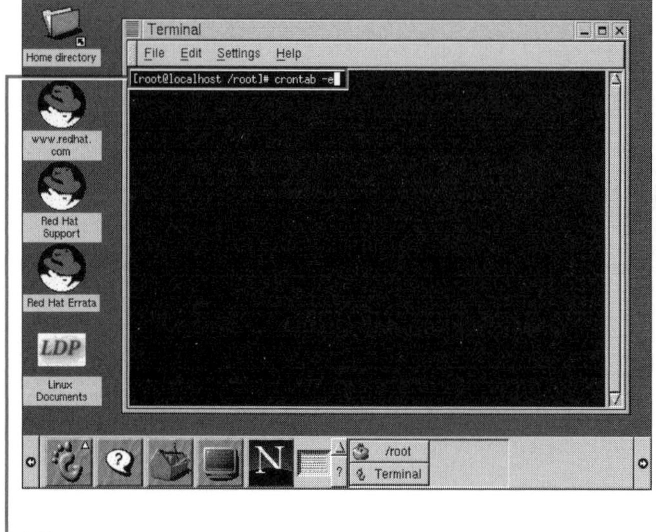

1 Type **crontab -e** to edit the crontab.

2 Press Enter.

■ The vi editor appears. Because no cron jobs were input yet, it's completely empty.

3 Press **I** to enter the INSERT mode.

4 Add the time according to the six fields listed above.

Note: Leave a space between each field. Placing an asterisk in the Day Of Month and Month columns shows this task will run on every week, every month of the year.

What should I do if my cron program ran at the wrong time?

✔ Double-check the time you've entered into the `crontab`. The most common mistake is where people neglect to adjust the time to a military standard. 04 is not four in the afternoon; it's four in the morning. 16 denotes four in the afternoon.

What do I do if the time is set correctly and the job still is done at the wrong time?

✔ What's probably happening is that `cron` is running fine, but the system time it's tracking is wrong. You can check what time your computer thinks it is by typing `date` and pressing Enter. The `date` program displays your system time. If it's off, change the time setting to the one that you want.

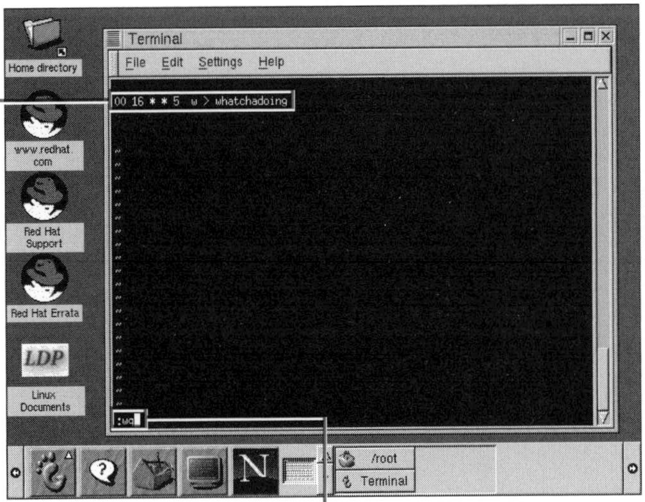

5 Type **w > whatchadoing** to redirect the w output into the file.

6 Press Esc to return to Command mode.

7 Type **:wq** to exit and save your entry.

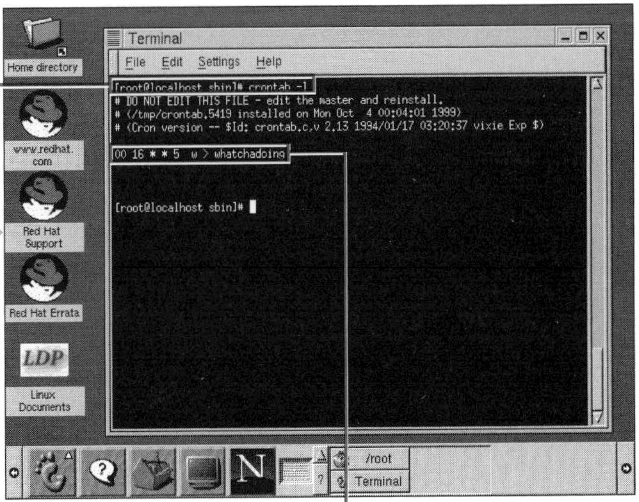

8 Check the results by typing **crontab -l**.

9 Press Enter.

■ The `crontab` lists the job you entered.

■ Check whether the `whatchadoing` file was created and written.

USE THE GNOME LINUXCONF TOOL

LinuxConf is the main tool you use to do most of the administrative work in the GNOME GUI system. You use LinuxConf to create user accounts, edit system information, set up e-mail aliases, and a multitude of other functions. If you're from the Windows world, this tool is the combined equivalent of the various management tools available on your Windows NT Server.

LinuxConf stands for — as you might guess — Linux Configuration. Although other users on the system can view the settings you create and select in LinuxConf, only the root administrative account can actually make a permanent change in this administration tool.

While useful, the LinuxConf tool can be initially confusing for many new administrators. Before jumping directly into user and group administration, I go over the basics of how to use and get around in the LinuxConf tool.

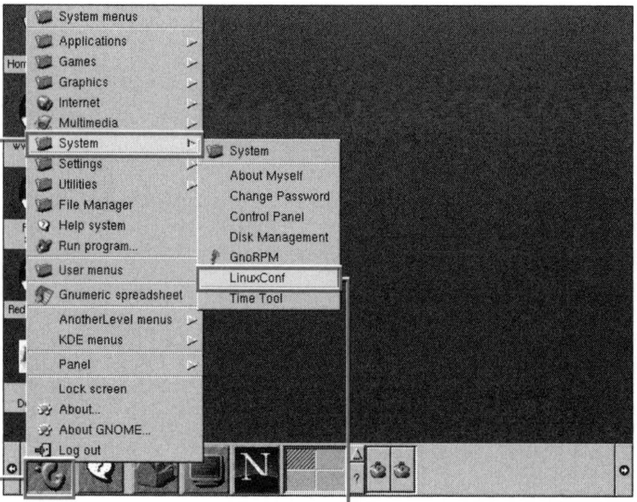

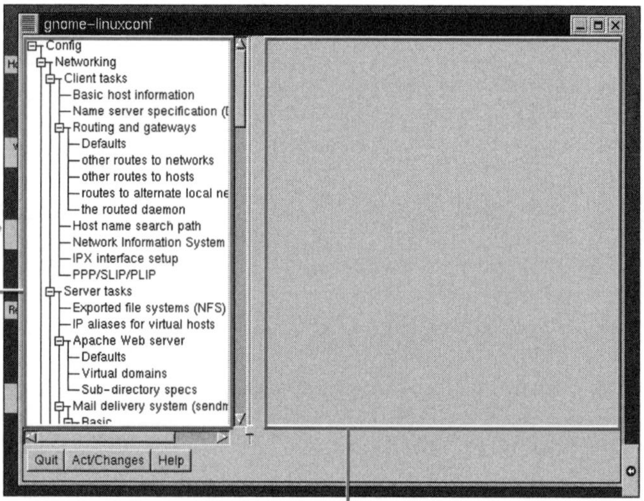

OPEN THE LINUXCONF

1 Click the Main Menu button.

2 Move the mouse pointer to System.

3 Move the pointer to LinuxConf.

4 Click LinuxConf.

■ The gnome-linuxconf window appears.

■ You can control (edit) the GNOME-based LinuxConf in the left pane.

■ LinuxConf displays your control panels' feature in the right pane.

What if I don't see the date & time of Features sections in the left-hand frame of the window?

- You should scroll all the way down to the bottom and you see the last two features you can edit: date & time and the Features setting itself.

Is there any way I can avoid having to scroll down through the list of features that LinuxConf can edit?

- You can "shrink" the list of features in the left-hand pane by clicking the little + and – boxes to the left of certain LinuxConf features, such as Networking or Server Tasks. Clicking the box so that a + sign appears closes the feature and hides all of the settings you can configure under it. Clicking the same box again so that a – sign appears on the box opens the feature again.

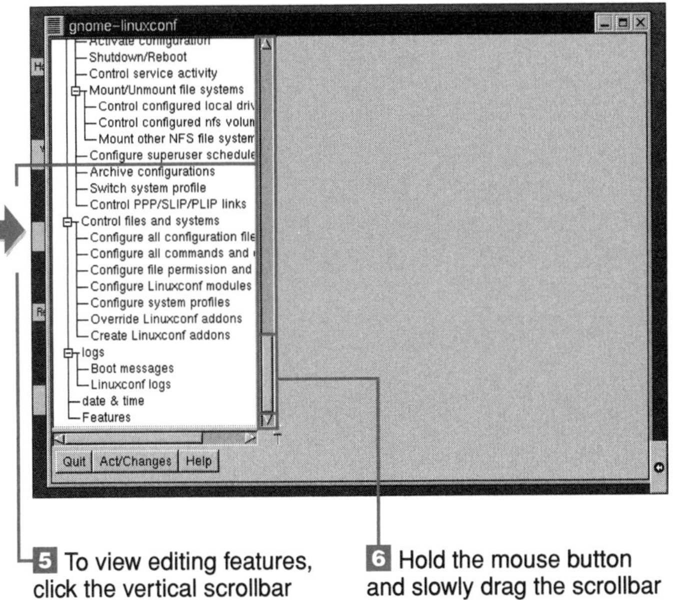

5 To view editing features, click the vertical scrollbar located between the left and right pane of the gnome-linuxconf window.

6 Hold the mouse button and slowly drag the scrollbar button toward the bottom.

■ The features that you can edit appears.

EDIT THE DATE & TIME FEATURE

1 Click the date & time feature in the left pane.

■ The right pane displays the Workstation date & time control panel.

CONTINUED

USE THE GNOME LINUXCONF TOOL

CONTINUED

You can change and configure each separate element of a given feature in the LinuxConf utility with the feature's panels. When you click a given object on the left-hand pane, such as date & time, feature, or Basic Host Information, the panel appears in the right-hand pane.

The objects displayed in the right hand portion of the gnome-linuxconf window are called *panels*, not terminals or windows, because they don't have scrollbars or independent movement outside of LinuxConf. You can't click a panel and resize it, or drag it off to a different portion of the screen.

In addition, each panel has a tab at its upper left-hand corner that serves as both a label and a place-holder. If you have multiple panels open, you can quickly bring one panel to the foreground by clicking its tab.

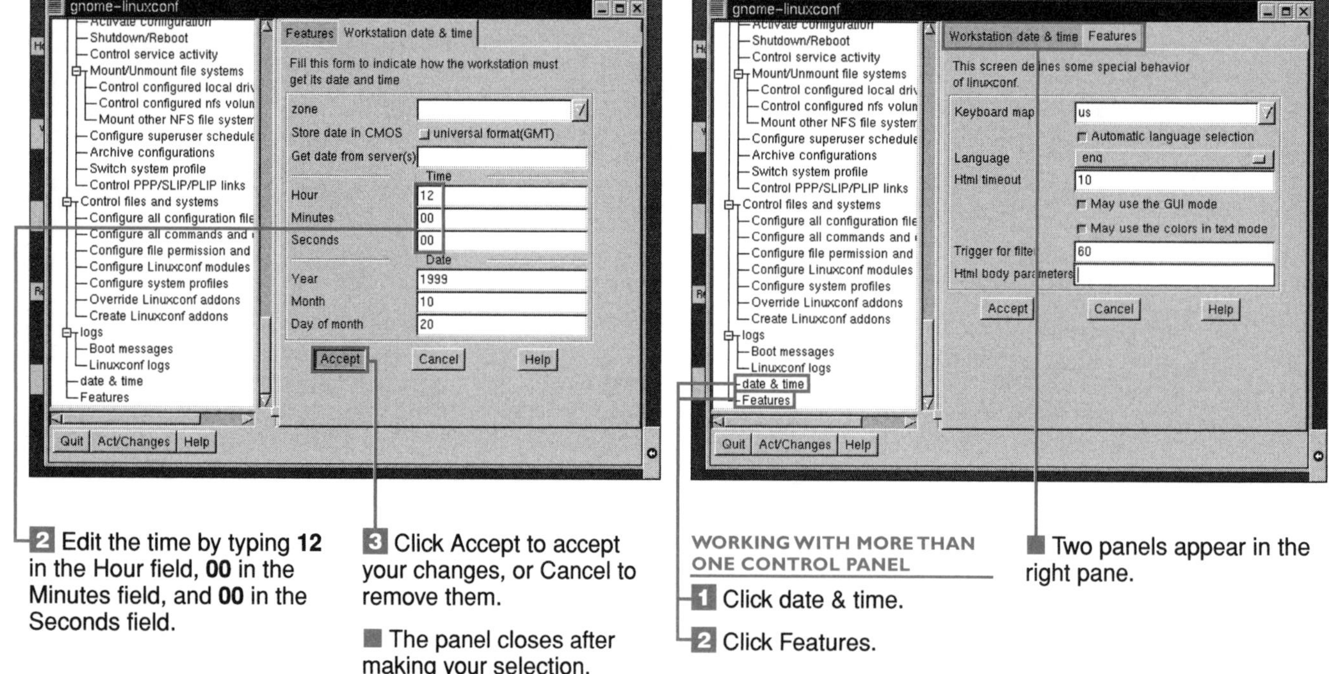

2 Edit the time by typing **12** in the Hour field, **00** in the Minutes field, and **00** in the Seconds field.

3 Click Accept to accept your changes, or Cancel to remove them.

■ The panel closes after making your selection.

WORKING WITH MORE THAN ONE CONTROL PANEL

1 Click date & time.

2 Click Features.

■ Two panels appear in the right pane.

What do I do if I have so many panels open that the right-hand window can't display them all?

- When you have more than six or seven panels open, LinuxConf displays a pair of arrow buttons in the upper-right. Click the arrow buttons to move back and forth through the list of open panels. However, using this feature can get confusing, so try not to use it.

I opened LinuxConf, but the window says it's linuxconf in all lowercase! Does this mean anything?

- This doesn't mean anything. Although Linux is normally case sensitive to the extreme, this is one of LinuxConf's strange little quirks.

What happens if I just click the Quit button when the final LinuxConf screen asks me if I want to Accept, Preview, or Don't Quit?

- LinuxConf exits with no complaint. All of your changes are discarded, not applied.

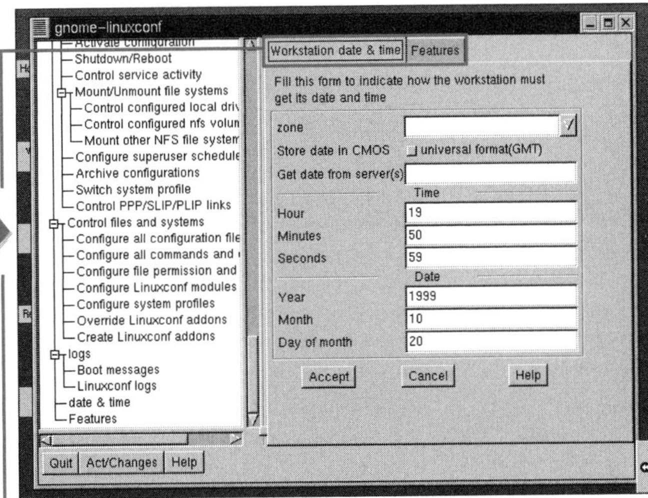

■ To switch between the two panels, click tabs at the top of each panel.

3 Click the Workstation date & time tab.

■ The Workstation date & time panel appears in the foreground.

■ When a panel is in the foreground, it is active.

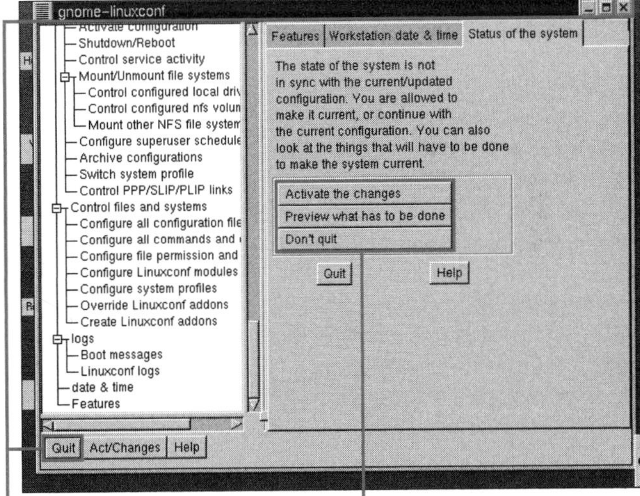

LEAVE LINUXCONF

1 To leave LinuxConf, click Quit or the X button in the upper-right corner of the window.

■ A Status of the system panel appears if you made any changes.

2 Click the appropriate button.

■ If you click Activate the changes, you apply your changes to the system and leave LinuxConf.

LIST USER ACCOUNTS

You can use LinuxConf to easily view the entire list of user accounts on your system. LinuxConf enables you to view the account listings in alphabetical order in a friendly, graphic mode. When you do this, keep in mind that you're seeing every single account that's been created on your Linux system — not every user account that is currently logged in. Note also that a user account may or may not have a person attached to it.

For example, you may see the user account xfs in the xfs group. Xfs is simply the dummy account that the system uses when accessing the X Font server, so you shouldn't go off and try to locate the user who logs in with xfs.

Whenever the operating system needs to perform an automated task on the X Font server, it uses the dummy account to do the work.

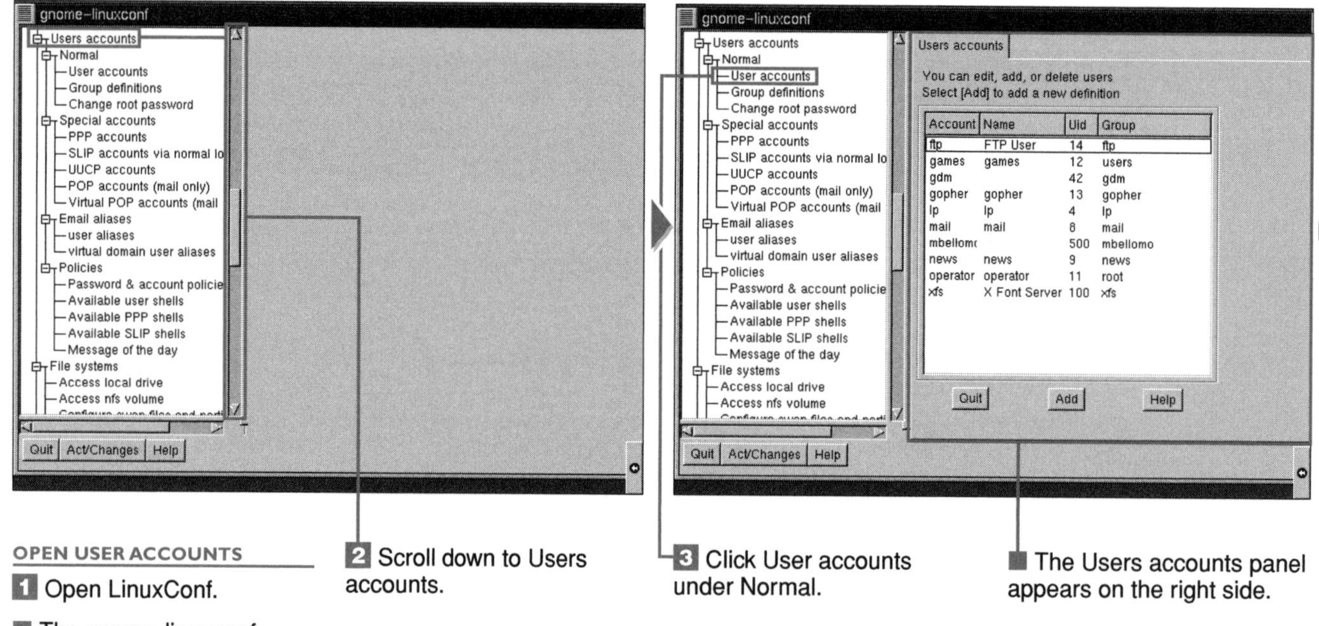

OPEN USER ACCOUNTS

1 Open LinuxConf.

■ The gnome-linuxconf window appears.

2 Scroll down to Users accounts.

3 Click User accounts under Normal.

■ The Users accounts panel appears on the right side.

How can I list users by UID (User ID) or Name instead of Account?

- Unfortunately, LinuxConf's User Account panel isn't quite as flexible as its nearest Windows counterpart. To find where a user is listed, scroll down the alphabetical list to locate the entry.

I have some users listed like mbellomo and gdm in your example: They have a listing under the Account field but not under the Name field. Does this affect anything important?

- This doesn't affect anything important. The Name field is occasionally used when searching or listing accounts, and is displayed in some e-mail programs.

How can I fix this?

- When you click mbellomo to list more information on that account, the Full name Field appears blank. Simply click the field to place the cursor in it, and then type the name of the user.

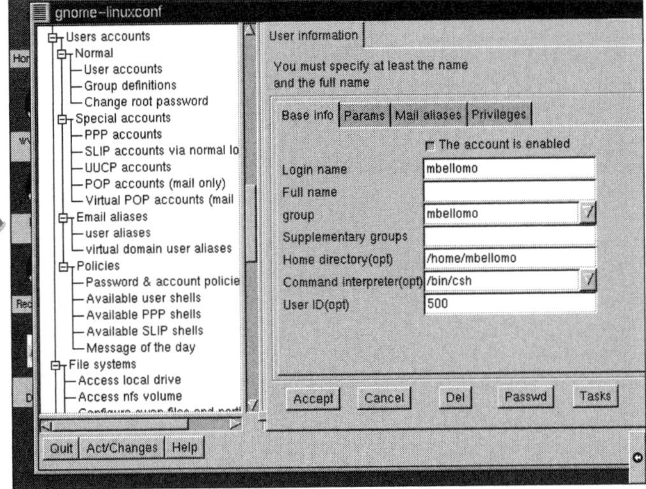

4 Click the name mbellomo to see the details on the user account.

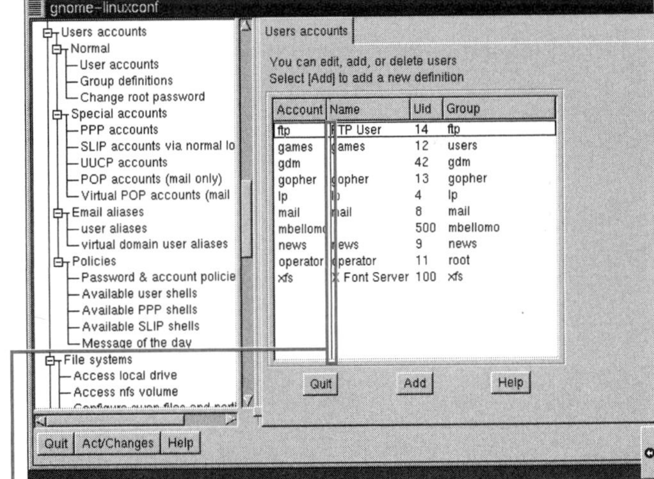

INCREASING THE SIZE OF A FIELD

1 To expand the column's width, click the line that separates the Account and Name fields.

2 Hold the mouse button and drag the line to the right.

■ Crosshairs mark the new border.

3 Release the mouse button after you pull the Account field over as far as you want.

ADD USER ACCOUNTS

One of the most basic of all administrative functions in Linux is adding users. And if you work on a network with more than a few users, you know that adding users is a common task. Luckily, LinuxConf is designed to handle adding new users with ease.

As with the majority of the functions in the Linux configuration tool, only the root user may add a new user account. After the account is created, the user may re-configure his account, unless the administrator decides to disable it.

Note that there is no set ratio between users and user accounts. Because user accounts are simply the method by which a user can log into a Linux system, a single user can have one or multiple user accounts. However, it's best not to grant more than one account to any user. This limits the possible security breaches from an illegally gained password.

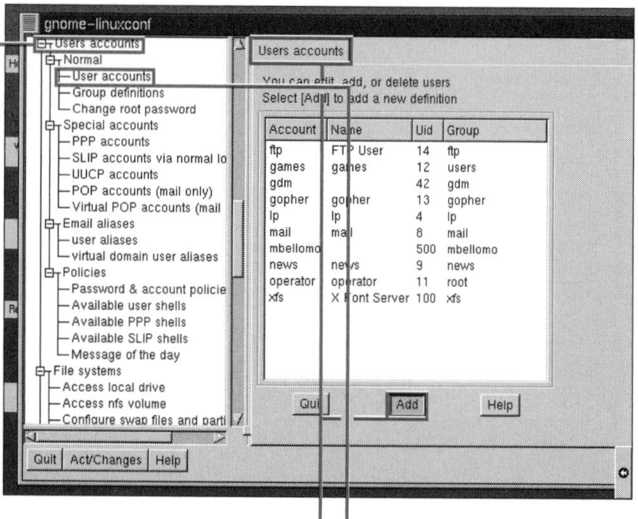

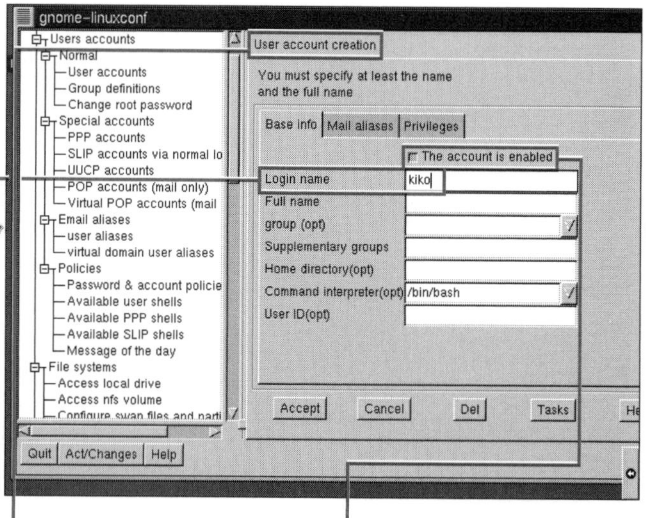

ADD A NEW USER

1 Open LinuxConf.

■ The gnome-linuxconf window appears.

2 Scroll down to Users accounts.

3 Click User accounts under Normal.

■ The Users accounts panel appears in the right pane.

4 Click the Add button.

■ The User account creation panel appears.

5 Type **kiko** in the Login name field.

■ By default, The account is enabled is depressed. If not, click it to activate the account.

TIPS

Why do I need to click the Account Enabled button when I create an account? Isn't it automatically active when I create it?

- By default, an account is normally active when created. The enabled setting exists to allow you to disable an account, as explained later in this chapter.

Why is the shell called the command interpreter in LinuxConf?

- This was a decision made by the creators of LinuxConf. Command Interpreter is a fancy name for a shell; it's the shell that actually takes and applies (or interprets) the commands you give to Linux.

Which command interpreter should I select for my users?

- For consistency, you should continue to use the shell that is predominant on your system. However, if you're starting from scratch, you're probably best off selecting the default setting in Linux, the Bourne-again shell (bash) due to the large number of utilities available to it.

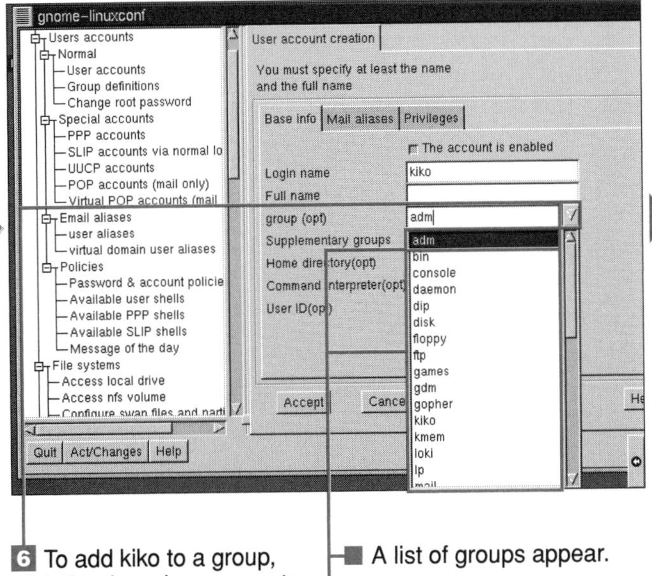

6 To add kiko to a group, click the drop-down arrow to the right of the group (opt) field.

■ A list of groups appear.

7 Click to select a group.

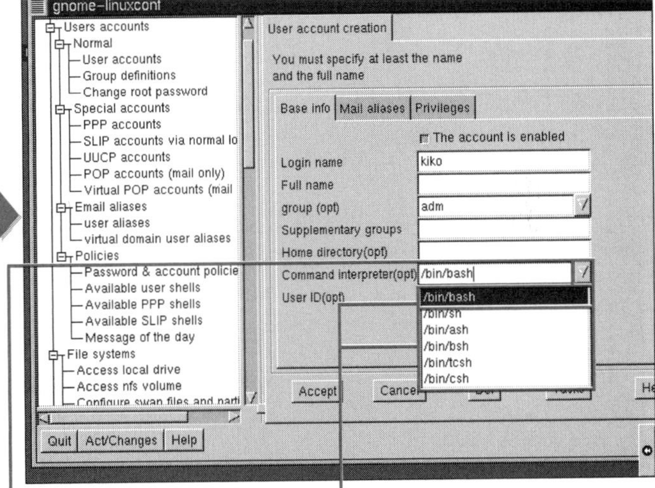

8 To select a shell for this account, click the arrow to the right of the Command interpreter (opt) field.

■ A drop-down menu appears.

9 Click to select a shell.

CONTINUED

ADD USER ACCOUNTS CONTINUED

You have a built-in safeguard against typing mistakes whenever you add user account passwords in Red Hat Linux. Whenever you add a new user, you're prompted to type their password twice. Although you may make a typo when typing a password the first time, it's highly unlikely that you'll make the exact same mistake twice.

The passwords you give to each user depends on the naming scheme you have on your system. Because the majority of Linux users prefer to set their own passwords after you set up their account, it's usually best to assign the user an obvious password they can remember, such as their first name, until they decide to change the password to something else. Of course, if more security is needed, simply assign a password that is harder to remember but is not easy for someone else to guess.

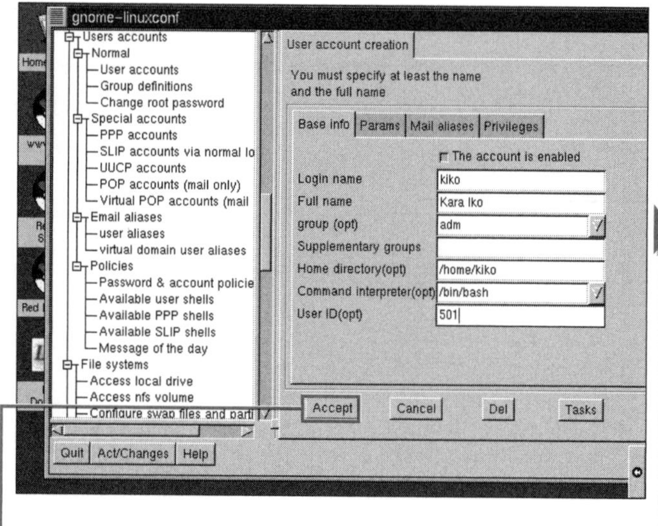

10 Click the Accept button when done.

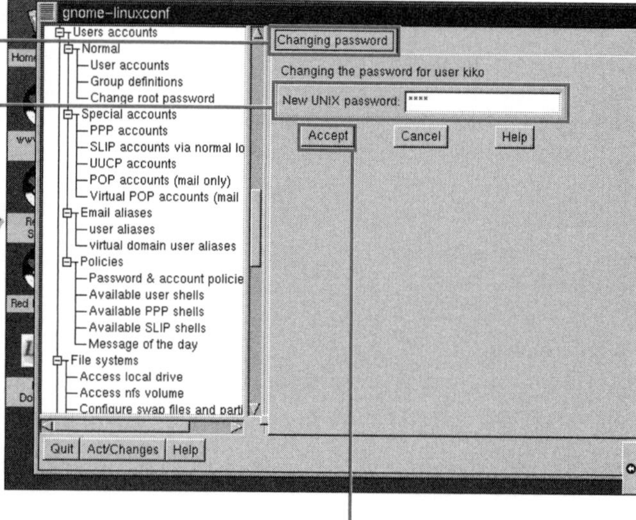

■ The Changing password panel appears.

11 Type the password for kiko in the New UNIX password field.

12 Click Accept.

What does the (opt) listing to the right of certain settings in the User account creation panel mean?

- *Opt* stands for optional. If you choose to add a listing in these empty text fields, you may, but it's not required. The user accounts run properly if these fields are left blank.

Should I take the time to type the optional information into each text field in the User account creation panel?

- It's best to add this data if you have time. For example, entering the user's real name in the User ID field helps you remember who owns what account.

Which group should I select for my users?

- Most users should be put in the user group. The important point here is to never put users in the root group. This grants them administrative authority, which is not what you want on a secure system.

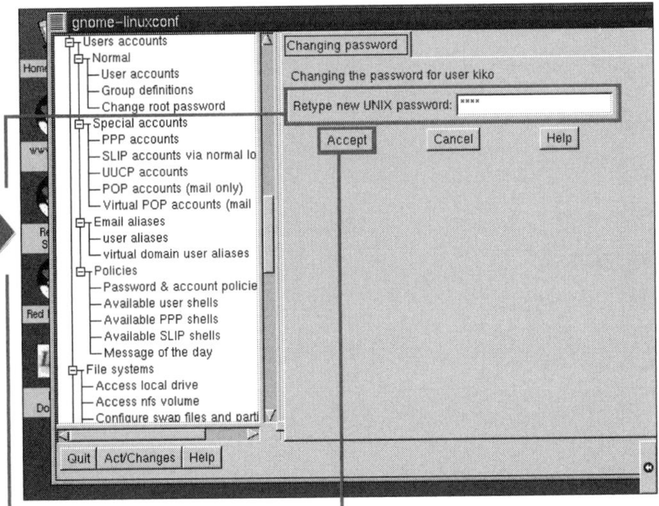

13 Retype the password in the Retype new UNIX password field.

■ For privacy, your new password appears as asterisks.

14 Click Accept when you're done.

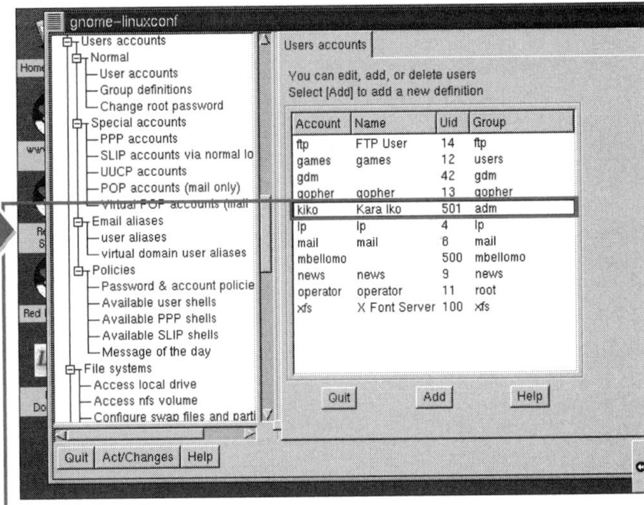

■ The Users accounts panel appears displaying the new account.

EDIT USER ACCOUNTS

You can edit user account information from LinuxConf's Users Accounts screen. Depending on how you permission your system, users may be able to change their password and pertinent information. If you want to keep all administrative information at your fingertips alone, you can be the sole point of contact for change. Be warned, however that in this circumstance, you can easily become swamped by relatively mundane administration chores.

For example, say that a new user needs to be added to the games group. Furthermore, the user has changed his name, so you have to change the user's account name to reflect this. Another user needs her mail aliases changed, and a fourth wants you to change his password to something more obscure. If you have to continually do this for a large user community, you're spending too much time administering user accounts.

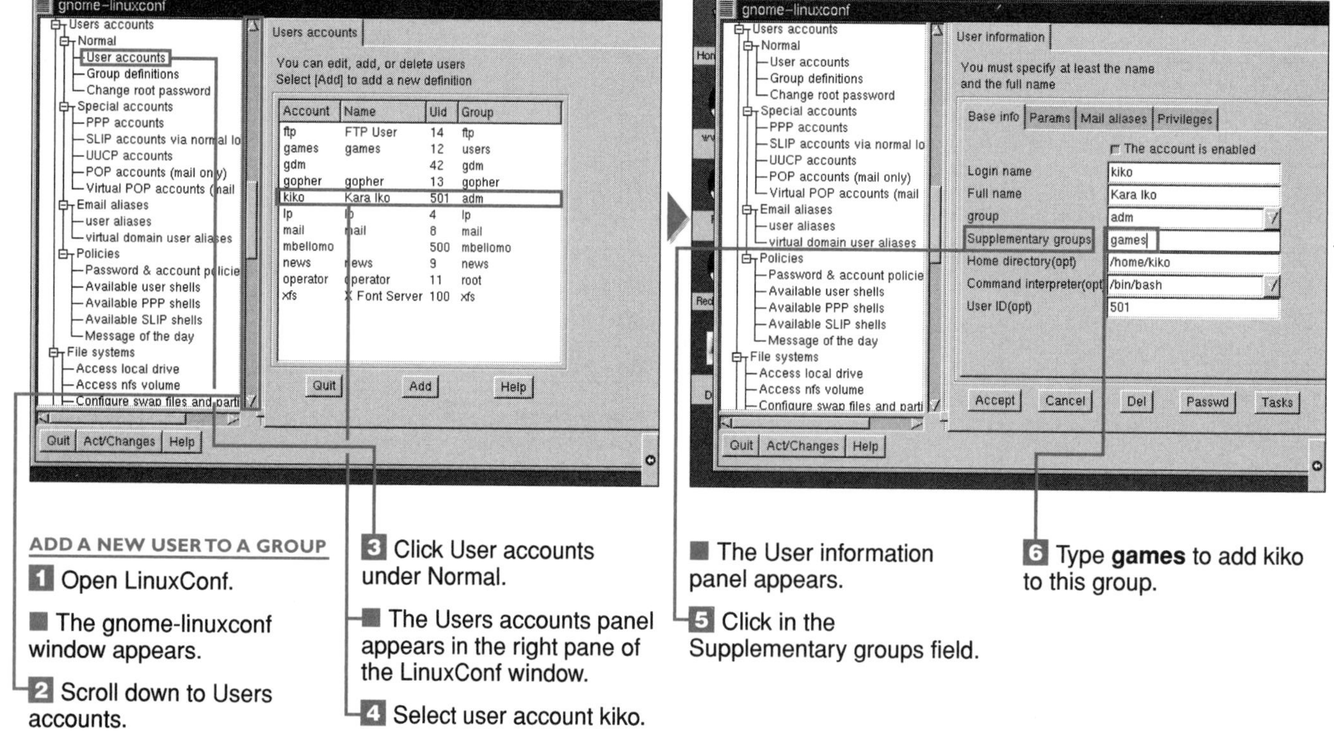

ADD A NEW USER TO A GROUP

1 Open LinuxConf.

■ The gnome-linuxconf window appears.

2 Scroll down to Users accounts.

3 Click User accounts under Normal.

■ The Users accounts panel appears in the right pane of the LinuxConf window.

4 Select user account kiko.

■ The User information panel appears.

5 Click in the Supplementary groups field.

6 Type **games** to add kiko to this group.

Are there any user account names that I shouldn't use?

- The first rule is that you always want to avoid duplication. The second rule is that you want to maintain a consistent naming scheme on your system if you have more than a few users. For example, a common scheme is to use a combination of the user's first initial and their last name, so John Smith's account name would be jsmith.

What advantages are there to having a consistent naming scheme?

- If you have a consistent naming scheme, it's easier to organize, locate, and recognize users on your system. For example, if you get a request for a password change from jsmith, you may know who this person is, what department they belong to, and what his needs might be. A similar message from user `THX1138` gives you no such clues.

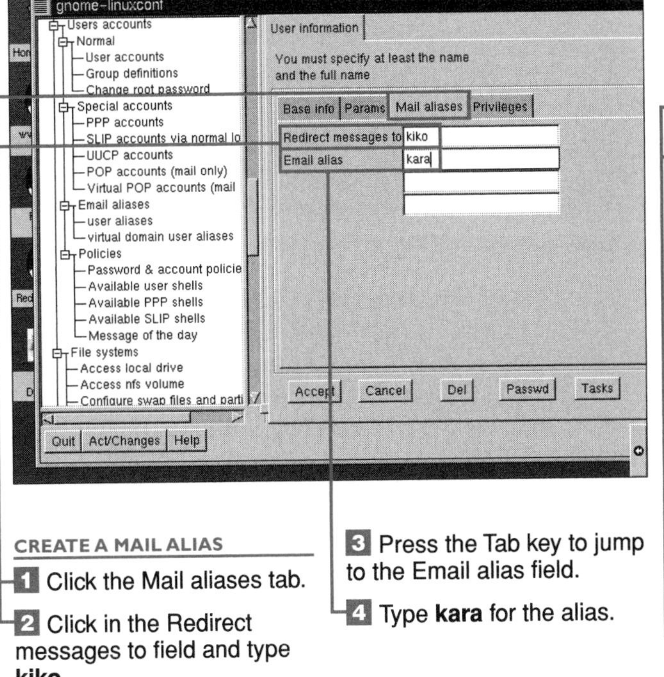

CREATE A MAIL ALIAS

1. Click the Mail aliases tab.
2. Click in the Redirect messages to field and type **kiko**.
3. Press the Tab key to jump to the Email alias field.
4. Type **kara** for the alias.

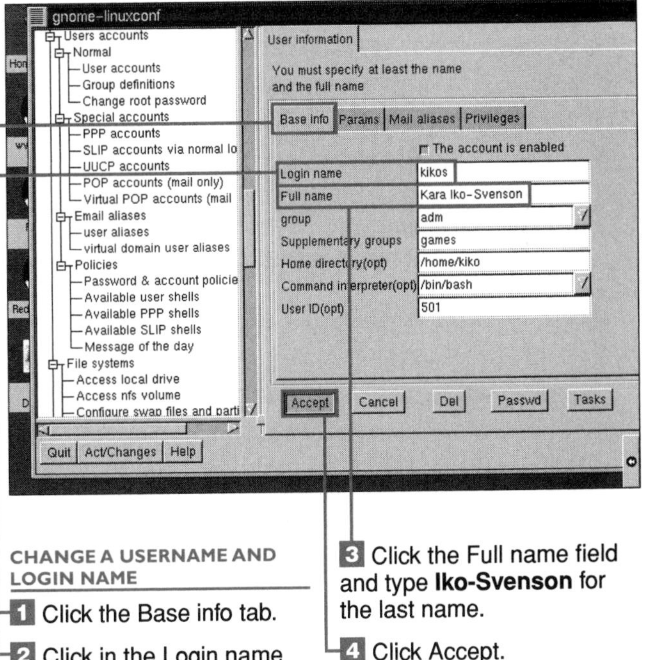

CHANGE A USERNAME AND LOGIN NAME

1. Click the Base info tab.
2. Click in the Login name field and type **s** after kiko.
3. Click the Full name field and type **Iko-Svenson** for the last name.
4. Click Accept.

CONTINUED

EDIT USER ACCOUNTS CONTINUED

You can easily change a user account's password in LinuxConf. As when you first created the account, you have a built-in safeguard that prevents you from entering in a password with typing errors. However, a key difference in the task of changing a user account's password now versus when you first created the account is that the user can also perform this task at any time. Root is the only account that can set a user's password at account creation time.

Because users can set their password whenever they want, you only have to edit their passwords in special situations. The most common case is when you're having a security problem because someone is *hacking* (gaining illegal access) onto your system through a specific user account. If the user is on vacation or is not using his account, it's up to you to make the password change.

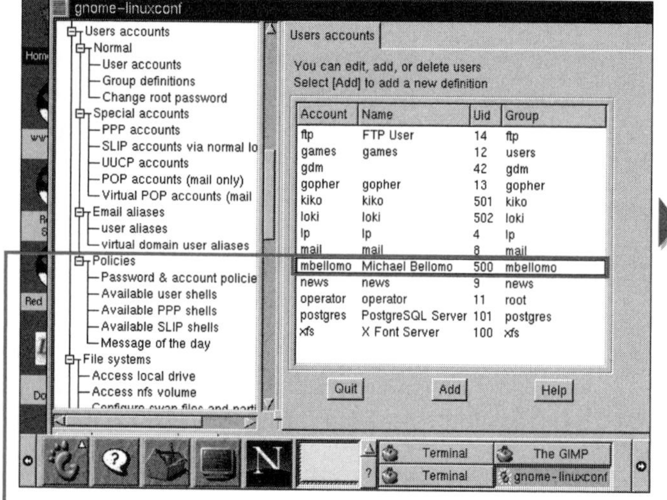

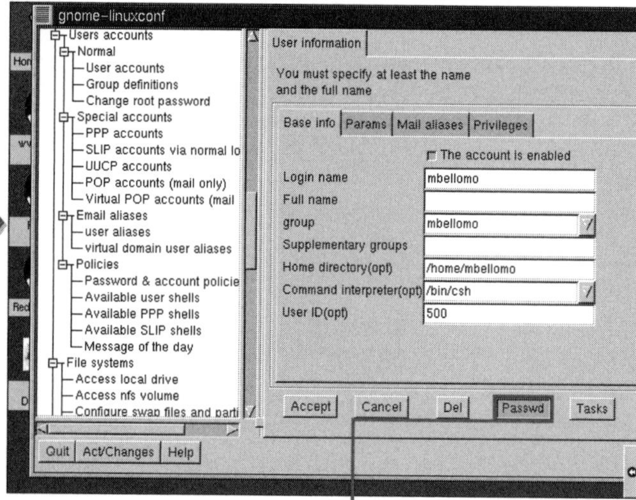

CHANGE A PASSWORD

1 Click the user account of mbellomo.

■ The Users information panel appears.

2 In the User information panel, click Passwd.

TIPS

How can I enable users on the system access to perform changes in LinuxConf?

- When you click the user's account name in LinuxConf, one of the tabs on the far right is the Privileges tab. The access privilege list is located there, and you can grant permission to a user to use LinuxConf. Be very cautious in doing this, however. It only takes one mistake from a user with administrative privileges to cause serious problems on your system.

One of my users wants to change his user account name to mail. Can I do this?

- You shouldn't enable users to change their names to duplicate system accounts. This could cause both Linux and a new administrator some confusion. User account names by necessity should be unique. In any case, LinuxConf has built-in safeguards that won't let you duplicate a user account name.

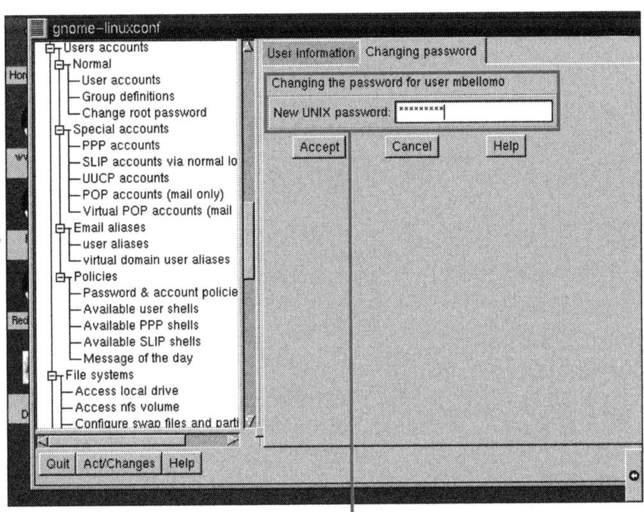

■ The Changing password panel appears.

3 Enter the new password in the New UNIX password field.

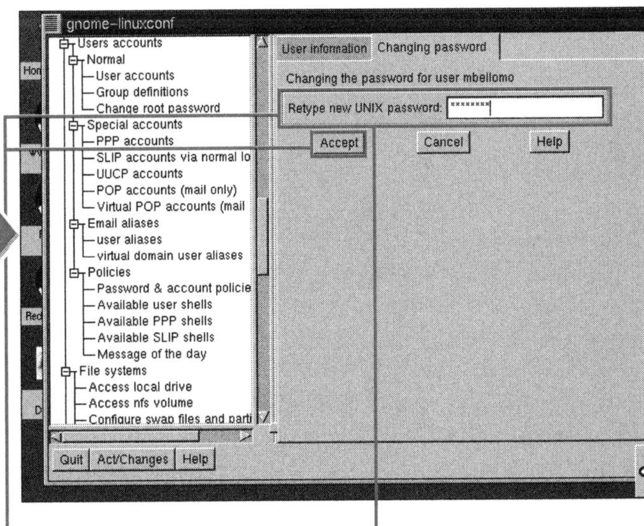

4 Enter the password twice to protect against typos.

5 Click Accept.

■ Your new password appears as asterisks.

DELETE USER ACCOUNTS

Deleting accounts from the Users Accounts screen in LinuxConf is as easy as the creation or editing of user accounts in GNOME-based Linux. An additional advantage is that in LinuxConf, deciding what level of account removal you want is easy. You can remove the account outright, archive the user's home directory and mail inbox, or simply leave it in place.

You should delete user accounts only in certain instances. If an employee leaves the company that owns the network, or if a student is graduating from the institution that runs the Linux installation, then the account should be removed as a matter of basic security.

On the other hand, you don't want to use account deletion as a cure-all. For example, if a user is going away for an extended vacation but will return, or if a given user is causing you serious problems, your best option is to disable the user account, not delete it.

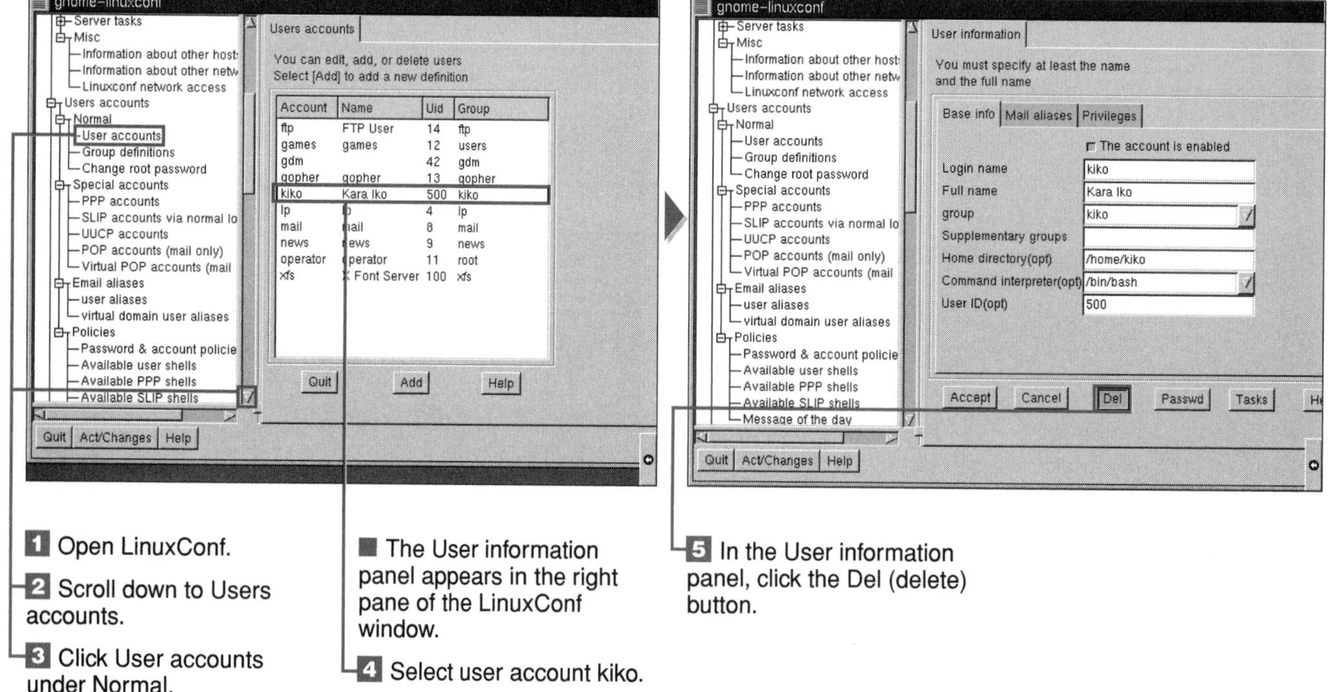

1 Open LinuxConf.

2 Scroll down to Users accounts.

3 Click User accounts under Normal.

■ The User information panel appears in the right pane of the LinuxConf window.

4 Select user account kiko.

5 In the User information panel, click the Del (delete) button.

TIPS

When should you select the Archive option when deleting a user account?

- This option is the default action taken by LinuxConf, simply because it can be most easily reversed. You should keep this default if you feel the user has information that you need in her mailbox or home directory, but you want to make it smaller to save space and prevent people from looking at it.

When should you select the Delete option when deleting a user account?

- Use this whenever you want to free up maximum space on the hard drive. It's the most commonly used option.

When should you select the Leave in Place option when deleting a user account?

- If you're sure that Kara Iko had files that should be made publicly available, or you want to preview what was in the home directory before deleting it all, this is your best option.

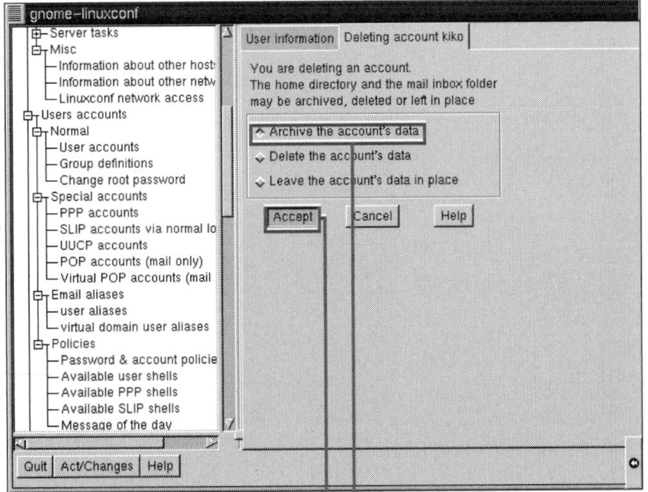

■ The Deleting account panel appears.

■ You can archive, delete, or leave kiko's home directory and mailbox alone.

6 Click Archive the account's data.

7 Click Accept.

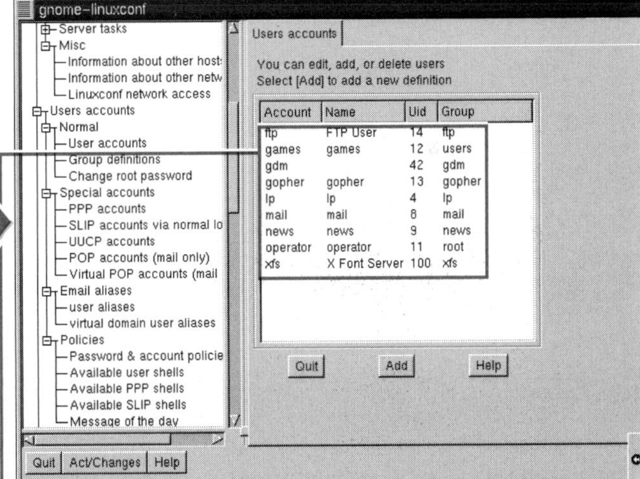

■ When you return to the Users accounts panel, kiko is deleted from the list of users.

DISABLE USER ACCOUNTS

You should be familiar with the process of disabling user accounts because this gives you more options when controlling members of your user community without deleting accounts. For example, if you plan to delete a user account every time a company employee goes on sabbatical, you're effectively doubling your work because you have to re-create the account each time.

If a user will not log in for several weeks or months, disabling the user's account to increase your system's security without increasing your work load.

Disabling user accounts gives you some middle ground when it comes to disciplining errant users. It's useful as a warning to a user who tries to cause trouble on your system. A user who tries to gain access to administrative files or root privileges is disabled until you consider him trustworthy.

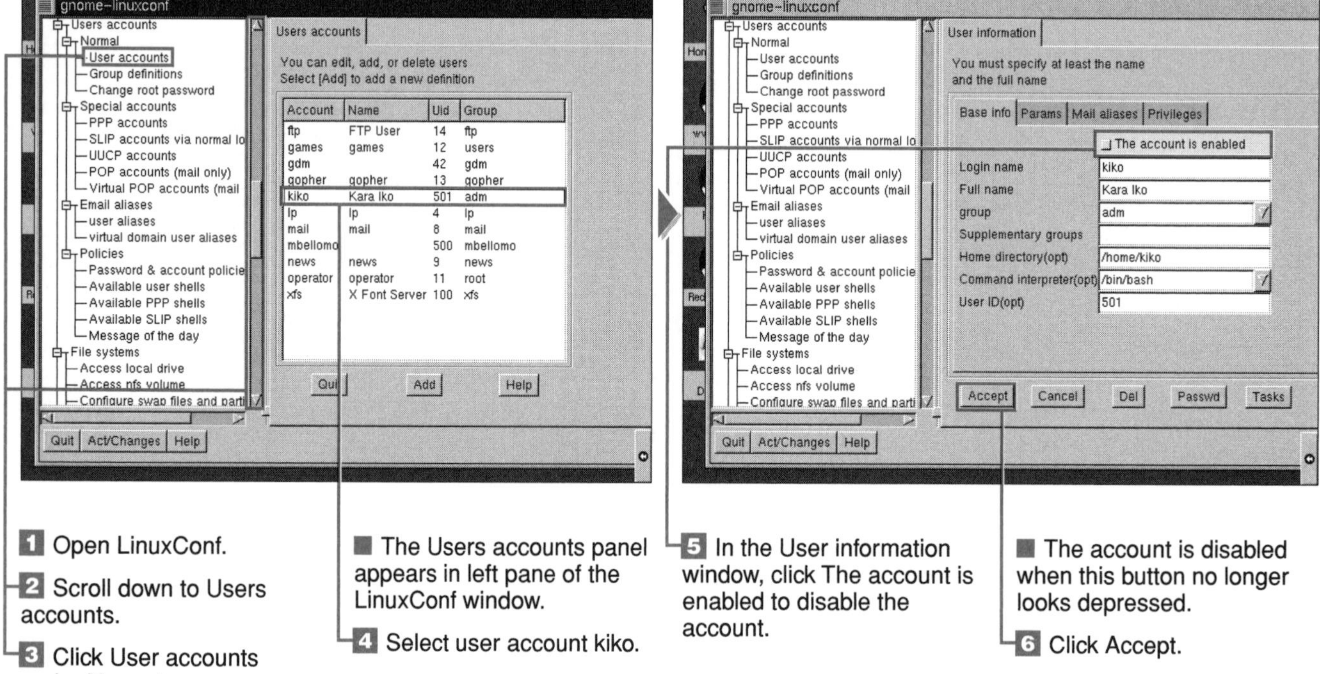

1 Open LinuxConf.

2 Scroll down to Users accounts.

3 Click User accounts under Normal.

■ The Users accounts panel appears in left pane of the LinuxConf window.

4 Select user account kiko.

5 In the User information window, click The account is enabled to disable the account.

■ The account is disabled when this button no longer looks depressed.

6 Click Accept.

One of my users is complaining that I disabled her account when I didn't do a thing. What's going on?

- Find out if the user recently changed his password. If not, then the person running the Linux system is responsible.

The user made some changes to the account, but he can't remember what he did. What can I do now?

- Take it in stages. First, try to give him a new password, using the procedure previously described. If that doesn't do the trick, you may have to delete the account and start from scratch. Try archiving or leaving the user's mailbox and home directory alone if the user has important files inside.

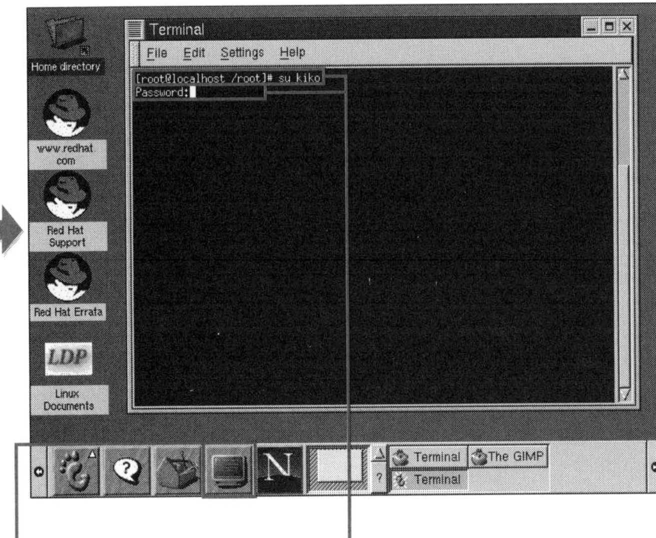

7 To test the disabling of the account, click the Terminal button at the bottom of the screen.

■ The Linux Terminal window appears.

8 Use the `su` or `switch user` command to log in as kiko's account.

9 Type **su kiko** at the prompt and press Enter.

10 Enter this user account's password and press Enter.

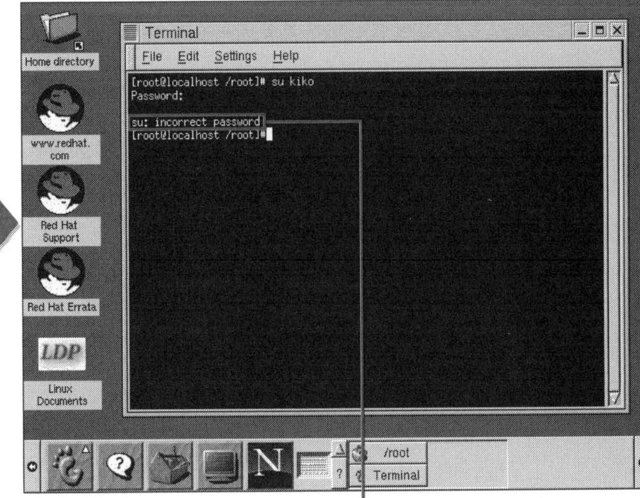

■ Linux complains that this password is incorrect.

■ This is the standard message that Linux gives when an account is disabled.

ADD USER ACCOUNTS IN THE LINUX TERMINAL

You can also add new user accounts without using the LinuxConf utility. Although using LinuxConf is slightly easier, especially if you're familiar with the Microsoft Windows environment, you can perform the same tasks from the Linux Terminal.

Knowing how to perform the account creation task without benefit of the LinuxConf utility is a useful skill. For example, if you are doing work in the Linux Terminal, switching between the GNOME GUI environment and the Linux Terminal becomes less convenient. Instead, you're better off doing the work in the Terminal proper and saving yourself some labor.

The Linux command to add new user accounts is `useradd`. The `useradd` command has the same default settings for account setup as LinuxConf, such as starting new accounts in the bash shell. If you want to make changes, creating the account with `useradd` and then editing the user account afterwards is easier.

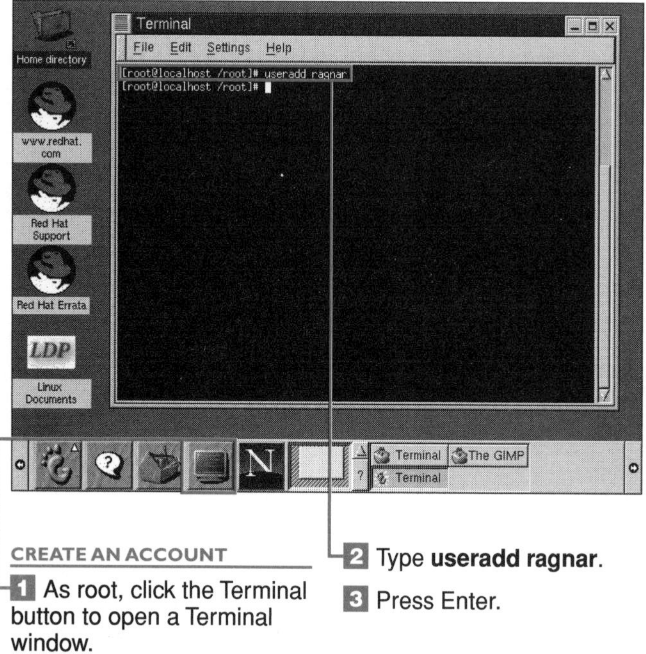

CREATE AN ACCOUNT

1 As root, click the Terminal button to open a Terminal window.

■ The Linux Terminal window appears.

2 Type **useradd ragnar**.

3 Press Enter.

SET THE PASSWORD

1 Type **passwd ragnar** and press Enter.

2 Type the password for the user.

Note: For security purposes, the password does not display on screen.

3 Press Enter.

How can I tell what the user account's defaults are set to?

- You can simply start up LinuxConf again, scroll down to Users accounts, and click User accounts under Normal. Select the user account from the list to get all the information at a glance.

How can I tell if the account creation process was successful without resorting to LinuxConf?

- If you want to stay in the Linux Terminal, you should view one of the files that Linux automatically edits when a new user is created. Use the `vi` editor to see the file `/etc/passwd`. This file lists all the user accounts, much like LinuxConf. Although the output may look more arcane than LinuxConf, if you see your user account listed, it was created and is available to the user.

4 To prevent typos, re-enter the password at the prompt.

5 Press Enter.

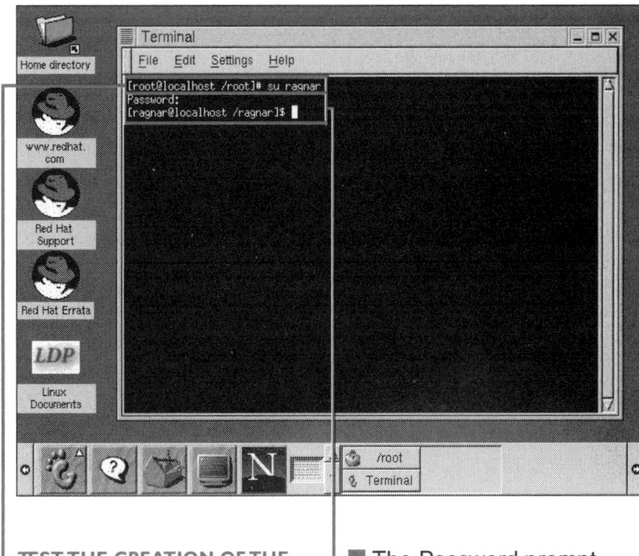

TEST THE CREATION OF THE ACCOUNT

1 Type **su ragnar** at the command line to log in as ragnar's account.

2 Press Enter.

■ The Password prompt appears.

3 Enter ragnar's password.

■ You can log in as this user.

EDIT USER ACCOUNTS IN THE LINUX TERMINAL

You can make changes to user accounts in the Linux Terminal as well as in the GNOME interface. Editing user accounts in the Linux Terminal comes with a couple advantages over working in GNOME.

For example, if you're already working on items in the Terminal window, you don't have to shift back and forth from the Linux Terminal to the GUI system. Another advantage is that when you are editing accounts in the terminal, your Linux skills are more transferable. This means that if you go to a slightly different Linux system (which does not have a GUI-based LinuxConf tool, Red Hat Linux), you can still sucessfully edit user accounts.

Keep in mind that a Linux expert needs to know how to perform tasks in both the GUI and the Linux Terminal. When editing accounts in the terminal, you will use the `vi` editor. See Chapter 6 for more information on using the `vi` editor.

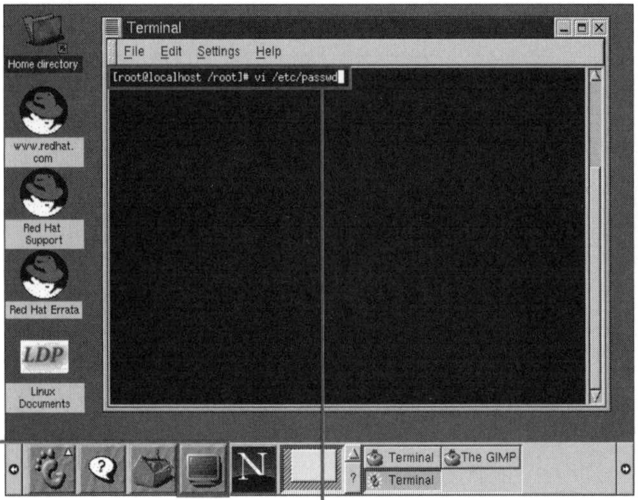

1 As root, click the Terminal button.

■ The Linux Terminal window comes up.

2 Type **vi /etc/passwd**.

3 Press Enter.

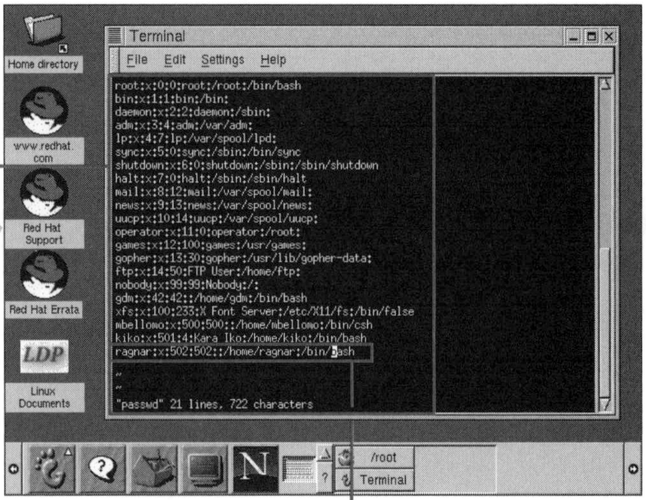

■ You are now in the `vi` editor screen.

■ The screen displays the contents of the `passwd` file.

4 Move the cursor to the bottom line so that you can edit the user account ragnar.

Why do I need to type a ! when saving and quitting the /etc/passwd file?

✔ You should always include a !, or bang sign, when editing the `passwd` or `group` files. Both of these files require this as an extra safety feature so that even a root account won't accidentally edit this file.

What do I do if I make a typo when I edit the passwd file?

✔ If you can't easily correct the error, then you should quit without saving and try again. To do this, type a colon, followed by a `q!`.

Can I use the Linux Terminal to edit an account name to match a system account?

✔ No. The same rules apply to accounts regardless of how you create them. Every account should have a unique name.

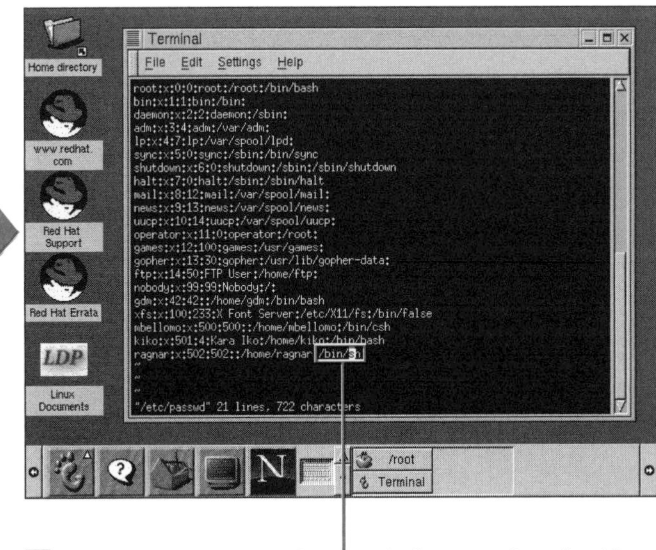

5 To change ragnar's shell from bash to the regular Bourne shell or `sh`, position the cursor over the `b` in `bash`.

6 Press X.

■ In Command mode, this deletes one character at a time.

7 Press X again.

■ The field now reads `/bin/sh`.

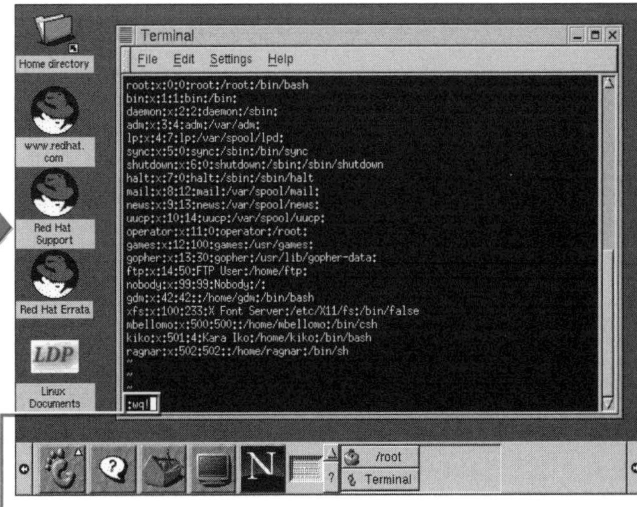

8 To save and quit the file, type a colon (:).

■ A colon appears at the bottom of the screen.

9 Type **wq!**.

10 Press Enter.

■ The `wq` writes (saves) your changes and quits `vi`.

DELETE AND DISABLE ACCOUNTS IN THE LINUX TERMINAL

Deleting and disabling user accounts relate directly to your Linux system's security. Because disabling accounts can involve taking immediate action against a user who is interfering with the operation of your system, you can disable accounts wherever working on the system, whether in the Linux Terminal or in LinuxConf.

Also, you need to know how to use the Linux Terminal for security purposes if there is damage to the system. If the GNOME Enlightenment windows program fails to start properly or is damaged by a system crash, then you can't afford to sit back while you have a security breach.

To complete these tasks, you need to use the `vi` editor. Using `vi`, you can lock an account by placing an asterisk in a user's password field in `/etc/passwd`. For a review of the `vi`-text editor, refer to Chapter 7.

OPEN THE PASSWD FILE

1 As root, click the Terminal button.

■ A Linux Terminal opens.

2 Type **vi /etc/passwd**.

3 Press Enter.

■ The `vi` editor screen displays the contents of the `passwd` file.

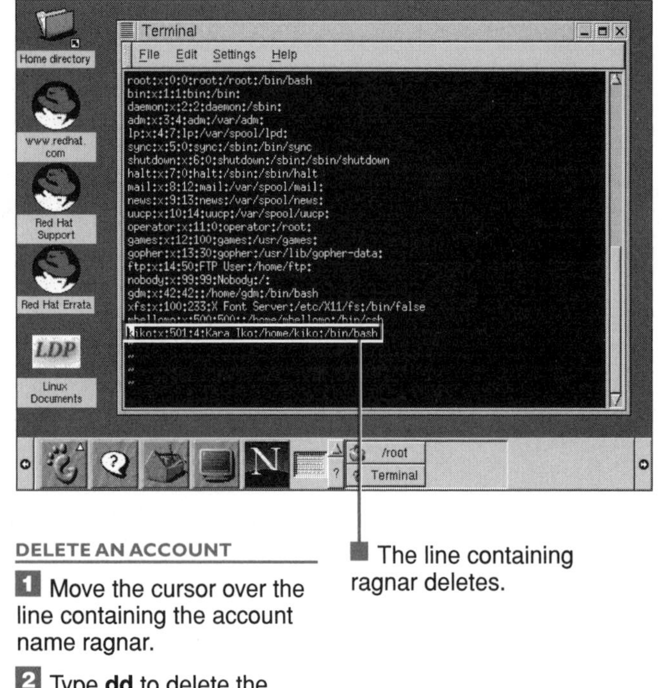

DELETE AN ACCOUNT

1 Move the cursor over the line containing the account name ragnar.

2 Type **dd** to delete the entire line.

■ The line containing ragnar deletes.

How do I re-activate an account?

- To do this, use the `vi` editor on the `/etc/passwd` file. Go to the password field and remove the asterisk. Don't type anything in its place. Exit and save your changes in the `vi` editor. Immediately have the user enter in a new password.

Why does the user have to enter a new password immediately?

- When you remove the asterisk in the password field, you are left with two colons side by side. To Linux, this means the field is empty, so no one needs a password for this account to get on your system! This is a security hazard to the first degree.

Why can't I type the new password into the /etc/passwd file?

- Linux stores passwords not as characters of the alphabet, but as code. The `passwd` command is the only way that Linux can properly translate your password into that code.

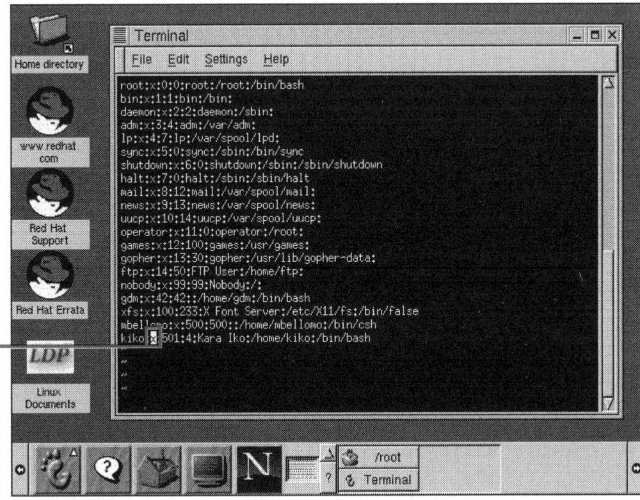

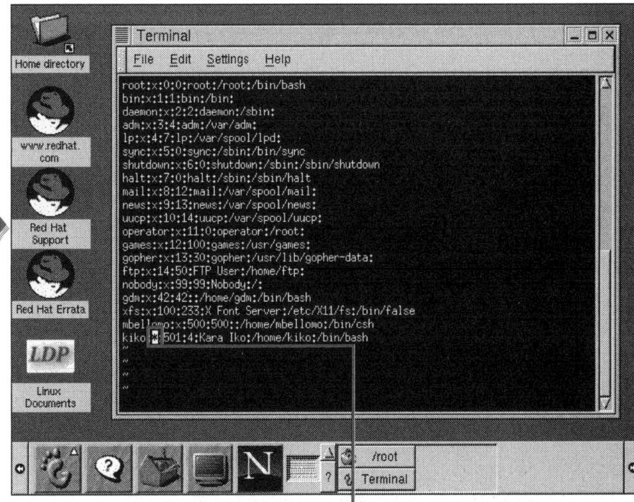

DISABLE AN ACCOUNT

1 Move the cursor to the second field in kiko's account row.

■ The fields in the `/etc/passwd` file are separated by colons.

Note: The password field for all accounts is an x.

2 Delete the X in the field.

3 Insert an asterisk in its place.

LIST USER GROUPS

You can use the LinuxConf tool to view the entire list of user groups on your system.

A *user group* is a logical collection of user accounts. As a user, you are part of a group of accounts that share file permissions, e-mail aliases, and probably the same slice of hard disk that holds data.

LinuxConf enables you to view this group information in alphabetical order in a friendly, graphic mode.

Note also that when LinuxConf lists all groups, it's not just listing groups that users belong to. LinuxConf is showing you all the groups, which may or may not have users attached to them.

For example, say you have a user group called games that has no users in the group. Just because there are no users in the group doesn't mean that the group ceases to exist — it's simply an empty logical container that you can place users into.

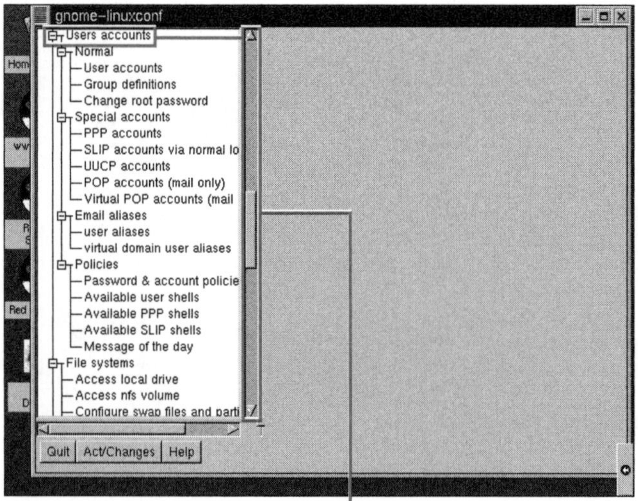

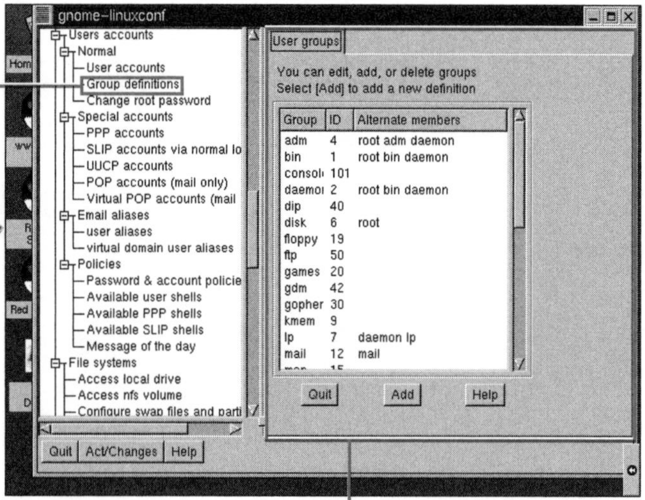

1 Open LinuxConf.

■ The gnome-linuxconf window appears.

2 Scroll down to Users accounts.

3 Click Group definitions under Normal.

■ The User groups panel appears in the right pane.

■ The last letters of the groups console and daemon are slightly cut off in the first field.

Can I list users by Group ID (GID) or Members alphabetically?

- No. LinuxConf's User Account panel isn't quite as flexible as its Microsoft Windows counterpart. To find where a group is listed, scroll down the alphabetical list in the Groups field to locate the entry.

I have some users listed like daemon. However, I didn't create this account; why is it here?

- Accounts like daemon, adm, and lp are automatically created during the Linux installation. Linux uses these accounts (sometimes called "dummy" accounts) to run systems processes and maintenance procedures like disk defragmentation. These accounts are sometimes parts of these groups and are listed in LinuxConf.

Can I name a group after a user?

- You can, but you shouldn't get into the habit of doing that. It causes you no end of confusion if you have to start remembering who is called what.

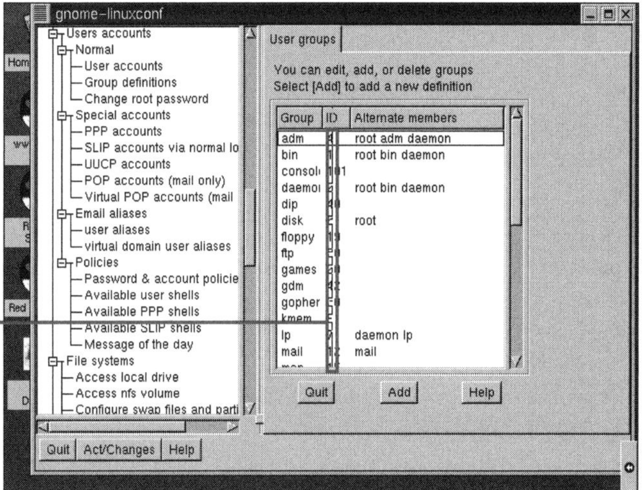

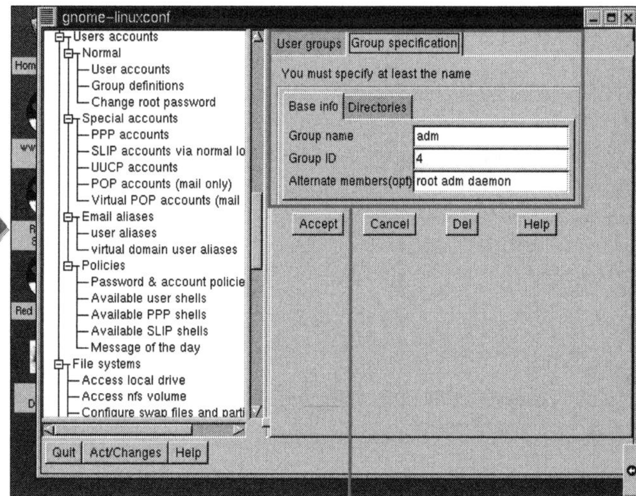

4 Drag the line that separates the Group field from the ID field to the right.

■ The new border is marked with crosshair to show you where it goes.

5 Release the mouse button after setting your border.

■ The other fields shift to the right to allow the Group column more room.

6 Click the name of a group.

■ The details on the user group appears.

ADD USER GROUPS

If you work on a network with more than a few user accounts, it is good to know how to add new user groups.

Creating new user groups helps you to keep your users organized. Normally, the root account organizes the groups by the name of their departments, such as Accounting, Marketing, or Research.

As with the majority of the functions in the Linux configuration tool, only the root user may add a new user group. After the group is created, you can add or delete members from it at your leisure.

No set ratio exists between users and user groups. Because user accounts are simply the method by which a user can log into a Linux system, a single user can have one or multiple user groups. Similarly, a group can have one user, two users, a million users, or no users at all — the logical grouping still exists and works just as well.

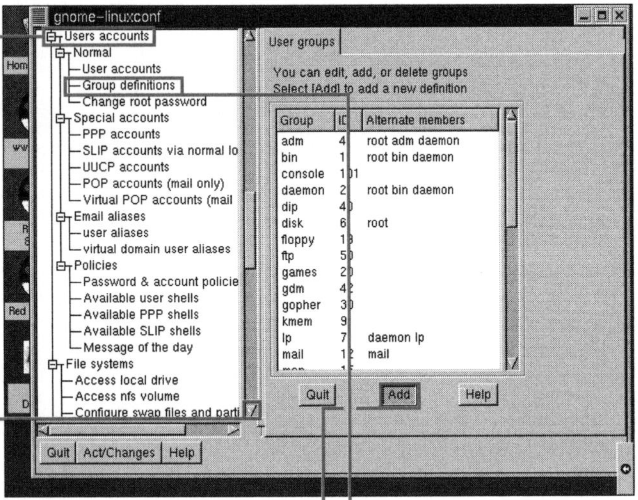

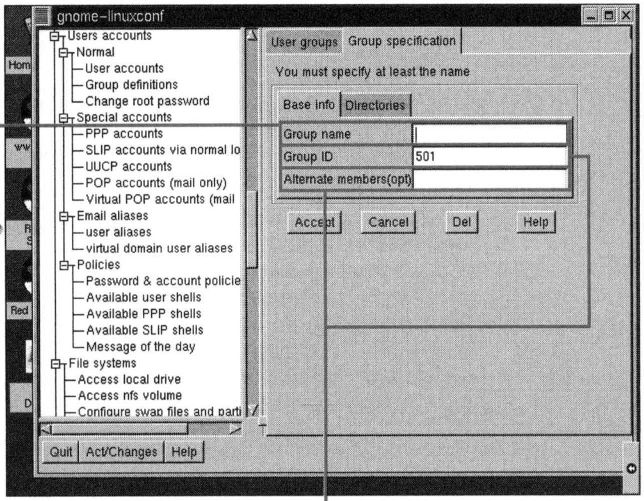

1 Open LinuxConf.

■ The gnome-linuxconf window appears.

2 Scroll down to Users accounts.

3 Click Group definitions under Normal.

■ The User groups panel appears in the right pane.

4 Click the Add button.

■ The Group specification panel appears.

5 Click the Group name field.

6 Type **accounting**.

7 Press the Tab key twice to jump to the Alternate members (opt) field.

8 Type **kiko**.

■ Linux assigns a unique number to the Group ID field.

Why is the root account part of several groups, such as disk, root, and wheel?

- These are groups that specifically relate to administrative functions. Root is placed in these groups to note this fact.

Should I delete groups with no users in them?

- As a rule, you shouldn't do this unless you're sure that *you* created the group. Having an extra group doesn't affect anything. Worse, you could end up deleting a group that's important to the system and really cause some problems. For example, deleting the lp group, which controls print functions, could leave you without the ability to send documents to your printer.

Which group should I select for my users?

- Most users should be put in the user group. The important point here is to never put users in the root group because doing so would give them administrative authority, which is not what you want on a secure system.

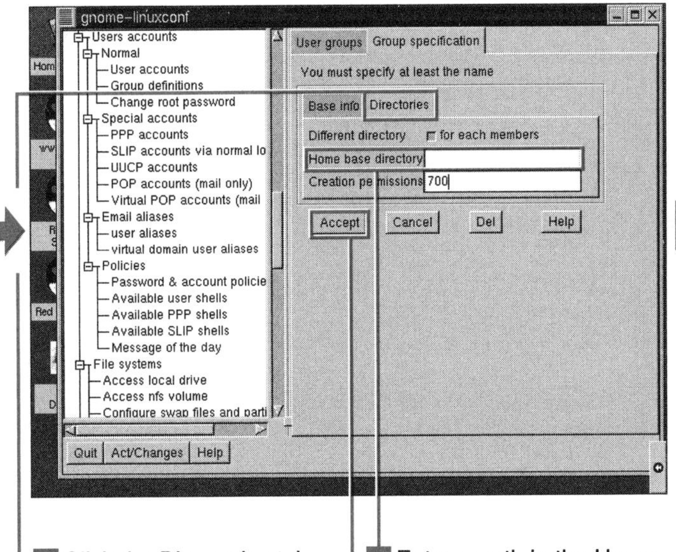

9 Click the Directories tab.

10 Enter a path in the Home base directory field to place accounting in a different location than the default.

11 Click Accept.

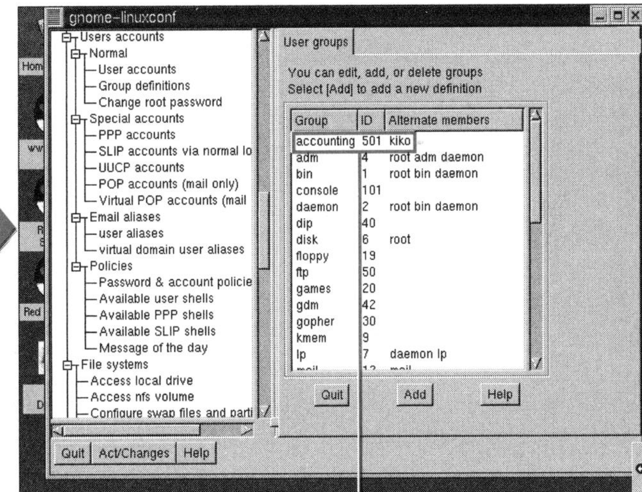

■ You return to the User groups list.

■ At the top of the list is accounting with the list of users in the accounting group — in this case, user kiko.

EDIT USER GROUPS

You can edit user group information from LinuxConf. Editing user group information in Linux is substantially simpler than editing user account information because you have fewer options to choose from. Also, you don't need to change basic group information on a weekly or daily basis, unless your organization is very large and is undergoing major changes.

Most of what you do with user group administration revolves around making minor changes to the user groups on your system. For example, if your company or university has eliminated the accounting or research department, you might have to change or delete a group name.

If you're reorganizing departments, you could end up needing to change the group's GID (Group Identification number). Most importantly, if your organization has gained, lost, or transferred personnel, you must edit the membership of the group itself. LinuxConf makes each of these tasks easy to accomplish.

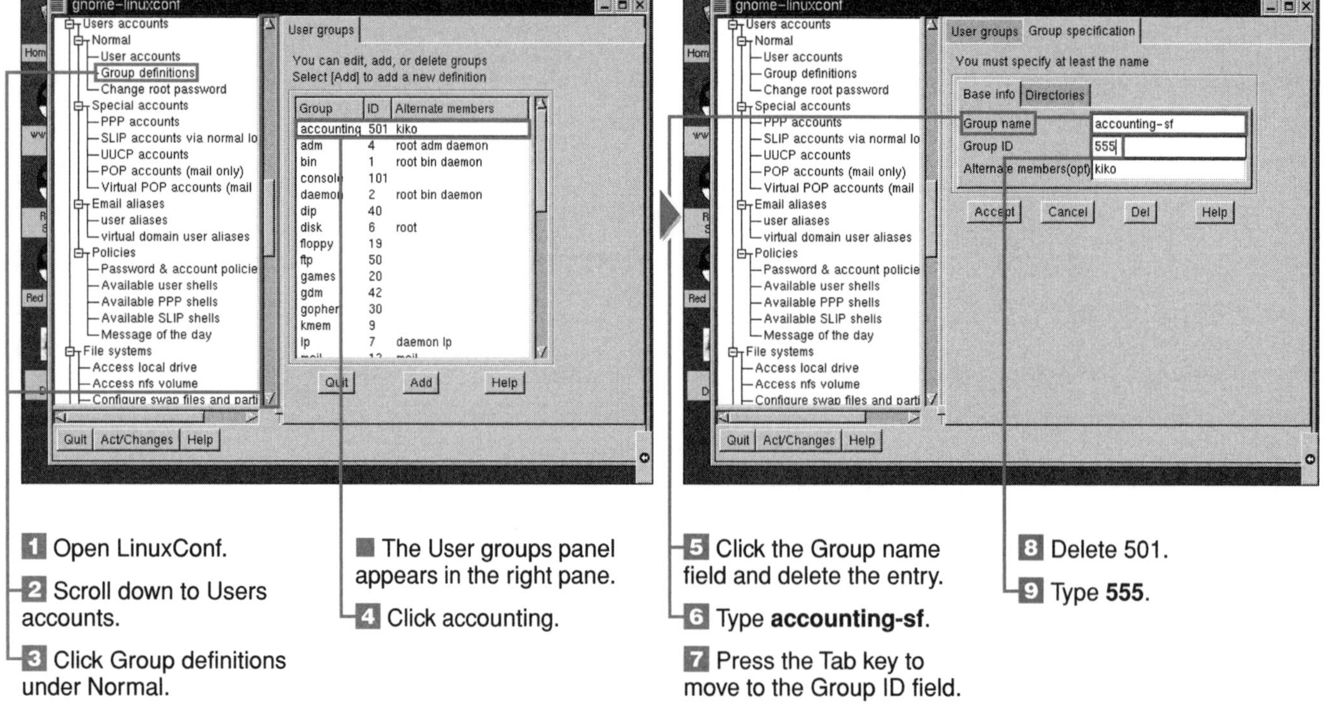

1 Open LinuxConf.

2 Scroll down to Users accounts.

3 Click Group definitions under Normal.

■ The User groups panel appears in the right pane.

4 Click accounting.

5 Click the Group name field and delete the entry.

6 Type **accounting-sf**.

7 Press the Tab key to move to the Group ID field.

8 Delete 501.

9 Type **555**.

How can I enable users on the system access to perform group changes in LinuxConf?

- Changing, adding, or deleting group memberships is a role that only the root account should have. Because it's administrative, you're better off performing this task.

Why would I want to add or delete a user from a certain group?

- In many cases, if you make one change to a file that affects a number of people, a given user should also be affected. For example, if you make the `account-data` file available to everyone in the accounting group, it doesn't help anyone who needs accounting data if they're not in the group!

Does adding root to a group give root permissions to all accounts in the group?

- No, the presence of root doesn't confer administrative privileges. However, you should keep other accounts out of the root group.

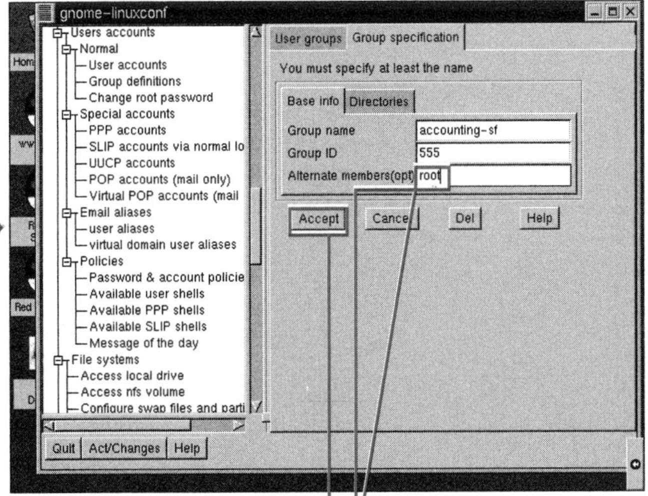

10 Press the Tab key to move to the Alternate members (opt) field.

11 Delete kiko.

12 Type **root**.

13 Click Accept.

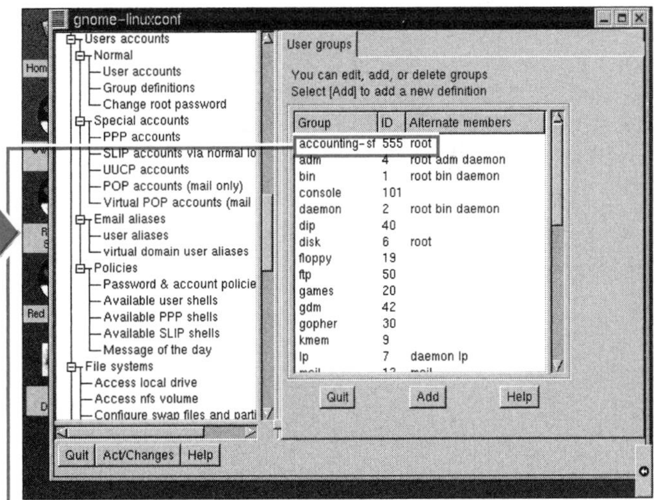

■ The changes appear when you return to the User groups panel.

DELETE USER GROUPS

Deleting groups from the User groups screen in LinuxConf is as easy as the creation or editing of user groups in GNOME-based Linux. However, you should delete user groups only in certain specific instances.

For example, say that you're part of a company that has two accounting groups — one in San Francisco and one in Los Angeles. Because the branch in L.A. is closing, you might consolidate accounting-sf and accounting-la into the plain-vanilla group accountants.

On the other hand, you don't want to use group deletion indiscriminately. For example, don't delete the group consultants just because your consultants have completed their tasks and moved on. Chances are that someday you'll need this group again if your company decides to hire more consulting services. You should delete a group when you have more than three or four groups that have no users in them. This prevents your `/etc/groups` file from getting cluttered.

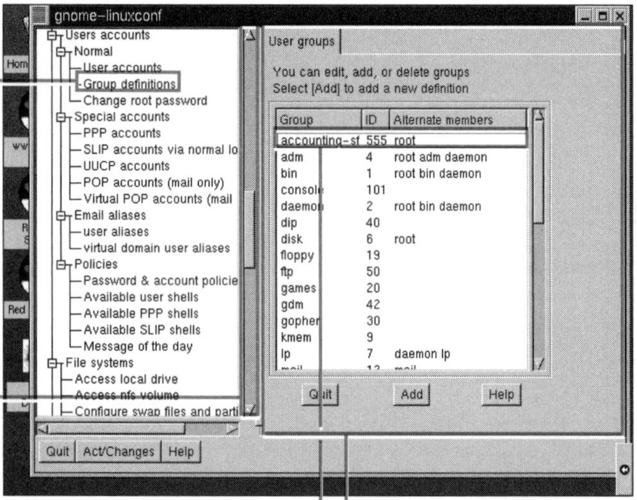

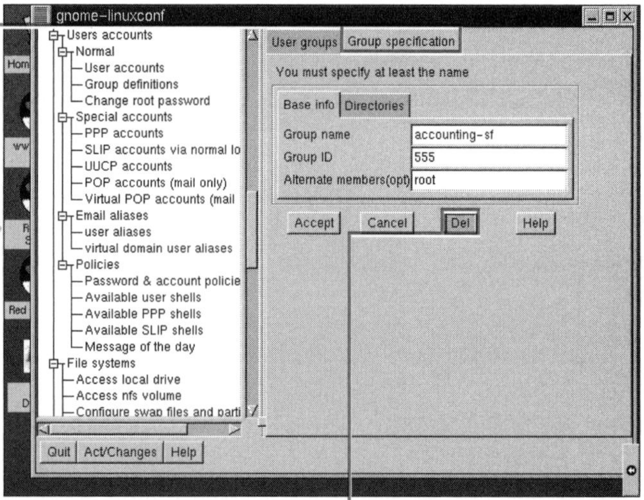

1 Open LinuxConf.

2 Scroll down to Users accounts.

3 Click Group definitions under Normal.

■ The User groups panel appears in the right pane.

4 Click accounting-sf.

■ The Group specification panel appears.

5 Click the Del button.

TIPS

Can you disable a user group the way you disable a user account?

- User groups serve a different function than user accounts. User groups don't contain actual data in and of themselves, so you can't put them into stasis the way you can with a user account. Being a logical grouping file, the best you can do is to delete it or leave it alone.

If I don't want to delete a group but I want to come as close as possible to disabling it, what can you do?

- Your best bet in this case would be to remove every user account that's in the group, leaving it empty.

What if I accidentally delete a group?

- You can't restore a user group — though you can re-create it.

If I delete a group, do I delete the user accounts in it?

- You delete the logical grouping of the accounts that make up that group. But don't worry, you don't delete the user accounts.

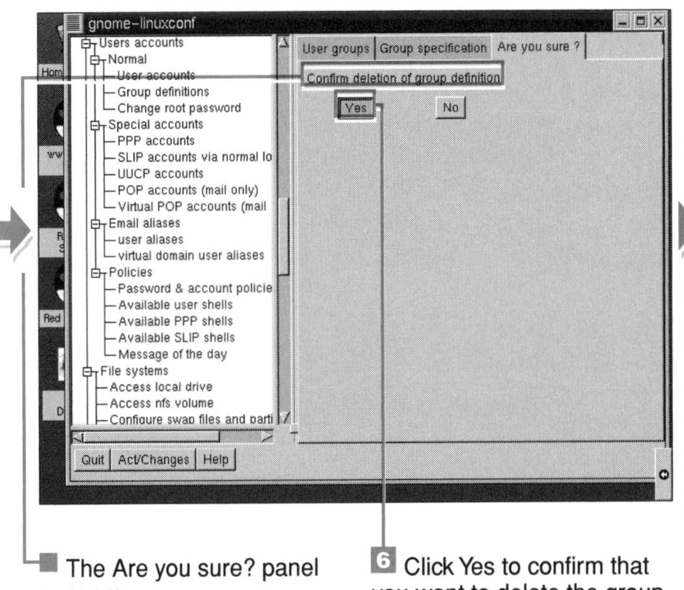

■ The Are you sure? panel appears.

6 Click Yes to confirm that you want to delete the group.

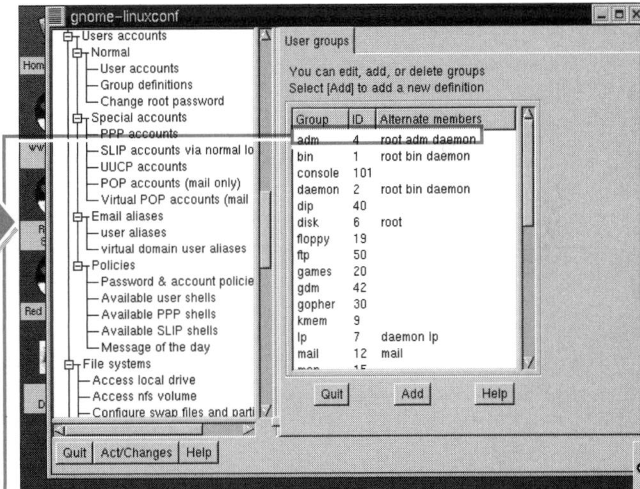

■ The group accounting-sf is deleted.

ADD USER GROUPS IN THE LINUX TERMINAL

You can add new user groups from the Linux Terminal.

Knowing how to perform the account creation task without benefit of the LinuxConf utility is a useful skill. For example, if you are doing work that requires you to be in the Linux Terminal, it becomes less convenient to switch between the GNOME GUI and the Terminal. You're better off doing the work in the Terminal proper and saving yourself some labor.

The Linux command for adding new user groups is `groupadd`. The `groupadd` command pulls the same default settings for group setup as LinuxConf. If you want to make changes to the group's ID number or membership, creating the group with `groupadd` and editing the user account afterwards is easier than changing the information as you create the group. Separating the two tasks is always a good idea because it reduces the chance that you may make an error during the add process.

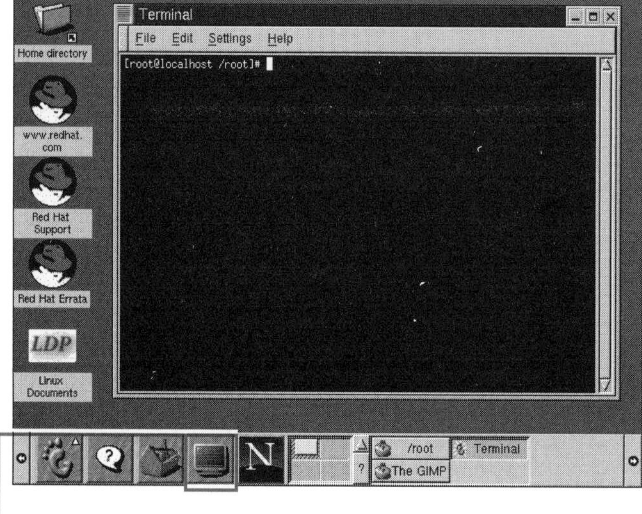

1 As root, click the Terminal button to open a Terminal window.

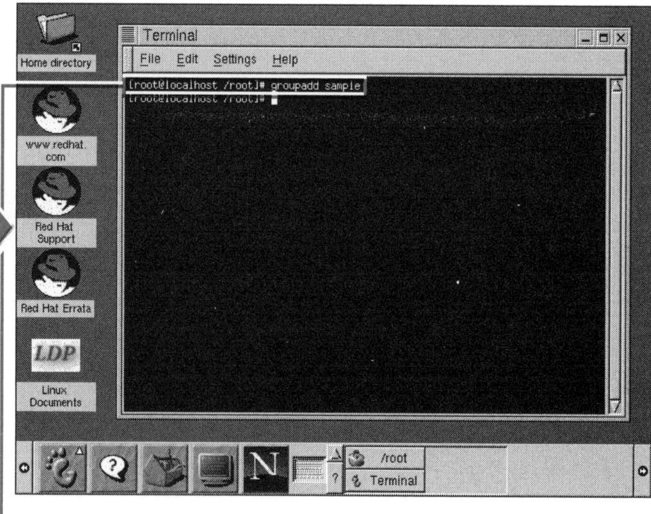

2 Type **groupadd sample** to add group sample.

3 Press Enter.

Who is placed in a new group by default?

- By default, no accounts — not even root, administration accounts — are placed in a newly created group. If you want to add users, see the section, "Edit User Groups in the Linux Terminal."

What if I don't want to add users but I want this group to own files?

- If you wish to add files to this group's ownership, use the **chgrp** command, discussed in Chapter 6.

Can I tell if the group creation process was successful by resorting to LinuxConf?

- If you want to stay in the Linux Terminal, you should view one of the files that Linux automatically edits when a new user is created. However, if you like the look and feel of LinuxConf, simply start it up as discussed throughout this chapter and you should see the group in the group listings.

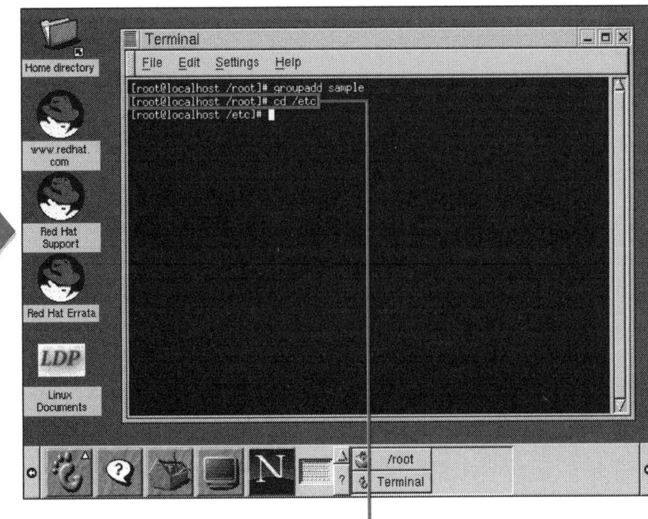

■ Check to ensure that the group has been created by changing directories and viewing the file `/etc/group`.

4 Type the command **cd /etc**.

5 Press Enter.

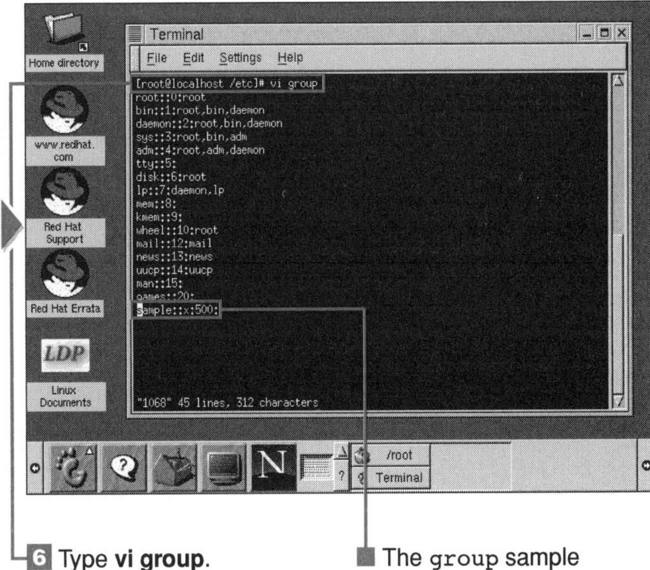

6 Type **vi group**.

7 Press Enter.

■ The `group` sample appears on the bottom line.

EDIT USER GROUPS IN THE LINUX TERMINAL

You should be able to edit groups in the Linux Terminal as well as in the GNOME interface. If you're already working on items in the Terminal window, you won't have the extra steps of having to shift back and forth from the Linux Terminal to the GUI system.

An additional bonus of learning how to edit groups outside of the LinuxConf tool is making your skills transferable. If you have a 100 percent Red Hat Linux installation at your site and you don't plan to ever move elsewhere, then this doesn't concern you. But if you go to a slightly different Linux system, the GUI-based LinuxConf may not be available.

Overall, a true Linux administrator should know how to use both a GUI and Terminal. Make sure that you remember the lessons from Chapter 7 on the `vi` editor, and you're ready to edit groups.

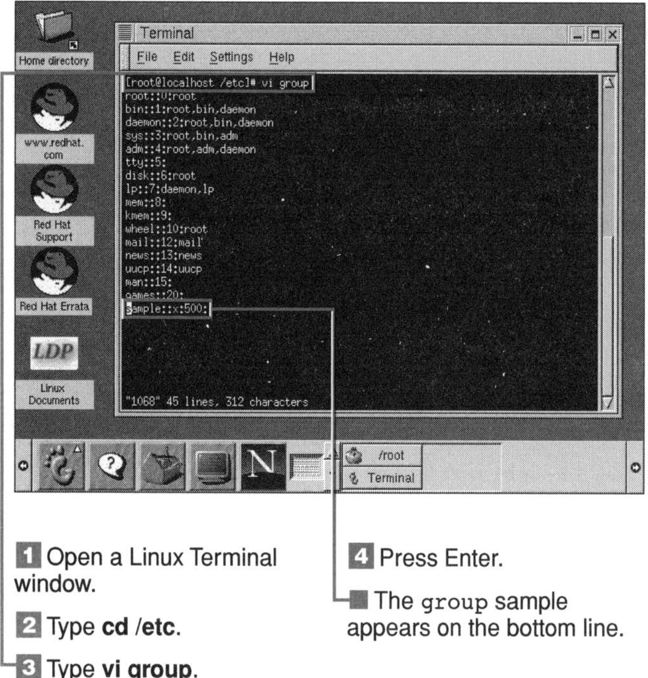

1 Open a Linux Terminal window.

2 Type **cd /etc**.

3 Type **vi group**.

4 Press Enter.

■ The `group` sample appears on the bottom line.

5 Move the cursor to the start of the bottom line.

6 Press X twice to delete sa.

If I don't see any users in groups, such as tty, ftp, and nobody, can I delete these groups?

- You should not delete these groups. All of these groups were automatically created when you installed Linux. While they may not have any members listed, they perform the same functions as system accounts in the `/etc/passwd` file — they help your Linux system perform routine, automated system maintenance.

Can I merge two groups in Linux if I just give each group the same Group Identification Number?

- Even though it seems like a good idea, you shouldn't do this. Giving two groups the same GID (Group Identification number) doesn't fool the Linux system into thinking that the groups are one and the same. Instead, you're likely to confuse the computer so that it ends up ignoring the users listed in both of the groups.

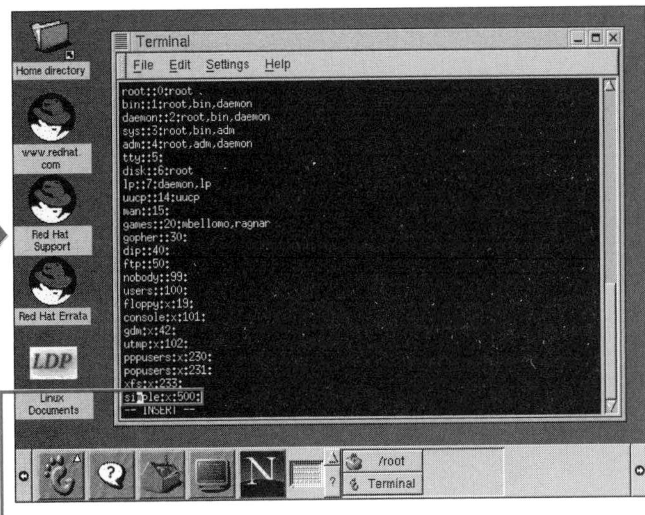

7 Press I to get to INSERT mode.

8 Type **si** to change `sample` to `simple`.

9 Press Esc to return to Command mode.

10 Move the cursor to the end of the simple line.

11 Press A to insert text.

■ Use an A instead of an I here to append text to the end of this line.

12 Type **mbellomo** at the end of the line.

■ The colon acts as a field delimiter, as it does in `/etc/passwd`.

CONTINUED

EDIT USER GROUPS IN THE LINUX TERMINAL CONTINUED

You should be aware that editing user groups in the Linux Terminal with the `vi` editor is slightly different than typing in the text fields of the LinuxConf utility. For starters, you must make sure that when you add multiple users to a certain group in the `/etc/group` file, the members are separated by commas.

More importantly, you have to make sure that no spaces lie between the two names and the comma. Where a properly formatted piece of text in a gnotepad+ or WordPerfect for Linux document might read as `kiko, mbellomo`, in the `/etc/group` file these two users should be entered as `kiko,mbellomo`. Linux does not interpret a space in the groups file as any kind of character at all. Therefore, when you use a space, Linux assumes that the list of users ends right at that point.

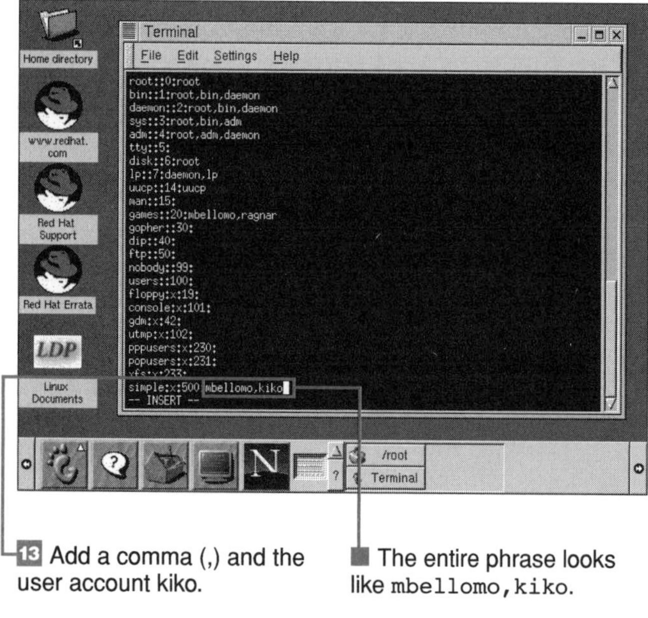

13 Add a comma (,) and the user account kiko.

■ The entire phrase looks like `mbellomo,kiko`.

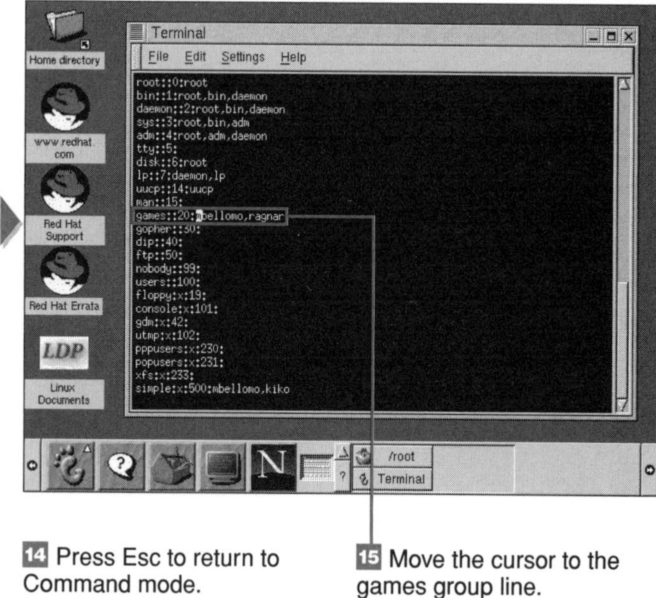

14 Press Esc to return to Command mode.

15 Move the cursor to the games group line.

16 Place the cursor over the m in mbellomo.

If I have multiple users in a group, can I separate them with a colon instead of a comma?

- Linux interprets the colon in the `/etc/groups` file as a field delimiter, while a comma tells Linux that the text after the comma is part of a list. If you separate users with colons, Linux assumes that it is supposed to ignore anything after the colon as not part of the same list or field.

What happens if I delete a user account but forget to remove the account from the /etc/groups file?

- If you forget to remove the account from the `groups` file, it won't affect your system negatively. However, you should take the time to go back and clean up the `/etc/groups` file every now and then so that it doesn't get too heavily cluttered with defunct user account names.

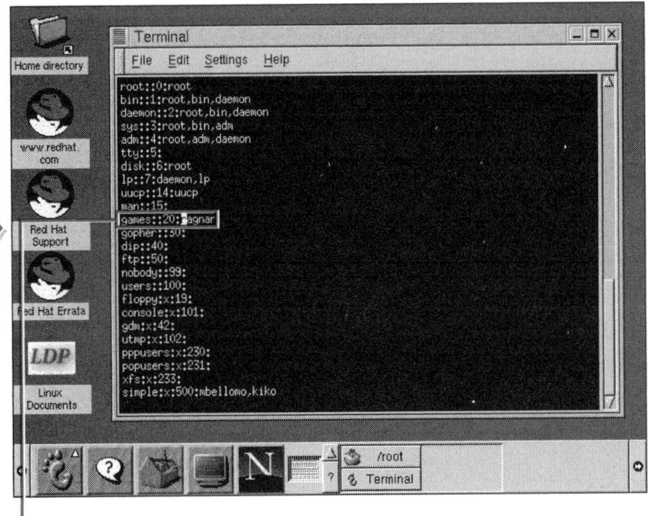

17 Press X until the word deletes.

■ Delete the comma between `mbellomo` and `ragnar`, but don't delete the colon, which is the field delimiter.

18 To save and quit the file, type a colon (:).

■ A colon appears at the bottom of the screen.

19 Type **wq!**.

20 Press Enter.

■ The `wq` writes (save) your changes and quits `vi`.

DELETE USER GROUPS IN THE LINUX TERMINAL

You need to know how to delete a group in the Linux Terminal as well as in LinuxConf. Working on the `/etc/group` file in the Terminal enables you to perform several tasks (such as deletion) more quickly than in the GUI, because a few keystrokes replace a half-dozen mouse clicks and window openings.

Knowing how to do this is also useful in case you need to perform repairs to the group file when the system is malfunctioning. If you're unable to get the GNOME desktop to work properly or if LinuxConf won't let you get to where you can edit groups, working in the Terminal is a useful advantage.

To complete these tasks, you need to use the `vi` editor. If you need to, review Chapter 7 on the `vi` editor before you begin to edit the group file, `/etc/group`.

1 As root, click the Terminal button to open a Linux Terminal.

2 Type **vi /etc/group**.

3 Press Enter.

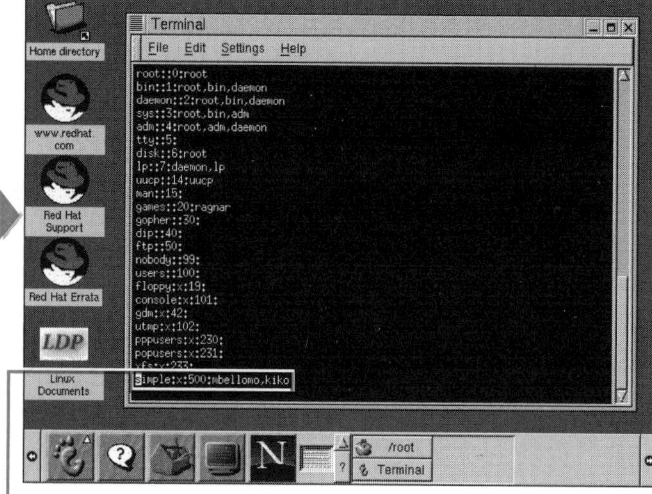

4 Move the cursor to the line containing the group name simple.

Is there any way to disable a group the way you can disable a user account?

- Not really. Groups and accounts serve completely different purposes because one is a gateway to access your system, while the other is simply a logical grouping.

What if I delete the entire groups file?

- Then your users are all groupless! Although this doesn't cripple your system immediately, as things continue to run, you are in serious straits. Immediately restore this file with a backed-up copy.

What if I don't have a backup of the /etc/groups file?

- Check to see if any copies exist locally. If your user groups weren't a big concern, at least restore the system groups (root, lp, and so on) by referencing a machine on a different network and `vi`'ing a new group file. In the worst case scenario, you have to reinstall Red Hat. Be sure to back up all files if you're going to that extreme.

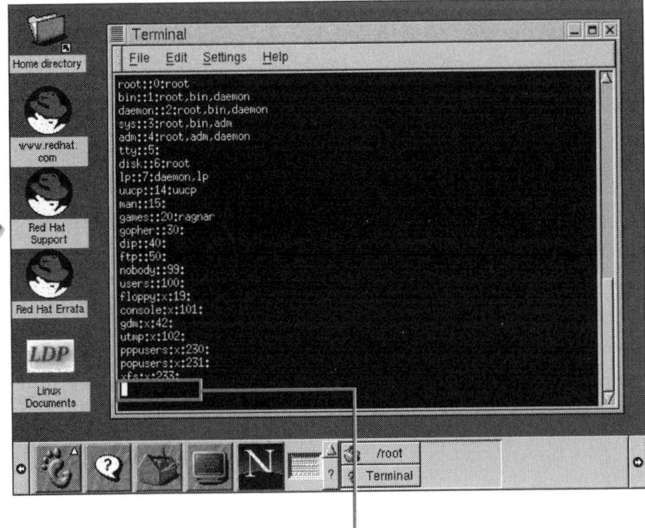

5 Type **dd** to delete the entire line.

■ The line disappears.

6 To save and quit the file, type a colon (:).

■ A colon appears at the bottom of the screen.

7 Type **wq!**.

8 Press Enter.

■ The `wq` writes (saves) your changes and quits `vi`.

SHARE FILES AND DIRECTORIES

You work with files and file systems constantly when you perform basic administrative or user tasks. To the Linux operating system, everything — graphic objects, directories, text — is a file. Because of this, all objects under Linux behave in roughly the same way.

Your job is to master the management, distribution, and mounting of file systems in your Linux environment. One of the most basic but important tasks you need to perform is changing permissions on files and directories. Although files themselves and the directories that contain them serve different purposes, when it comes to changing permissions to share them with other groups, they're exactly the same.

By sharing a file, all members of the group that the file belongs to can read and write to it. By sharing a directory, all members can read, write, and enter it.

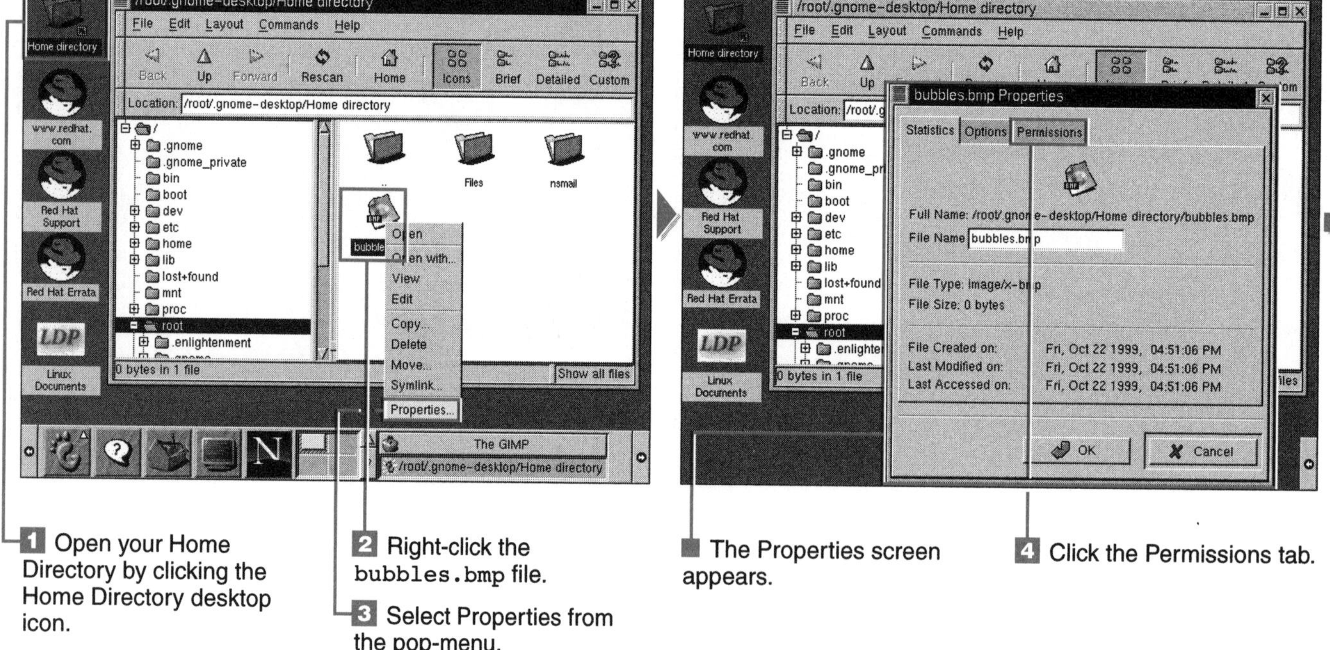

1 Open your Home Directory by clicking the Home Directory desktop icon.

2 Right-click the `bubbles.bmp` file.

3 Select Properties from the pop-menu.

■ The Properties screen appears.

4 Click the Permissions tab.

How can I double-check to make sure that the changes took place?

- Open a Linux terminal and `cd` to the directory in which the file resides. Type `ls-l` to get the full, long listing and permissions associated with the file.

How can I make a file executable with this method?

- Files that are executable are called *scripts* because they command the computer to take a series of actions depending on what was written in the script. Select the Executable button (labeled as Exec in the Permissions Panel) to make a file executable.

If directories are executable, are they scripts?

- Directories aren't scripts; they're special files in Linux that allow you to group other files or scripts underneath them. When you execute a directory, you move into its structure so that you can view other files beneath it.

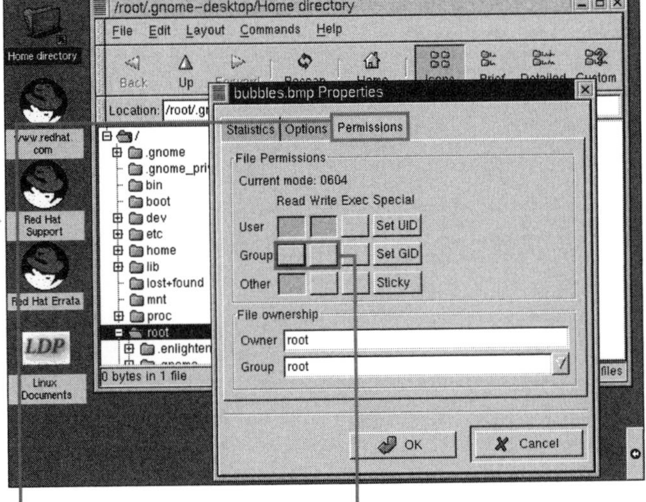

■ The Permissions panel comes to the foreground.

5 Click the Read and Write buttons for this file's Group settings.

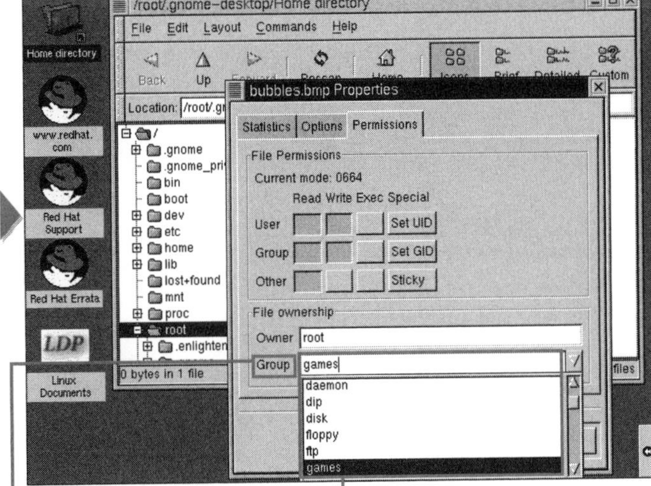

■ You can select the group ownership of this file at the bottom of the Panel, in the field labeled Group.

■ You can delete root and type a different group name in the field, but you can use a different method.

6 Click the down-arrow button beside the Group field.

7 Select root.

8 Click OK to apply the changes.

LIST YOUR FILE SYSTEMS WITH LINUXCONF

Your most important items to manage are the Linux file systems themselves. The file systems are the defining structure of your entire Linux machine, determining where the directories that reside under them are placed on the hard drive.

You'll either be manually setting these file systems on separate slices of the hard drive when you install Linux, or you'll be accepting pre-programmed system defaults. In either case, it's very helpful to know what files you have, where they're located, and what directories you have on each slice of your hard drive.

The easiest way to view these settings is to use the GNOME tool LinuxConf. If you've just read through Chapter 10, you're familiar with the use of this tool. If not, then you should be aware that this GUI-based tool is one of the most useful GNOME has to offer, allowing you to configure file systems, user permissioning, and a multitude of other functions.

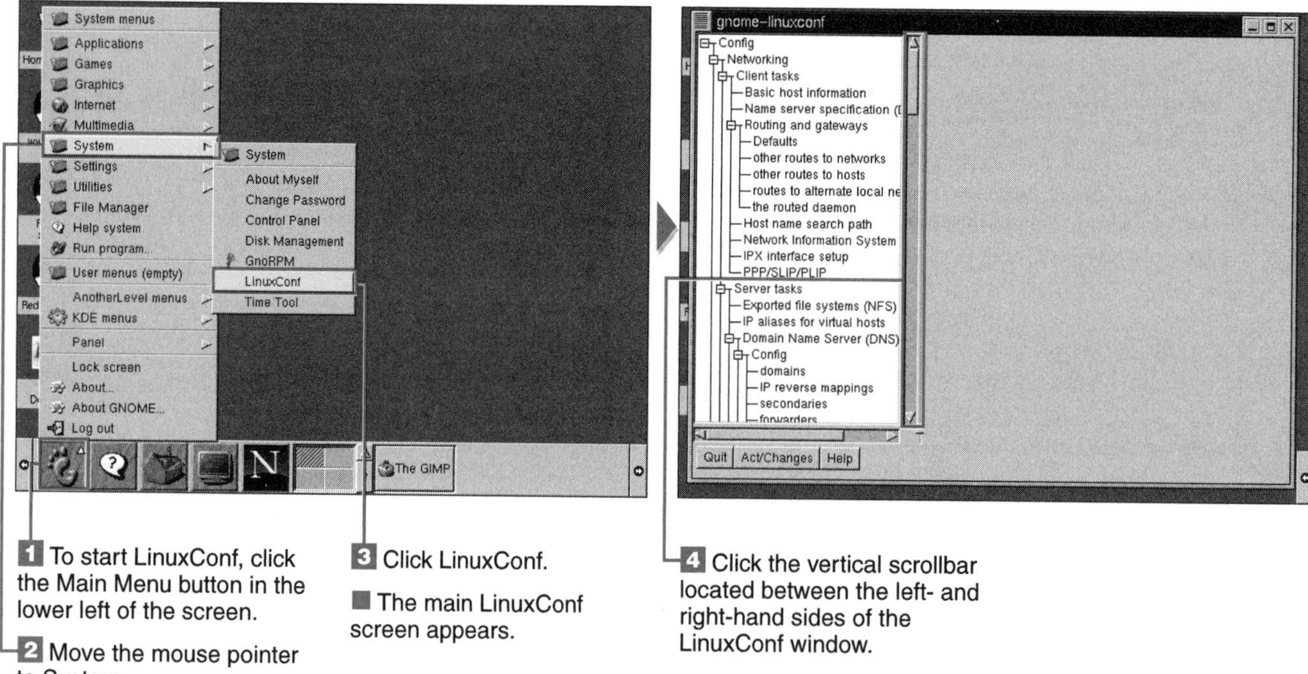

1 To start LinuxConf, click the Main Menu button in the lower left of the screen.

2 Move the mouse pointer to System.

3 Click LinuxConf.

■ The main LinuxConf screen appears.

4 Click the vertical scrollbar located between the left- and right-hand sides of the LinuxConf window.

How do I check what is mounted if I'm not using the Linuxconf utility?

- If you're in the Linux terminal instead of the LinuxConf GUI system, use the `mount` command. `Mount` shows all the file systems that are currently available to you. For example, if you don't see /dev/fd0 among them, you know that you won't be able to access your floppy drive.

If I'm not using the Red Hat CD-ROMs that come with this book for my Linux installation, do I have the Linuxconf utility to perform these actions?

- You may or may not have `Linuxconf` available to you. The `Linuxconf` utility is not unique to Red Hat Installations of Linux. Instead, you can use LinuxConf in any Linux installation that uses the GNOME envronment. This includes the latest releases of Red Hat and Debian, among other Linux releases.

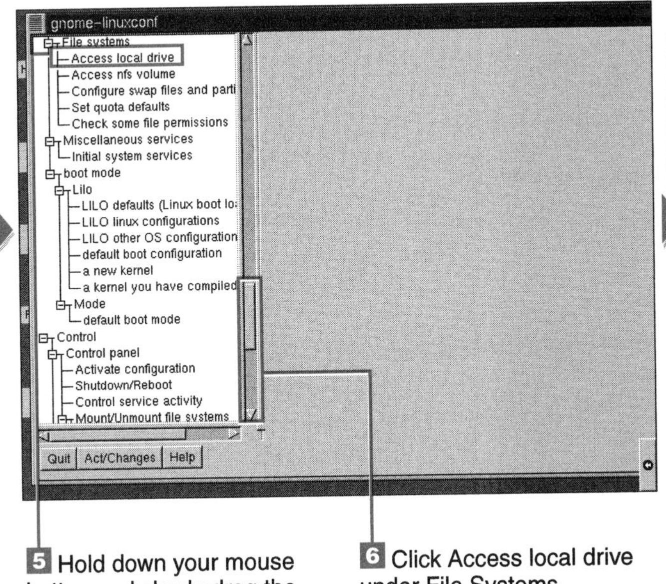

gnome-linuxconf

Local volume

You can edit, add, or delete mounts
Select [Add] to add a new definition

Source	Mount point	FsType	Size	Partition type	Status
/dev/sda5	/	ext2	768M	Linux(83)	Mounted
/dev/sda8	/home	ext2	258M	Linux(83)	Mounted
/dev/sda1	/tmp	ext2	23M	Linux(83)	Mounted
/dev/sda6	/usr	ext2	768M	Linux(83)	Mounted
/dev/sda7	/var	ext2	258M	Linux(83)	Mounted
/dev/fd0	/mnt/floppy	msdos			
/dev/cdrom	/mnt/cdrom	iso9660			
none	/dev/pts	devpts			Mounted

Quit | Add | Help

5 Hold down your mouse button and slowly drag the scrollbar toward the bottom.

6 Click Access local drive under File Systems.

■ The panel that opens on the right side lists the available file systems in detail.

DETERMINE ALLOCATED AND FREE SWAP SPACE

You can determine how much swap space — and how much you're in need of it — by using the System Info utility in the Linux GNOME GUI. Swap space is a portion of your hard drive that has been allocated specifically for swapping, or extra processing power, instead of holding file systems and their attendant files.

Swap space is used by your computer to gain a little extra power when it's under a lot of strain running multiple processes. When your system is being heavily used, with many users and multiple processes taking up a lot of memory, the system may begin utilizing the swap space.

While your system — particularly if you're on a stand-alone machine — may never need swap space, most networked systems should have a partition allocated to swap. Allocating the partition needs to be done during the installation of Linux, but for now, you can at least see how much swap space you have, and if you actually need to allocate more.

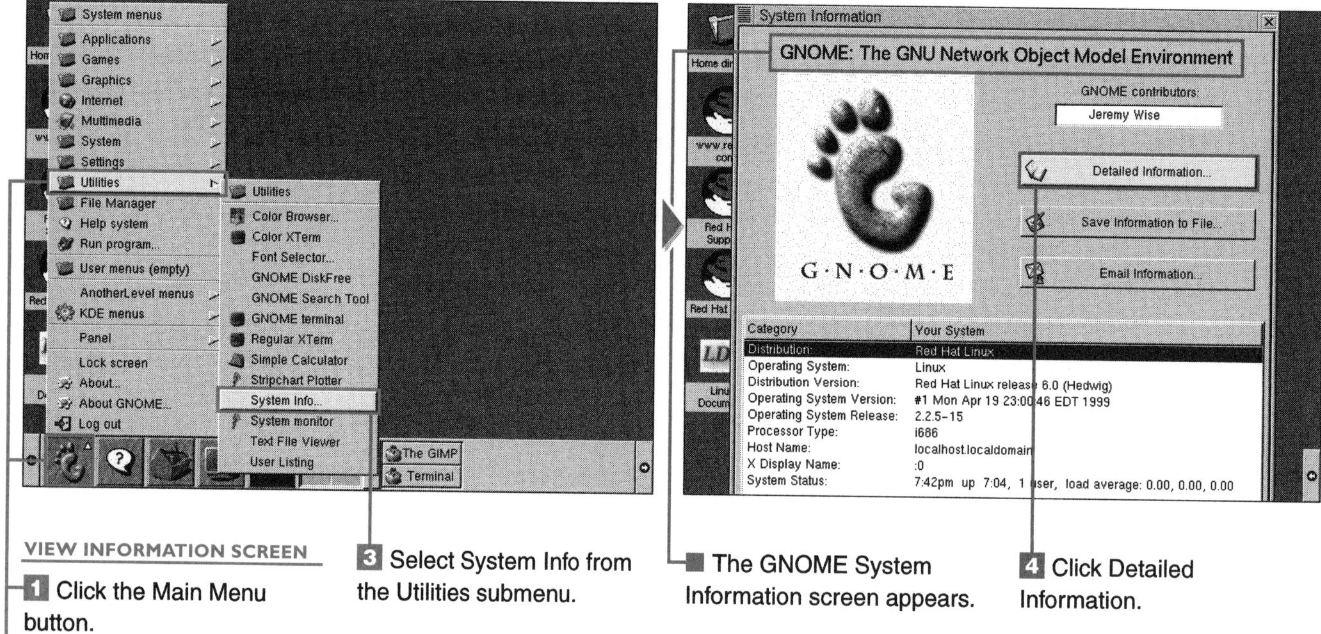

VIEW INFORMATION SCREEN

1 Click the Main Menu button.

2 Move the mouse pointer to Utilities.

3 Select System Info from the Utilities submenu.

■ The GNOME System Information screen appears.

4 Click Detailed Information.

In the above example, why did it look like the computer had no swap space?

- Because in the above example, this computer wasn't allocated any swap space at all! If you run System Info on any of your networked machines and see this situation, you should consider re-allocating space to swap.

Is it good that my system is actively using swap space?

- If your system is actively dipping into its swap, then you're suffering severe speed penalties as it accesses the hard disk for processes that should run entirely off the hard disk. So, if you're swapping regularly, consider adding more memory to your machine. (Add physical memory like RAM, not just more swap.)

When's the easiest time to allocate more swap space?

- When you install or re-install the Linux operating system, if you select a custom install, you can allocate space to all of your file systems, including a partition for swap.

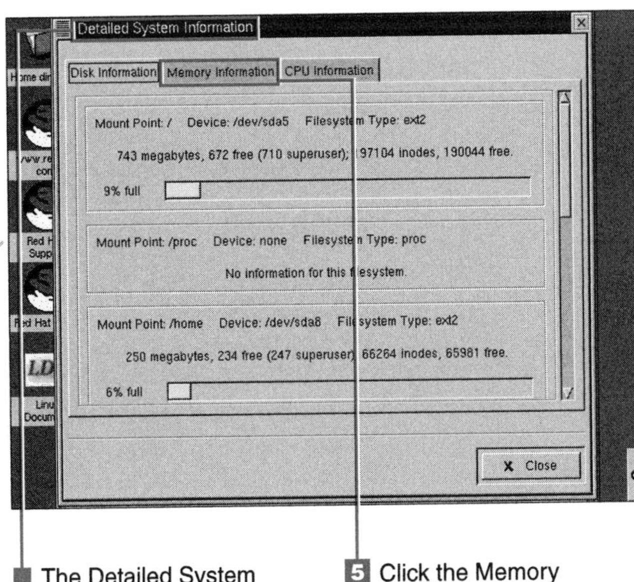

■ The Detailed System Information screen appears.

5 Click the Memory Information tab.

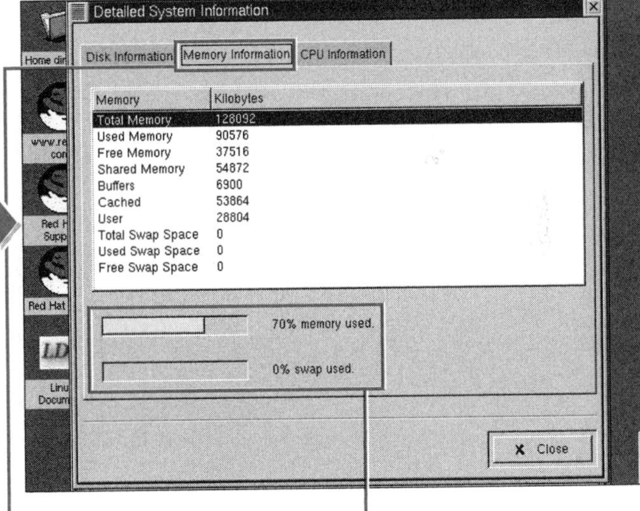

■ The Memory Information panel comes to the foreground

■ You can view swap information in two locations.

CONTINUED

DETERMINE ALLOCATED AND FREE SWAP SPACE CONTINUED

You can also determine how much swap space — and how much you need — outside the Linux GNOME GUI. If you're in the Linux terminal, you can get a similar readout to determine the level of swap you've been using and how much you have available.

When your system is being heavily used, the system may begin utilizing the swap space. You'll most likely notice the heavy swapping when users begin complaining that the system starts to bog down during peak times.

While your system may never need to use swap space, most networked systems do run into periods of exceptionally heavy use, such as when a user downloads a large file from the Internet. For that reason, you should be able to determine inside or outside the Linux terminal how much you need that extra margin of swap space.

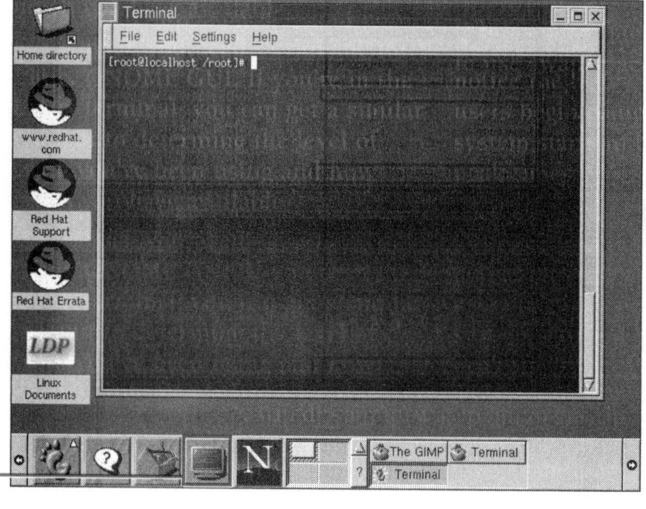

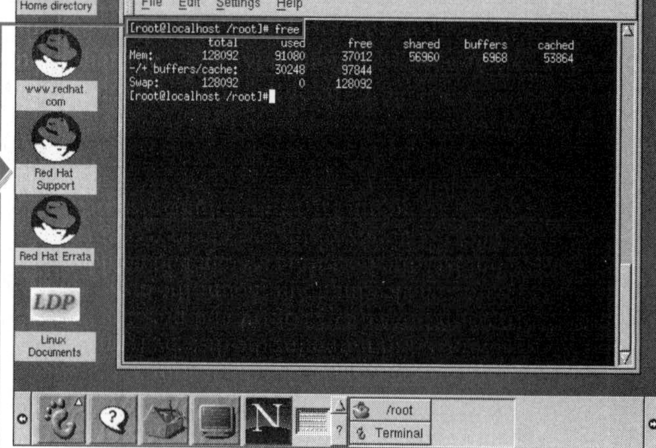

VIEW MEMORY AND SWAP NUMBERS

1 Click the Linux Terminal button to open the Linux Terminal.

2 As root, type **free** to view the memory and swap numbers in kilobytes.

■ *Total* is the complete amount of Memory (Mem) and Swap you have on this machine.

■ *Used* is the amount being utilized right now

■ *Free* is the amount of space left to use.

The free command is very useful, but why won't it work on my friend's computer, which runs Solaris, Sun's version of UNIX?

- UNIX, although it's a close cousin to Linux, is not 100 percent the same. To list swap space on Solaris, use the `swap -l` command.

If I'm running Linux on a mixed network of Linux and UNIX machines, does the 'free' command work on all of the machines?

- UNIX, although a close cousin to Linux, is not 100 percent the same. For example, if you wanted to list swap space on Solaris, you would use the `swap -l` command, not `free`. However, you can use `free` on any brand of Linux you work with.

How can I increase the size of the swap partition if I'm out of hard disk space?

- Swap space can't be created from nothing, so you'll need to either re-partition the disk and trim down a file system that is taking up unused space, or you'll have to add a new hard drive with more space.

How can I make sure that I install swap by default?

- When you install or re-install the Linux operating system, selecting the Automatic Install allocates space to all of your file systems, including a partition for swap.

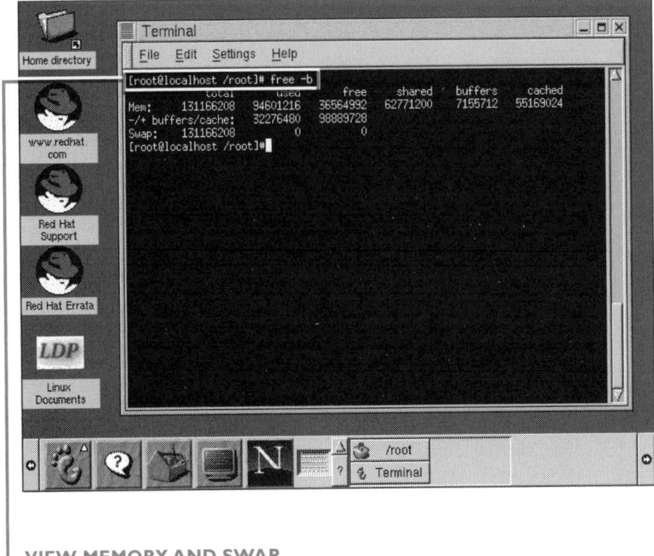

VIEW MEMORY AND SWAP NUMBERS IN BYTES

1 Type **free -b** to display the totals in bytes.

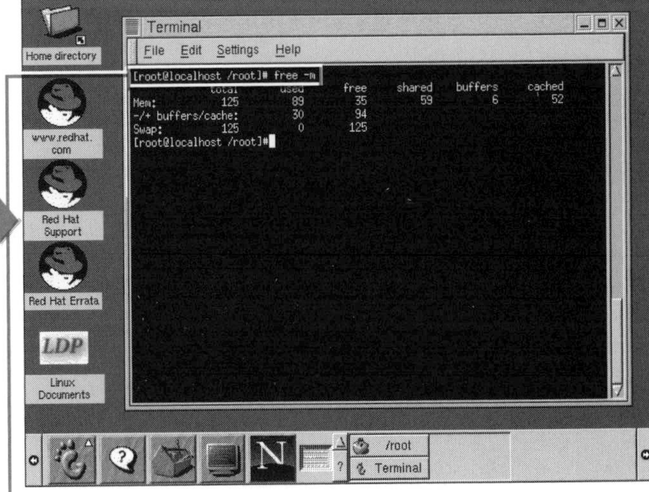

2 Type **free -m** to display the totals in megabytes.

CREATE A LINUX FLOPPY DRIVE

You usually have to configure the floppy drive on a new Linux machine. You have two choices when it comes to formatting the floppy drive. You can configure it to handle disks to transfer data from one Linux machine to another, or you can configure the drive to handle data that can be transferred between Linux machines, as well as PCs.

The key to this difference is the type of file system that you set up for the floppy disk drive. The ext2 file system can only be easily read by another Linux system — or a system that is running a varient of UNIX, such as Solaris or Irix.

Your best bet (for flexibility) is to configure a drive to handle both kinds of information. But if you only plan to store and transfer data between Linux machines, then this configuration is what you need.

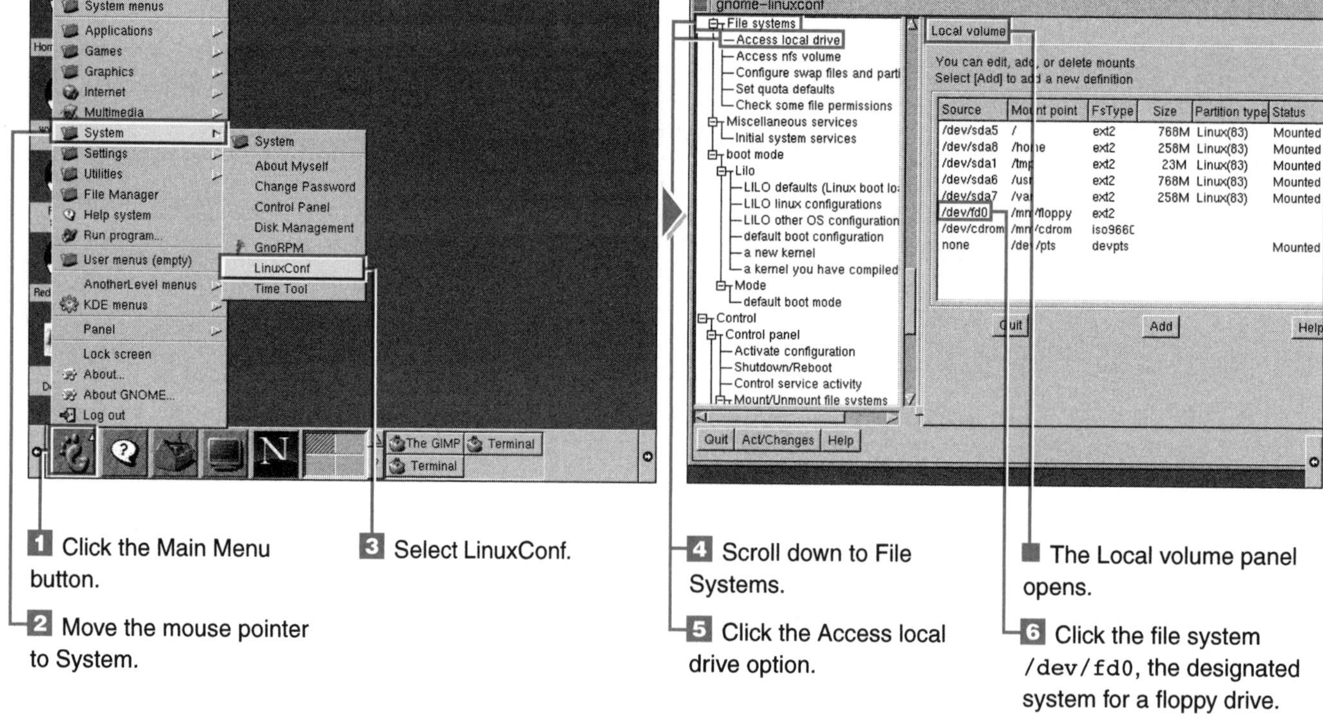

1 Click the Main Menu button.

2 Move the mouse pointer to System.

3 Select LinuxConf.

4 Scroll down to File Systems.

5 Click the Access local drive option.

■ The Local volume panel opens.

6 Click the file system `/dev/fd0`, the designated system for a floppy drive.

What are the advantages in creating a floppy drive to only handle floppy disks formatted with the Linux file system?

- There are two main advantages in creating a floppy drive that handles only Linux disks. First, floppy disks configured with the Linux file system ext2 can store slightly more data because of the design of the ext2 file system. Second, floppy drives configured to handle only Linux disks gain a slight speed boost, again because of the design of the file system.

If I configure the floppy drive to handle Linux-only disks and later change my mind, can I reconfigure the drive?

- Absolutely. When you configure the floppy drive to handle certain types of file systems on a floppy disk, the changes are not permanent. If you want to reconfigure the drive to handle PC-compatible disks, this task is described later in this chapter.

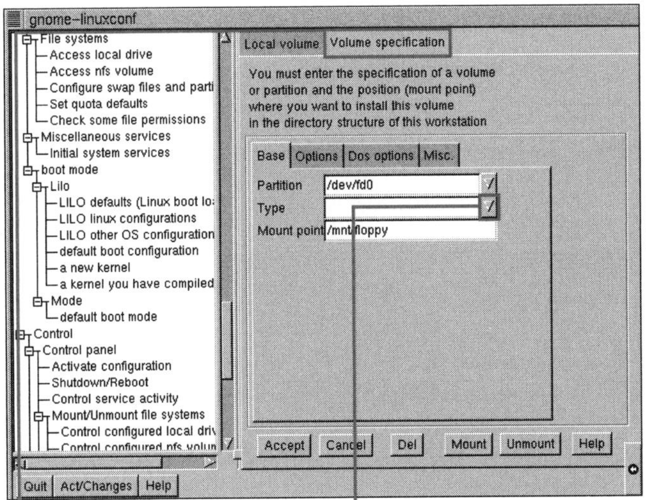

■ The Volume Specification panel opens.

7 In the Base panel, click the arrow button to the right of the Type field.

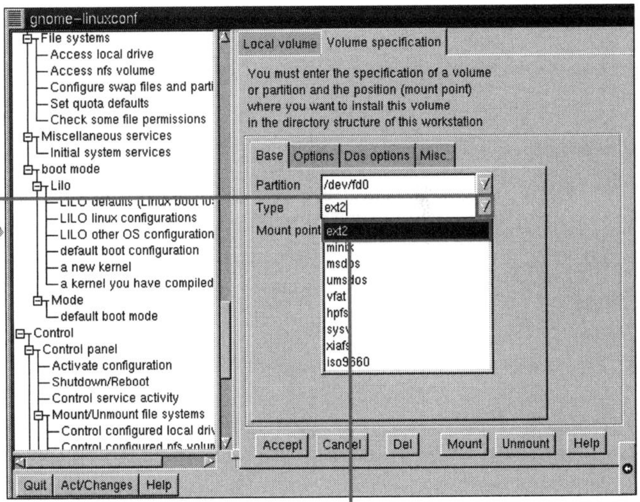

■ A new pop-up menu appears.

8 To make this drive handle Linux disks, select type `ext2`.

CONTINUED

CREATE A LINUX FLOPPY DRIVE

CONTINUED

You can also configure more detailed settings on your Linux floppy drive. In the `Linuxconf` utility, you can select the Options screen under the Volume Specification panel to select read options, user mounting, and whether the drive should be mounted when the system is restarted.

Be sure to turn on the Read Only option if you want to make sure that no one accidentally writes over information you've saved on a disk in the floppy drive. Read Only prevents you from copying data from the hard drive onto a floppy disk, even if the floppy disk has adequate space to hold more information.

This option is rarely used, however. Most of the time, you'll want to be able to save information or documents from your Linux machine onto a floppy drive to back up the information or to transfer it to another machine.

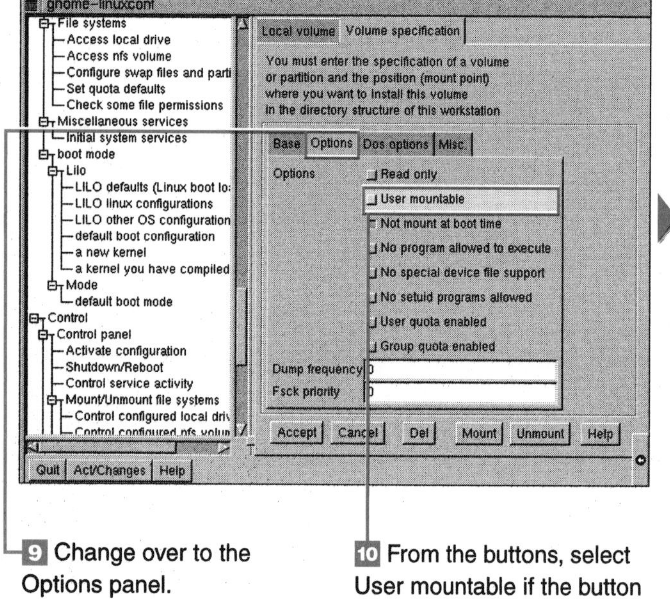

9 Change over to the Options panel.

10 From the buttons, select User mountable if the button is not already depressed.

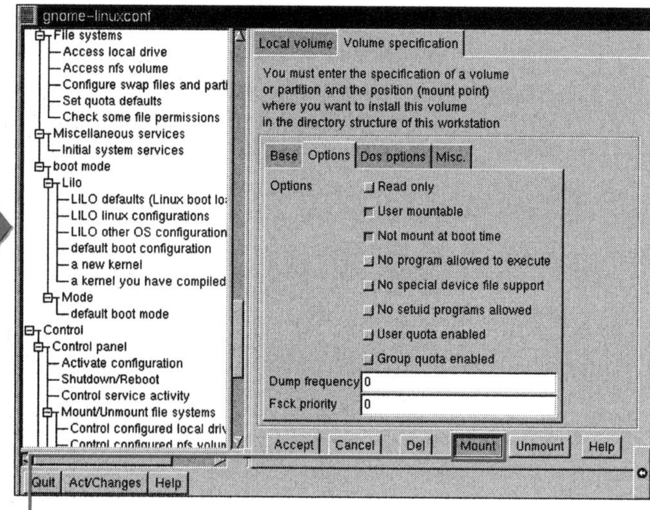

11 Click the Mount button at the bottom of the screen to mount this drive.

How can I format a floppy disk to be Linux only?

✔ Floppy disks in Linux, unlike for the Mac, are always readable by Linux, as well as PCs. However, depending on the format in which you save it, one system is able to read the data easier than the other.

Can I mount the floppy drive somewhere else besides /mnt/floppy?

✔ You can create a mount point anywhere you like on the system because a mount point — like everything else in Linux — is just a file. But be warned: Straying from the system defaults confuses the operating system and causes you more problems than you need. It's best to stick to the defaults.

Why should I turn on the user mountable option?

✔ This allows other users to mount the floppy drive instead of just the root administrative account. Centralizing control to the degree that requires you to be on hand each time someone wants to mount a drive is unwieldy and slightly ridiculous.

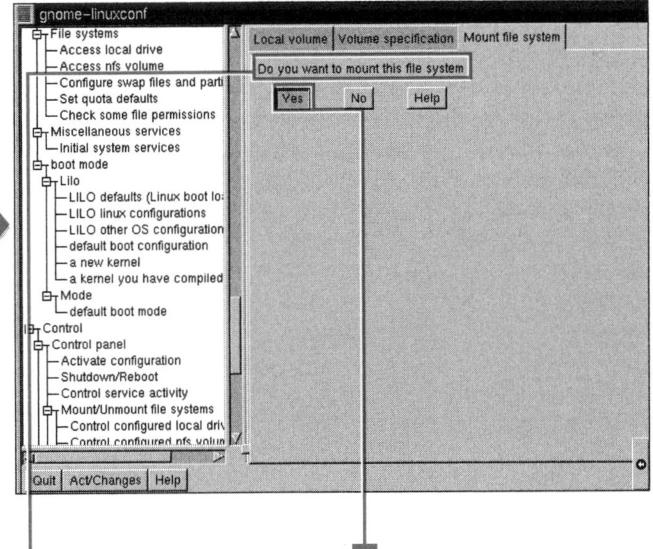

■ A new panel appears.

12 Click Yes to confirm that you want to mount this drive.

■ After the drive mounts, a confirmation panel appears.

13 Click OK.

■ You return to the Local Volume panel, where `/dev/fd0` is listed as mounted.

CREATE A DOS FLOPPY DRIVE

As mentioned in the preceding section, your second option when configuring your Linux machine's floppy drive is to make it an msdos file system. The msdos file system's chief advantage is that files saved under this system can be easily transferred between Linux machines and PCs.

For a floppy drive to be most useful to a PC, it should be based on msdos, the precursor and base program of Microsoft Windows for Workgroups, 3.1, 95, 98, and NT. This is why an msdos floppy drive is best suited to reading and storing information on disks that can be read on both PCs and Linux machines. You can format disks yourself to handle the msdos file system, or you can purchase them preformatted to use the msdos file system.

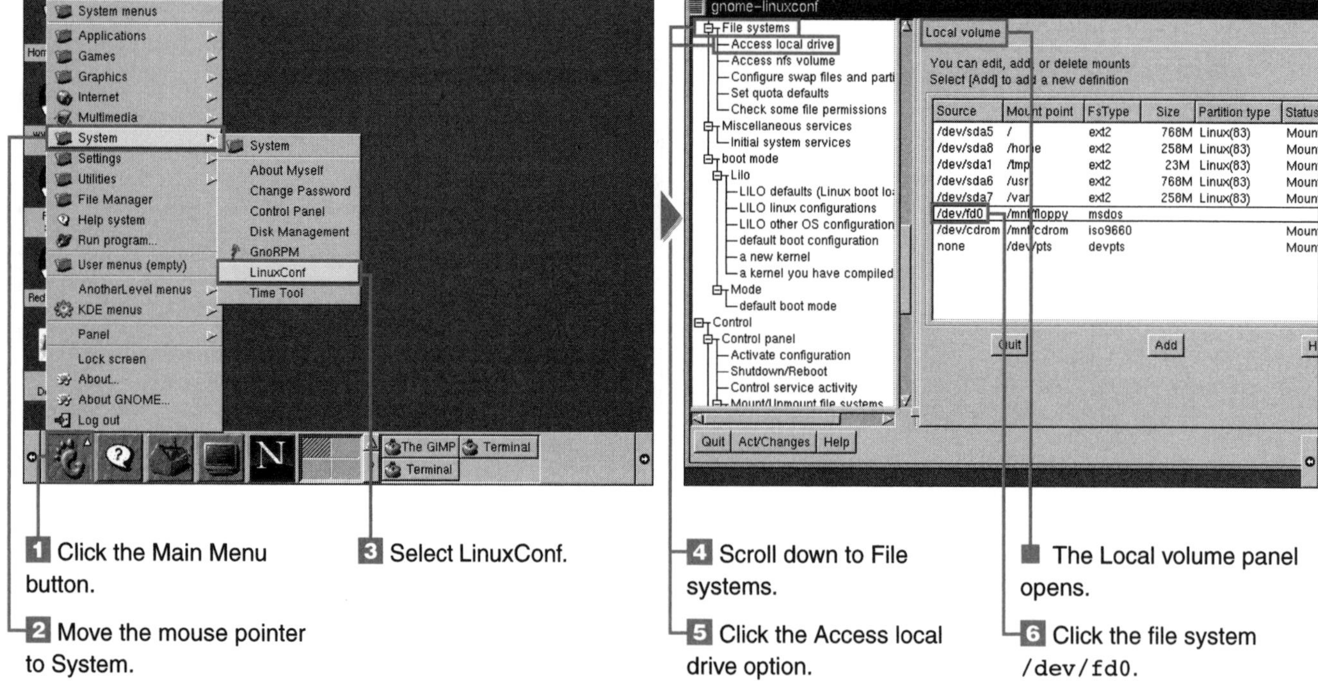

1 Click the Main Menu button.

2 Move the mouse pointer to System.

3 Select LinuxConf.

4 Scroll down to File systems.

5 Click the Access local drive option.

■ The Local volume panel opens.

6 Click the file system `/dev/fd0`.

TIPS

I just bought a new external hard drive. Can I hook it up and mount it?

- You can't mount an external drive — or an internal one, for that matter — until the system sees and recognizes it. Installing new hardware should always be considered a major upgrade. If you're running a Linux network and the machine is a server of some sort, first notify your user community; then set aside downtime to hook the drive up and re-boot the machine so that the start-up processes can detect it.

What should I do when the drive refuses to mount?

- Occasionally, the GUI system insists that it has done the deed although you still can't access the drive. Check to make sure that you have a disk in the drive and that the drive is functioning normally. If so, then try and bypass the GUI by mounting the drive from the Linux terminal.

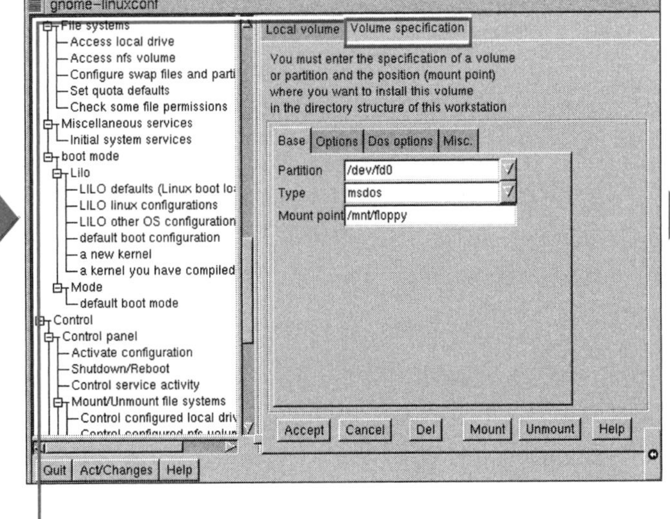

■ The Volume specification panel opens.

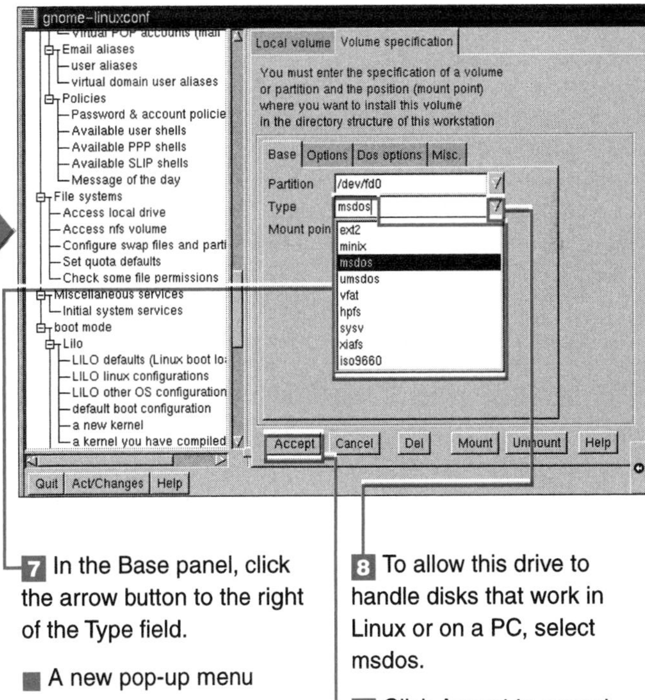

7 In the Base panel, click the arrow button to the right of the Type field.

■ A new pop-up menu appears.

8 To allow this drive to handle disks that work in Linux or on a PC, select msdos.

9 Click Accept to accept your changes.

MOUNT THE FLOPPY DRIVE FROM THE LINUX TERMINAL

After your drive has been configured to run either as a Linux-only file system or as a PC-compatible msdos drive, you need to mount the drive to use it. Although you can do this easily with the Linux GNOME tools, such as the GUI-based Disk Manager, you can also do this from the Linux terminal.

Knowing how to mount the drive from the Linux terminal saves you time if you happen to already be working in the Linux terminal. In addition, less advanced versions of Linux or UNIX are still GUI-free, so you need to know how to mount drives if you happen to be working on such a system.

To perform mount functions in the Linux terminal, you'll be using the `mount` command. This command is one of the most basic in all of UNIX or Linux and is found on all systems.

1 Click the Terminal button to open a Linux Terminal.

2 At the command prompt, type **mount**.

- This list of mounted systems appears.
- You should see all of your major systems, but not `/dev/fd0`, your floppy drive.

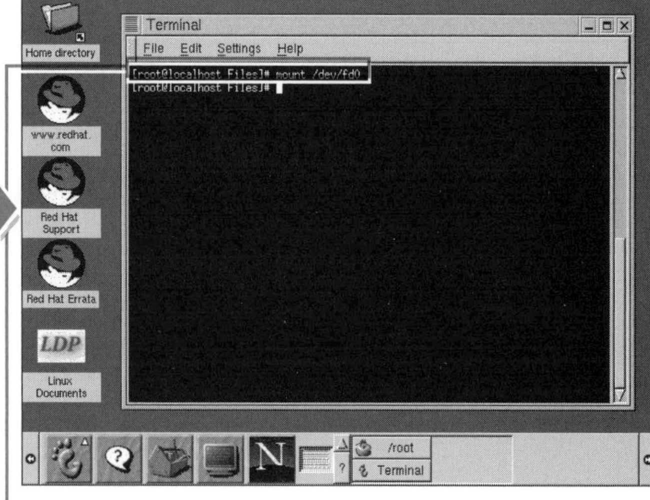

3 Insert a floppy disk into your disk drive.

4 At the command prompt, type **mount /dev/fd0**.

5 Press Enter.

Should I unmount the drive when I remove the disk?

- Yes. Unlike the Microsoft Windows system where disks can be popped in and out at will, you always need to unmount the floppy drive before removing the disk. In the Linux terminal, use the `umount` command to unmount the disk by typing `umount /mnt/floppy` and pressing Enter. Neglecting to unmount the disk confuses the operating system and could affect the ability of the system to recognize a disk to mount later on. A hung disk drive is no fun matter.

What if I want to hook up a Zip drive to my Linux machine?

- Reports vary: Some say that Zip drives can be configured like any other piece of hardware. However, it is also likely that your Linux machine won't have the right drivers to interface with the Zip drive.

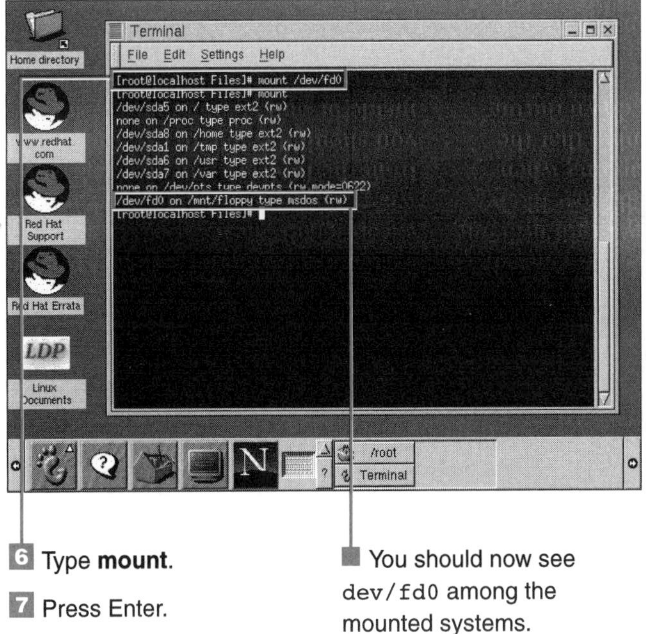

6 Type **mount**.

7 Press Enter.

■ You should now see `dev/fd0` among the mounted systems.

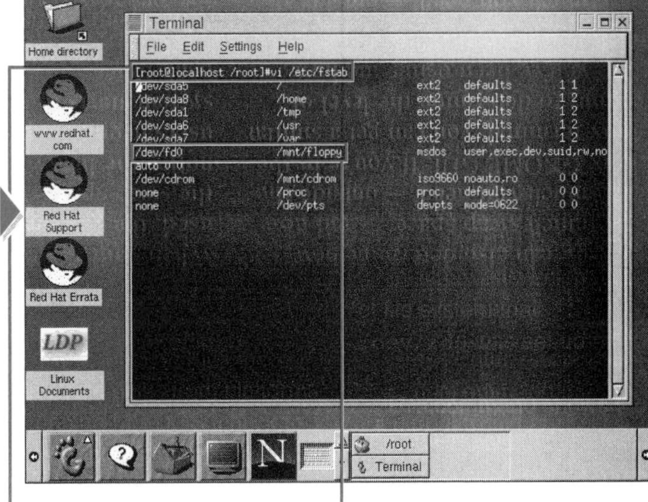

■ If you have problems reading disks from platforms running MS-DOS, check to see what kind of file system `/dev/fd0` is set to.

8 Type **vi /etc/fstab**.

9 Press Enter.

■ This command shows the contents of your file system table. Linux lists which types of file system that `/dev/fd0` was set up as.

READ FROM THE FLOPPY DISK

You can view files, directories, and information on a floppy disk from the Linux GNOME interface with ease. It's actually easier to view the contents of a floppy disk from GNOME than from a Linux Terminal because GNOME can present the contents of the floppy disk graphically.

One quirk to keep in mind is that in Linux, the location of the mount point for a floppy disk can be quite different from where you would actually copy files from the hard drive to the floppy. *A mount point* is simply an area where the machine recognizes that the floppy disk exists.

The file system location of the mount point for a floppy is `/mnt/floppy`. However, if you search for readable files on the floppy, you'll find them located at `/mnt/floppy` or, in some cases, at `/mnt/msdos`.

Because of this, when you perform a `mount` command in the Linux terminal to determine whether the floppy is mounted, you see `/dev/fd0`, not `/mnt/floppy`.

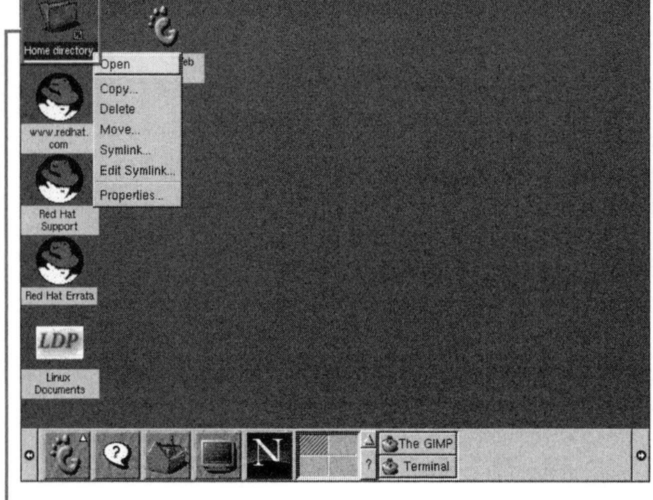

1 Double-click your Home Directory icon on your desktop.

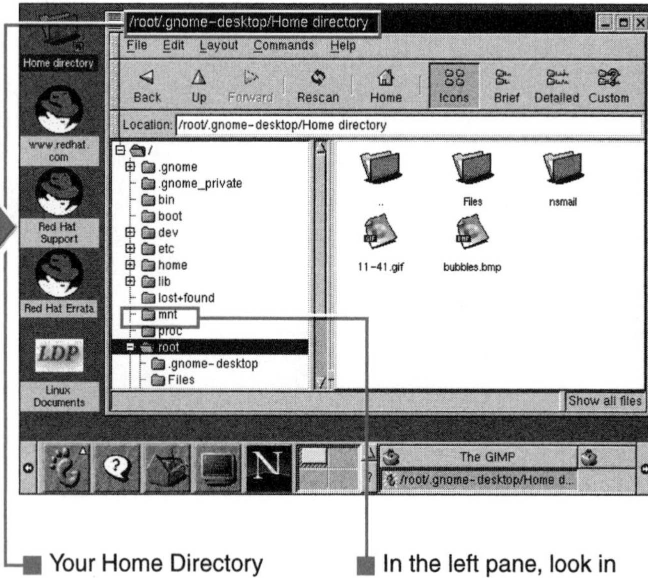

■ Your Home Directory appears.

■ In the left pane, look in the directory tree for `mnt`.

How can I display the files on my floppy more compactly so I can see them all?

✔ The method of file display from a floppy is controlled by your Monitor display, not the floppy. Use the display controls in the floppy's Window the same way you'd use it for your home directory. Set the display to List or Small Icons, and you'll get more space.

Why can't I locate the files off my floppy disk at /mnt/floppy?

✔ If the disk is in the drive and appears to be properly mounted, look in `/mnt/msdos`. On some systems, when allocating the floppy drive to the msdos system, a separate directory is created for msdos disks, as opposed to Linux system disks. Clicking the **`msdos`** directory will likely turn up the files.

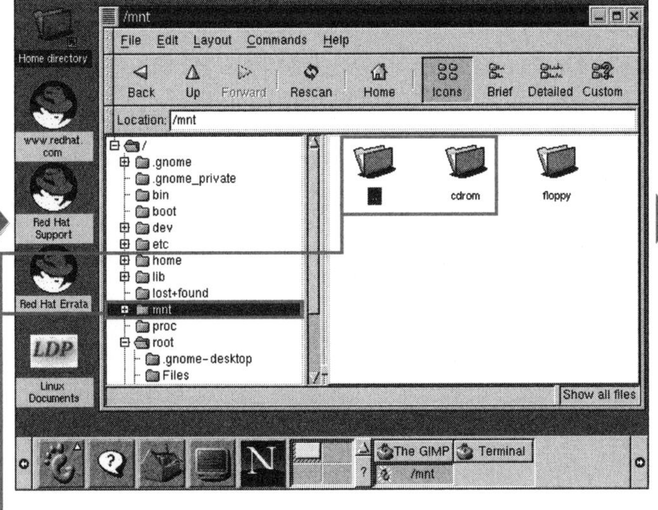

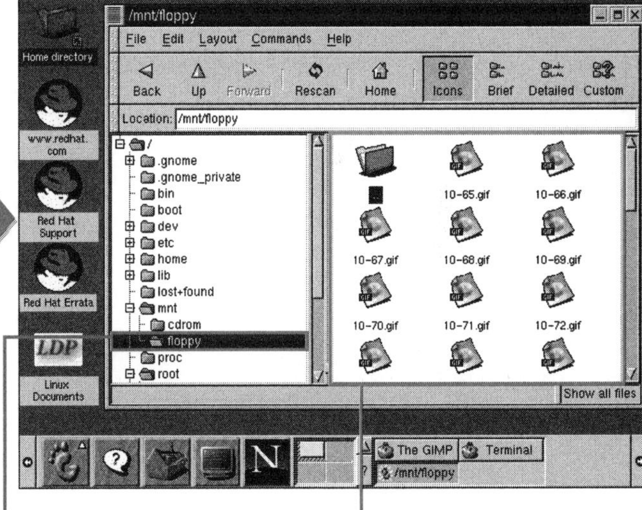

2 Click `mnt`.

■ In the right-hand pane display, you'll typically have two folder icons.

3 Insert a floppy disk in the drive, mounting according to the instructions in this chapter.

4 Click the floppy folder icon.

■ If the disk is mounted and you have files inside, the files display graphically.

COPY FILES TO THE FLOPPY DISK

You can copy files to the floppy disk for transporting data to machines that aren't on your Linux network, or you can copy files to a floppy as a simple, efficient form of backup as long as you don't need to save more than a single megabyte of data. When you start stacking up the floppies, it's time to invest in a tape drive.

You can select a file to copy with a single click. If you want to select a whole range of files to copy at one time and they're in the same directory, simply click and drag the mouse over the entire group of files you want to copy. You'll be able to easily tell which files are selected because they'll be highlighted. After you select the files, you can copy them to the location you want.

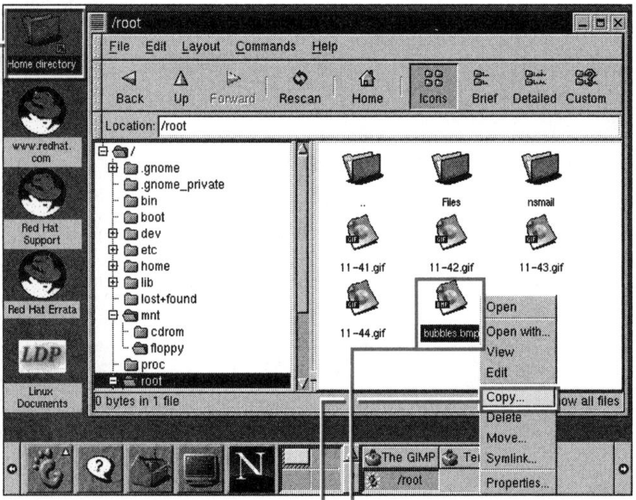

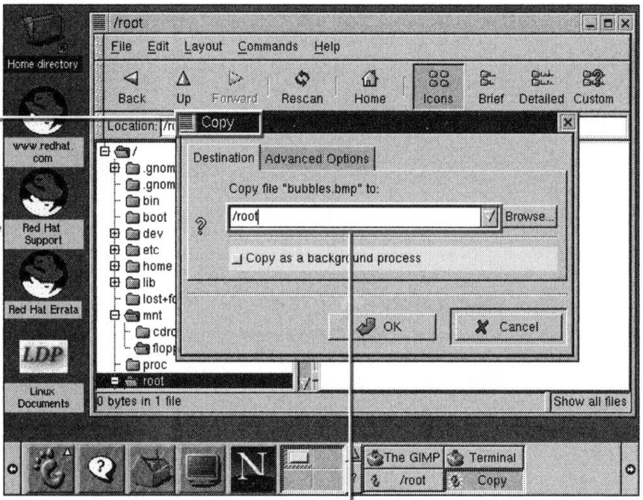

CHANGING COPY LOCATION WITH THE DOWN-ARROW BUTTON

1 Open your Home Directory.

2 Right-click the `bubbles.bmp` file.

3 Select Copy from the pop-up menu.

■ The Copy Screen appears.

■ By default, your Home Directory appears as the copy destination.

TIPS

If I'm not sure where I want to keep a copied file, where is a good default place to store the file?

- Your best bet if you're undecided where to store a given file is to save it to the `/tmp` directory. `/tmp` stands for temporary. This directory is nothing more than a holding area for files that you may want to erase or move to a floppy disk in the future.

Should I just store all of my files in this directory?

- This isn't a good idea. The `/tmp` directory has a unique characteristic that gives the directory its name. Files in that directory are only temporarily held there because files in `/tmp` are automatically erased every time the computer is shut down and restarted. If your files are valuable for any reason, move them out of the `/tmp` directory as soon as possible.

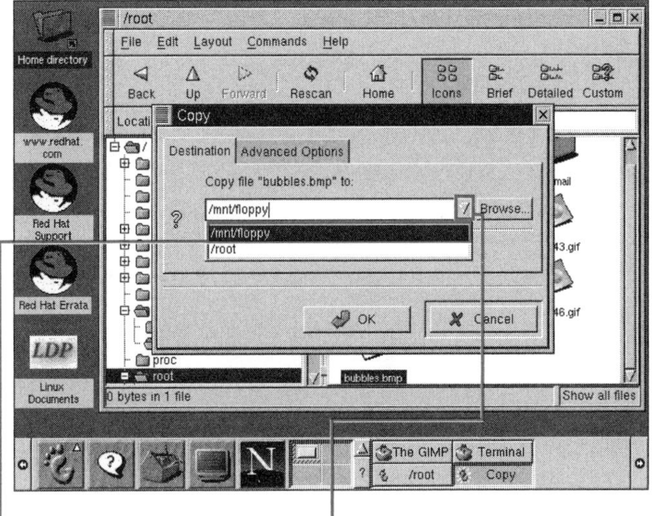

4 Click the down-arrow button to the right of the copy location field.

■ Linux stores the last few copy locations you've used.

■ A pop-up menu appears showing the last few copy destinations.

5 Click the one you want.

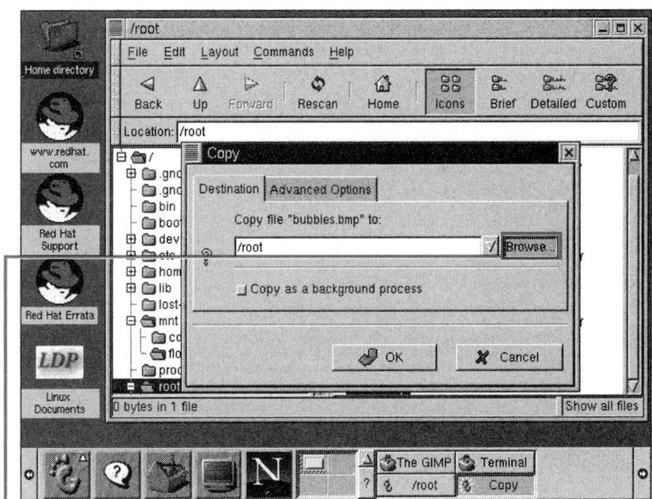

CHANGE LOCATION USING THE BROWSE BUTTON

1 Click the Browse button to the right of the copy location field.

CONTINUED

COPY FILES TO THE FLOPPY DISK

CONTINUED

You can select any part of the Linux file system as the destination for copying files. If you know the exact directory to which you want to copy, you can type it in the appropriate text box. On the other hand, if you only have a general idea of where you want to store a file, you should use the Browse button at the Find Destination Folder screen.

By using the Find Destination Folder screen, you can navigate to each of the directories on your Linux machine to determine where you want to save a particular file.

However, keep in mind that although this screen shows you multiple destinations to which you can copy material, how much space left in any given directory is not shown. If the file you plan to copy is larger than the space available, the copy process can't be completed.

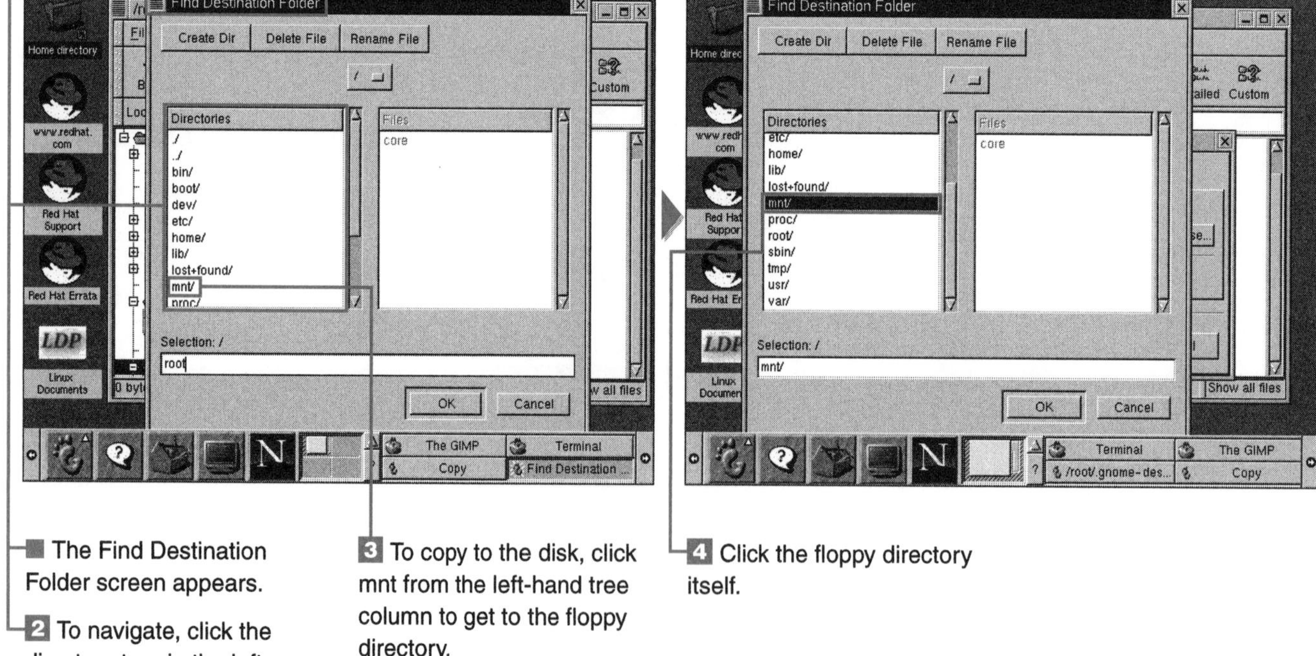

■ The Find Destination Folder screen appears.

2 To navigate, click the directory tree in the left pane.

3 To copy to the disk, click mnt from the left-hand tree column to get to the floppy directory.

4 Click the floppy directory itself.

If I'm working in Microsoft Word or WordPerfect, how can I save a document that works on a Linux machine?

- Word processors insert a lot of data behind the scenes when you save a document in Word or WordPerfect. This data is usually translated by text editors, such as Linux's Gnotepad, as garbage characters. You're best off saving a document to a disk in Text format.

If I create a document in Linux using the Gnotepad+ text editor (for information on Gnotepad+, see Chapter 14), can I paste pictures into it and still transfer the document to Microsoft Word or WordPerfect on a PC?

- You'll have difficulty. PC-based word processors have trouble working with documents created in Linux unless they're saved as plain text. Save the Linux document as plain text, and then add pictures when you transfer the document to Microsoft Word or WordPerfect.

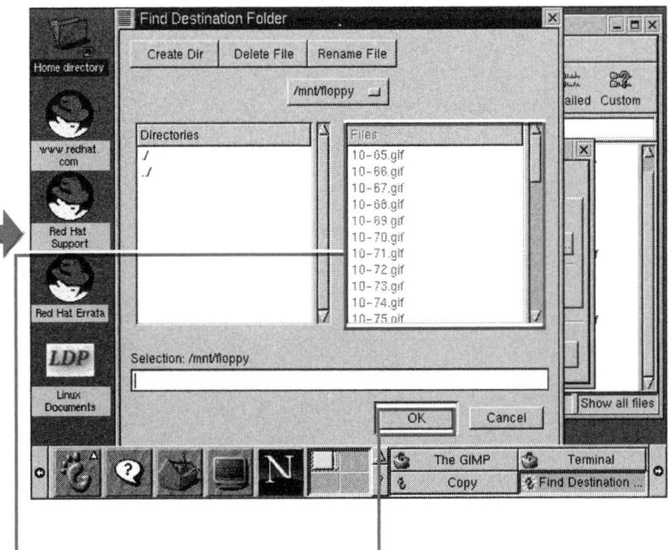

■ If your disk is in the drive and properly mounted, any contents of the disk are shown in the right-hand pane.

5 Click OK to select this copy location.

■ The Copy screen appears with the selected destination in the Copy Location field.

6 Click OK to begin copying files to the disk.

FORMAT FLOPPY DISKS

You have to format a floppy disk before you can store information on one. You can buy some floppies pre-formatted. However, most disks fresh out of the box need to be formatted. Formatting prepares the disk for data copying and storage.

A disk formatted for a PC is already formatted properly for your Linux machine, as long as you're using an msdos-configured floppy drive. If you're using a Macintosh formatted disk, you'll have to reformat it for your use.

Of course, if you're formatting a disk you've already used, be aware that the format process erases all the data on the disk. Unless you've pulled the disk right out of the box, check out the disk's contents before formatting.

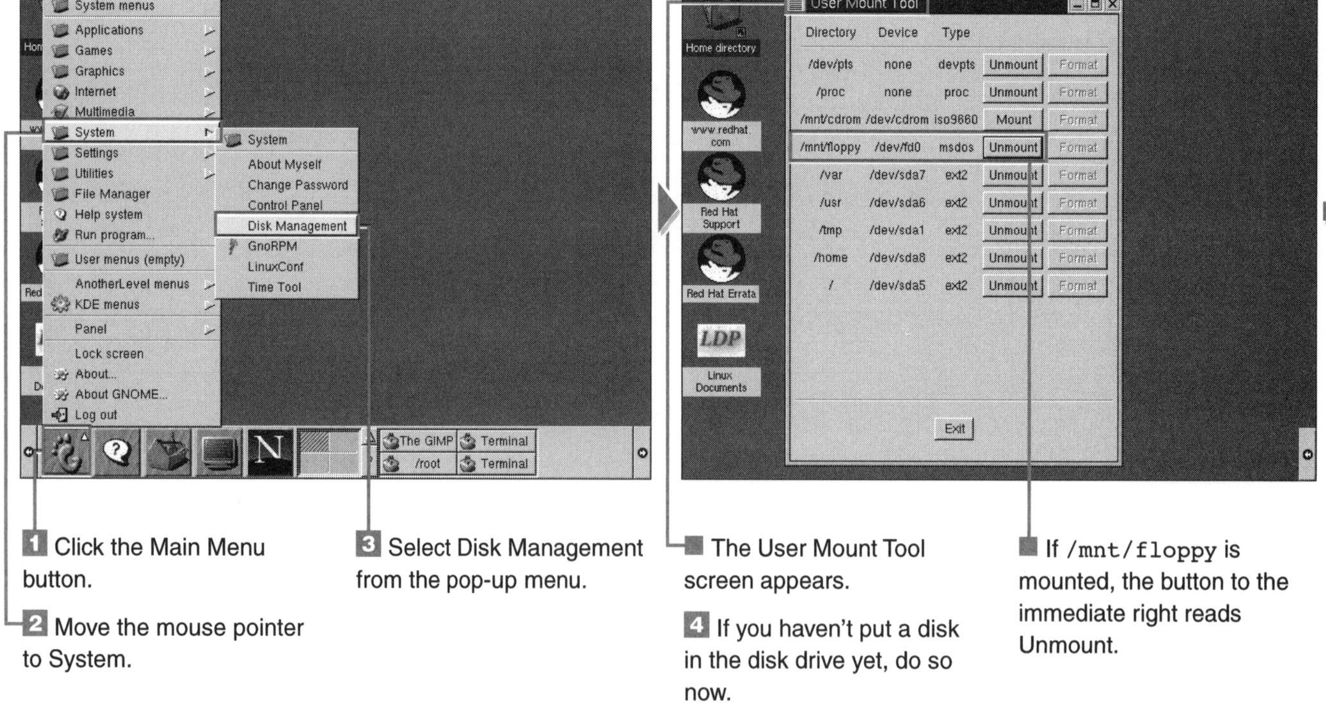

1 Click the Main Menu button.

2 Move the mouse pointer to System.

3 Select Disk Management from the pop-up menu.

■ The User Mount Tool screen appears.

4 If you haven't put a disk in the disk drive yet, do so now.

■ If `/mnt/floppy` is mounted, the button to the immediate right reads Unmount.

TIPS

What should I do if a computer running Windows for Workgroups, 3.1, 95, 98, or NT doesn't recognize my Linux disk?

- Disks storing Linux and PC information should work equally well on either system; it's only the format and the types of files stored that cause problems. If your PC doesn't recognize the disk and asks permission to format it, don't agree unless you can afford to lose the data on the disk. Instead, try a different floppy and see if the PC's drive is at fault.

When should I use a low-level format?

- A low-level format is similar to an erase command. This format process erases data from a disk but won't format it completely. This is useful when the disk is already formatted the way you want but you want a quick, thorough erase.

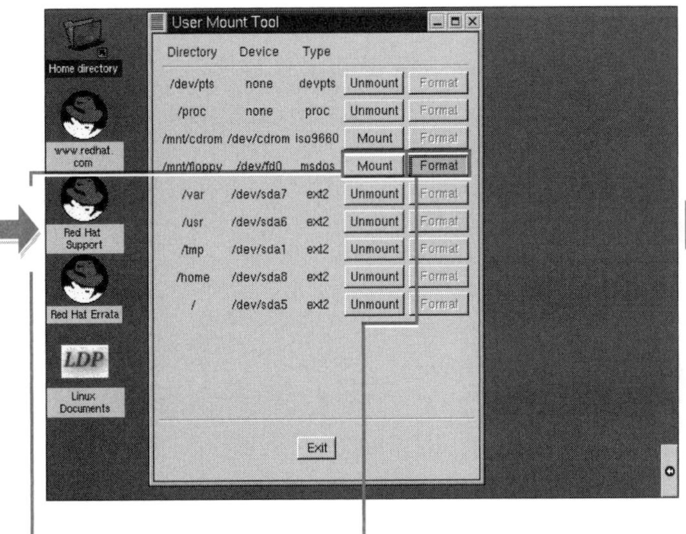

5 Click Unmount.

■ The drive is unmounted.

■ The button changes to Mount and the Format button is no longer grayed out, allowing you to format the disk.

6 Press Format to format the disk.

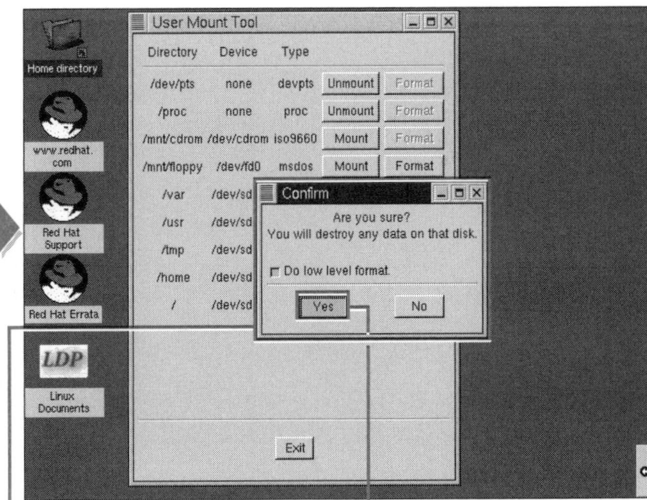

■ The Disk Manager asks you to confirm, because Formatting destroys all data on the disk.

7 If you're sure, click Yes.

■ When the formatting process is complete, you return to the User Mount Tool.

CONFIGURE THE CD-ROM DRIVE

Your CD-ROM drive is an integral part of your Linux system because it's a major avenue of information and data for installations, upgrades, and information storage. Even though many of these functions can be accomplished over the network today, it's hard to beat the speed and reliability of a local CD-ROM drive.

You need to configure your CD-ROM drive to accept all properly formatted CD-ROM media. Thanks to advances in CDs over the last decade, this process is a lot less confusing because media has been standardized.

You should be able to perform this simple configuration without any system downtime. Of course, if you need to hook up an external CD-ROM drive or replace the internal CD-ROM drive, you may need to reboot the machine for it to locate and recognize the new drive.

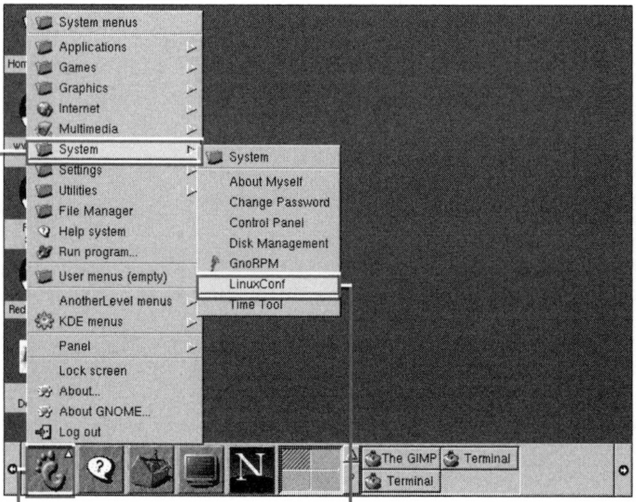

1 Click the Main Menu button.

2 Move the mouse pointer to System.

3 Select LinuxConf.

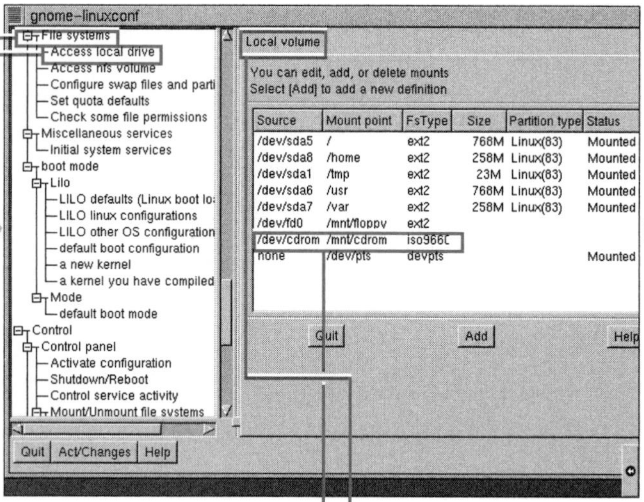

4 Scroll down to File Systems.

5 Click the Access Local Drive option.

■ The Local Volume panel opens.

6 Click the file system `/dev/cdrom`.

What other settings can I select for my CD-ROM drive in the Type area of the Volume Specification panel?

✔ The only other selection that enables a CD-ROM drive to run properly is the `hpfs` setting. *`hpfs`* stands for High Performance File System and is occasionally used on Linux and UNIX systems for installing programs. However, this setting is not recommended as it doesn't enable your CD-ROM drive to read CD-ROMs formatted for the PC.

Can a CD-ROM drive type set to iso9660 read a Macintosh CD-ROM?

✔ Because the ISO9660 setting has become the industry standard, you will be able to read a Macintosh CD-ROM. However, because the Macintosh file system is so different from Linux, you may not be able to copy files from the CD-ROM onto your hard drive, let alone run any programs from the CD-ROM.

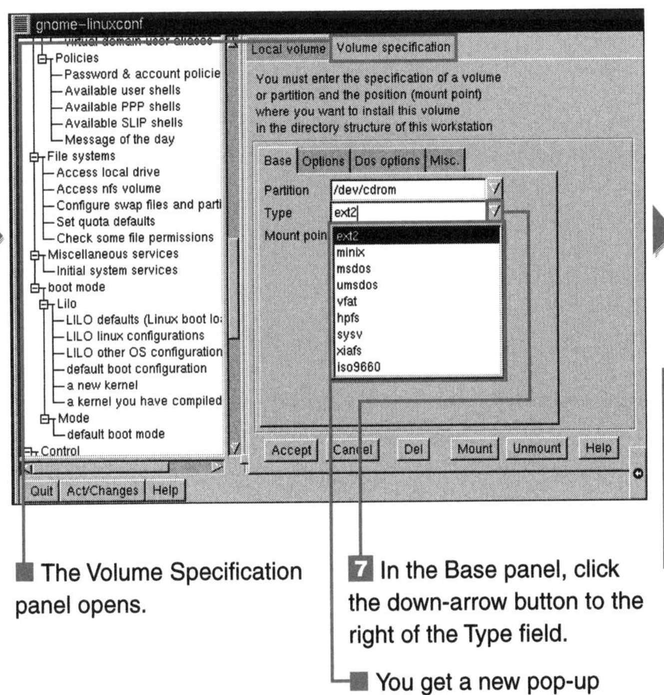

■ The Volume Specification panel opens.

7 In the Base panel, click the down-arrow button to the right of the Type field.

■ You get a new pop-up menu.

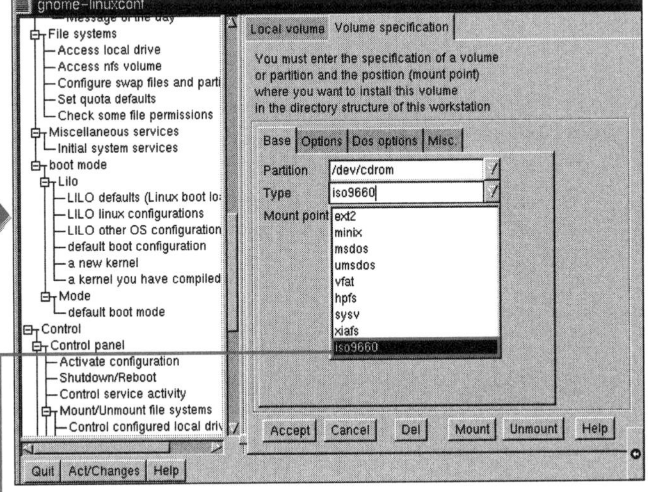

8 To enable this drive to handle CD-ROMs that work in either Linux or on a PC, select iso9660.

CONTINUED

CONFIGURE THE CD-ROM DRIVE

CONTINUED

You can configure the CD-ROM drive in such a way that any user can mount it. By default, any CD-ROM drive you add and configure is set in this way, although you should double-check to make sure that it's properly set.

You want to enable other users to mount the CD-ROM drive on the machine. Enabling users to mount their own CD-ROMs reduces your workload because you get fewer requests to do this basic task. Also, it allows your users to be more independent and make better use of the Linux system because they can use CD-ROMs to download Linux utilities or graphics files that they can use in their everyday work.

As long as your users don't have root privileges, you don't have to worry about users installing files that could affect the operation of your system.

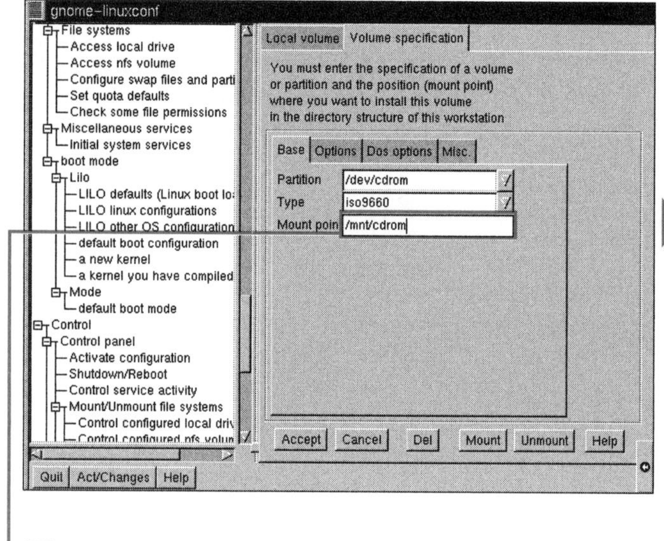

9 If the Mount point field is empty, type **/mnt/cdrom**.

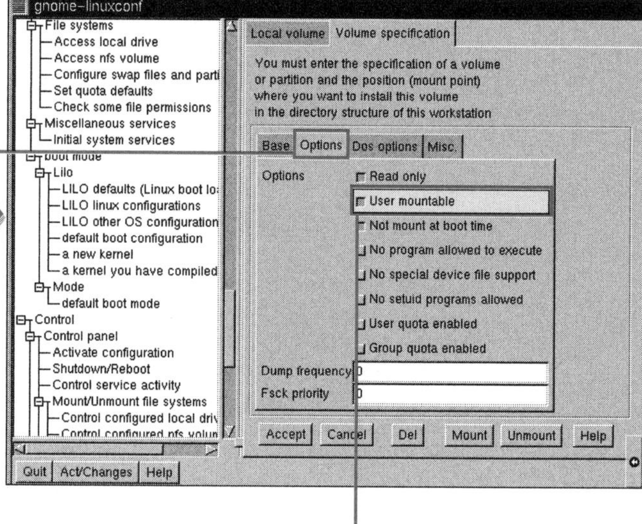

10 Click the Options panel.

11 From the buttons, select User mountable if the button is not already depressed.

Should I unmount the drive when I remove the CD?

- Yes. Unlike the Microsoft Windows system in which CDs can be popped in and out at will, you always need to unmount the drive before removing the CD. Not doing this confuses the operating system and could affect the ability of the system to recognize a disk to mount later on.

What should I do if the CD-ROM drive refuses to mount and starts making a high-pitched whine?

- On most systems, this is a sign that the CD-ROM is spinning but is unbalanced. The drive is refusing to mount because of this. In the vast majority of cases, the cause of the unbalanced CD-ROM is that the CD was placed in the drive upside down. Eject the CD-ROM, turn it over, and place it back in the drive to try again.

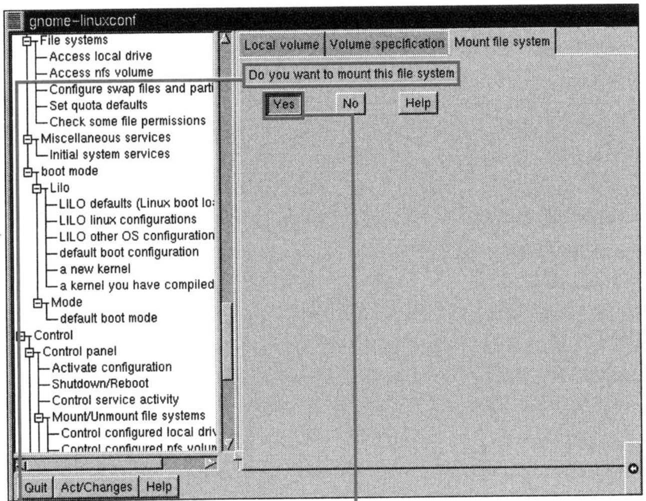

■ A new panel appears asking you to confirm whether you want to mount this drive.

12 Click Yes.

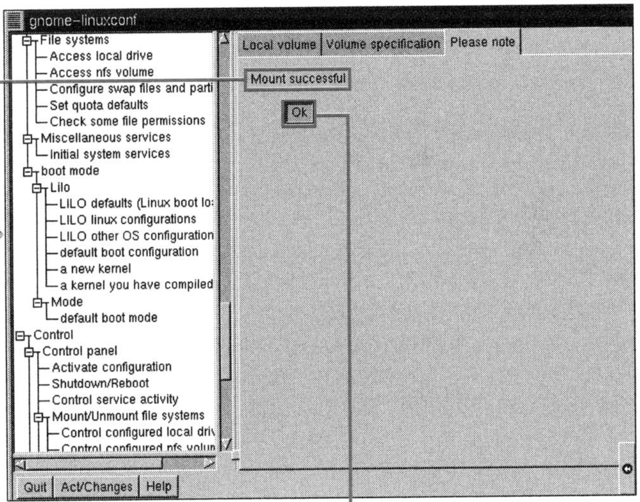

■ A confirmation panel appears.

13 Click OK.

■ The Local Volume screen reappears, listing `/dev/cdrom` as mounted.

MOUNT THE CD-ROM DRIVE

You can mount the CD-ROM drive in order to access the text, graphics, and other files stored on the CD. *Mounting* tells the Linux operating system that the disk drive is recognized as a functioning piece of hardware that it can properly read. As with the Linux floppy disk drive, you need to mount the CD-ROM drive in order to access the data on the CD itself.

Compared with the Microsoft PC world, the CD-ROM drive does not always stay mounted and ready for use in Linux. Also unlike on a PC, you can't put CDs into the drive or remove them without going through the mount process.

Granted, this sounds more cumbersome than it really is, especially compared with a PC.

However, Linux is based on UNIX, an operating system that radically pre-dates CD-ROMs, Zip drives, and even cathode-ray screens (monitors)!

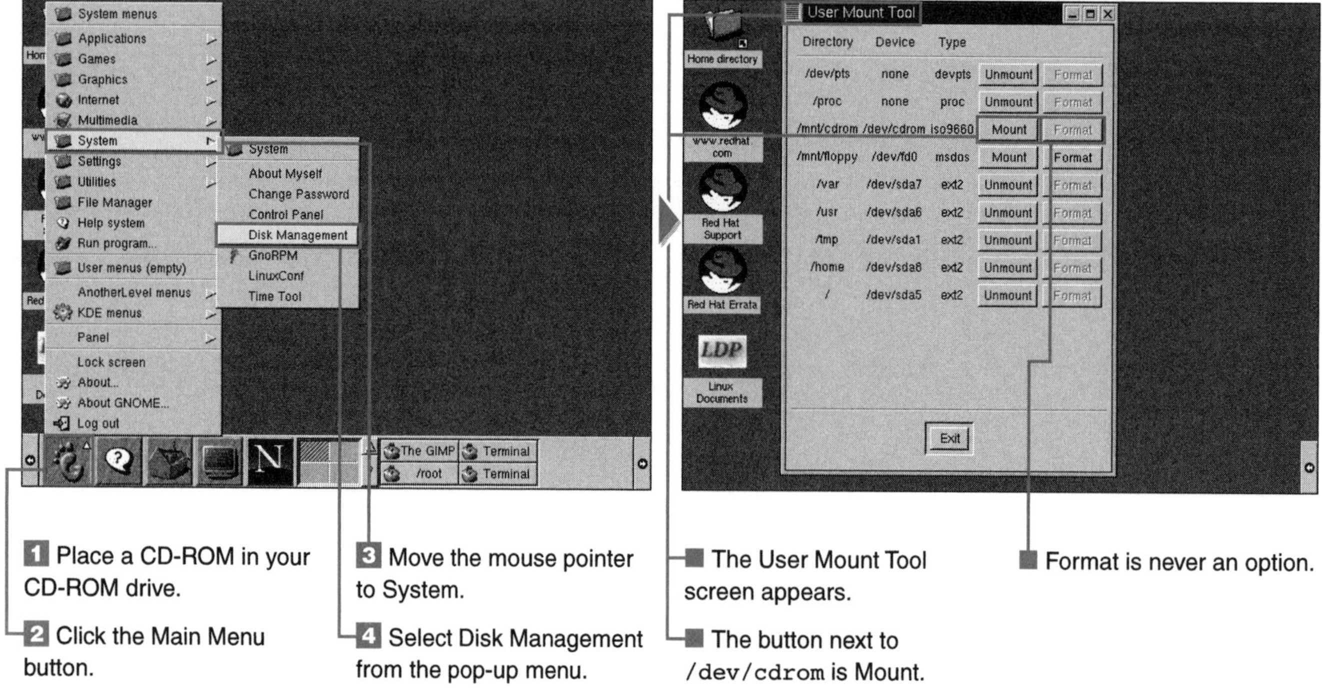

1 Place a CD-ROM in your CD-ROM drive.

2 Click the Main Menu button.

3 Move the mouse pointer to System.

4 Select Disk Management from the pop-up menu.

■ The User Mount Tool screen appears.

■ The button next to `/dev/cdrom` is Mount.

■ Format is never an option.

What do I do if I accidentally click Format in the User Mount Tool screen for the CD-ROM drive?

- Don't worry. Unlike a floppy disk, unless you have a CD-R (Recordable CD-ROM), you won't be able to erase the information contained on the CD. In the near future, of course, this will change.

What if the User Mount Tool can't mount my CD-ROM drive?

- The most common cause of this problem is a bad cable connection. Don't just check the plug connections by wiggling them in the socket. You should test out the entire cable by trying a different one. When you discover a bad cable, cut it in half immediately. Otherwise, you run the risk of forgetting which cable is the defective one when you're running a typical computer lab, which often has dozens of similar looking cables lying around.

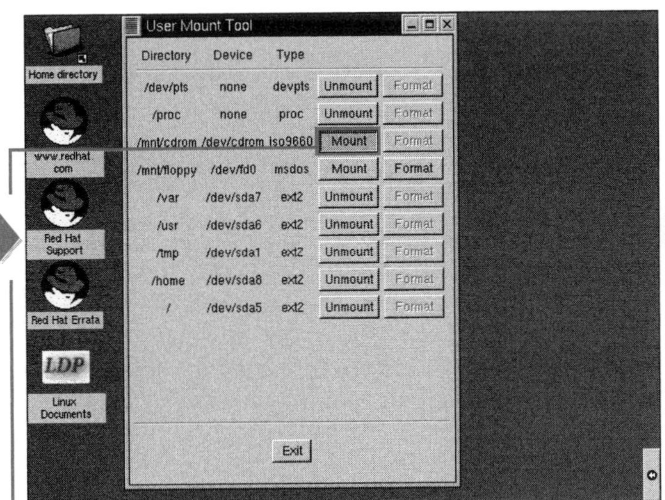

5 Click the Mount Button to the right of the `/dev/cdrom` listing.

■ When the CD-ROM drive is fully mounted, the button reads Unmount.

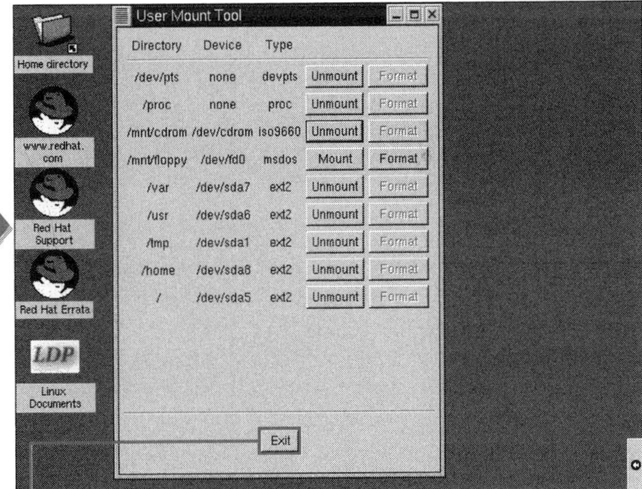

6 Click Exit to close the User Mount Tool screen.

■ The user can access the CD-ROM drive and the contents of the CD.

MOUNT THE CD-ROM DRIVE FROM THE LINUX TERMINAL

You can mount the CD-ROM drive by using the vi editor in the Linux terminal. Although mounting the CD-ROM drive in the terminal is not as quick and easy as completing this task in the GNOME desktop, you have the added bonus of viewing all of the file systems that your system is capable of mounting.

Use the `vi fstab` command to show the contents of your file system table, fstab. As long as the `/dev/cdrom` file system is set up as ISO9600, your CD-ROM will work properly.

Remember that to perform mount functions in the terminal, use the mount command, just as if you were mounting a floppy disk drive. This command is one of the most basic in all of UNIX or Linux and is found on all systems, so you'll be able to use it anywhere.

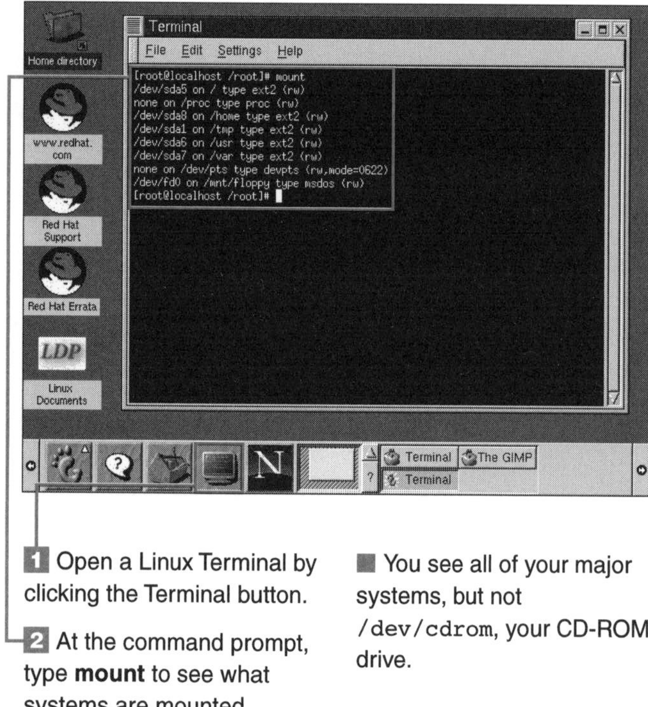

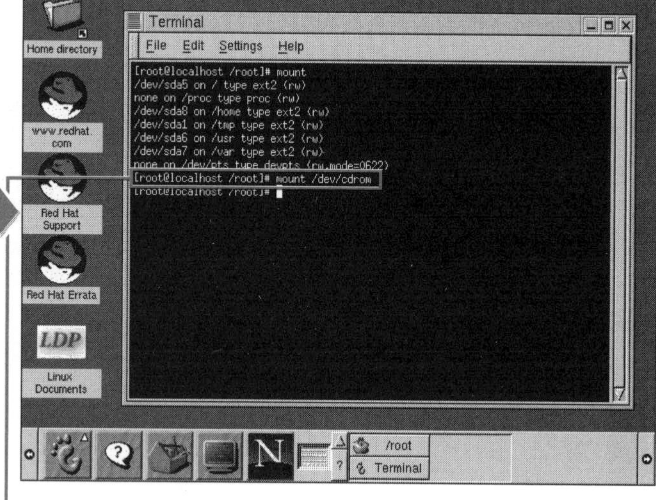

1 Open a Linux Terminal by clicking the Terminal button.

2 At the command prompt, type **mount** to see what systems are mounted.

■ You see all of your major systems, but not `/dev/cdrom`, your CD-ROM drive.

3 Insert a CD-ROM into your CD drive.

4 At the command prompt, type **mount /mnt/cdrom**.

5 Press Enter.

TIPS

What if I want to use a different system than ISO9600?

- You're best off sticking with the ISO system. Over the last 10 years, CD-ROMs have been standardized so that 99 percent of them operate properly under the ISO standard. Changing this radically increases the chance that you'll run into a problem.

If I've set all the CD-ROM parameters that have been recommended in this chapter and I still have problems with the CD-ROM drive, what should I do?

- If you continue to have problems reading CD-ROMs, check to see what kind of filesystem `/dev/cdrom` is set to in the `/etc/fstab` file. Most errors are from editing — but not saving — changes to this file.

What should I do if I accidentally edit the /etc/fstab file?

- This is a serious problem. Immediately exit the vi editor without saving your unintended changes. Remember: Go to the Command Mode and type `:wq!` to exit.

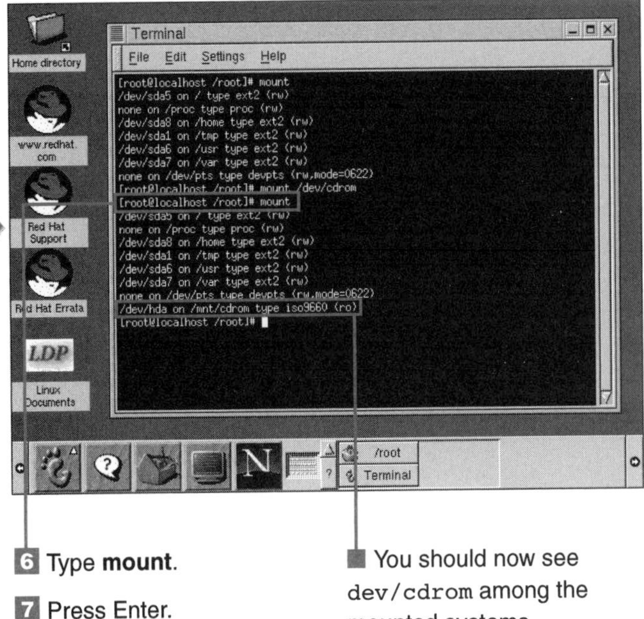

6 Type **mount**.

7 Press Enter.

■ You should now see `dev/cdrom` among the mounted systems.

8 At the command prompt, type **vi /etc/fstab**.

9 Press Enter.

READ AND COPY FILES FROM THE CD-ROM

You can view and copy the information on a CD from the Linux GNOME interface with ease. Keep in mind that like the floppy disk location, the site of the CD-ROM files also differ between the mount location and the location of the files when reading the disc.

The file system location of the mount point for a CD is `/dev/cdrom`. However, when you search for readable files from the floppy, you'll find that they're located at /mnt/cdrom. Because of this, when you perform a `mount` command in the Linux terminal to determine whether the CD is mounted, you'll see `/dev/cdrom`, not `/mnt/cdrom`.

In addition, you should always prepare for longer copy times when moving files from the CD-ROM to your local hard drive. This can be partly due to a slow drive. Also, most of the time, you'll be copying over larger files from a CD-ROM, even whole applications.

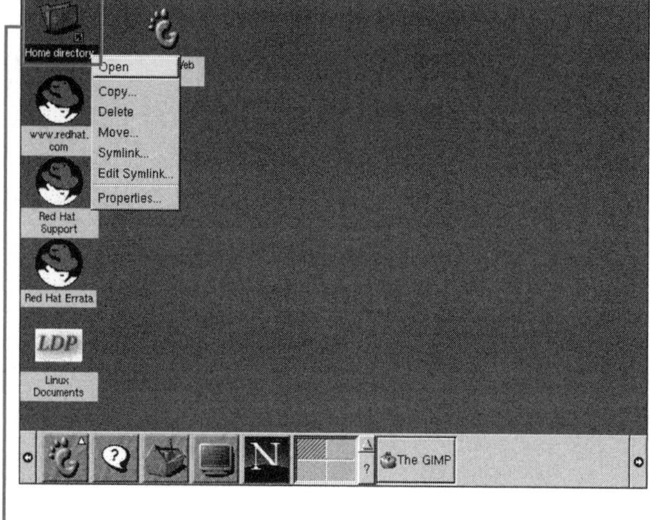

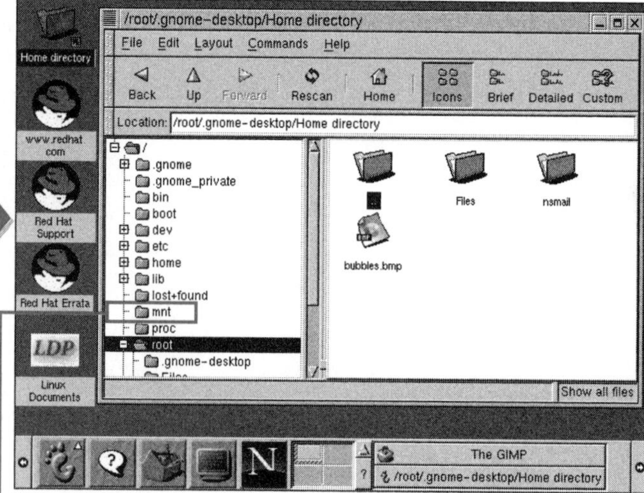

READING FILES

1 On your desktop, open your Home Directory.

2 In the left-hand pane, look in the directory tree for mnt.

■ The directories under mnt are allocated for mounting external devices, such as a CD-ROM drive or floppy disk.

TIPS

What if I don't see a cdrom directory icon in the /mnt directory?

- If for some reason you don't see a `cdrom` directory icon under `/mnt`, then the directory may have been accidentally deleted or improperly installed. You'll need to create a `cdrom` directory here in order to read or copy files from a CD-ROM. See Chapter 4 if you need to review how to create a new directory.

Are there any files from a CD-ROM that should not be copied to a Linux machine?

- Certain files can cause your machine to become confused if you copy them from a CD-ROM to your machine's hard drive. Don't copy multiple installations of the Linux operating system to your hard drive. Also, don't copy any Microsoft Windows files to your hard drive. Either of these files can cause your system problems when booting up.

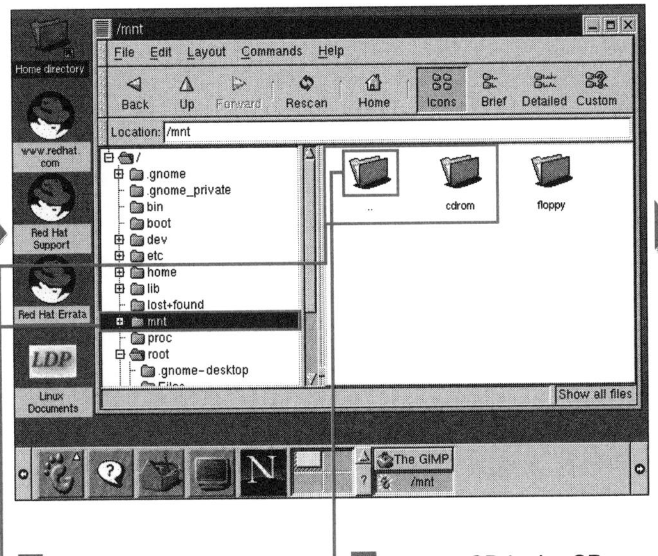

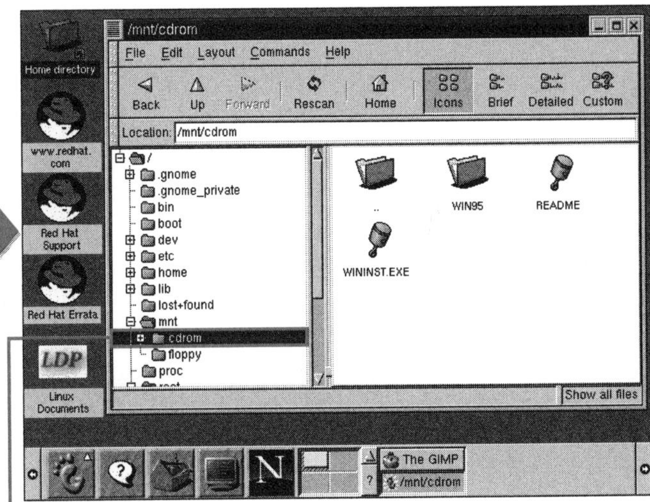

3 Click `mnt`.

■ In the right-hand pane display, you typically see two folder icons, `cdrom` and `floppy`.

4 Insert a CD in the CD-ROM drive and be sure it's mounted.

5 Click the `cdrom` folder icon.

■ If the disk is mounted and you have files inside, they are displayed.

CONTINUED

READ AND COPY FILES FROM THE CD-ROM CONTINUED

You copy files from a CD-ROM in the same way that you copy files from one place on your GNOME desktop to another. By using your mouse, you can click and drag items to different locations on the desktop or into a directory's desktop icon.

This method is efficient compared with copying files from the CD-ROM in the Linux terminal. When copying files from the CD-ROM in the Linux terminal, you often have to type long strings of text to specify certain subdirectories that are buried beneath other directories to get to the files you need. For example, a quick series of click-and-drag motions can be completed more quickly than typing `cp /mnt/cdrom/linux/utility` multiple times. Also, you can transfer entire directories from a CD-ROM by clicking its directory icon and dragging it to its destination on your desktop.

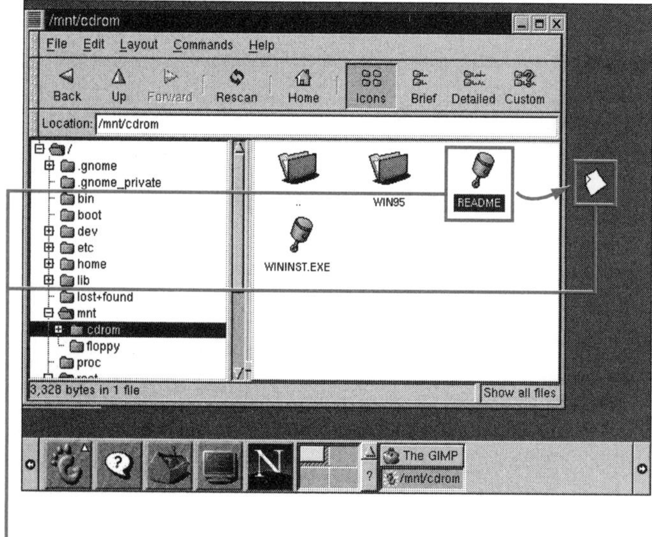

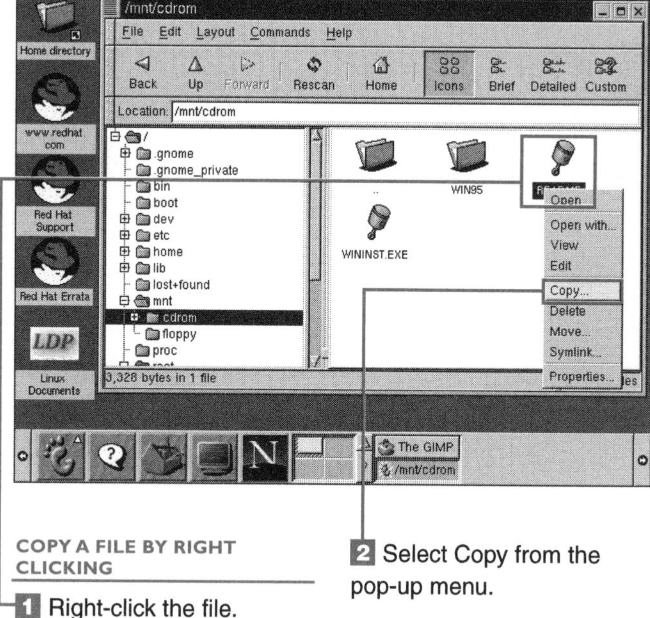

COPY FILES USING CLICK AND DRAG

1 Click the README file to copy it from the CD-ROM.

2 Drag the file to your desktop.

■ Your pointer icon looks like a sheet of paper.

■ The file you copy is available to you on your desktop.

COPY A FILE BY RIGHT CLICKING

1 Right-click the file.

2 Select Copy from the pop-up menu.

Why is the copy process from the CD-ROM taking so long?

- There can be a number of reasons. Not all CD-ROM drives are created equal! Remember that if you have an old, double-speed drive, you'll be looking at a much longer copy time than if you have a faster speed CD-ROM. Generally, you get the best speed gains if you have a 10X or 20X speed CD-ROM drive or better.

I just installed a cutting edge CD-ROM drive. Why is it still so slow?

- If you pop a super fast CD-ROM drive into a slow machine, you may just transfer the data bottleneck from one area to another. If you have an old information bus or a small amount of RAM, you could be memory bound. (Of course, if you have a fast machine and a slow CD-ROM drive, you're drive bound.)

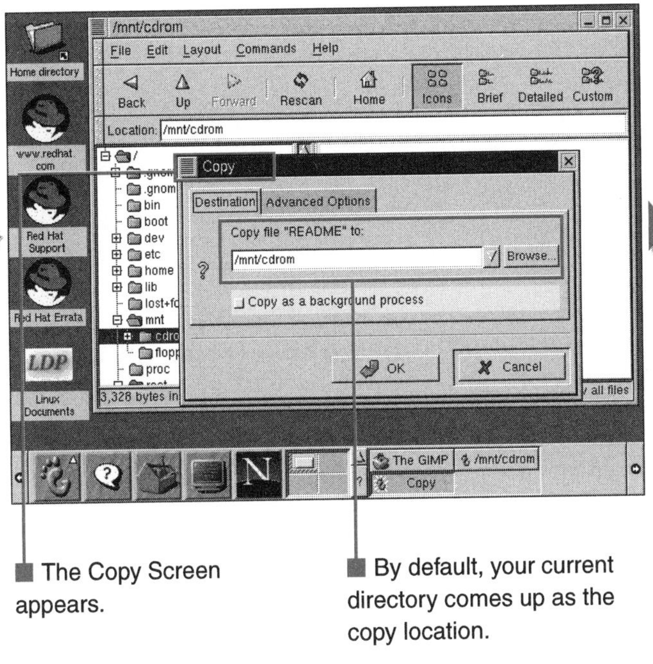

■ The Copy Screen appears.

■ By default, your current directory comes up as the copy location.

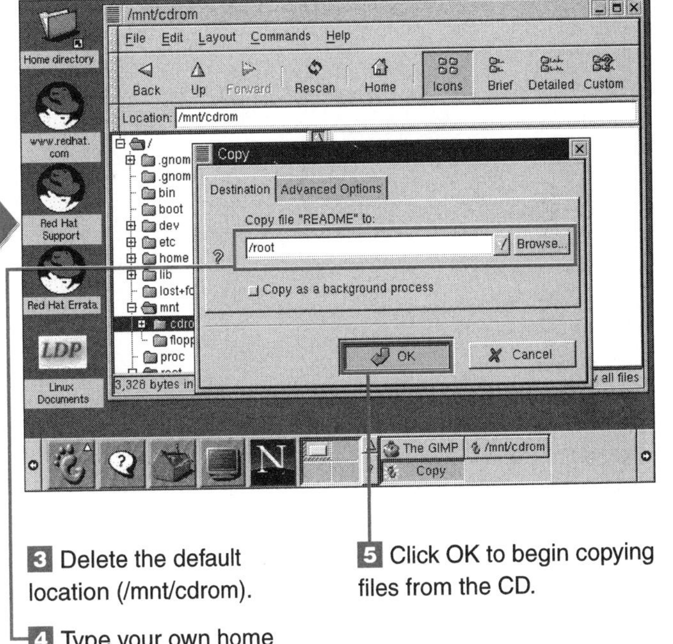

3 Delete the default location (/mnt/cdrom).

4 Type your own home directory — /**root**.

5 Click OK to begin copying files from the CD.

EJECT FLOPPY DISKS AND CD-ROMS

Remember that although you're using floppy disks and compact discs, you're not using a standard PC with a Linux system. The eject process is more complex than with the simple pop-and-go philosophy of a PC. In this case, the GNOME system makes your life much easier by placing these functions on a tool, the Disk Manager.

By placing the functions you need on the label of a button, preparing a floppy or compact disc drive for mounting or unmounting has never been easier. Of course, you should be aware of how to accomplish this in the Linux Terminal outside of the GUI, in case you need to do this on a non-GUI Linux or UNIX system. Ejecting the CD-ROM in the Linux terminal requires that you type `eject -r` at the command prompt and press Enter.

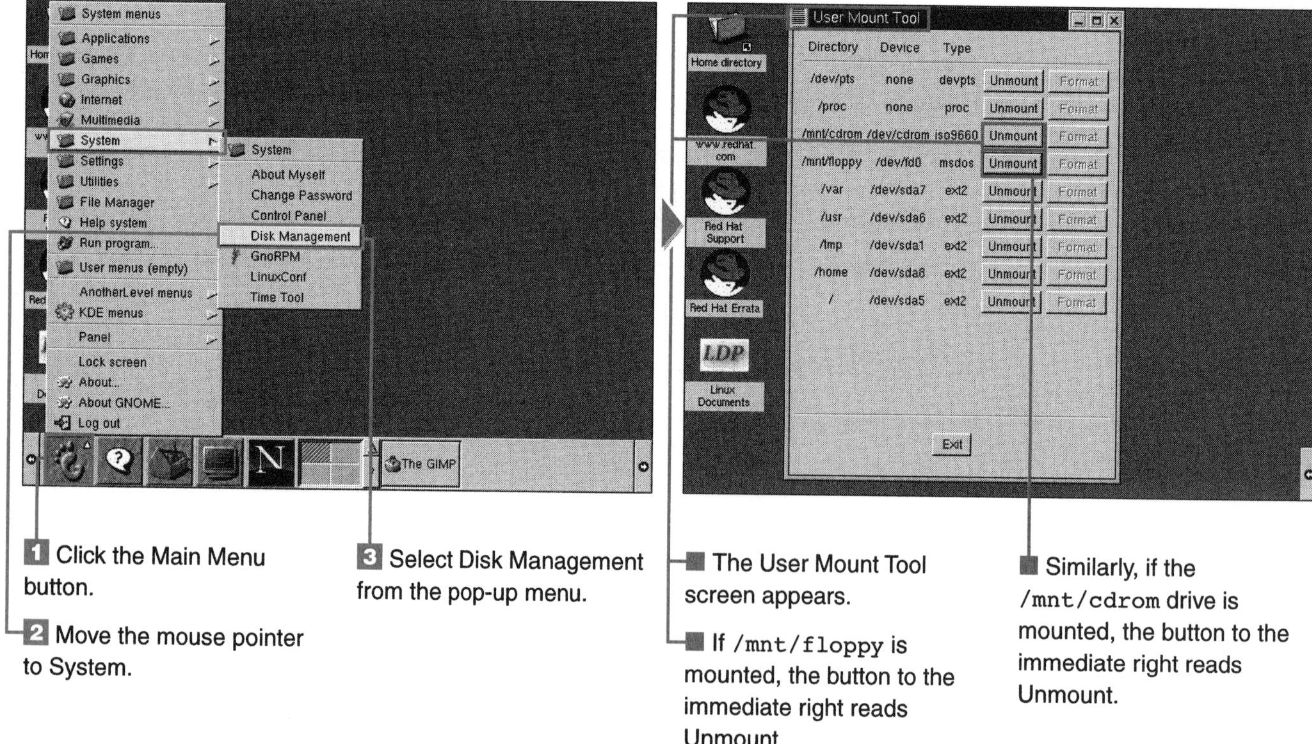

1 Click the Main Menu button.

2 Move the mouse pointer to System.

3 Select Disk Management from the pop-up menu.

■ The User Mount Tool screen appears.

■ If `/mnt/floppy` is mounted, the button to the immediate right reads Unmount.

■ Similarly, if the `/mnt/cdrom` drive is mounted, the button to the immediate right reads Unmount.

How can I get my floppy disk back if the drive refuses to unmount?

- Of course, all Linux and PC-based Linux machines have a physical method to eject the disk. If your system is having constant trouble in this area, perform a backup of the system before continuing. Reboot the system and see if the trouble persists. If you're running Linux on a Mac, you'll need a paper-clip or thin pencil to force-eject the floppy disk.

How can I get my CD-ROM back if the CD-ROM drive tray refuses to open?

- Immediately back up your system before proceeding any further. See if any lights on the drive are flashing when you press the reset button on the CPU. If you do, make doubly sure that the drive has been dismounted. If not, the drive may be hung, and you'll have to reboot the machine to free it up.

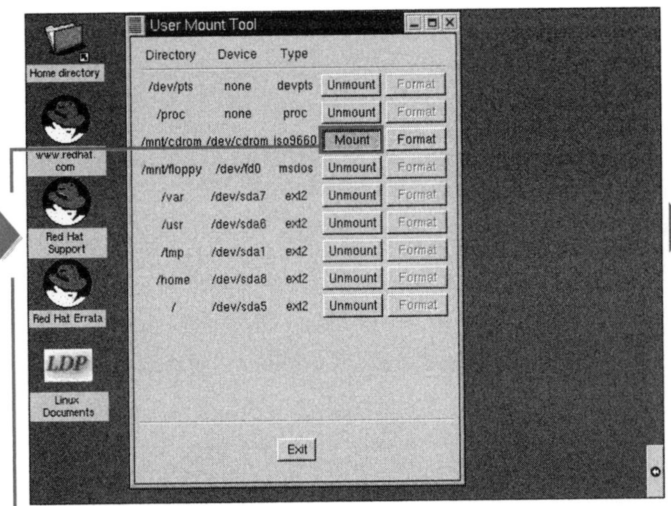

4 Click Unmount next to /mnt/cdrom.

- The drive is unmounted.
- The button changes to Mount.
- You are now able to remove the CD from the drive safely.

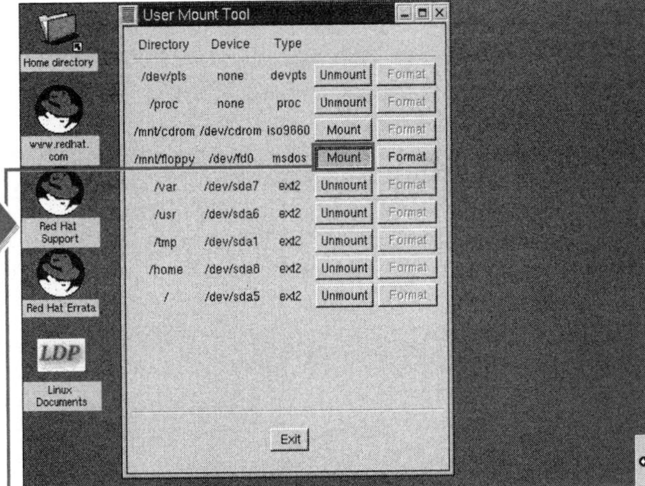

5 Click Unmount next to /mnt/floppy.

- The drive is unmounted.
- The button changes to Mount.
- You can remove the floppy from the drive safely.

VERIFY AVAILABLE DISK SPACE

Always determine how much space you have available on your computer's hard drive partitions before you attempt to install or upgrade a major program. Obviously, it causes your system no end of trouble if your installation process freezes in the middle of the work because of space shortage.

As a rule, allow yourself about ten percent of your partition's size for breathing room before it fills up. This gives you some leeway in case a process starts growing too quickly and begins filling up the drive. A 100 percent full drive will almost always lead to a system slowdown and crash.

You can determine how much space — and how much you are in need of it — with the tools provided by GNOME's GUI. The most useful of the tools is the System Info tool, found under the LINUX system's Utilities.

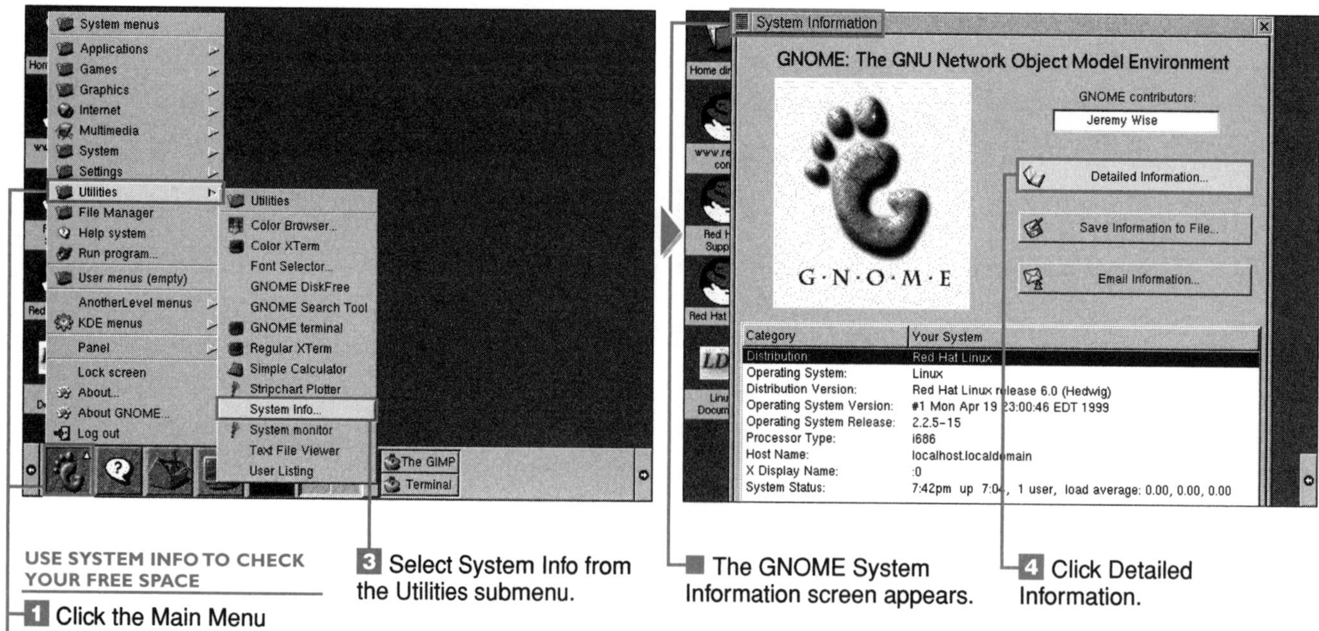

USE SYSTEM INFO TO CHECK YOUR FREE SPACE

1 Click the Main Menu button.

2 Move the mouse pointer to Utilities.

3 Select System Info from the Utilities submenu.

■ The GNOME System Information screen appears.

4 Click Detailed Information.

TIPS

What kind of problem could cause the disk to fill up rapidly?

- A disk fills up in the span of a few hours most often because of a runaway process that writes a log file to part of the hard disk. After the disk fills up and there is no room to save any more information, all work on the computer can grind to a halt, forcing you to reboot the computer.

If I have a stable number of users and no problems with my system, can the disk still fill up?

- Absolutely. Just because you are not adding new users does not mean that you are not going to gradually use more space. As people work on the system, they tend to save their text and graphics files on the hard disk. Although the process is slow, you can run out of space in months or years.

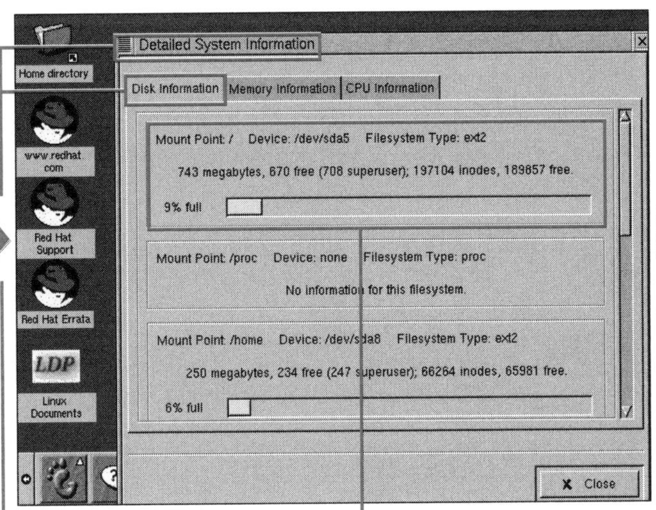

- The Detailed System Information screen appears.
- The numbers you need are on the Disk Information default panel.
- The amount of free space displays as a number and a bar graph
- The main mount point of the system (/ or `root`) is 9% full, or 91% free.

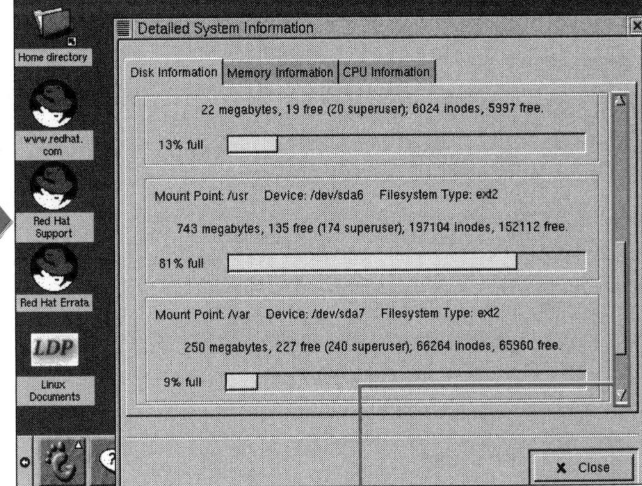

- Disk Information runs off the screen and reports on the other mount points.

5 Click and drag the slide bar down to see more readings.

CONTINUED

VERIFY AVAILABLE DISK SPACE
CONTINUED

You can monitor the amount of available hard disk space you have on your Linux system. After you have collected the relevant system information for your computer, be sure to store the results for future reference. For added security, consider storing the information on a floppy disk in case your hard drive suffers a failure.

Use the GNOME disk utility called Disk Free; it gives you a good idea how much space you have available on your system for saving files, graphics, software installations, and application upgrades.

This is especially important when you are running a computer that several people use. It is also a critical task if you plan to install a lot of new software on your computer because running out of disk space during an install could cause system errors and force you to reboot the computer.

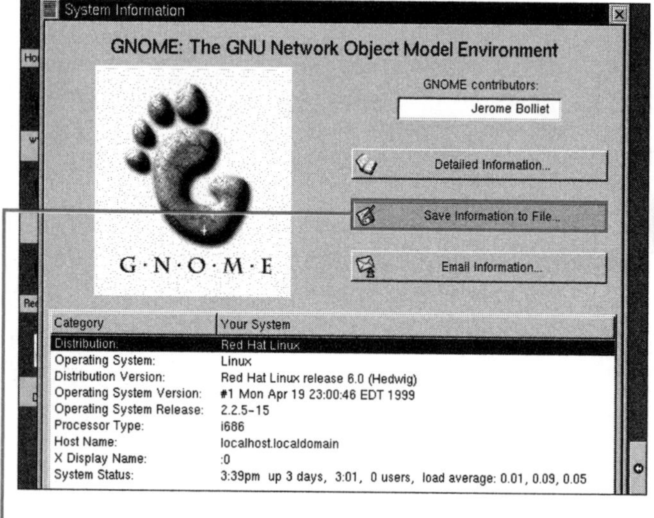

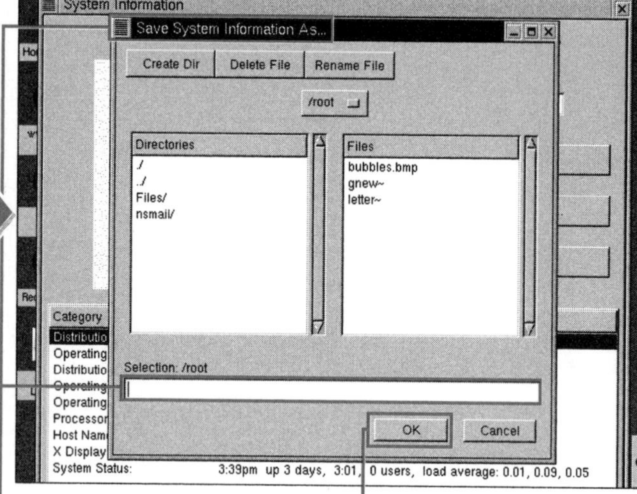

SAVE SYSTEM INFORMATION TO A FILE

1 On the GNOME System Information screen, click the Save Information to File button.

■ The Save System Info As screen appears.

2 Type the name of the file you would like to save the info under.

3 Press the OK button.

When should I use System Info instead of Disk Free?

- System Info provides you with additional data on physical and virtual memory, CPU, and RAM. Aside from that, you should decide which to use based on what you find more user-friendly: rotary dials or bar graphs.

What if I want to send system information to a manufacturer or to a new system administrator?

- There is a button — you can find it directly on the System Info screen — that enables you to e-mail the data listed in the System Info tools to whomever you want. Click the button to have the information packaged for you; type the address you want to send it to. Of course, if you do not want to use this option, you can always save the information as a file and send it as an e-mail attachment.

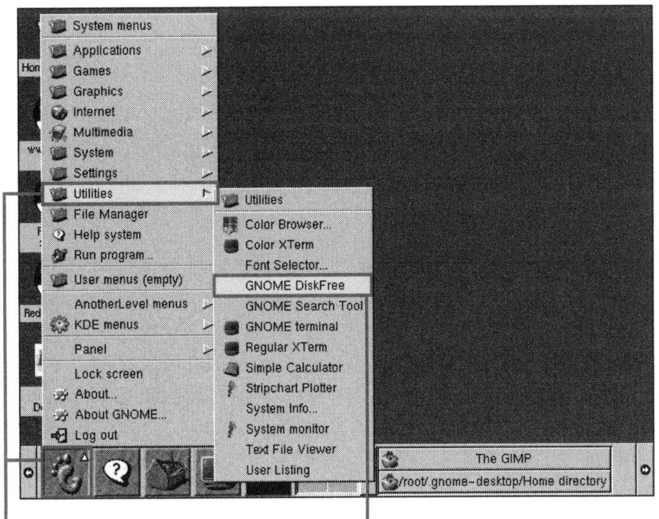

USE DISK FREE TO CHECK YOUR FREE SPACE

1 Click the Main Menu button.

2 Move the mouse pointer to Utilities.

3 Select GNOME DiskFree from the Utilities submenu.

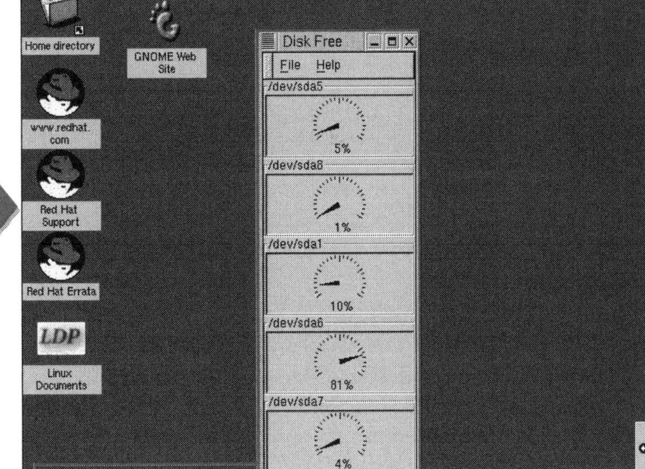

■ The Disk Free information screen appears.

■ *Note: The readings on these dials indicate how much free space is left, not how much of the disk is full.*

START THE GNOME RED HAT PACKAGE MANAGER

You can use the Red Hat Package Manager to install new utilities and to upgrade existing ones. RPM is a complex, versatile process — whole books have been written on the topic. However, GNOME has again simplfied the core processes of RPM by providing a GUI front end for it, namely GnoRPM — the GNOME Red Hat Package Manager. A GUI-based front end added to an application means that the software designers have designed screens, buttons, and icons that make the program more user friendly and intuitive.

Knowing how to work with the GnoRPM is helpful because the majority of your package installations come to you on CD-ROM. For example, the Red Hat CD-ROMs that come with this book are chock-full of utilities that you can use, including new graphics programs and an excellent version of the Apache Linux Web Server.

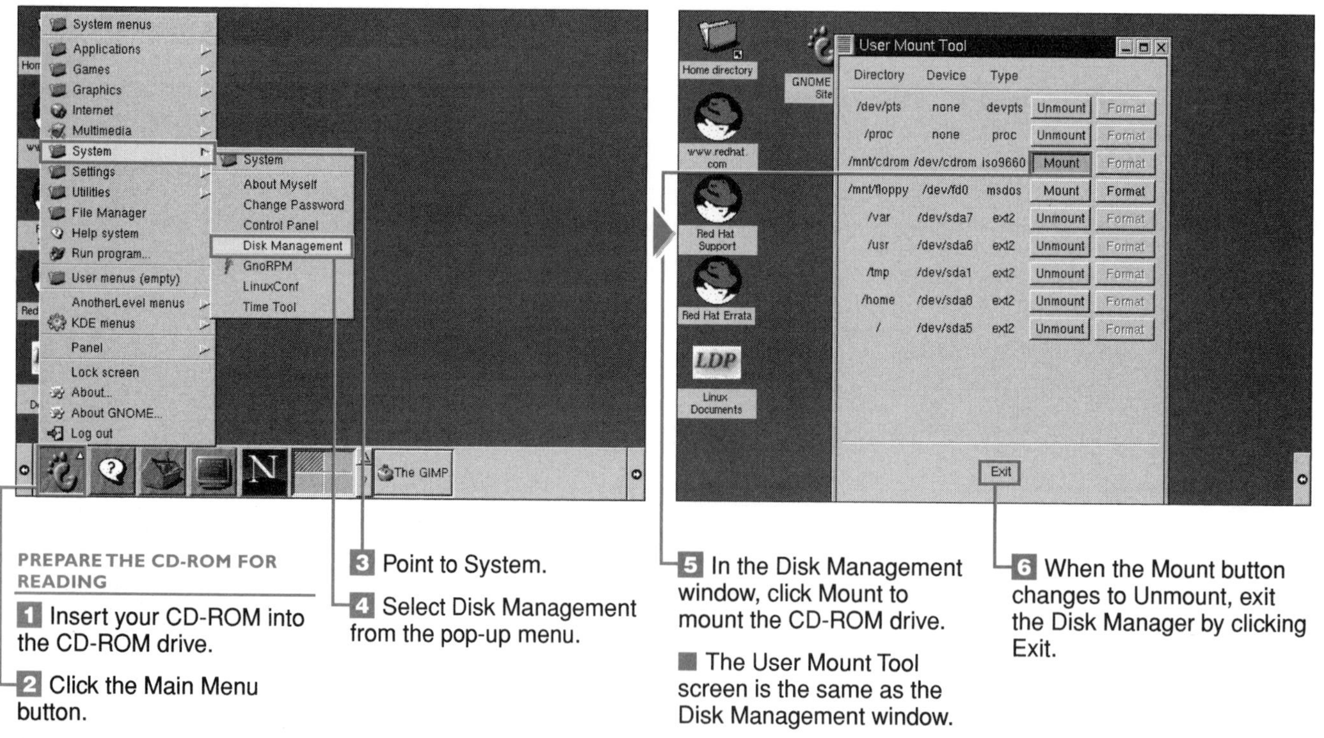

PREPARE THE CD-ROM FOR READING

1 Insert your CD-ROM into the CD-ROM drive.

2 Click the Main Menu button.

3 Point to System.

4 Select Disk Management from the pop-up menu.

5 In the Disk Management window, click Mount to mount the CD-ROM drive.

■ The User Mount Tool screen is the same as the Disk Management window.

6 When the Mount button changes to Unmount, exit the Disk Manager by clicking Exit.

TIPS

How do I use GnoRPM if I am downloading a new module or utility from the Web?

✔ You do not have to make any changes when you are using GnoRPM while downloading files from a Web site. Your first priority is to get the files from the network to a location local to the computer. Once there, uncompress or `untar` the file so that it is usable. (For info on downloading and uncompressing, see Chapter 27.) When the file is local, run GnoRPM and be sure to specify the local directory containing the new file.

How is RPM different than pkgadd or any of the other UNIX/Linux commands for software package administration?

✔ RPM and GnoRPM are designed specifically to work with Red Hat Linux. While this does not do much for other flavors of UNIX or Linux, it helps make a more seamless transition between upgrades and installs than with other flavors.

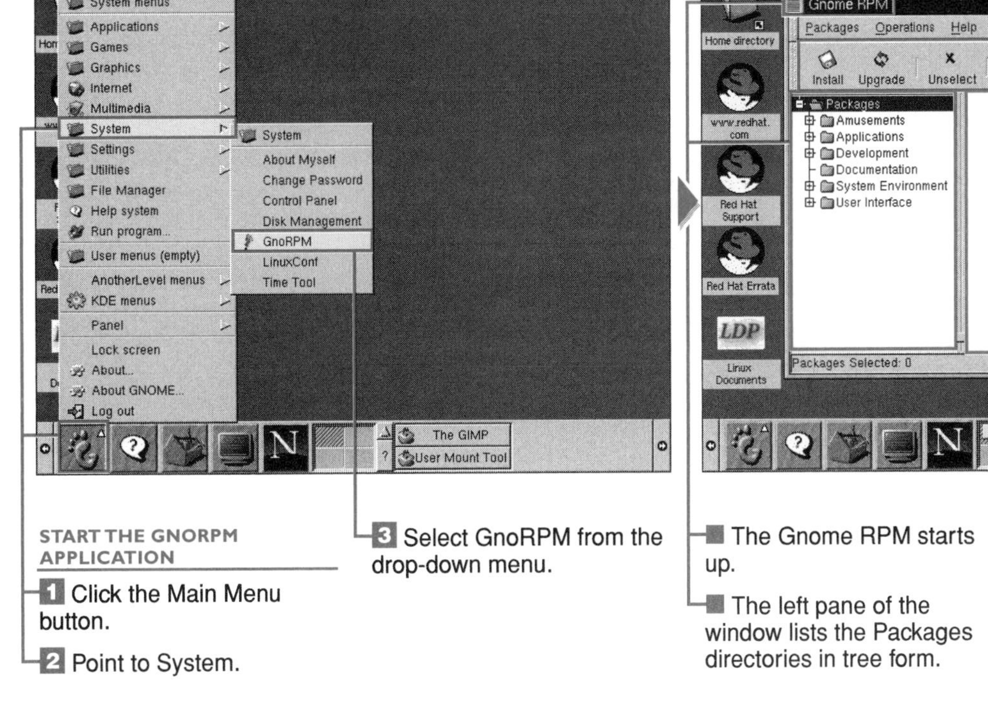

START THE GNORPM APPLICATION

1 Click the Main Menu button.

2 Point to System.

3 Select GnoRPM from the drop-down menu.

■ The Gnome RPM starts up.

■ The left pane of the window lists the Packages directories in tree form.

■ The right pane lists the contents of these directories when you clicked on them.

■ The RPM toolbar lists the main features of the RPM GUI.

VERIFY PACKAGES WITH RPM

You can verify software packages using GnoRPM as the `root` user. Verification is a useful tool; it ensures that your application has been completely installed, with no missing modules. If you are having on-again, off-again problems with a Linux utility, verifying packages can be a good way to eliminate one possibility — your program cannot be short a few nuts and bolts to work properly.

Verification is particularly helpful with installs that you have performed by downloading programs over the World Wide Web or the local network. On a busy network, traffic may cause some sensitive material to drop out or become corrupted. That is, when information is sent over a network, it is broken up into small packets of information that the network can handle. If a few packets of information that are critical to how well a program function are lost, the program may appear complete upon arrival, but instead is badly flawed. Verification of completeness is even more important in these cases.

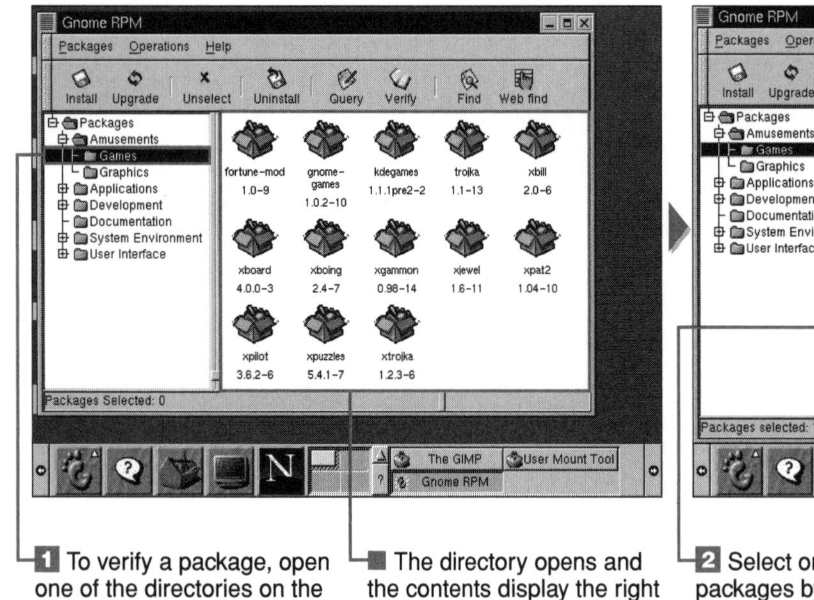

1 To verify a package, open one of the directories on the left pane of the Gnome RPM screen.

■ The directory opens and the contents display the right pane.

2 Select one of the packages by right-clicking it.

3 Select Query from the pop-up menu.

Why do I need to verify a package after I have queried it?

✔ A software query simply gives you more information on the contents of the file, the programmers, and the software version — it does not tell you the condition of the file's contents, whether a piece is missing, or whether a file has been corrupted. Never substitute verification with a query.

What should I do if I discover evidence of file corruption?

✔ In these cases, perform a complete reinstall rather than fix the problem piece by piece. Run GnoRPM to uninstall the package (per the Remove Software Packages with RPM task later in the chapter) to remove the package. From there, reinstall the software from scratch.

What should I do if I discover evidence of file incompleteness?

✔ An incomplete file is one that did not install properly. Immediately reinstall the package.

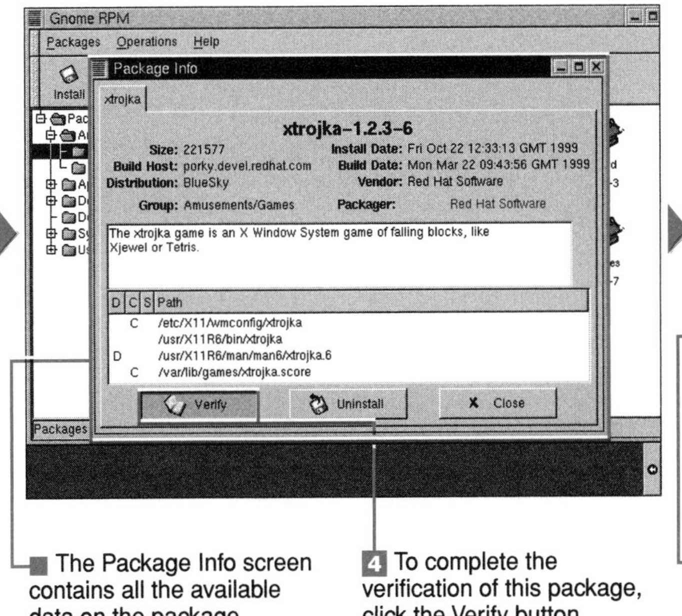

■ The Package Info screen contains all the available data on the package.

4 To complete the verification of this package, click the Verify button.

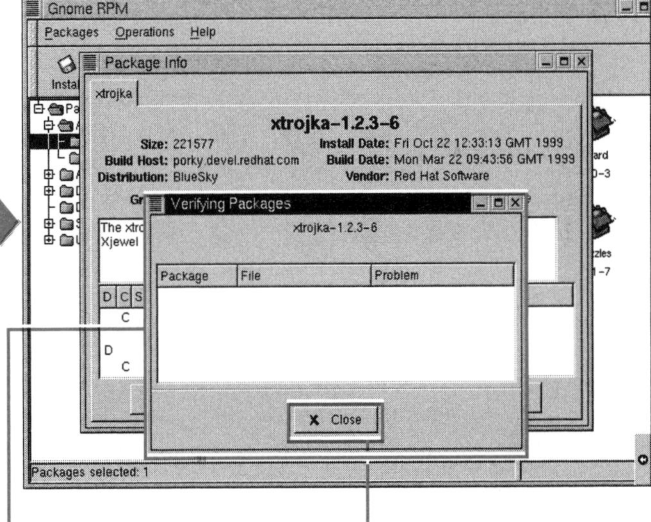

■ The Verifying Packages screen appears.

■ Since there are no comments indicating that the file is corrupt, its health is verified.

5 Click Close to return to the Query screen.

INSTALL SOFTWARE PACKAGES WITH RPM

You can use GnoRPM to easily and seamlessly install new or upgraded software packages. Although GnoRPM works best with new software, and more easily with software that has been written specifically for Linux (especially Red Hat Linux), it can install most any Linux software package.

If you want to install software on your Linux system from a UNIX system, you may run into difficulty. UNIX comes in many more flavors, or brands, than does Linux. For instance, Solaris or HPUX are two UNIX examples. Unfortunately, there is no way to reliably determine which software from the different kinds of UNIX will work with your system.

The GnoRPM Add function is one quirk to be aware of when installing new programs. If you click the Add button more than once, you end up listing the same program to be installed twice. Use the Unselect option or button to keep the list down to its particulars.

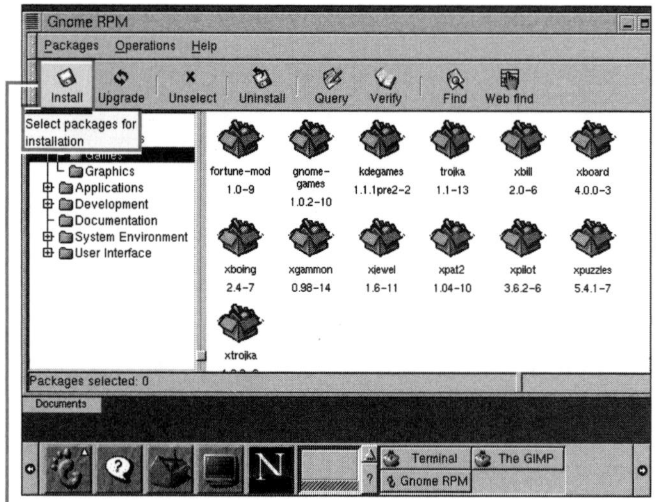

1 In the GNOME RPM, click Install from the toolbar menu.

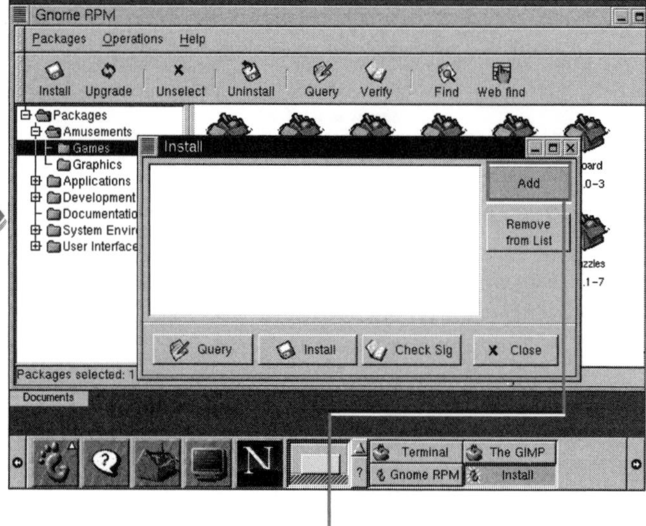

2 When the Install screen appears, click the Add button.

Why will GnoRPM not install a UNIX package on my Linux system?

- Some software packages from proprietary vendors will not install properly on Red Hat Linux; therefore, GnoRPM does not recognize them. If it did, then you might be stuck with a mess of applications that either would not work or would interfere with applications that did work.

How similar is the procedure to performing a software upgrade?

- The process is almost exactly the same. Instead of selecting Install from the toolbar, you select the icon to the right of that: Upgrade. From that point, the selection process and confirmation dialog box is exactly the same.

I mounted the CD-ROM drive and navigated to /mnt/cdrom in the GnoRPM application, but there are no files listed. What is wrong?

- It is likely that the CD-ROM is scratched or dusty, preventing it from being read. Eject the CD-ROM and check it for physical problems.

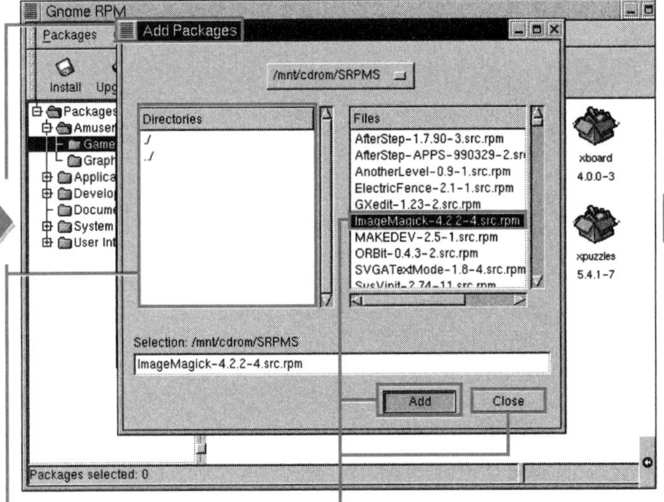

- The Add Packages screen appears.
- Using the left panel, you can navigate to `/mnt/cdrom` to view the packages available for installation.

3 Choose the packages from the list in the right pane; click those you want.

4 Click Add to add the package to the install list.

5 Click Close to return to the Install screen.

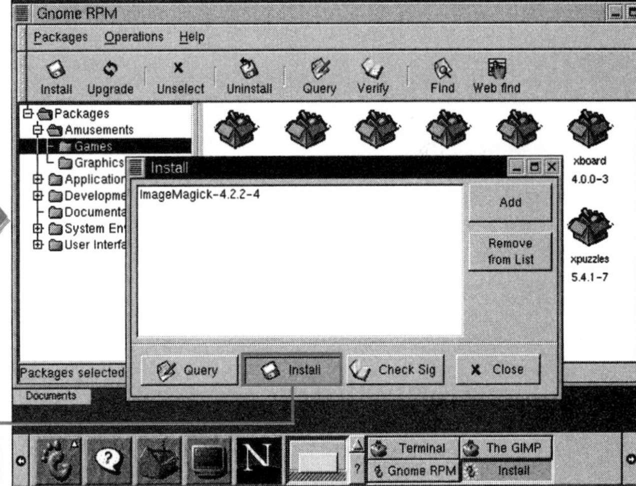

6 Click the Install button when you are returned to the Install screen.

- GNOME RPM installs the package and returns you to the Install screen after it completes the install.

REMOVE SOFTWARE PACKAGES WITH RPM

You can use GnoRPM to remove Linux software packages easily and without leaving code debris behind to take up hard drive space. Though GnoRPM works best with new software, and more easily with software that has been written specifically for Linux (especially Red Hat Linux), it can remove most Linux or UNIX software packages.

You should use software removal sparingly despite the fact that Red Hat Linux provides a dialog box that confirms that you want to remove a given package. Always schedule downtime for a software overhaul; expect problems if the install and removal do not go exactly perfectly. Also keep in mind that programs are often hooked into common files that can cause problems when the hooks are removed. Be prepared to track down any difficulties that you find as soon as you have removed software from your system. Otherwise, these problems can trouble your system long after the software in question has been removed.

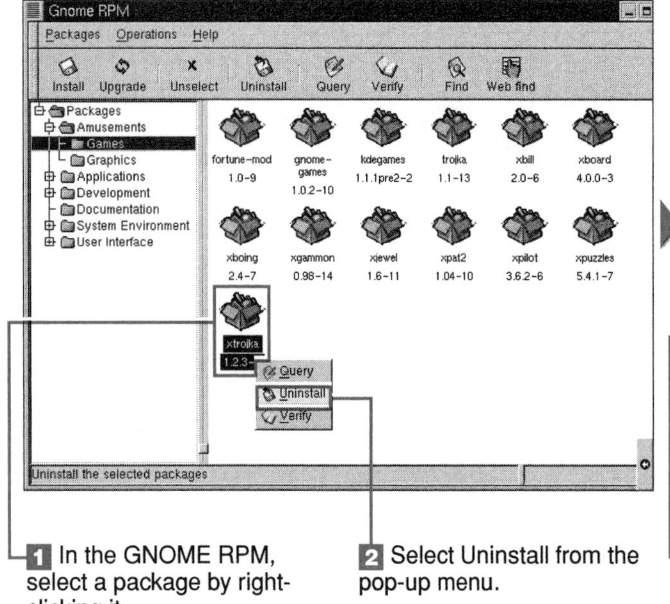

1 In the GNOME RPM, select a package by right-clicking it.

2 Select Uninstall from the pop-up menu.

■ As an alternative, in the GNOME RPM, select a package by clicking it once to highlight.

Should I use rm (the file removal command) or uninstall in GnoRPM for most file deletions?

- As long as you have the GNOME environment available, `uninstall` is much better than `rm`, which is designed to zap files. `uninstall` is designed to dig for all the small programs that feed into a major installed application, and it removes them more cleanly.

How can I check for leftover files after completing a major software removal?

- The GnoRPM `verify` command is useful after performing an `uninstall`; the `verify` command checks for debris that may be left behind. If the command complains that it is finding only portions of the program available, you must go into the file system and use `rm` or `vi` to delete these last portions.

If I temporarily remove a Red Hat Linux package, will I have problems reinstalling it?

- You should not have problems. GnoRPM is designed to make smooth repeat installations and deletions.

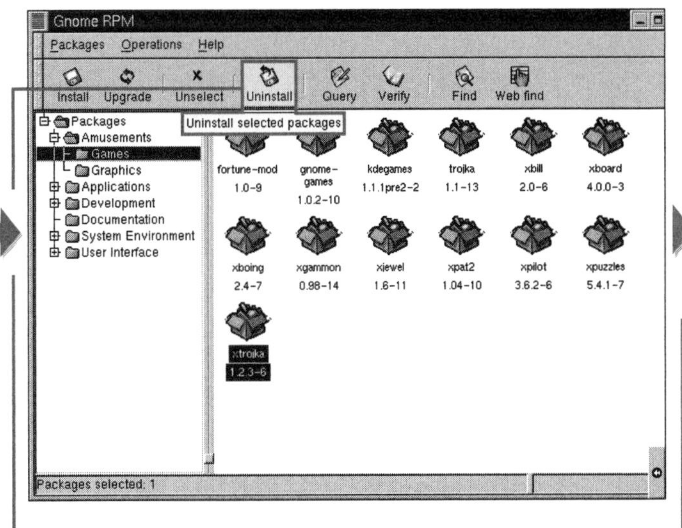

■ Then, click the Uninstall button on the toolbar.

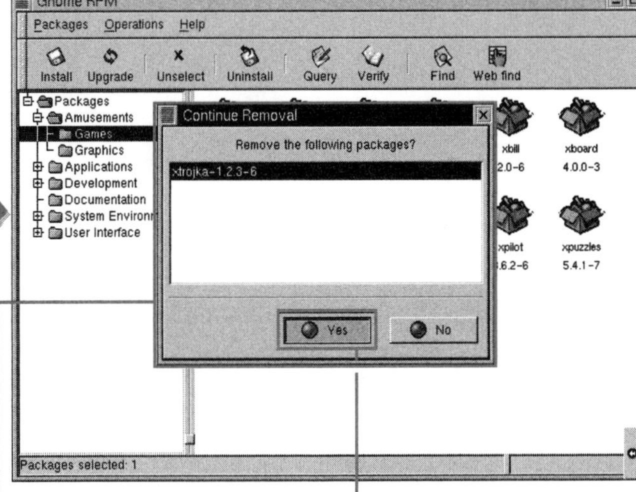

■ The Continue Removal screen appears and GNOME RPM asks you for a final confirmation.

3 Click Yes if you are sure you want to remove this package.

■ The package and its icon disappear.

START AND EXIT GNOTEPAD+

Gnotepad+ is a word processing program that comes with all Red Hat Linux installations. Although gnotepad+ doesn't have all the options that come with Microsoft Word, it's on the same par with WordPad in Windows and can produce a quality office document, memo, or resume.

Word processing on your Linux machine—or any computer—is much like composing on a typewriter. However, you can edit multiple documents on the fly, undo mistakes, and cut or paste whole sections of text in a way that typewriters simply cannot match.

As in most word processors, you have several ways to exit gnotepad+ after editing your document. Because gnotepad+ works with the GNOME graphics-based desktop, you can use the menu button, the Close button, or an icon on the toolbar to close gnotepad+.

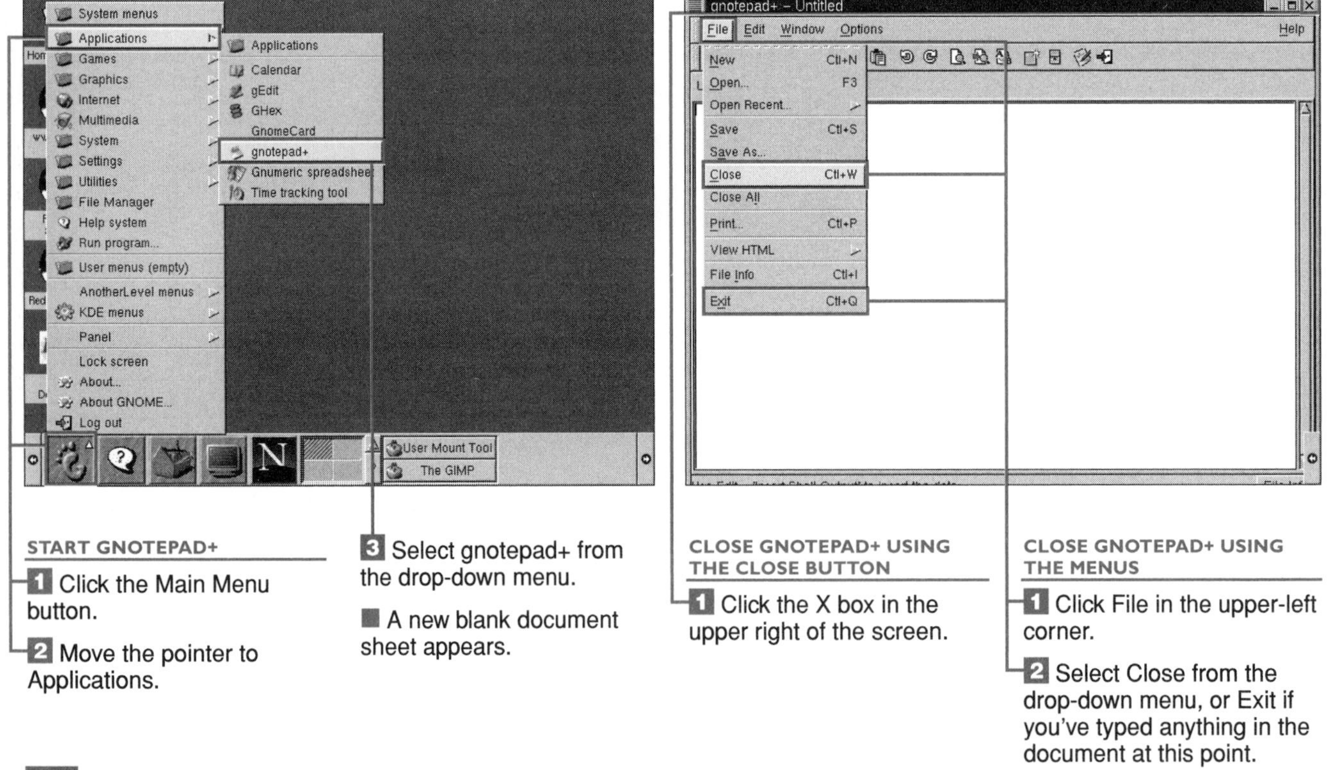

START GNOTEPAD+

1 Click the Main Menu button.

2 Move the pointer to Applications.

3 Select gnotepad+ from the drop-down menu.

■ A new blank document sheet appears.

CLOSE GNOTEPAD+ USING THE CLOSE BUTTON

1 Click the X box in the upper right of the screen.

CLOSE GNOTEPAD+ USING THE MENUS

1 Click File in the upper-left corner.

2 Select Close from the drop-down menu, or Exit if you've typed anything in the document at this point.

TIPS

How can I transfer my gnotepad+ document to another machine?

- Save your document to a mounted floppy disk. You can then take the document on disk to edit on another machine. If the machine is on the same network, you may consider copying it there instead.

Why can't I save my document in places like the / directory?

- You're probably not logged in as the root administrator account, who owns those areas. Remember, unless you have write permissions in a directory — as yourself, your group, or for everyone — you cannot save a document there.

Which style of commands should I use— the toolbar buttons or the drop-down menus?

- Either method works. Whichever you choose to use is purely a matter of personal preference.

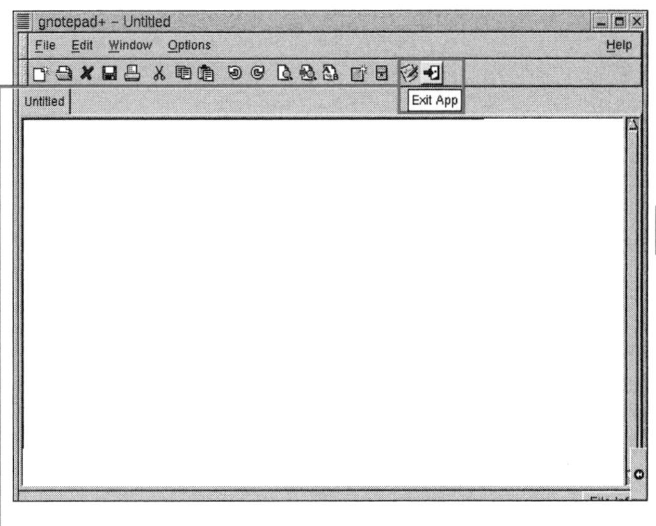

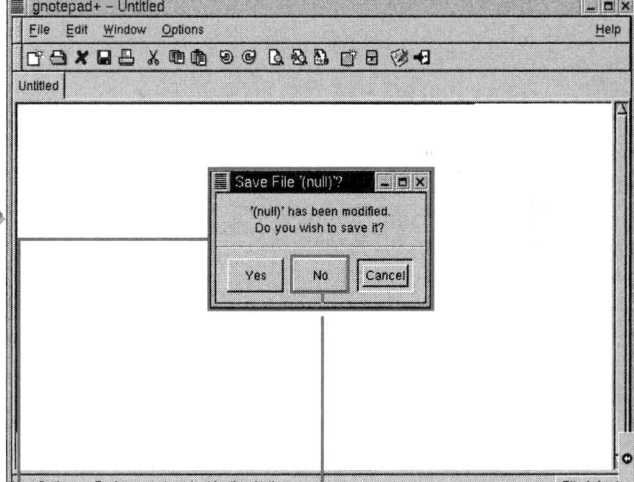

CLOSE GNOTEPAD+ USING THE TOOLBAR ICON

1 Click the Exit App (Exit Application) icon.

■ If you hold the mouse pointer over the icon for a few seconds, a label pops up, telling you the button's function.

■ If you've edited the document in any way, gnotepad+ warns you that the document was modified and asks you if you want to save it.

2 Click No if you don't want to save any changes and exit the program.

CREATE AND SAVE NEW DOCUMENTS

You can create new documents whenever you want to make note of a procedure, put together a job report, or send a letter to a friend. gnotepad+ is extremely easy to use, especially if you are familiar with other, more esoteric text editors such as `ex` or `vi`.

Save your new documents for future use and editing. In addition, timely backups reduce lost productivity — and frayed nerves — if there is a disk crash or power outage at the wrong time.

Of course, nothing equals the importance of a good disk or tape backup of the entire system, but as an individual user make an effort to save your work as you type. And as an administrator, it's the least you can do to keep copies of the more sensitive Linux files on tape or, failing that, a floppy disk.

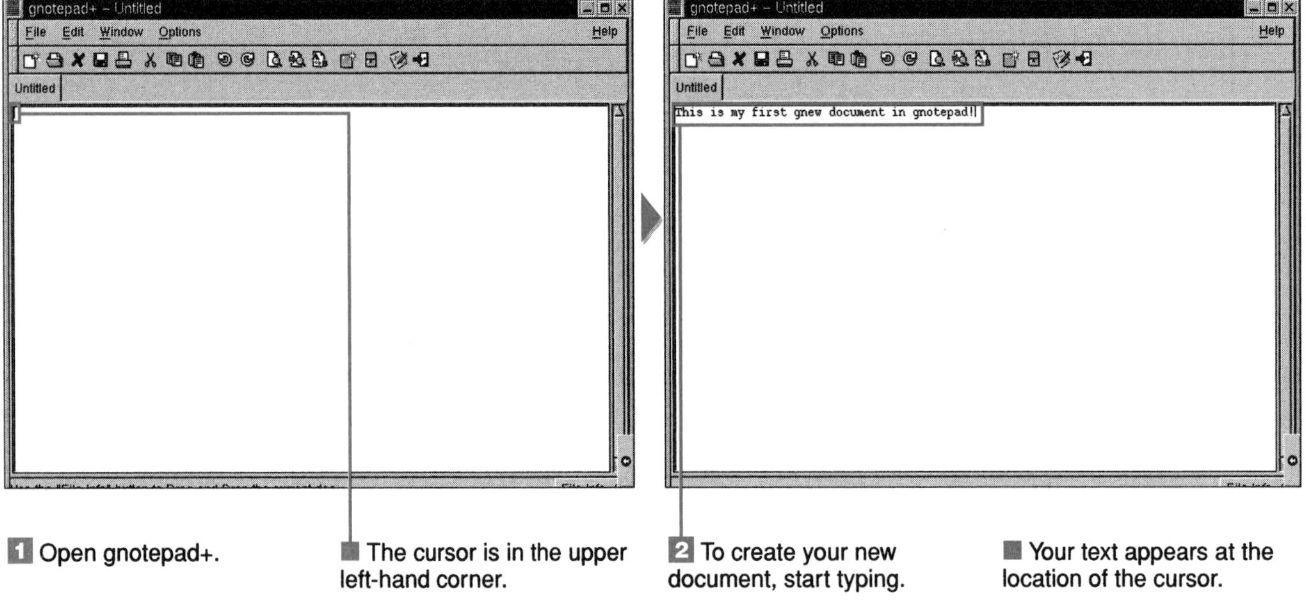

1 Open gnotepad+.

■ The cursor is in the upper left-hand corner.

2 To create your new document, start typing.

■ Your text appears at the location of the cursor.

What's the advantage of using Save versus Save As?

- The first time you save a document, it doesn't matter which command you use, because you are prompted to pick a name for your new document. On subsequent saves, it does matter. Selecting Save re-writes the file to disk with your new changes. Save As creates a new file for you to name, which consists of the old file with your new changes added in.

How can I transfer text documents between gnotepad+ and other programs?

- Save and transfer files as Plain Text. This option is the default in gnotepad+ and a selection available to you in Microsoft Word.

Is there another way to save a document besides clicking the Save toolbar button?

- Alternatively, you can click File and select Save or Save As from the drop-down menu.

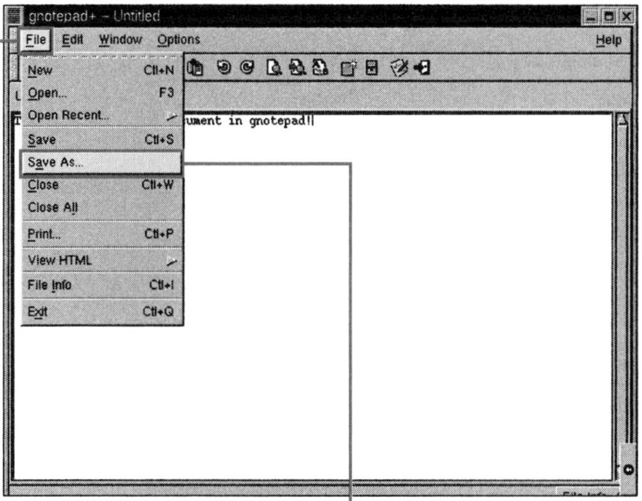

3 Click File.

4 Click Save As.

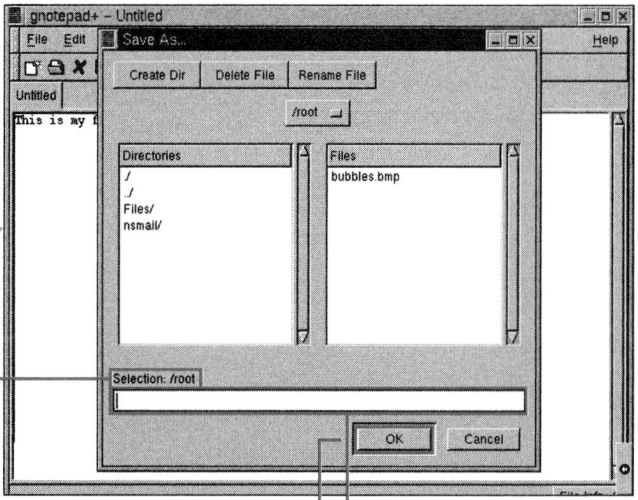

■ The Save As screen appears.

■ By default, your document is saved to your home directory unless you specify otherwise.

4 Type a name for your file in the Selection: /root field at the bottom of the Save As screen.

5 Click OK.

OPEN NEW DOCUMENTS

You can open existing documents to edit in gnotepad+ when you want to add, delete, or just re-word a piece of text. When you decide to open a document, you must be sure that you know its location. For example, if you plan to open and edit a document that exists only on a floppy, mount the floppy before you search for the file in `/mnt/floppy`.

Due to the inconvenience in hunting for files to edit, it's best to establish an area (usually your home directory) where you can find all of your files. In addition, consider copying a file from a floppy directly to the hard drive if you'll edit it on a regular basis. This avoids the slow access time from a floppy disk and allows you to work faster.

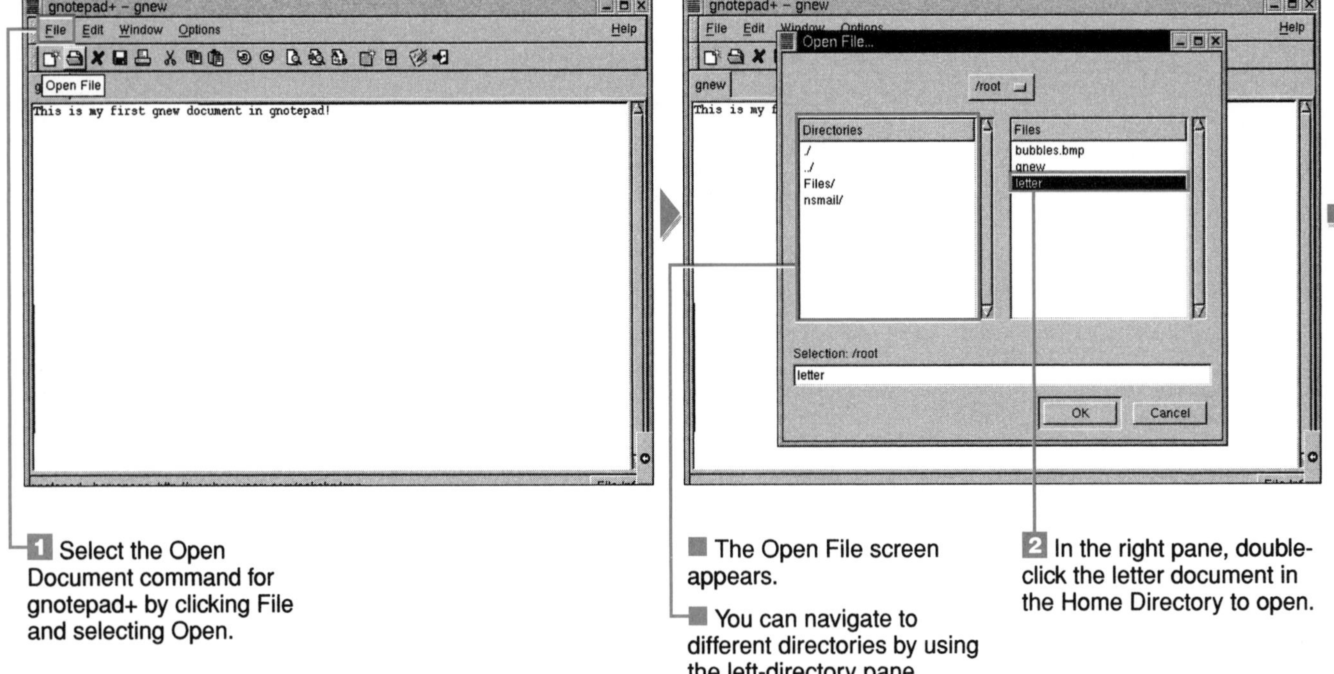

1 Select the Open Document command for gnotepad+ by clicking File and selecting Open.

■ The Open File screen appears.

■ You can navigate to different directories by using the left-directory pane.

2 In the right pane, double-click the letter document in the Home Directory to open.

Is there a faster way to open a document?

- If you've been saving the file regularly in the same location and you've just worked with it recently, there is. Under the Open selection in the drop-down menu, you can get an additional menu to pop up, listing the last 4 or 5 files you edited. Select one by clicking it.

Do I have to use the drop-down menus to open a document?

- You can open a document by clicking the Open icon on the toolbar, which is shaped like a piece of paper in an opening folder.

Why can't I see the document I want to edit in the Open window?

- Either you saved the document elsewhere, or you may have opened the Open window in a new location. Use the left pane to navigate if you're in a different location.

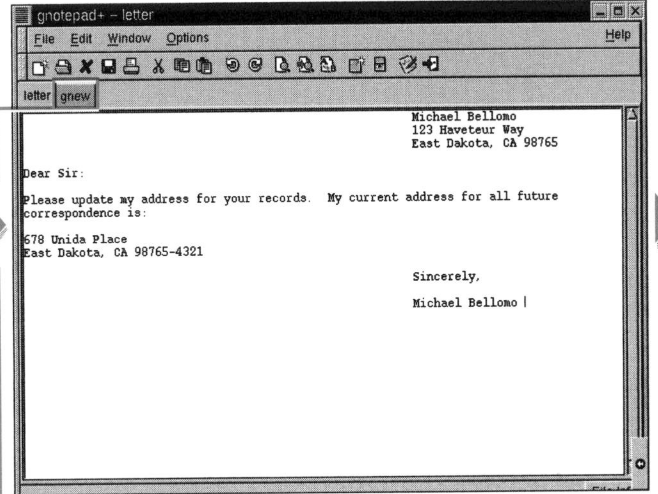

■ When the letter document opens, the older document, gnew, hasn't been overwritten or hidden. Instead, it's in the background, accessible via a tab.

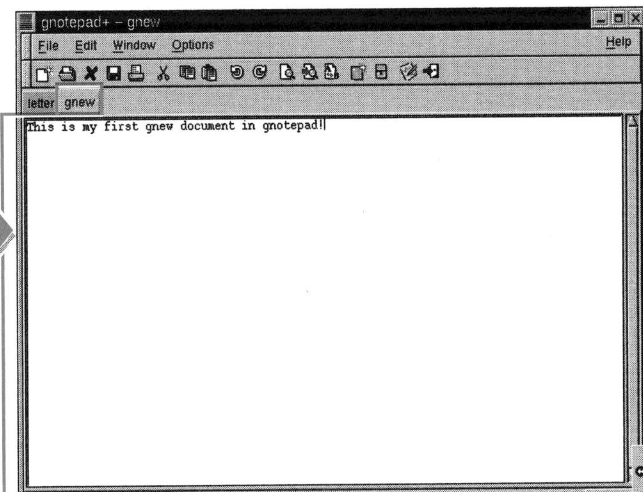

3 To get gnew back to the foreground, click the gnew tab.

■ Gnew moves to the front while letter moves to the background.

INSERT AND DELETE TEXT

You can insert text into any word processing document and delete it at will. gnotepad+ offers you more choices than many of the text editors in Linux, and it doesn't require you to remember if you're in Command Mode or Insert Mode when you do so.

The differences in text insertion and deletion among text editors center on specific conventions in gnotepad+. For example, no other text processor contains a wrap-around notation. Also, most of the options available to you for inserting and deleting text differ in the location of the action—to the right or left of the cursor.

Keep in mind that if you want to insert or delete a large block of text, these aren't the commands you want. See the commands for Moving and Pasting text later in this chapter.

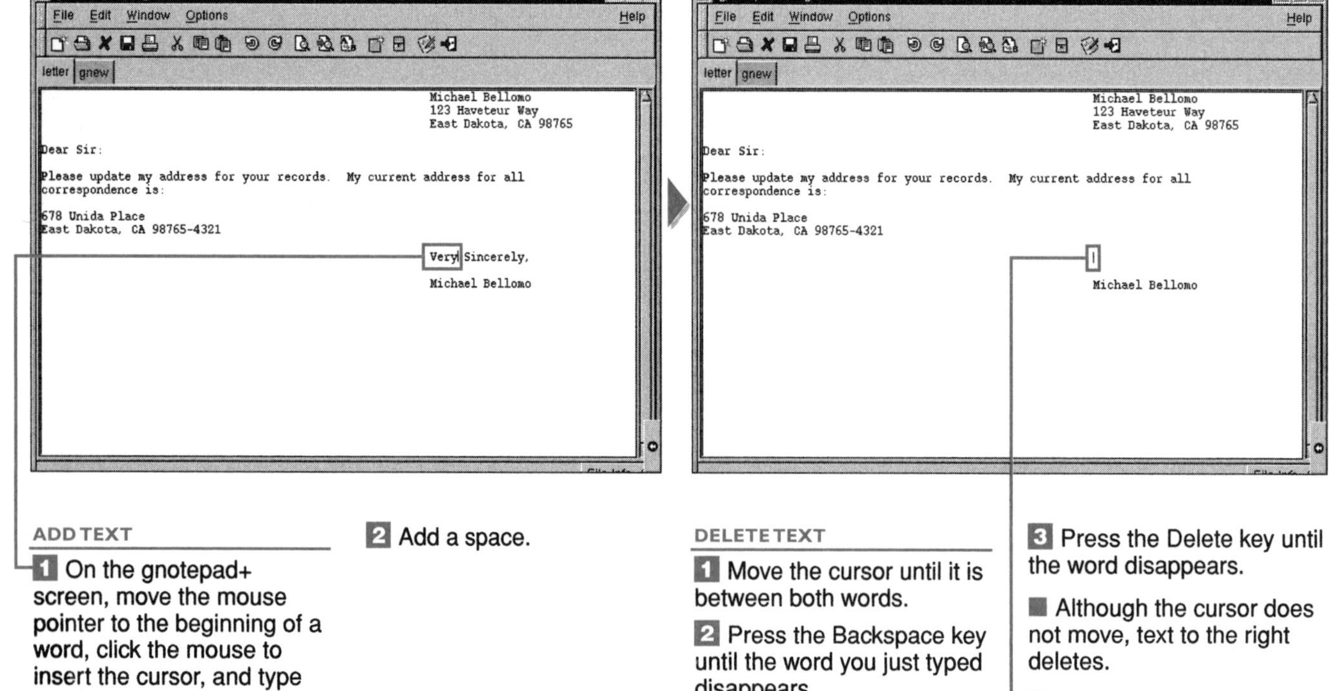

ADD TEXT

1 On the gnotepad+ screen, move the mouse pointer to the beginning of a word, click the mouse to insert the cursor, and type another word in front.

2 Add a space.

DELETE TEXT

1 Move the cursor until it is between both words.

2 Press the Backspace key until the word you just typed disappears.

Note: The cursor moves to the left, deleting text as it moves.

3 Press the Delete key until the word disappears.

■ Although the cursor does not move, text to the right deletes.

■ The line that contained the two words is blank.

How can I delete an entire line of text?

- Unlike the `vi` editor, there is no command to delete a whole line. However, if you click and drag the mouse to select a line, pressing the delete or backspace key will delete the entire line.

How can I select a word with the mouse?

- Aside from clicking and dragging, placing the cursor inside the boundaries of the word with a click and then clicking a second time will highlight the entire word. Pressing the Backspace or Delete key removes the offending word at a moment's notice.

How can I delete all of the text in a single document?

- Click the Edit menu and then click Select All. This will highlight the entire document. Press the delete or backspace key to remove all the highlighted text.

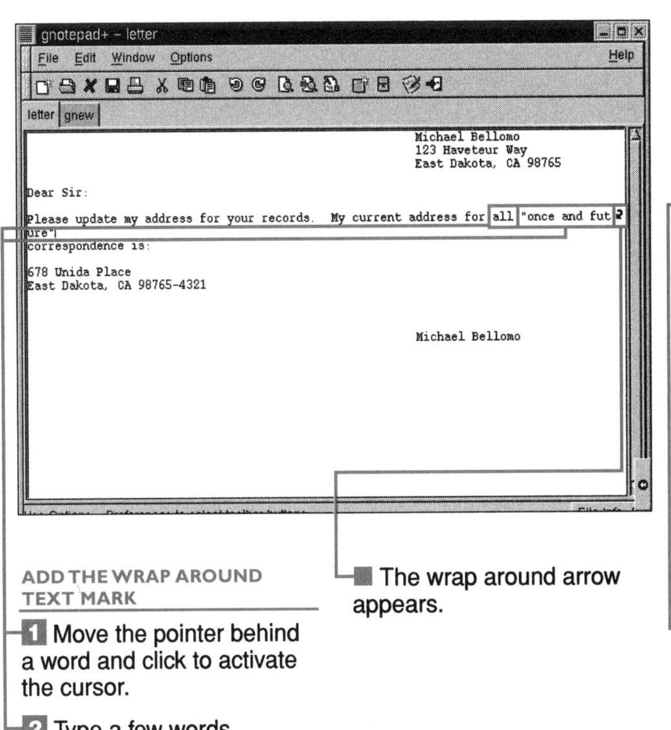

ADD THE WRAP AROUND TEXT MARK

1 Move the pointer behind a word and click to activate the cursor.

2 Type a few words.

■ The wrap around arrow appears.

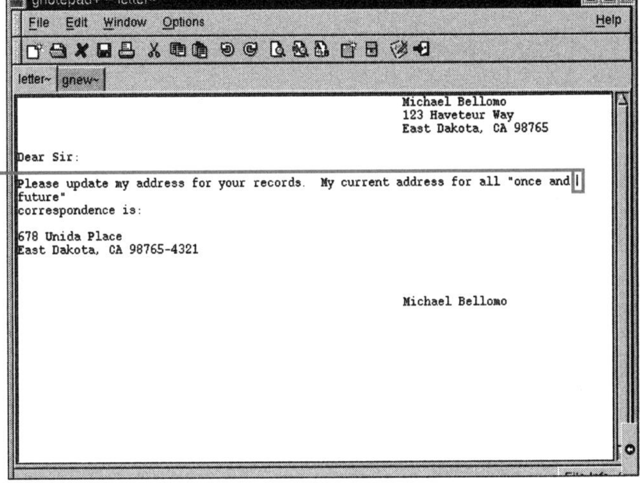

REMOVE THE WRAP AROUND TEXT MARK

1 Click the cursor where you want to break the line — after the word — and press Enter.

■ This adds an extra Carriage Return to break the line.

MOVE AND COPY TEXT

You can use the Cut, Copy, and Paste buttons to move and copy text in gnotepad+. As with other graphics-based text processors like WordPerfect or Microsoft Word, the mouse is useful for positioning the cursor and dragging it over large bodies of text to highlight or select.

When you use the mouse along with the Cut and Paste functions in gnotepad+, you have unprecedented mobility when it comes to text placement.

When you either cut or copy text, it is placed in a special buffer or clipboard until you decide to paste it somewhere.

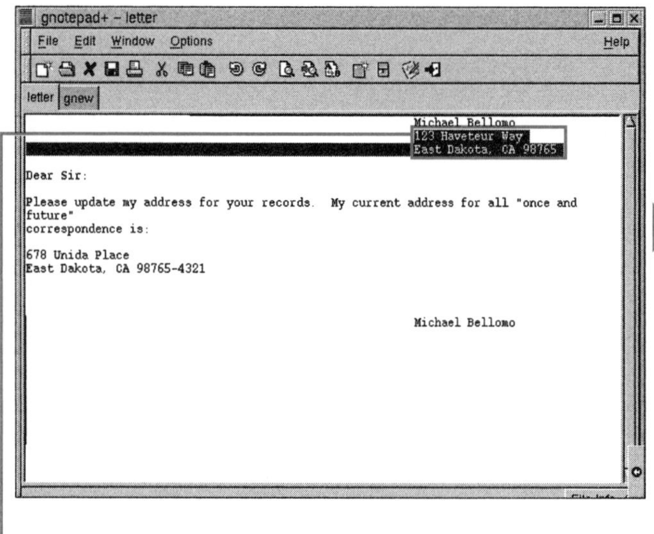

1 Move your mouse pointer to the start of a two-line sentence.

2 Click and drag to highlight both lines.

■ You can cut, copy, or paste the highlighted section.

3 Select Cut from the Edit drop-down menu to cut this text.

How can I use Cut and Paste to make multiple copies of a text pattern?

- Simply Copy or Cut the text pattern you want. Move the cursor to a location you want, or open a new document. For each copy of the pattern you want, press Paste (or type **Ctrl+V**). If you need large quantities of the pattern, you can paste five copies; and then select and copy that pattern of five.

How can I use the text that's on the clipboard?

- If you want to use or re-use this text, you can open a new document and paste it onto the blank page. In addition, Linux normally notifies you if you have more than one page of text on the clipboard when you attempt to close gnotepad+. You are given the option of putting the text somewhere off the clipboard, or letting Linux automatically delete the text once gnotepad+ closes.

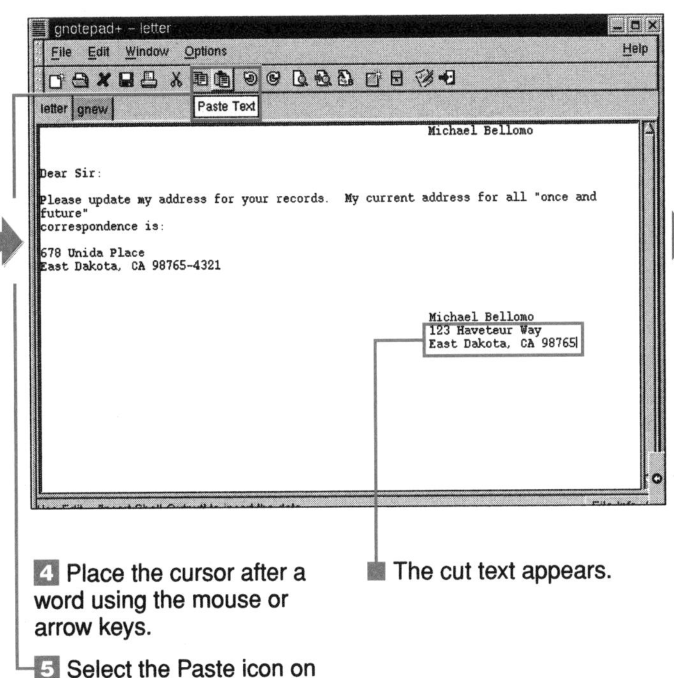

4 Place the cursor after a word using the mouse or arrow keys.

5 Select the Paste icon on the toolbar.

■ The cut text appears.

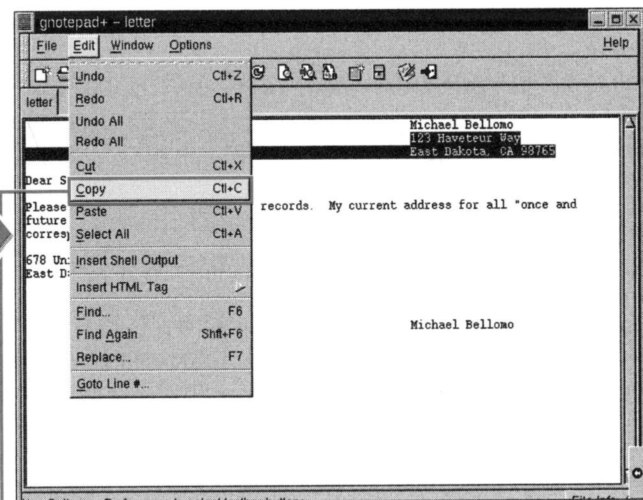

6 You can copy this text by highlighting it and selecting Copy from the Edit drop-down menu.

7 Paste this text by moving the cursor to a new location and select Paste from the Edit menu.

UNDO AND REDO CHANGES

You can undo or replace a change to a gnotepad+ document by using the Undo and Redo menu commands. The Undo and Redo menu commands are simple to use and very important if you've made a major mistake that threatens to wipe out a large amount of text.

The Undo and Redo menu commands in gnotepad+ are sophisticated enough so that, like with more mainstream word processors, it has multiple levels of undo and redo. You can even undo an action that occurred several keystrokes or commands ago.

Finally, if you can't remember the exact sequence of events, use the new menu commands Undo All and Redo All. The entire sequence of events leading to the problem is undone and you can start anew without having to search for an older copy of the document. It is wise to save your document regularly to prevent problems like this.

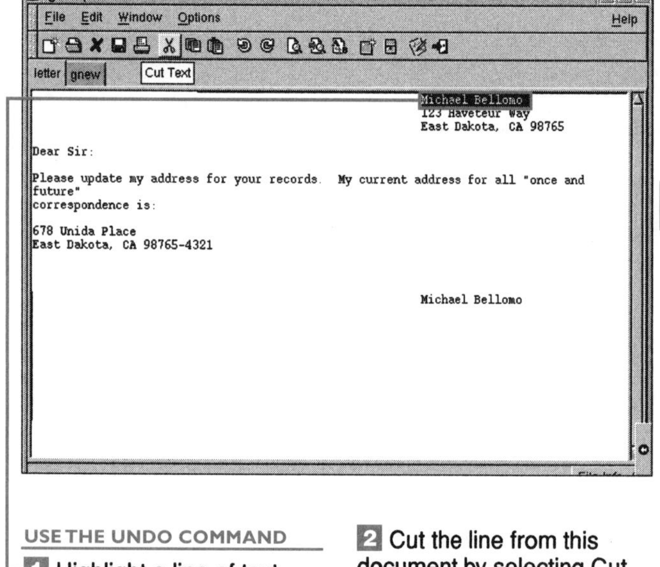

USE THE UNDO COMMAND

1 Highlight a line of text.

2 Cut the line from this document by selecting Cut from the Edit menu.

3 Select Undo from the Edit drop-down menu.

■ Selecting Undo once undoes the last action.

■ You need to select the command once for each action that you want to undo.

TIPS

How do I remember which icon is Undo and which is Redo?

- You can move the mouse pointer over one of the buttons and see which notification screen pops up. An easier way to remember is that as you type text, the cursor moves from left to right across the screen. The Undo arrow turns counter-clockwise (to the left) against the flow of text, as if it were turning back the typed event.

Can I close and open the document instead of using Undo All and Redo All?

- You can, but then you have the extra steps of opening and closing the document. Furthermore, gnotepad+ will delay you even more by asking if you want to save your changes. If you accidentally click Yes, then you have no way of turning back the mistake.

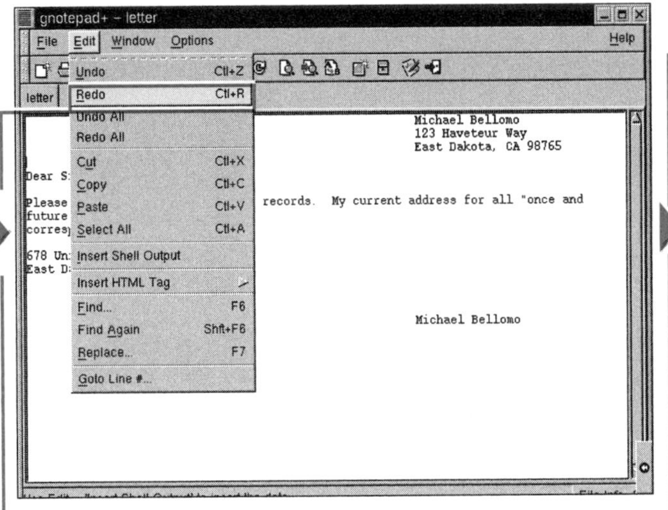

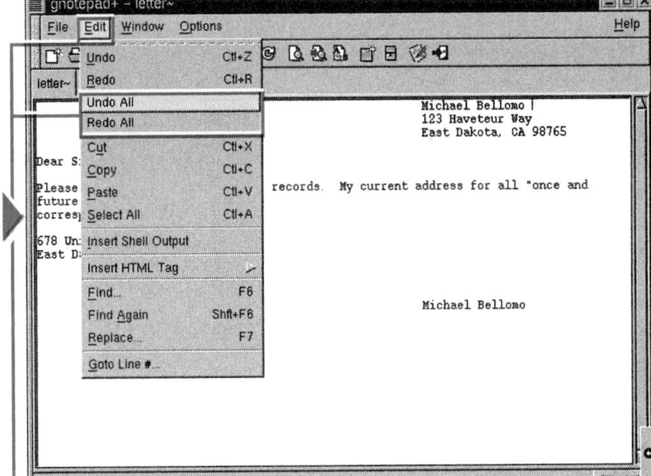

4 If you repeat your last action, select Redo from the Edit drop-down menu.

■ Selecting Redo once redoes the last action.

■ You need to select the command once for each action that you want to redo.

USE UNDO ALL AND REDO ALL

1 Click the Edit Menu.

2 Select Undo All or Redo All.

■ There are no icons or Ctrl keys to activate these commands.

SEARCH AND REPLACE TEXT IN A DOCUMENT

You have a wide range of tools available to you in Linux's gnotepad+ when it comes to finding and replacing old text patterns with new ones. Depending on whether you want to simply search for patterns or make sweeping edits, you can choose different options accordingly.

Searching menu commands are very useful if you want to edit a specific passage, or want to come to a portion of a long document that is hard to find. The Find menu works particularly well on long, dense passages where it's difficult to pick out what you're looking for.

Replacement commands, particularly the Replace All, is the most incredibly efficient way to make multiple, identical changes to a document. Instead of having to scroll through the document and select each instance, a single click of the mouse does all the work for you.

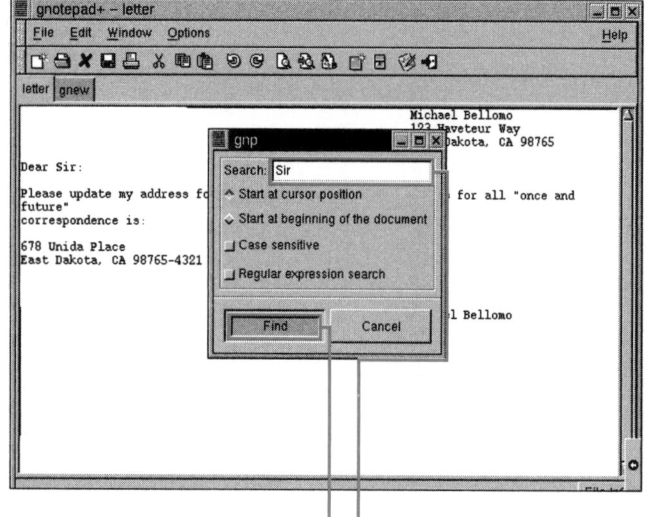

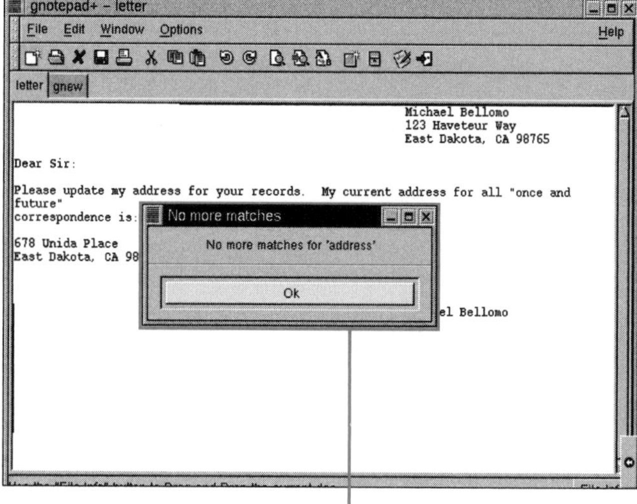

USE FIND

1 Select Find from the Edit menu.

■ The Find screen appears.

■ The Find button is grayed out until you type a pattern to search for.

2 Type a text pattern in the Search text box.

3 Click Find.

■ You are taken to the first occurrence of the pattern.

USE FIND AGAIN

1 Select Find Again from the Edit menu.

■ Find Again searches for the next occurrence of the pattern until it no longer finds the pattern. The command notifies you when there are no more matches.

How can I find a specific, but common pattern like "the" in a document?

- If you're searching for a specific "the" in a document that could have a dozen "the" patterns, you need to get more specific. The Find menu command in gnotepad+ can search for text patterns the size of phrases. So if you really mean to find the sentence "The morning was passing," you can put the whole phrase in and avoid finding all the other "the" patterns in the way.

How can I search for a pattern in a series of documents?

- While there is no text searcher for multiple documents like Linux's **`grep`** command in gnotepad+, there is an alternative. Open all the documents you want to search in gnotepad+. You can move from one document to the next by clicking on the Tab labels. On each document, perform a Find.

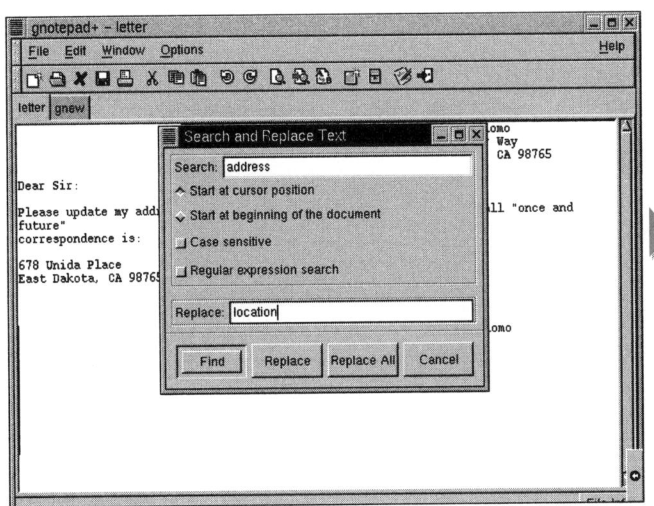

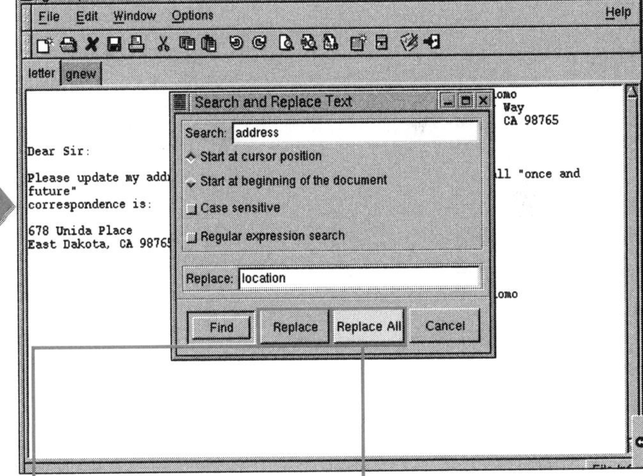

USE REPLACE

1 Select Replace from the Edit menu.

■ The Search and Replace Text screen appears.

■ The button selections are grayed out until you type a pattern to search for.

2 Type a pattern in the Search text box and Replace text box.

3 Click Replace.

■ This action replaces the first occurrence of a word with another.

4 Click Replace All.

■ This action searches the entire document and replaces all text patterns that match the search pattern.

PRINT DOCUMENTS

You can send a copy of your work to a print device like a laser printer or ink jet plotter from gnotepad+ at any time during your work. You don't need to save the document to print it. Unlike more sophisticated word processors, you cannot select a default printer for the program. Instead, each time you first print a document, you must put the printer name in.

From then on, each time you want to change to a different printer, you must type a new printer name. This is an uncommon situation, but it can lead you to change the order of your print jobs. In addition, gnotepad+ offers very limited ability to print documents in landscape or horizontal mode. gnotepad+ printing is pretty much limited to letters, memos, and other basic documents.

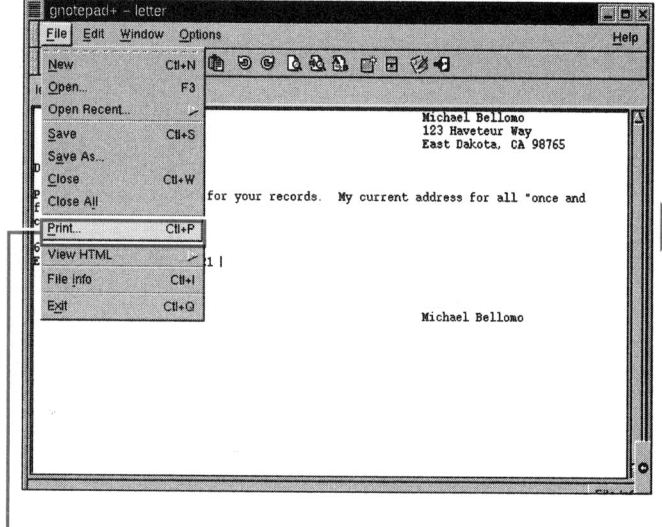

1 Select Print from the File menu.

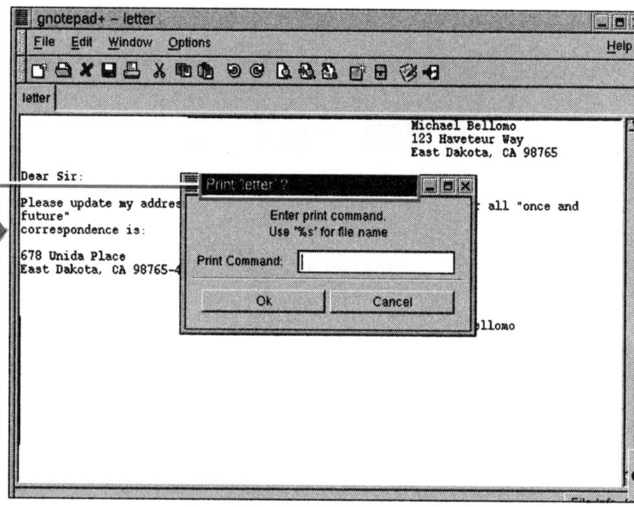

■ The Print screen appears.

How can I print out something in Landscape mode in Linux?

- In GNOME, open a graphics program like GIMP or Electric Eyes and bring up your document as a picture. You now have more control over the printing direction.

What if I can't bring it up as a graphic in these programs?

- Copy or e-mail it as an attachment to a PC with a more sophisticated word processor that can handle more esoteric print jobs. You can also make it available to any Linux box with a copy of WordStar or WordPerfect for Linux.

Is there a command for printing on the toolbar that I can use to print a document?

- Yes. Click the Print icon on the toolbar. This icon looks like a printer with a piece of paper coming out.

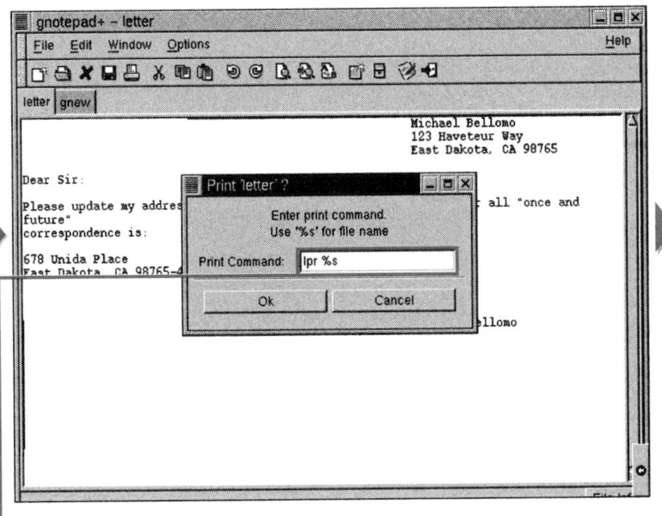

2 Unless you have a default printer set up from LinuxConf, type **lpr** and then the name of the printer you want in the Print Command field.

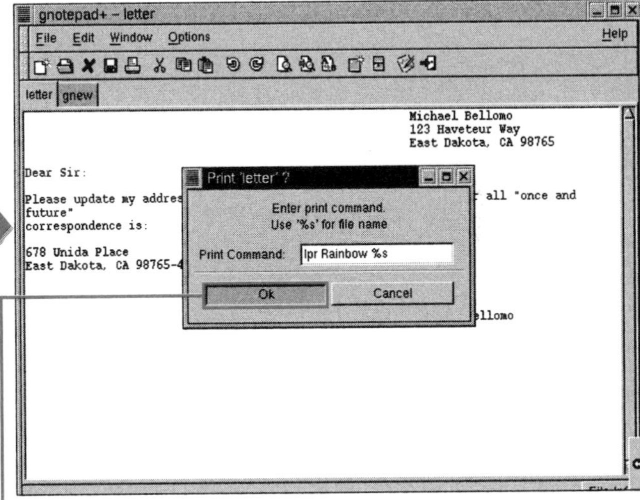

3 Click OK to start the print job.

PREFERENCES FOR GNOTEPAD+

You can change critical settings in your gnotepad+ application by editing the Preferences menu in the program. With Preferences, you can customize four major aspects of the program: the default font, print style, point size, and toolbar appearance. You can enlarge the default font, print style, and point size to make gnotepad+ easier to read or shrink it to save screen space. And you can change the toolbar appearance settings to include or exclude HTML.

Additionally, you can edit the default height of the gnotepad+ application window. If you want to play with formatting even further, you can reposition the Tab settings in the document as if you were moving the metal levers on a typewriter.

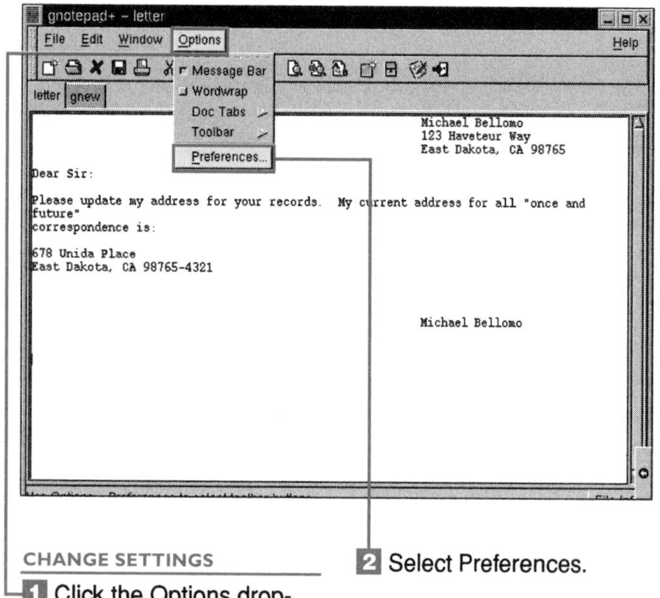

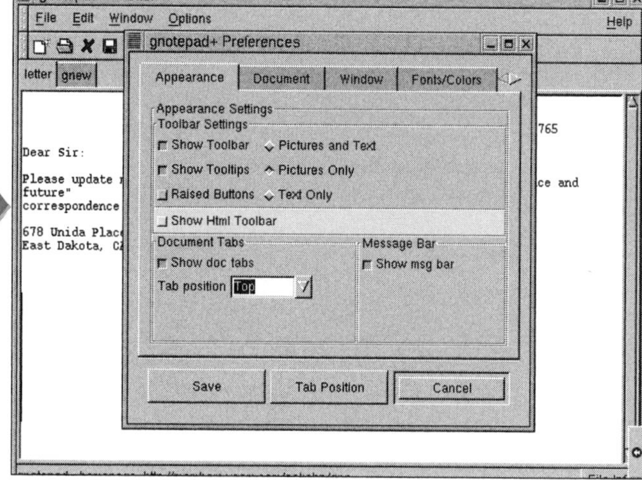

CHANGE SETTINGS

1 Click the Options drop-down menu.

2 Select Preferences.

■ The Preferences menu and its four panels appear.

When I open gnotepad+, why can't I find my document in the Recent Documents list?

- Your document may have been opened too long ago, so that it is no longer on the list. Note that time itself is not the determining factor as to whether your document is on the list. The number of different documents that have been opened since the last time you opened your own document is the determining factor.

How many recently opened documents are kept on the Recent Documents list?

- By default, gnotepad+ doesn't keep more than the last five documents you opened on the list.

Ideally, what should I set the Autosave setting to?

- This is a matter of personal preference. Don't set your computer to save your document automatically every minute; it is a drag on system resources. However, Autosave your documents at least once per hour to protect against random power outages.

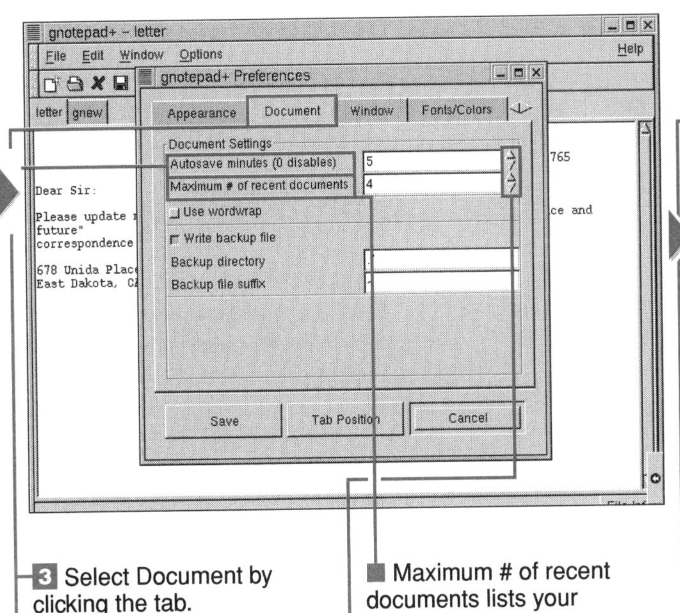

3 Select Document by clicking the tab.

■ AutoSave starts a timed save process to minimize disruption if you lose your document.

■ Maximum # of recent documents lists your recently edited documents from the File drop-down menu.

4 Change these settings by clicking the arrows to the

5 Select the Window by clicking the tab.

6 Click the arrows to the immediate right of the window height, width, or default positions fields to make any change

CONTINUED

PREFERENCES FOR GNOTEPAD+

CONTINUED

You can change the fonts used by default in your gnotepad+ documents with the Font Selection panel in the gnotepad+ preferences. Similarly, you can use the Preferences screen to change the foreground or background color in your document.

Whichever fonts you select depends on your preferences or needs. For example, if you have a dark screen or you find yourself straining your eyes to read the text in your gnotepad+ documents, increase the size of the font used in the gnotepad+ documents.

For example, if you find that you're working in the gnotepad+ application several hours, consider which font and font size you will use. Decide if you want to use a font with small letters, such as Courier, or a font with curly, busy letters such as Gothic. Changing to a cleaner font like Times, or enlarging Courier from 12 to14-point size helps avoid eyestrain.

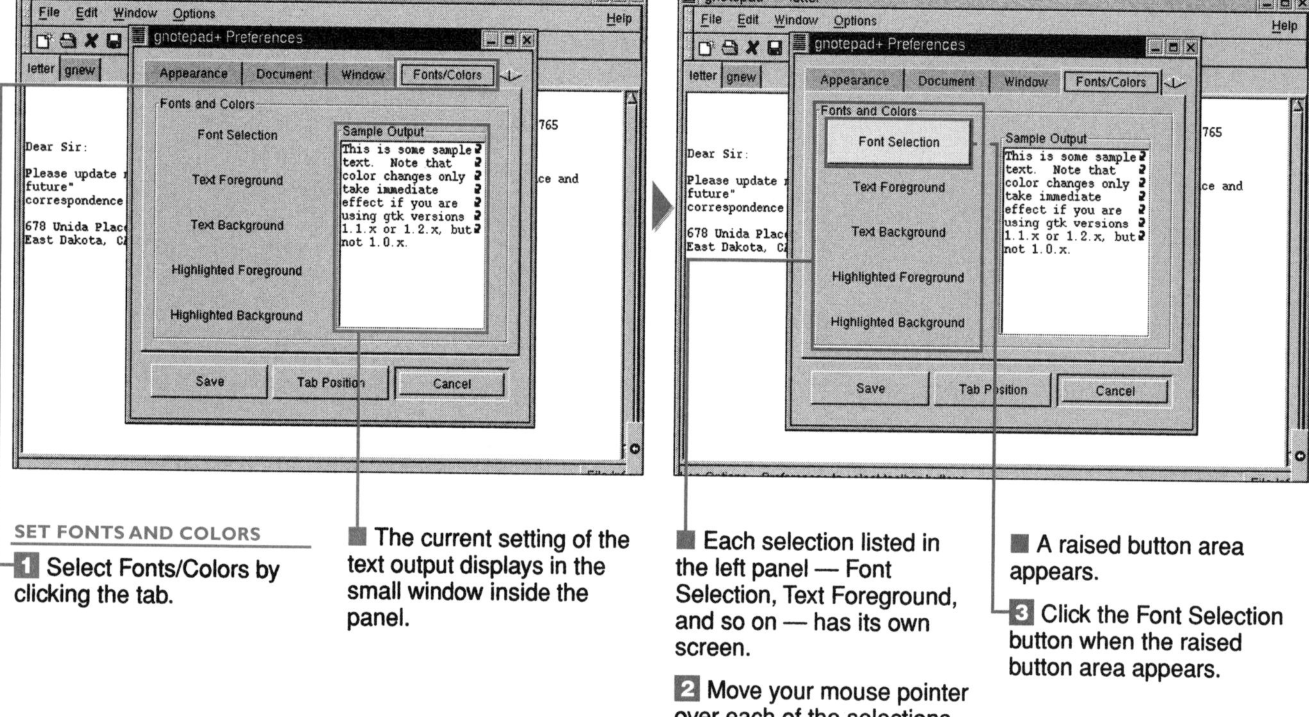

SET FONTS AND COLORS

1 Select Fonts/Colors by clicking the tab.

■ The current setting of the text output displays in the small window inside the panel.

■ Each selection listed in the left panel — Font Selection, Text Foreground, and so on — has its own screen.

2 Move your mouse pointer over each of the selections.

■ A raised button area appears.

3 Click the Font Selection button when the raised button area appears.

TIPS

Can I call up the gnotepad+ Preferences from the application's toolbar?

- Yes, by clicking the Checklist icon on the toolbar. The icon is the second one from the right

How can I reduce the size of my toolbar if I'm short on screen space?

- In the Preferences window, under the Appearance panel, you can select the types of toolbars available and change the look of the existing ones. To save space, you can request that the toolbar display text only, text and pictures together to help you remember what the icons are for, or the default, which is pictures only.

What is the recommended font type and size for a gnotepad+ document?

- All fonts and sizes are acceptable. However, for ease on the eyes, a 12-point Courier or Times font seems to be best.

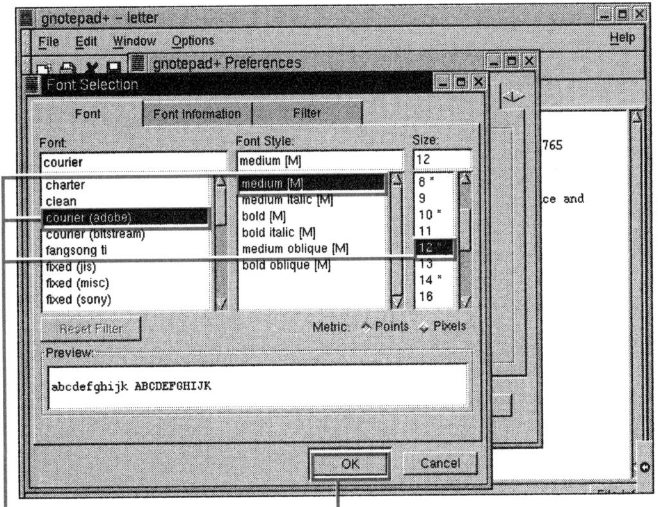

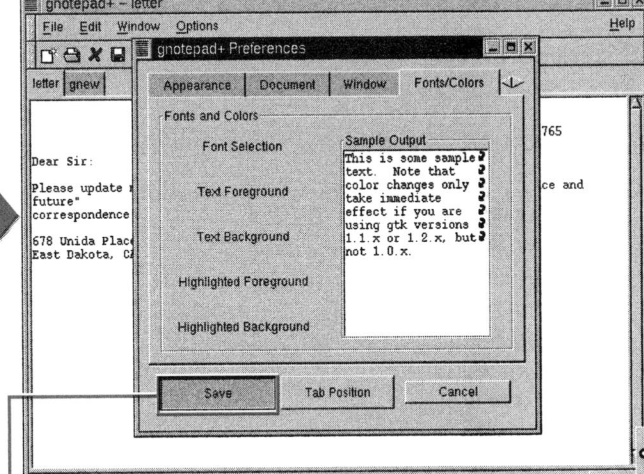

■ The Font Selection screen appears.

4 To select a given font style, font, and size, click the selection you want in each window field.

■ The Preview is located in a small window at the bottom of the panel.

5 After you finish, click OK.

■ You return to the Preferences window.

6 To make sure the system accepts your changes, click Save in the Preferences window.

TEAR-OFF MENUS

You can make use of a surprising little feature that exists in many of the Red Hat Linux programs in the GNOME environment if you're short on screen space. Many of the programs come with tear-off menus that you can move to different parts of the screen as needed.

Tear-off menus come with a dotted line that you can select in its drop-down mode. Once selected, the menu is detached from the gnotepad+ toolbar and left open on the screen.

You can then move the menu to different locations on the screen by clicking the menu with the mouse and dragging it. If you're selecting options from this menu many times, keeping a tear-off menu is convenient because you don't have to click File, Edit, or another command from the window's toolbar to 'pull down' the menu each time. This enables you to select options without having to click the menu continually to access a function on the drop-down menu.

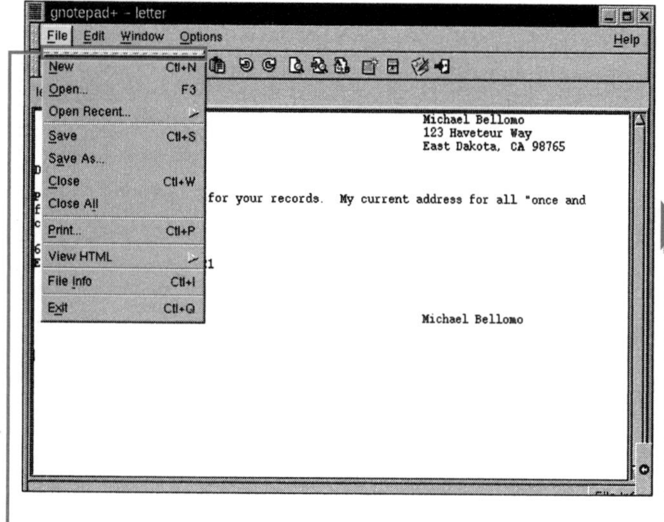

■ Tear-off menus are indicated by their dotted cut-away.

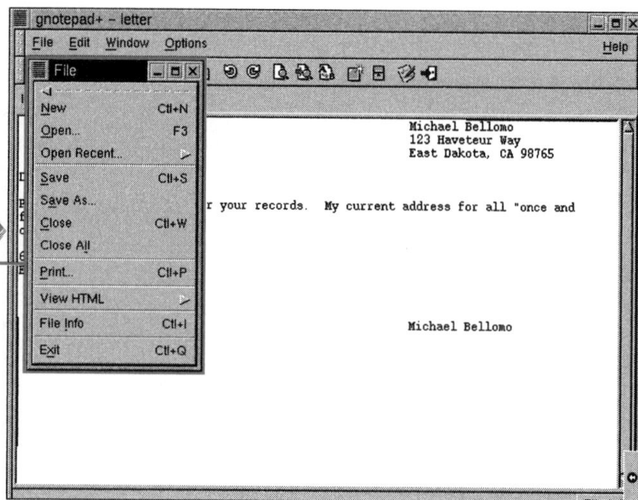

■ After you click the tear-off menu, the menu detaches itself from the drop-down area.

■ You can still execute commands from the menu.

I've lost one of my tear-off menus. Where did it go?

- You can't lose a tear-off menu. If you've lost sight of it, it's slipped behind another application's window. If you minimize program application screens one at a time, it will pop back into the foreground.

How do I remove one of the tear-off menus when I'm done with it?

- A tear-off menu is simply a graphical representation of the commands available to you. By clicking the X box on the upper right of the menu, the menu reverts to a drop-down menu.

Are there any other ways that I can close a tear-off menu that I've torn off?

- If you can't get to the X box on the menu's upper right-hand corner, you can click the left-facing arrow in the menu's upper left-hand corner to make the tear-off menu disappear.

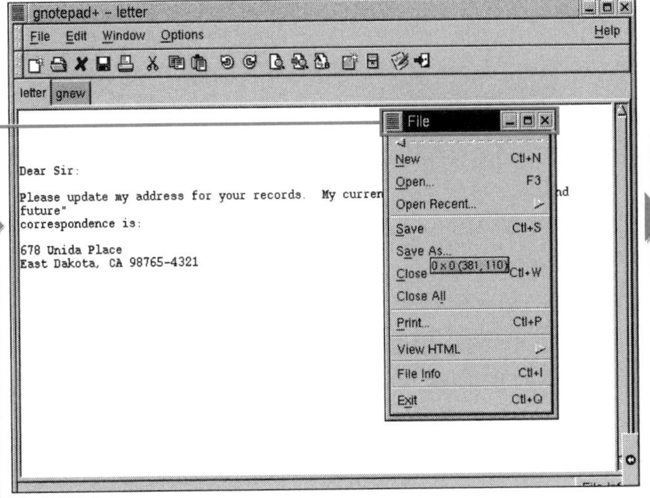

1 Click the blue border region of the detached menu.

2 Drag the menu to a new location.

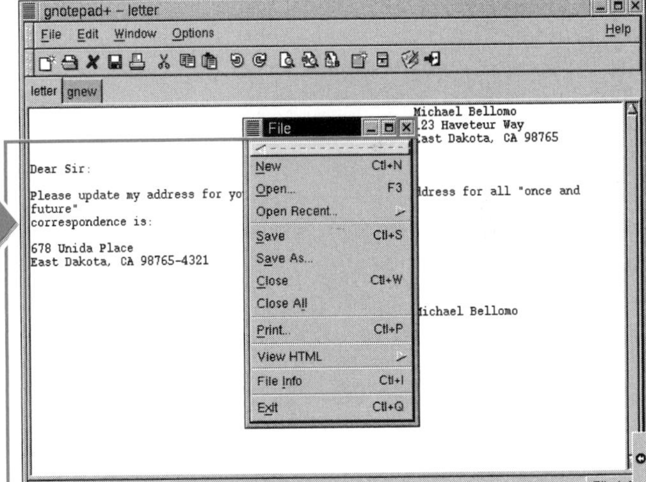

3 To close a tear-off, click the X box.

SECTION IV

14) NETWORKING IN THE LINUX GNOME ENVIRONMENT

Get Basic Host Information 322
Check Network Connectivity with ping 324
Set Up Default Gateways 326
Set Up the Routed Daemon 328

15) REMOTELY LOGGING INTO OTHER MACHINES

Log In Remotely with rlogin 330
rlogin with the -l Option 332
Use rsh — THE REMOTE SHELL 334
Log In with telnet 336
Give Remote Commands to a Remote Machine 338

16) COPYING FILES TO AND FROM OTHER MACHINES

Copy Files with uucp 340
Copy Files with rcp 342
Copy Files with ftp 344
Transfer Files with Different FTP Options 346
Change Directories while in FTP Mode 350

THE LINUX NETWORK—THE WORLD BEYOND YOUR COMPUTER

GET BASIC HOST INFORMATION

You can start to administer networking information from your Linux machine if you are connected to a group of machines. These machines can be running UNIX, Linux, Windows, or the Macintosh operating system. Upon installing Linux, you start with the default host and domain names: localhost and localdomain. Normally, you would have to go into the Linux terminal and use the `vi` editor to change the host and domain default name to the one you want.

However, with the addition of GNOME to the latest versions of Red Hat Linux, there is now a GUI front end to the process. Using the LinuxConf tool, you can start performing increasingly complex networking-setup tasks for your Linux system.

These tasks involve the Networking section of the LinuxConf tool. On some systems, the Networking portion of the directory tree is collapsed so that you cannot see the details.

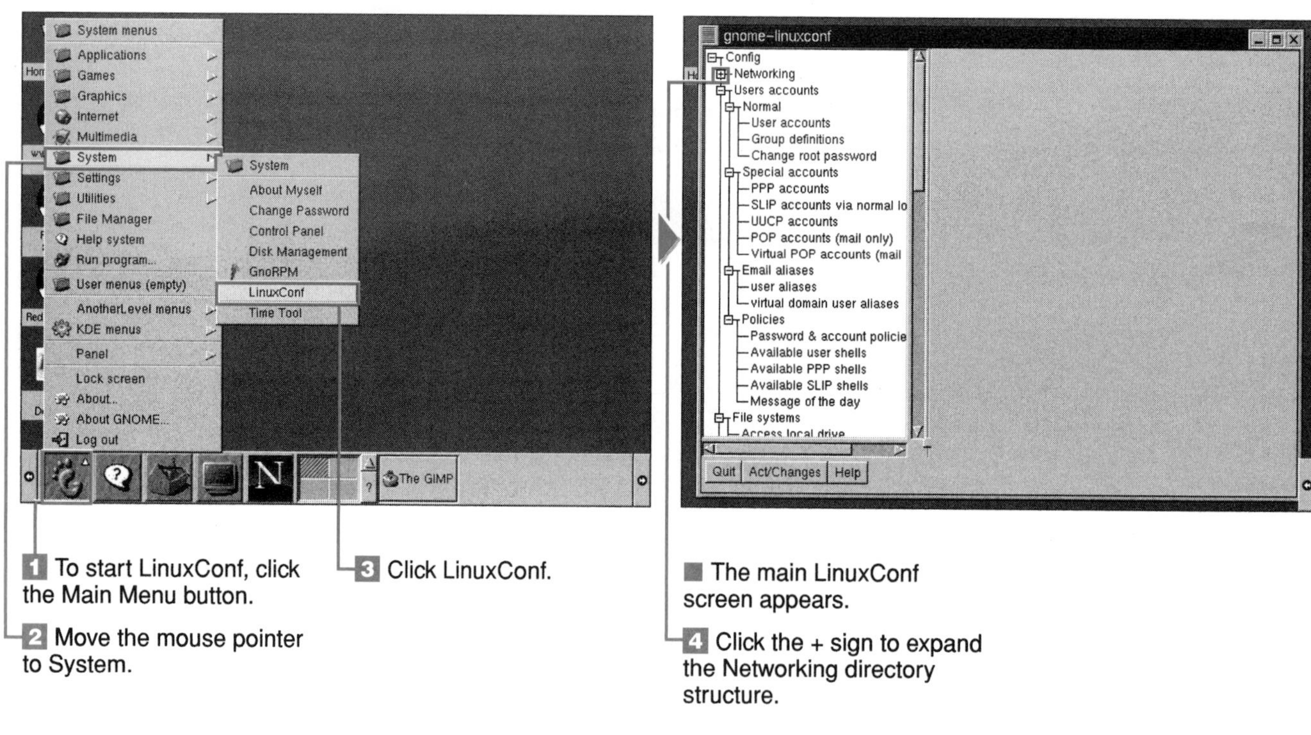

1 To start LinuxConf, click the Main Menu button.

2 Move the mouse pointer to System.

3 Click LinuxConf.

■ The main LinuxConf screen appears.

4 Click the + sign to expand the Networking directory structure.

TIPS

Where do I check for local host information if LinuxConf isn't working?

- Your best bet is to bring up a Linux Terminal. Change directories to `/etc`, and `vi` the hosts file. The first entry in the file will be the local host's address, host name, and domain.

What guidelines should I follow when changing the host name?

- Don't include any characters besides numbers and letters. Your best bet is to stick to letters only, and if you have a group of machines, name them by a theme. For example, you could name all your mail servers after islands or all client machines after movie stars. Be sure not to make names too long. Having to retype **sea_of_tranquility** multiple times is very awkward.

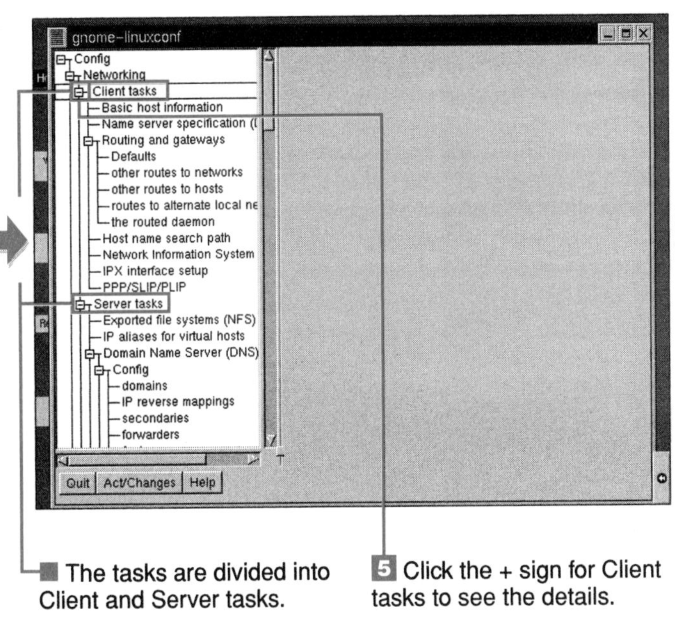

■ The tasks are divided into Client and Server tasks.

5 Click the + sign for Client tasks to see the details.

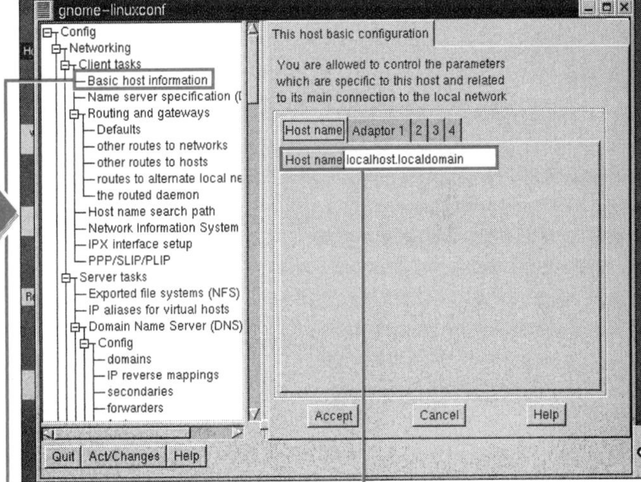

6 Click Basic host information.

■ The default panel lists the host name and domain of your machine.

■ You can change this setting later if you wish, but for right now, this information helps when and if you make other network changes.

CHECK NETWORK CONNECTIVITY WITH PING

You can see if your networked computers are able to send messages to each other properly in Linux. When checking on or hooking up machines to your network, you need a utility to check whether there is connectivity between two machines on your network. That utility is `ping`, one of the oldest and most useful commands in Linux or UNIX.

The `ping` command sends a series of TCP packets between two selected machines on your network. The TCP (Transport Control Protocol) packet is also called the virtual circuit because it provides feedback after its destination receives it. `ping` harnesses the power of a TCP response mechanism to report whether a host is up and working. If a destination is unable to reply, `ping` notifies you that it is unable to complete the TCP circuit.

You will use the properties of TCP in the `ping` command to check network connectivity between machines.

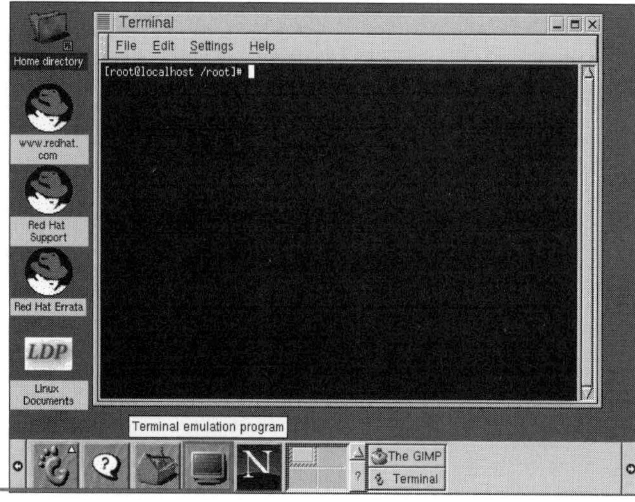

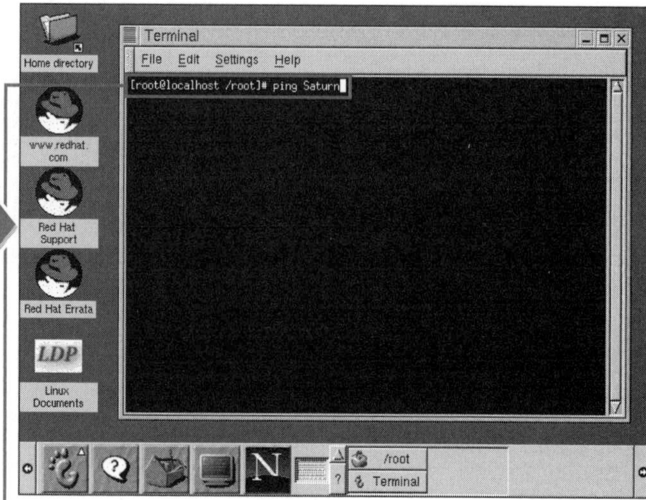

PING VIA HOST NAME

1 As root, click the Terminal button to open a Linux Terminal.

2 When the Linux Terminal window opens, type **ping Saturn**.

3 Press Enter.

What kinds of machine connectivity can I check with ping?

- You can check any machine that hooks up to another machine with `ping`. You can `ping` from PCs, Linux servers, and laptops to routers, mail servers, and remote hosts. As a rough rule, if you can remotely log into it, you can `ping` it.

What other information can I glean from ping?

- If you use `ping –v` for text output, you'll get network statistics that help you estimate the speed of your network and whether it's bogging down. Packet transmission times are usually recorded in milliseconds.

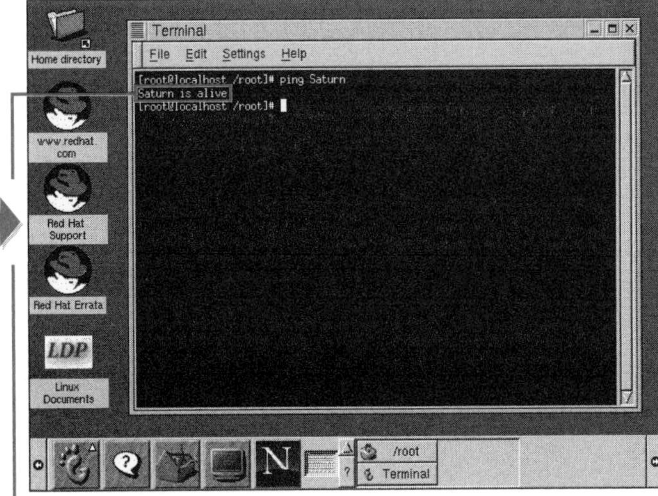

■ If the machine is up and functioning properly on the network, a message appears, similar to `Saturn is alive`, or `'PING Saturn: 56 data bytes`.

■ If not, you may get a host of error messages, including `Saturn not responding` `Saturn unavailable`, and the like.

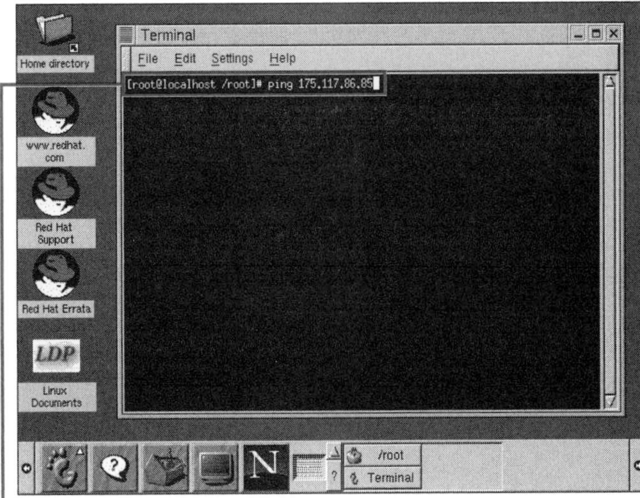

PING VIA IP ADDRESS

1 Type the following at the command line: **ping 175.117.86.85**

2 Press Enter.

■ You get the same response back from this method as you would from `ping`ing a host name.

SET UP DEFAULT GATEWAYS

Your Linux machine needs to talk to a specific machine on the network if you are connecting to the Internet, or a large group of networked computers. This machine is normally a piece of hardware called a *router* or a *bridge*. A router or a bridge passes your messages and requests for information to other computers.

Because a router or bridge helps you talk to other computers, it's also called *gateways*. In this section, you set up the "default" gateway, which is the first router or bridge to which your computer will try to talk. If your computer is unable to make contact with the default gateway due to network traffic or an inoperative router, it will look for a secondary gateway.

Normally, you need to set up a default gateway for your computer to use. That is, on most small networks, only one router or bridge exists. If the bridge is down, it is easy to locate and fix the problem.

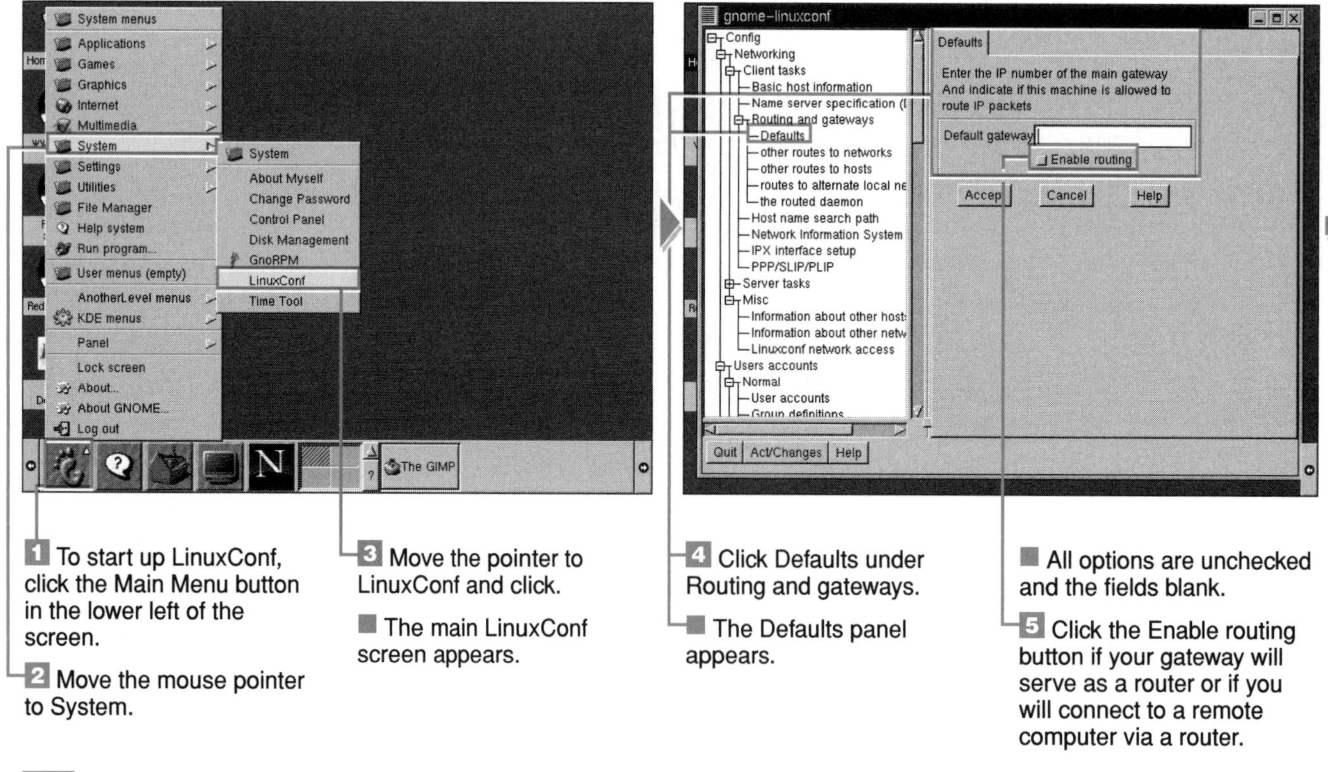

1 To start up LinuxConf, click the Main Menu button in the lower left of the screen.

2 Move the mouse pointer to System.

3 Move the pointer to LinuxConf and click.

■ The main LinuxConf screen appears.

4 Click Defaults under Routing and gateways.

■ The Defaults panel appears.

■ All options are unchecked and the fields blank.

5 Click the Enable routing button if your gateway will serve as a router or if you will connect to a remote computer via a router.

How do I find out the IP address of the machine or router I'm setting up as my default gateway?

- If you set up the gateway machine yourself, you should have records to refer to. By default, you must set IP addresses on machines that have been set up to be gateways. If you weren't the one who set the machine up, you're best off speaking with the person who did, or see the machine itself. Often, the machine will be labeled with the address for reference purposes.

I've correctly set up the gateway, but I'm not able to send packets beyond it. What could be wrong?

- If you've double-checked the address on your machine, then check to make sure that you can send packets (via `ping`) to other machines on your local subnet. If so, then `ping` the gateway machine itself. If you get no response, the machine could be having problems.

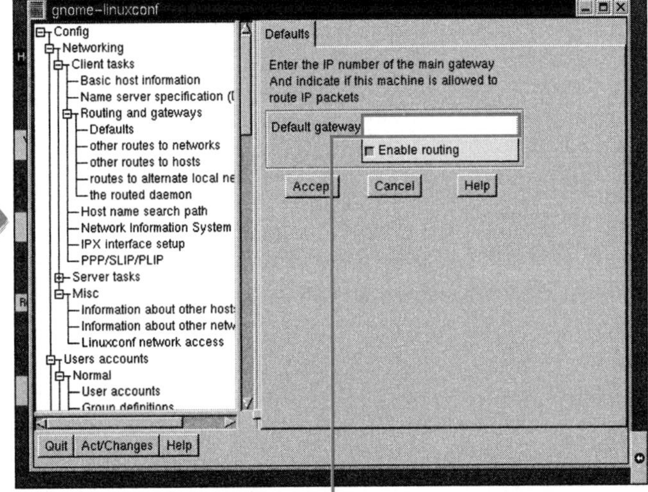

6 Type the IP address of your default gateway (usually a router or a bridge) in the Default gateway field.

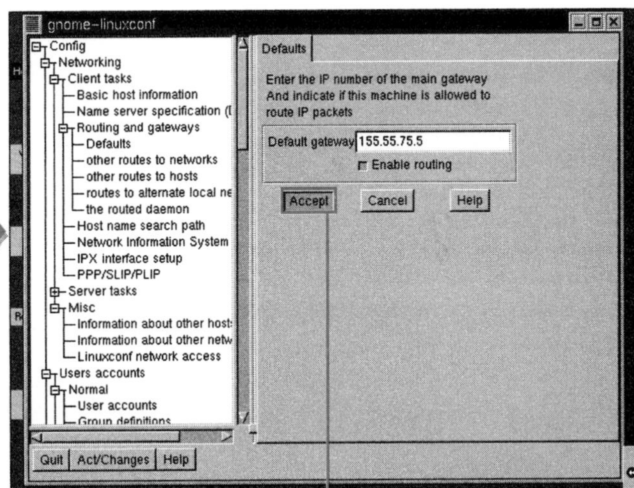

7 Click Accept when you are ready to input your data.

SET UP THE ROUTED DAEMON

Your *Route Daemon*, or Routed, maintains dynamic information about the networks that your system communicates with to determine which routes it can efficiently transfer data across. Routed is smart enough to switch the routes when needed; this is known as *dynamic routing*.

Static routing is an older system in which the routes, or pathways, that the data follows do not change. In a static system, a file called the *routing table* tells the computer how to send information. No deviation is permitted.

Because the world is trending toward more and more complex, larger networks, by default the Routed daemon on your system is set up to handle dynamic routing — instead of static routing. You can configure the Routed daemon to export the default route. This can change or remain in silent mode and not export the route.

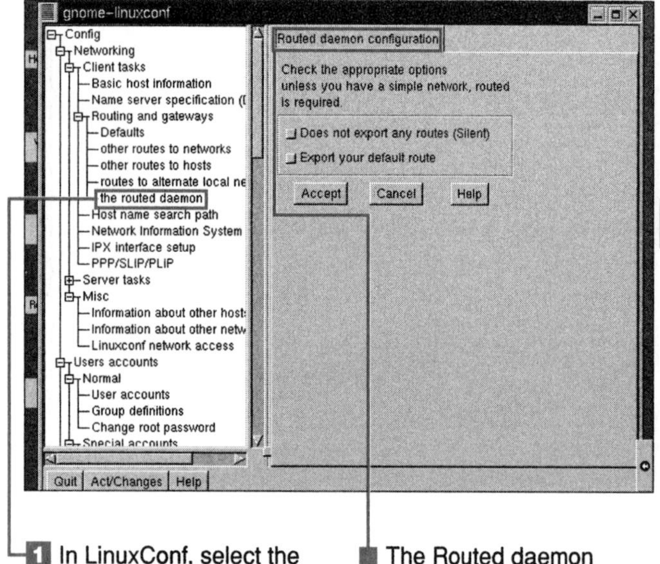

1 In LinuxConf, select the routed daemon under Routing and gateways.

■ The Routed daemon configuration panel appears.

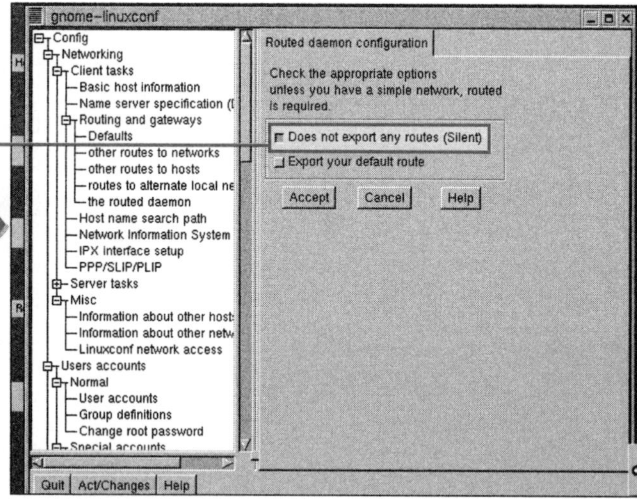

2 Select an export option.

■ If you want the Routed daemon to avoid exporting your routes by default, click the top button.

A friend's UNIX network has a gated daemon, but no Routed daemon. Should I be running both daemons?

- *Gated* stands for Gate Routing Daemon and performs similar tasks to Routed. Running them together confuses them and the system, causing problems.

How can I find the command options that I can use with routed?

- Routed has a number of command options which you can explore by typing **man routed** at the command line and pressing Enter. Be aware that most of these options are extremely technical and rarely used.

How can I add a static route to my machine?

- You would use the **`route add`** command on the Linux Terminal. Open a Terminal and type the command and the IP address of the host to which you want to make a static link at the command prompt. For example, for host 178.78.18.8, type **route add 178.78.18.8** and press Enter to accept the change.

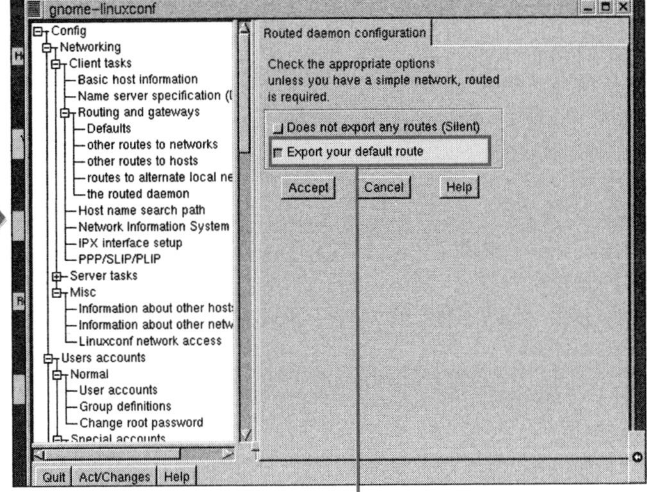

■ Click the bottom button, Export your default route, if you want to export the route.

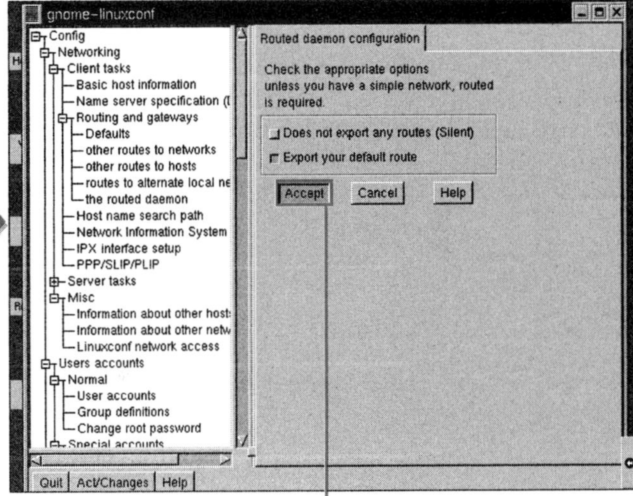

3 Click Accept to implement your settings.

LOG IN REMOTELY WITH RLOGIN

You can connect to other Linux clients and servers on your network, list their files, and even give them commands remotely. With a remote login, you have complete access to all the remote computer's resources — it is as if you are sitting at the keyboard, even if you are a continent away. The most commonly used remote login tool in the Linux/UNIX world is `rlogin`, or `remote login`.

`rlogin` is automatically installed on your Linux network as part of the TCP/IP connection protocols. `rlogin` is also fairly well automated. Your machine starts up a connection daemon, called rlogind, from the moment you execute the `rlogin` command from the Linux Terminal.

This daemon handles the specific byte-to-byte operations of setting up an `rlogin` session with the remote host of your choice. The `rlogin` `daemons` also automatically ends a connection if the remote machine suffers a system crash so that you're not left with a hung network connection. Finally, when you are finished with your remote login session, `rlogind` shuts itself down without further assistance.

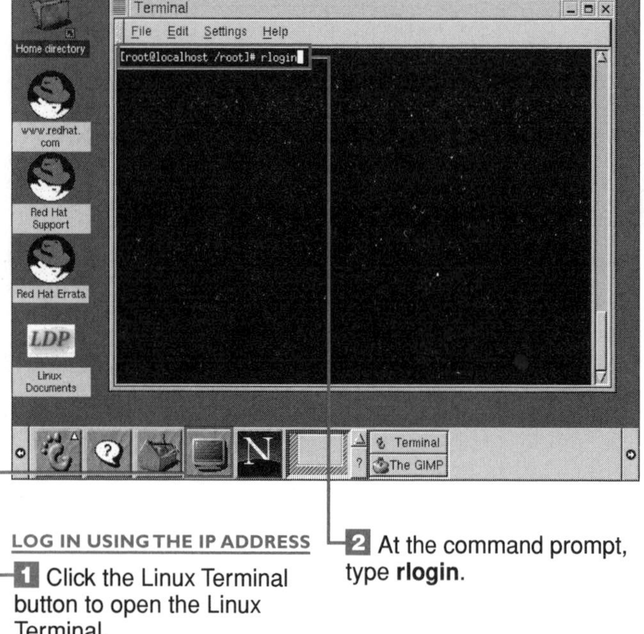

LOG IN USING THE IP ADDRESS

1 Click the Linux Terminal button to open the Linux Terminal.

2 At the command prompt, type **rlogin**.

3 Type the name of the machine or the IP address after the `rlogin` command.

4 Press Enter to begin the `rlogin` process.

I want to connect to a machine on my network that runs the Kerberos authentication system. Is there a way I can log in to the machine that bypasses the Kerberos authentication system?

✓ `rlogin` comes with a way to turn off all Kerberos authentication. At the command line, type **rlogin –K <hostname>**. The `K` command option effectively bypasses the program's authentication by shutting it down.

What should I do if rlogin hangs?

✓ If the `rlogin` prompt stays on the screen without connecting, it will not give return command prompt. You can either wait five minutes for the `rlogin` process to automatically time out or you can attempt to `kill` the process. To kill the process, use the `kill` command, which is discussed in Chapter 6. You might also try pressing Ctrl+C to see if you can cancel the `rlogin` process from the screen.

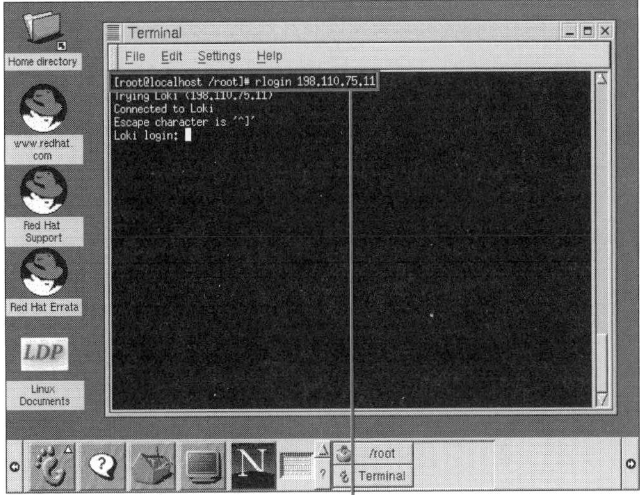

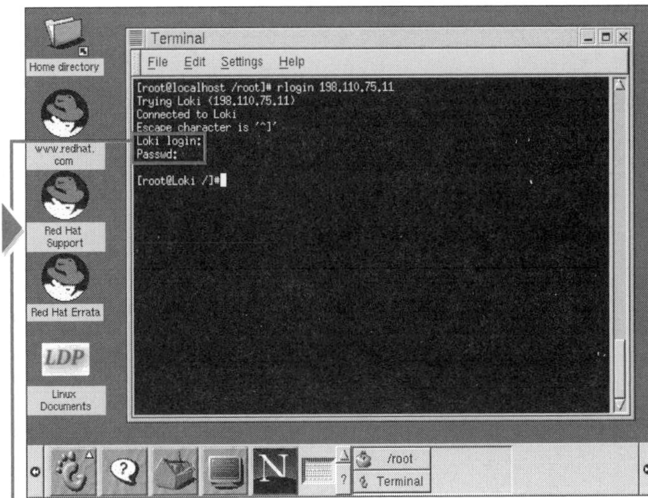

LOG IN USING THE ADDRESS

■ Alternatively, if you do not know the machine's host name but you do know the IP address, you can `rlogin` using this address.

1 Type **rlogin** and the four-part address after the `rlogin` command.

2 Press Enter to begin the `rlogin` process.

3 Enter your username and password.

■ You are allowed to log in if your account is recognized.

RLOGIN WITH THE -L OPTION

You can connect to other Linux machines as the `root` administrator account, even if you are currently logged in as a mere user. This is possible thanks to the most powerful of the `rlogin` command options: `l`.

The `-l` option allows you to log in to remote machines with a completely different user account and privileges. If you `rlogin` to clients and servers on your network as `root`, you can give commands remotely that only the administrative account is allowed.

For example, if you are logged in as a user and want to edit the `/etc/passwd` files on a remote machine, you need to log in as `root`. By using the `-l` option, you can actually log in to that computer as the `root` account (provided you have the password) and edit the `passwd` file without touching the remote machine.

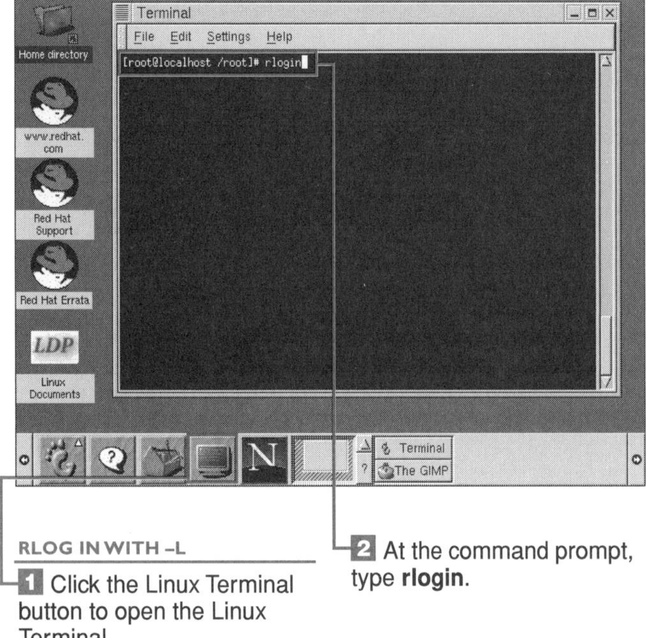

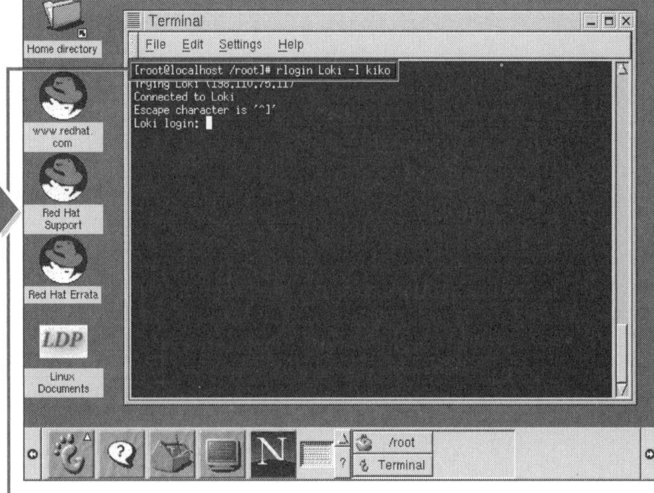

RLOG IN WITH -L

1 Click the Linux Terminal button to open the Linux Terminal.

2 At the command prompt, type **rlogin**.

3 After `rlogin`, type the name or IP address of themachine you want to log into, followed by **-l** and the new username.

4 Press Enter to begin the `rlogin` process.

Why does rlogin not seem to work for some machines?

- Linux machines can be set up as restricted hosts that, although they are on the network, refuse remote logins. This option was more valuable when there were not as many security safeguards to implement, but today it is more of an inconvenience.

I need to perform administrative tasks on a remote host. What if I forget to use l when logging in?

- Instead of backing out and wasting time connecting again, use the `su` command to become the `superuser` account.

What should I do if rlogin freezes and will not continue the login process?

- This condition means that there is something wrong with the network connection on the machine you are trying to log in to. `rlogin` times out and stops trying to log in after a while. Wait 15 to 20 seconds and `rlogin` will unfreeze.

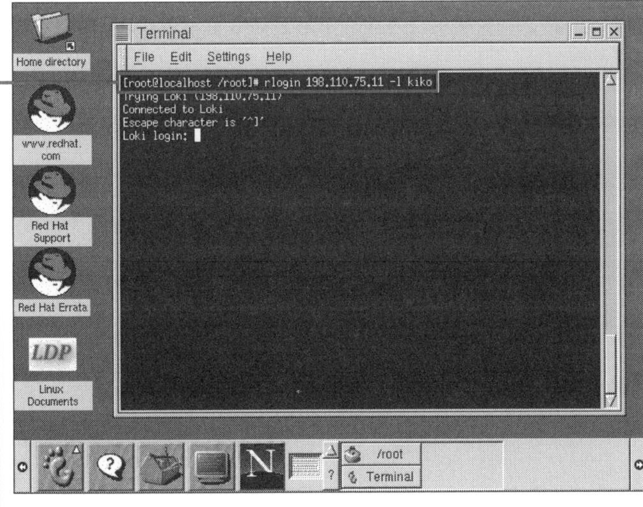

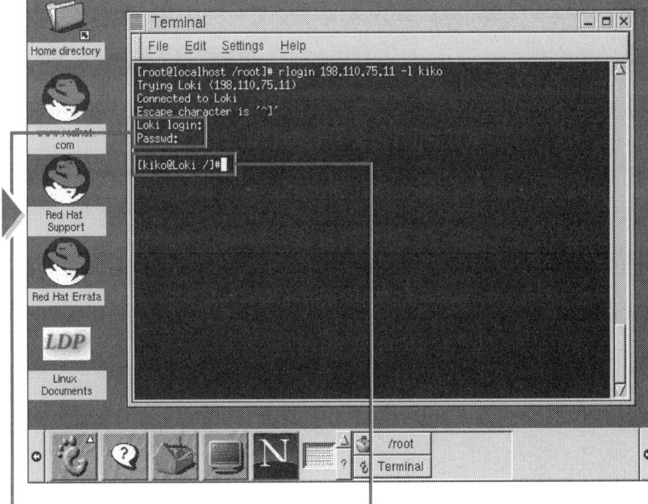

RLOG IN WITH –L PASSWORD

1 Alternatively, after `rlogin`, type the IP address of the machine you want to log into, followed by **-l** and the username.

2 Press Enter to begin the `rlogin` process.

■ The authentication process asks for the password of the new user.

3 Type your password.

4 Press Enter.

USE RSH — THE REMOTE SHELL

You can use rsh (the command Remote Shell) to execute a single command on a remote host. By typing **rsh <hostname>**, your one allowed command logs you in to the machine and lets you do more work remotely. Although rsh is less sophisticated than telnet or rlogin, you can use it for a quick login and limited remote work on other machines.

rsh is used less commonly than the other commands, and mostly on intrasystem remote logins (within the network) versus intersystem logins (outside the network). rsh works particularly well when trying to log in to machines running Linux and other variants of the UNIX operating system. This is because rsh was originally developed as a utility to help UNIX machines talk to each other on the first primitive networks.

On the flip side, the rsh origins are in UNIX, so you will be unable to rsh into a machine that runs Windows 95, 98, or NT.

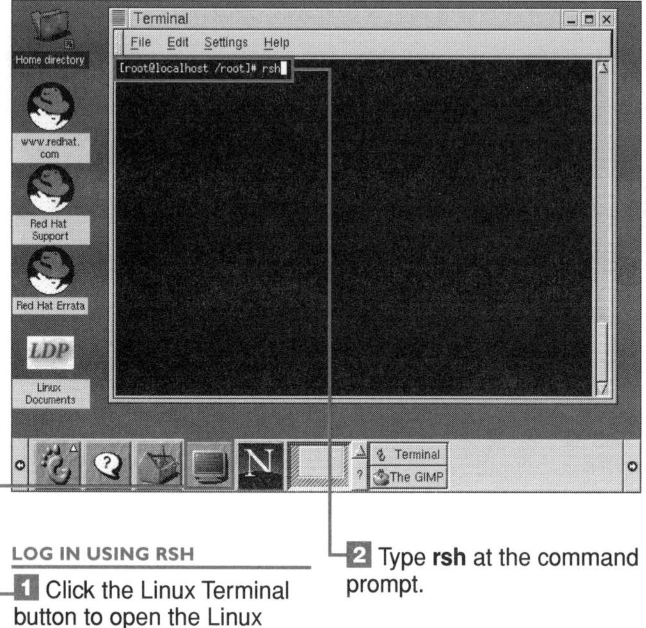

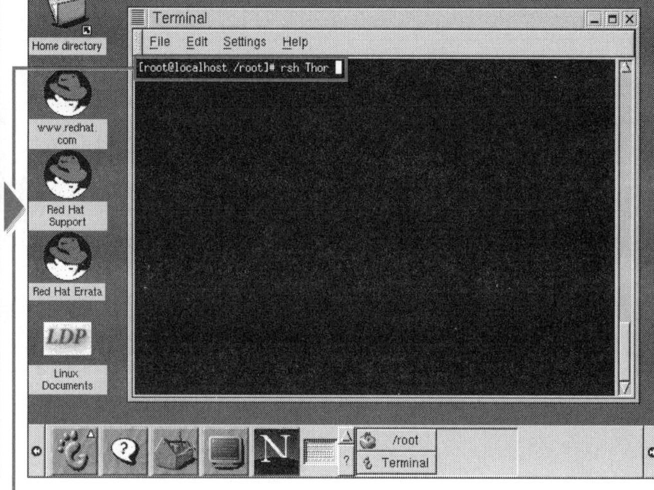

LOG IN USING RSH

1 Click the Linux Terminal button to open the Linux Terminal.

2 Type **rsh** at the command prompt.

3 Type either the machine name or the IP address after the rsh command.

4 Press Enter to log in.

TIPS

Is it true that rsh is similar to rlogin in some of its command options?

- `rsh` and `rlogin` do have some similar command options, but they are not related. `rlogin` is a fairly complex utility and `rsh` is little more than a glorified command.

Can I specify a different username when I execute remote commands with rsh?

- This is another case where `rsh` is similar to `rlogin`. Using the `-l` option with `rsh` allows you to send a command to a remote host as a different user.

Why am I not allowed to use the vi editor on a machine that I just logged in to?

- This is a well-known bug in `rsh` which, for some reason, has never been fixed. If you want to use the `vi` editor on a remote machine, log in using `rlogin`.

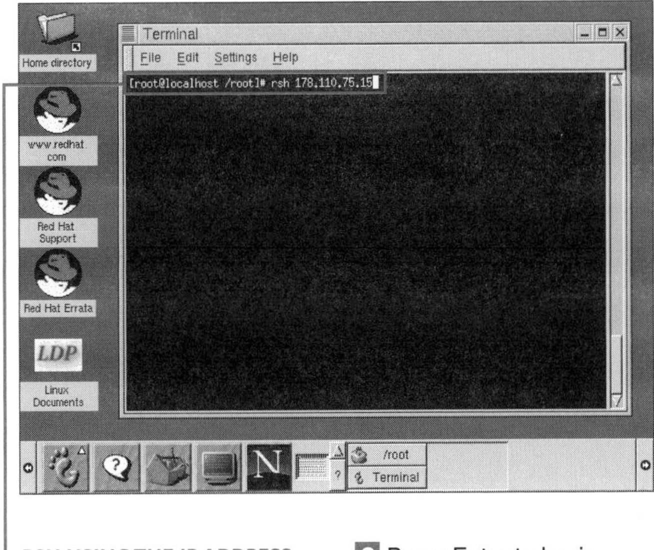

RSH USING THE IP ADDRESS

1 Type **rsh** and the four-part address after the `rlogin` command.

2 Press Enter to log in.

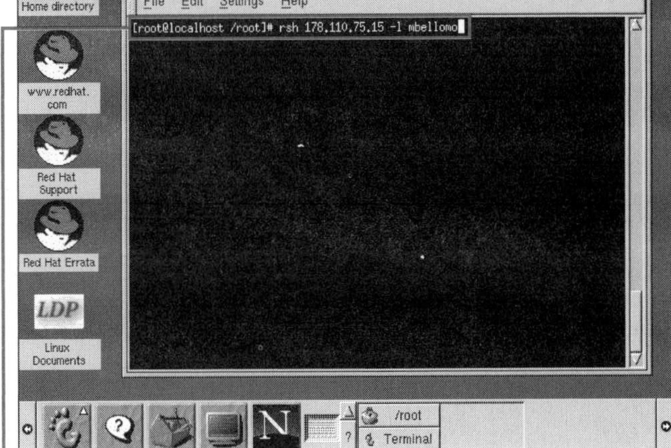

LOG IN AS A DIFFERENT USER WITH -L OPTION AND RSH

1 For example, if you are root and want to log in as mbellomo, type **rsh –l mbellomo**.

LOG IN WITH TELNET

You can use telnet as an alternate method of remotely logging into other machines. Like rlogin, telnet is automatically installed on your Linux network as a remote connection system. When you execute the telnet command, your Linux box starts a daemon (telnetd), which handles the specific byte-to-byte operations of setting up a Telnet session with the remote host of your choice.

On the whole, telnet is more popular than rlogin or rsh. The reason is due to the command becoming a standard piece of software to include with an operating system. Computers running UNIX, Macintosh, Windows 95, 98, and NT all come with the telnet utility. rlogin and rsh may not allow you to connect Linux to other kinds of computers, so it's not as flexible as telnet.

Because telnet is simple, reliable, and easy to use, TCP/IP-based telnet sessions have become the most widely accepted method of opening communication between different computers.

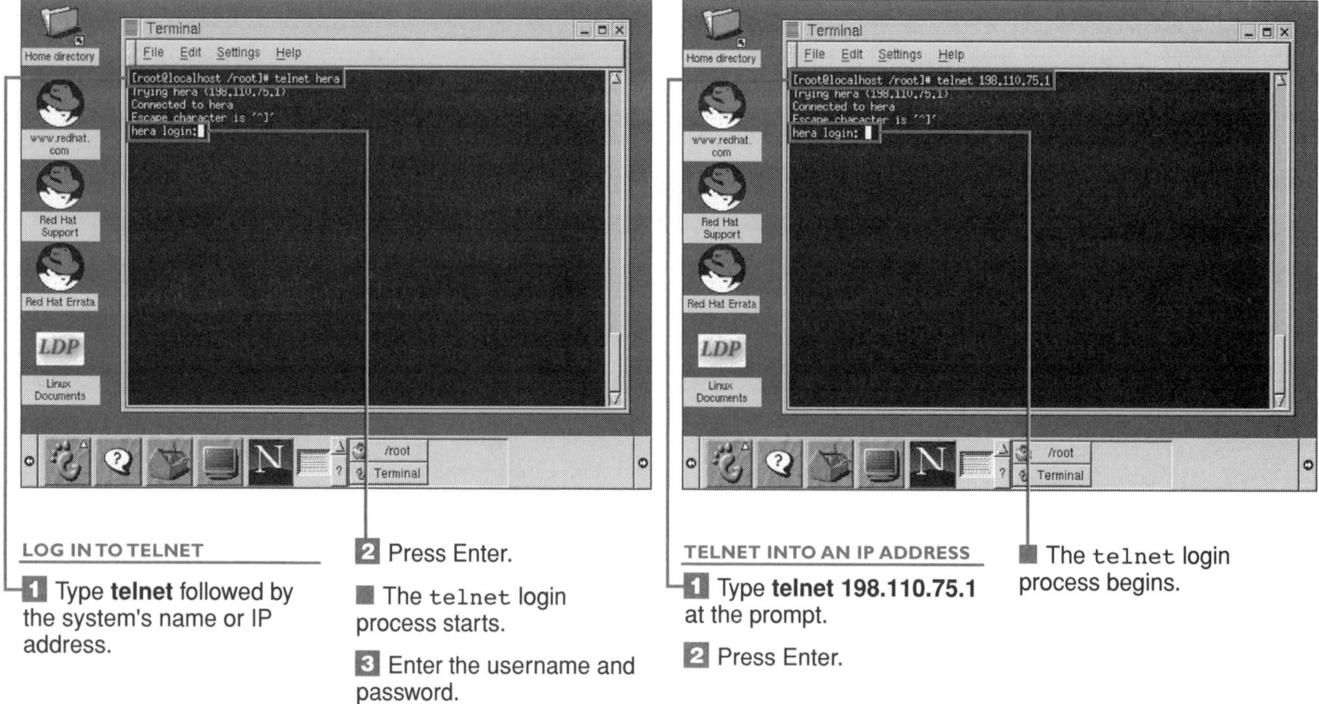

LOG IN TO TELNET

1 Type **telnet** followed by the system's name or IP address.

2 Press Enter.

■ The telnet login process starts.

3 Enter the username and password.

TELNET INTO AN IP ADDRESS

1 Type **telnet 198.110.75.1** at the prompt.

2 Press Enter.

■ The telnet login process begins.

I accidentally typed telnet and pressed Enter without specifying a host. Why do I now get telnet> where my prompt used to be?

- `telnet` is a more complete program than `rlogin`. When typed by itself and activated, it comes up with its own command prompt. To begin a login session, type a host name or IP address. To exit the `telnet` prompt, type exit or quit.

Is there an equivalent to rlogin –l in telnet?

- `telnet` has a way to attempt an automatic login, though it is not exactly the same as `rlogin –l`. Typing `telnet` with the `-a` option attempts an automatic login to a remote machine you specify, but with the same username.

Is the Hyperterminal utility on some Windows machines the same thing as telnet?

- Not really. `Hyperterminal` is a Windows specific communications utility. Continue to use `telnet` if you want to log in to a Linux machine.

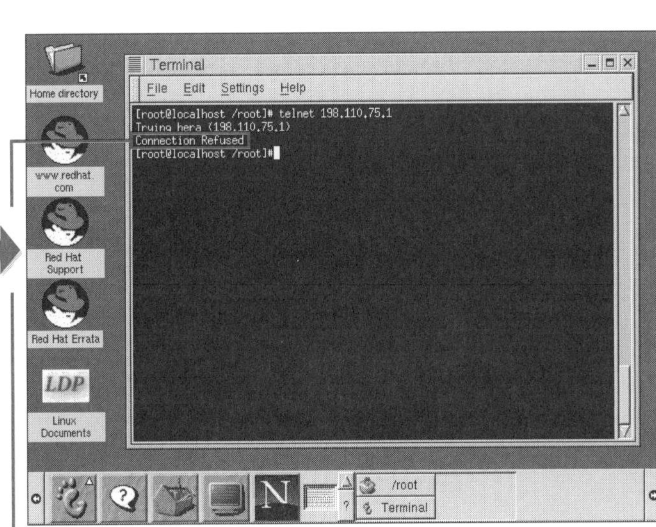

■ Sometimes, a system is set up to refuse `telnet` connections except through a single selected port.

■ If you try to log in on the default `telnet` port, you see this message.

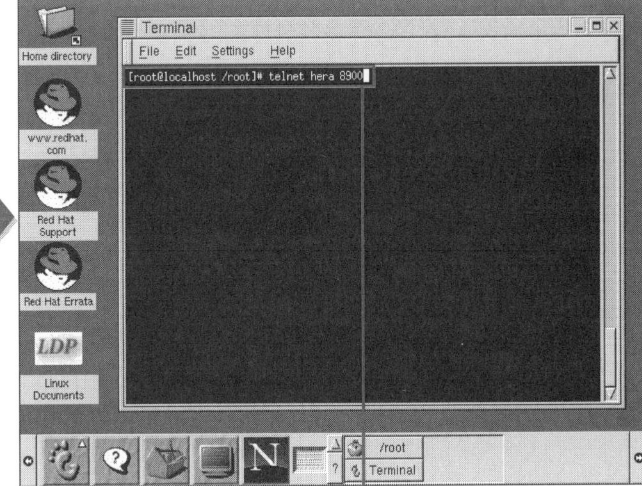

Note: To `telnet` onto a system, specify the port number after the telnet command.

3 To `telnet` into a system, type **telnet hera <port number>**.

4 Press Enter to begin the `telnet` login process.

GIVE REMOTE COMMANDS TO A REMOTE MACHINE

After you have used `telnet` or `rlogin` to log in to a remote computer, the remote machine responds just as if it were your own machine in the same room. If you are in the U.S. and the remote machine is in another country, you can command it list directories, start Web browsers, and even print a copy of its text files. Also, you can remotely log into a second remote machine off the first one by using the `telnet` or `rlogin` command a second time.

Remote logins give you a *transparent interface* with the machine you are logged in to. This means you should not notice major differences between being logged in to the remote machine and logged in to your local machine.

About the only difference you may notice is that when the remote machine is sitting an ocean away, there might be a time lag between what you type and what the remote machine does.

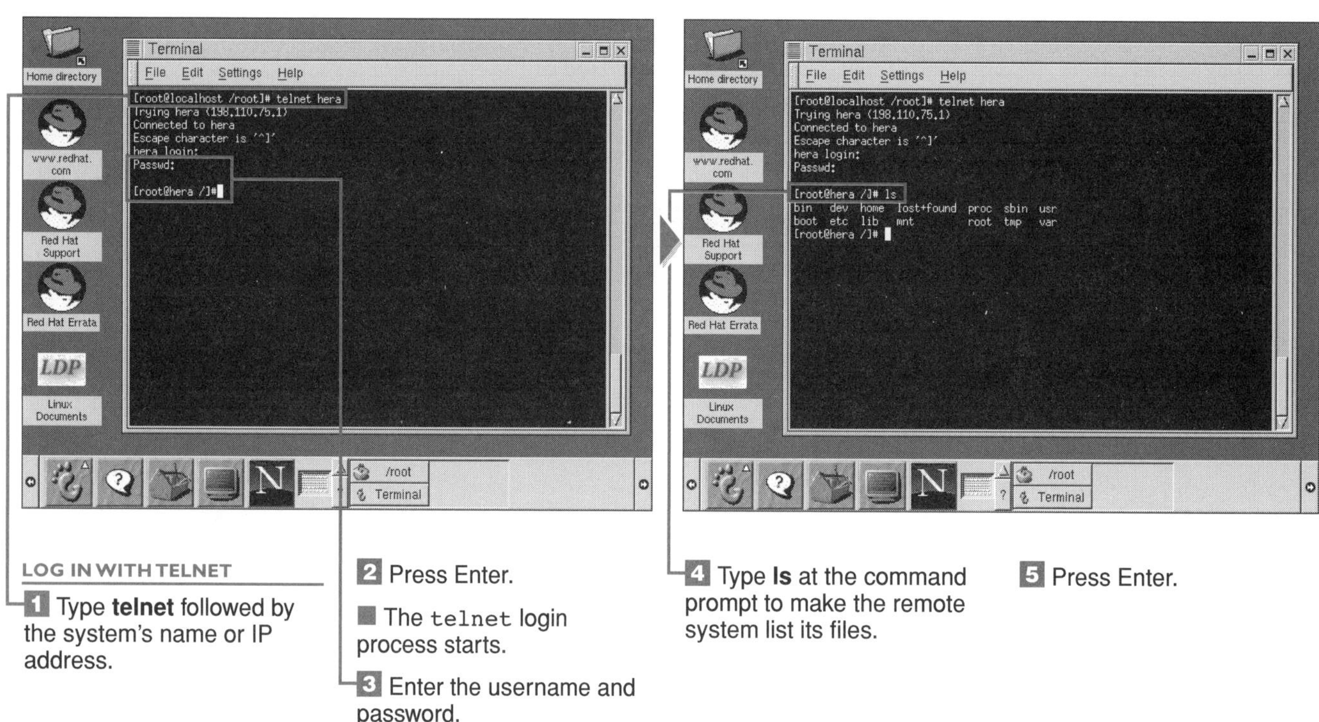

LOG IN WITH TELNET

1 Type **telnet** followed by the system's name or IP address.

2 Press Enter.

■ The `telnet` login process starts.

3 Enter the username and password.

4 Type **ls** at the command prompt to make the remote system list its files.

5 Press Enter.

How many rlogins can you chain along from one computer to the next?

- In theory, this is limited only by the number of times you can stand to type `rlogin`. However, in practice, it is like laying out more and more phone lines behind you. Your connection becomes slower and more vulnerable to a disruption. Try to avoid logging in to a machine that is more than two `rlogins` away.

What should I do if the remote machine is ignoring my Linux commands?

- You may have connected to a machine that does not use Linux. When you remotely log in to a machine, you automatically begin using its local operating system. Although your screen looks the same, you could be connecting to a computer that uses Solaris or HPUX, where the commands may be different.

What are my options if I can't log into the remote machine?

- The most common reason why you can't log into a remote machine is high network traffic. Try to log in remotely when the network is less busy.

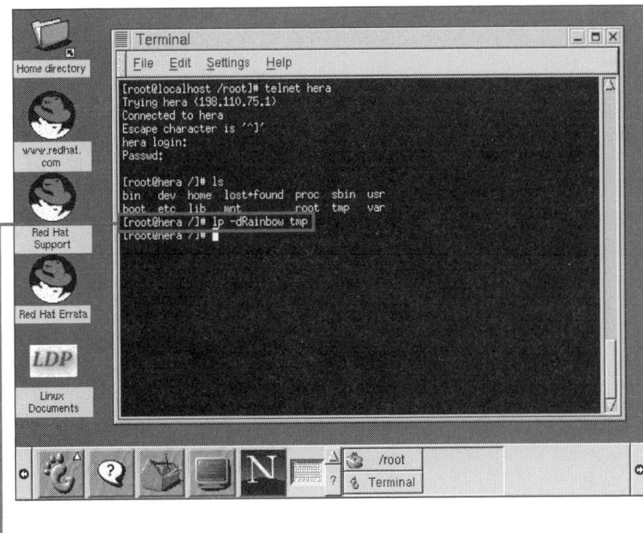

PRINT A FILE

1 Type **lp -dRainbow tmp** at the command prompt, specifying `Rainbow` as the printer and `tmp` as the file.

2 Press Enter.

Note: The printer `Rainbow` is local or remote. The only limitation here is that the system `hera` has to recognize this printer as being on the network.

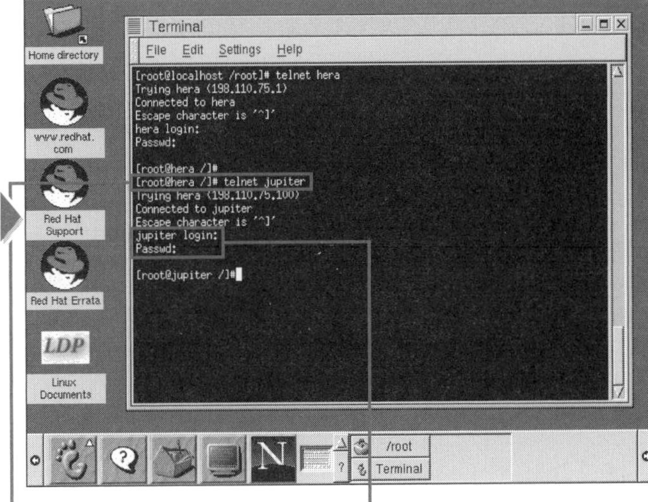

CONNECTO TO HERA TO PRINT

1 Type **telnet jupiter** at the command prompt.

2 Press Enter.

3 Follow the exact same login procedure that you used for logging into `hera`.

COPY FILES WITH UUCP

Copying in the graphical user interface (GUI) is a straightforward business: You simply click and drag icons from a networked drive to your disk, directory, or desktop. You have a few more options in the Linux Terminal. `uucp` (UNIX-to-UNIX copy) is one of the oldest but most reliable ways to copy from one Linux machine to another.

`uucp` is limited in that it can transfer files between only UNIX and Linux machines. Although it is an old network communications war horse, `uucp` has been upgraded over the years to perform vastly greater functions, such as handling mail and news. This sections shows you the most common uses of `uucp` — transferring large files between machines.

For example, -R is the command option most commonly used with `uucp`. It lets you copy over a directory and all of its contents, recursively.

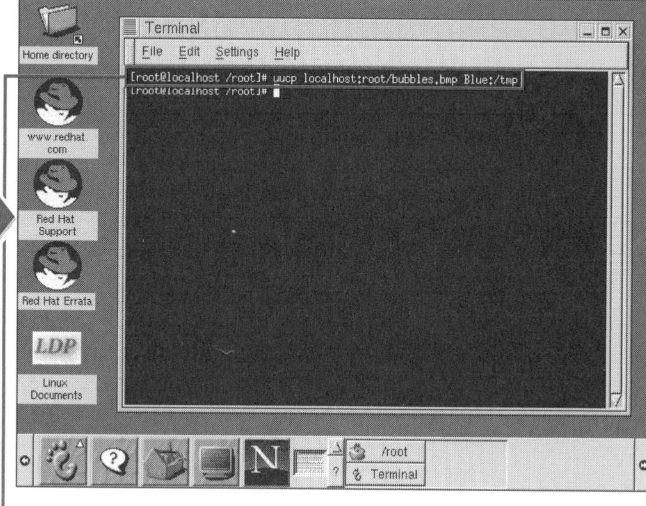

COPY A FILE TO A DIRECTORY

1 Click the Linux Terminal button to open the Linux Terminal.

2 Type the following at the command line:

uucp localhost:root/bubbles.bmp Blue:/tmp

■ This command copies the file `bubbles.bmp` from `/root` on the system `localhost` to the `/tmp` directory on the Linux machine Blue.

3 Press Enter.

Why does uucp seem unable to immediately carry out my copy requests?

- uucp does carry out most of its copy jobs immediately, especially if the job is very large. uucp starts up the uucio daemon, which acts as a sort of queuing method, allowing uucp to perform its function when enough resources are available to begin the large task.

How can I make sure that uucp copies all the contents of a directory?

- To make doubly sure that all the subdirectories of a given selection are copied, use the -R, or recursive, command option when running uucp.

Can I set up uucp to notify me when it is done with a large copy job?

- Start uucp with the -n option. Add the –n <username> option when copying files, specifying your user account; you will be e-mailed when the job is completed.

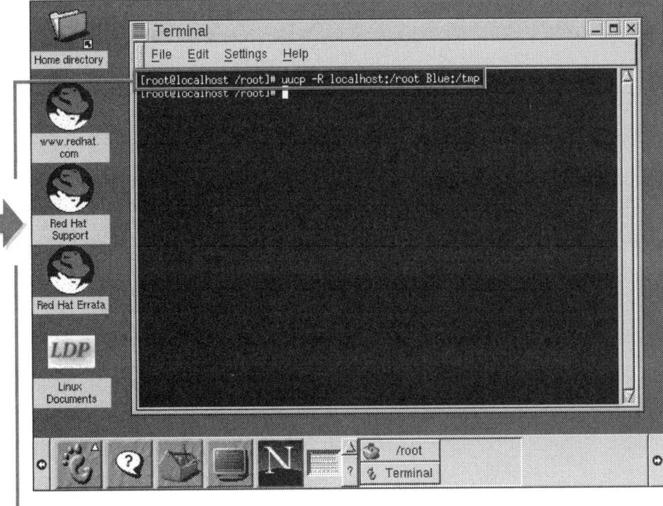

4 Type the following at the command line:

uucp -R localhost:/root Blue:/tmp

■ This command copies the /root directory on the machine localhost into the /tmp directory on the Linux machine Blue

5 Press Enter.

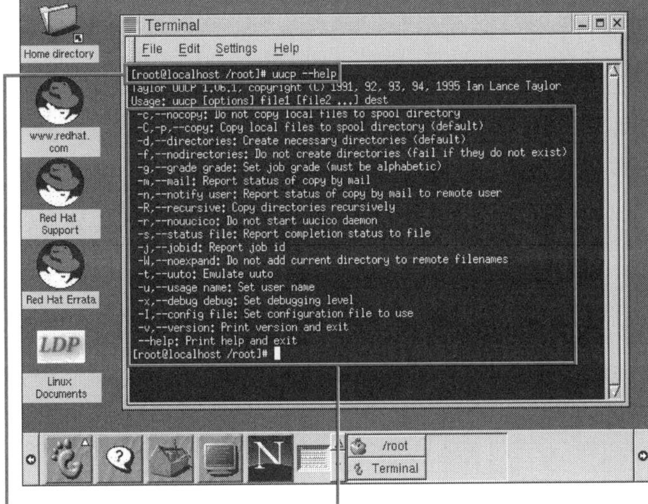

VIEW A LIST OF COMMAND OPTIONS TO USE WITH UUCP

1 Type **uucp --help** at the command line.

Note: The double dash distinguishes help from the -h command option.

2 Press Enter.

■ You get an entire list of the command options, complete with explanations.

COPY FILES WITH RCP

You can use `rcp` (remote copy) between Linux and UNIX machines on an intranet. The advantage to using `rcp` is that it is probably the fastest, most stable method of transferring small-to-medium-sized files across the network.

On the other hand, the command syntax is a little tricky at times and is limited by the fact that the copying function is restricted to Linux and UNIX machines, like `uucp`. `rcp` is, like `rsh`, less of a standalone utility and more of a glorified command or extension of the UNIX command `cp` (`copy`).

When you're ready to perform a remote copy, be sure that you're in the directory where the file resides. In the following example, if the file `gnew` is located in the `/Gnew2` directory, you should change directories to `/Gnew2`.

However, when you perform recursuve copies of entire directories, change directories so that you are one level above the directory you want to copy. Reasoning is, you can't recursively copy a directory if you're in it at the time.

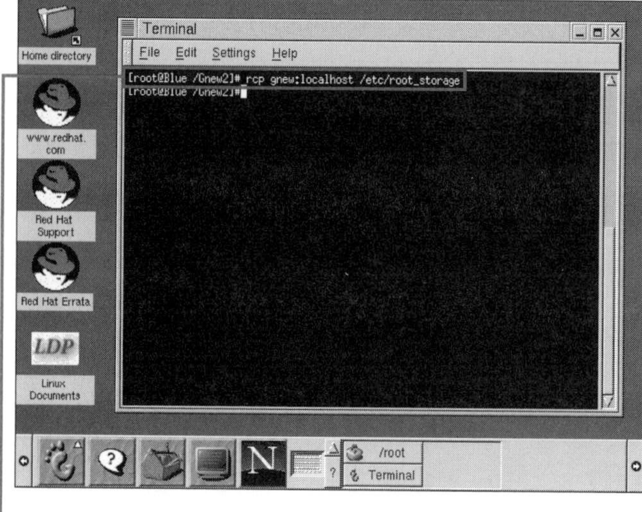

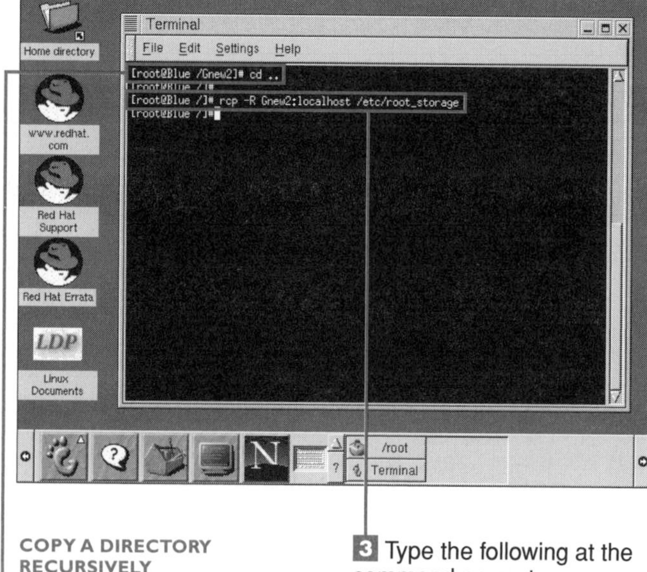

COPY FILES

1 Click the Linux Terminal button to open the Linux Terminal.

2 Type: **cp gnew:localhost /etc/root_storage** at the command line.

3 Press Enter.

■ Linux makes the connection and copies the file.

COPY A DIRECTORY RECURSIVELY

1 Type two periods (**..**).

2 Press Enter.

3 Type the following at the command prompt:

rcp –R Gnew2:localhost /etc/root_storage.

4 Press Enter.

rcp does not prompt me for passwords when copying files from remote machines. Why not?

- `rcp` does not ask you for authentication again because it acts like a one-shot login, just as `rsh` does. When logged in to the remote machine, you can use `rcp` as often as you like.

What happens if I get an rcp refused message when running remote copy?

- You get an `rcp refused` message if you are running into network problems. Stop your copying immediately, log out of the remote machine, and attempt to log back in.

Why I am unable to copy the files I want from one machine to the other?

- `rcp` is such a simple command that there is not much that can go wrong. If you are not allowed to copy files, it is most likely a matter of file permissioning. Make sure you have write permissions for both your target file and the directory you are copying to.

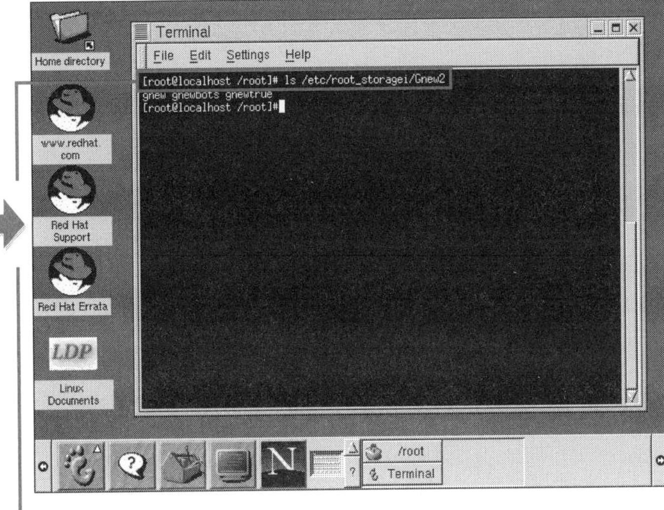

5 Perform an `ls l` on the new directory `Gnew2` under `/etc/root_storage`.

■ You find that `gnew`, as well as all othe files and directories underneath `Gnew2` were copied.

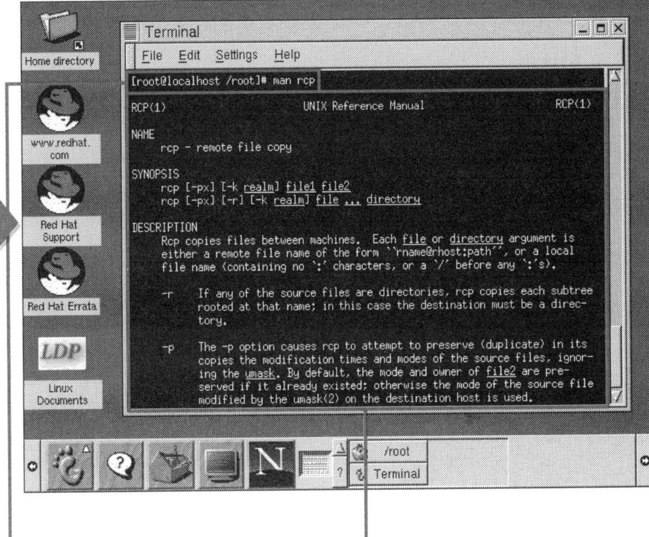

6 To find other options that you can use with rcp, type **man rcp** at the command prompt.

7 Press Enter.

■ You get the first of a series of `man` pages detailing the options for `rcp`.

COPY FILES WITH FTP

The most common choice for copying files from a Linux machine to a PC (and from a Linux machine to other networked machines) is by `ftp`. File Transfer Protocol (FTP) has become the new standard in file transfers because of its stability, speed, and greater flexibility in communicating with non-UNIX machines. You can also copy files with the `cp` command, but this does not work on `copygin` files between machines. Also, `uucp` (UNIX-to-UNIX copy) is a more stable method of transferring files between Linux machines if the files are larger than 500MB. However, you will rarely transfer files of that size on a regular basis.

FTP is, like Telnet, a more complete program unto itself. Activating it actually brings up a new `ftp` command prompt with special FTP commands that allow you to list files, change directories, and upload/download files between computers. This example shows how to connect to a networked file server called `ftp.idg.org`.

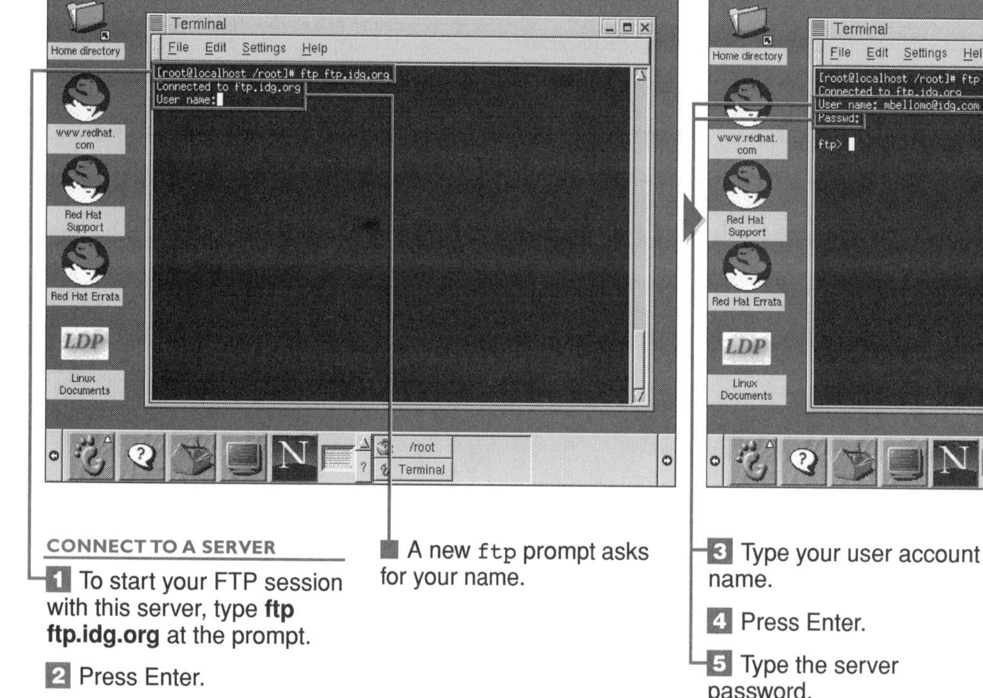

CONNECT TO A SERVER

1 To start your FTP session with this server, type **ftp ftp.idg.org** at the prompt.

2 Press Enter.

■ A new `ftp` prompt asks for your name.

3 Type your user account name.

4 Press Enter.

5 Type the server password.

6 Press Enter.

■ Your username and password may not display.

■ You can get any file in the directory that you are logged into.

How do get and put equate to the network terms upload and download?

- As a rule, `get` is the equivalent of download and `put` is the equivalent to upload. Traditionally, network diagrams show most data consumers (client machines) as below the servers. You therefore `get` a file and pull it down to the client machine, and vice versa.

Why am I unable to copy a file to the FTP server?

- It is a question of permissions. Unless you have write permissions for the target directory on the FTP server (which is rare on a secure server), you are not allowed to put or upload files to the server at all.

Can I log in to a secure FTP server?

- To use a secure FTP server, you must have a user account name and password that the server recognizes. However, most secure servers let you log in with the user account name `guest`.

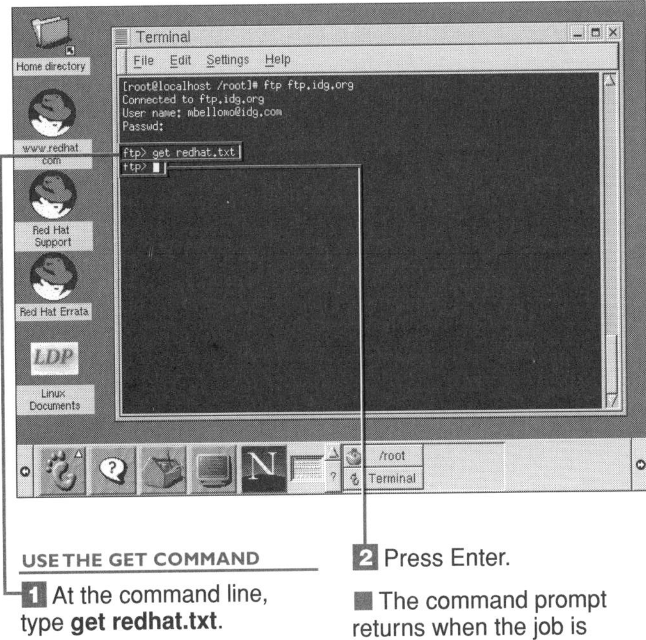

USE THE GET COMMAND

1 At the command line, type **get redhat.txt**.

■ This command allows you to `ftp` to a file called `redhat.txt`

2 Press Enter.

■ The command prompt returns when the job is complete, allowing you to enter new commands.

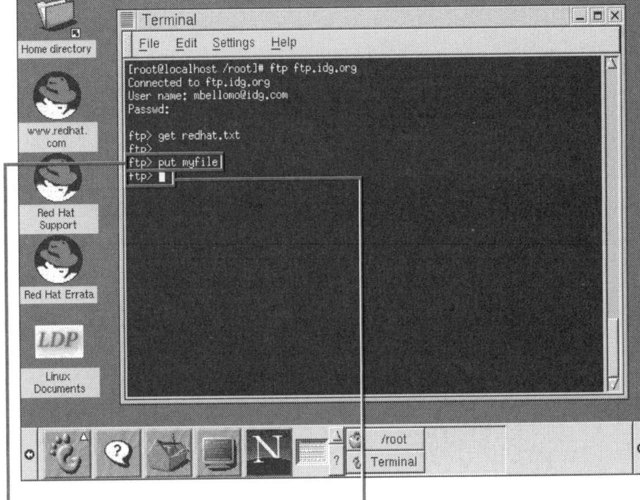

USE THE PUT COMMAND TO COPY FILES TO THE FTP SERVER

1 At the `ftp` command prompt, type **put myfile**.

■ This command puts the file `myfile` on the server.

2 Press Enter.

■ The command prompt returns when the job is complete.

TRANSFER FILES WITH DIFFERENT FTP OPTIONS

Several additional FTP options can make the program more useful and flexible.

For example, when FTP is in the process of transferring a gigantic file, how can you tell whether the computer is busy working or is frozen? Use the `hash` command at the `ftp` prompt. The `hash` command makes your computer print a string of # characters (called *hash signs* by those in the UNIX and Linux world) while FTP copies the file you specified.

FTP does have limitations: One is that you cannot transfer an entire directory at one time. You use `mget` (`multiple get`) to transfer multiple files *to* your machine. You use `mput` (`multiple put`) to transfer multiple files *from* your machine to the server.

When you want to transfer multiple files, you can use wildcards in your `ftp` command instead of laboriously typing each filename.

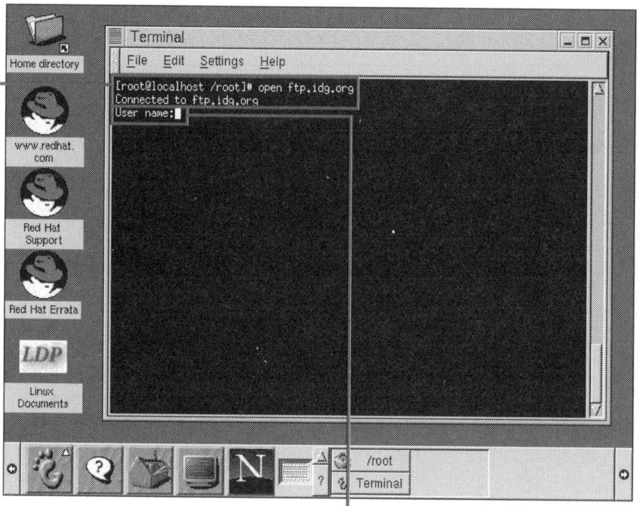

CONNECT TO FTP SERVER

1 At the command prompt, type **open ftp.idg.org**.

2 Press Enter.

■ A new `ftp` prompt asks for your name.

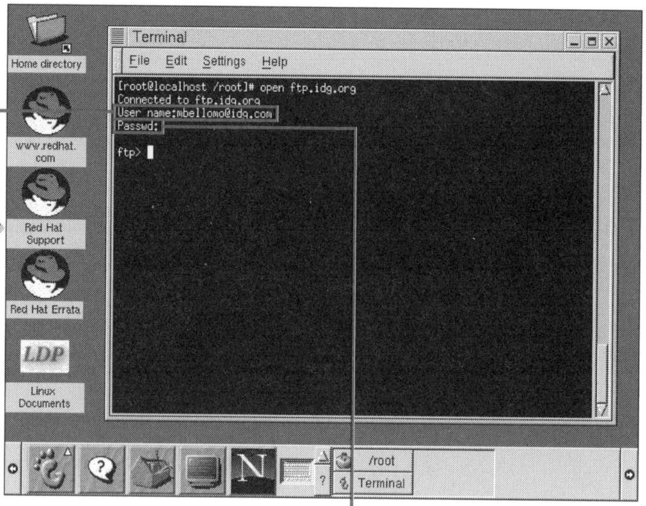

3 Type in your user account name.

4 Press Enter.

5 Type the server password.

6 Press Enter.

How can I turn hash marking off without exiting FTP?

- If you do not want to exit FTP, type **hash** at the `ftp` prompt a second time to turn the hash switch back off.

Will the hash mark setting work if I am transferring very small files between machines?

- After you switch the hash mark setting on, it works for all files big and small. Of course, it takes so little time to transfer a small file in FTP that you may see only a single hash mark appear on your screen before the transfer is complete.

What happens if I transfer a binary file without switching FTP to the binary mode?

- A binary file is a program that runs in Linux. If you transfer a binary file without switching to binary mode, then the file is incorrectly copied as a text file. The program will not start when you try to run it.

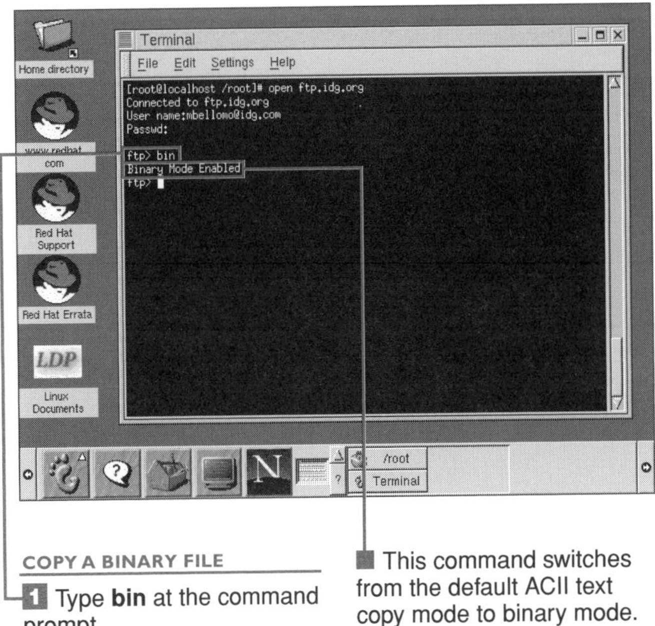

COPY A BINARY FILE

1 Type **bin** at the command prompt.

2 Press Enter.

■ This command switches from the default ACII text copy mode to binary mode.

■ Some machines notify you that the change has taken place.

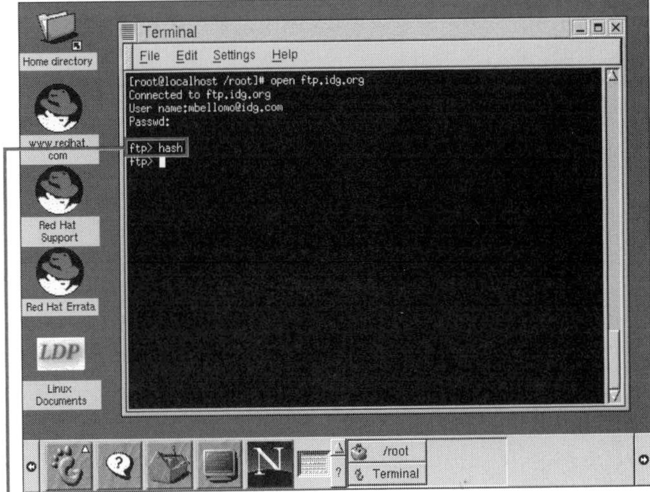

TURN HASH ON

1 By default, `hash` is off. To turn it on, type **hash** at the `ftp` command prompt.

2 Press Enter.

CONTINUED

TRANSFER FILES WITH DIFFERENT FTP OPTIONS CONTINUED

You can copy multiple files at one time with FTP. Because FTP is not part of a graphics-based system, you cannot use a mouse to click and drag over an area of the desktop to select multiple files. Instead, you have to select multiple files as a range of names or letters. For example, you can have FTP copy all files that begin with `M`, or all files that end with `012`.

You need two components when copying multiples files in FTP this way. First, you need to use the `mget` or `mput` command (the `multiple get` or `multiple put` commands). Second, you need to use a wildcard character to specify a range of filenames you want to transfer. For example, if you want to transfer files called `Report`, `Reprise`, and `Re-entry`, you would request a copy of multiple files of the name `Re*`.

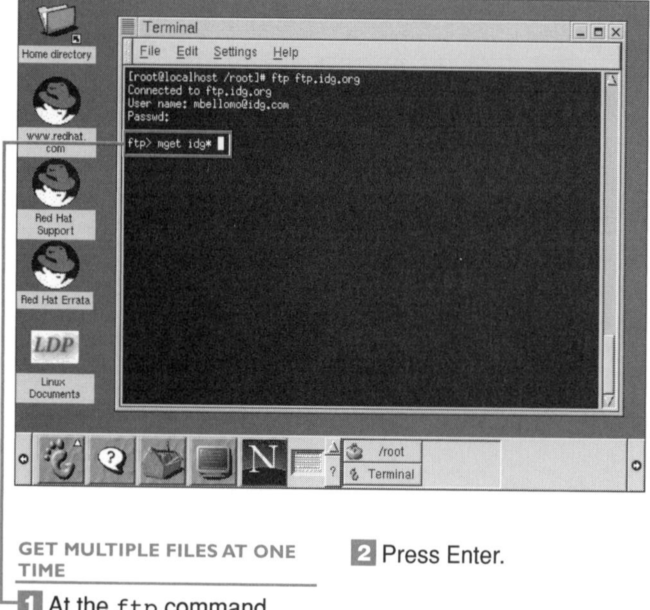

GET MULTIPLE FILES AT ONE TIME

1 At the `ftp` command prompt, type **mget idg***.

2 Press Enter.

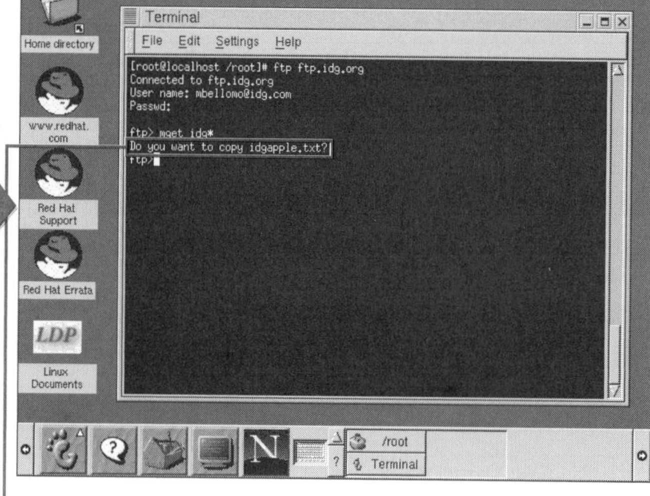

■ The system wants to know whether you want to copy the first of the files.

Can I use any other wildcards with FTP?

✓ You can also use brackets: `[ ]`. Brackets match any single character contained within. For example, `[Idg]` matches an uppercase I, or a lowercase d, or a lowercase g.

Can I use a wildcard like the asterisk in the middle of a filename, instead of at the beginning or the end?

✓ You can, but it is useful in very limited situations. For example, typing `mget blue*color` would cover files `blue1color`, `blue-color`, and `bluedcolor`, but it would not copy over the file `blue1colors`.

Can I bypass the interactive prompting during an mget process? How can I do so?

✓ You can bypass the need to type Y (to indicate yes) or N (to indicate no) in a multiple `get` or `put` process. Start FTP with the `-i` command option, which turns off the interactive prompting.

3 If this file is one of those you want, press Y.

4 Press Enter.

■ Linux copies this file and moves to the next, querying you at each file. This prevents duplication of unwanted files in a series.

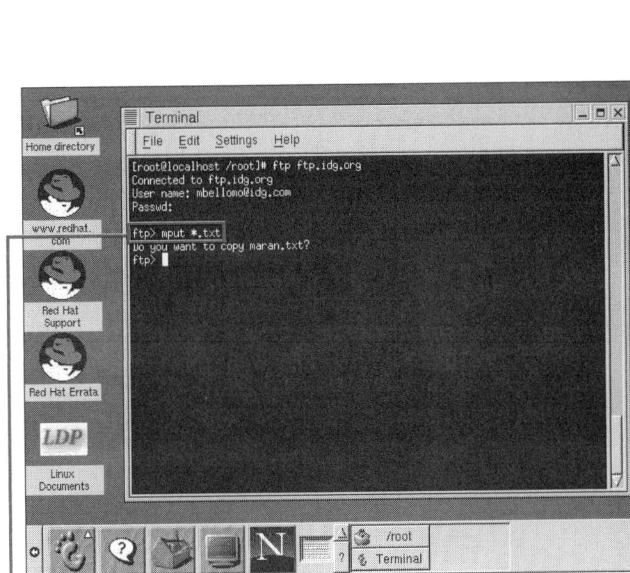

PUT MULTIPLE FILES AT ONCE

1 At the `ftp` command prompt, type **mget *txt**.

2 Press Enter.

■ All files that end with `txt` are put on the server.

CHANGE DIRECTORIES WHILE IN FTP MODE

You have one final set of options with the FTP program that make it more flexible for your purposes. These options allow you to access the files that you want to transfer from one machine to another with greater ease and flexibility.

For example, the `cd` command used in the `ftp` prompt allows you to change the directory in which you are searching for files to transfer. When you use `cd`, you are changing directories on the FTP server machine. It is particularly useful to use `cd` at the `ftp` prompt, rather than to log in and out to get to a new location on the server machine.

Want the opposite effect? Use the `lcd` command at the `ftp` prompt. `lcd`, or `local change directory`, to change the target directory on your home machine (where the files sent via FTP files are going to end up).

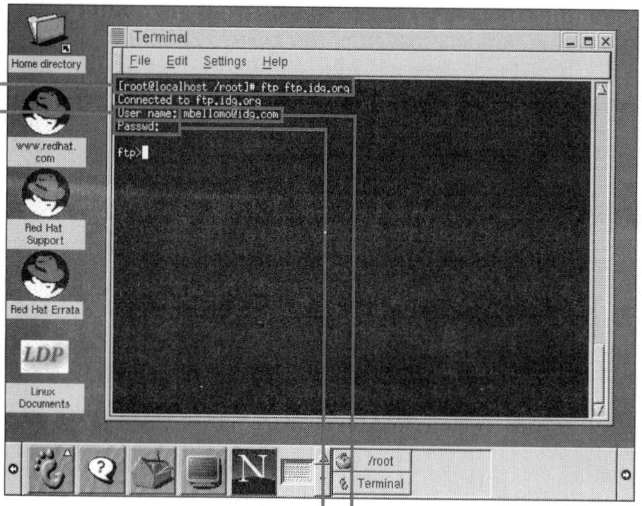

1 At the command prompt, type **ftp ftp.idg.org**.

2 Press Enter.

■ A new ftp prompt asks for your name.

3 Type your user account name.

4 Press Enter.

5 Type the server password.

6 Press Enter.

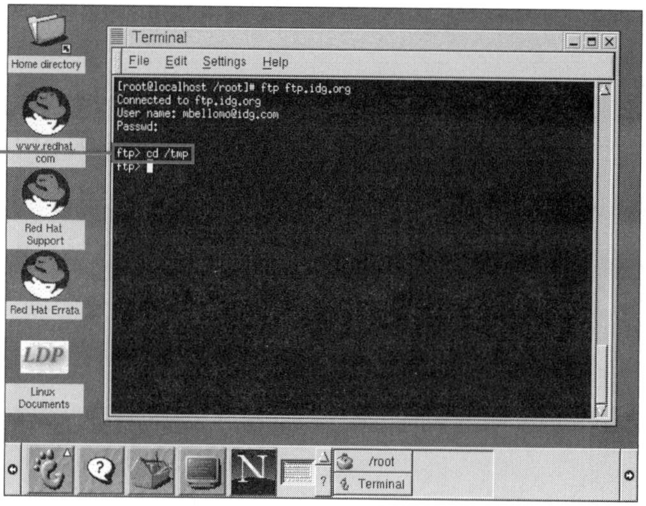

CHANGE THE SERVER'S DIRECTORY

1 At the `ftp` command prompt, type **cd /tmp**.

2 Press Enter.

■ You change to the server's `/tmp` directory.

Why am I unable to find lcd as a command by my regular Linux command prompt?

- `lcd` is an FTP-specific command. You will not find it in use on the system as a whole because it is designed for only one function — to work with FTP. You can only execute it from the `ftp` prompt.

Can I get file transfer statistics from FTP?

- By default, FTP should show you — in bytes and seconds — some transfer statistics. However, use the `v` (`verbose ftp`) command option if you need more information.

Can I exit from FTP by typing exit or quit?

- `exit` and `quit` allow you to exit from FTP in the version of FTP that comes with Red Hat Linux. However, FTP has a quirk that comes to pass on other Linux or UNIX machines: It only allows you to exit the program using the `close` and `disconnect` commands.

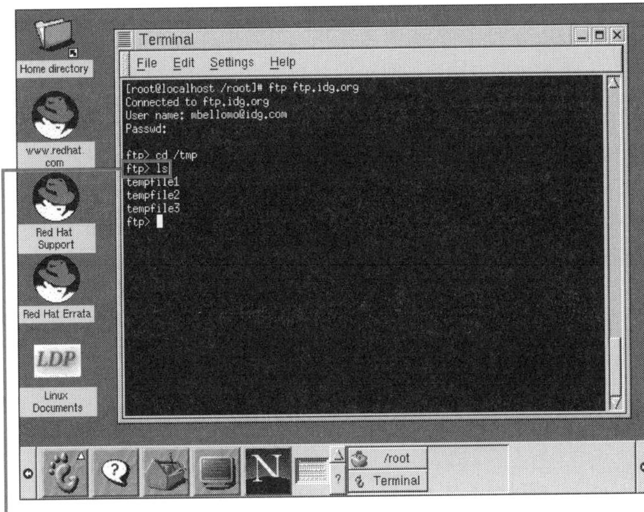

LIST THE CONTENTS OF THE SERVER'S /TMP DIRECTORY

1 Type **ls** at the `ftp` command prompt.

2 Press Enter.

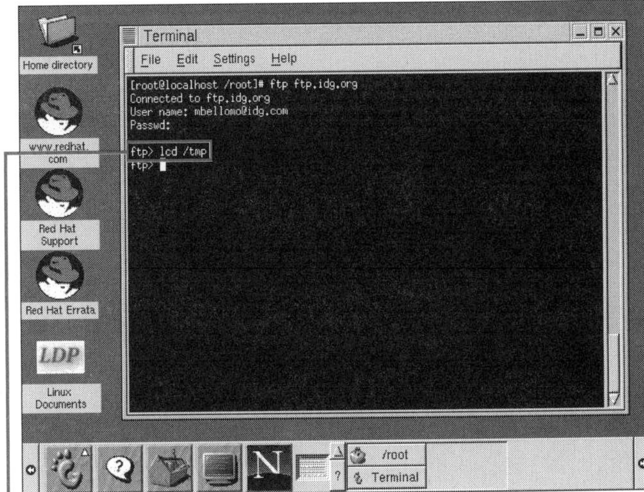

CHANGE THE LOCAL DIRECTORY ON YOUR CLIENT MACHINE

1 Type **lcd /tmp** at the command prompt.

2 Press Enter.

■ You are changed to the `/tmp` directory on the machine on which you originally started the FTP session.

SECTION V

17) SETTING UP NETWORK PRINTERS

Open the Linux Print System Manager 354
Add a Local Printer 356
Add Remote UNIX Printers 358
Add Windows or NetWare Printers 360
Delete Printers 362
Edit and Test Printers 364

18) THE NETWORK FILE SYSTEM

View NFS Settings in GNOME 368
Add and Delete Exported File Systems 370
Add, Mount, and Remove a Remote NFS File System 374
Select Mounting Options for Exported Systems 380
Select NFS Options for Exported Systems 382

19) THE NETWORK INFORMATION SYSTEM

Configure the NIS Client 384
Set Up a Samba Server 388
Connect Your Machine as a Samba Client 394

20) SETTING UP NETWORKED DATABASE USERS

Install PostgreSQL, the Linux Database 396
Add the PostgreSQL User 400
Initialize Your PostgreSQL Server 404

SHARING FILES AND MACHINES OVER THE NETWORK

OPEN THE LINUX PRINT SYSTEM MANAGER

Next to actually starting the Linux operating system, effectively administering your printer and Print Manager is the most important task in running a Linux network. The reason is that the volume of printing in any given office, college, or laboratory far outweighs any other kind of request. Because of this, it's worthwhile to learn how to effectively add and configure printers in Linux.

Printers are external hardware devices that punch, spray, or burn ink onto paper. Although printers are commonly referred to by their method of printing — inkjet, dot matrix, laser — that is not important to an administrator. The types of printers you come in contact with are related to their physical location (local or remote) or by the type of operating system they're designed to work with, such as NetWare, Linux, or Microsoft Windows 95, 98, NT, or 2000.

To handle all of these types of printers, you'll be using the Print System Manager utility, which is part of the GNOME graphic interface.

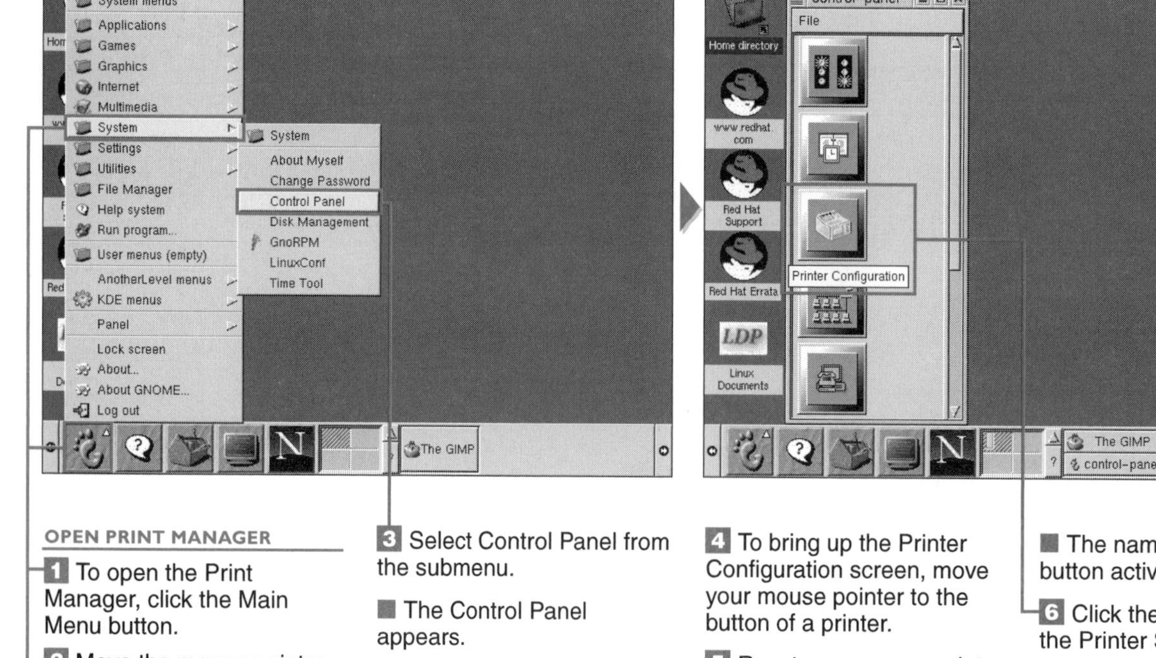

OPEN PRINT MANAGER

1 To open the Print Manager, click the Main Menu button.

2 Move the mouse pointer to System.

3 Select Control Panel from the submenu.

■ The Control Panel appears.

4 To bring up the Printer Configuration screen, move your mouse pointer to the button of a printer.

5 Reset your mouse pointer on the button.

■ The name of the utility the button activates display.

6 Click the button to start the Printer System Manager.

TIPS

Why is my Control Panel labeled Con . . . el or some other odd name?

- It's a form of automatic compression of the Control Panel name, designed to save space. If you want to, you can stretch the Panel out by clicking one of the window borders and dragging it out. As you drag it, the full name Control Panel becomes visible.

Why can't I use my terminal after I start the Control Panel?

- When you start the Control Panel from the terminal, you can't use that specific terminal again. To Linux, the Control Panel is using that terminal to run. If you want to use a Linux terminal, you have to create a new one.

When I close the terminal, I lose my Control Panel!

- The terminal and Control Panel are linked when you use one to start the other. Killing the terminal kills the Control Panel process. However, killing the Control Panel does not kill the terminal.

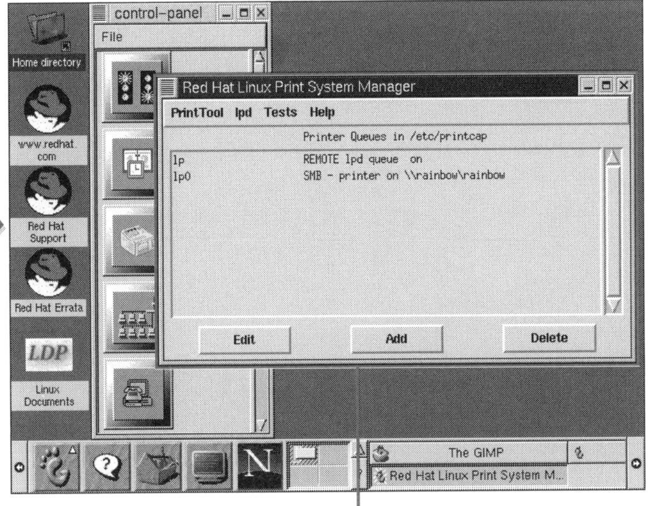

■ The Printer Configuration tool starts up.

7 Make the tool active by clicking anywhere in the window of the tool.

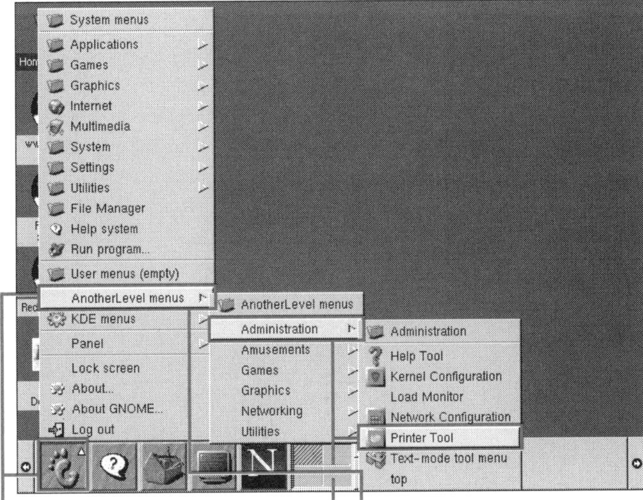

ALTERNATIVE WAY TO OPEN THE PRINT SYSTEM MANAGER

1 Click the Main Menu button.

2 Point to AnotherLevel menus.

3 Point to Administration submenu.

4 Click Printer Tool submenu.

ADD A LOCAL PRINTER

A local printer is one that you connect directly to a given machine. Although the name *local* implies that the printer handles only print jobs generated from the computer it is attached to, that is not the case. You can have a local printer, but as a networked printer, the printer can receive print jobs from all corners of the network.

You primarily work with local printers if you work on a small, single-office network, or if you only take care of only a few users.

Finally, you likely work with local printers most when running Linux at home, on a stand-alone system. Because you don't have a network in place (except perhaps one or two machines you've linked together), your printer additions through the Printer Manager are all local ones.

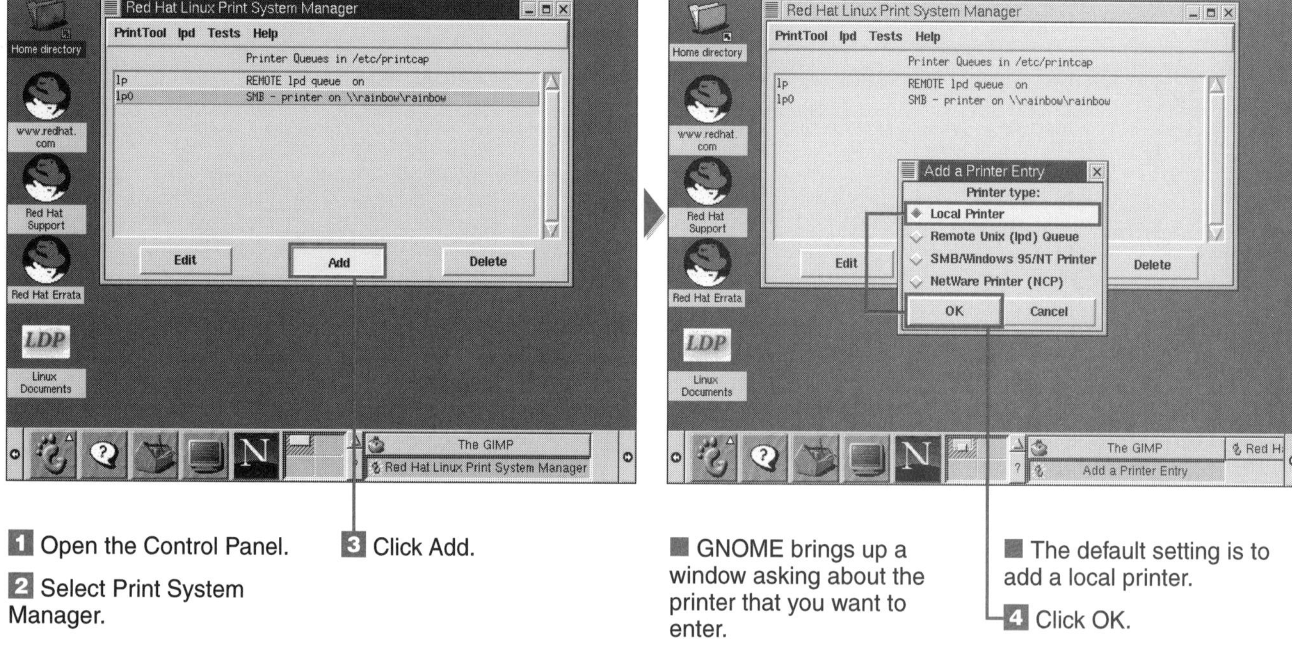

1 Open the Control Panel.

2 Select Print System Manager.

3 Click Add.

■ GNOME brings up a window asking about the printer that you want to enter.

■ The default setting is to add a local printer.

4 Click OK.

TIPS

If the Auto-Detection Information screen appears, does that mean I did something wrong?

There's a good possibility that nothing has gone wrong. Just because the printer was not automatically detected doesn't mean that something is awry. You may be using a serial printer (which connects via your machine's round serial port as opposed to the rectangular parallel port) or you may be using Sparc or Alpha architectures.

If my printer isn't detected automatically, what procedure should I follow?

1. Check the printer cables. Often, one end or the other is loose.
2. If that doesn't work, restart the computer.
3. If you still don't see the printer, try replacing the printer cables. Restart and try again.
4. Finally, check the printer on another machine to isolate the problem. You could have a 100-percent perfect Linux machine but a malfunctioning printer.

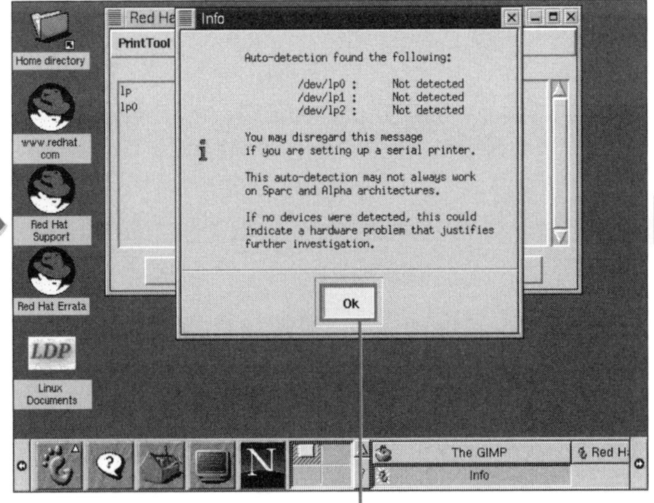

■ The Info screen appears.

5 Click OK.

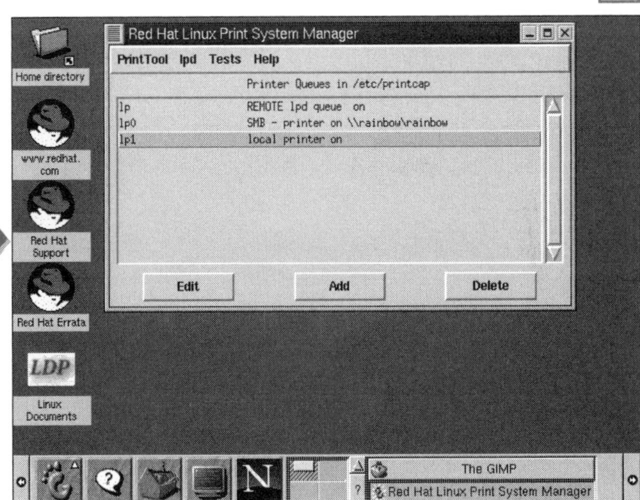

■ In the Printer System Manager window, the new printer appears.

ADD REMOTE UNIX PRINTERS

A *remote printer* is connected to a machine other than your own. By definition, a remote printer is networked and able to receive print jobs from all over the network.

You primarily work with remote printers if you're in an environment with many machines or users who are geographically spread out. Keep in mind that a remote printer doesn't necessarily mean that it is located in a different city or country. Our network could have multiple printers in the same room, which may not be able to plug into one machine at the same time.

Of course, you could be working in an environment where the level of printing demands that you have multiple printers spread throughout departments in different areas, perhaps even different countries. In such a case, most of your printer additions through the Printer Manager will be remote ones.

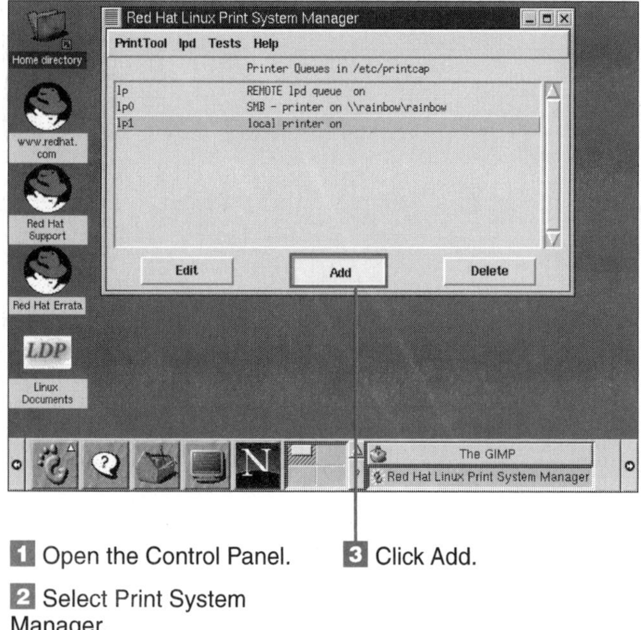

1 Open the Control Panel.

2 Select Print System Manager.

3 Click Add.

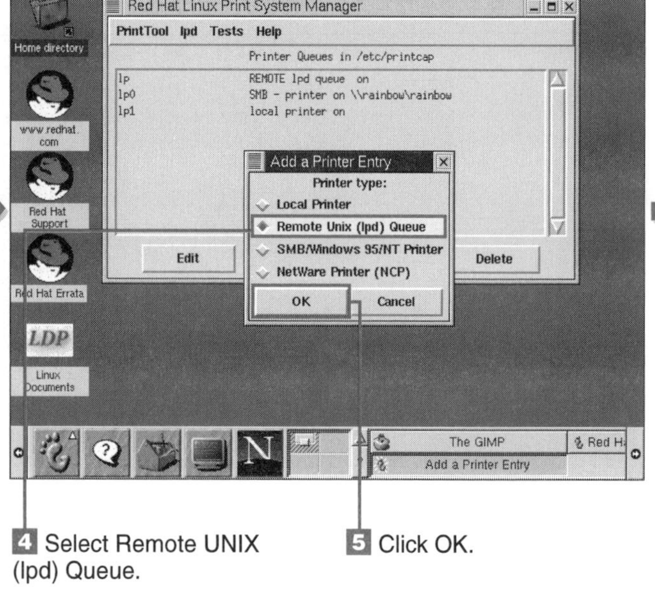

4 Select Remote UNIX (lpd) Queue.

5 Click OK.

Why should my printers follow the naming scheme of the computers to which they're attached?

Matching the printer names to the computer names serves as a quick memory guide to where specific printers are located. For example, say your company has named two print servers on different floors—California and New York. If you name the printers after universities in these states (Berkeley for one, Cornell for the other), you can know exactly where to go when someone reports a problem.

What is the function of the Suppress Headers option in the Edit screen?

When you suppress a header, you tell the machine to ignore the header file that starts off a document. On some networks, a header file may be an entire sheet of paper with the print requester's name on it, to help keep separate print jobs from overlapping in the paper tray.

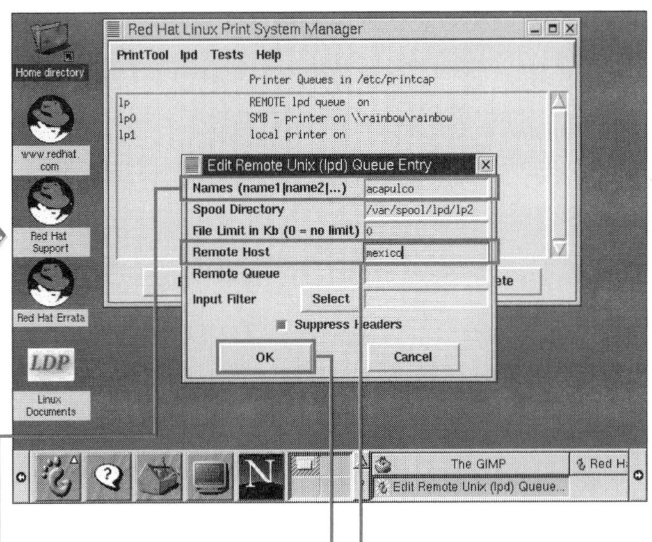

6 Delete the default printer name.

■ By default, Linux assigns a name that a server recognizes, such as `lp1` or `lp2`.

7 Type a new name.

8 Click the Remote Host field.

9 Type the name in the field.

10 Click OK to apply your edits.

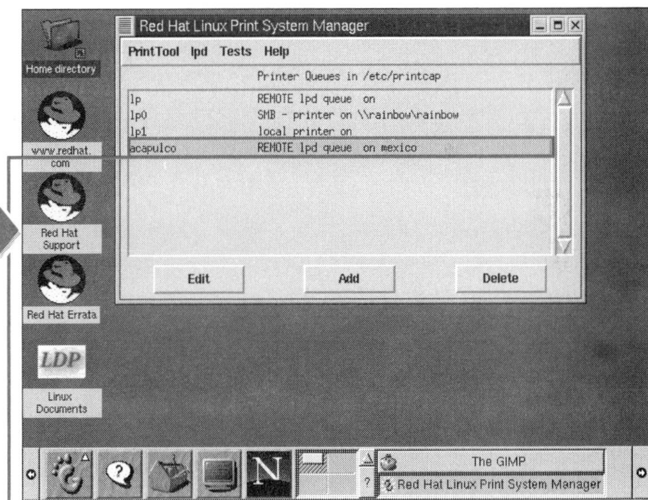

■ The Printer System Manager window shows the new printer, acapulco.

ADD WINDOWS OR NETWARE PRINTERS

In today's corporate and collegiate world, more often than not, you'll be running a mixed computing environment. In a mixed environment, you may be running 20 Linux machines with a dozen other computers running Microsoft Windows (in its various incarnations) or NetWare.

Although all can talk to each other on the same network via the same network protocols, certain functions between the different operating systems are more difficult and require special configurations. One example of this is adding printers that are configured to run with Windows or NetWare.

Use the Print System Manager to add these printers properly. As long as the Manager utility knows that the printers you are adding come from the NetWare or Windows world, the Manager can translate and send jobs effectively to any kind of printer. If you don't properly configure these printer additions, print jobs will either stack up or get lost.

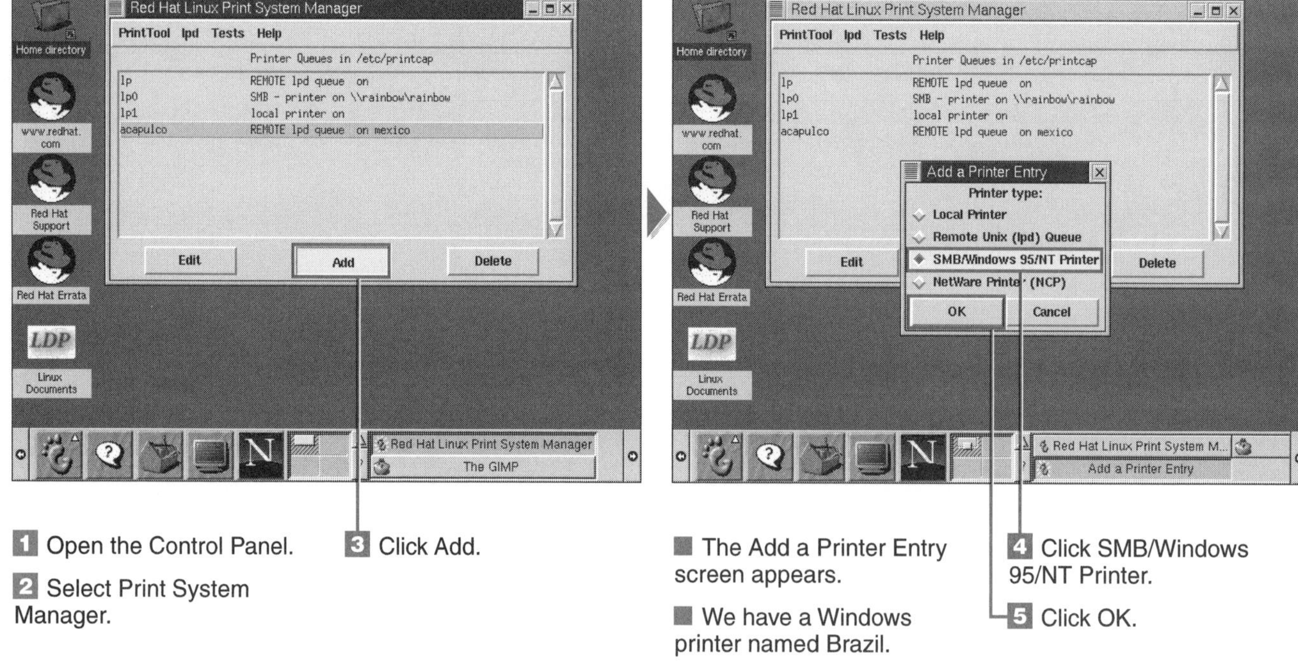

1 Open the Control Panel.

2 Select Print System Manager.

3 Click Add.

■ The Add a Printer Entry screen appears.

■ We have a Windows printer named Brazil.

4 Click SMB/Windows 95/NT Printer.

5 Click OK.

Why can't I read my information screen? The window extends off the main screen!

- This is a flaw in GNOME. When you click OK on the Add Printer Entry Screen, the Information screen is plotted to begin about four inches above it. To correct for this flaw, drag your Add Printer Entry Screen down a couple of inches so you can read the entire information screen if you so desire.

Why is this considered a flaw and not a bug?

- A bug is a mistake in the code of a program that leads to significant, often insoluble problems. The positioning of the information screen is a flaw, simply because it happens on screens that are of a specific brand or size, and it is easily corrected.

Can I run my engineering plotter off my Linux machine?

- You might have more luck attaching your plotter locally to the Linux print server. There have been reports that Windows print servers have difficulties dealing with older engineering plotters.

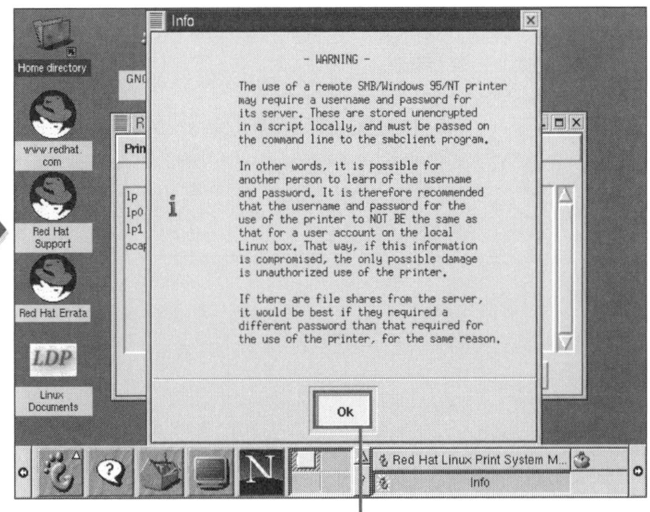

■ A screen appears telling you that, in the Windows or NetWare world, you may need a username and password for the server.

6 Click OK when you finish reading this information.

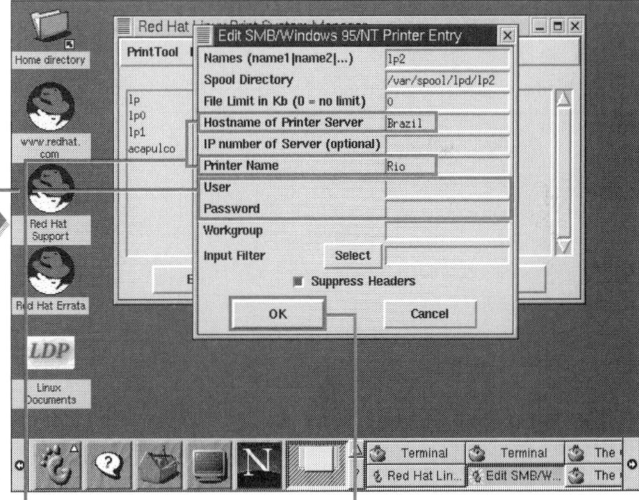

7 Enter a Name, Printer Name, and Hostname of the printer server, by clicking the field and typing.

8 Type a User and Password entry if you want to enable/change the printer settings.

9 Click OK after you finish.

■ In the Printer System Manager window, the new printer Rio appears.

DELETE PRINTERS

If a printer is broken, has been replaced, or has been moved to another network, you need to remove it from the printer list. Otherwise, people may still see it as a viable printer and send print jobs to it. Also, some of the more advanced word processors that work actively with printer servers by balancing printing jobs across a network may send print jobs to it.

In such a situation, a more equal portion of the printing traffic gets jammed up on a printer that is broken or non-existent. So once a printer is scheduled for temporary or permanent down time, remove it from the Print System Manager screens as soon as possible. Luckily, the Manager makes this task exceptionally easy.

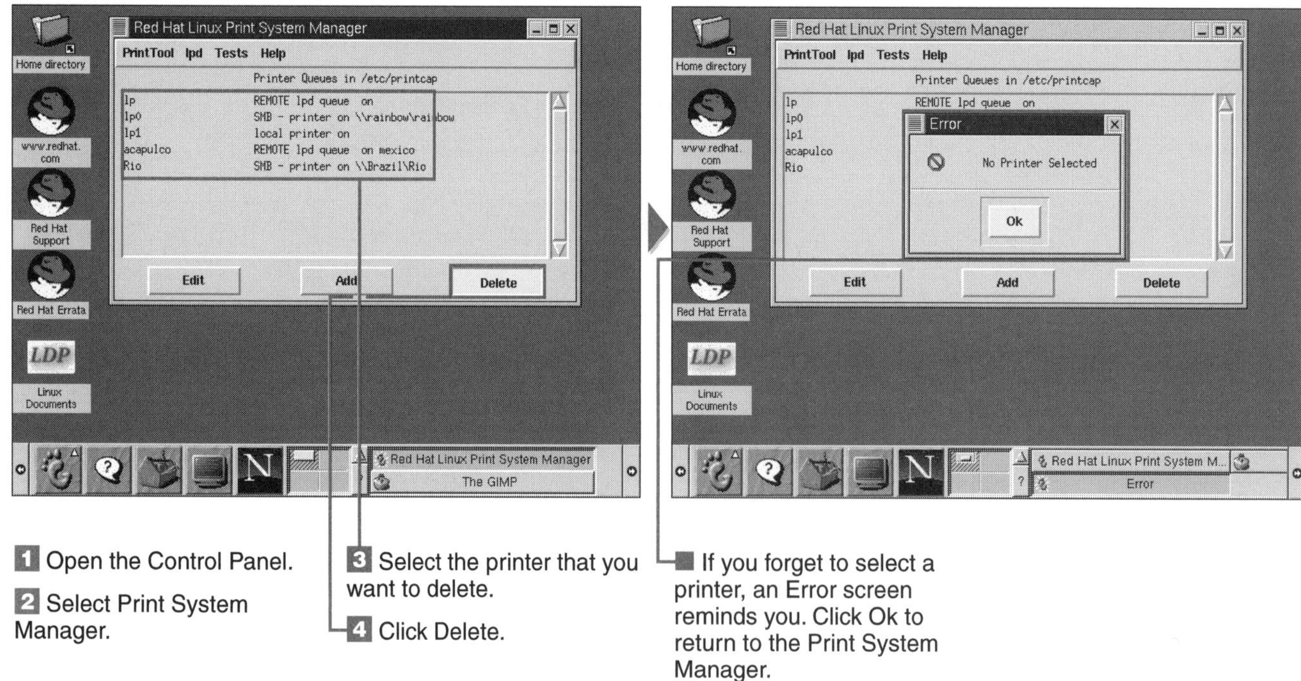

1 Open the Control Panel.

2 Select Print System Manager.

3 Select the printer that you want to delete.

4 Click Delete.

■ If you forget to select a printer, an Error screen reminds you. Click Ok to return to the Print System Manager.

The delete notice asks if I'm sure I want to delete Rio from /etc/printcap. What does this mean?

- The `printcap` is a Linux file that serves the same purpose as the Print System Manager. In effect, the Print System Manager is simply a graphical front end that enables you to edit this file without resorting to the `vi` editor.

What happens to the print jobs stacked up on a broken or nonexistent printer?

- Often times, these jobs don't just go away or get reassigned automatically. If your system logs indicate a loss of disk space for no discernible reason, check your print queues to ensure that nothing is getting backed up.

What happens to the print jobs stacked up on a broken printer after the printer has been removed?

- Once a printer has been removed, it has no print queue. All print jobs stored in that queue are permanently deleted.

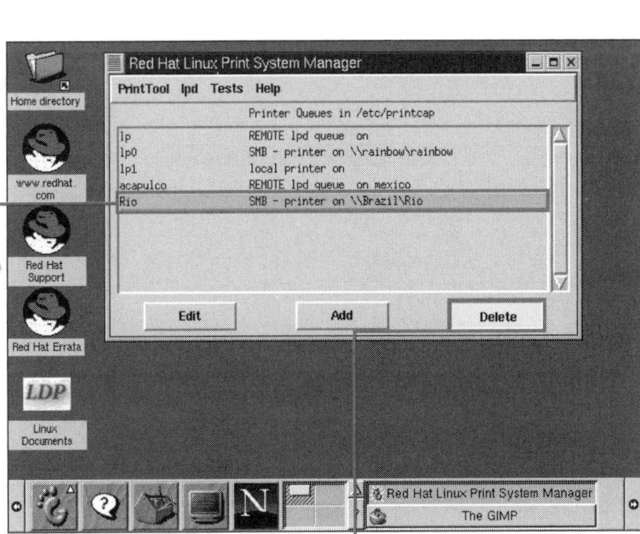

5 Select the printer you want to delete by clicking in the Print Manager Screen.

■ The printer you select appears highlighted.

6 Click the Delete button to continue.

■ Linux queries you to make sure that you want to delete the printer.

■ By default, the selection is Cancel.

7 Click Continue if you're sure you want to delete this printer.

■ The printer is removed from the Print System Manager.

EDIT AND TEST PRINTERS

Once you've successfully added a printer and decided not to delete it, the final two steps are to edit its configuration in the Print System Manager and print a test page from the server to ensure that the connectivity is in order.

You should make special modifications to your printers to make maximum use of your space, or to take advantage of special options that brand of printer may have, such as an increased level of resolution. If you're short on disk space, you can limit the size of the print spool or queue, which is the space on the hard disk where the print server stores documents that are waiting to print.

Similarly, you may be running a specific brand of printer, such as Epson or HP, which has special features. To ensure that you're running a printer driver program to take advantage of these features, edit the Printer through the Manager Utility. Finally, be sure and test the connections you've made between computer and printer by utilizing the Test Page facility.

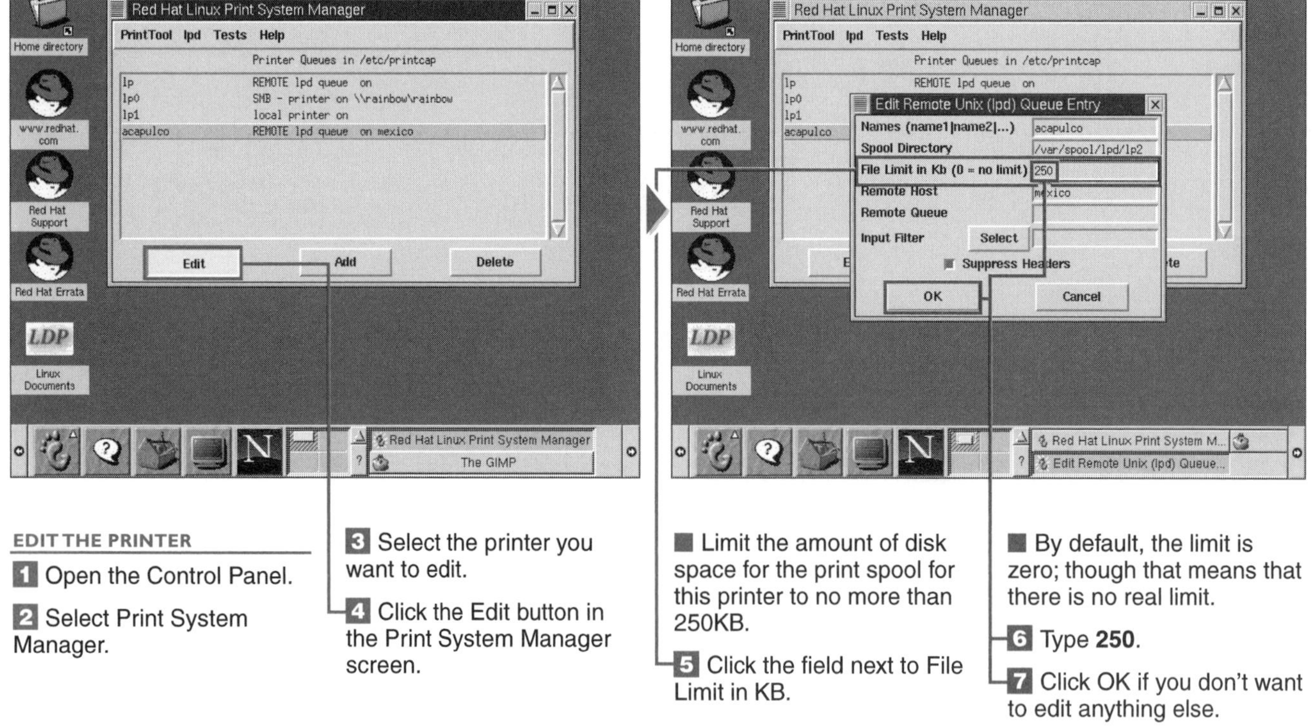

EDIT THE PRINTER

1 Open the Control Panel.

2 Select Print System Manager.

3 Select the printer you want to edit.

4 Click the Edit button in the Print System Manager screen.

■ Limit the amount of disk space for the print spool for this printer to no more than 250KB.

5 Click the field next to File Limit in KB.

■ By default, the limit is zero; though that means that there is no real limit.

6 Type **250**.

7 Click OK if you don't want to edit anything else.

TIPS

Where should I put my print spool if I'm short on space?

- By default, the print spool is normally stored in the /var directory. If the disk partition where /var is located is getting full, you can try moving the print spool to /tmp. The advantage to doing this is that /tmp is automatically emptied whenever you restart your computer, which helps prevent /tmp from filling up.

How do I change the print spool's location?

- Click any printer in the Print Manager. When the Edit screen appears, type a new location (like /tmp) in the Spool Directory text field.

What else can I do to keep the print spool from getting too large?

- If you don't want to set print spool size limits, your best bet is to e-mail your users and ask them not to print out documents longer than 50 pages during peak hours.

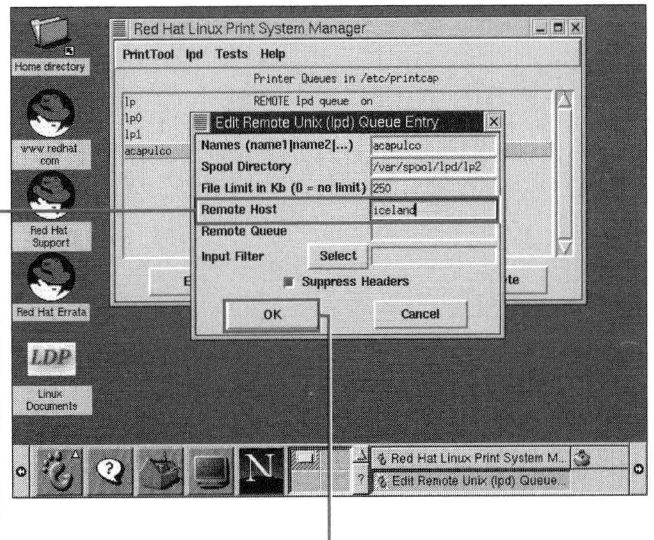

EDIT THE HOST FIELD

1. In the Edit screen, click the Remote Host field.
2. Delete the host name.
3. Type the new remote host name.
4. Click OK if you don't want to edit anything else.

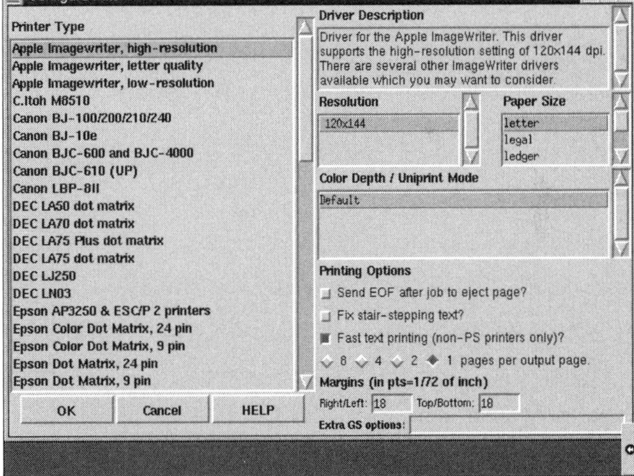

SWITCH THE CONFIGURATIONS FOR A PRINTER

1. Click the Select button in the Edit screen.

■ The Configure Filter screen appears.

CONTINUED

EDIT AND TEST PRINTERS CONTINUED

You can configure even the very small details of the printers that you add to your network with the Print System Manager. These detailed preferences are selected in the Configure Filter screen.

The Configure Filter screen lists over 40 different types of printers in detail. You can read a description of the printer's *driver*, the software that the printer uses to communicate with the computer. You can select the size of paper that the printer will be handling, from legal-size paper to letter size.

You can even set the resolution of text that the printer places on the page. If you have multiple resolution choices, remember that the higher the resolution, the longer the print job takes and the more ink it uses. Heavy ink usage can become an important issue on a system with many users.

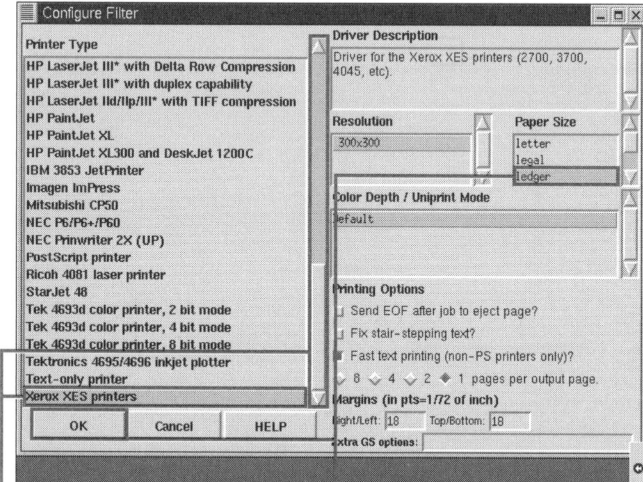

2 Click and drag the vertical scrollbar to the right of the Printer Type column.

3 Click Xerox XES printers to select it.

4 Move your mouse to the Paper Size field.

5 Click Ledger.

6 Click OK if you are done with your selections.

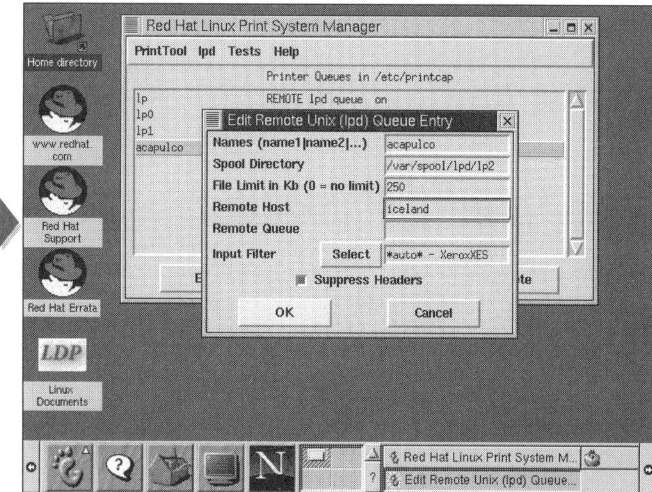

■ The Edit screen appears.

What's the difference between printing an ASCII test page and a Postscript test page and printing directly to a port?

- ASCII and Postscript are distinct systems, and certain types of printers handle one or the other best. You may end up using the default printer port setting (Print ASCII Directly to Port), which works best for local printers on a small or stand-alone machine only.

Where can I go for further instructions and help?

- You can find more documentation that might help you through a common printing problem by clicking the Help button. Once you've done that, you're free to select General Help or Troubleshooting, depending on your need.

What are SMB (Samba) and NCP (NetWare) printers?

- SMB stands for Samba, which means you're dealing with software that enables you to run Windows machines on your Linux network. NCP stands for NetWare Control Protocol, which means that you're dealing with a NetWare print server.

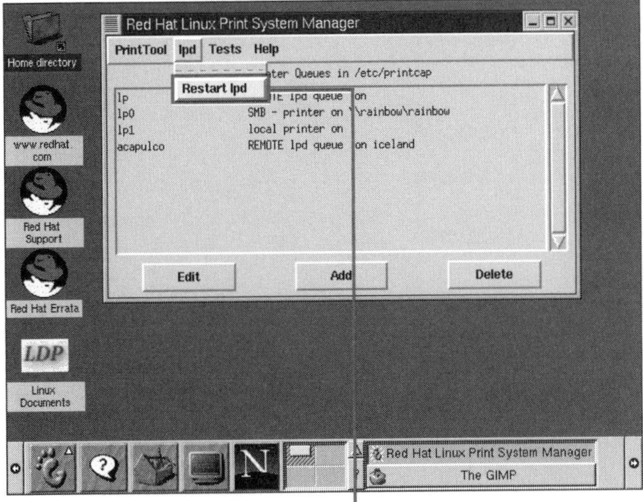

RESTART THE DAEMON

1 Select Print System Manager from the Control Panel and then select lpd on the Print System Manager toolbar.

2 Select Restart lpd from the drop-down menu.

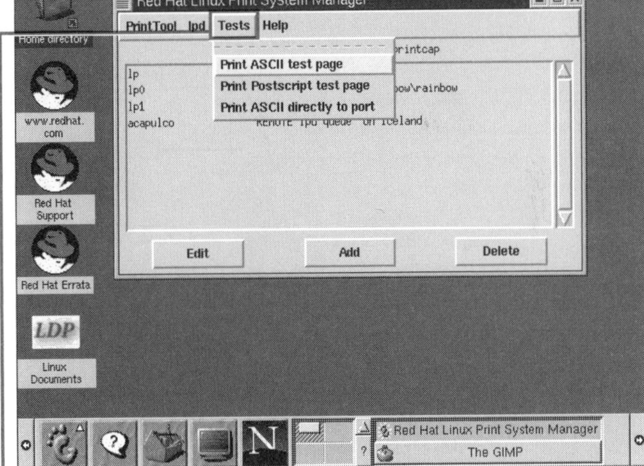

PRINT A TEST PAGE

1 Select Tests on the Print System Manager toolbar.

2 Click the print selection that you want from the drop-down menu.

■ You can print either an ASCII or Postscript test page.

VIEW NFS SETTINGS IN GNOME

You can view directories and files on other networked computers by using NFS, the Network File System. *NFS* mounts (makes available) file systems on other computers. These file systems contain the directories and files that you can access from your local computer with the NFS utility.

NFS also allows you to export file systems. Exporting file systems means that you're making selected directories and files on your local machine available to other people on the network through the NFS utility. By default, exported file systems are accessible to all users on your network.

In order to effectively edit and administer the `Network File System` utility, you need to view the NFS settings that are already in place. You can see NFS settings from the Linux Terminal window or from the `Linuxconf` utility. If the settings are blank, they are not set up yet to export file systems for public consumption.

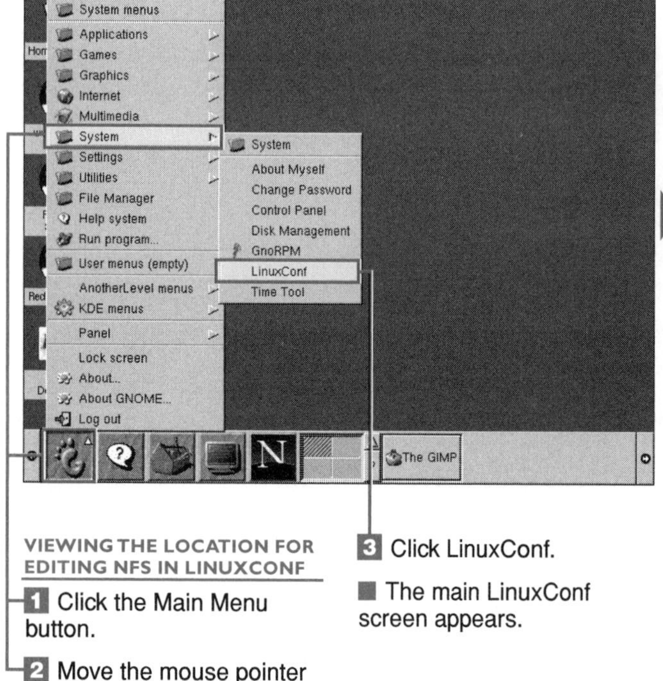

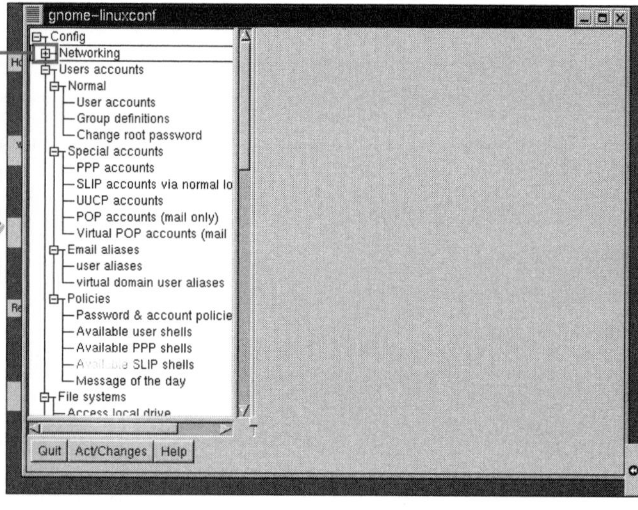

VIEWING THE LOCATION FOR EDITING NFS IN LINUXCONF

1. Click the Main Menu button.

2. Move the mouse pointer to System.

3. Click LinuxConf.

■ The main LinuxConf screen appears.

4. Click the plus sign (+) to the right of Networking to expand the directory structure.

TIPS

How can I tell if the Network File System utility is available on my Linux machine?

- You can use NFS on your machine if the Exported File Systems setting under Server Tasks in LinuxConf and the NFS daemon, also known as nfsd, are available.

If I don't have the Exported File Systems setting in LinuxConf, how can I install it?

- Unfortunately, you can only install NFS components when you install the Linux operating system. Your only option is to backup any files you may have created on your computer and then re-install Linux.

I can find Exported file systems by opening LinuxConf, but how can I tell if I have the NFS daemon?

- By default, the NFS daemon starts up each time you reboot your computer. You can double-check to make sure it's running by using the `process search` command, which is covered in Chapter 6.

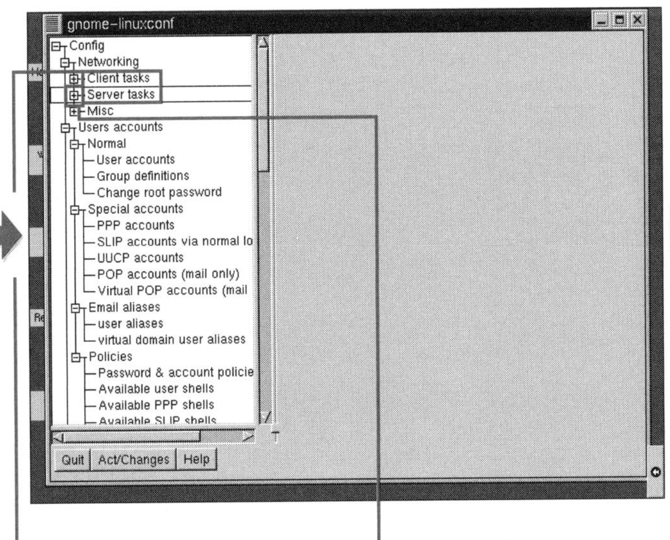

■ The Networking tasks are divided into Client and Server tasks.

5 Click the + sign for Server to see the details.

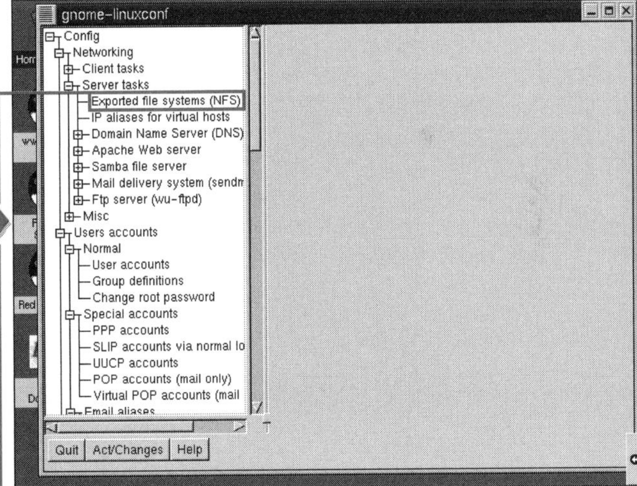

■ By default, the NFS screen for exporting file systems is available.

ADD AND DELETE EXPORTED FILE SYSTEMS

Once you're set up to use the Network File System, you can begin exporting file systems across your entire network. An exported file system acts much like a virtual file system. Although a user can edit and save to an exported file system, the file system doesn't reside locally on his or her machine.

A Linux administrator can conserve both disk space and funds needed to buy more disk space. An exported file system that is mounted doesn't take up any space on the remote system. Instead, the user gets the full benefit of the file system at the price of some slightly heavier network traffic. The only downside to running an NFS system is that the failure of an NFS server has a much greater impact on the network as a whole. If this happens, your primary goal is to return the NFS server to service as soon as possible before attempting to add or delete any more file systems.

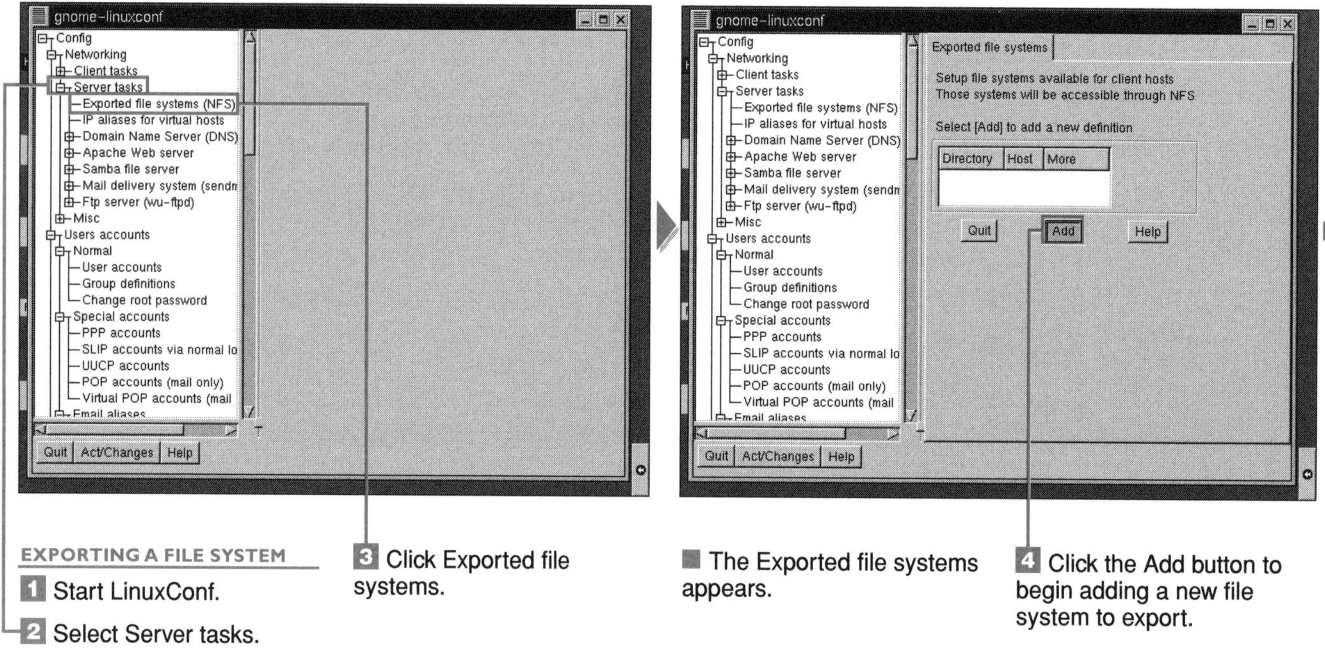

EXPORTING A FILE SYSTEM

1 Start LinuxConf.

2 Select Server tasks.

3 Click Exported file systems.

■ The Exported file systems appears.

4 Click the Add button to begin adding a new file system to export.

When can I select the request access from secure port option in LinuxConf?

- You can select this option for files you want to keep secure and if your system is connected to the Internet via any kind of network connection. When selected, only users who know the Secure port setting can dial in, reducing the chance of an outsider illegally logging into your system and doing damage.

When can I select the translate symbolic links option?

- Select this option to allow users to use files that link one file to another in a different location. This is helpful if you have links to files that exist outside the exported file system.

If I decide to enter text in the Comment field under Path to Export, what do I type?

- Try to enter some short notes in the Comment text field that will refresh your memory as to what you have exported. Another option is to jot down a note to remind yourself why you're exporting these particular files on the Network File System.

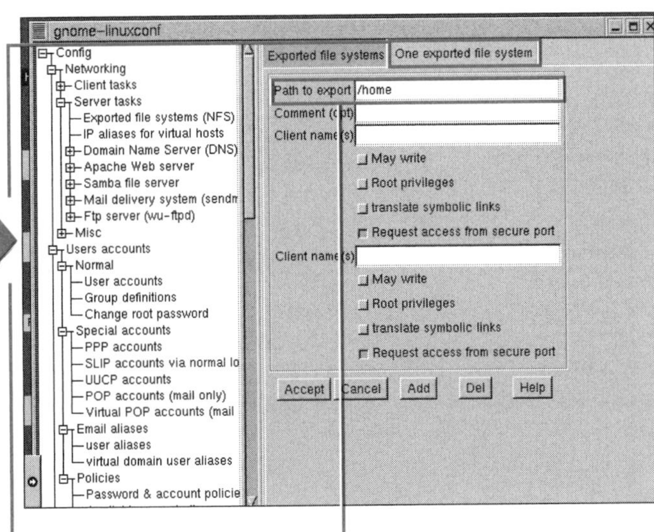

■ The One exported file system appears.

5 Click the Path to export field.

6 Type the file system you want to export.

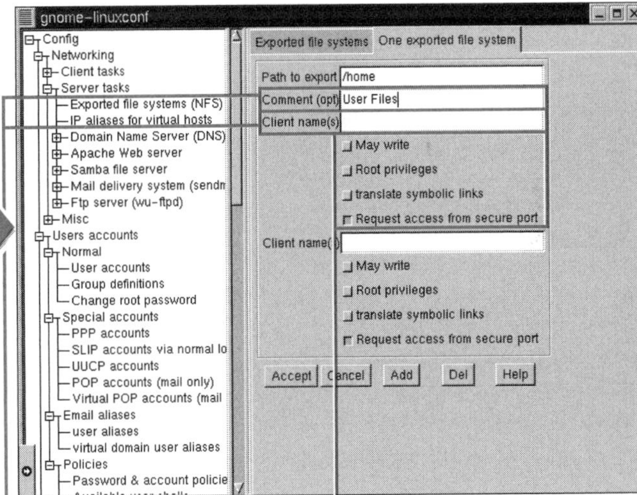

7 Type your comment in the Comment (opt) field to remind you what you're exporting.

8 Click the Client name(s) field if you want to specify clients.

9 For maximum access, leaving this blank allows any remote host on your network to access the exported file system. Type the machine names to restrict access.

CONTINUED

ADD AND DELETE EXPORTED FILE SYSTEMS CONTINUED

You can have a degree of control over the parameters of the `Network File System` utility if you choose to selectively grant access to files by directory or machine. Exporting any file system under NFS is automatically recursive.

A *recursive export* means that when you export `/home`, the Network File System automatically exports the entire file structure underneath `/home`. Since `/home` normally contains user accounts, the entire contents of `/home/mbellomo` or `/home/kiko` will become available for everyone to view unless these users change their file permissions to prevent access.

You can actually grant access permissions to specific machines in NFS. If you prefer to have access to a given file system for security reasons, you can specify which machines these are by adding their names to the Client name field under the `Linuxconf` utility.

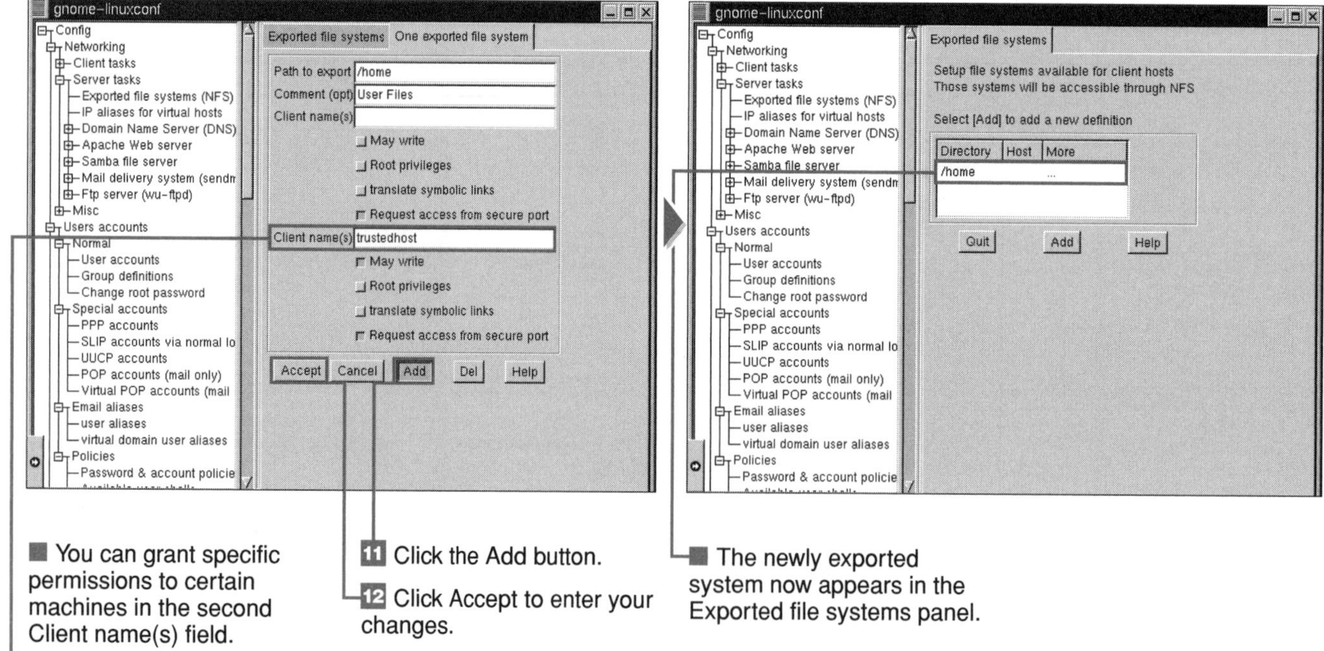

■ You can grant specific permissions to certain machines in the second Client name(s) field.

10 Click in the second Client name(s) field and type the name of a machine.

11 Click the Add button.

12 Click Accept to enter your changes.

■ The newly exported system now appears in the Exported file systems panel.

Is there any way to block access to a subdirectory that has been exported along with a higher level directory?

- If you export `/home`, there is no way to prevent `/home/mbellomo` from being exported as well. However, you can block access to this directory if the root administrative account or the directory owner changes the file permissions to prevent users from reading, writing, or executing any files in it.

What can I do if I delete a file system, but it still appears in LinuxConf's Exported file systems panel?

- Close the `Linuxconf` utility and start it again. Go to the Exported file systems panel and check the display again. If the file system still shows up, you may need to delete the file system again.

When should I grant May write privileges for a file system?

- It's best if you never grant this privilege in order to prevent someone from tampering or accidentally erasing your files.

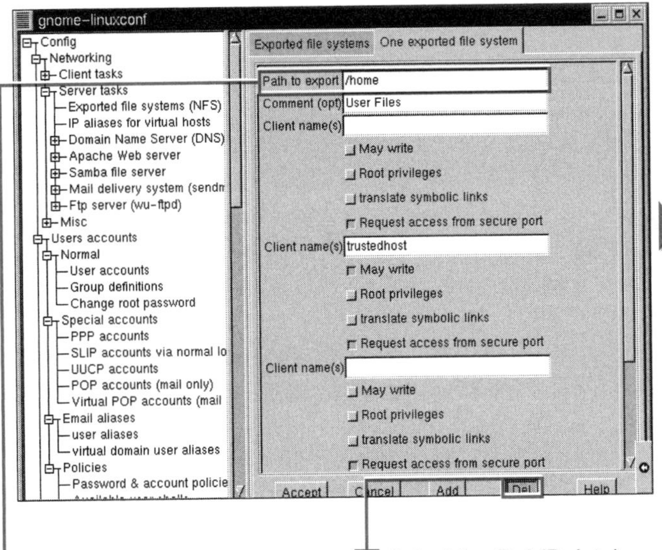

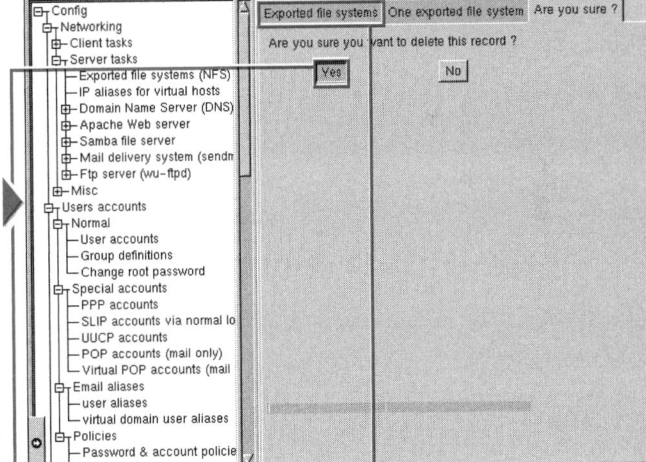

DELETE AN EXPORTED FILE SYSTEM

1 Open the Exported file systems panel.

2 Click the file system that you want to delete.

3 Select the Del (Delete) button.

■ A message appears, asking if you really want to delete this record.

4 Click Yes if you want to complete this action.

5 Check the Exported file systems panel.

■ If the deletion process was successful, the exported file system no longer appears in the field.

ADD, MOUNT, AND REMOVE A REMOTE NFS FILE SYSTEM

You need to know how to perform three actions when you administer a remote NFS system. First, you need to know how to add a newly exported volume. Second, you need to know how to mount the volume once it has been added to the list so that others can access the data on it. Finally, you need to know how to remove the file system once it's no longer needed.

Removing an NFS entry is also important if the exported file system resides on a hard drive that is down or in for repairs. An NFS server can easily hang due to inappropriate or inaccurate information in the `Linuxconf` utility. Of course, if the disk is replaced, it's in your interest to get the file system mounted again for your user community as soon as possible. Make sure that the new disk is working properly by copying files to it and viewing the contents of the disk. Once this has been done, you are ready to add the file system back into the NFS area.

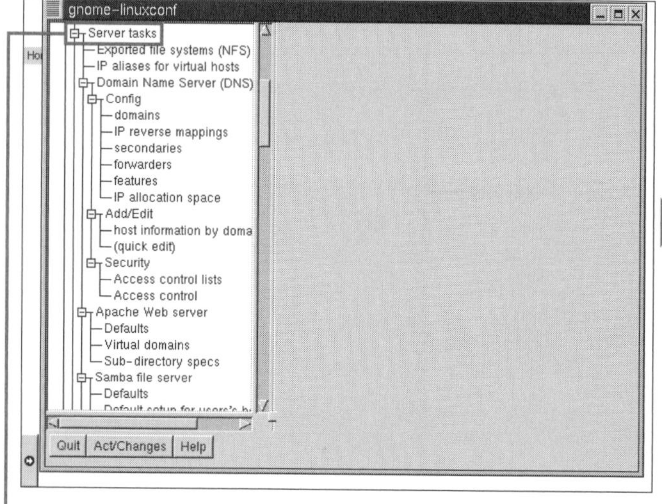

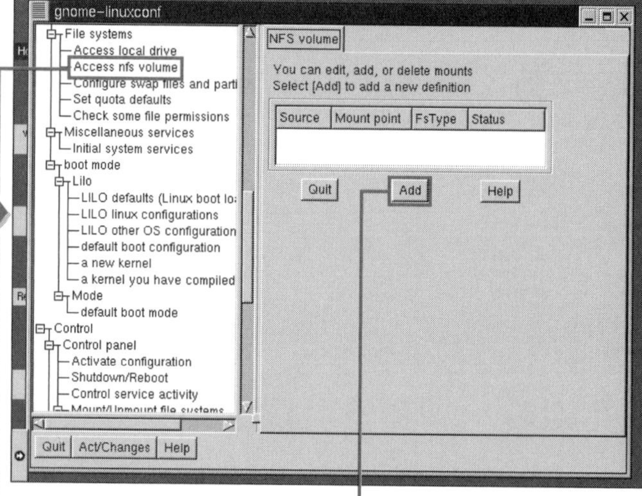

1 Start LinuxConf.

2 Select Server tasks from the left pane.

3 Scroll down to File systems and click the + sign to open the File systems panel.

4 Click Access nfs volume to open the NFS volume panel.

5 Click Add to add an exported volume.

What if my computer doesn't recognize the server machine I enter in the Server text field portion of the Volume specification panel?

- It's rare, but sometimes your computer may not officially recognize a machine's name when you're setting up NFS. Most likely, you have a network connection problem. Check the physical cable connections on the server you're trying to connect to and test the network connection with the `ping` command, covered in Chapter 14.

If the network connections check out, then can I connect to a server via the IP address?

- This is another workable solution. Every networked machine is assigned an IP or Internet protocol address, which is a four-part number like 160.101.40.82. Typing this number in the Server field is acceptable. If you haven't set up the server machine, you'll need to ask the server's administrator for the machine's IP address.

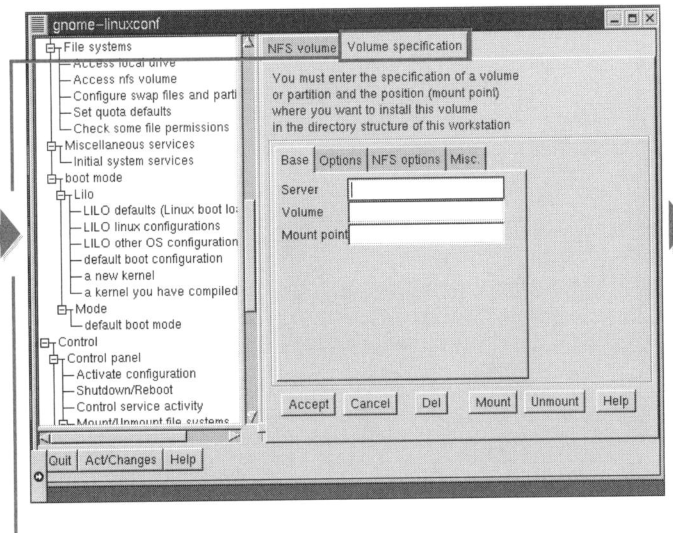

■ The Volume specification panel appears.

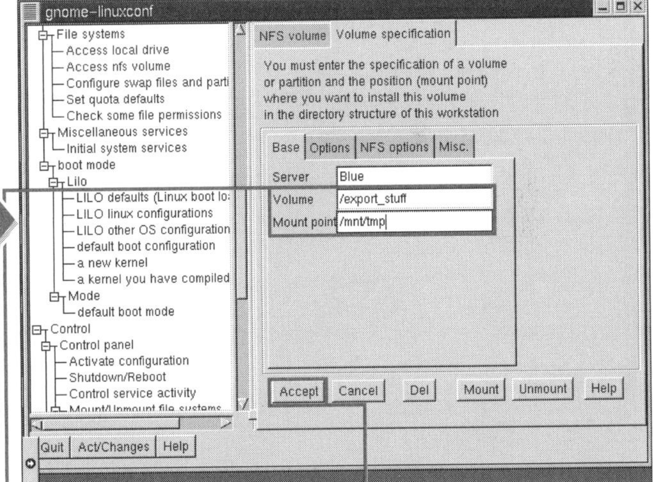

6 In the appropriate fields, type the name of the server that is exporting the volume, the name of the volume (for example, **/export_stuff**), and the mount point you plan to use, (for example, **/mnt/tmp**).

7 Click Accept to add this information to the NFS Volume list.

CONTINUED

ADD, MOUNT, AND REMOVE A REMOTE NFS FILE SYSTEM CONTINUED

You can add new file systems to the Network File System list in the Linuxconf utility at any time. The number of file systems you can add to the NFS volume list is, in theory, without limit.

Speaking practically, you're probably better off not adding more than six or seven file systems to the NFS volume list if you have a slow (pre-Pentium) computer.

With a more up-to-date machine, don't add more than one or two dozen file systems to the NFS volume list. Otherwise, your machine starts to bog down with increased network traffic as it handles requests for information from the listed file systems.

Therefore, be judicious in adding new file systems to the NFS volume list. Also keep in mind that before you can read the files in a newly added file system, you must first make sure that the file system has been mounted.

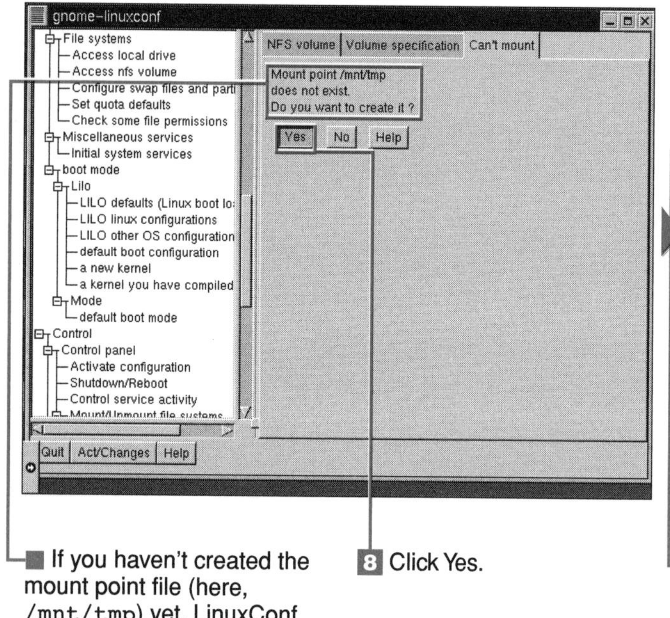

■ If you haven't created the mount point file (here, `/mnt/tmp`) yet, LinuxConf will prompt you to do so automatically.

8 Click Yes.

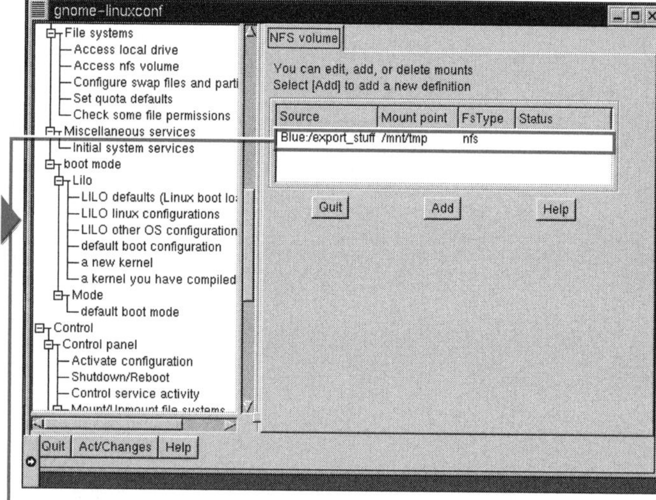

■ The file system you added appears in the NFS volume panel.

By default, can I read, edit, and execute files that are exported through the Network File System utility?

- Unless the file permissions are set to restrict you, or the Read Only option has been selected in the Options tab of the Volume specification panel, you can do all the above by default. The idea behind the Network File System is to make file systems on remote computers look and act exactly as if they are stored on your local hard drive.

Instead of using Linuxconf to add the file system and then mount the file system, can I mount the file system first and then add it?

- You can't mount and then add a file system in that order. The reason is that Linuxconf can't mount any file system in NFS unless it's been added to the NFS volume list.

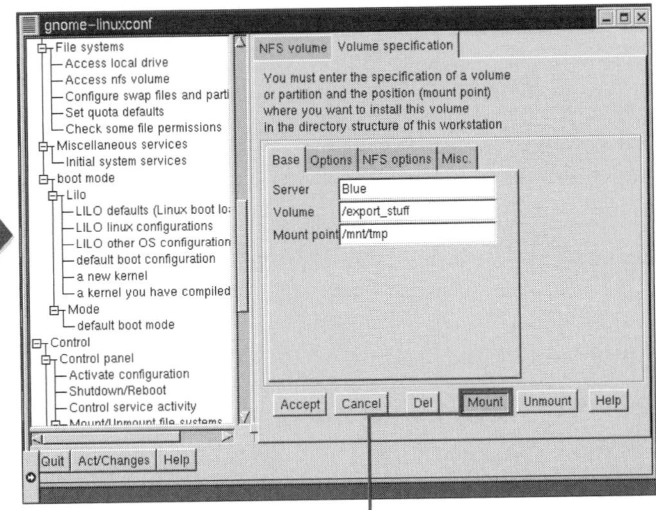

■ You can't access the files in the exported directory because the file system isn't mounted yet.

9 Click Mount to mount this file system.

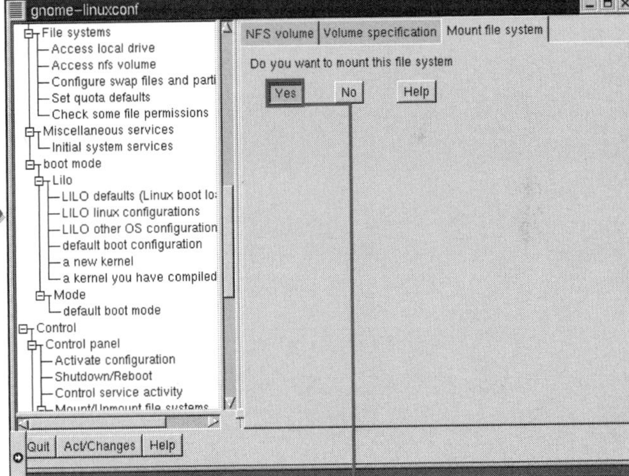

■ The confirmation screen appears.

10 Click Yes to proceed.

CONTINUED

ADD, MOUNT, AND REMOVE A REMOTE NFS FILE SYSTEM CONTINUED

You can check which file systems have been mounted successfully, as well as the status of your mounted file systems with the `mount` command. *`mount`* is a Linux command that pre-dates the GNOME desktop environment, so it can only be accessed through a Linux Terminal screen.

`mount` is especially useful as a tool to double-check the actions you've performed in LinuxConf. While the `Linuxconf` utility is extremely useful, one flaw in its design is that it rarely alerts you if an action you've ordered cannot be completed. Using `mount` is a good way to prevent confusion if you're under the impression that you've mounted a file system that you are unable to read or get to. For example, LinuxConf may insist that you mounted the file system `/mnt/floppy`. However, if this file system isn't listed when you run the `mount` command, the mount has informed you correctly.

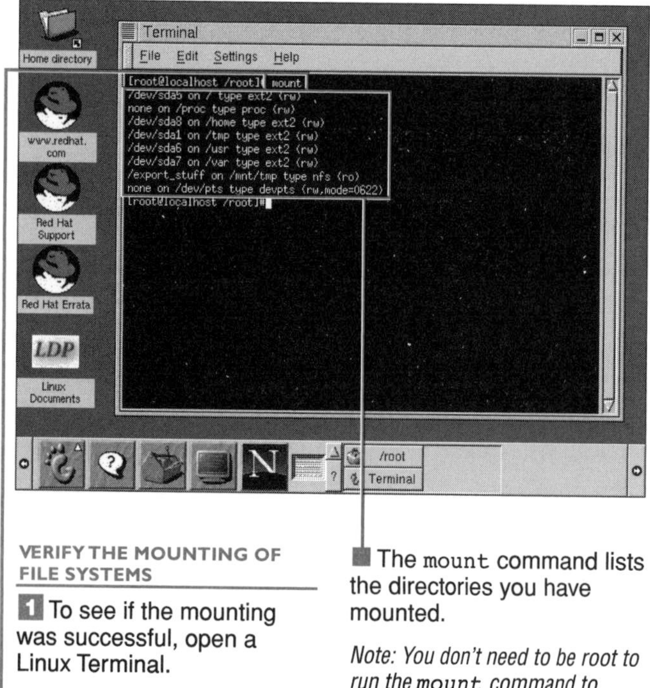

VERIFY THE MOUNTING OF FILE SYSTEMS

1 To see if the mounting was successful, open a Linux Terminal.

2 Type **mount** at the command line.

■ The `mount` command lists the directories you have mounted.

Note: You don't need to be root to run the `mount` command to check currently mounted file systems.

DELETE THE EXPORTED FILE SYSTEM

1 Go to the Volume specification panel.

2 Click Unmount.

■ The confirmation screen appears.

3 Click Yes to confirm this action.

Why the distinction between Accept and Mount on the volume Specification panel?

- Accepting options sets up the program to apply your new settings immediately. The next time you mount the file systems, the new options are in effect. If you select Mount, then your settings will not take affect until you are finished mounting and dismounting the system.

What if I don't know the name of the server?

- If you don't know the name or the alias of the server, double-check the IP address before you enter it. Use the `ping` utility in the Linux Terminal and see if you get a response.

Why double-check whether file systems have been mounted or unmounted in the Linux Terminal versus the LinuxConf?

- The Linux Terminal is more reliable than LinuxConf when it comes to telling you which file systems are mounted or unmounted.

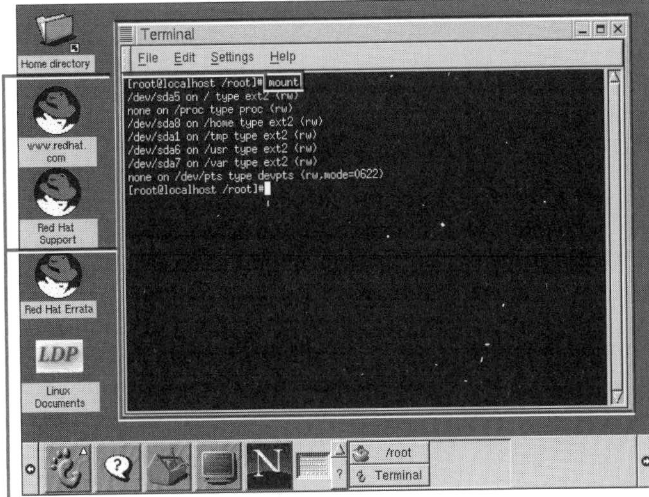

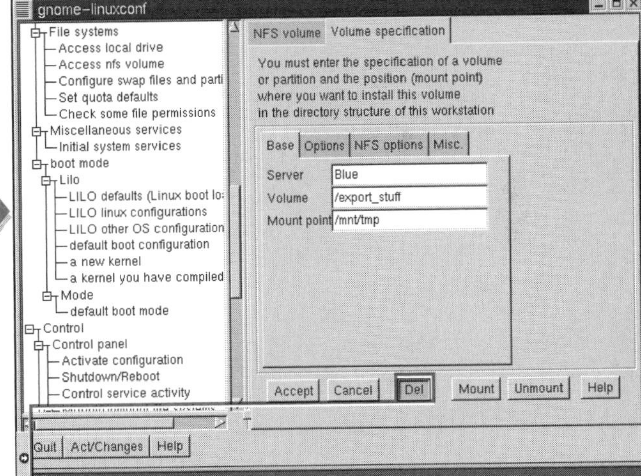

VERIFY THE UNMOUNTING

1 To double-check the unmount of a system, open a Linux Terminal.

2 Type **mount** at the command line.

■ If the exported file system doesn't appear in the list, it was successfully unmounted.

3 To delete the exported file system after it has been unmounted, go to the Volume specification panel and click Del (Delete) to remove the file system.

■ The confirmation screen appears.

4 Click Yes to confirm.

SELECT MOUNTING OPTIONS FOR EXPORTED SYSTEMS

You can select special options that affect how you mount the file systems you plan to export to other machines. These specialized options allow you to decide how much control users have on an exported system, and the amount of persistence that a system has when trying to mount an unresponsive file system.

For example, you can set the file system options so that users may only read files, not edit them. This adds additional protection for sensitive files in case the files were improperly permissioned, enabling users access to change them. You can also restrict access to all files in a file system by not selecting the user mountable option. This prevents users from manually accessing this file system in the first place.

As a rule, you do not want to use these specialized options too heavily unless you plan to do some heavy-duty NFS administration or file system export. For general security, file permissions are more effective in safeguarding your system.

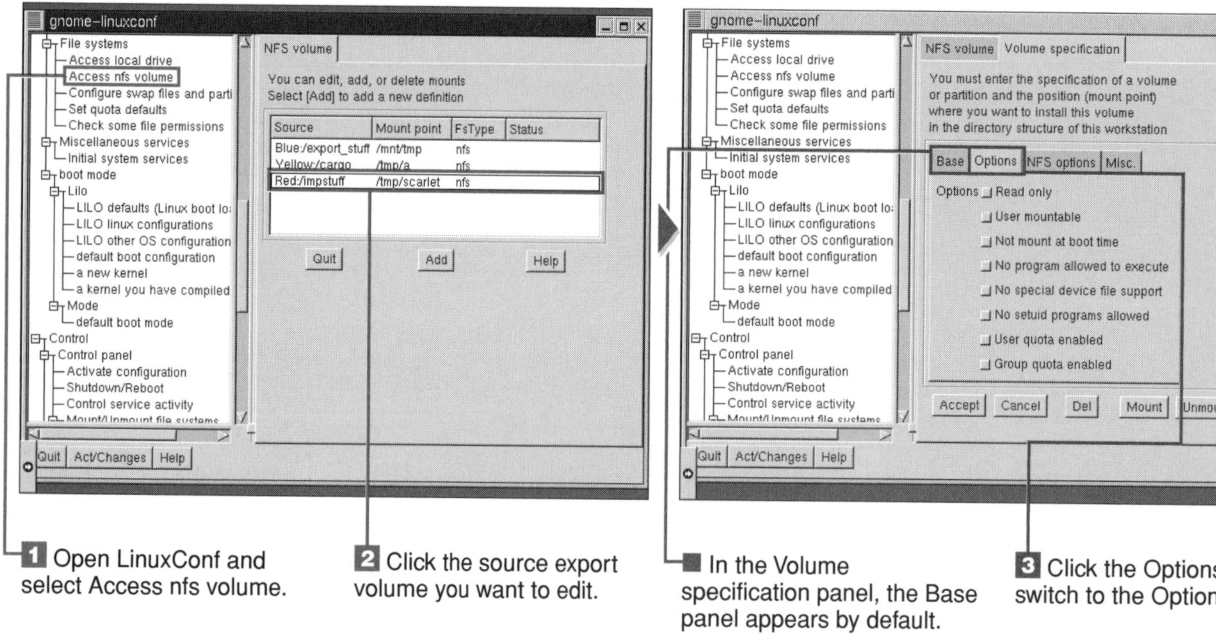

1 Open LinuxConf and select Access nfs volume.

2 Click the source export volume you want to edit.

■ In the Volume specification panel, the Base panel appears by default.

3 Click the Options tab to switch to the Options panel.

Why should you prevent the use of special devices and setuid programs?

- In both cases, particularly with a setuid program, a user can receive administrative privileges similar to the root account. This allows a user, who may be restricted from taking certain actions (such as creating new files) to bypass security and permissioning.

Is there a disadvantage of mounting multiple systems at boot time?

- If you have multiple file systems to mount at boot time, you're substantially increasing the time it takes for the machine to setup for operation. In the case of a server, you want to be up and running as soon as possible.

Where can I find more information on administering NFS?

- You can find more information on working with NFS in *Red Hat Linux Secrets,* by Naba Barkakati or *Linux Administration For Dummies,* by Michael Bellomo (both books published by IDG Books Worldwide, Inc.).

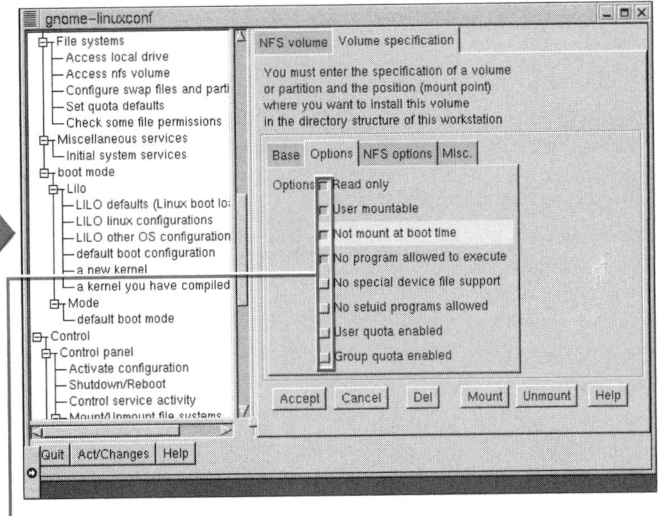

4 To select the options of your choice, click the button to the left of the option.

5 If the option is selected, you can deselect it by clicking the depressed button.

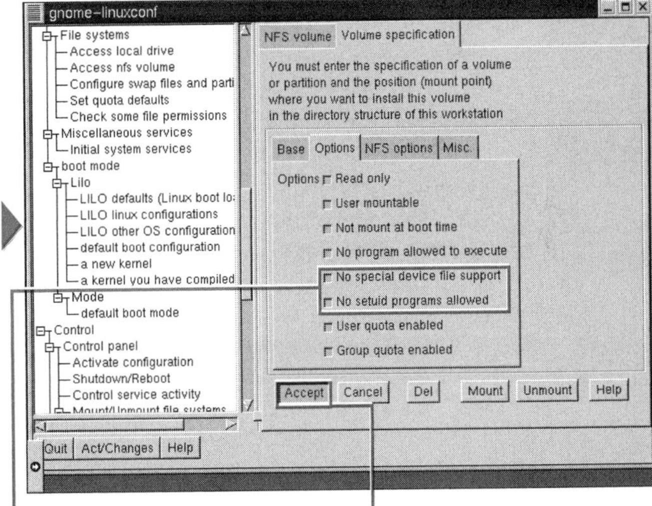

6 To prohibit special permissions on the exported system, select No special device file support and No setuid programs.

7 Click Accept (not Mount) to have these changes take effect.

SELECT NFS OPTIONS FOR EXPORTED SYSTEMS

You can tailor your NFS options to increase file accessibility for some groups while restricting it for others. For example, while allowing everyone in the company to view accounting rolls is nice, it's probably better if the information is restricted to the hosts in the account department only.

By selecting the proper options for the varied file systems, you can guarantee exported accounting data to all the hosts in the accounting department, while denying access to the rest of the company.

In a less extreme example, you may want to ensure that the files you do export are read-only, so that people cannot edit the files without your permission. Keep in mind that if you only want to restrict certain files or directories, instead of entire file systems, your best option is to change the file or directory permissions instead, as described in detail in Chapter 4.

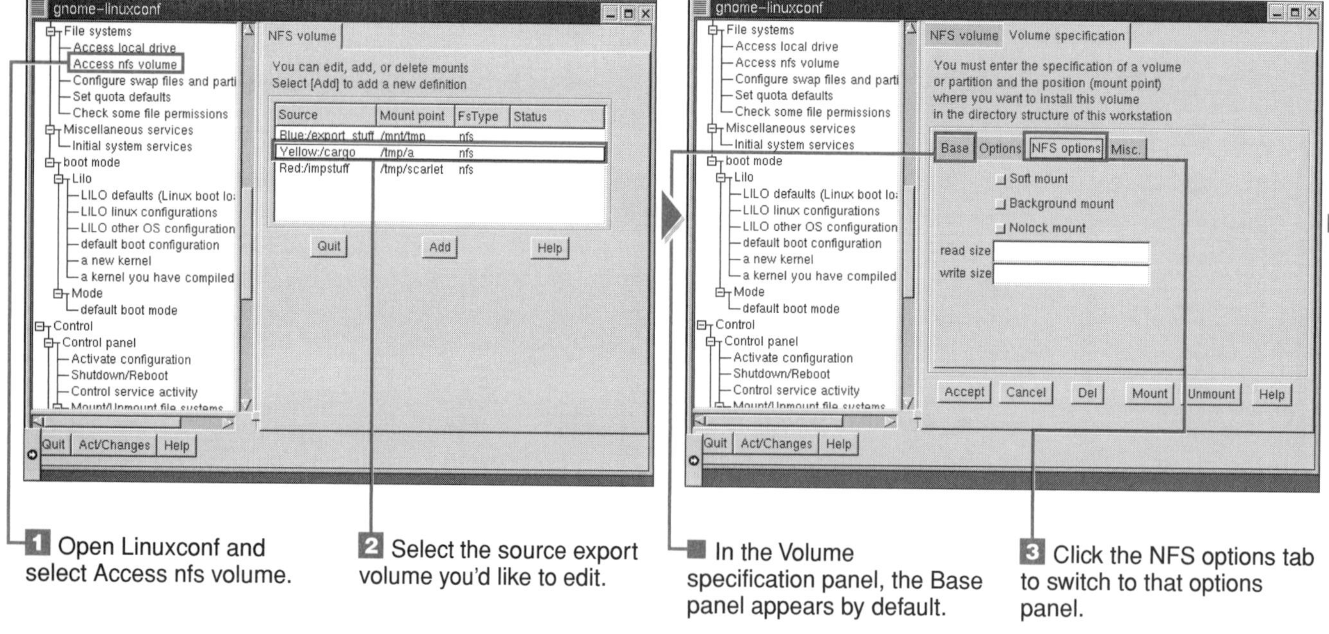

1 Open Linuxconf and select Access nfs volume.

2 Select the source export volume you'd like to edit.

■ In the Volume specification panel, the Base panel appears by default.

3 Click the NFS options tab to switch to that options panel.

When should I use the Background mount or Nolock mount options in the NFS options tab of the Volume specification panel?

- Background mounting is very rarely used and only by machines that are running short of processing power. This option doesn't mount file systems immediately, but waits for the level of system activity to slow down enough to complete the task.

  Nolock mounting prevents the computer from freezing if it cannot mount a file system after 60 seconds. However, you can avoid the problem altogether by selecting the Soft mount option instead.

Where can I find more information on NFS on my machine?

- You can find more information on the NFS daemon and other portions of NFS in the man pages. Open a Linux Terminal and type **man nfsd** to see more information on the nuts and bolts aspect of the parts that make up the Network File System.

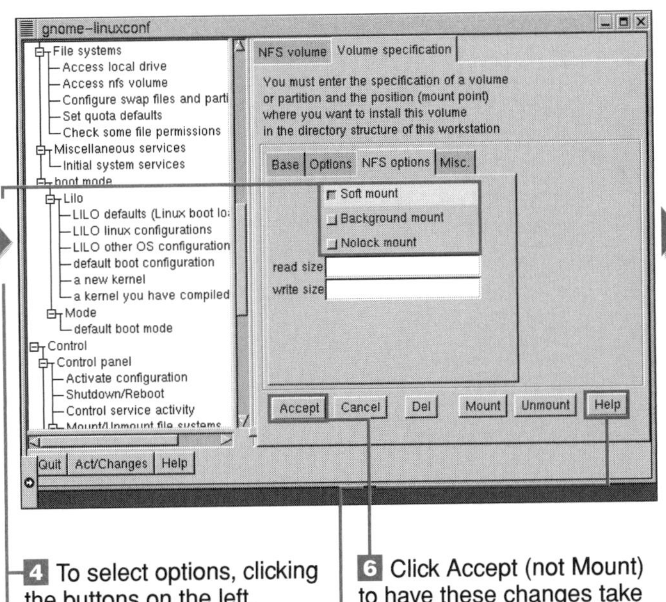

4 To select options, clicking the buttons on the left.

5 If the option is selected, you can deselect it by clicking the depressed button.

6 Click Accept (not Mount) to have these changes take effect.

■ If you get need help, simply click the Help button available in the NFS volume or Volume specification panels.

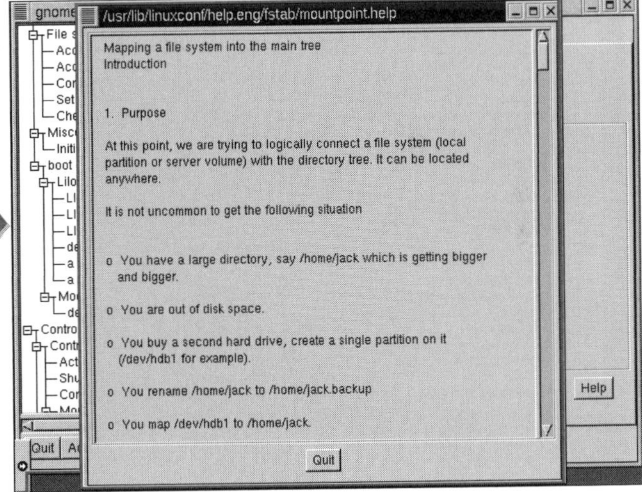

■ The Help screen appears.

CONFIGURE THE NIS CLIENT

You can configure your computer as an NIS client in the `Linuxconf` utility. NIS (Network Information System) is a distributed database system for common configuration files. First developed by Sun Microsystems and called the Yellow Pages, the name was switched to NIS for legal reasons. Occasionally, you see a file or daemon in NIS that 117 percent uses the prefix `yp`, such as `ypbind` or `ypserv`.

Using LinuxConf, you can set up any Linux machine on your network to run as an NIS client. When the NIS-configured client starts or reboots, it sends out a broadcast to the network, searching for an NIS server. The server then allows the client to access remote information without keeping a local copy. For example, the file `/etc/hosts` can be centrally managed by an NIS server without devoting space to it on each and every machine on your network.

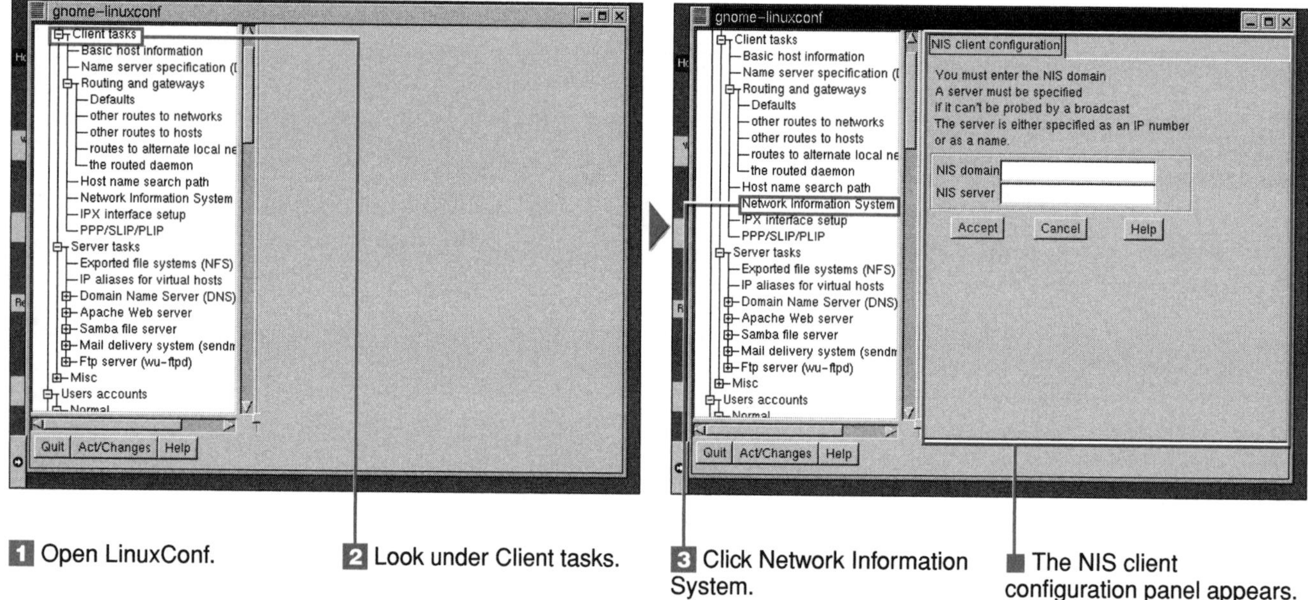

1 Open LinuxConf.

2 Look under Client tasks.

3 Click Network Information System.

■ The NIS client configuration panel appears.

I need to set up an NIS environment that is more complex (with multiple NIS servers for my client machine to connect to). Where can I get more information?

✓ While you can get more information on NIS from either the Sun Corporation itself (`www.sun.com`) or from Red Hat (`www.redhat.com`), you can find more detailed information from books rather than Web sites. The best work on the subject is *NFS and NIS Networking*, published by O'Reilly.

I have heard the term *domain* used a few times to describe working in NIS. What exactly is an NIS domain?

✓ A domain is really a logical grouping of machines that are bound together by a special networking system or software. For example, a group of machines that use NIS as clients that connect to an NIS server can be referred to as an NIS domain.

4 Click the open field by NIS domain.

5 Type the NIS domain name.

6 Click the open field by NIS server.

7 Enter the NIS server you want the client to connect to.

8 Click Accept to accept these changes.

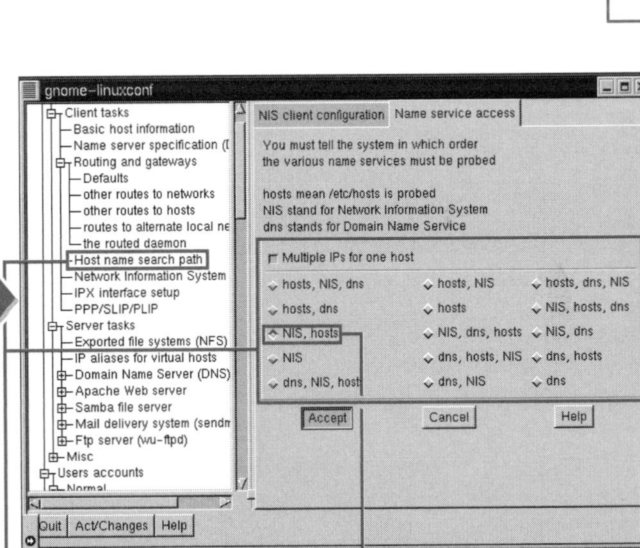

9 Click Host name search path.

■ Depending on what services you have and what action you want the machine to take, select one of the 15 combinations.

10 Select NIS, hosts.

■ The machine first tries to contact the NIS server, then alternate hosts on the network.

CONTINUED

CONFIGURE THE NIS CLIENT CONTINUED

You can complete your computer's configuration as an NIS client by taking care of two final items. You must first make sure that the ypbind daemon is running. You must then create a special subdirectory (yp) under the /var directory.

ypbind is the daemon that links your client to the ypserv daemon, which runs on an NIS server. ypbind must be running on your NIS client to connect and receive information from the NIS server. You can tell whether ypbind is running by using the process search command (ps). ypbind is listed on the screen when it is running.

Your second task is just as important. The NIS system creates and stores its information in a special directory called yp, which stands for yellow pages. Be sure to create it where NIS is programmed to look for it — in the /var directory.

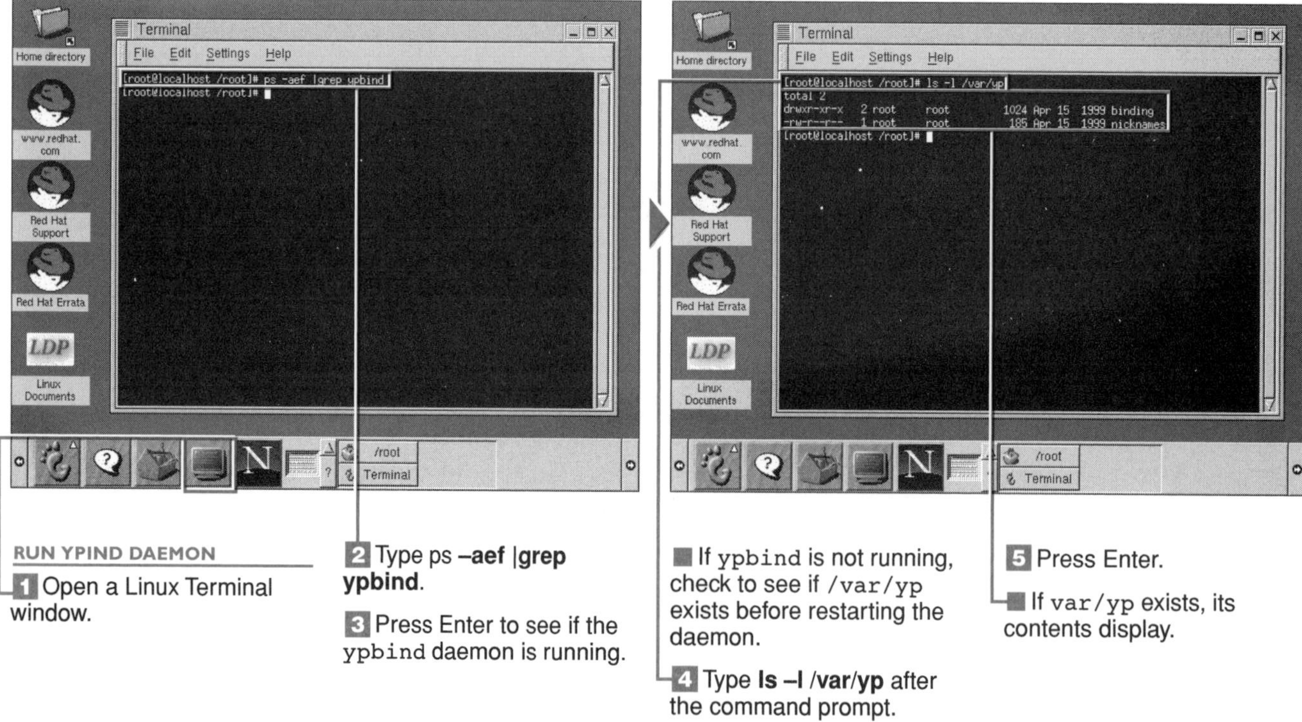

RUN YPIND DAEMON

1 Open a Linux Terminal window.

2 Type ps **–aef |grep ypbind**.

3 Press Enter to see if the ypbind daemon is running.

■ If ypbind is not running, check to see if /var/yp exists before restarting the daemon.

4 Type **ls –l /var/yp** after the command prompt.

5 Press Enter.

■ If var/yp exists, its contents display.

What is ypbind? What role does it play in NIS? Why am I unable to check ypbind in LinuxConf?

- NIS is not as native to Linux as some other systems (NFS, for instance), so the GNOME support via LinuxConf is more limited. You are best off working through the Linux Terminal for these tasks.

Does the ypbind daemon require a lot of computing power to run? I am running Linux on an old PC (x486 chip) and wonder if I should run NIS at all.

- The `ypbind` daemon was built specifically to work on any machine that is powerful enough to run Linux, no matter how old. You should not have a problem.

Can I create the /var/yp directory somewhere else to save space?

- You could create a symbolic link in the `/var` directory to lead to `/yp` on a different system such as `/etc`, but that might confuse the NIS system. As a rule, it is best to leave the NIS defaults alone.

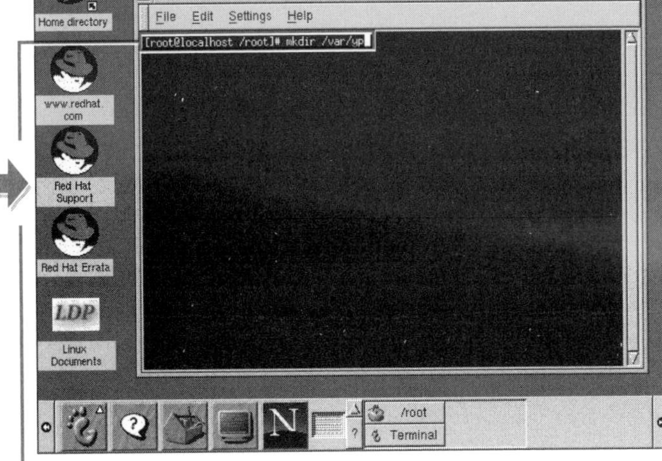

6 If `/var/yp` has not been created, type **mkdir /var/yp** after the prompt.

7 Press Enter.

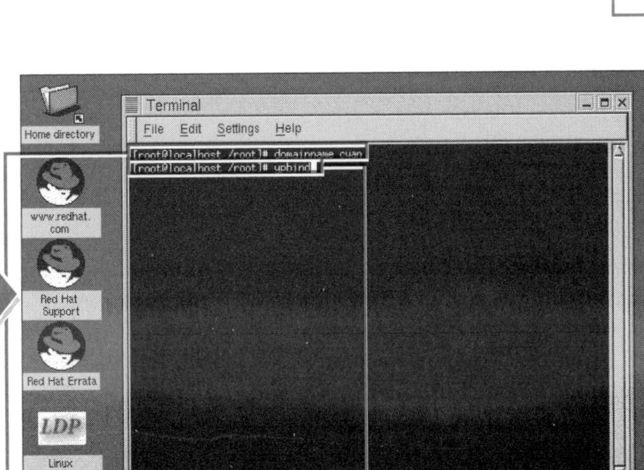

8 Type **domainname <name of domain>** after the prompt.

9 To restart the `ypbind` daemon, type **ypbind** and pressing Enter.

SET UP A SAMBA SERVER

Microsoft products use a networking protocol called SMB, or Server Message Block. While primarily used in Windows networking, this protocol is used by or can be adapted to many different networking systems. For example, Windows clients on your Linux network can communicate with your Linux machines. In order to do this, the Windows clients must be using SMB, and your Linux clients must be using an offshoot of SMB called Samba.

Samba is useful if you have clients running variants of Microsoft Windows and you want them to be able to access files and print servers on the Linux side of the network (and vice versa). Keep in mind that Samba administration is a unit separate from NFS or any other kind of networking you have set up on your system. You may need a different set of passwords to work in Samba to link your Windows and Linux machines.

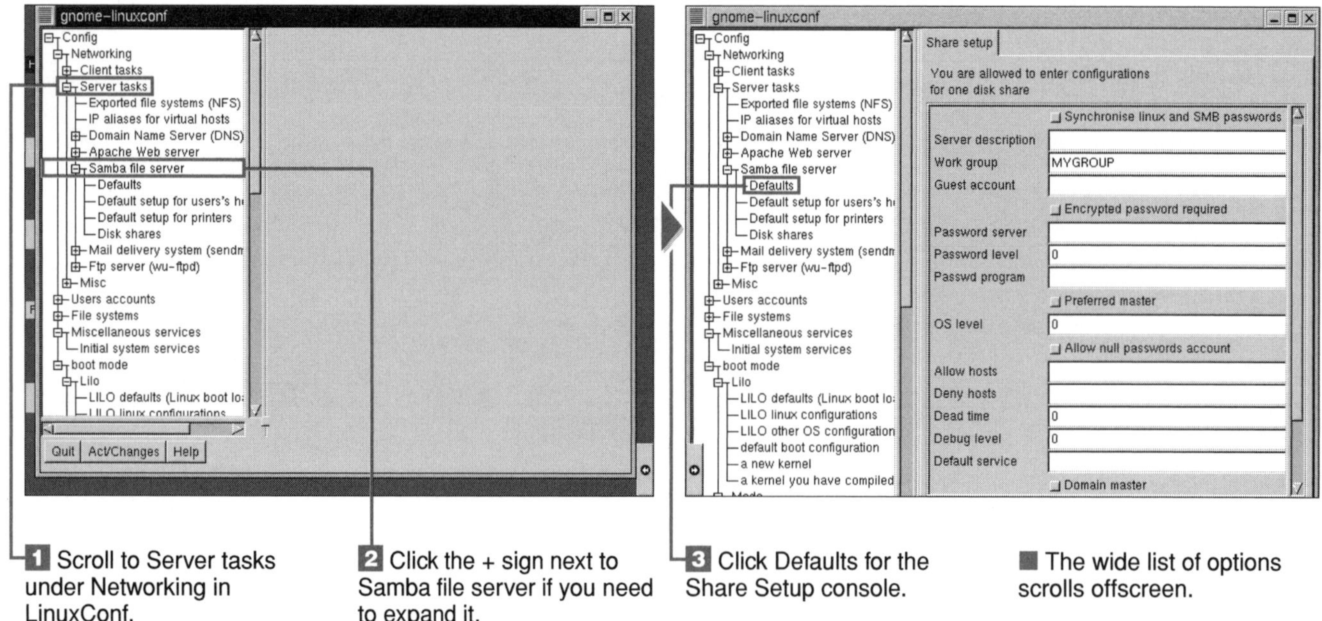

1 Scroll to Server tasks under Networking in LinuxConf.

2 Click the + sign next to Samba file server if you need to expand it.

3 Click Defaults for the Share Setup console.

■ The wide list of options scrolls offscreen.

When should I use the Synchronize Linux and SMB Passwords setting?

- You should always use this option. The only time you might want to leave this option switched off is when you are running Linux on an old, slow machine, on which the synchronization process could slow it down further. If your machine is slowed down, you are best off installing more RAM.

Should I specify a specific password server in the Password Server text field in the Share Setup screen?

- This is not necessary unless you have a large number of users who will be using Samba multiple times in a given day. Even in that circumstance, you do not need to specify a specific password server to handle all of the password entries and requests unless you are running your Samba server on an exceptionally old or slow machine.

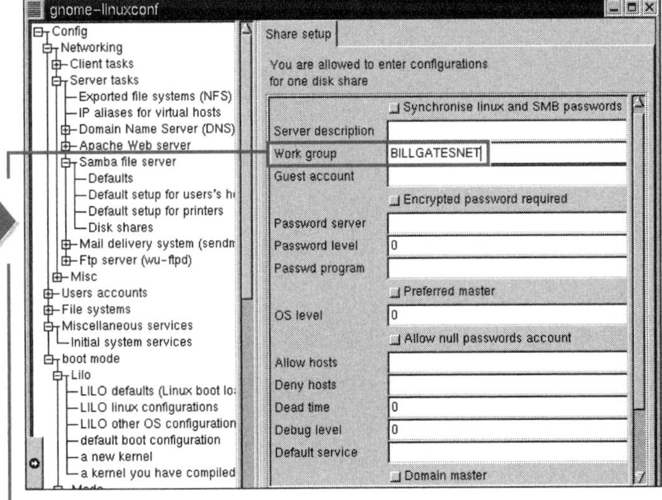

4 In the Work group field, enter the name of the Windows workgroup where your Windows clients reside.

5 Click the Synchronize Linux and SMB passwords button if you want to ensure that the Windows and Linux network passwords match.

CONTINUED

SET UP A SAMBA SERVER CONTINUED

You select which portions of your computer you want shared over Samba. This is done via the Disk Shares and Share Setup consoles in the Samba file server section of LinuxConf. The Disk Share console asks you to define multiple independent entry points in your file server. This means that you are at the point in the Samba setup when you need to decide what parts of the hard disk you will make available to the Samba clients.

In Samba, you actually specify the portion of the disk you want to make available under the Share Name field. Samba works this way because the files and directories you may want to share are kept in a given location, such as `/etc`, that correspond to a physical location on the hard disk itself. Defining the shared sections of the disk allows Samba to work efficiently.

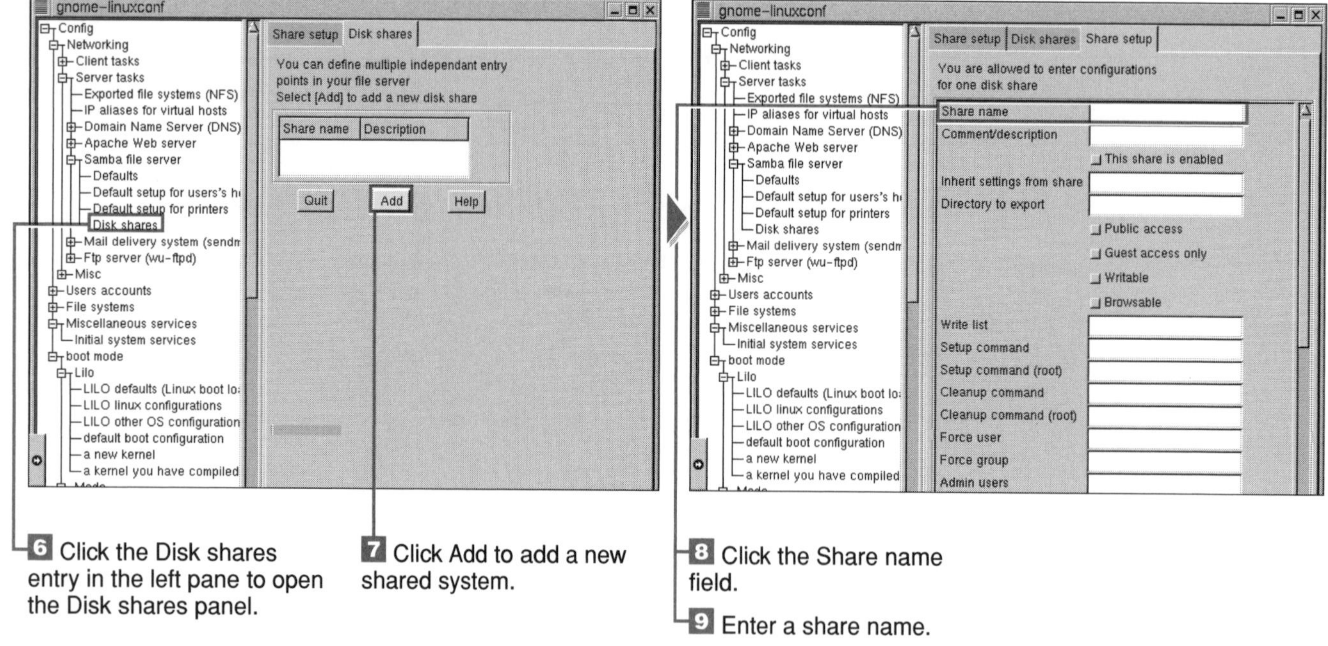

6 Click the Disk shares entry in the left pane to open the Disk shares panel.

7 Click Add to add a new shared system.

8 Click the Share name field.

9 Enter a share name.

What other information should I list under the Comment/Description text field in the Share Setup console?

- You should list enough of a description so that a quick glance at the field enables you to remember what you set up and why. For example, you might note that you are setting up `/Shareme` for the Accounting department, but only through the month of April.

Why does the Share Setup screen specify that I am allowed to enter configurations for only one disk share?

- The LinuxConf utility forces you to individually set up each portion of the disk to be shared; this helps avoid confusion for the computer and the Samba administrator. For example, a given share name might be `/Shareme`, but your Linux machine might be confused by a string of share names, such as `/Shareme`, `/Shareme2`, and `/Shareme3`.

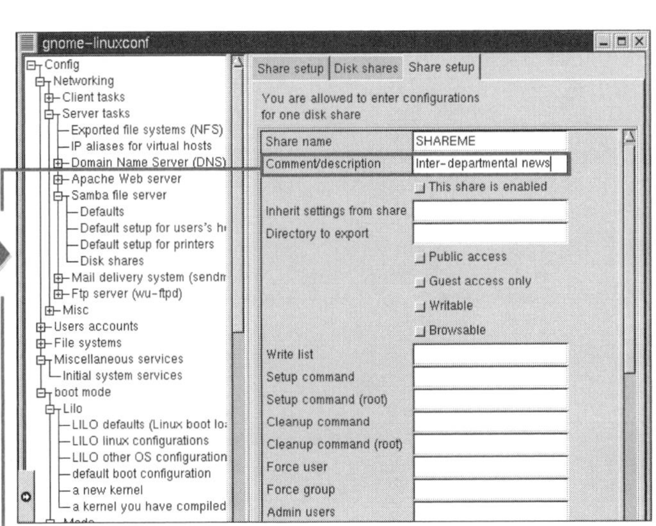

■ You may include a comment about the share name to help you keep track of the files you're sharing.

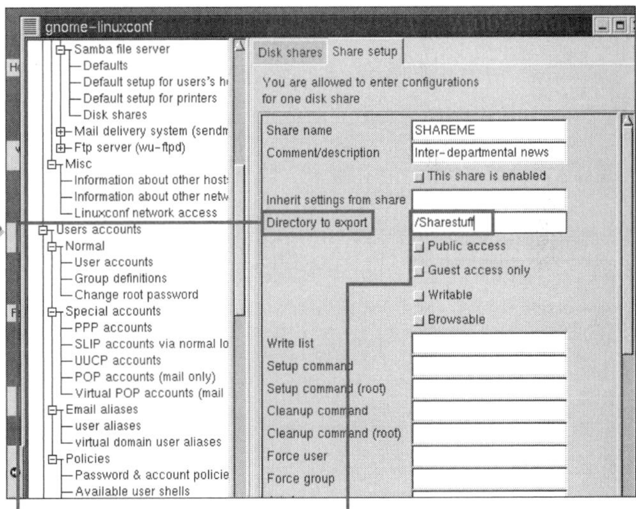

10 Click the Directory to Export field.

11 Type the name of the directory.

Note: All directories under the directory you export are shared out.

CONTINUED

SET UP A SAMBA SERVER CONTINUED

You can complete your Samba setup on your Linux computer by making sure that you are exporting the files that you want. Remember that in Linux, the term *export* means roughly the same thing as *making available*. When you export a file or directory under Samba, you are essentially making it available to all of the non-Linux or UNIX-based machines that are also set up to run with the SMB protocol.

When you make a file or directory accessible by exporting it, be sure to decided how public you want the information to be. Much like deciding regular file permissions, you have to determine whether you will allow Samba clients to read or edit the file. Luckily, setting permissions on exported files is automatically recursive; if you export a directory, all of the files and subdirectories under it are set similarly.

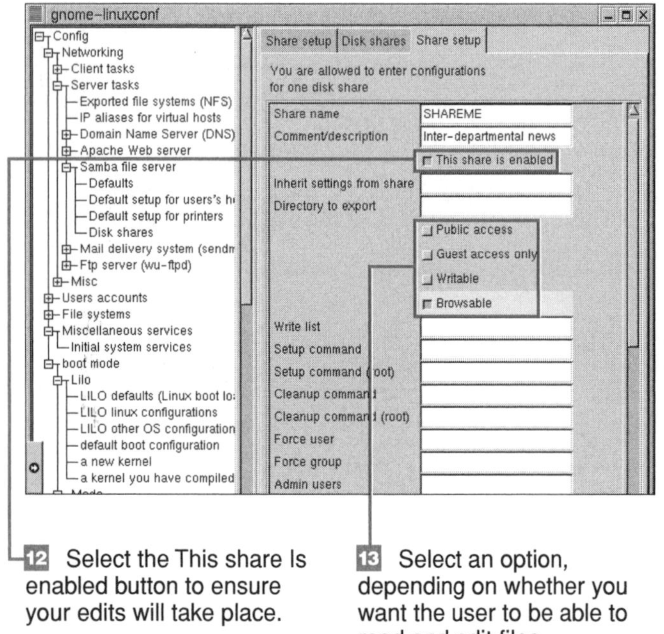

12 Select the This share Is enabled button to ensure your edits will take place.

13 Select an option, depending on whether you want the user to be able to read and edit files.

14 Click Accept.

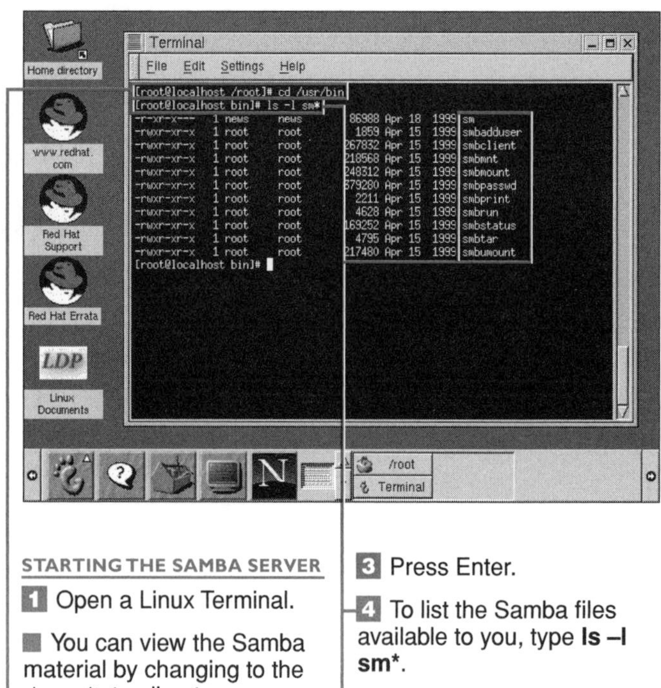

STARTING THE SAMBA SERVER

1 Open a Linux Terminal.

■ You can view the Samba material by changing to the /usr/bin directory.

2 Type **cd /usr/bin**.

3 Press Enter.

4 To list the Samba files available to you, type **ls –l sm***.

■ All the Samba files begin with sm.

Are these all of the procedures needed to connect SMB and Samba machines?

- This is what you need to do on the Linux end. In all likelihood, you must still configure your Windows clients to connect to the Samba-enabled Linux machines. Note also that it is likely that configuring your Windows clients may require them to reboot. If this is the case, be sure that the Windows clients are not running anything critical on your network or user community.

How can I get more information on setting up my Windows clients?

- For this and more information on Samba, see `www.samba.org`. If you want more information specifically on how to set up Windows clients to use SMB and talk to Samba-enabled Linux machines, see *Networking For Dummies*, 4th Edition, by Doug Lowe, (IDG Books Worldwide, Inc.).

5 To start the Samba server, type **/etc/rc.d/init.d/smb restart**.

6 Press Enter.

Note: Samba has a curious quirk under Linux. After you start it the first time, it fails to shut down and then starts!

CONNECT YOUR MACHINE AS A SAMBA CLIENT

When you have set up your network so that Microsoft and Linux machines are ready to speak SMB and Samba to each other, you may want to set up your machine to connect to an SMB server as a Samba client.

SMB and Samba are a set of protocols that a Microsoft and a Linux or UNIX machine use to communicate with each other. This is helpful if you are running a Linux machine but your print server is running Microsoft Windows. This is also a useful task to perform if your network is predominantly Windows-based, instead of primarily Linux-based.

Although the latest versions of Samba have proven to be fast and trouble-free, use caution when using older machines that may use an older variation of the SMB-Samba interface. You may find that because of the translation process between machines, your network speed has been reduced a significant degree.

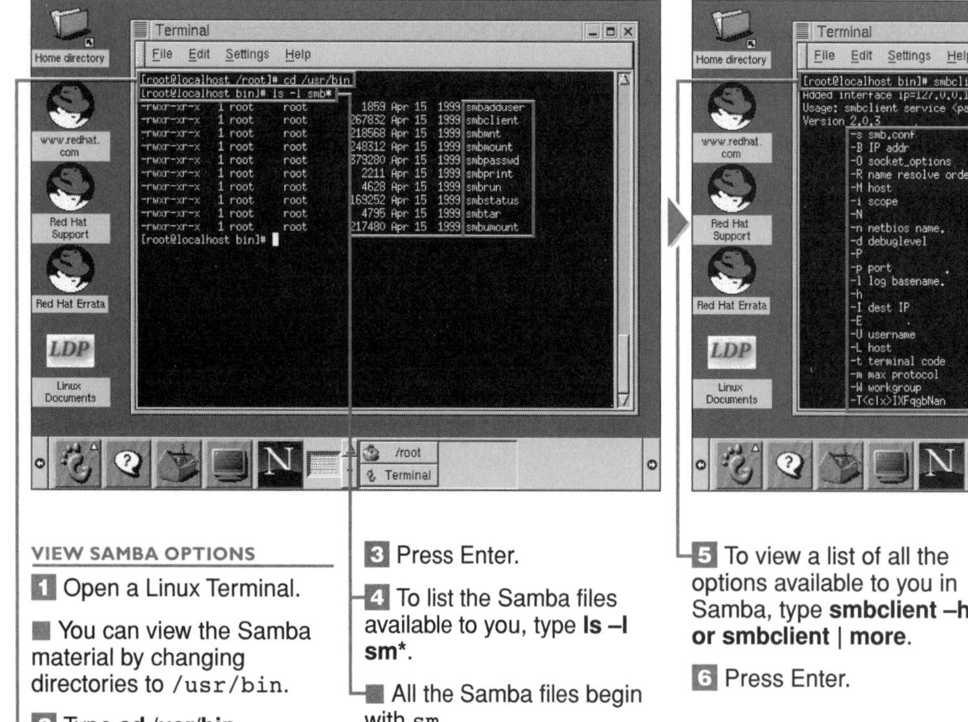

VIEW SAMBA OPTIONS

1 Open a Linux Terminal.

■ You can view the Samba material by changing directories to `/usr/bin`.

2 Type **cd /usr/bin**.

3 Press Enter.

4 To list the Samba files available to you, type **ls –l sm***.

■ All the Samba files begin with `sm`.

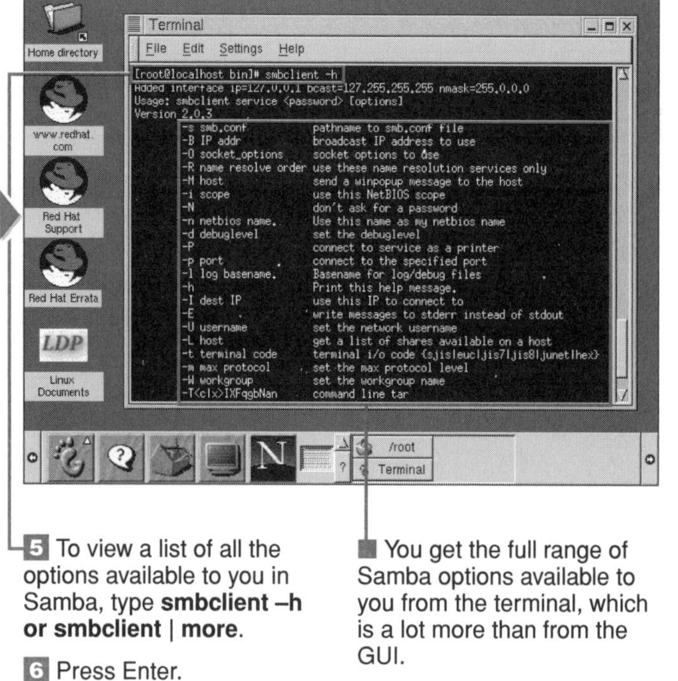

5 To view a list of all the options available to you in Samba, type **smbclient –h or smbclient | more**.

6 Press Enter.

■ You get the full range of Samba options available to you from the terminal, which is a lot more than from the GUI.

Where, other than the Web site, can I find more information on Samba?

- Samba is another topic that needs a full book to do it justice. Luckily, there are several good titles out on the market for working with Samba. For information on Samba networking problems and solutions, check out *Samba For Dummies*, by George D. Haberberger, (IDG Books Worldwide, Inc.).

Why do the Samba files in Linux begin with sm?

- Samba is a variant of the protocol used by Microsoft Windows, SMB. Therefore, all Samba files tend to follow this naming convention and go by names like `smbclient`.

Can I configure Samba parameters at all in the Linux Terminal?

- You can work with Samba parameters by opening a Linux Terminal and using the `vi` editor on `/etc/smb.conf`. Although it looks a bit obscure, there are plenty of helpful comments and samples to help you configure it properly.

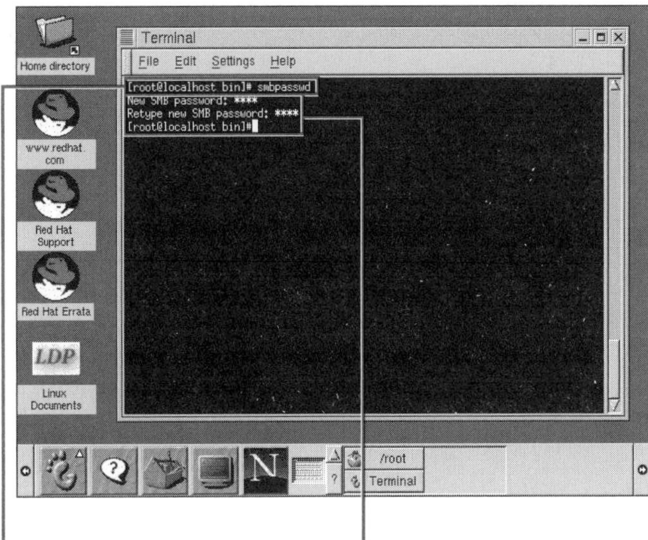

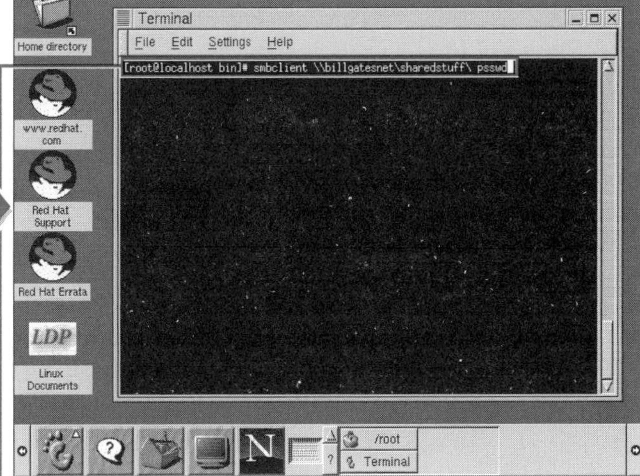

USE A NEW PASSWORD SPECIFICALLY FOR A SAMBA CONNECTION

1 Type **smbpasswd** at the prompt.

2 Press Enter.

3 Follow the prompts to choose a password for the user account you are currently logged in as.

Note: Use the new password the next time you log in to Samba.

4 Type the following at the command prompt:

smbclient \\billgatesnet\sharedstuff\ passwd

■ Be sure to alter the command syntax depending on the server you are logging in to.

5 Press Enter to complete the login process.

INSTALL POSTGRESQL, THE LINUX DATABASE

If you want to use a database application that is 100 percent native to Red Hat Linux, the PostgreSQL product is for you. This database falls somewhere between Microsoft Access and the higher-level databases, such as Informix or Sybase. On the plus side, this means that you can store large tables and databases. On the minus side, relatively few people use this kind of database, and so it is rarely installed on a standard Linux installation.

This chapter covers installing and initializing the database. For any information beyond that, you must look to other books.

Your primary consideration is to know SQL, the Structure Query Language that runs all major databases, before attempting to work with PostgreSQL. You will use Linux commands to locate, install, and initialize the database server itself on your system. However, when it comes to manipulating the lines and tables of data in the database itself, use SQL to complete your tasks.

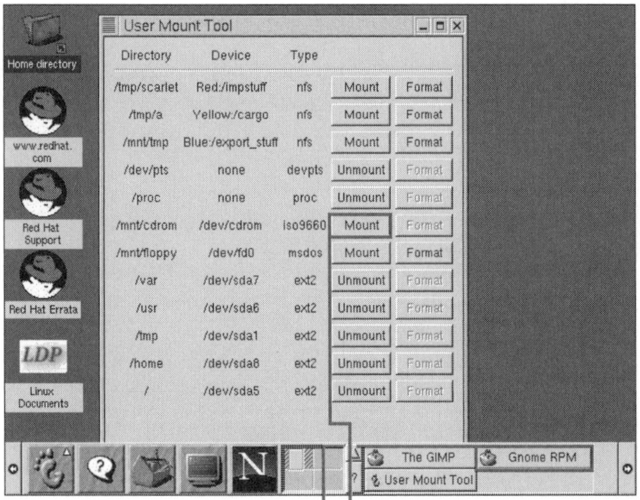

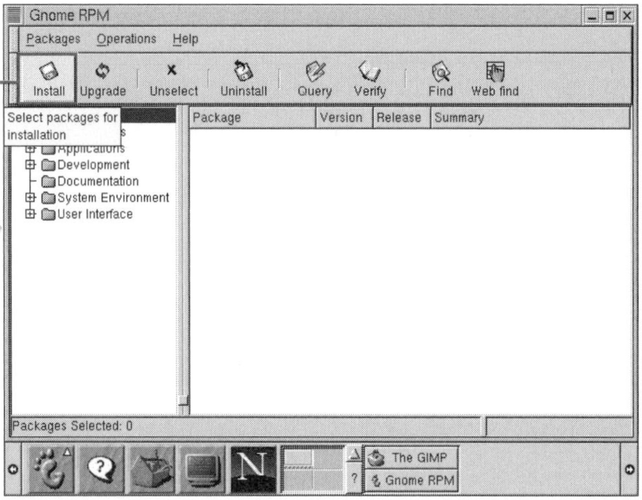

1 Insert your Red Hat CD-ROM into your computer.

2 Open the Disk Management tool.

■ The User Mount tool panel appears on the desktop.

3 Click Mount next to the CD-ROM drive.

4 Open Gnome RPM, the Red Hat Package Manager.

5 Click the Install button on the top toolbar.

I cannot find the database installation information on my CD-ROMs or disks. Where can I go next?

- If you cannot find PostgreSQL on your hard disk or on your installation media (disks or CD-ROMs), you can install it from the Web. Download the database software from the Web site at `www.postgresql.org`. For more information on downloading, consult Chapter 22 on setting up your Web browser.

I need to install a database program on my Linux machine, but I want to use Sybase, Informix, or Oracle's database instead of PostgreSQL. Can I do this in Linux?

- You can for Informix and Oracle. Informix was the first major database company to make a version of their program available in Linux. Oracle has followed in their footsteps and produced their own Linux version. Sybase has not produced a Linux version of their database at this time.

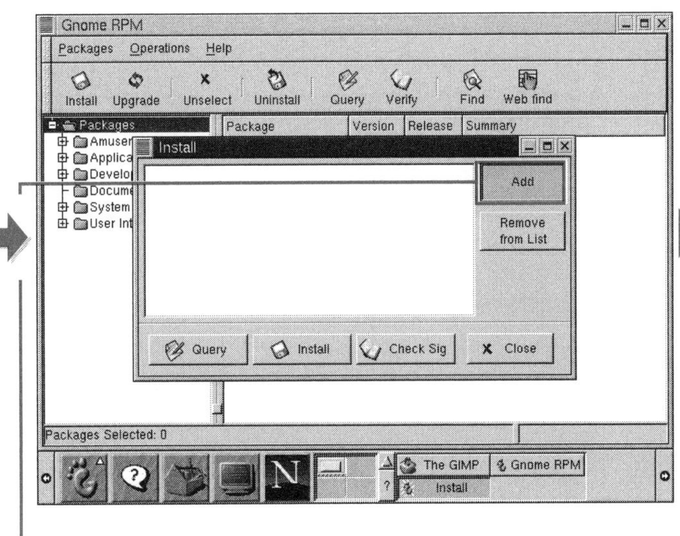

6 In the Install screen, click Add.

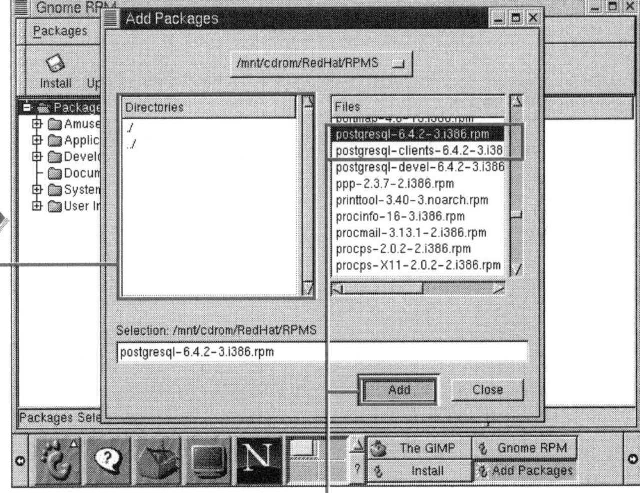

7 In the Add Packages screen, use the left pane to navigate to `/mnt/cdrom`.

■ You are looking at files on the CD-ROM itself.

8 Continue to navigate to `/RedHat/RPMS`.

9 Scroll down to Postgresql and Postgresql-clients.

10 Click each module to select it.

11 Click Add.

CONTINUED

INSTALL POSTGRESQL, THE LINUX DATABASE CONTINUED

You have several advantages over most database administrators if you choose to run the PostgreSQL program over the offerings from Oracle or Informix. First, PostgreSQL is written specifically for Linux. Therefore, it is much more stable than the other, more commercially available programs, which have only recently come out with Linux versions.

Second, PostgreSQL is built to run on machines that can run Linux, which means it can run on computers much less powerful than can larger database programs such as Access. Finally, it takes up less disk space than an equivalent installation of Informix, Oracle, or other database program.

You should be able to add some of your own code to PostgreSQL if you are interested in programming. While PostgreSQL is not public domain software, the University of California (who owns the copyrights) had granted permission to use, copy, modify, and distribute PostgreSQL to all of its users.

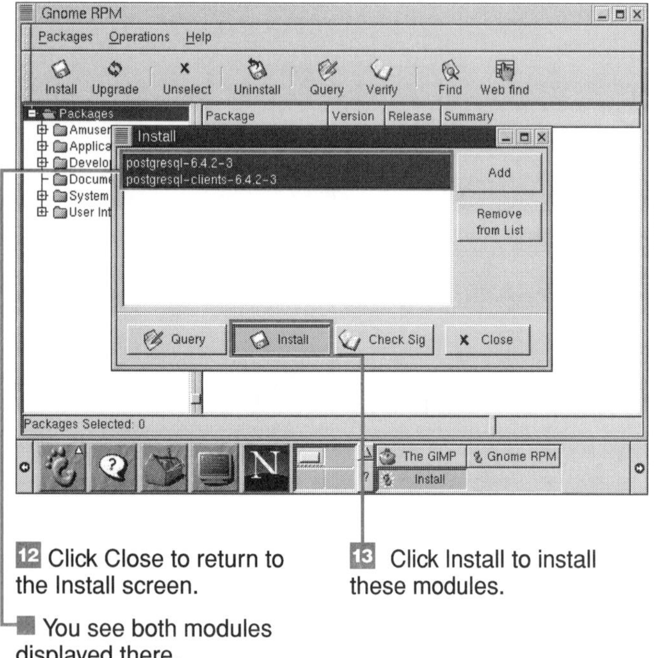

12 Click Close to return to the Install screen.

■ You see both modules displayed there.

13 Click Install to install these modules.

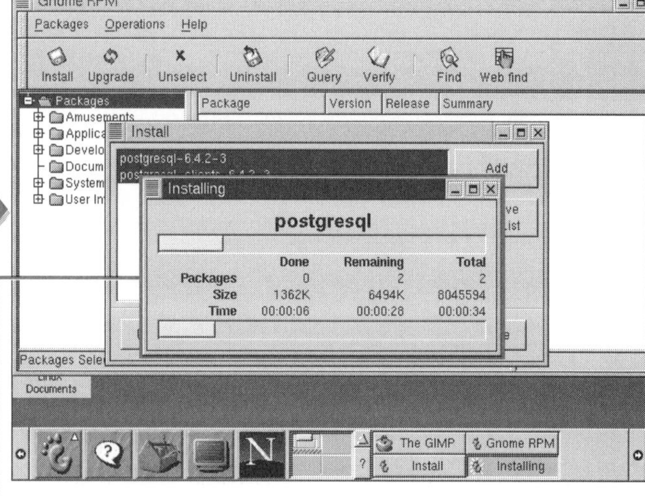

■ Due to the large size of these modules, a bar graph displays the progress of the installation.

I am familiar with Microsoft Access and Excel. Can I store tables and graphs from these programs in PostgreSQL?

- Unfortunately not. PostgreSQL is a pure database program, with little in the way of a graphical user interface or a translation device to add Access or Excel data. Again, if you truly want to tap into the power of this application, you need experience as a database administrator and knowledge of SQL.

Where can I get more information on other Linux database products such as Microsoft Access, Informix's IDS Server, or the Linux version of Oracle?

- Informix has an excellent series of user and installation guides that you can download from this Web address: `www.informix.com/informix/products/linux`. You can get information on Oracle at `platforms.oracle.com/linux`. Of course, if you want information on Access, visit `www.microsoft.com`. Check back with the Red Hat Corporation at `www.redhat.com` from time to time for pointers on the latest database products.

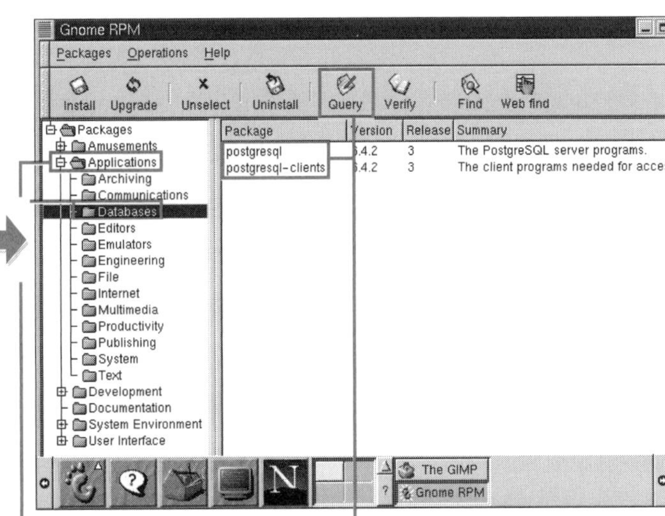

14 To check the installation, expand the `Applications` directory in the `Gnome RPM` utility.

15 Click the folder Databases.

16 Click both database applications to select.

17 Click the Query toolbar button to query the contents of each database application.

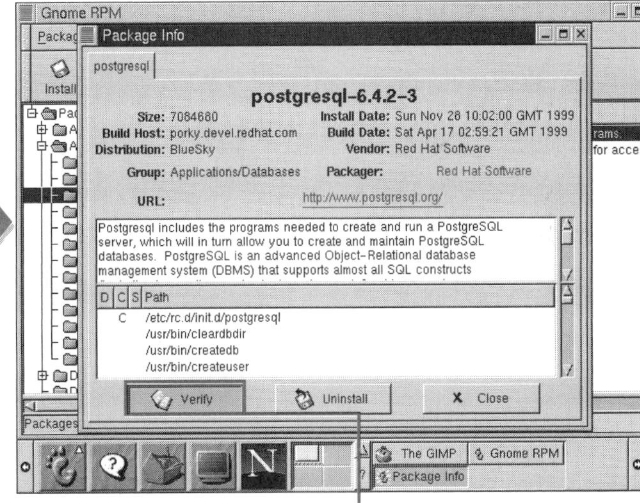

■ You get the Package Information screen.

18 Click the Verify button to ensure that there were no errors in the copy process.

ADD THE POSTGRESQL USER

The PostgreSQL server must be run by the specially created user account `postgres`. The PostgreSQL program is designed this way in order to increase security; this limits access to the program to this one user account. Although sometimes this account is automatically created when you install the PostgreSQL program, you may have to manually create the account yourself before you are able to use the database application.

Even if the user `postgres` has been created, be sure to change the password. Most of the time, you will install the PostgreSQL server from the `root` account. The files and user account that you create could inherit the `root` account permissions.

Because of this, you need to make doubly sure that the `postgres` account has a different password than the `root` account. Otherwise, you will leave yourself with a major security gap.

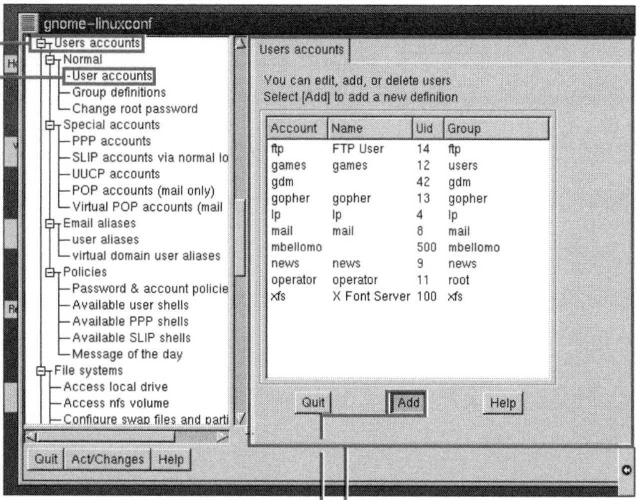

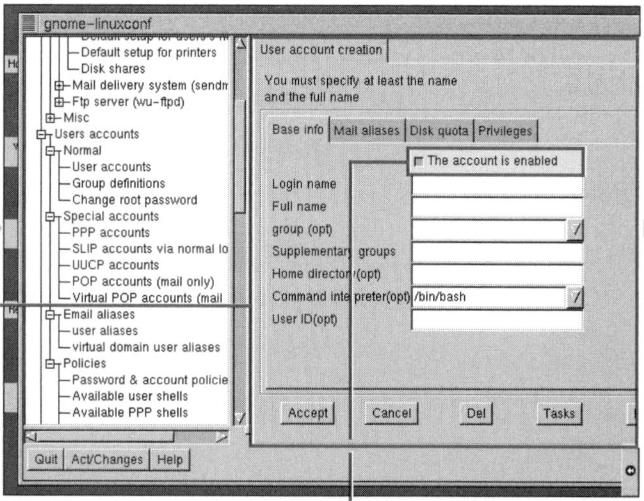

ADD A NEW USER ACCOUNT POSTGRES

1 Open LinuxConf and scroll down to User accounts.

2 Click User accounts under Normal.

■ The User accounts panel appears in the right pane of the LinuxConf window.

3 Click Add.

■ The User account creation screen appears.

Note: By default, The account is enabled button is depressed.

4 If The account is enabled button is not depressed, click it to activate your new account.

Where can I go to get more information on the utility used here to add user accounts, LinuxConf?

- If you have come to this section of the book before using LinuxConf in Red Hat Linux first, go to Chapter 10 for additional information on add user accounts.

Instead of /var/lib/pgsql, can I select a different area for the PostgreSQL user's home directory, such as /home/postgres?

- The `/var/lib/pgsql` directory setting should not be changed when you create the PostgreSQL user account. When PostgreSQL starts on your Linux machine, it is designed to look for the `potsgres` home directory in only that location. If you change the location, the database program becomes confused and will not start properly. It may even cause your system to freeze, meaning that you have to reboot your computer.

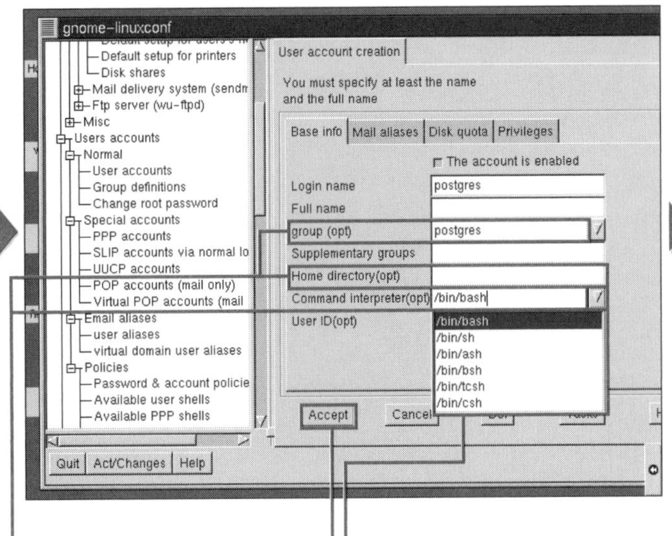

5 Click the Group field.

6 Type **postgres**.

7 Type **/var/lib/pgsql** in the Home directory field.

8 Click the arrow button to the right of the Command interpreter field.

■ A drop-down menu appears, allowing you to select the interpreter you prefer.

9 Select the interpreter you want.

10 Click Accept.

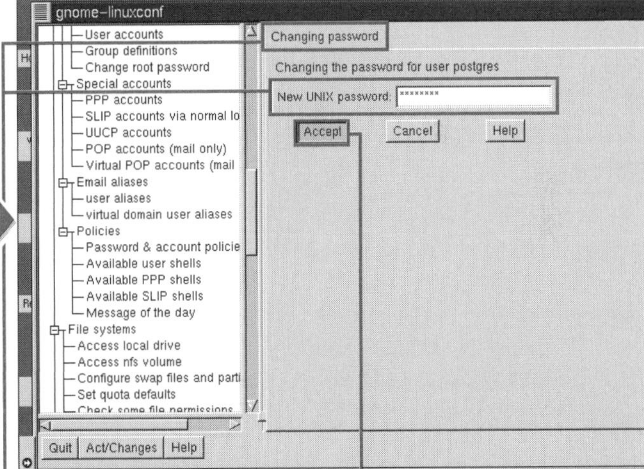

■ The Changing password screen appears.

11 Type the password you selected for postgres in the open field.

12 Click Accept.

■ You are taken back to the User Account screen, where the new account is listed.

CONTINUED

ADD THE POSTGRESQL USER CONTINUED

You can check to see if the `postgres` user account has been created during the installation of the PostgreSQL program by checking the User Accounts setting under the LinuxConf utility. However, the majority of the time, you need to create the account yourself.

The `postgres` user account is also sometimes called the PostgreSQL superuser. This is a slightly misleading term for two reasons. First, the name may lead you to believe that you should allow this account to have `root` privileges. You should not do this, as it creates possible security problems.

Second, while `postgres` can be compared with `root` in that both are administrative accounts, they differ in one vital aspect: The Linux `root` account protects system files against tampering by restricting edit and read permissions. The `postgres` account protects database files by being the only user account that can work with them through the PostgreSQL program.

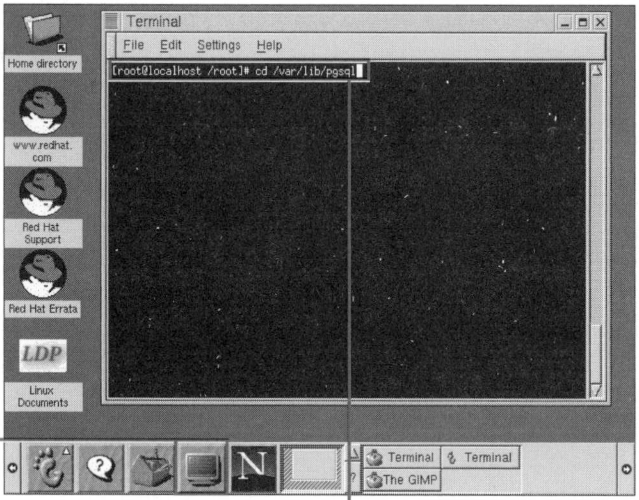

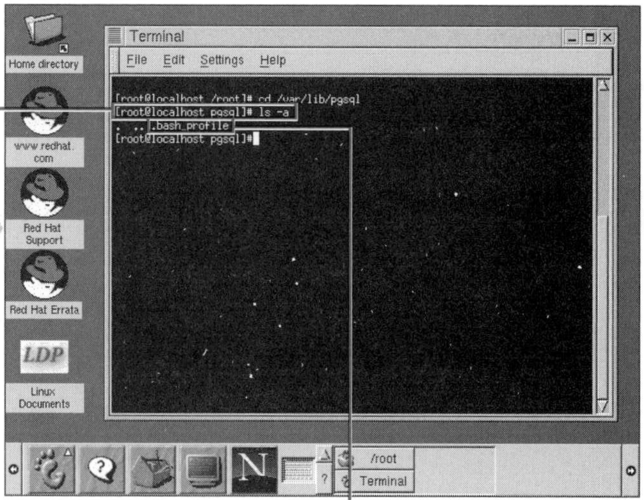

ADD NEW ENVIRONMENTAL VARIABLES FOR THIS ACCOUNT

1 Open a Linux Terminal.

2 Type **cd /var/lib/pgsql**.

3 Press Enter.

■ The file you want to edit is hidden.

4 Type **ls –a** to list all files in the directory, including hidden ones.

■ You should see the file `bash_profile`.

Does PostgreSQL use SQL, DDL, DML, or DCL?

- Being a database program, it uses all four. SQL (Structured Query Language) is a standardized language that all database programs use in one form or another. DDL, DML, and DCL are actually language components of SQL. They stand for

DDL:	Data Definition Language
DML:	Data Manipulation Language
DCL:	Data Control Language

What is the PGLIB system variable that I added to the bash_profile of the postgres user account?

- PGLIB stands for PostgreSQL Library, a file that contains all of the critical data that the database application needs for performing its functions. The application will not even start — let alone run — without knowing the location of its library.

Can I use the postgres account like I can any other user account on my system?

- Yes, but it is not recommended. This account is configured for only one function — working with PostgreSQL.

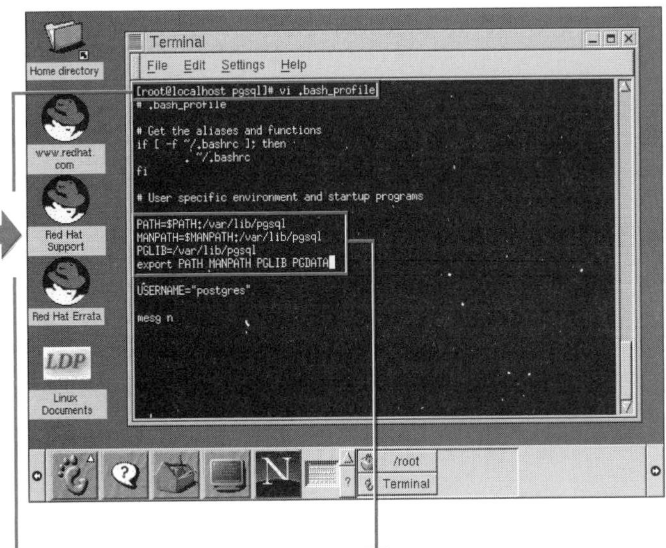

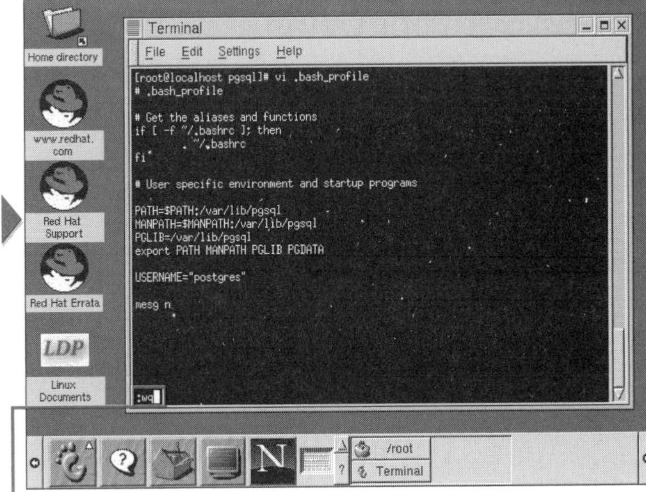

5 Type **vi .bash_profile**.

6 Press Enter to edit the file.

7 Add the following lines:

PATH=$PATH:/var/lib/pgsql

MANPATH =$MANPATH:/var/lib/pgsql

PGLIB=/var/lib/pgsql

export PATH MANPATH PGLIB PGDATA

8 Type **wq**.

9 Press Enter to finish.

INITIALIZE YOUR POSTGRESQL SERVER

After you have completed installing, verifying, configuring, and adding users to work with the PostgreSQL product, it is time to initialize the server. Initializing is similar to starting a program that gets the application or database ready to receive or edit data. Because PostgreSQL acts more like a server than a typical application, its initialization is a bit more complex than simply double-clicking a desktop icon.

The daemon program that runs the database server is called the `Postmaster` daemon. You start this program each time you want to initialize the server. Keep in mind that after you start the server in a Linux Terminal window, you may not use the Terminal for anything else until the database session has been concluded. If you want to work on other tasks in the Terminal window, open a second Terminal. To avoid typing in the PostgreSQL Terminal window, consider minimizing the window so that you can freely work on your desktop.

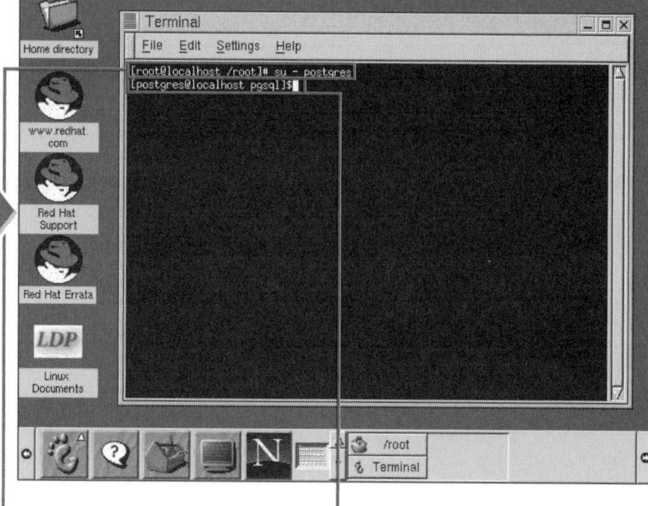

1 Open a Linux Terminal.

Note: You are in as the `root` account, which is not the account that can effectively use the server application.

2 Use the command `su - postgres` to change to the `postgres` user account.

Note: The hyphen after the `su` tells Linux to use the environment variables that PostgreSQL needs to run.

3 Press Enter.

■ The prompt for the user `postgres` appears.

Where can I find more information on how to effectively use the PostgreSQL product?

✔ Your best bet (especially if you already have some database experience) is to visit the PostgreSQL Web site at `www.postgresql.org`. You can join the mailing list or simply ask questions via e-mail if you have concerns or queries about a certain aspect of the database.

How can I enable the database program to begin automatically upon startup?

✔ Visit `www.postgresql.org`. The main document, *The PostgreSQL Administration Guide,* describes how to set up this feature.

Where can I find a good source for starting to learn more about SQL?

✔ IDG Books Worldwide publishes a number of good books that start your learning process. Among others, *SQL For Dummies* (written by Allen G. Taylor) is a good place if your knowledge of SQL is at the novice level.

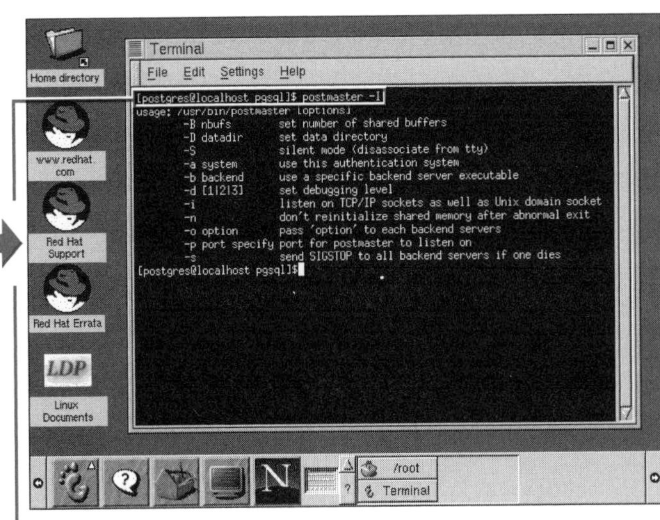

4 At the command prompt, type **postmaster –I** to initialize the server for the first time.

5 Press Enter.

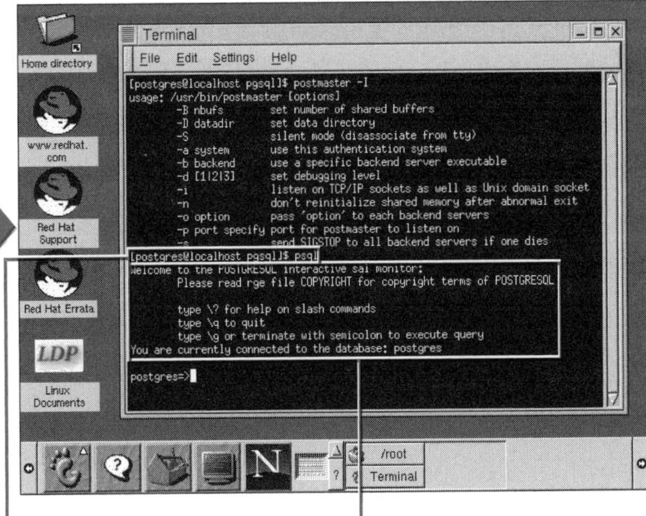

6 Once PostgreSQL is running, type **psql** at the prompt.

7 Press Enter to connect.

■ You come to the entry screen, complete with a list of commands on how to proceed or access help files.

SECTION VI

21) ESTABLISHING NETWORK CONNECTIVITY

Start the Control Panel's Modem & Network Utilities 408
Configure a Modem 410
Enter DNS Information 412
Add and Delete a PPP Interface 414
Configure a Direct Connection 420

22) SETTING UP YOUR NETSCAPE BROWSER

Launch the Netscape Web Browser 424
Browse the Web with Netscape 426
Configure Netscape Appearance and Navigation 428
Configure New Web Page Settings 430
Configure Netscape's Advanced Network Settings 432
Set Up Netscape to Send E-mail 434
Set Up Netscape to Receive E-mail and News 436
Send and Receive E-mail in Netscape 438

23) INSTALLING AND CONFIGURING APACHE

Install the Apache Web Server 440
Configure Apache 444

24) SENDING AND RECEIVING MAIL IN THE LINUX TERMINAL

Open Pine Mail 448
Compose E-mail in Pine 449
Receive E-mail in Pine 450
Delete E-mail in Pine 452
Save E-mail in Pine 453
Navigate and Administer Your Folders 454
Exit the Pine Mail Program 458

START THE CONTROL PANEL'S MODEM & NETWORK UTILITIES

You can configure your modem and network setup with the GNOME Control Panel. This is a special graphical interface that can configure several aspects of your Red Hat Linux system.

The Control Panel differs from the `Linuxconf` utility in a couple ways. First, it's more graphically based. For example, the button you press to get to the Modem configuration actually has a picture of a telephone on it. In `Linuxconf`, you would have to search for the PPP/SLIP/PLIP text entry in LinuxConf's left pane.

Second, the Control Panel does not affect most of the deeper functions of your Linux machine, such as file systems and routing. Instead, most of what you can find on the Control Panel deals with setting system time, printers, and modems.

However, these *are* important functions to your user community, and you can only administer them via the Linux Terminal or the GNOME Control Panel.

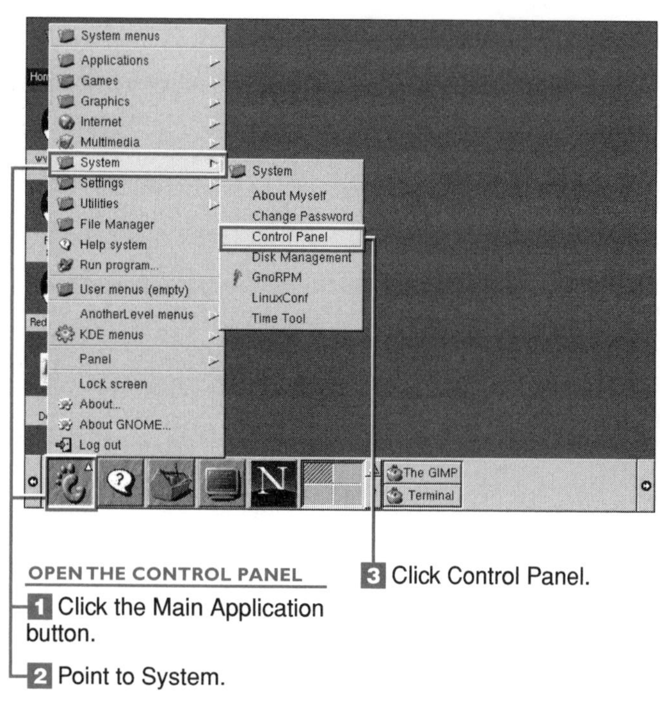

OPEN THE CONTROL PANEL

1 Click the Main Application button.

2 Point to System.

3 Click Control Panel.

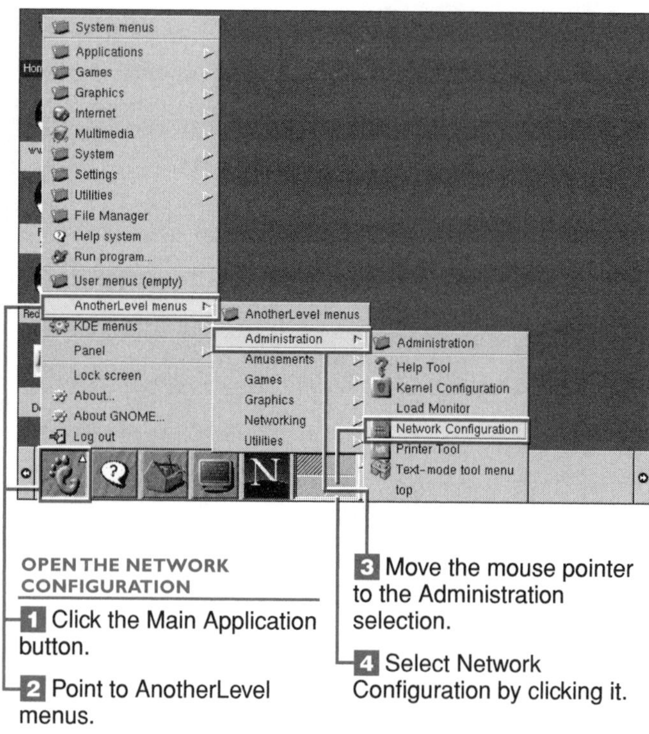

OPEN THE NETWORK CONFIGURATION

1 Click the Main Application button.

2 Point to AnotherLevel menus.

3 Move the mouse pointer to the Administration selection.

4 Select Network Configuration by clicking it.

Why are the Control Panel screens so much more picture-oriented than the functions of the Linuxconf utility?

- `Linuxconf` is designed to present a simple, graphic desktop environment. The GNOME Control Panel, on the other hand, runs with the help of small, separate programs called applets—small applications, which are more self-contained, so they can offer more services.

Why can't I find a function on the Control Panel that I'm looking for?

- Note that the Control Panel by default does not expand to its full size. The Control Panel has a scrollbar that runs alongside one of its faces. Click and drag along this scrollbar to reveal more buttons that may be hidden when you initially open the Control Panel. You can also click and drag the border of the Control Panel to increase its size, the way you would enlarge a window.

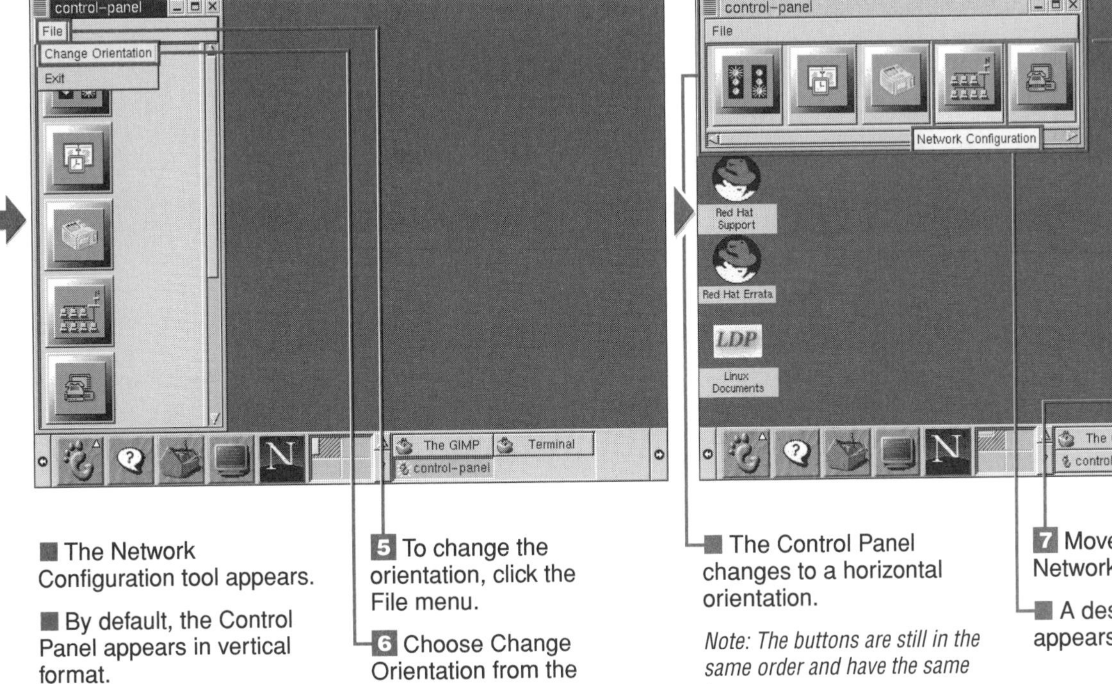

■ The Network Configuration tool appears.

■ By default, the Control Panel appears in vertical format.

5 To change the orientation, click the File menu.

6 Choose Change Orientation from the drop-down menu.

■ The Control Panel changes to a horizontal orientation.

Note: The buttons are still in the same order and have the same icons.

7 Move the pointer over the Network Configuration icon.

■ A description of the button appears.

CONFIGURE A MODEM

A modem is a communication device that connects your computer via a telephone jack to the outside world, the network, and the World Wide Web. If you run an older system, you might have an external modem, which can look like anything from a cigar box to a radar detector. On more modern systems, modems are installed internally, and your computer has a telephone-style jack.

You'll use your modem as the force to connect to the Internet. In order to make sure your computer knows the location of its modem communication port and to ensure that you're operating the modem at the correct speed, you need to configure it. The Control Panel applet can help you complete all these tasks without much difficulty.

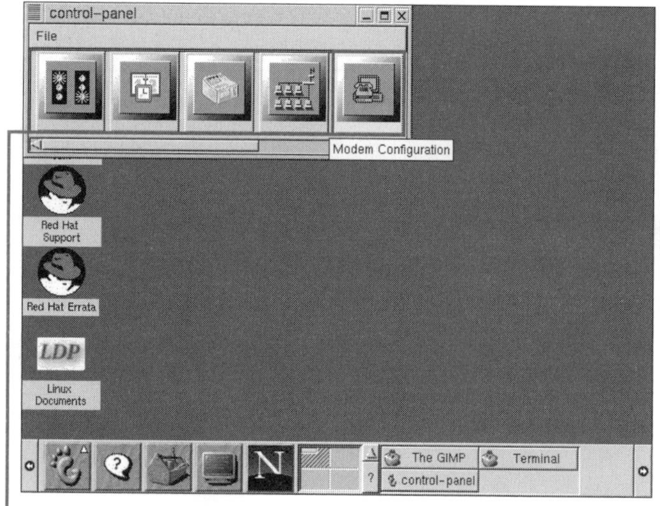

1 Click the Modem Configuration button.

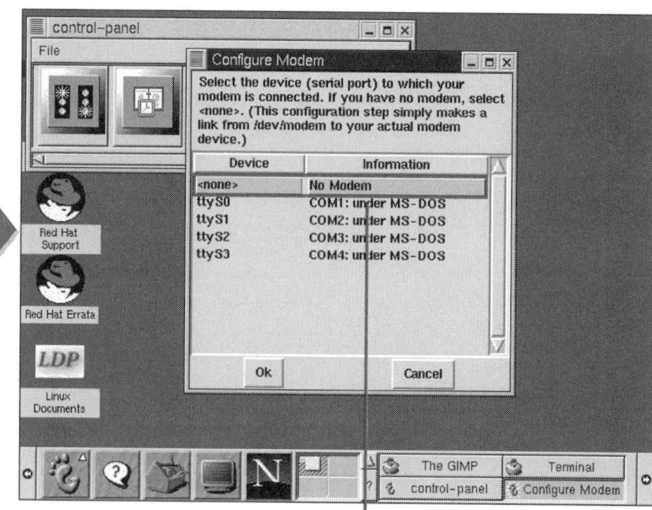

■ The Configure Modem screen appears.

■ By default, No Modem is selected.

TIPS

I'm at home, and I have only one phone line. Does using the modem hog that line?

- Telephone lines are one-purpose items, as opposed to a multitasking line. When you actually use a modem, the phone line is busy transmitting and receiving data on the line, and no other impulses can get through. This is true even if you have a splitter plug that allows you to hook your modem and telephone into the jack at the same time. Therefore, if you're using your modem to connect to the Internet, you cannot receive incoming or make outgoing calls.

How do I know if I've selected the right modem port?

- When you first try to connect to the outside world, you'll know that you have the right port when you hear the high-pitched modem sound as it tries to connect. (Expert opinion says it sounds like a duck choking on a kazoo.) Even if you fail to connect, the fact that it makes the sounds means that your machine knows that it has a modem and is using it.

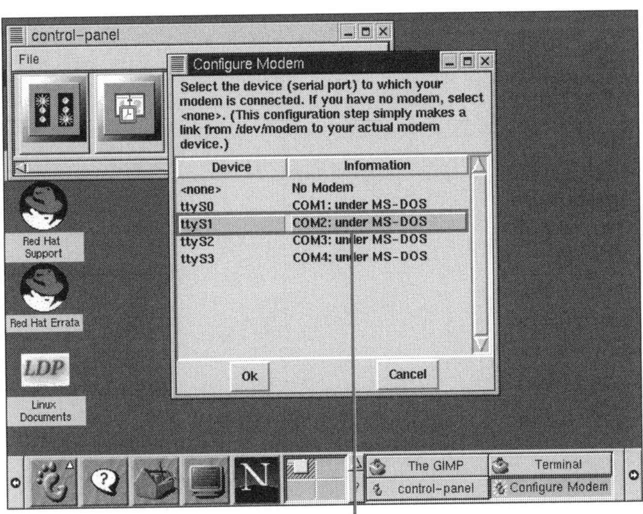

■ The most common serial port for a modem is COM2, also known as ttyS1.

2 Click this setting in the Configure Modem screen.

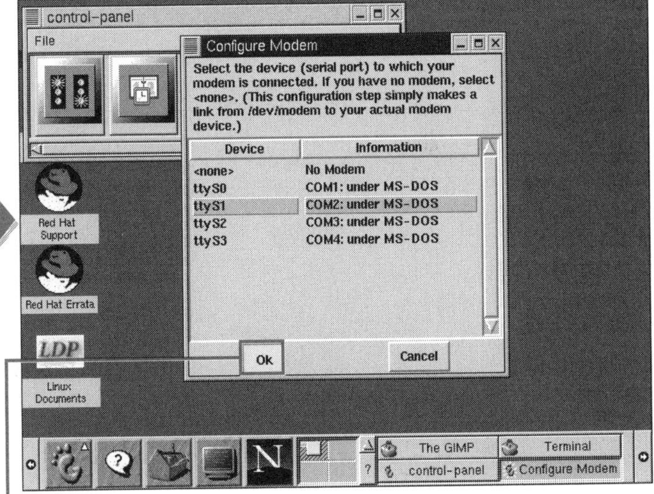

3 Click OK to accept this setting and to exit the Configure Modem process.

ENTER DNS INFORMATION

You need to enter DNS information into your connection configuration. DNS information allows your system to translate a computer's network address into a recognizable Web site address, such as www.samplesite.com. These addresses are also called URLs (Uniform Resource Locators). *DNS* (Domain Name Servers) are computers designated to look up Internet locations based on the text URL you request from them.

You also need the DNS server to translate the Web site www.samplesite.com into a number that the machine can understand and connect to, such as 165.36.55.21. This number is the IP (Internet Protocol) address of the machine. This address translates to its URL, www.samplesite.com. The number set itself is called a *tuplet*. The DNS information you enter is a tuplet, or pair of tuplets, that allow your machine to automatically get to the DNS server through a PPP, or Point to Point connection.

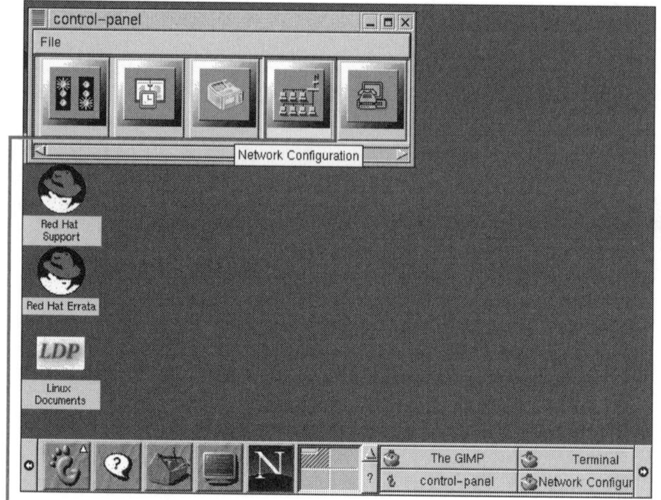

1 Click the Network Configuration button to get to the Network Configurator screen.

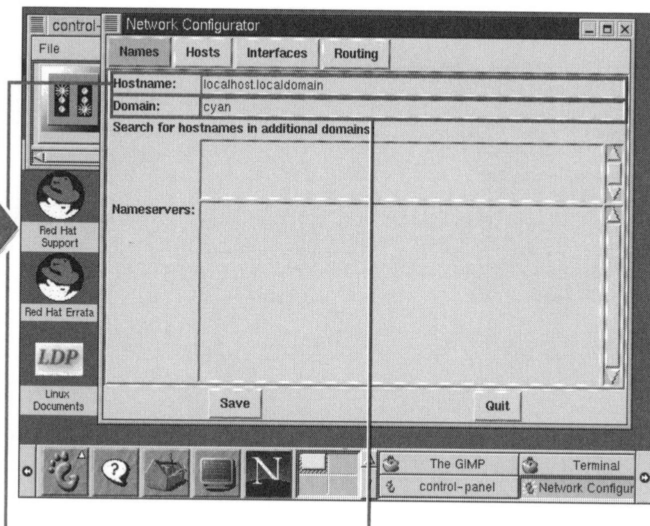

■ The hostname of your machine is by default listed in the hostname field.

2 Click the Domain field and type the name of the domain if it is different from the one listed as part of your hostname.

Why has my ISP given me two tuplets to use?

- ISPs know that during peak times, their primary DNS server will become overloaded and slow down or start dropping connections. It's in their interest and yours to have a backup DNS tuplet that your machine can fall back on and try to connect to when the primary is too busy. Be sure to enter both tuplets in the configuration tool.

If I'm running Windows clients on my Linux network, where else should I add the DNS information?

- If you're running in a mixed environment, it's easiest if you enter the DNS information directly on the Windows machine rather than remotely. You'll need to add the tuplets to the machine's Network Neighborhood, by right-clicking the icon and selecting Properties. On the Configuration tab, add the TCP/IP information.

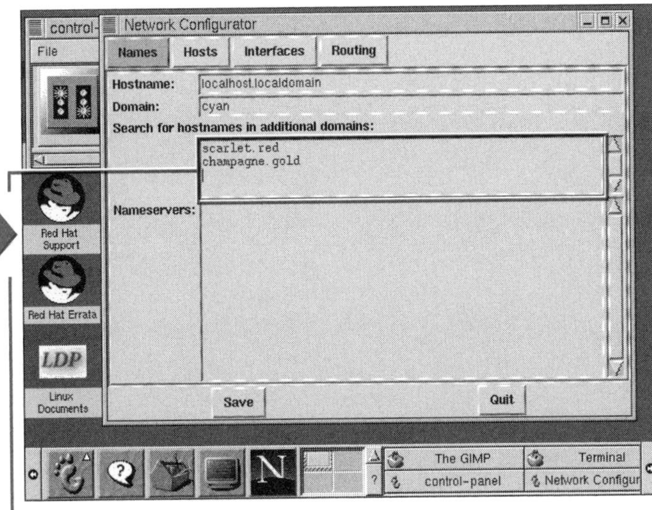

3 Click the Search for hostnames in additional domains field. If you have any hostnames to search for, enter them here.

■ This field searches for hostnames in different domains, resolving them (so that the computer can use them) as IP addresses.

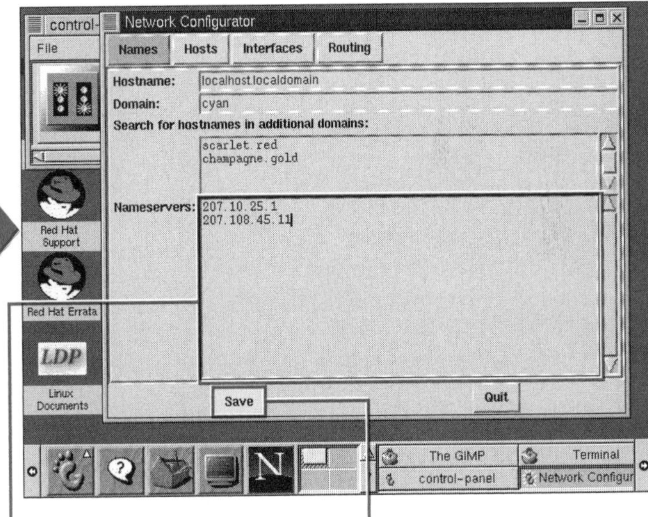

4 Click the Nameservers field and type the Internet Protocol address(es) of the DNS servers that belong to you or your ISP (Internet service provider).

5 Click Save to save this information.

■ Do not click Quit unless you've already configured a PPP connection.

ADD AND DELETE A PPP INTERFACE

You can use a PPP interface to connect to your Internet Service Provider. PPP is only one of many types of connections you can create to access your ISP and the World Wide Web, but it's one of the simplest and most common. It's also relatively easy to set up when you use the Control Panel's network configuration manager.

PPP is not the way you want to set up your computer if you're only planning on connecting to an office or company Ethernet-based network. PPP is more commonly used and more suited to use in a stand-alone system or networked system that is talking to the outside world via a properly configured modem. This is because PPP is slightly slower to connect and make software handshakes, but it shuts down cleaner than most other types of connections.

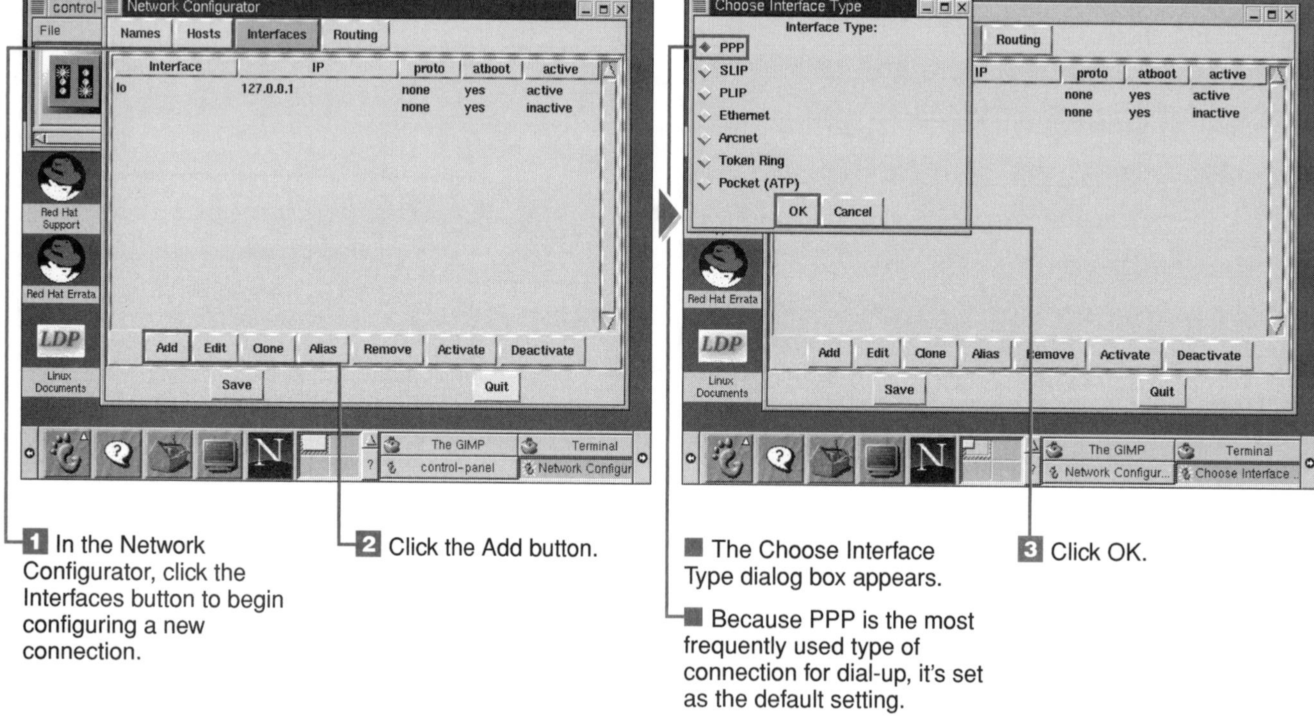

1 In the Network Configurator, click the Interfaces button to begin configuring a new connection.

2 Click the Add button.

■ The Choose Interface Type dialog box appears.

■ Because PPP is the most frequently used type of connection for dial-up, it's set as the default setting.

3 Click OK.

Is PPP the most efficient kind of interface connection, or should I be using a different kind?

✔ PPP is one of the most efficient connections when you're using any kind of telephonic device, such as a dial-up modem, to connect to a network. Because of its efficiency and compatibility with many kinds of hardware, PPP is the most frequently used type of connection for dial-up.

When I enter my ISP's phone number in the Phone Number text box in the Create PPP Interface dialog box, should I include the area code?

✔ If your ISP is located in a different area code, you must enter the area code. However, if the phone company classifies a call to your Internet service provider as long distance, you could drastically increase the cost of your phone bill.

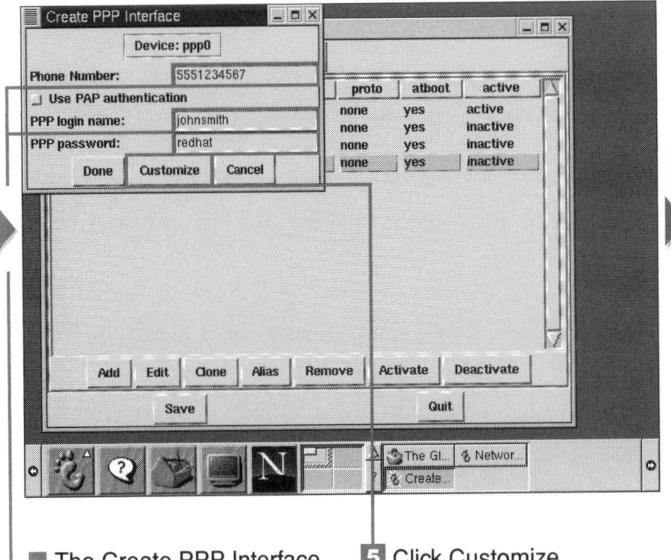

■ The Create PPP Interface dialog box appears.

4 Enter your ISP's phone number, your login name, and password in the appropriate field.

5 Click Customize.

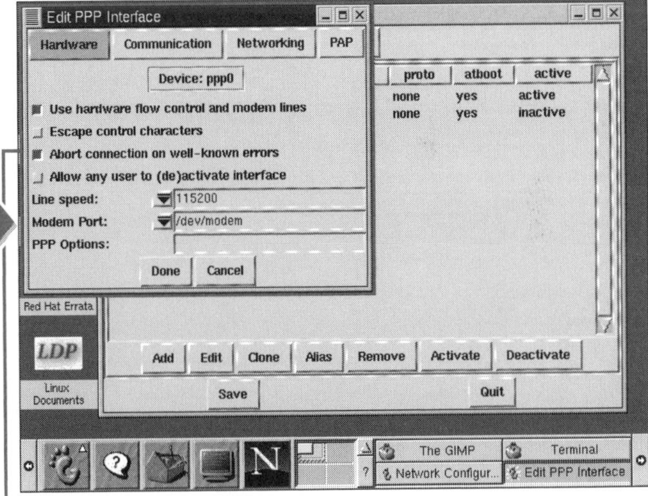

■ The Edit PPP Interface screen appears.

CONTINUED

ADD AND DELETE A PPP INTERFACE
CONTINUED

You can configure the making of a PPP connection in the Edit PPP Interface screen. A PPP, or Point to Point Protocol, cannot be made without a hardware device to connect to the network. This hardware device can be a network card, a telephone modem, or even a cable modem.

The most important aspect to consider when configuring hardware involved in a PPP connection is line speed. In the Edit PPP Interface screen, you can set line speed at anywhere from 1,200 baud (also known as bps or bytes per second) to 115,200.

Although you can leave the line speed at the highest setting, older, slower modems may get confused if you leave it there. If you have a slow modem (9,600 baud or slower), it's best to set the line speed to match the top data transfer speed that your modem can handle.

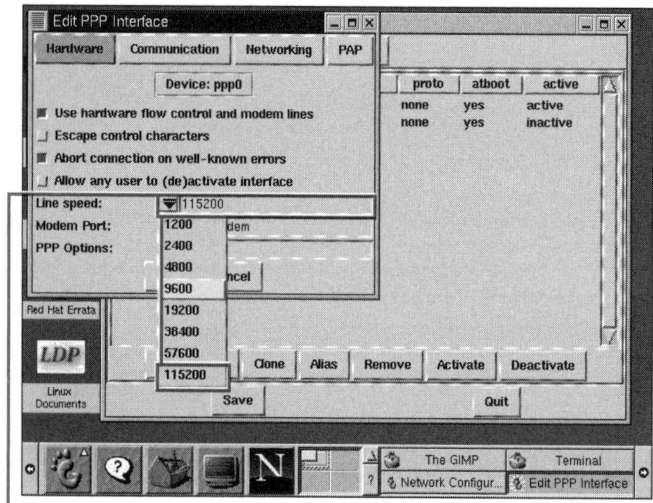

■ By default, the modem's line speed (which affects the speed of transmitting data) is set to the highest level.

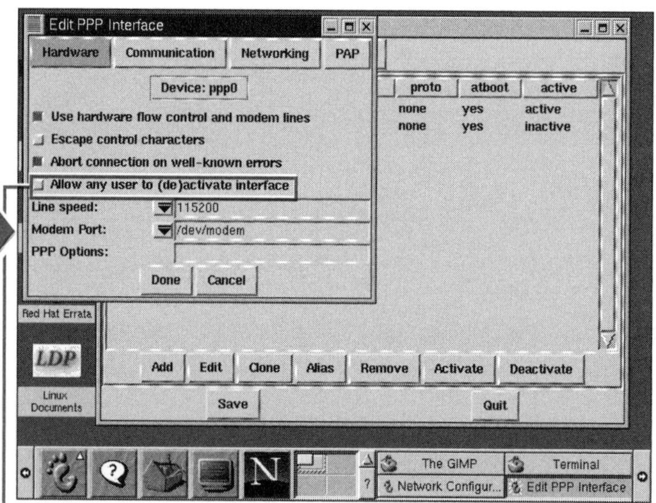

6 For maximum flexibility, click the button next to Allow any user to (de)activate Interface to select.

■ This enables any user to connect or disconnect from the ISP at will.

TIPS

Because a slow modem will get confused if you set the line speed to a higher setting, will a fast modem get confused if you set the line speed too slow?

- Fast modems won't get confused if you set the line speed below their fastest rates. However, you'll lose the benefit of having the faster modem. For example, if you set your line speed to 9600, a 56K modem will run only at a maximum speed of 9600.

Is there any difference in setting the line speed if your modem is an internal versus an external one?

- There is no difference when setting the line speed in the Network Configurator. However, an external modem, which sits outside of your computer's case, usually can change to a slower or faster speed with a button or switch. An internal modem, which is installed inside your computer, lacks this capability.

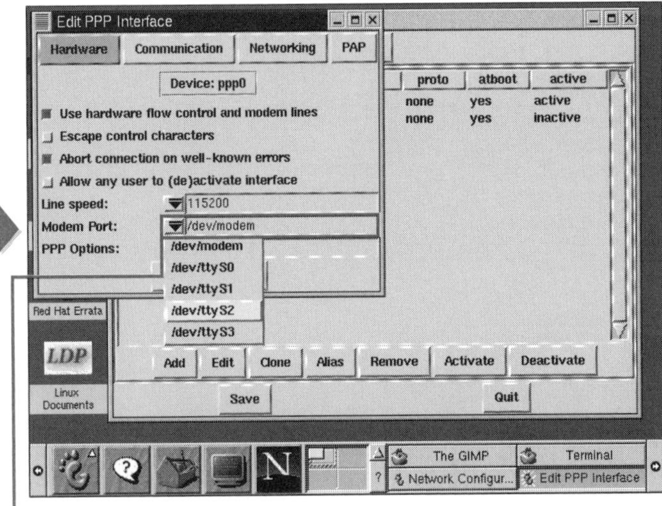

7 To change the default modem port, click the down-arrow in the Modem Port field and click to select.

Note: Do not click Done until you have edited the remaining tabs to your satisfaction.

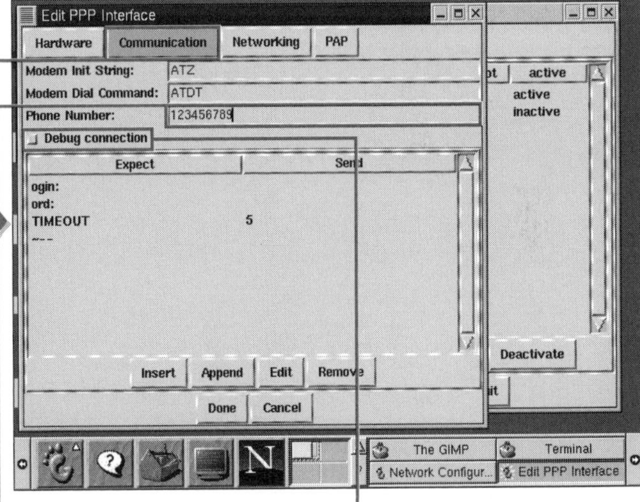

8 Click the Communication tab to move to the next panel.

9 Enter the Phone number for your modem.

10 Select Debug connection only if you are experiencing problems and you are familiar with modem debugging techniques.

CONTINUED

ADD AND DELETE A PPP INTERFACE

CONTINUED

You can prevent your computer from freezing, otherwise known as hanging, if it encounters a broken PPP connection or simply gets no answer at all from the computer it is trying to connect to. Depending on the type of connection and the computer that you're trying to talk to, your machine may stop working for up to a minute as it tries to complete its PPP connection.

Your computer will eventually return to normal after the attempted PPP connection allotted timeframe. The timeout procedure allots a given amount of time for your machine to form the point-to-point connection. If the connection is not made within that timeframe, the connection is deemed unusable and the attempt is given up. The timeout value is normally 60 seconds. If you don't want to wait around for a full 60 seconds for the timeout to occur, you can set these values in the Networking portion of the Edit PPP Interface screen.

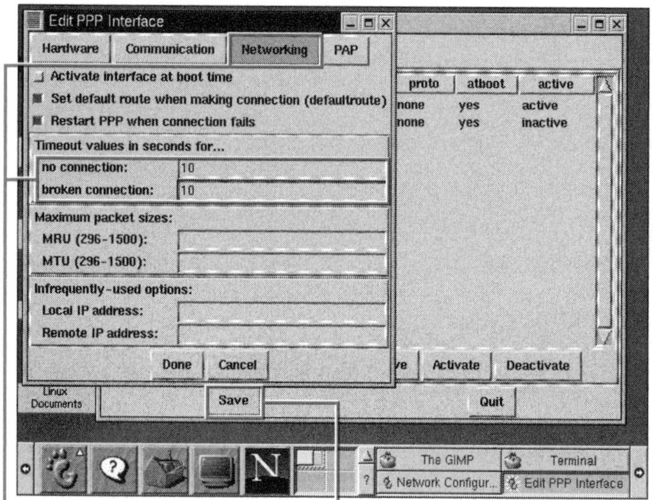

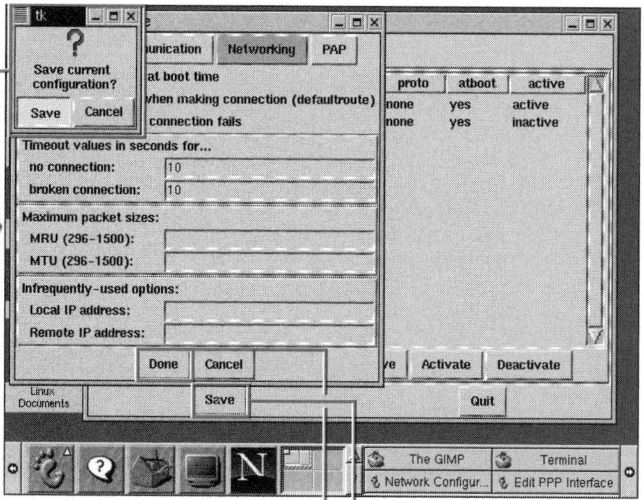

11 Click the Networking tab to move to the next panel.

12 Set timeout values in the no connection and broken connection fields.

■ Default timeouts are usually five seconds, but you can extend or reduce the time as you wish.

13 Click Save to save the results.

■ A dialog box appears asking if you wish to save these settings.

14 Click Save to save these settings.

15 Click Done to return to the Network Configurator screen.

TIPS

What do the Activate and Deactivate buttons in the Interfaces console have to do with my network connection?

- Just because you create a connection, doesn't mean that you have to keep it in use. For example, if you connect at one time or another to different Internet service providers, you might use one type of connection for one ISP and a different one for the second. To prevent problems, you could de-activate one or the other at any given time.

How can I use the Clone button in the Interfaces console?

- If you want to create a new connection with only a different name or port connection, you can clone a given connection you've already created. *Cloning* means to make a duplicate copy of a connection's properties. You can then change the name or port connection. This will save you some typing while you're duplicating the settings.

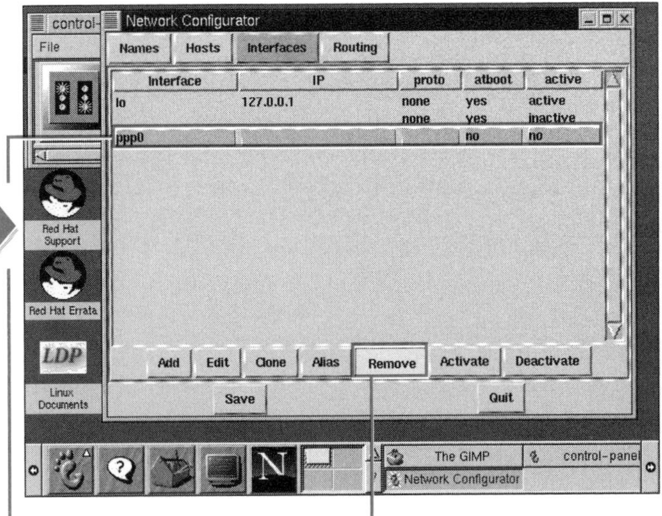

■ On the Network Configurator screen, the new interface appears.

16 If you want to delete this interface, click to highlight.

17 Click the Remove button.

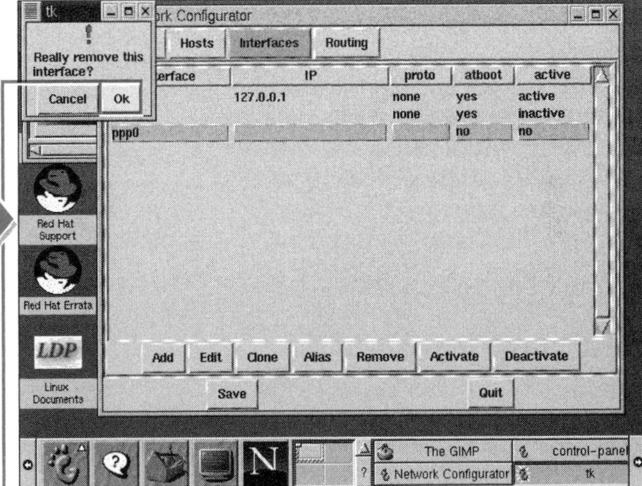

■ A dialog box appears asking if you really want to delete the interface.

18 Click OK.

■ The interface is removed from the Interfaces panel.

CONFIGURE A DIRECT CONNECTION

You have a direct connection setup if you log into the World Wide Web via a LAN (Local Area Network) or if you use one of the more popular cable modems. This kind of connection is also called broadband, due to the increased amount of network traffic you can handle in this manner.

Setting up a broadband, or direct connection to the Internet requires you to make a few unique changes within the Interfaces panel. Although you may be using a cable modem or other forms of access, you must select Ethernet as your connection type. This is because broadband connections most closely emulate the connection you get from running a standard inter-office Ethernet card.

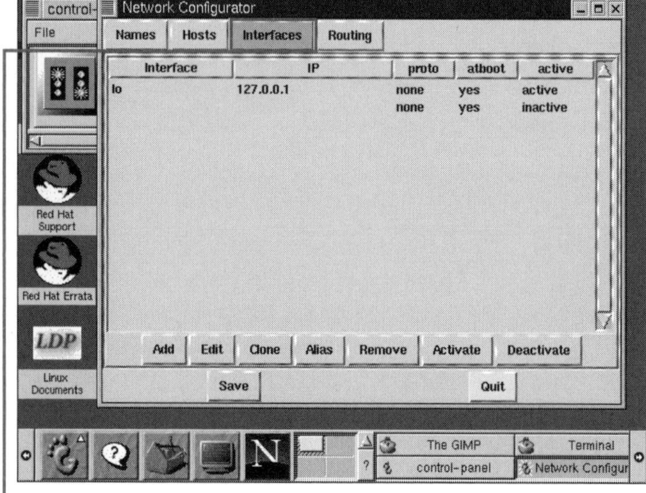

1 In the Network Configurator, click the Interfaces button to begin configuring a new connection.

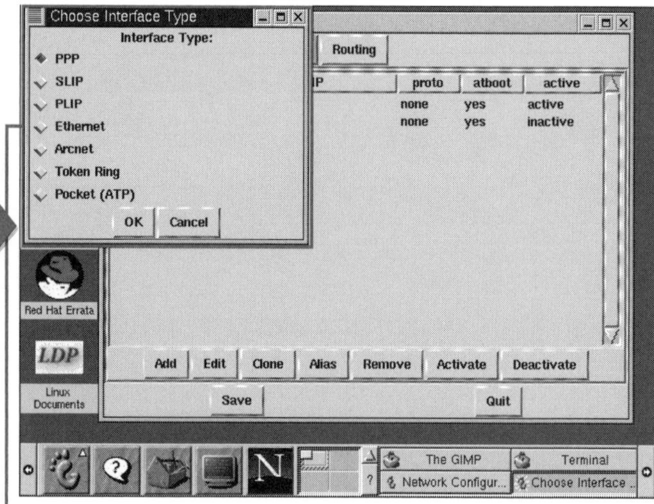

2 Click the Add button.

■ The Choose Interface Type dialog box appears.

Why are Ethernet connections the default setting whenever you add new interfaces in the Network Configurator?

- Ethernet is the default setting when adding new interfaces because it's the most popular and flexible form of network interface on the market. Due to its popularity, Ethernet is the de facto standard interface for the majority of systems.

What's the advantage of allowing any user to activate or deactivate a network interface?

- The advantage of allowing users to complete these tasks is that they can activate network connections without having to come to you. Users who are working on the machine will also respond more quickly when you need to deactivate a network interface, such as when network traffic begins to slow the computer down. On the other hand, users who aren't experienced in this procedure are likely to damage or delete the interface, so this setting isn't recommended.

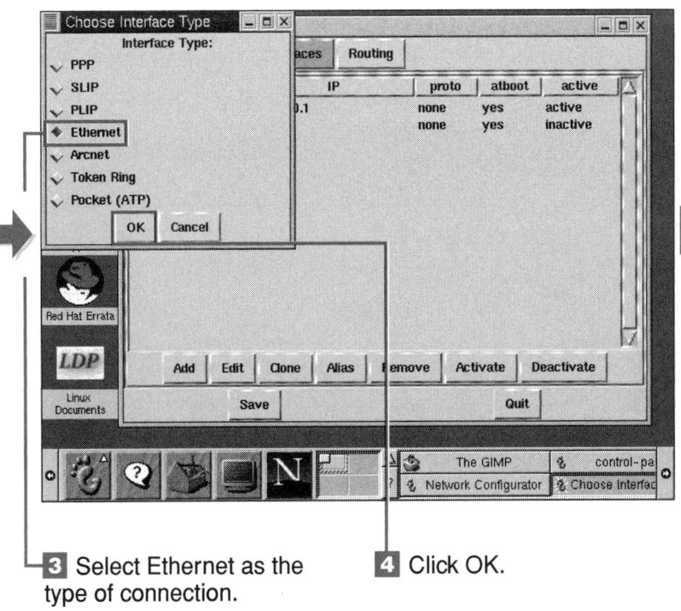

3 Select Ethernet as the type of connection.

4 Click OK.

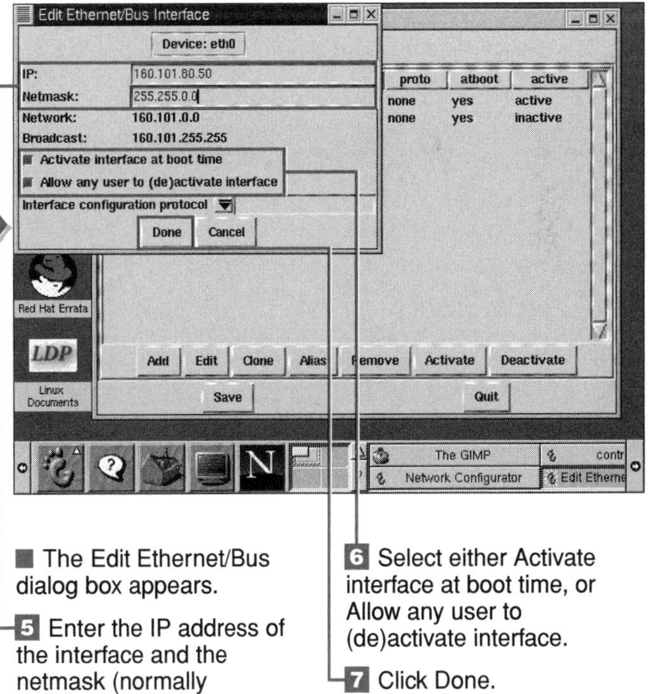

■ The Edit Ethernet/Bus dialog box appears.

5 Enter the IP address of the interface and the netmask (normally 225.0.0.0).

6 Select either Activate interface at boot time, or Allow any user to (de)activate interface.

7 Click Done.

CONTINUED

CONFIGURE A DIRECT CONNECTION

CONTINUED

You can use the Control Panel's `Network Configurator` utility to add the names of the domains you want to access. In the Names screen of the Network Configurator, you can specify that the computer search for hostnames in other domains.

This feature is very helpful if your company or computer group has just re-organized the network. If the machine you want to connect to has been moved into a different domain — but has kept the same hostname — you can reconnect by specifying the machine's new domain in the Network Configurator.

You can also specify the machine that will act as the default gateway for your computer in the Routing screen. The gateway is a machine that your computer automatically talks to when you attempt to connect to a network like the Internet.

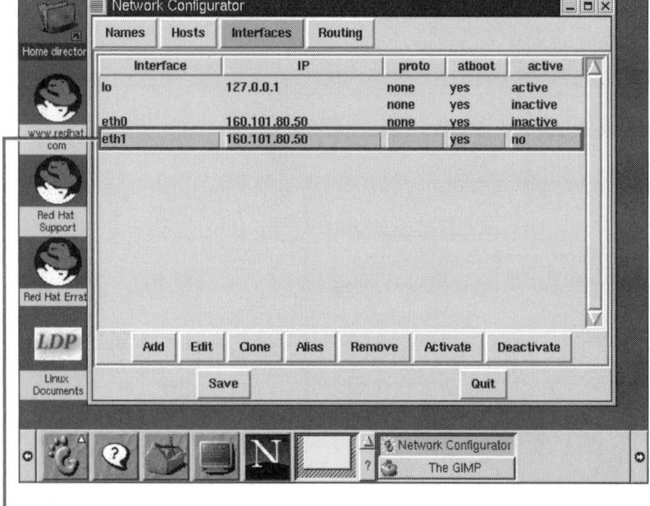

■ The new interface appears in the Interface panel.

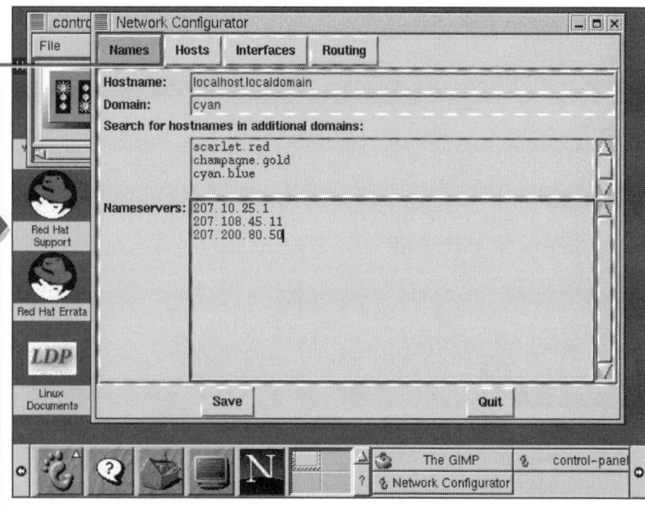

8 Click the Names tab and then click the Save button to save your work.

What if I need to specify different routers and gateways for my different interface functions?

- Your best bet in that kind of situation is to set up your connections with a more powerful configuration tool outside of the Control Panels. Use the Routers page from the `Linuxconf` utility to configure these settings.

I changed the IP address of the Default Gateway. Why am I still connecting to the old default gateway?

- When you change your default gateway settings, you must click the Save button, not the Quit button. Clicking Quit discards your changes.

Are there any circumstances where I can use the other Interface types?

- You'll rarely use these Interface types. For example, the token ring connection is a type of network structure that, by today's standards, is quite antiquated—so you'll likely find it only if you're connecting to or running a very old network.

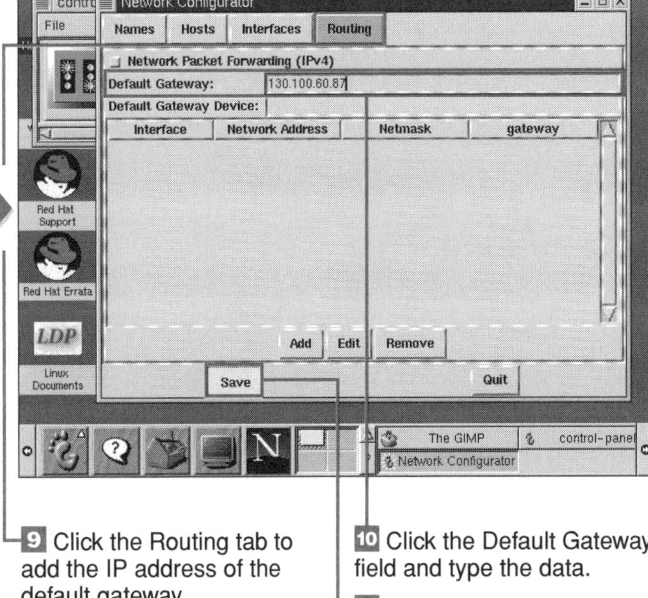

9 Click the Routing tab to add the IP address of the default gateway.

10 Click the Default Gateway field and type the data.

11 Click Save.

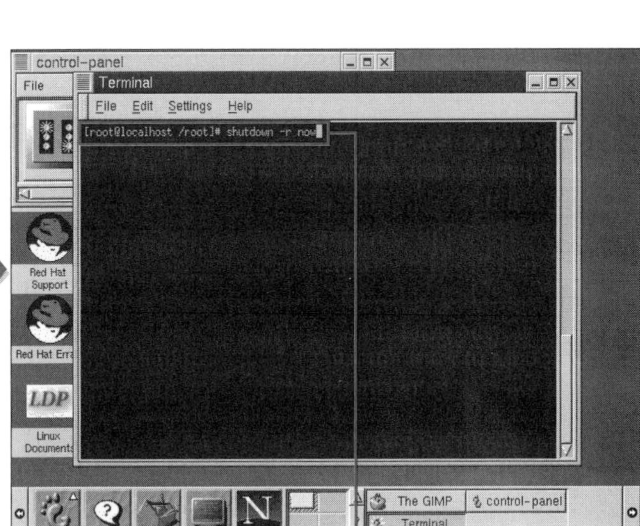

■ For these settings to take effect, you must reboot your machine.

12 You can choose to use the Logout menu prompt, or you can open a Linux Terminal and type **shutdown –r now** and press enter to reboot your machine.

LAUNCH THE NETSCAPE WEB BROWSER

Your Netscape Web browser is by far the greatest freebie you have available to you in your Red Hat Linux package. Although it doesn't run any of the core programs or parameters that make your Linux machine work, it's the most useful and fun tool to use on your system because it enables you to surf the Web.

To start working with this amazing tool, you need to activate, or launch, it. Your Red Hat Linux installation provides you with a myriad of ways you can access Netscape. Be sure to take your time and read the Netscape agreement when it comes up the first time you activate your new browser. As a whole, you'll find that Netscape is as easy — if not easier — to use than the Web browsing program from that other company in Seattle, Washington.

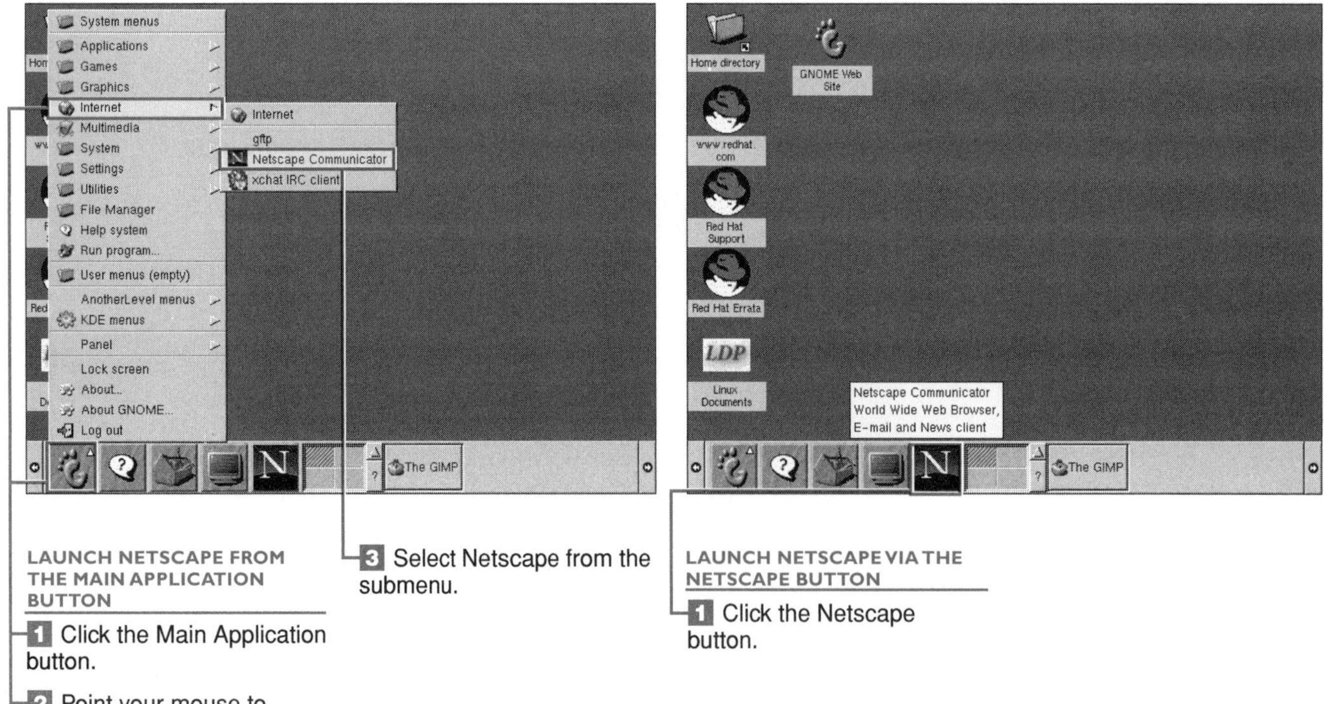

LAUNCH NETSCAPE FROM THE MAIN APPLICATION BUTTON

1 Click the Main Application button.

2 Point your mouse to Internet.

3 Select Netscape from the submenu.

LAUNCH NETSCAPE VIA THE NETSCAPE BUTTON

1 Click the Netscape button.

Can I launch Netscape from the Linux terminal window?

- Normally, you can. To launch Netscape from the terminal window, type `netscape` at the command prompt and press Enter. After a few seconds, the Netscape window appears on your desktop.

What if Netscape won't launch from the terminal?

- If Netscape refuses to launch, check your $PATH variable. Compare it to the location of the Netscape binary. If, for example, the Netscape binary were in `/etc/netscape`, you should make sure that your PATH includes `/etc` or `/etc/netscape`.

Why can't I use my terminal after I launch Netscape?

- After you start Netscape from the terminal, it acts like a newly started daemon, refusing to relinquish the screen until you shut Netscape down. Your best bet is to simply work in another Linux terminal window, or to start Netscape by typing `netscape &`, which runs Netscape in the background, freeing up the terminal.

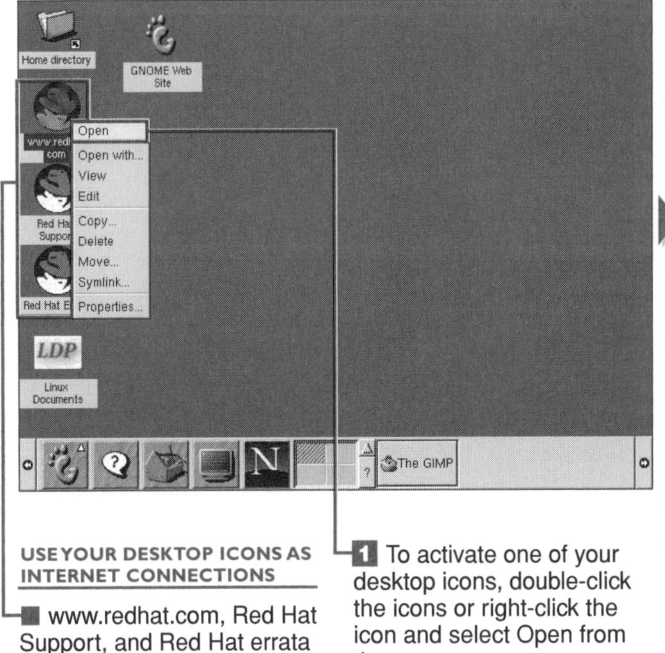

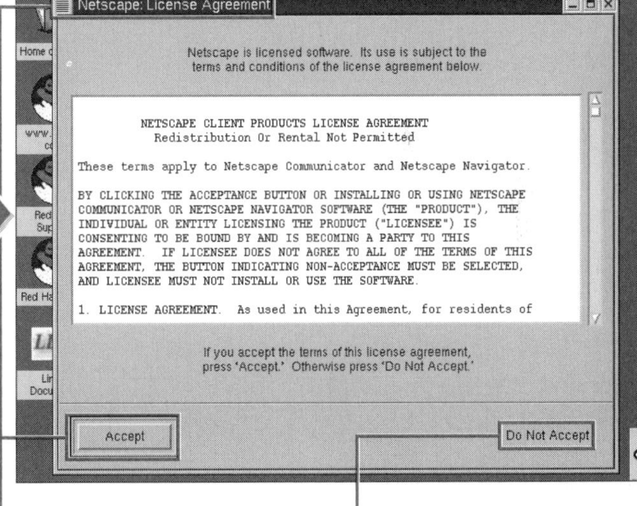

USE YOUR DESKTOP ICONS AS INTERNET CONNECTIONS

■ www.redhat.com, Red Hat Support, and Red Hat errata start your Web connection.

1 To activate one of your desktop icons, double-click the icons or right-click the icon and select Open from the pop-up menu.

■ The Netscape License Agreement appears.

2 Read the license agreement usage carefully.

3 If you agree, click Accept and the Web browser will start.

■ If you click Do Not Accept, you return to the desktop.

BROWSE THE WEB WITH NETSCAPE

A Web browser is a graphical interface that you use when you connect to the Internet. By clicking the appropriate fields and buttons, you can navigate to any given point or Web site on the World Wide Web, search for any kind of information, or bookmark a site that you liked so that you can return to it with a single click.

Also, when you've browsed or surfed through several Web sites, your Netscape Web browser will keep a cache (a list) of the sites you've visited. By clicking the Back or Forward buttons, you're moving to different points on the list, saving you from bookmarking every single site or typing it in again and again. Like your GNOME control panel, Netscape tries extra-hard to be user friendly, so look for button icons like the forward and back arrows, or the printer picture on the Print button.

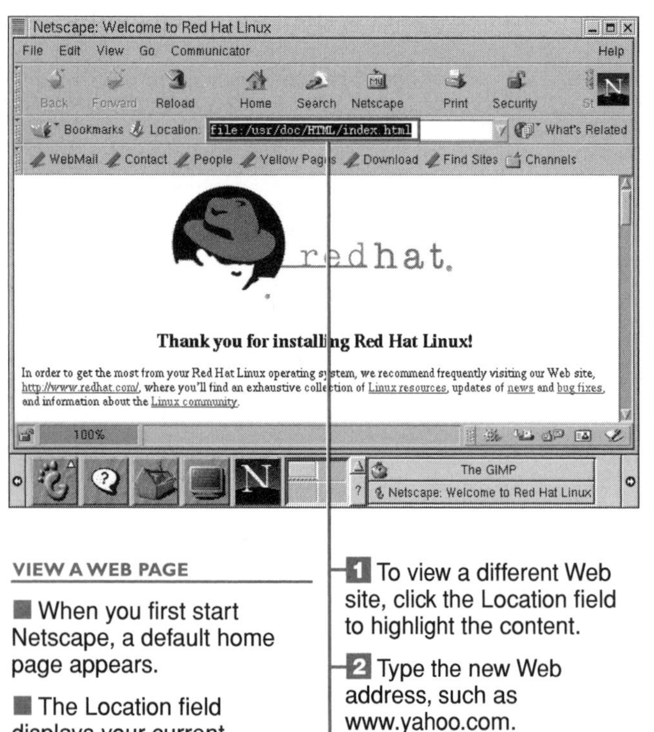

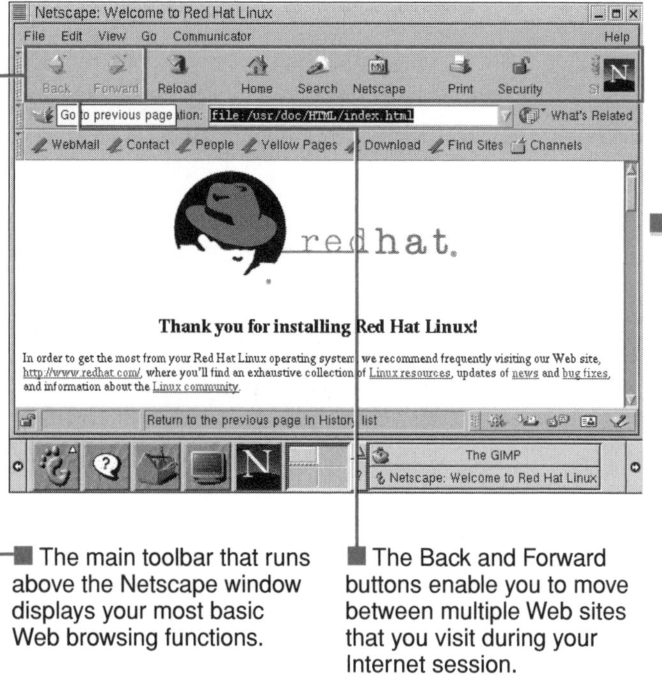

VIEW A WEB PAGE

■ When you first start Netscape, a default home page appears.

■ The Location field displays your current location on the Web.

1 To view a different Web site, click the Location field to highlight the content.

2 Type the new Web address, such as www.yahoo.com.

3 Press Enter.

■ The main toolbar that runs above the Netscape window displays your most basic Web browsing functions.

■ The Back and Forward buttons enable you to move between multiple Web sites that you visit during your Internet session.

What if I want to jump to a site I visited three or four sites back?

- You have two options available. You can either hit the Back button three or four times, or you can take the simpler method that requires more mouse dexterity. On the Back and Forward buttons in Netscape are small, indented arrows. Move the mouse pointer over one of these arrows for a second, then click once. You get a drop-down menu listing all of the sites stored in the cache. Select the site off the name list and you'll be taken directly there.

Where did all those other bookmarks in the Bookmark utility come from? I didn't put them there!

- The Bookmark utility comes pre-loaded with sites that Netscape thinks you'll find useful. For example, under Travel, you may find sites linked to agencies or airplane reservations.

■ The Reload button is useful if the site you're downloading has been interrupted by a network failure on your side, or if you think that the server at the other end has gone to sleep or otherwise suffered a glitch in delivering your data.

BOOKMARK A SITE

■ If you come across a site you may want to revisit, bookmark it.

1 To bookmark a site, click Bookmarks.

2 Select Add Bookmark from the drop-down menu.

■ The next time you click the Bookmarks tab, you can select the site and jump right to it.

CONFIGURE NETSCAPE APPEARANCE AND NAVIGATION

You can alter the look and feel of your Netscape Navigator program by changing the settings that control the style of font, the size of the lettering, and even the colors of the background, hypertext, and document letters.

Also, you can change the settings that you use to create your own Web page. Most ISPs allow you a certain amount of space to post your own creation — your Web page, complete with your text, graphics, and perhaps a scanned picture or two.

Finally, you want to use these settings to change how you browse the Web itself. Each time you connect, you'll want to return to your special home page. Even if you haven't built a custom one, always try and start off your Internet session on a page that you find full of valuable information.

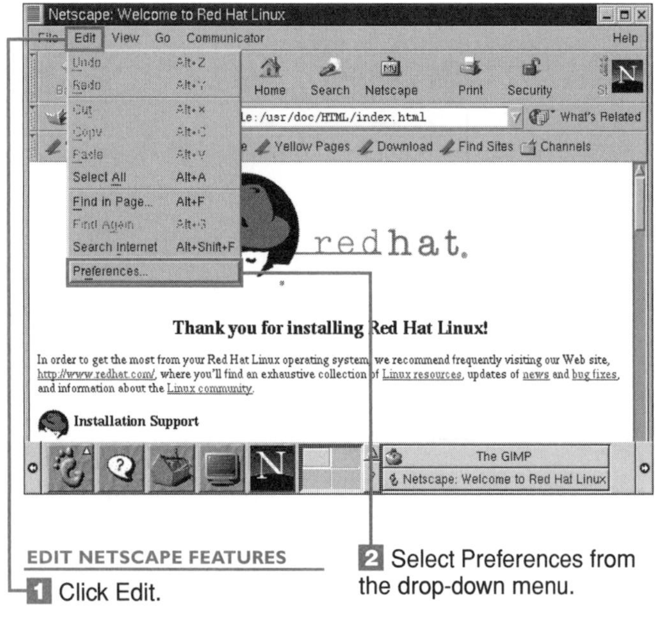

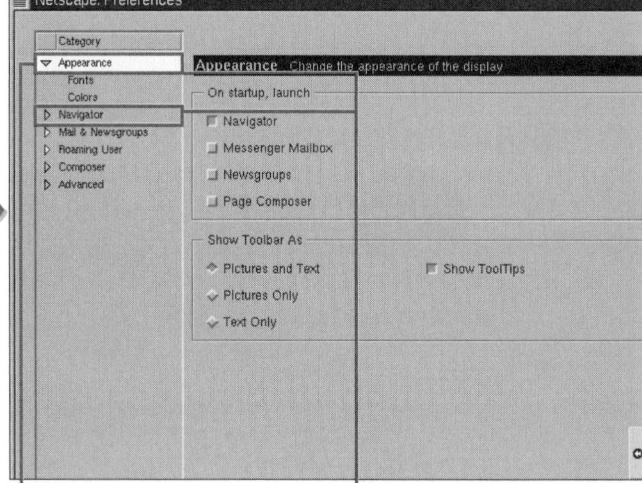

EDIT NETSCAPE FEATURES

1 Click Edit.

2 Select Preferences from the drop-down menu.

■ By default, the Appearance category displays.

■ You can select toolbar settings, fonts, and colors in your Web browser by clicking the appropriate buttons.

■ A downward-facing arrow displays submenus, while a right-facing arrow hides menus. When you double-click an arrow, the submenus appear automatically as the arrow changes orientation.

Why should I pick a specific location for my downloaded files?

✓ This depends on the nature of your system and what you plan to download. If you download small, important files that you plan to use right away, you can choose to download files directly into your home directory or onto the desktop. On the other hand, if you download huge files like long MP3s and you're short of space, it's best to download to someplace noncritical, like the `/tmp` directory.

What Web site should I select as my home page?

✓ Ideally, if you've decided to compose your own Web page on the Internet, then that should be your home page. However, if you just want a convenient starting point for your Web browsing, you should pick either a page on a topic that interests you or a Web search engine, such as Yahoo!, Excite, or AltaVista.

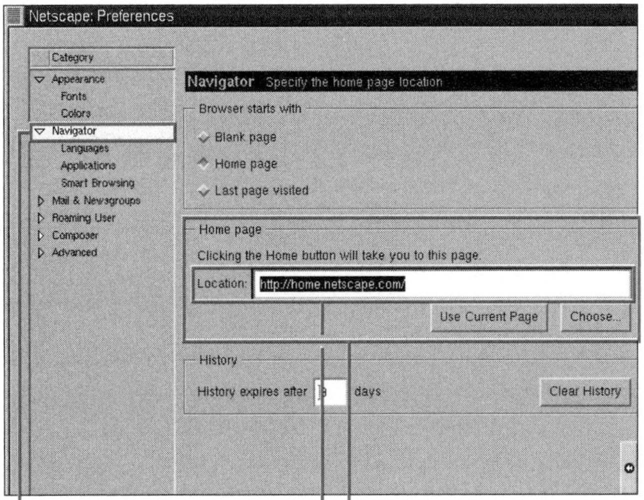

3 Click Navigator to get to the Navigation panel.

■ The main setting to edit is the Home page field.

4 Change your Netscape startup home page by typing in a new address in the location field.

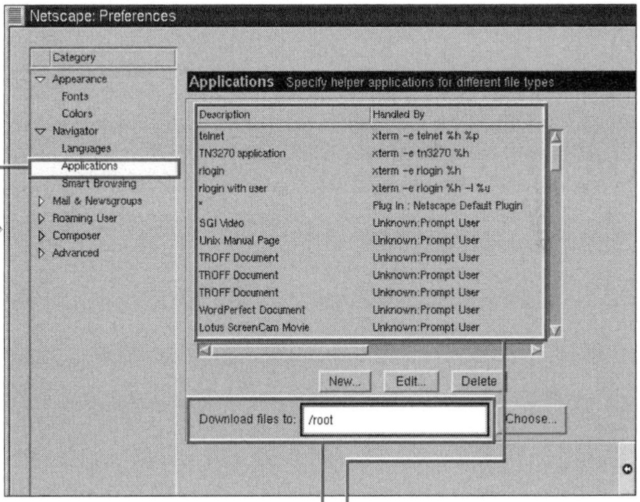

■ This setting appears when you click the Home button.

5 Select Applications in the left pane.

■ In this window, you can determine each specific application function in Netscape, and where to download your new files.

6 Click the Download files To field to type where you want to place Internet files.

CONFIGURE NEW WEB PAGE SETTINGS

You can configure your Netscape preferences to enable you to compose new Web pages according to a specific *template*. A template is a Web page that has already been designed — you've just selected it to act as a model or a guide for constructing your own pages. You can choose a template from a number of default types that Netscape provides, or you can find a page on the Web that you want to emulate.

You can also select a special color scheme for your Web page compositions. For example, by default, Web text *hyperlinks*, which are pieces of text that you can click to jump to another Web page, are colored blue. If you want to use a shade of blue for your Web page's background color, you're best off selecting a different one for your hypertext links.

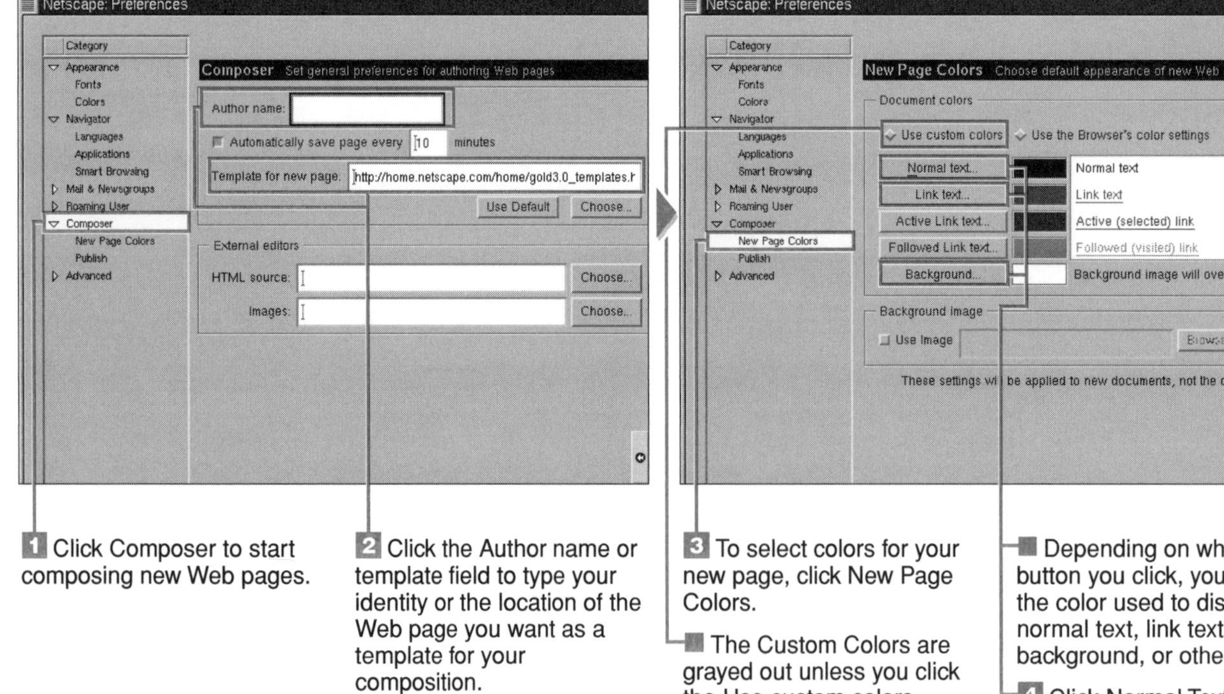

1 Click Composer to start composing new Web pages.

2 Click the Author name or template field to type your identity or the location of the Web page you want as a template for your composition.

3 To select colors for your new page, click New Page Colors.

■ The Custom Colors are grayed out unless you click the Use custom colors button.

■ Depending on which button you click, you can edit the color used to display normal text, link text, background, or other effects.

4 Click Normal Text to change the text display color.

When should I select the Custom Colors setting under the New Page Color screen?

- You can choose Custom Colors whenever you want to add a bit more originality to your Web page. There is no limitation. However, keep in mind that if you have a monitor that displays only 256 colors, what you select may look very different on a screen that can display more colors.

Is it better for my publishing location to be from an FTP or an HTTP server?

- That depends on the planned use of your Web page. HTTP servers are more commonly used for Web pages because they are more efficient at taking requests for text and picture files. On the other hand, an FTP server is much faster at transferring large quantities of data. If your Web page provides large documents, sound or graphics files, an FTP server is the better choice.

■ The Set Colors/option box appears.

5 Use the Old and New color swatches to compare color between the old setting and the new setting.

6 Select a color by clicking its square.

7 Click OK to finish and return to the New Page Colors screen.

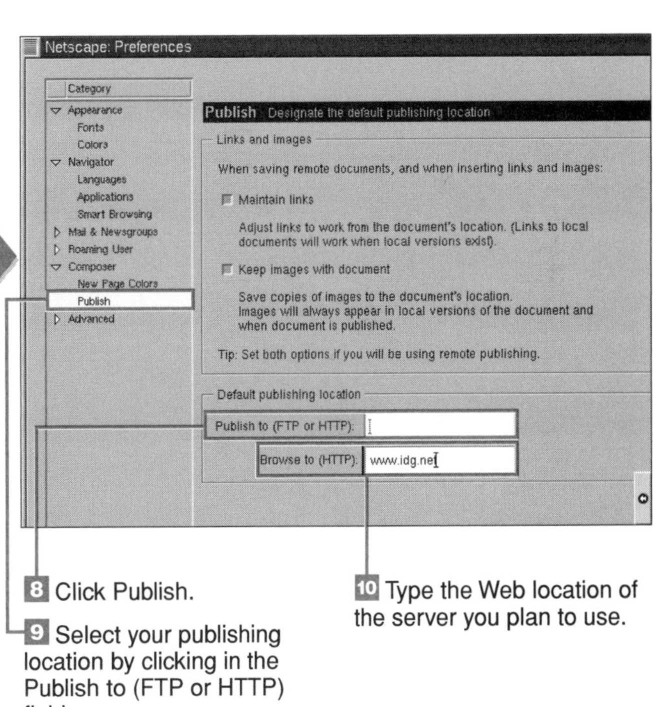

8 Click Publish.

9 Select your publishing location by clicking in the Publish to (FTP or HTTP) field.

10 Type the Web location of the server you plan to use.

CONFIGURE NETSCAPE'S ADVANCED NETWORK SETTINGS

You can edit and change the most advanced, detailed settings that affect your Netscape Web browser's ability to handle and process Internet data. One choice that you may make for speed and space purposes is to deactivate the automatic use of both Java and cookies, both of which increase the versatility of a Web site but slow you down and take up disk space.

Also, you may choose to expand or decrease the *cache*, or amount of disk space allocated by your Web browser to store Web site information. When you visit a Web site, your Web browser stores the site's pictures and text in this cache. If you return to the same Web site after visiting others, your Web browser can pull the images off this cache, speeding up your access time.

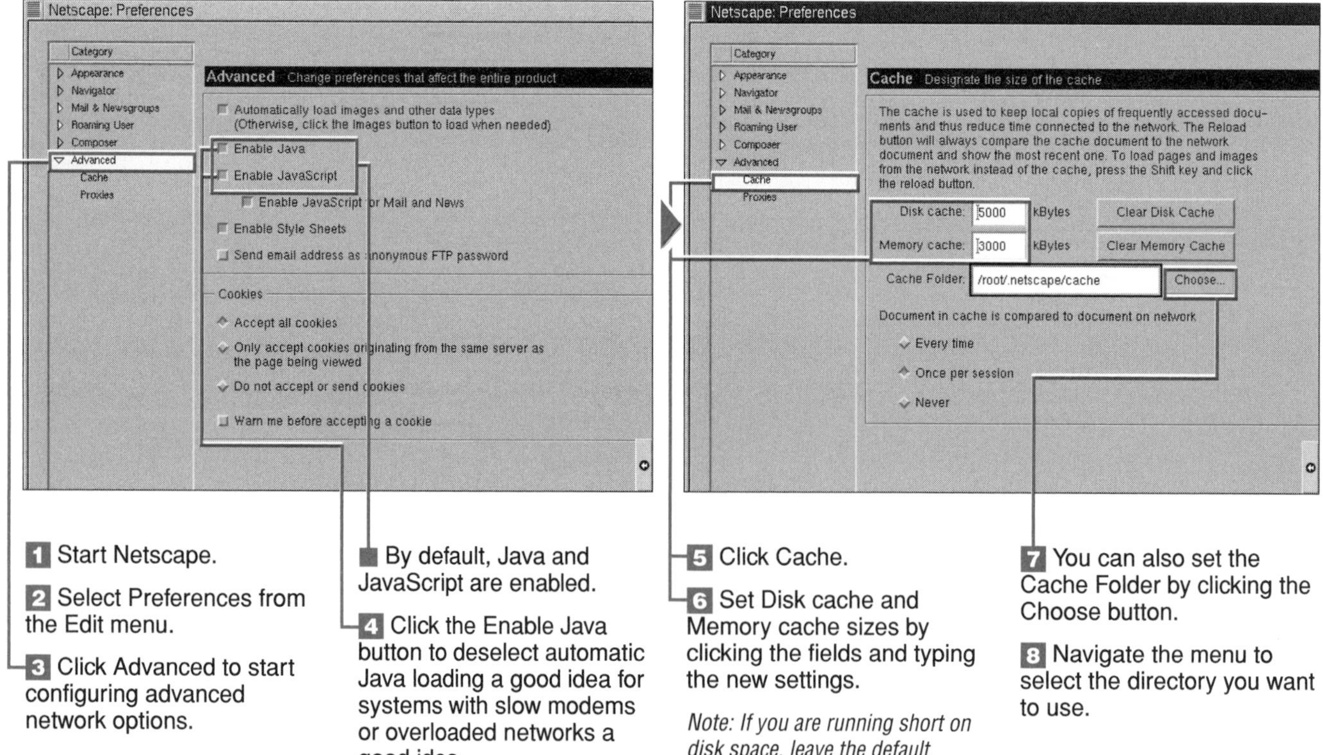

1 Start Netscape.

2 Select Preferences from the Edit menu.

3 Click Advanced to start configuring advanced network options.

■ By default, Java and JavaScript are enabled.

4 Click the Enable Java button to deselect automatic Java loading a good idea for systems with slow modems or overloaded networks a good idea.

5 Click Cache.

6 Set Disk cache and Memory cache sizes by clicking the fields and typing the new settings.

Note: If you are running short on disk space, leave the default settings alone.

7 You can also set the Cache Folder by clicking the Choose button.

8 Navigate the menu to select the directory you want to use.

Should I change my Web browser cache settings from the defaults?

- Much like the download location for your files, this depends on the nature of your system. If you have no shortage of disk space but you plan to do a lot of Web surfing, then you might want to keep or increase your cache settings. On the other hand, if you're short of space on your hard drive, you're better off scaling down your limits.

Why do large networks use proxy servers?

- Networks with large user groups and demands use *proxy servers* as a way to spread out network load and increase access speed for all sorts of uses. Rather than overload one server that needs to handle network printing, FTP facilitation, and Web access, many organizations spread out these functions by allocating one machine per use.

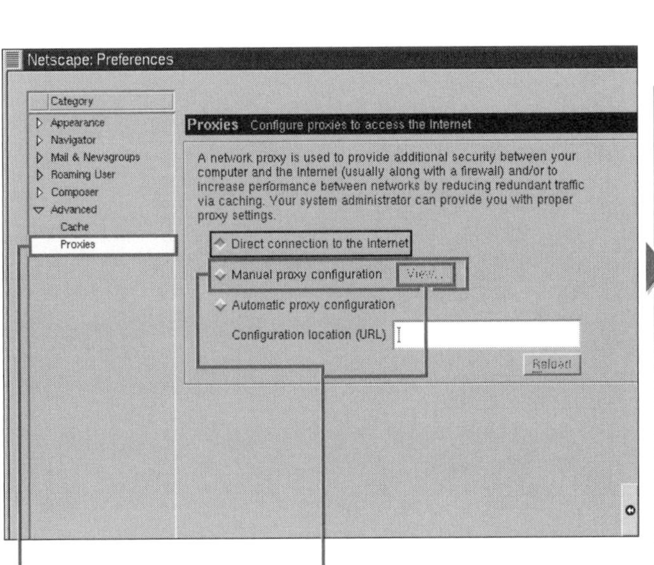

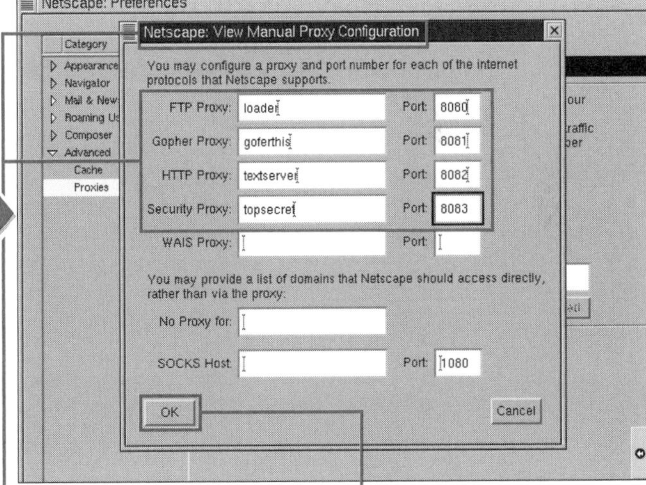

9 Click Proxies.

■ If you're on a large network, you may have divided each service into a different machine or network port.

10 Click the Manual proxy configuration button.

■ The View button is no longer grayed out.

11 Click the View button.

■ The View Manual Proxy Configuration screen appears.

12 Select the proxy machines and the ports by clicking each field and typing the entry in.

13 Click OK to return to the main Preferences screen.

SET UP NETSCAPE TO SEND E-MAIL

You can also configure Netscape to handle your electronic mail (e-mail) for you, both sending and receiving e-mail. Although not as efficient as some UNIX-based e-mail programs that come with Linux, most people find the graphical style easier to use.

In order to send and receive e-mail, your Web browser must be set up to connect to a specific machine that is set up to handle e-mail, normally called a *mail server*. This kind of server is also called a *POP server* because of the specific kinds of protocols it uses to hold and send e-mail.

In this configuration area, you can also edit what identity you plan to give out over the Web via e-mail.

Although you won't be able to send out e-mail anonymously, you can choose to remove your given name or (on the other extreme) provide detailed personal or business information.

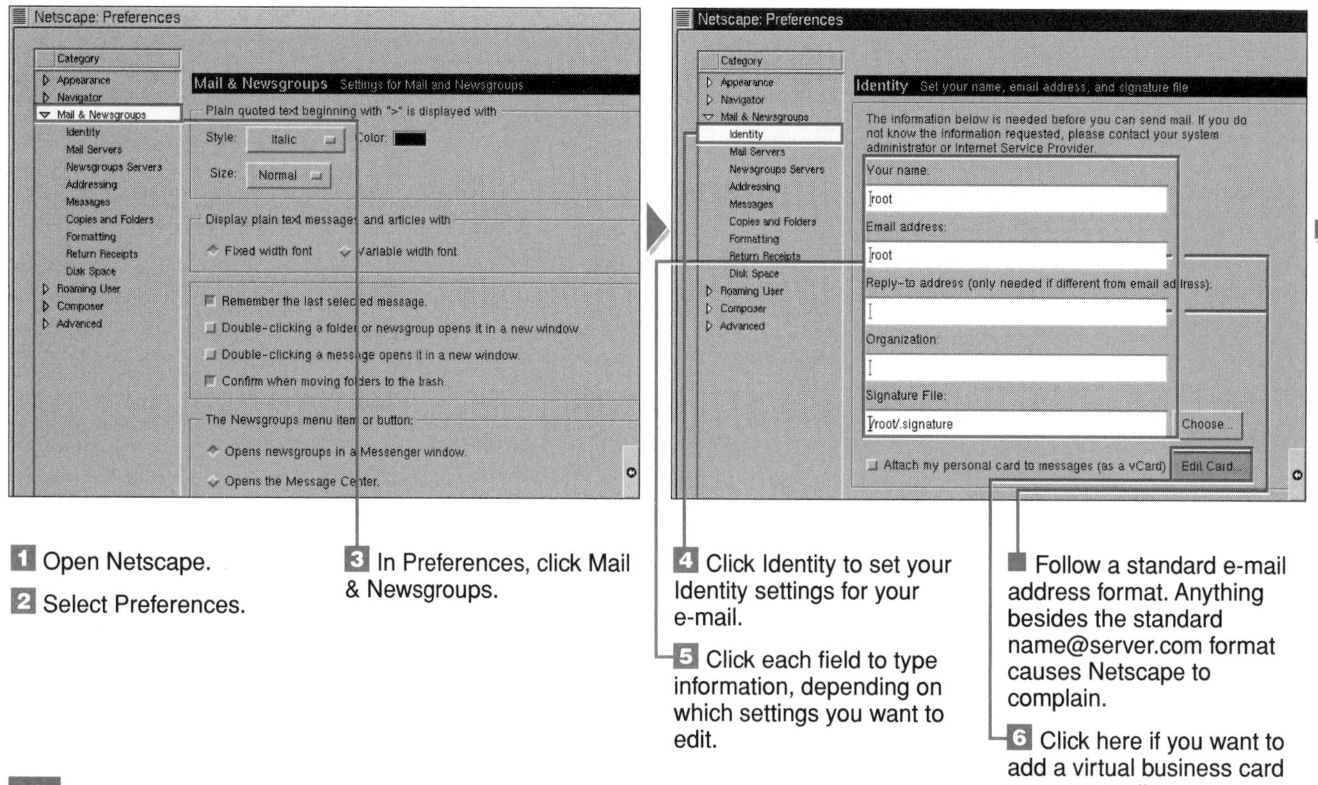

1 Open Netscape.

2 Select Preferences.

3 In Preferences, click Mail & Newsgroups.

4 Click Identity to set your Identity settings for your e-mail.

5 Click each field to type information, depending on which settings you want to edit.

■ Follow a standard e-mail address format. Anything besides the standard name@server.com format causes Netscape to complain.

6 Click here if you want to add a virtual business card to your e-mails

Why do some e-mail servers send me e-mail that asks for a return receipt?

✔ Certain e-mail programs, such as Eudora, enable you to attach a reply receipt, allowing you to rate a given e-mail with a priority message, such as high, medium, or highest. This allows business users to zero in on messages that may be very time sensitive.

If I plan to connect my Linux machine to a mail server set up by my ISP (Internet Service Provider), how can I find out the name of the server machine?

✔ Unfortunately, you can't determine the name of the server machine from Netscape, or anywhere else in Linux. You have to call your ISP to get that information. Of course, when you subscribe to an ISP, you should be given this information at the time you sign up.

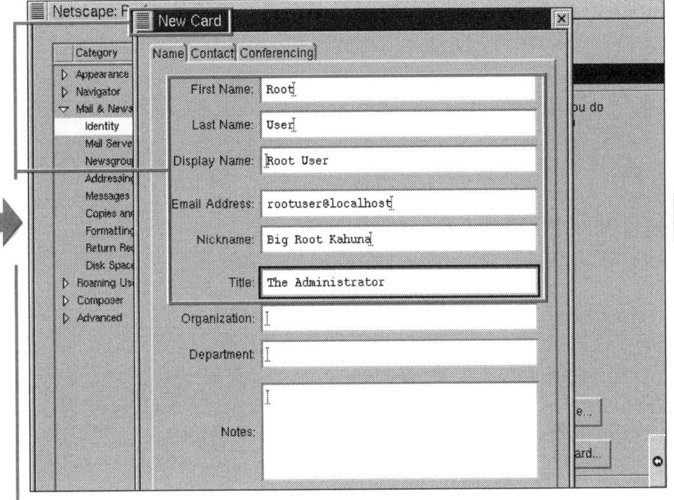

■ You're taken to the New Card screen.

7 Click each field to type the relevant information.

8 Press Enter to return to the Identify and Preferences screens.

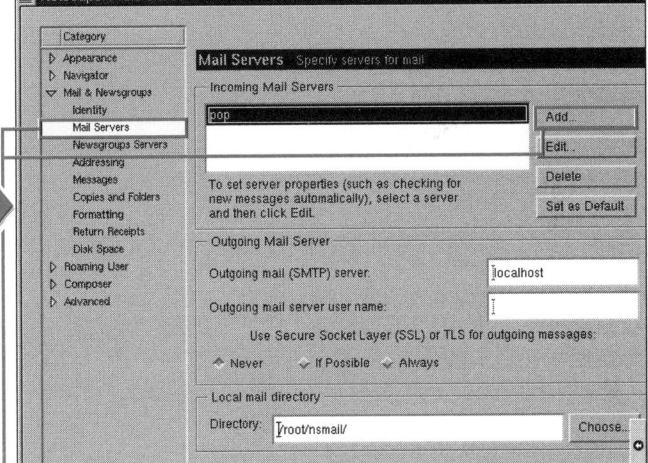

9 Click Mail Servers.

10 If you don't see an incoming mail server allocated to you in the Incoming Mail Servers field, click Add.

11 Type the name of your mail server machine.

12 Press Enter to return to Preferences.

SET UP NETSCAPE TO RECEIVE E-MAIL AND NEWS

You can change the location of the directory where your Netscape Web browser stores your e-mail and newsgroup messages. This is done in the Netscape Preferences screens. By default, Netscape stores e-mail messages in the directory `/root/nsmail` and newsgroup messages in `/root`.

Your Netscape Web browser also comes with a built-in safeguard to prevent your hard drive from filling up with extremely long e-mails, or e-mails with large sound or graphics attachments. The default setting here is 50 kilobytes (K). However, if you want to be able to receive large e-mails — for example, if your friends routinely send music or sound effects files to you via e-mail — you can increase this limit to as high as you want. If you're running short of disk space, you can also shrink this setting to prevent filling up your hard drive.

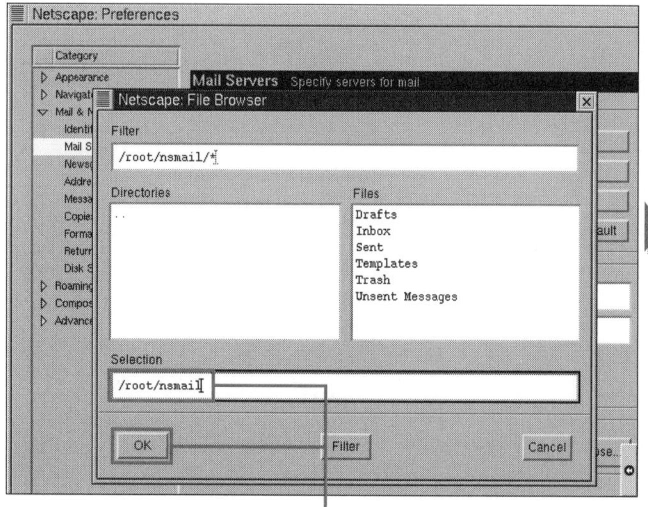

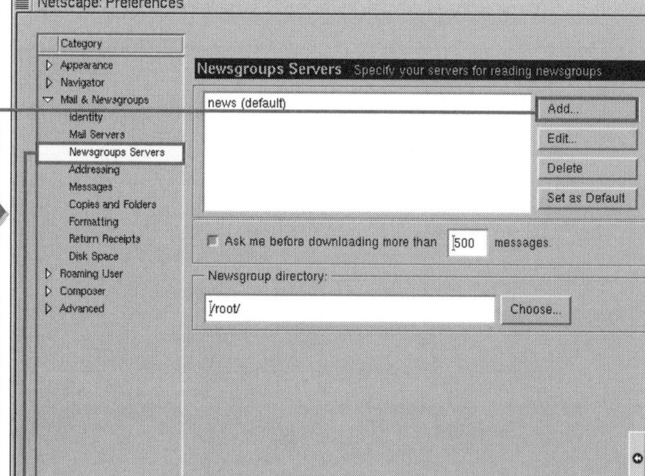

1 Select Preferences, Mail & Newsgroups, and then Mail Servers.

2 If you want to change the directory where you store your e-mail, click Choose in the Mail Servers dialog box.

■ The File Browser screen appears.

3 Select a location by clicking in the right pane, or type the location in the Selection field.

4 Click OK to return to Preferences.

5 Click Newsgroups Servers.

6 If you don't see an incoming news server allocated to you in the Newsgroups Servers field, click Add to the right of the field.

7 Type the name of your news server machine.

8 Press Enter to return to Preferences.

What can I do if I'm running short of disk space to store e-mail messages?

- Click Disk Space under Mail And Newsgroups and type in the maximum size message you want stored in the Do Not Store Messages Locally That Are Larger Than field.

How should I set the Disk Space parameter?

- If your hard drive is overflowing constantly, reduce this setting to only 10K. You should also plan to buy a larger hard drive.

If I plan to connect to a news server run by my ISP (Internet Service Provider), how can I find out the name of the news server machine?

- You won't be able to find out the news server name from your Linux machine. Call your ISP to find this out. If they're not immediately available, try using the name of your ISP's mail server. Often, the same machine will handle news and e-mail.

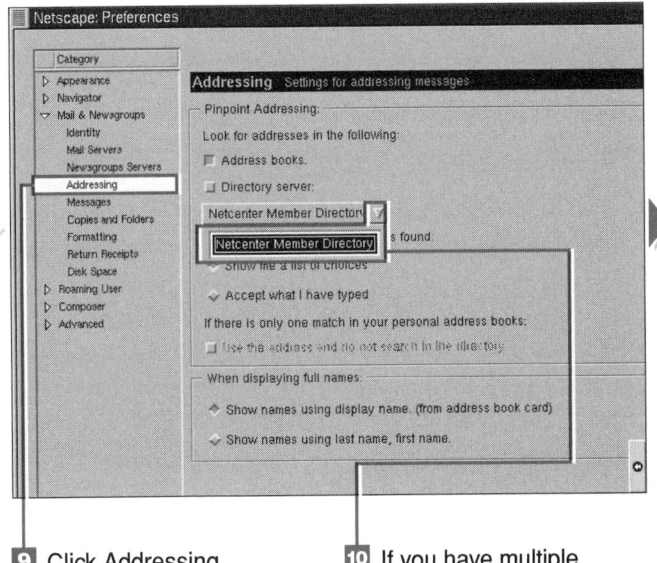

9 Click Addressing.

10 If you have multiple directory servers, you can choose one by clicking the arrow to the right of the Netcenter Member Directory field and selecting one from the drop-down menu.

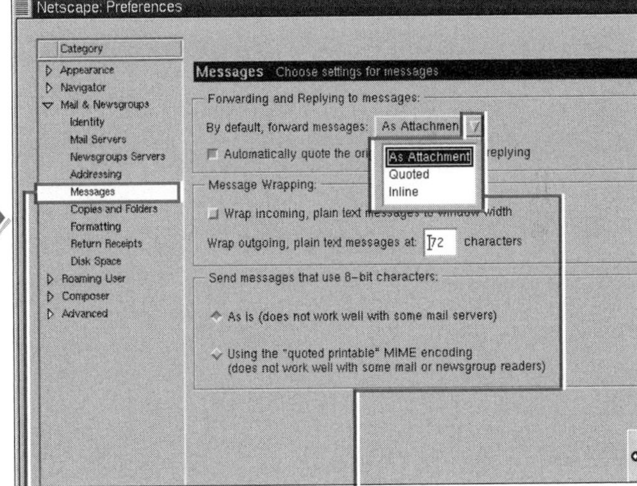

11 Click Messages.

12 If you want to send forwarded messages as anything besides attachments, click the arrow to the right of the default As Attachments and select your choice from the drop-down menu.

SEND AND RECEIVE E-MAIL IN NETSCAPE

Once you've completed setting up Netscape to connect to the Internet, browsed the Web, and located a mail server, you're ready to begin the pleasurable pastime of sending out and receiving e-mail. Receiving mail in the Netscape Messenger utility is a very simple task, only requiring a couple clicks of the mouse and some reasonable typing skills to put together a letter.

Unlike some e-mail programs, Netscape on Linux will not actively get your mail. In order to save CPU cycles and reduce your annoyance level, Netscape won't pull mail from the mail server every 10 to 15 minutes. Instead, if you want to check for mail, you need to click the Get Mail button on the toolbar. The disadvantage to this method is that if you're in a fast-paced network environment, you may not get urgent messages until you feel like checking your mail queue.

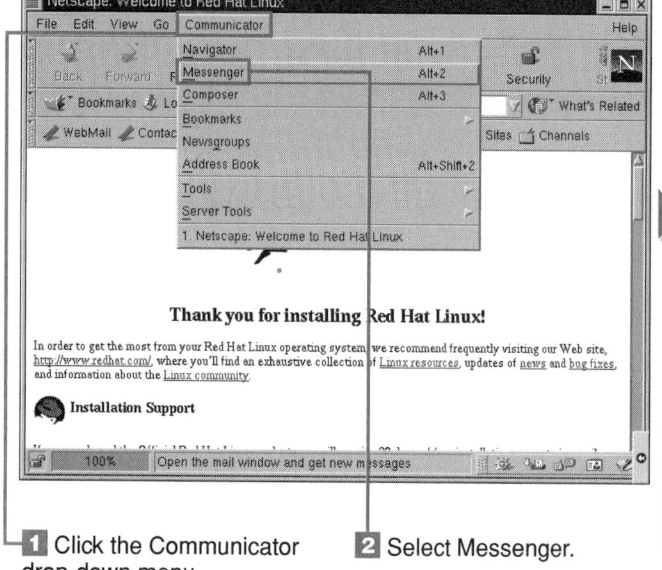

1 Click the Communicator drop-down menu.

2 Select Messenger.

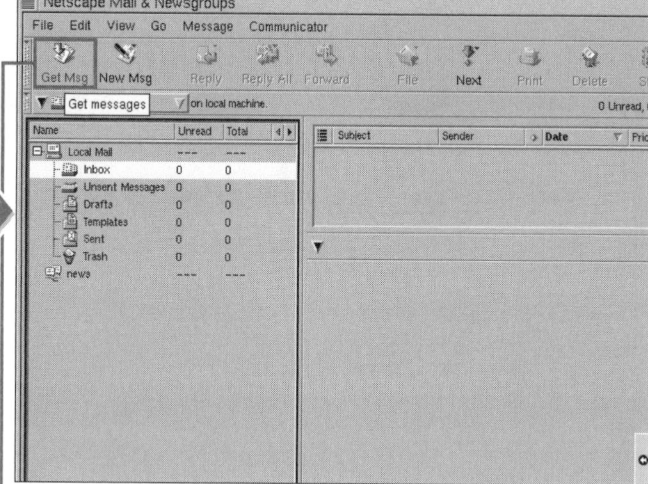

3 Click the Get Msg button to receive e-mail.

■ Any e-mail that has been sent to you since the last time you checked is downloaded from the mail server and sent to you locally.

■ The first time you use this service a prompt may appear asking for your user password.

Are there other ways to get to the Messenger from the main Netscape screen?

- The lower right-hand corner of your Netscape window contains an icon that looks like a letter in a slot. Click this icon to bring up the Netscape Messenger.

What is an e-mail attachment?

- An attachment is a picture or file that you choose to send with your e-mail. Think of it as an extra document you paper clip to your message. Attachments can be of any size (although big ones can slow you down) and in any number.

How can I attach a picture or file to an e-mail?

- When composing e-mail, click the paper clip icon below and to the left of where your recipient's e-mail address is entered. A blank field comes up to the right of the paper clip icon. Click anywhere in this field to be taken to a navigation screen where you can select the file to attach by clicking it once. When you click the Send button, Netscape sends both your message and the file you've attached.

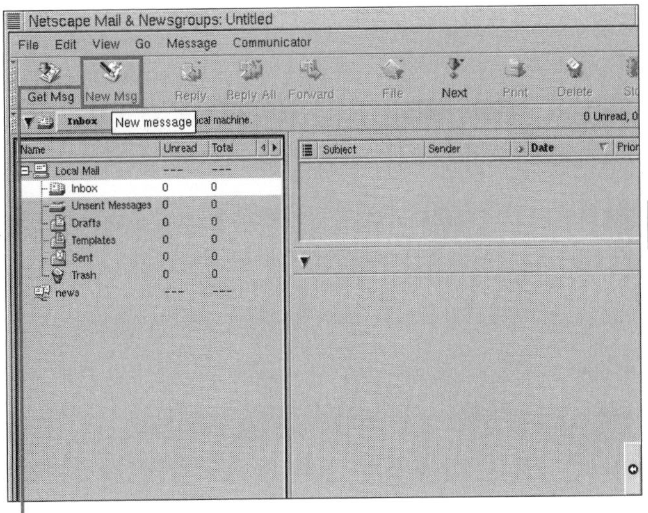

4 To send a message, click the New Msg button.

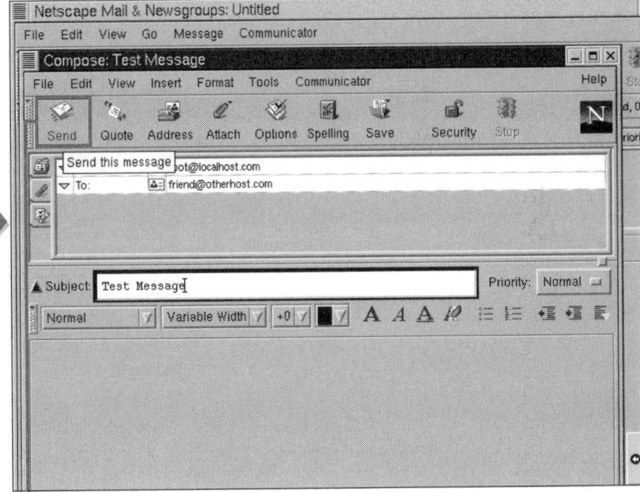

5 After you compose your message, click the Send button on the composition to send.

INSTALL THE APACHE WEB SERVER

You can install the Apache Web Server software on your Linux machine if you plan to use it as a Web server. A Web server is a computer that handles requests for data that come in from the Internet. The data that is sent back consists of text and graphics that make up a Web page. If you plan to make your computer a Web server, you can still run other programs on the computer. However, your computer may run slower during periods when there's a large number of Web page requests.

Apache is the dominant enterprise-class Web server in the independent ISP (Internet service provider) market. You can use Apache for a wide range of Web-based operations, from simple Web page posting to larger, Web farm operations. Also, Apache is amazingly stable and low budget when it comes to draining CPU cycles.

Even if you are not administering the Apache software itself, you can take care of the machine and the operating system it runs on.

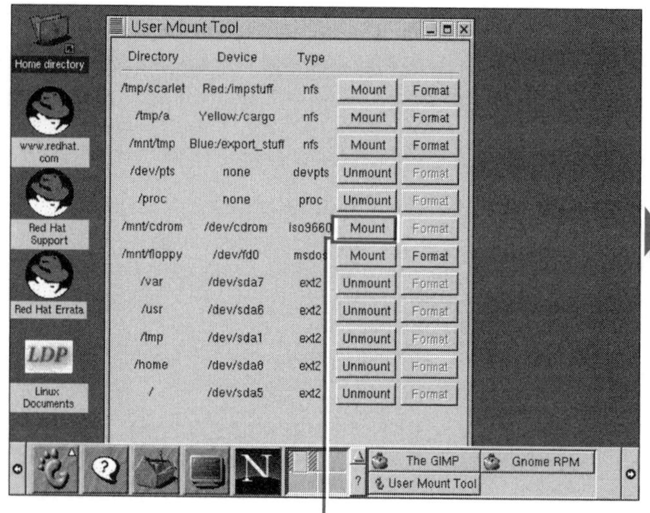

1 Insert your Red Hat CD-ROM into the CD-ROM drive.

2 Click the Main Application button.

3 Highlight System and click Disk Management.

■ The User Mount Tool screen appears.

4 Click Mount next to the CD-ROM drive.

5 Click the Main Application button.

6 In the drop-down menu, highlight System and click GnoRPM, the Red Hat Package Manager.

7 Click the Install button.

TIPS

Is the latest version of the Apache Web server on the CD-ROM in the back of this book?

✓ The CD-ROMs that come with this book contain the latest commercially available version of Apache. Of course, the Apache Web server, like the Linux operating system, is constantly being upgraded, so eventually you may want to install a more recent version. Generally, a major release of an application is worth moving to on an annual basis.

If I'm using a version of Red Hat Linux that didn't come with this book, can I still use these instructions to install Apache?

✓ It's not a guarantee. Red Hat 6.0 is the first version of Red Hat Linux to incorporate the Apache Web server into the LinuxConf utility. If you're using an older version of Red Hat, these instructions may not be as helpful.

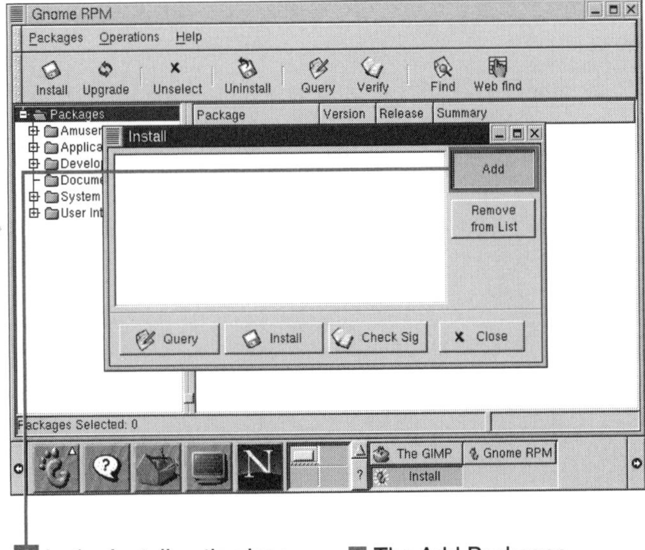

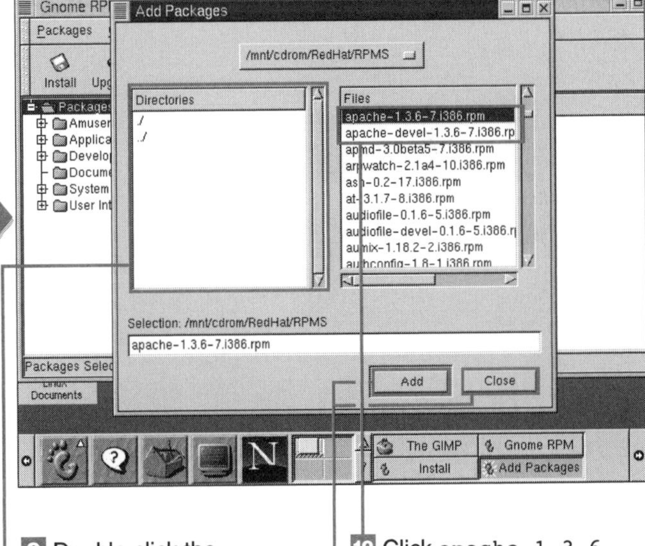

8 In the Install option box, click Add.

■ The Add Packages options box appears.

9 Double-click the directories until you reach `mnt/cdrom/RedHat/RPM`.

■ The `apache` and `apache-devel` files appear in the Files selection box.

10 Click `apache-1.3.6-7.i386.rpm` and `apache-devel-1.3.6-7.i386.rpm` in the right pane.

11 Click Add.

12 Click Close.

CONTINUED

INSTALL THE APACHE WEB SERVER
CONTINUED

You can check to make sure the installation was a success in one of three ways. After the Gnome RPM (Gnome Red Hat Package Manager) has completed installing the selected Apache components, you can then start up the `Linuxconf` utility to view the Apache components on the desktop.

A second way to check on the installation of the Apache components is to locate the `directory /etc/httpd` in the GNOME file manager. You can also navigate to this point using the Linux Terminal and the `cd` (change directory) command by typing **cd /etc/httpd** at the command prompt and pressing Enter.

Finally, you can check on the installation of the Apache Web server components by starting Netscape Navigator. If the components are in their proper places, Netscape shows you a special screen to inform you of this.

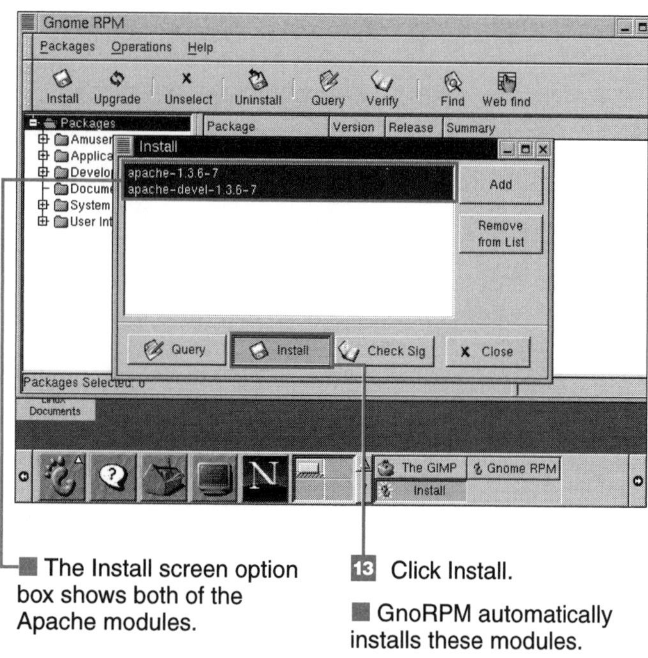

■ The Install screen option box shows both of the Apache modules.

13 Click Install.

■ GnoRPM automatically installs these modules.

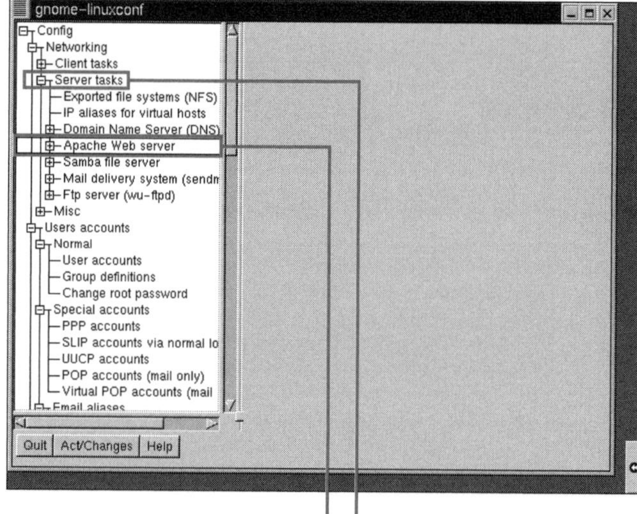

CHECK LINUXCONF UTILITY

1 To check the Apache installation, click the Main Application button.

2 In the drop-down menu, highlight System and click LinuxConf.

3 Click the + sign next to Server tasks to show all the submenus.

■ Apache Web server appears in the directory if it is installed.

TIPS

After I install Apache, do I need to start the http daemon?

- The http daemon (httpd) controls most of the Web-based aspects of the Apache server, so you need to have it running for proper Internet access. You shouldn't have to start this daemon. However, if you do, restart your computer to crank it up because httpd normally starts by default. To see if the httpd daemon is running, use the process `search (ps)` command discussed in Chapter 6. If httpd is running, you see it in the readout printed on-screen by the process search command.

Can I use the Powered by Apache Web logo on my site?

- The Apache Project has graciously allowed any user of its product to prominently display their logo on any site. Be wary of displaying any other kind of corporate logo, however, as you could run into copyright infringements.

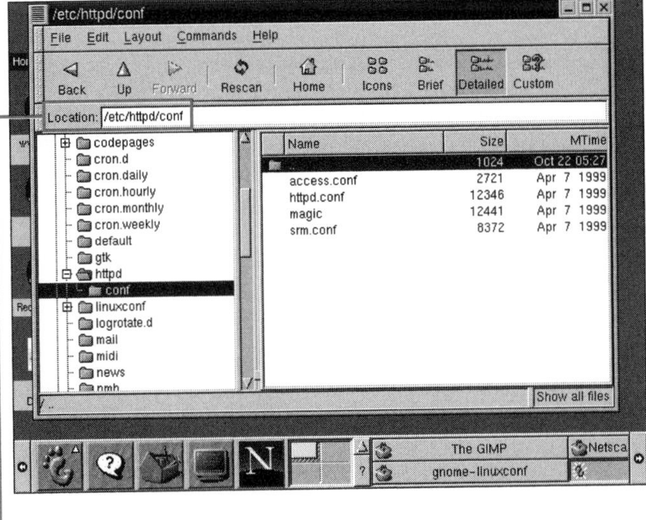

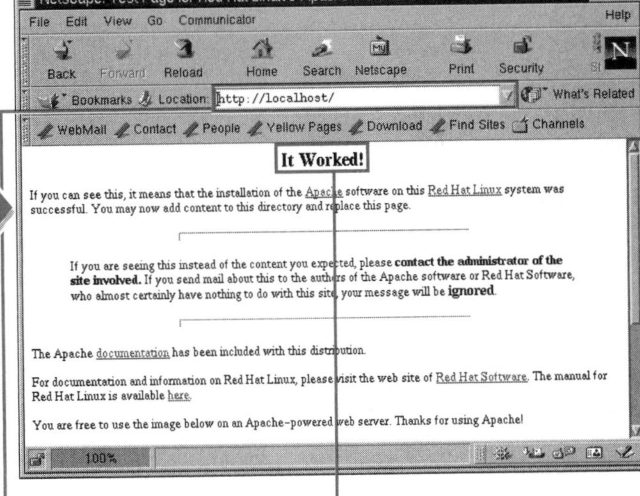

CHECK THE GNOME FILE SYSTEM

1 Click your Home Directory icon to open the GNOME file system.

2 Double-click the directory in the left pane to navigate to `/etc/httpd`.

■ Apache Web server appears in the directory if it is installed.

CHECK THE APACHE INSTALLATION VIA NETSCAPE NAVIGATOR

1 Click the Application or Netscape button to open Netscape Navigator.

2 Type **http://localhost/** in the Location bar.

3 Press Enter.

■ A note appears in the Web browser notifying you if the installation was a success.

CONFIGURE APACHE

You can configure your Apache Web server specifically for your computer setup. Red Hat includes an array of administrative tools that in the GNOME package that works with the Apache server. For example, under the `Linuxconf` utility, you can specify virtual hosts, domains, and even where you like the log files written to in specific areas. Use `Linuxconf` to administer your Web server unless you need to work at a much higher and detailed level.

If you plan to run a Web server that will receive more than a dozen hits, or requests for Web information per day, then make sure to send your server's error log to the `/tmp` directory. This way, Apache can log, or record, all errors made during each request to a file. If a error log gets too large, it can fill up a disk partition and cause the computer to crash. Placing the log in `/tmp` helps prevents this, since the `/tmp` directory is automatically emptied whenever the computer reboots.

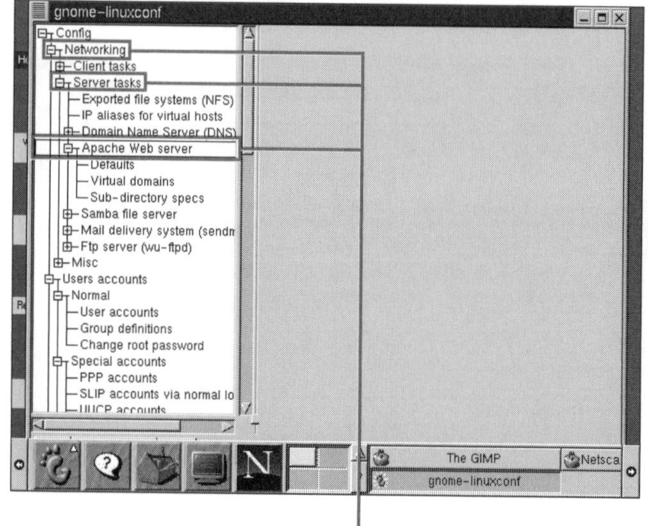

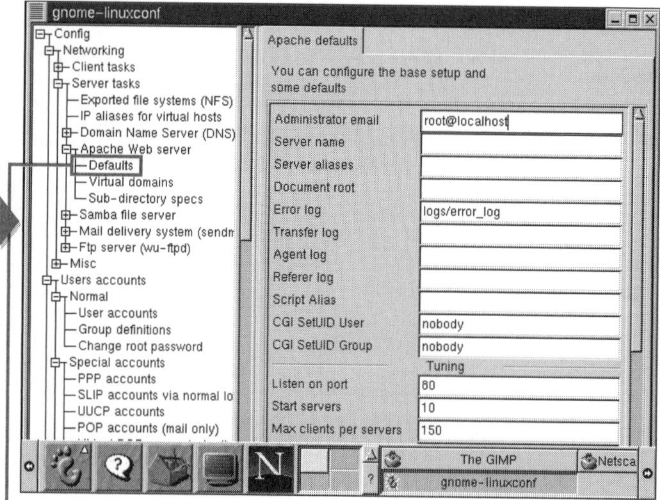

1 Click the Main Application button.

2 In the drop-down menu, highlight System and click LinuxConf.

3 Click Networking, Server tasks, and then Apache Web server to open the Apache Web.

■ Click the + sign if you need to expand the Apache Web server directory.

4 Click Defaults to open the default settings screen.

Why should I send the Apache error log to /tmp?

- You should specify that all application error logs be written to `/tmp`. The `/tmp` directory, or *temporary directory,* is set aside specifically to store nonessential data. It also has less of a chance of filling up, as it is automatically empties when you shut down or restart your computer.

Can I send the Apache server log to a different location?

- You can specify that Apache write its logs to any directory on the computer that you want. Typing in the error log location in the Error log text field under the Apache Defaults panel instructs Apache accordingly.

Can I change the Administrator e-mail address in the Apache defaults panel?

- Yes. By default, Apache sends error messages via e-mail to the `root@localhost` e-mail address. However, you can specify any e-mail address you wish in this field.

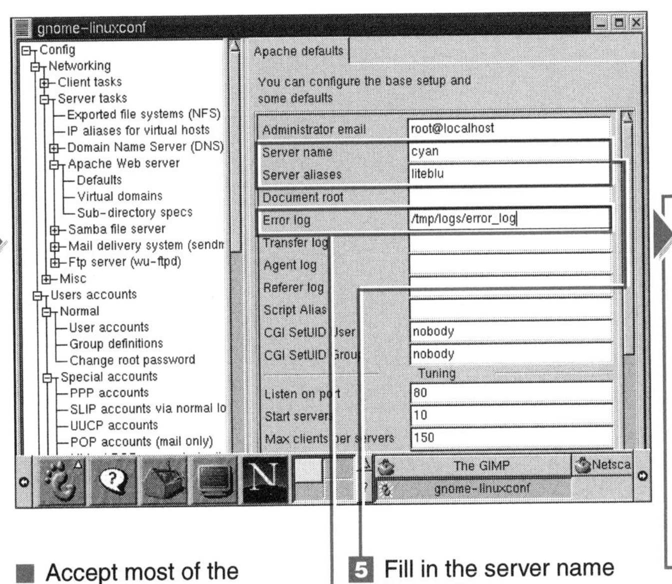

■ Accept most of the defaults, which are set the way the majority of Apache Web servers handle Web information.

5 Fill in the server name and any aliases.

6 Send the error log to `/tmp`.

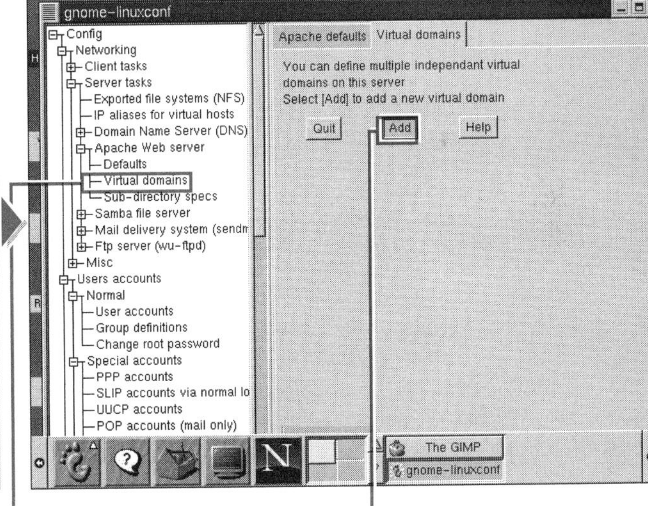

7 Click Virtual domains in the left pane to open the option box.

8 Click the Add button in the right pane.

CONTINUED

CONFIGURE APACHE CONTINUED

You can configure Apache to handle multiple Web sites by adding the names of different computers via the Virtual Host Setup screen in `Linuxconf`. In a virtual host setup, your Linux machine that runs the Apache Web server passes requests for data to other machines that store Web pages, and sends the data back to the user who requested the information.

In this manner, Apache allows your computer to act as a sort of clearinghouse for Web-based information like HTML pages and .GIF files. This process is also called *virtual hosting*. The key to successful Web hosting is that the machine running the Web server application is both stable and able to handle network traffic with a minimum of difficulty. The Linux operating system excels in both of these characteristics, making it a logical and popular choice for a virtual host Web server.

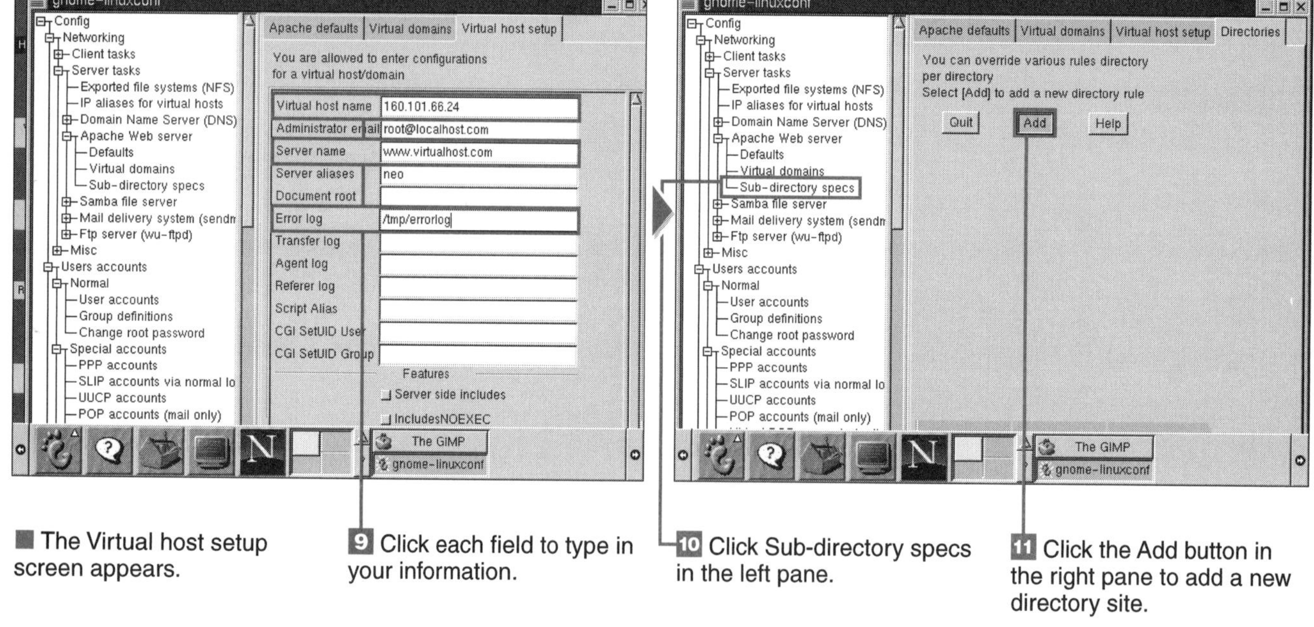

■ The Virtual host setup screen appears.

9 Click each field to type in your information.

10 Click Sub-directory specs in the left pane.

11 Click the Add button in the right pane to add a new directory site.

Do I have to be on the Internet before my site is ready for prime time or can I build the site in private?

- If you select the defaults when configuring Apache, just start constructing your site. Because you're not having Apache respond to any named host yet, no one will see your site as it emerges from construction.

How can I choose a domain name?

- Domain names now come with legal rights, much like a copyright. If you want to register a domain name or see if one is available, check out the Internic site at `www.internic.net`. The Internic acts as a sort of Web registry and copyright protection resource.

Where can I get more information on Apache software?

- The Apache software is developed, debugged, and maintained by the Apache Project, a collaborative, volunteer development effort you can access at `www.apache.org`.

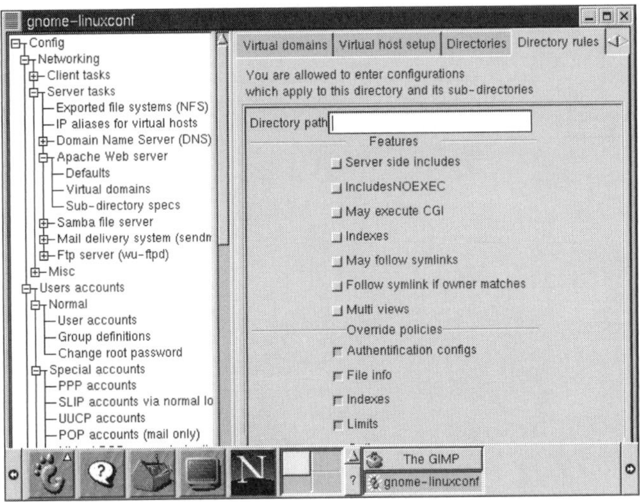

■ The Directory rules screen appears.

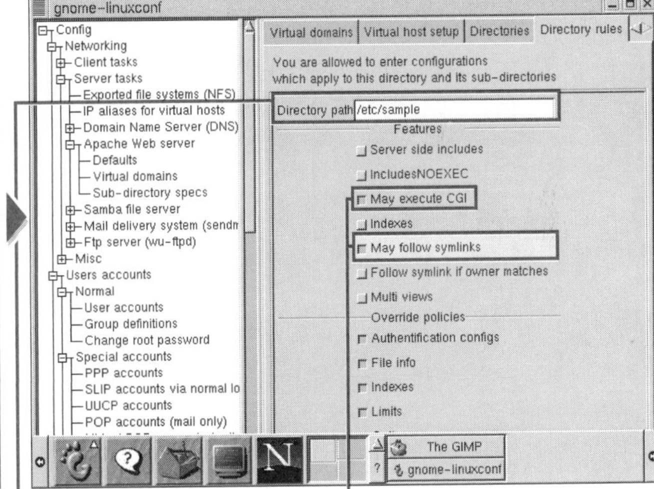

12 To edit this screen, click the Directory path field and type the path you want.

13 Select the options you want for the Directory path by clicking the buttons to the left of the options.

■ The May execute CGI and May follow symlinks options increase functionality and flexibility.

OPEN PINE MAIL

An alternative to Netscape mail is pine mail. pine is the name of an e-mail program that works in the Linux Terminal. You can use it as an alternative to Netscape Messenger if you want to keep your Web browsing program and your e-mail program separate. pine predates Netscape's mail program, and does not even use a GUI of any sort — you type in commands or press keys, but you do not use your mouse to work any part of pine mail.

What is the advantage of choosing pine as your e-mail program? It is native to Linux, making it much more stable than Netscape mail. It is also faster, on average, than Netscape mail because it has no graphics to display. On the other hand, you may experience difficulties when receiving graphics as e-mail attachments in pine mail, so if you get a lot of `.jpgs` or `.bmp` files, you may want to use Netscape Messenger instead.

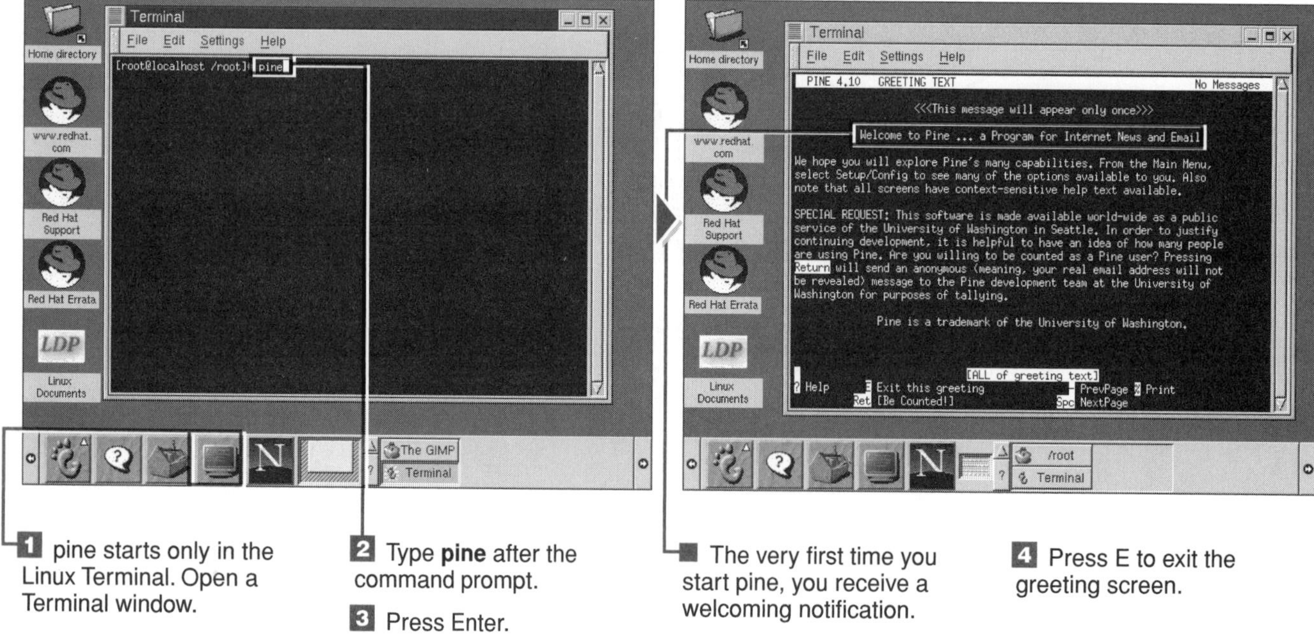

1. pine starts only in the Linux Terminal. Open a Terminal window.
2. Type **pine** after the command prompt.
3. Press Enter.

■ The very first time you start pine, you receive a welcoming notification.

4. Press E to exit the greeting screen.

COMPOSE E-MAIL IN PINE

You can compose e-mail in pine just as if you were using any graphics-based e-mail program, such as Eudora, Netscape Mail, or Microsoft's Internet Explorer's Mail tool. However, instead of clicking the mouse pointer on different text fields to select them (Subject, From, To, and other fields), you press the Enter or Tab key to move from one field to the next. If you need to back track to a field, continue pressing Enter or the Tab key until the cursor cycles back to the field you want.

Because pine is used in the Linux Terminal, many new Linux operating system users become confused when editing text in this mail program. You can write letters in pine, and therefore it is a text editor. However, it does not use the same commands or keys as the `vi` editor, the other major text-editing program in the Linux Terminal. Instead, pine uses keystrokes similar to that of a regular text editor, such as Word or Wordperfect.

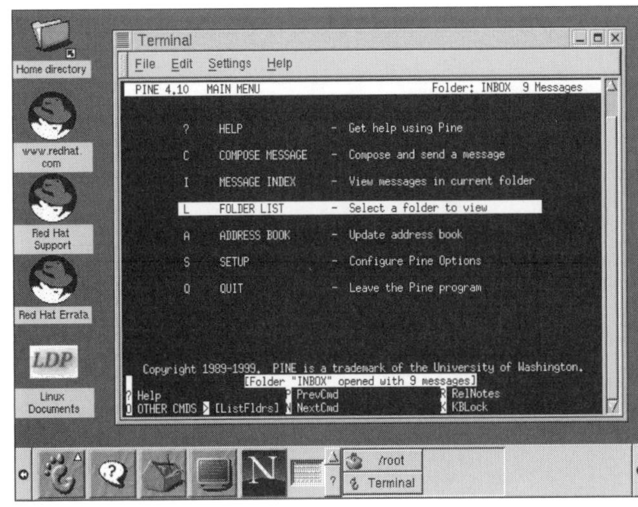

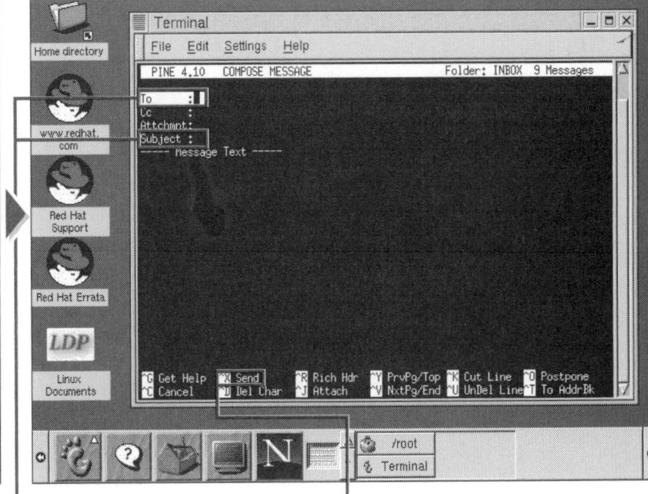

1 Type **pine** at the command prompt and press Enter.

■ Pine Main Menu appears. You can select an option by typing the letter or using the arrow keys to highlighted the roll.

2 Press C.

3 Press Enter.

■ The Compose Message screen appears.

4 Type the destination e-mail address in the To field and press Enter twice.

5 Type the subject of the e-mail and press Enter.

6 Type your message in the body.

7 Press Ctrl+X to send the message.

RECEIVE E-MAIL IN PINE

You can receive and store mail in the location of your choice when you work in pine. Of course, you can delete e-mail that you no longer want or need, and you can view what you decided to delete after you have made your decisions.

pine has its own conventions for receiving and deleting e-mail. pine works with a notification program called biff, which beeps whenever mail comes in. You also see a message at the base of the screen telling you that a message has arrived. When it comes to deleting mail, pine will not remove mail you have selected to delete until you actually exit the program. Even at that point, it asks for confirmation.

Keep in mind that unlike the Recycle Bin option in Microsoft Windows, once you confirm that you want a message deleted, it is no longer retrievable. If you receive a high volume of important e-mail, it's worthwhile to double-check what you're deleteing before comfirming that you want the e-mail removed.

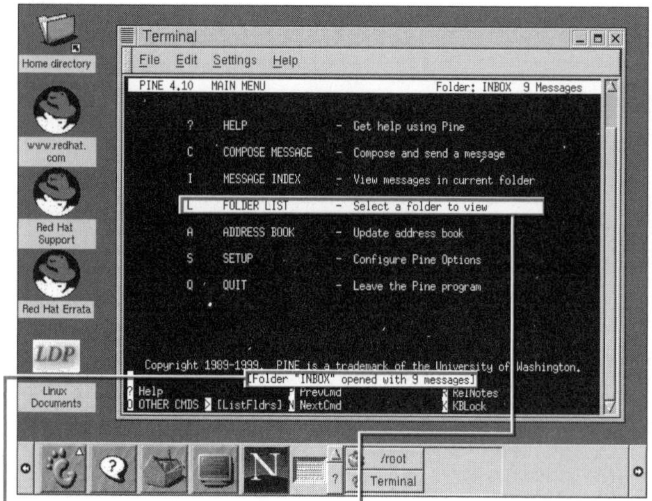

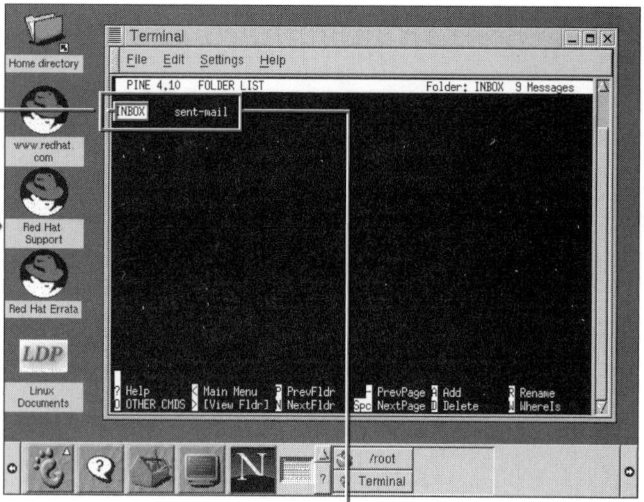

1 Type **pine** at the command prompt and press Enter.

■ If you see a message on the screen that says you have messages, you got mail in that folder.

■ By default, the selection bar highlights the Folder List.

2 Press Enter or the letter L to go to the Folder screen.

3 To view mail in your Inbox, use your arrow keys to highlight the Inbox and press Enter.

■ The two folders you see most often are Inbox and Sent. The Sent box stores all e-mail that you have mailed electronically.

How can I change the order of the messages in my Inbox?

- Unlike newer, GUI-based mail programs, you cannot change the order of the messages to organize them by username, priority, or reverse chronology. pine displays messages stored in the Inbox — or in any of its folders — strictly by chronological order. E-mail is marked according to the date on the sender's machine when the e-mail is sent, not when it is received. If you receive e-mails that are out of date, it means that messages were delayed between your mail server and the sender's.

Why am I unable to see Save under the menu options at the base of the Terminal screen?

- Because pine is not a GUI-based program, it does not have drop-down menus. The designers could only put in a dozen commands at the base of the screen. If you press Ctrl+O for other commands, you see the next dozen commands displayed. Note that the commands do not have to be on the screen at any time for you to use them.

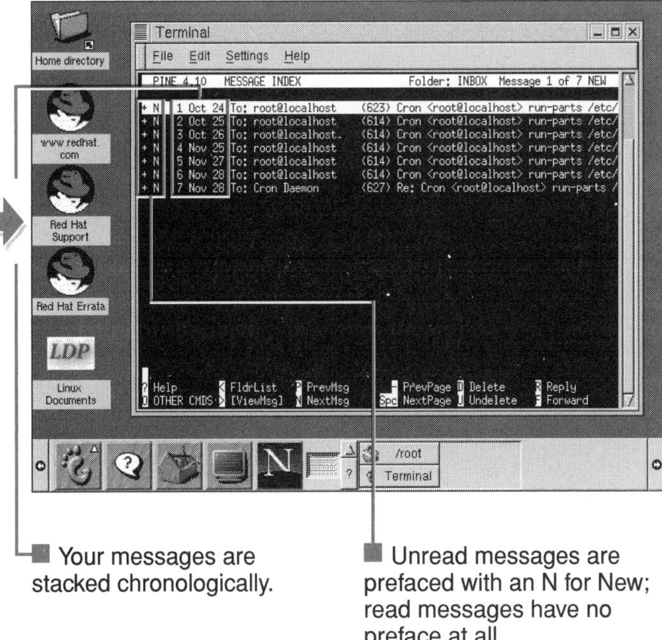

- Your messages are stacked chronologically.
- Unread messages are prefaced with an N for New; read messages have no preface at all.

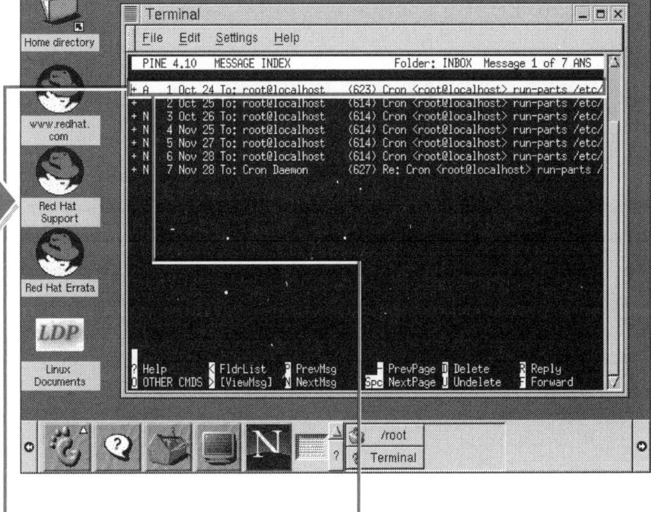

4. To read a message, use the arrow keys to highlight the message and press Enter.
5. Press I (Index Messages) to return to the Inbox screen or R to Reply to the message.

- After you reply, the N in front a message is replaced by an A for answered.

DELETE E-MAIL IN PINE

You can delete e-mail messages in the pine mail program with a single keystroke. Depending on how many e-mails you get in a given day, you should consider deleting the majority of your messages after reading them. Of course, an exception to this rule is when the message contains important information that you may need later in the day.

Deleting e-mail when you are done reading it is a good habit to get into when you first begin using the Linux operating system and its pine mail utility. Having dozens of messages that you do not need in your mail screen is visual clutter, and you may even have to scroll down through these messages to get to the new, more important ones. In addition, valuable disk storage space is wasted if you store previously read messages. Keep in mind that disk space is not freed up until the messages are actually deleted, which takes place when you exit the mail program.

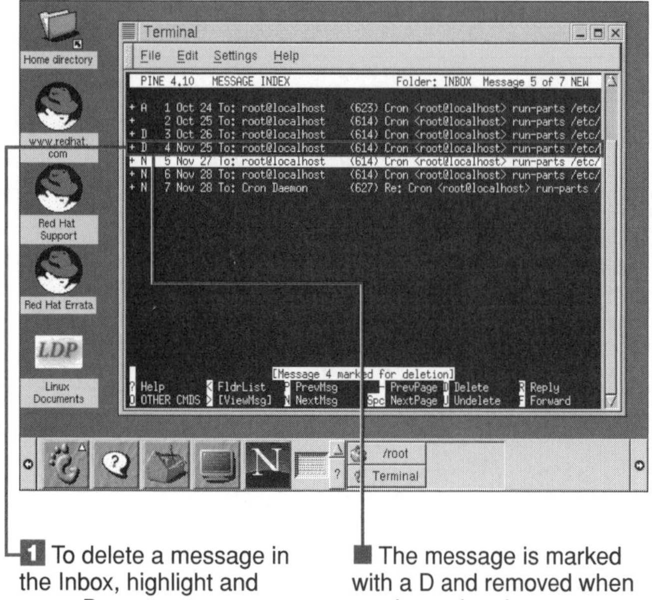

1 To delete a message in the Inbox, highlight and press D.

■ The message is marked with a D and removed when you leave the pine program.

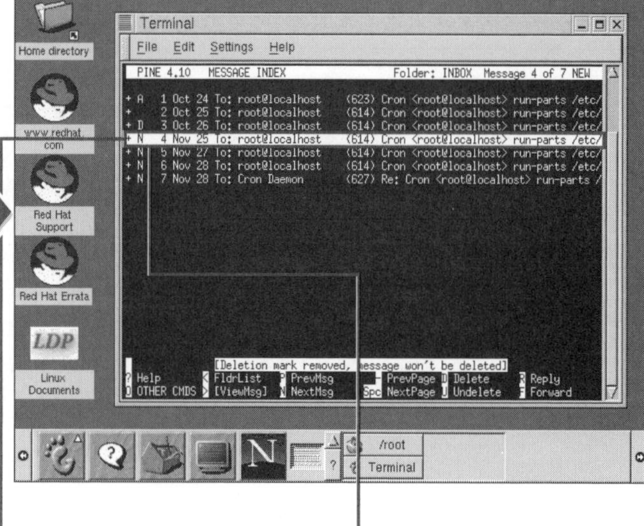

2 If you change your mind, highlight the item and press U for undelete.

■ The D disappears.

SAVE E-MAIL IN PINE

You can save selected e-mail messages for later reading in the pine mail utility. Although you should get into the habit of deleting e-mails when you are done with them, you may consider saving certain e-mails that are of personal value, list a valuable bit of information, or contain a helpful reminder.

Consider creating a series of mail folders in pine where you can save your e-mail by category. For example, you might have separate folders for work and home. If you are a student, you could create chemistry, geography, and calculus folders to store different reports or assignments in separate locations.

Finally, remember that whenever you save an e-mail, pine automatically marks the message as deleted. Pine does this regardless of whether you save your e-mail in the default saved-messages folder that comes with pine, or in a custom mail folder, such as Work or Home.

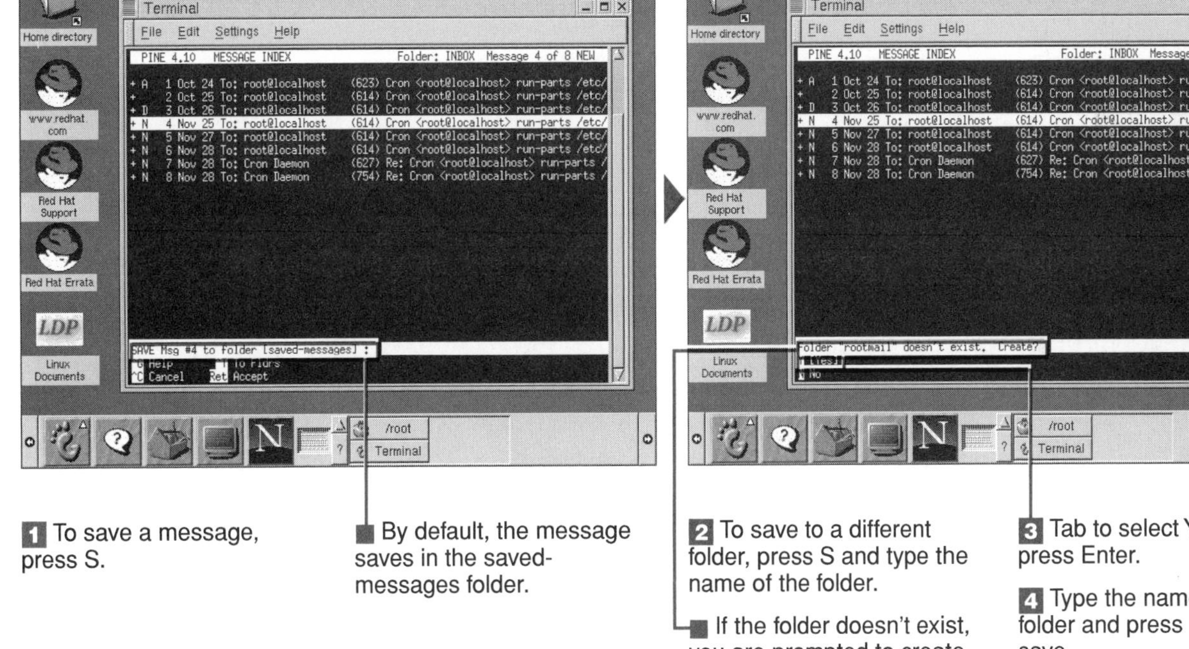

1 To save a message, press S.

■ By default, the message saves in the saved-messages folder.

2 To save to a different folder, press S and type the name of the folder.

■ If the folder doesn't exist, you are prompted to create this folder.

3 Tab to select Yes and press Enter.

4 Type the name of the new folder and press Enter to save.

NAVIGATE AND ADMINISTER YOUR FOLDERS

You can easily and quickly move between mail folders in your pine mail program from the Folder List screen. When you begin working with pine, you will find that creating multiple folders containing different kinds of mail makes your life easier. For example, you can divide mail from the Inbox into folders labeled by priority (High, Medium, and Low) or by function (Sysadmin, Users, and Managers).

In the Folder List screen, you can highlight a folder by selecting it with the arrow keys and pressing Enter to view the list of e-mails within the folder. Inside each folder, the messages display in chronological order on a Mail Index screen as in the default Inbox. You can answer, forward, attach, and delete e-mail messages using the same commands that you use in the Inbox Index screen.

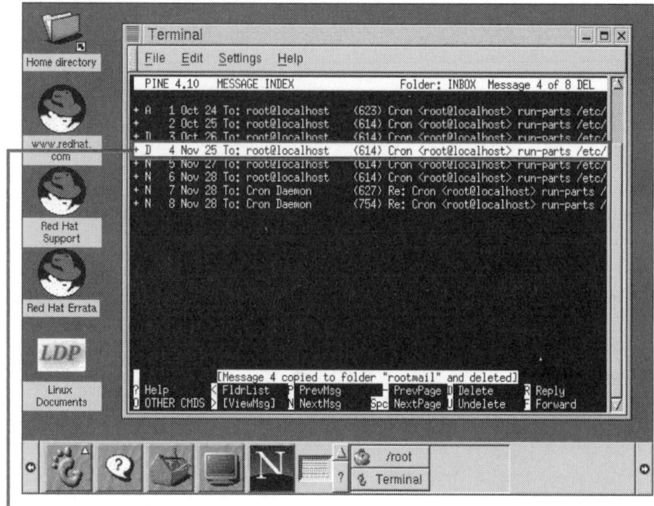

■ When you save a message, it is automatically marked with a D for deletion after you exit pine.

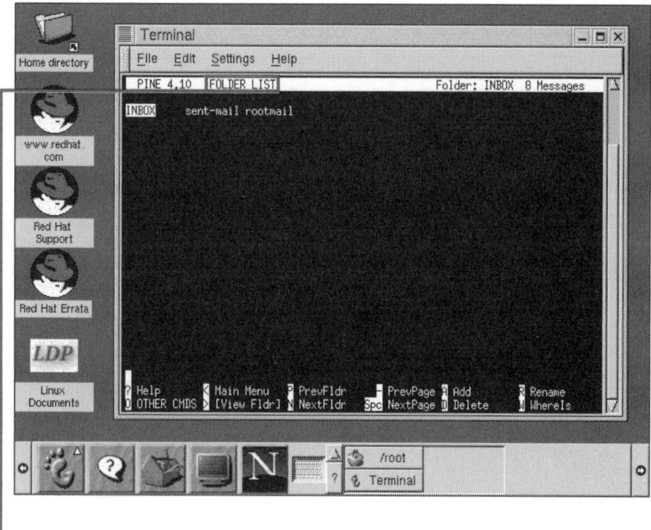

NAVIGATE BETWEEN FOLDERS

1 Press L to get to the Folder List screen.

When I move e-mail messages to another folder, they are marked deleted. How can I prevent these messages from being deleted?

- Use the arrow keys to highlight the e-mail and press U for undelete. Be sure to do this before you exit pine or your mail will be irretrievably lost!

Does pine have a limit to the number of folders I can create?

- There is no theoretical limit, but when you start using more than nine or ten folders, the system starts getting complicated and cumbersome. You are best off not using more than six or seven folders at a time.

Can I create folders inside the folders?

- pine does not allow you to create subfolders. If you need to sort closely related mail messages, create two separate folders with derivative names. For example, separate departmental mail into the folders accountingmail and engineeringmail.

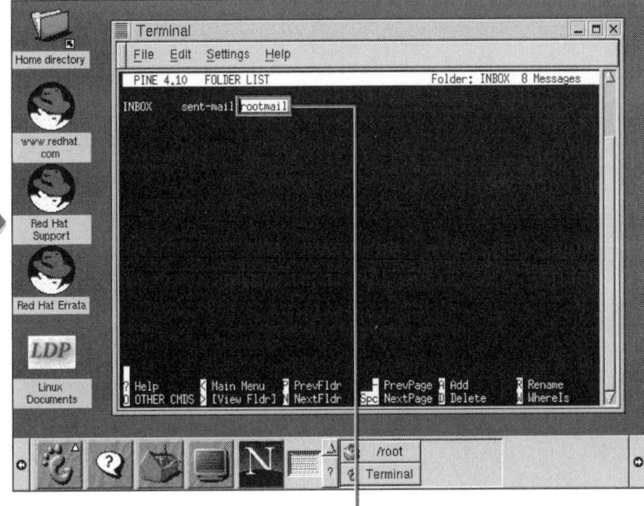

2 To view the contents of another folder, use the arrow keys to move to the folder you want.

3 Press Enter.

■ Another Index screen, with a different list of messages, depending on what you have stored.

DELETE A FOLDER

1 Go to the Folder List screen.

2 Use your arrow keys to highlight the folder.

3 Press D for delete.

■ A verification request appears.

4 Press Y for yes or N for no

■ The deletion takes place in your current pine session.

EXIT THE PINE MAIL PROGRAM

You should quit the pine mail program when you are not using it. Doing so prevents extra CPU cycles from being taken up on a busy network, and it lessens the chance of a malicious prankster sending out rude or inappropriate e-mails from your pine mail account.

pine is unique among mail programs in that it does not delete any e-mail that you want to get rid of until you exit the program. Before you quit pine, any messages you want to delete are only marked as deleted. This was a decision made by pine's original designers, who felt that the program would run more efficiently if it did not waste CPU cycles deleting e-mail while you were still viewing messages.

When exiting pine, you are always asked if you want to get rid of the e-mails marked for deletion. This prevents you from accidentally deleting e-mail you may want to save.

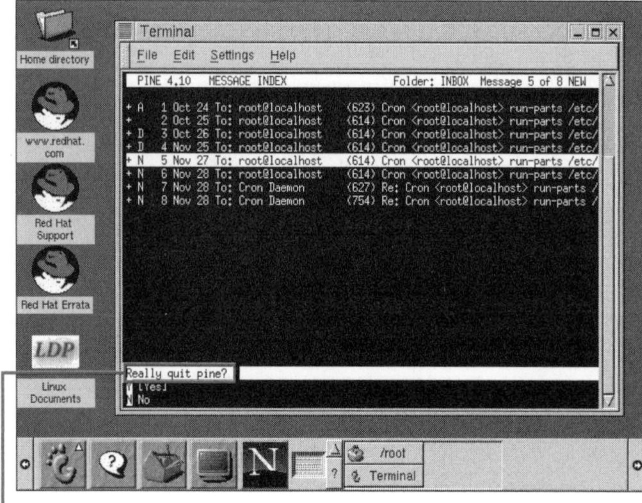

1 Press Q to exit the folder and leave pine.

■ A verification request appears.

2 Press Enter to confirm.

■ Confirm whether you want to delete the e-mails.

3 Press Y for yes or N for no.

Where do the files go if I decide not to delete any messages before I complete my pine shutdown?

- The files are not stored anywhere special — they remain in the Inbox. For example, if you deleted a message in the Inbox and then changed your mind as you left pine, the message would stay in the Inbox, minus the deletion mark.

pine has no set limit to the number of e-mails I can store. Should I just leave them where they are instead of deleting them?

- pine does not have limits. However, your system may have space quotas or other limits set outside pine. Furthermore, if you start holding a few hundred messages, your program will start noticeably slowing down. Back up e-mail to tape or floppy, then start trimming your stored e-mails to keep pine moving quickly.

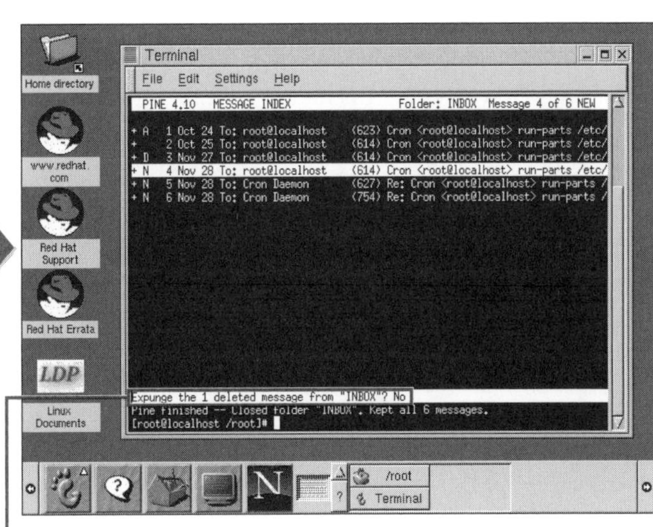

■ If you choose no, the command prompt returns and the messages remain in their current location. The D is removed when you restart pine.

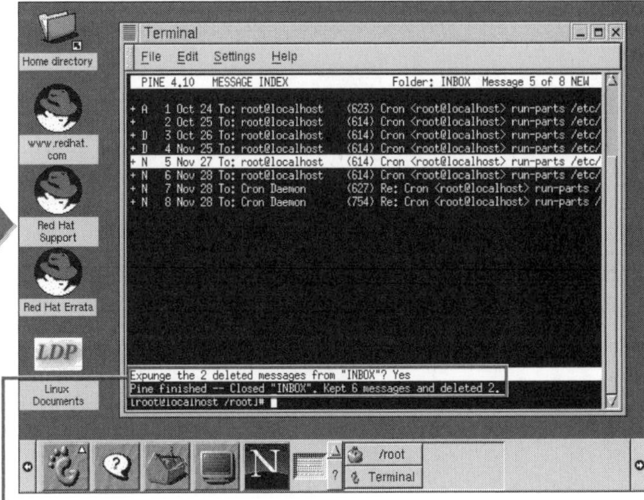

■ If you choose yes, the number of messages for deletion appears, as well as the number kept.

■ The Linux Terminal command prompt appears.

SECTION VII

25) YOUR SECURITY SCHEME

Change the User Account Password 460
Set Up Screen Savers to Increase Security 464
Set Password and File Permission Policies 466
Set File Permissions in GNOME 468
Set File Permissions in the Linux Terminal 469

26) TRACK USERS ON YOUR SYSTEM

Find out Who's on the Machine 470
Retrieve User Information 471
Determine User Activity 472

27) REPAIRING A SECURITY BREACH

Check System Permissions 474
Check Configuration Logs 478
Shut Down System Daemons 479
Using the Schema Manager 480

CHANGE THE USER ACCOUNT PASSWORD

Your first, best line of defense against unscrupulous users or cyber-saboteurs is the proper changing of user account passwords on your system. An open, guessed, or stolen password is as good as handing the keys of your house or car to a burglar. Depending on your system's security needs, you may want to insist that users change their passwords on a quarterly or yearly basis, or whenever you require your users to do so.

Two kinds of people exist from whom you want to protect your system: fellow users who may want to play around with your system under another's account name, and crackers.

A *hacker* is simply someone who likes to work with computers. In contrast, a *cracker* is someone who tries to crack your system so he or she can vandalize or do other kinds of malicious damage.

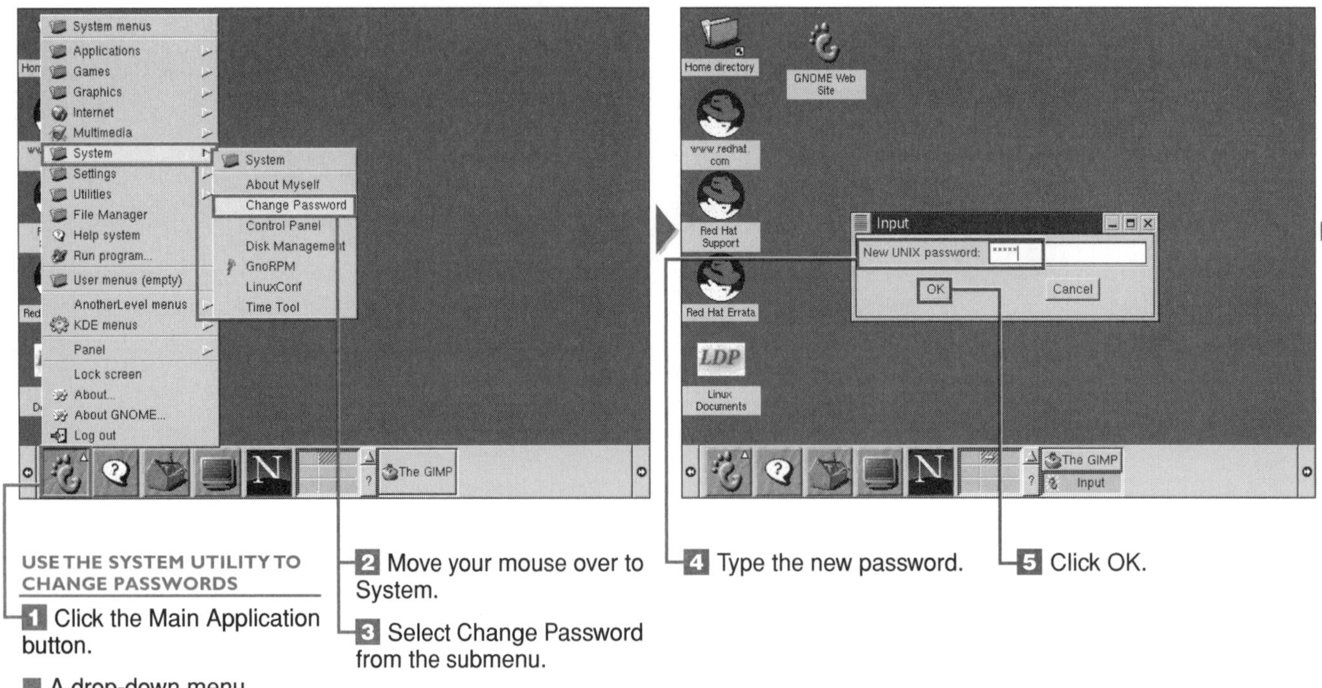

USE THE SYSTEM UTILITY TO CHANGE PASSWORDS

1 Click the Main Application button.

■ A drop-down menu appears.

2 Move your mouse over to System.

3 Select Change Password from the submenu.

4 Type the new password.

5 Click OK.

Why is the Changing Password screen labeled the 'New UNIX Password' field?

- Remember that Linux is an offshoot of the older UNIX operating system. Because of their deeply shared roots, Linux shares a large number of similar files. It also shares a number of naming conventions, which is why this screen is labeled UNIX.

Can regular users set their account passwords with this utility?

- Regular users cannot use this utility to set their passwords. Only the root (the administrative account) can access the System menu and the utilities under it.

If so, then how can regular users change their passwords?

- Regular users can change their password by opening a Linux Terminal and typing the `passwd` command. This command prompts them to enter in their old password and the new one they want to use. The changes they make will take effect immediately.

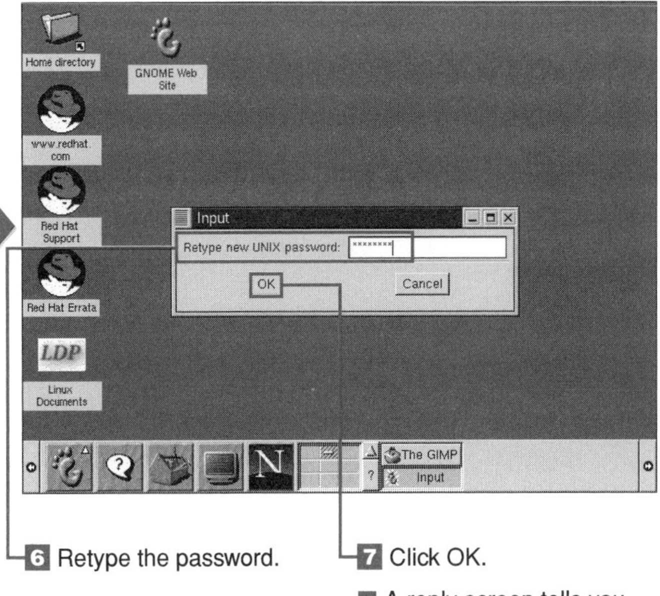

6 Retype the password.

7 Click OK.

■ A reply screen tells you the change was made.

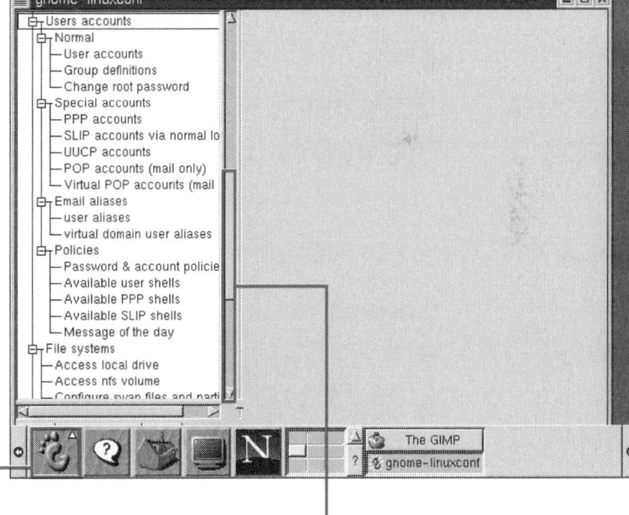

USE LINUXCONF TO CHANGE USER ACCOUNT PASSWORDS

1 Click the Main Application button.

2 Move your mouse over System to highlight

3 Select LinuxConf.

4 Scroll down to Users accounts.

CONTINUED

CHANGE THE USER ACCOUNT PASSWORD CONTINUED

You can also use the `LinuxConf` utility to change passwords for your users' accounts. Your main advantage in using LinuxConf to do this is the built-in screening feature that is part of the Passwords & account policies panel.

LinuxConf screens each password that you enter and warns you if the password you've chosen to enter is too short, too long, or a word that can be found in a standard dictionary. By default, LinuxConf requires that you choose a password that is at least six characters long. There is no upper limit to how long you can make your password.

You can choose to set up more stringent standards for choosing a password in LinuxConf. For example, you can require that the minimum length of a password be eight or ten letters long, and that at least one of these characters must be a number instead of a letter.

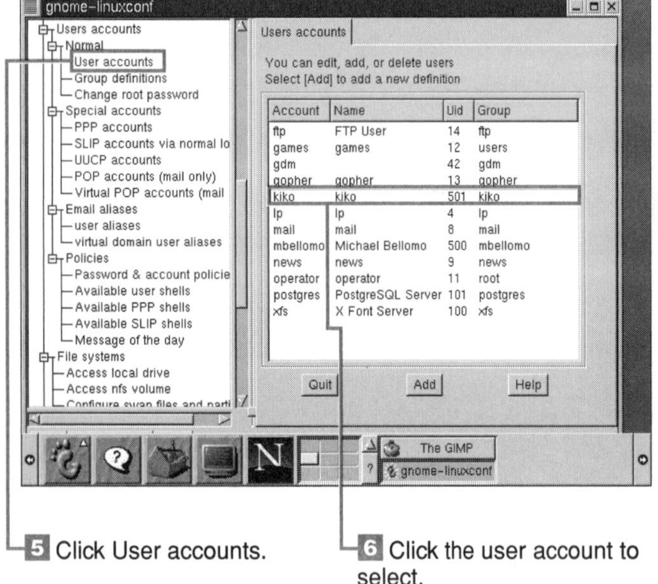

5 Click User accounts.

6 Click the user account to select.

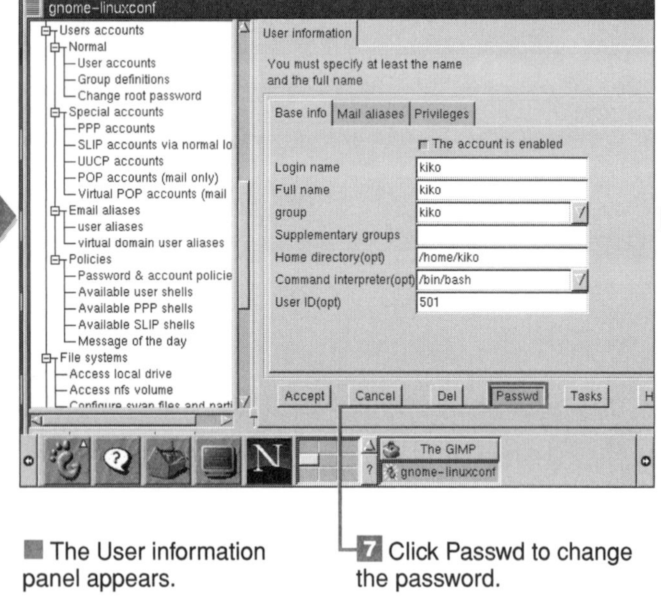

■ The User information panel appears.

7 Click Passwd to change the password.

If I use LinuxConf to change a password, why doesn't it ask me to type the old password?

- Since only root can run the `LinuxConf` utility, the extra step of verifying that the user has permission to edit this file is not needed.

Why does Linux complain that a given password is too close to a dictionary term?

- Because many people pick passwords that are regular, everyday expressions, many cracking programs start by running the password against a dictionary of words. Therefore, you shouldn't pick a word you can find in a standard dictionary as your user account password.

What if I want to use a 'dictionary' word as my password anyway?

- If you insist on using a password that is a word you can find in the dictionary, LinuxConf can't stop you. It only reminds you that choosing such a word decreases your system's security.

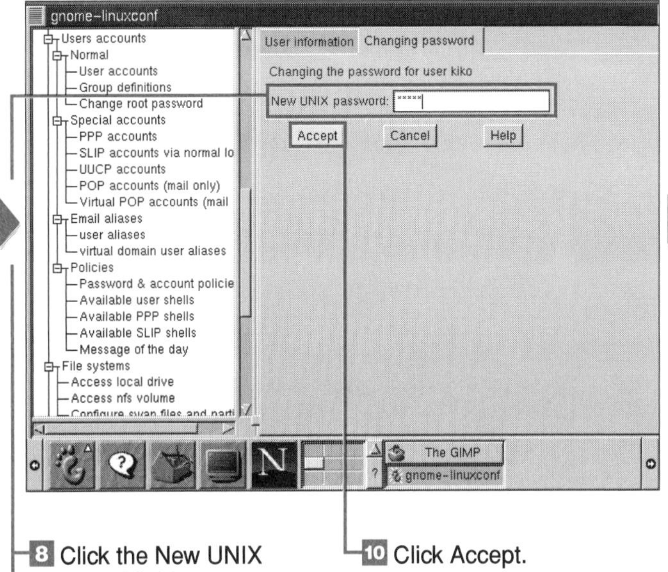

8 Click the New UNIX password field.

9 Type the new password you want to assign to the user.

10 Click Accept.

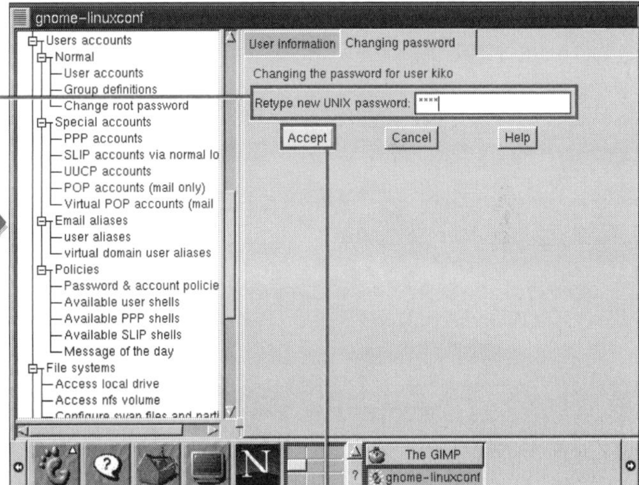

11 Retype the password to confirm it.

12 Press Enter.

SET UP SCREEN SAVERS TO INCREASE SECURITY

You can use your screen saver to enhance your everyday level of security by making sure that your screen saver is set up to lock your screen.

A *screen saver* is a program that activates when you leave your computer inactive for any length of time. It usually blanks your desktop out and plays some sort of moving pattern or picture until you touch the keyboard or move the mouse again.

The original reason for a screen saver was to prevent screen burn-in. The phosphorous dots that make up the screen image actually can be burned into your monitor, causing a ghost image on the screen, if the image is displayed for days at a time.

You can set the screen saver so that it requires you to enter your password to get back to the desktop. This increases your system's security with minimal effort.

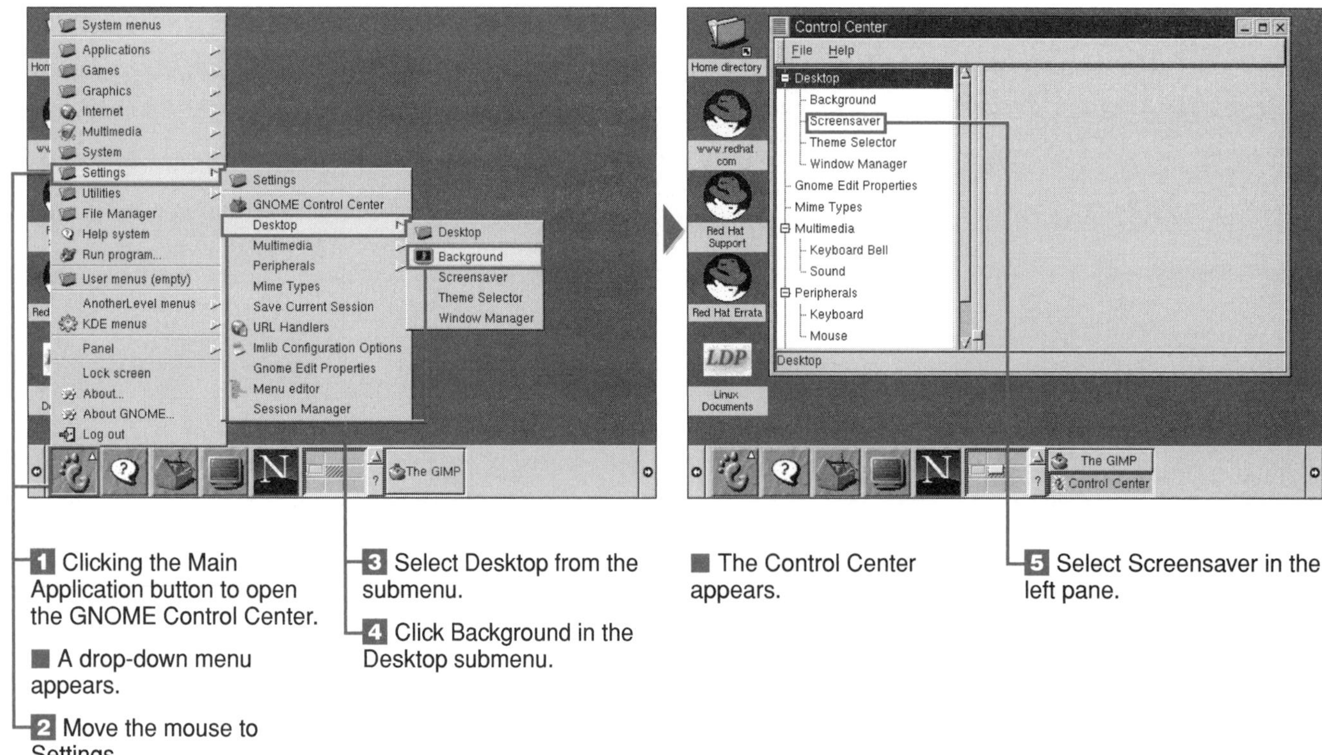

1 Clicking the Main Application button to open the GNOME Control Center.

■ A drop-down menu appears.

2 Move the mouse to Settings.

3 Select Desktop from the submenu.

4 Click Background in the Desktop submenu.

■ The Control Center appears.

5 Select Screensaver in the left pane.

When I select 'Require Password,' do I need to create a new password to unlock the screen saver?

- No. The screen saver will require you to enter the same password you already use to log into the computer.

How do I get back to the desktop if the screen saver locks the computer?

- When you next move the mouse or touch the keyboard, the screen saver freezes and asks you for your username and password. If you make a mistake, the screen saver warns you and lets you try again.

How long should I let my computer sit idle before the screen saver activates?

- If your security needs are high, then consider setting it to five minutes or less. If you leave your machine logged in all day and your security needs are low, set it for 10 or 20 minutes.

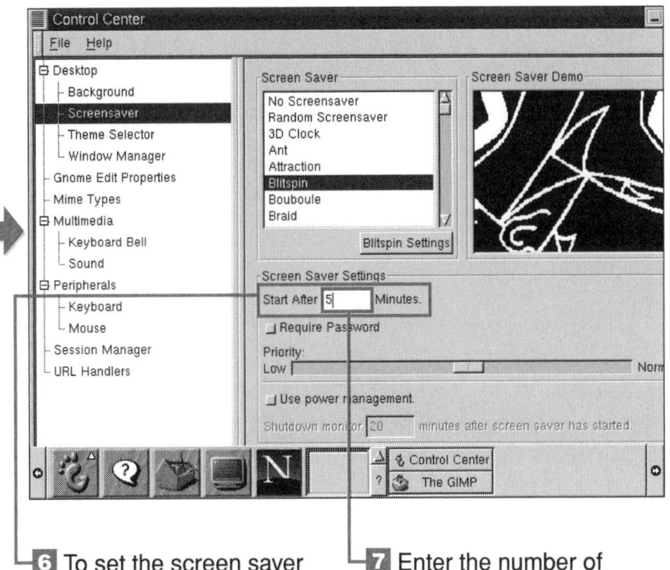

6 To set the screen saver timer, click the Start After Minutes field.

7 Enter the number of minutes for the setting.

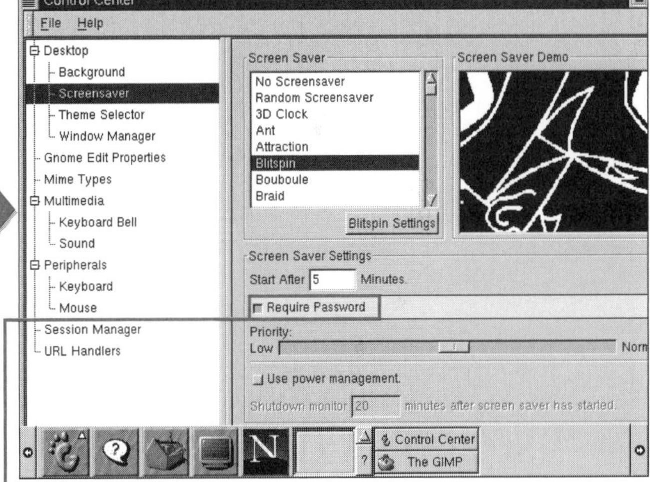

8 To set the security measure on your screen saver, click Require Password.

9 Click the OK button to exit.

SET PASSWORD AND FILE PERMISSION POLICIES

You can set the default policies for your system's file permissions and user passwords in the `LinuxConf` utility. By doing this, you free yourself from having to enforce your methods across the system because the files and user passwords have to conform to the standard that you set. This will allow you to raise the general level of security and reduce access to sensitive parts of the Linux operating system.

For example, if you note that lazy users are entering passwords like *hi* or *go*, then you can change the requirement for password length. You can also make sure that your users aren't simply picking words out of the dictionary by requiring that they use one or more non-alpha numeric characters are used in their passwords.

For example, if a user decides to use an easily cracked password such as *tools*, the system reject it. Instead, if you specify that a user must use at least one non-alphanumeric character, the user can use *too!s* or *tool$*, which are much harder passwords to crack.

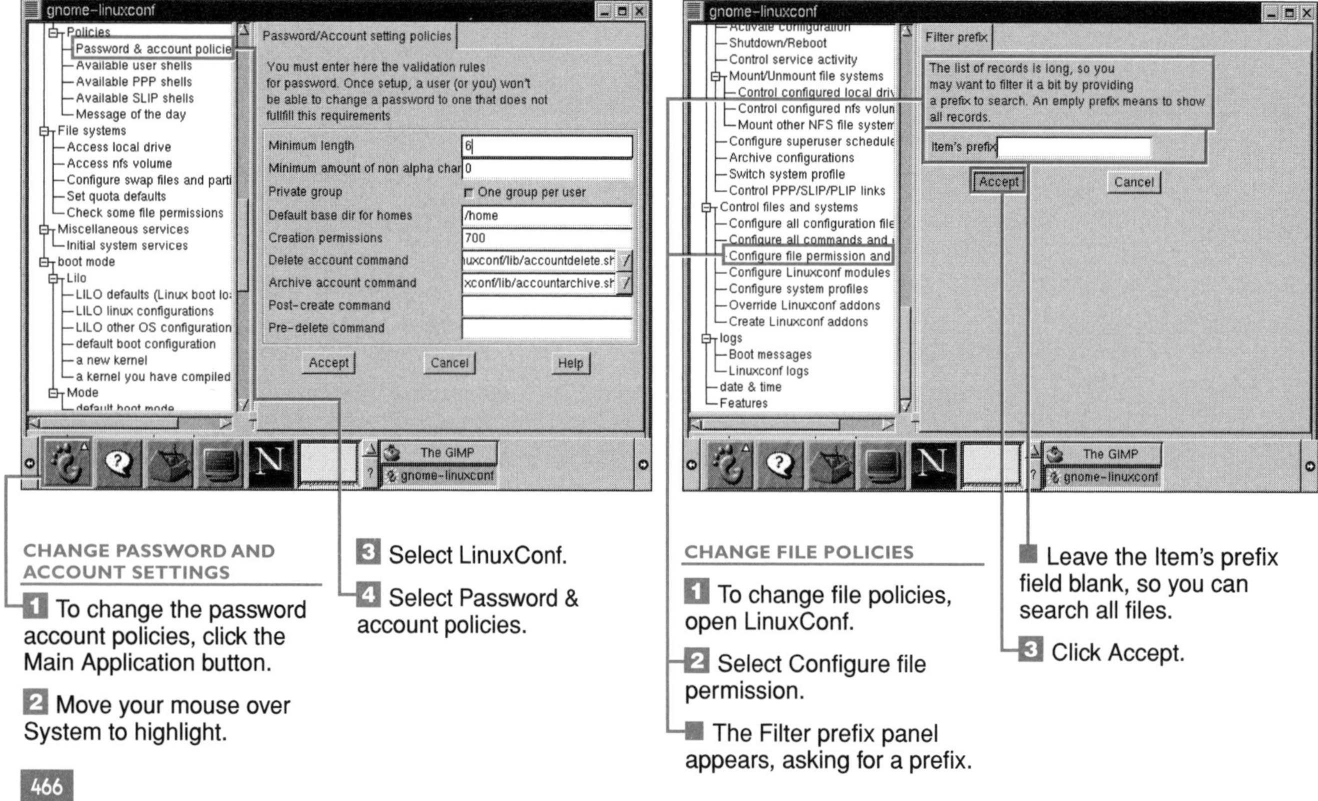

CHANGE PASSWORD AND ACCOUNT SETTINGS

1 To change the password account policies, click the Main Application button.

2 Move your mouse over System to highlight.

3 Select LinuxConf.

4 Select Password & account policies.

CHANGE FILE POLICIES

1 To change file policies, open LinuxConf.

2 Select Configure file permission.

■ The Filter prefix panel appears, asking for a prefix.

■ Leave the Item's prefix field blank, so you can search all files.

3 Click Accept.

When should the password policy settings be edited?

- Ideally, when you initially set up a Linux system, you should edit the policies at the start so that users coming on to your system immediately begin using your settings. However, if that's not possible, then you can change the settings whenever you feel the time is convenient, such as on a quarterly basis.

Will this affect current accounts?

- Unfortunately, if you have problems with users who have two or three letter passwords and you set the policy for six-letter passwords, users will not be forced to change their passwords until the next time they run the **passwd** command.

Should I just change a user's password by myself to avoid these problems?

- You certainly can, but this could cause friction between you and your users. Even if you're the administrator, you should try to take your users' wishes into account.

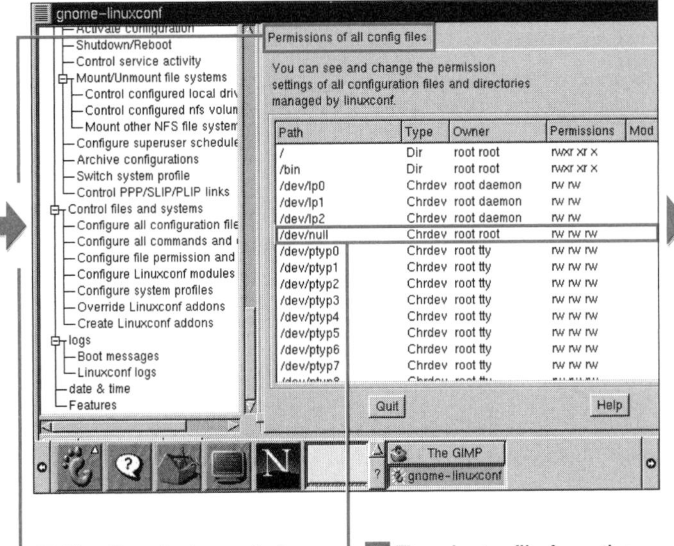

■ The Permissions of all config files screen appears.

4 To select a file from the list, click once.

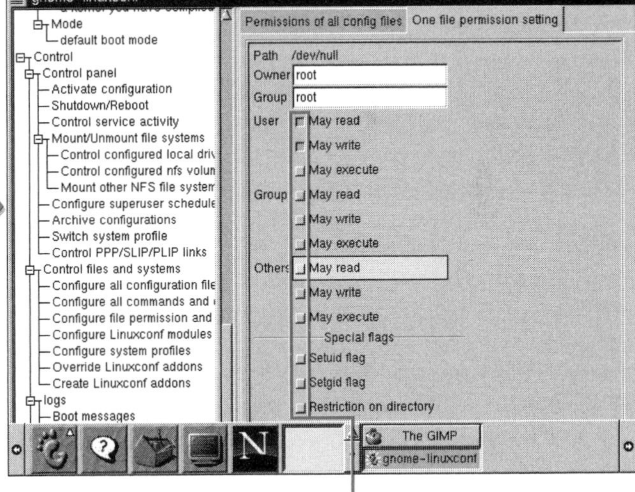

5 In the One file permission settings screen, click the permission buttons to select or de-select write and read privileges to the file.

SET FILE PERMISSIONS IN GNOME

You can also set read, write, and execute permissions on a file in the GNOME graphic desktop environment. By allowing you access to the Properties that make up a given file's parameters, you can make a file visible to only the user, the user and his or her group, or open the access to everyone on the system. The advantage to using the GNOME desktop for this task is that you can select permissions by clicking on a few buttons. Of course, you can also set these permissions in the Linux Terminal. When working with Linux files, you can use the `chmod` command to change or modify the permissions on any file that you own (see Chapter 4). Of course, if you're the root account, you automatically have permission to change the parameters of any file, regardless of ownership.

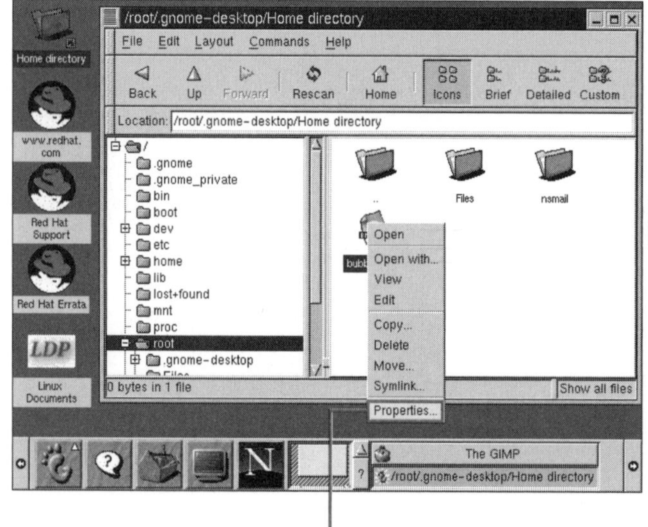

1 In your home directory on the GNOME desktop, right-click the icon of the file that you want to restrict read permissions for everyone but the user.

2 Select Properties from the pop-up menu.

3 Select the Permissions tab.

4 De-select the depressed buttons in the Read column for each row but the user.

SET FILE PERMISSIONS IN THE LINUX TERMINAL

You can set file permissions from within the Linux Terminal as well as from the GNOME desktop. Your first goal in restricting file permissions should be to determine which files need to be restricted so that your general user community cannot read them.

The most private files should be ones of a sensitive business or personal nature. A company stock report or payroll file should probably not be available for public consumption. Also, a user's mail files should not be on display in case there is a pertinent message that others shouldn't be reading.

Remember that no matter how restrictive you make the file permissions on a sensitive document, there is a way that the file is readable. The one account that can bypass all file security is the root account. Your top priority over file security should be the protection of the root password.

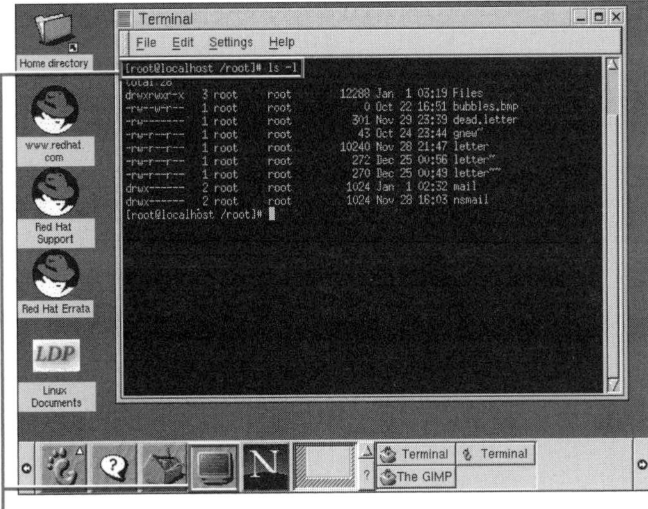

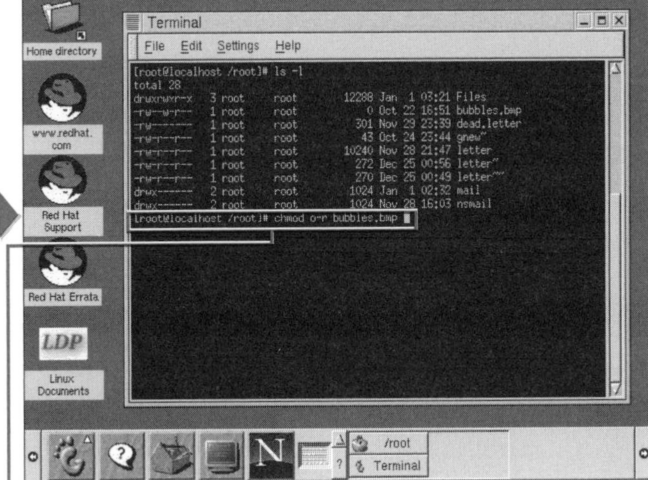

RESTRICT FILE PERMISSIONS FROM THE LINUX TERMINAL

1 Open a Linux Terminal window.

2 List files in long form by typing **ls –l** at the command prompt.

3 Press Enter for the listing.

4 Remove the read permissions from a file by typing **chmod o-r <filename>.**

5 Press Enter.

■ The file Read permissions is revoked for everyone but the user.

FIND OUT WHO'S ON THE MACHINE

You can keep tabs on who is logged into your Linux machine with the `who` utility. By monitoring user activity, you can usually stop trouble before it occurs. You can also use the same tools to locate the cause of an ongoing problem, such as a user account that is exhibiting suspicious behavior.

Suspicious behavior varies from system to system, depending on your level of security and the nature of your organization. However, most of the time, suspicious activity includes running programs that only `root` should be able to, editing system files (such as `/etc/passwd`) that affect the entire system, or hogging network connectivity by spawning multiple `rlogin`, `telnet`, or ftp processes.

Keep in mind that although you may see a user performing an illegal action, the user isn't necessarily the one doing the illegal activity. What you are viewing is a user account, not the user. The user's account could be stolen or commandeered by someone else with malicious purposes.

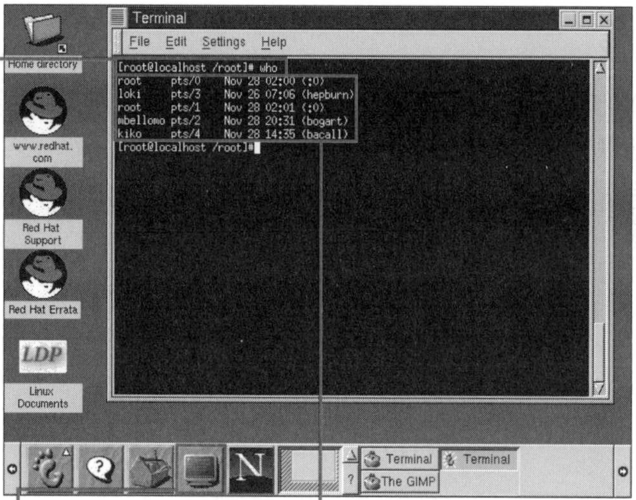
Terminal
File Edit Settings Help
[root@localhost /root]# who
root pts/0 Nov 28 02:00 (:0)
loki pts/3 Nov 26 07:06 (hepburn)
root pts/1 Nov 28 02:01 (:0)
mbellomo pts/2 Nov 28 20:31 (bogart)
kiko pts/4 Nov 28 14:35 (bacall)
[root@localhost /root]#
Home directory
www.redhat.com
Red Hat Support
Red Hat Errata
LDP
Linux Documents
Terminal
Terminal
The GIMP

1 To find out who is using your system, open a Linux Terminal.

2 Type **who** at the command prompt.

3 Press Enter.

■ The users' name appears on your network.

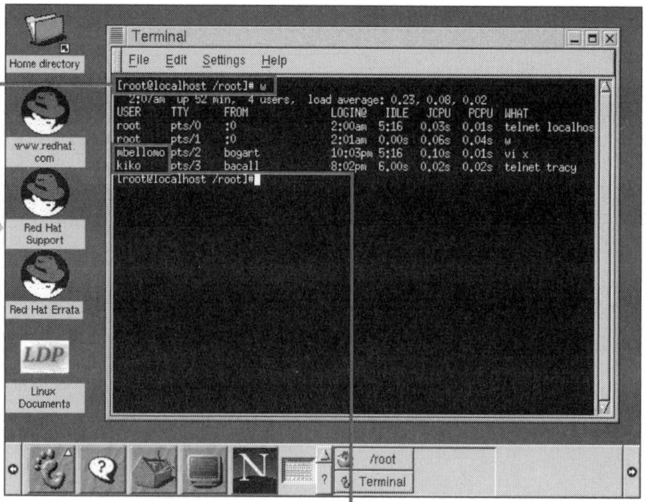
Terminal
File Edit Settings Help
[root@localhost /root]# w
2:07am up 52 min, 4 users, load average: 0.23, 0.08, 0.02
USER TTY FROM LOGIN@ IDLE JCPU PCPU WHAT
root pts/0 :0 2:00am 5:16 0.03s 0.01s telnet localhos
root pts/1 :0 2:01am 0.00s 0.06s 0.04s w
mbellomo pts/2 bogart 10:03pm 5:16 0.10s 0.01s vi x
kiko pts/3 bacall 8:02pm 6.00s 0.02s 0.02s telnet tracy
[root@localhost /root]#
Home directory
www.redhat.com
Red Hat Support
Red Hat Errata
LDP
Linux Documents
/root
Terminal

4 For more information about what the users are doing, press W.

■ User mbellomo is using the `vi` editor on file `x`, while kiko is telneting to a machine called tracy.

RETRIEVE USER INFORMATION

You can retrieve information about any user on your network with the `finger` command. `finger`, which runs in the Linux Terminal, allows you to see what is contained in the user's system files, including the user's account name, full (real) name, and any other information that they've put into their personal profile, such as a sample document, or even a picture.

The `finger` command is useful from the security administrator standpoint, as well, because it allows you to determine how long a user has been logged into a system. What's more, it allows you to find out how long the user has been on the system, but in an inactive state. As explored earlier, a logged-in account that is just sitting there is always a target for crackers or users who want to take an account for a joyride.

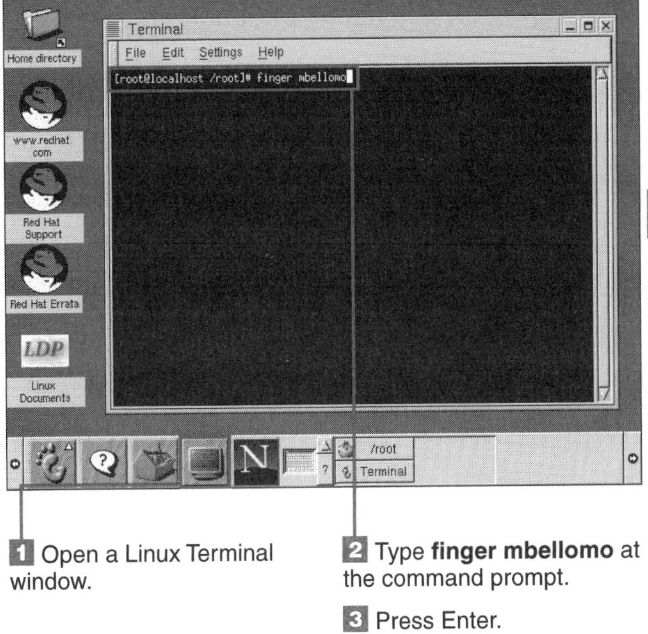

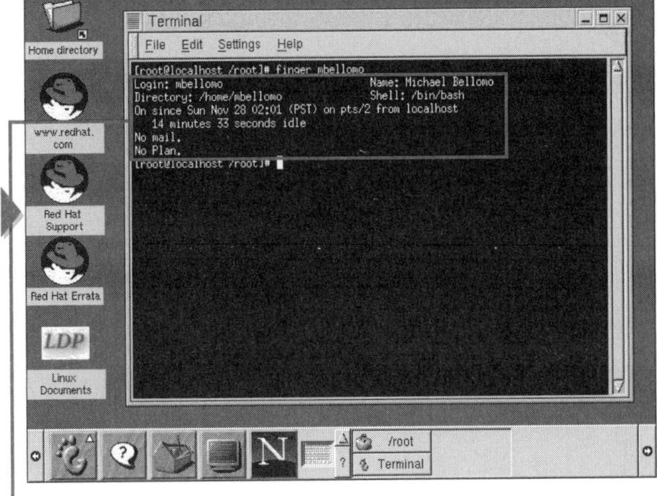

1 Open a Linux Terminal window.

2 Type **finger mbellomo** at the command prompt.

3 Press Enter.

■ The user's real name, home directory, the length of time online, and where the user's machine is located appears onscreen.

DETERMINE USER ACTIVITY

You can determine exactly what tasks a user is performing in Linux with the w command. You should use all the tools available to locate the user account causing the trouble, determine what he's up to, and stop the intruder in his tracks.

Be sure to see if the user has caused any damage or set any processes in motion that need to be stopped right away before they embarrass you, slow down the system, or worse. The majority of time, crackers won't do anything more than low-level vandalism or password changing on the sly. However, stopping this behavior before more significant damage occurs is a good idea.

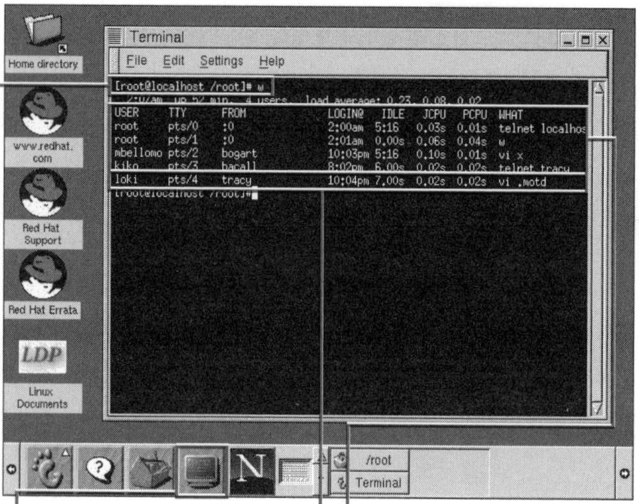

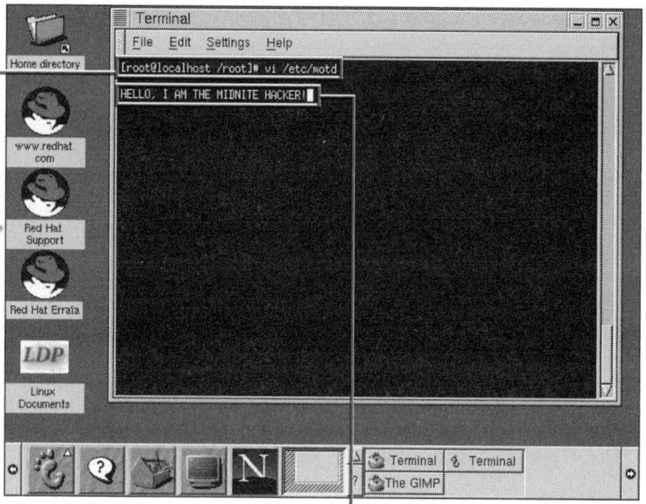

1 Open the Linux Terminal window.

2 Type **W** at the command prompt.

3 Press Enter.

■ Linux lists the users currently on the system and what they are doing.

■ The user is editing the `.motd` file, a file that is usually only accessible by root.

4 Type **vi /etc/.motd at the command prompt** to open the `.motd` file.

5 Press Enter.

■ The `.motd` file now reads, "Hello, I am the midnite hacker!" Obviously, this is unacceptable behavior, which you'll have to stop as soon as possible.

Is the .motd file a common target of crackers?

- The message of the day file is a common target of crackers, but only for the most juvenile ones. Since everyone who logs into your system from a Linux Terminal sees the message of the day displayed on their screen, it's a cheap way of notifying everyone that they broke the rules and got away with it.

What other files are common targets for crackers?

- The most common target files for unscrupulous users and crackers are the ones that control access and permissions on your Linux system. These include the `/etc/passwd` and `/etc/groups`. Once the password file is edited, you or your users may be unable to log into the system at all. If the groups file is edited, people may not be able to get to the files that they need.

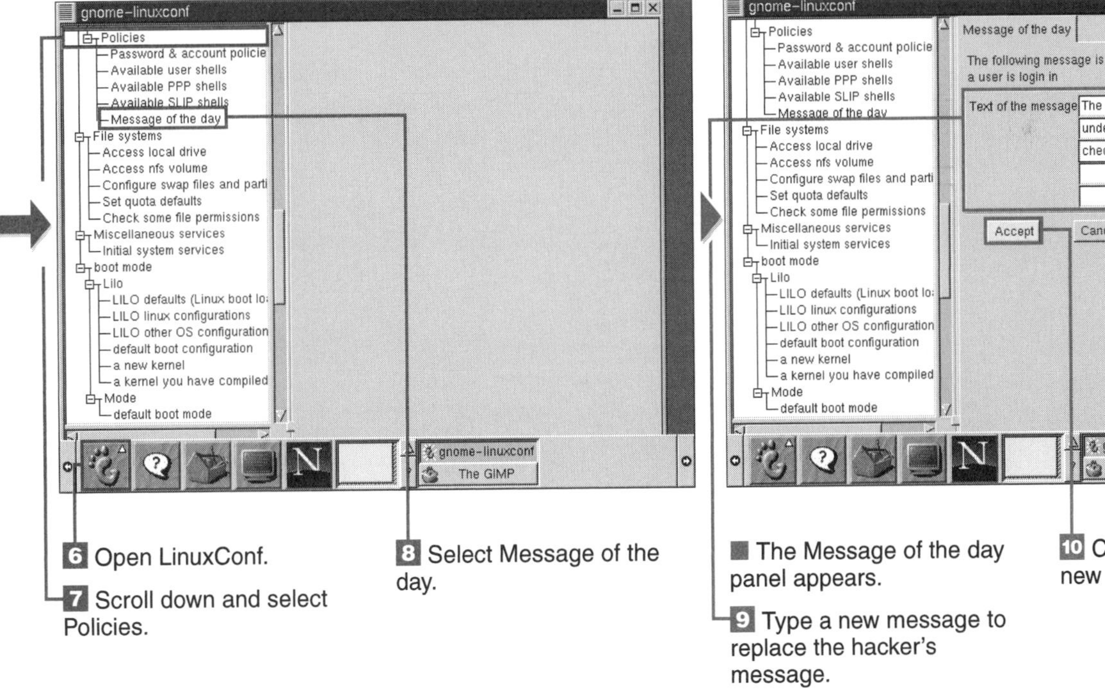

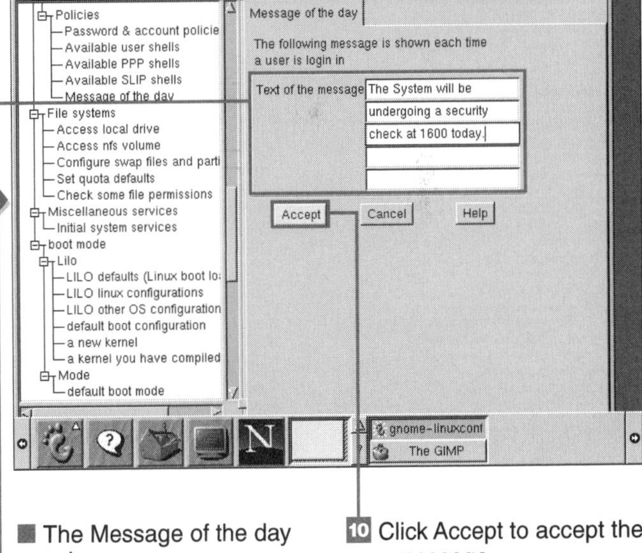

6 Open LinuxConf.

7 Scroll down and select Policies.

8 Select Message of the day.

■ The Message of the day panel appears.

9 Type a new message to replace the hacker's message.

10 Click Accept to accept the new message.

CHECK SYSTEM PERMISSIONS

You can check the permissions on your system files and user accounts after you've suffered a security breach in Linux. After you've evicted an intruder, cracker, or vandalistic user from your system, you should begin to repair the damage as quickly as possible.

Even when it appears that no lasting harm has been done to your system, you should never assume that you've gotten through the crisis with no damage. Often, a cracker or intruder will have meddled with files that could affect the long-term administration of your system. Symptoms of these problems might not appear for days, or even weeks after the initial entry onto your system. Because of this, it's always worthwhile to perform a check when you've run into problems.

To start, begin by checking out the aspects of your Linux system that are most susceptible to damage — the file systems and the user account areas. Several tools are available to help you do this. In the GUI, you can check on files and users to ensure that no damage occurred.

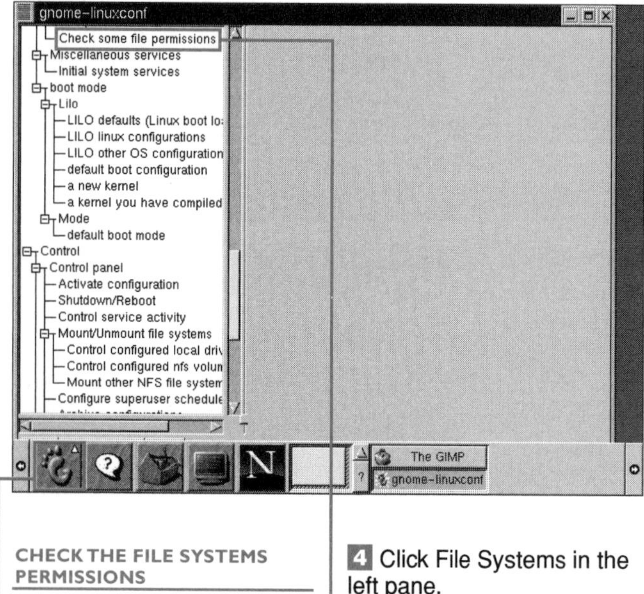

CHECK THE FILE SYSTEMS PERMISSIONS

1 Click the Main Application button.

2 Move your mouse over System to highlight

3 Select LinuxConf.

4 Click File Systems in the left pane.

5 Select Check some file permissions.

6 Press Enter.

■ The computer does an internal scan of the file system permissions.

■ If the scan verifies all the file system permissions are not corrupted, Linux flashes a message indicating that everything is okay.

7 Click Ok.

When editing a user's permissions under the Privileges tab, which privileges should I deny?

- The three privileges you should always deny to any user that is not the administrator are: May Use LinuxConf; May Activate Config Changes; and SuperUser Equivalence. You may also want to deny May Shutdown if you don't want users to turn off power to your computers.

When I edit a user's permissions under the Privileges tab, should I also deny May View System Logs'?

- This isn't absolutely necessary. While Linux users have no need to view the system logs, there's no way that the viewing the system logs can lead to a security breach.

Under Privileges, how can I deny the user the permission to administer the Apache Web Server?

- If you click the Services tab under Privileges, you can select the Denied button next to Apache administration.

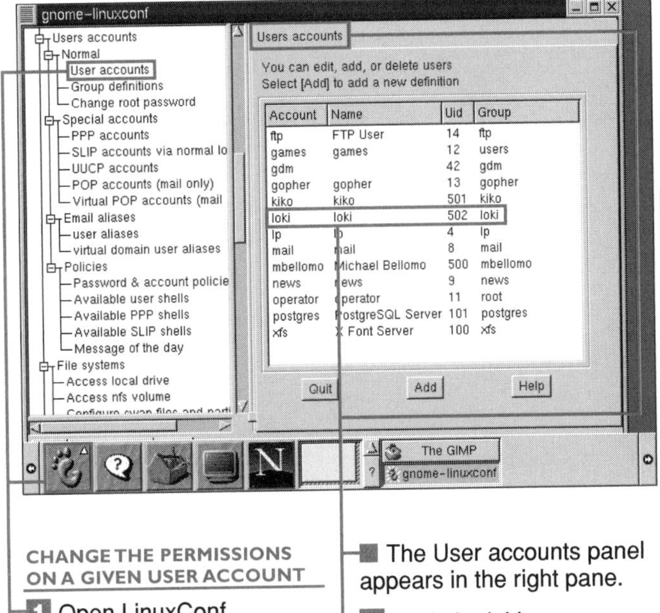

CHANGE THE PERMISSIONS ON A GIVEN USER ACCOUNT

1 Open LinuxConf.

2 Click User accounts in the left pane.

■ The User accounts panel appears in the right pane.

3 Click the loki user account.

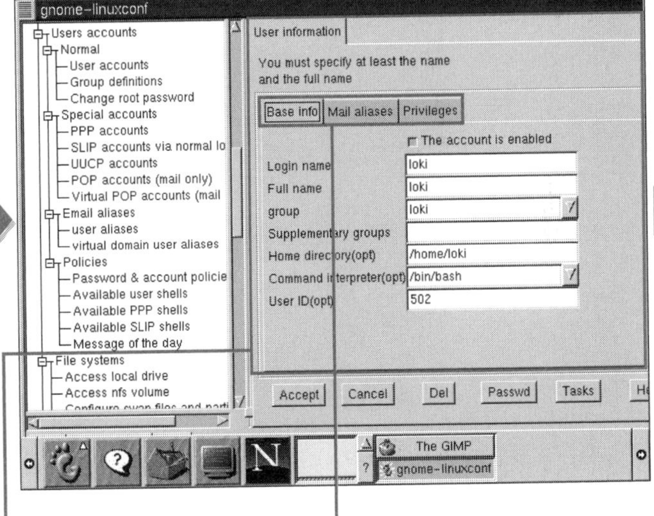

■ The User information panel appears in the right pane with loki's information.

4 Click the tabs to review the user account.

CONTINUED

CHECK SYSTEM PERMISSIONS CONTINUED

You can change the permissions on a user account if the user has created a security breach to grant himself root privileges. In the majority of cases where there has been a breach of security, a user has somehow gotten hold of the root password. Once you prevent the user from doing any damage, you need to change the root password so that the breach does not take place again.

In addition, you also need to change the user's permissions. If the user granted himself the same privileges as the administrative account, you need to return him back to the permissions of a regular user.

Finally, if this user has proven to be a problem in the past, you can lock that user's account. A locked account has not been removed from the system, but the owner of the account can no longer log onto the system.

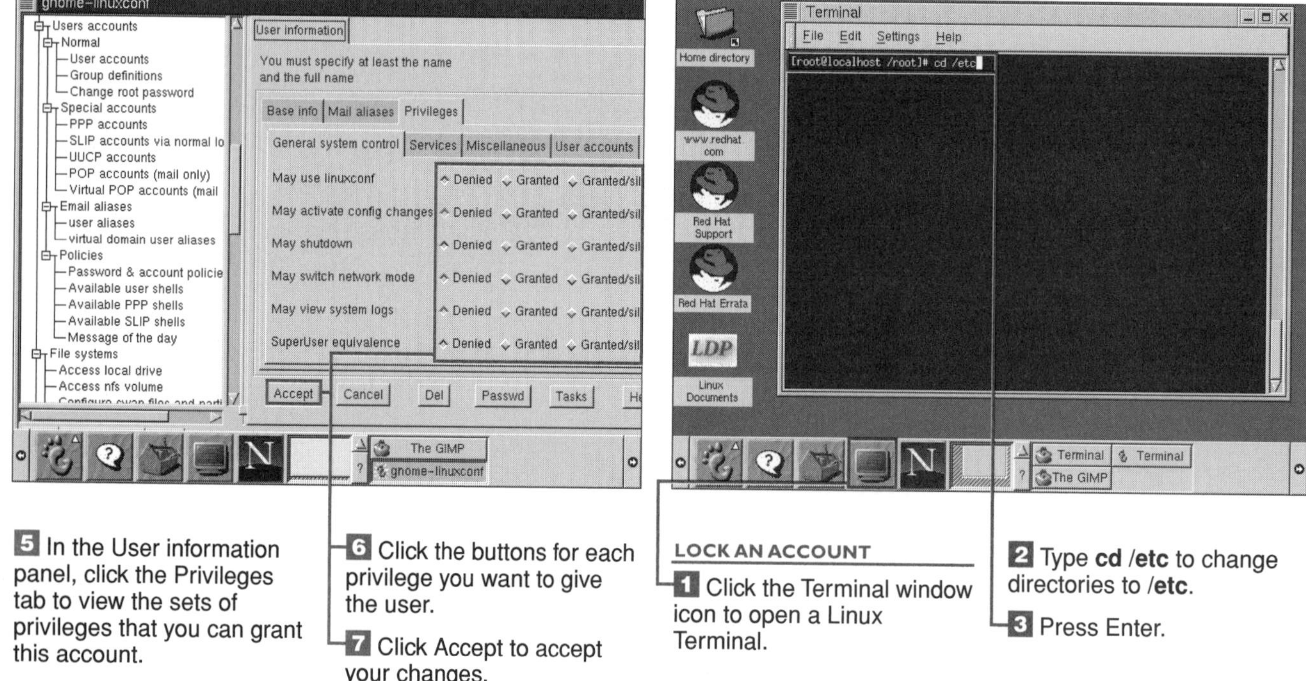

5 In the User information panel, click the Privileges tab to view the sets of privileges that you can grant this account.

6 Click the buttons for each privilege you want to give the user.

7 Click Accept to accept your changes.

LOCK AN ACCOUNT

1 Click the Terminal window icon to open a Linux Terminal.

2 Type **cd /etc** to change directories to **/etc**.

3 Press Enter.

Why does Linux use the asterix symbol to lock a user account? Isn't an asterix a wild card character?

- This is one of the quirks in the Linux operating system. In the `passed` file, an asterix tells the computer that the account is locked. In a different command, such as `ls`, the asterix means any single character, allowing you to search for a given file or text pattern.

What if the person who caused the security breach is still on the system as root?

- If this is the case, shut down all the network connections to the machine. This will ensure that anyone logged in as root before the password change took place cannot continue to use the account.

Is the Terminal or vi editor better for editing user account permissions and passwords?

- The answer depends on what you need done. Using the GUI reduces the risk of error and can be easier for those who aren't comfortable with the `vi` editor. However, the Terminal allows you to lock accounts or delete passwords much more easily.

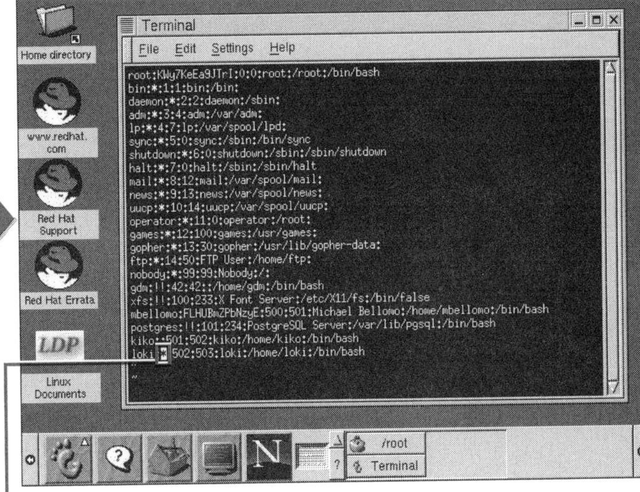

4 Type **vi passwd**.

5 Press Enter.

- The `password` file opens in the `vi` editor.

6 Enter an asterisk (*) in the password field of the user.

- Linux treats this account as locked, prohibiting the user from logging in.

CHECK CONFIGURATION LOGS

You can check the configuration logs on your Linux machine to ensure that you won't suffer further problems caused by a security breach. After you've completed changing the Linux environment to seal out the parties that hacked into your machine, you should begin damage control as soon as you can. You need to first determine what's been done to your system; some illegal users will only want to snoop around to see files they shouldn't. Other, more malicious types may have altered files, deleted data, or corrupted executables that the system needs to run.

In addition, you should check the current configuration of your Linux modules. During the security breach, alterations could have been made that will slow your system down or crash it. Checking the system configuration will make sure that no lasting changes will affect your system weeks or even months down the line.

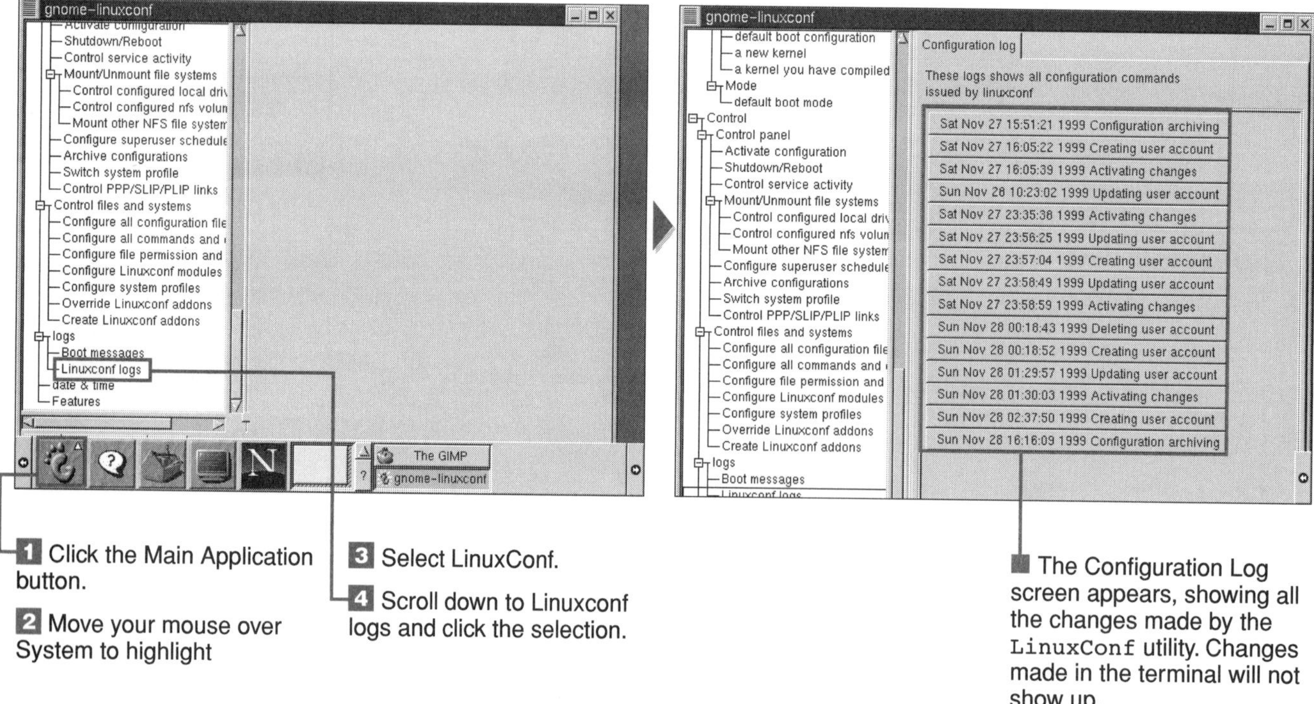

1 Click the Main Application button.

2 Move your mouse over System to highlight

3 Select LinuxConf.

4 Scroll down to Linuxconf logs and click the selection.

■ The Configuration Log screen appears, showing all the changes made by the `LinuxConf` utility. Changes made in the terminal will not show up.

SHUT DOWN SYSTEM DAEMONS

You can shut down the small programs that run your Linux system if they've been affected by a system security breach. These small programs, also called daemons, run everything from your network connections to managing your print queue. After you've finished checking the system configuration logs for a record of what was done, you can disable any daemons on your system if they are out of control.

A daemon is out of control on your system if it displays any one of three behaviors: if it is frozen, or not working; if it refuses to shut down when you use the `kill` command on it; or if it is spawning, or creating an unlimited number duplicate daemons just like itself. If left unchecked, the number of daemons running on a system can cause it to slow down or even crash.

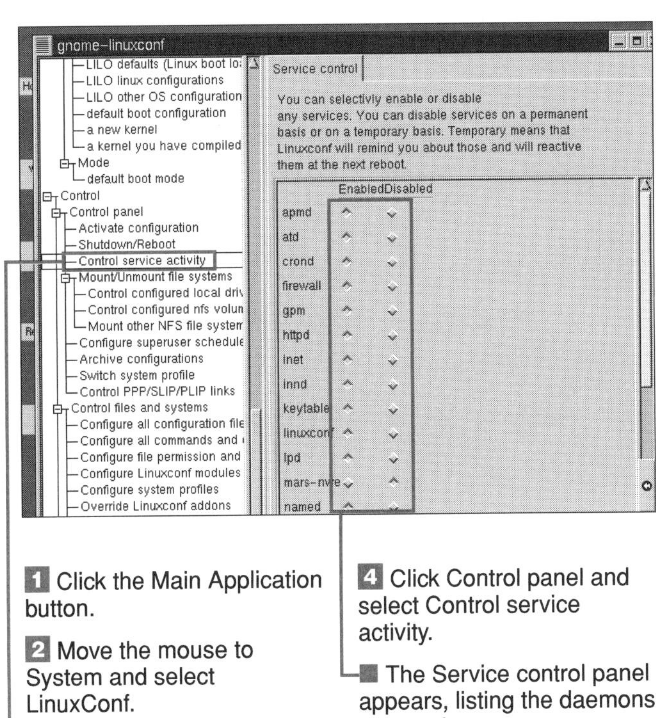

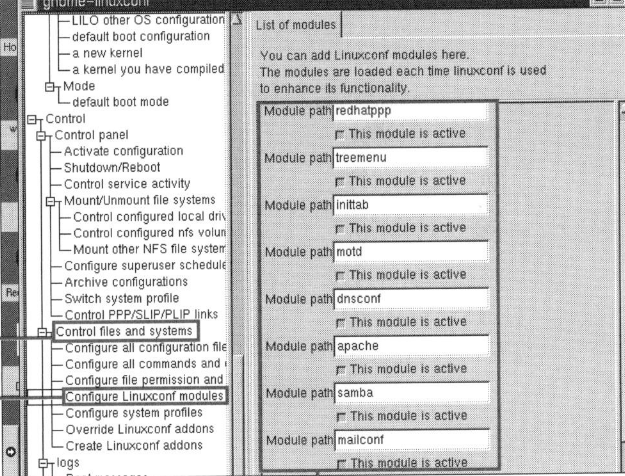

1 Click the Main Application button.

2 Move the mouse to System and select LinuxConf.

3 Scroll down to Control in the left pane.

4 Click Control panel and select Control service activity.

■ The Service control panel appears, listing the daemons it controls.

5 After enabling and disabling services, select Control files and systems under Control in the left pane.

6 Select Configure Linuxconf modules in the submenu.

■ The List of modules panel appears in the right pane.

7 To deactivate any module on the list, de-select the depressed button.

SECTION VIII

28) BACKING UP FILES

Create a Linux Boot Disk 482
Create a Linux Recovery Disk 484
Back Up Files with tar 486
Restore Files with tar 488
Compress Files with gzip 490

29) THE Y2038K BUG

Change the System Date 492
Test and Verify with GnomeRPM 496

30) TROUBLESHOOTING COMMON LINUX PROBLEMS

Reassign a Forgotten Root Password 500
Diagnose Device Problems on Reboot 502
Find Disk and CPU Hogs 504
Stop Hung or Spawned Processes....................506
Troubleshoot in the Gui 508

DISASTER PREPARATION AND RECOVERY

CREATE A LINUX BOOT DISK

You can create a Linux *boot disk* to back up your system. Although Linux is one of the most stable and reliable operating systems on the market, it is conceivable that something could happen to make the system go haywire and refuse to boot up. For example, a sudden loss of power, or surge from a nearby lightning strike while the system is in the middle of a delicate operation can cause a lock-up so severe that booting is not possible.

You might also run into this kind of problem if one of your hard drives is failing. In that case, booting up the system — even one more time — is crucial to salvage as many of the files on the old disk as possible. You'll only be able to perform this feat if you have a boot disk available.

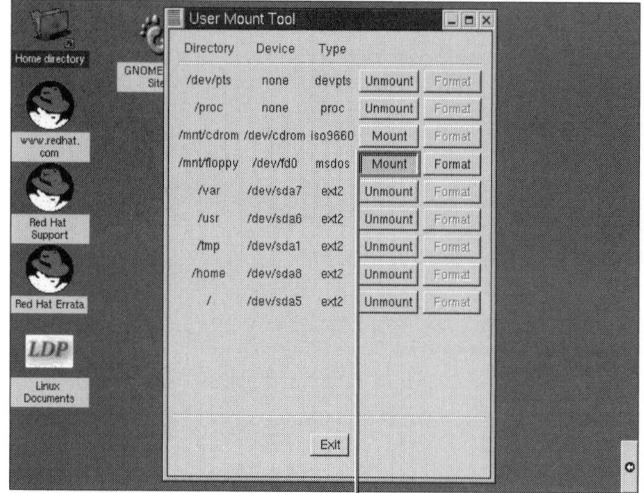

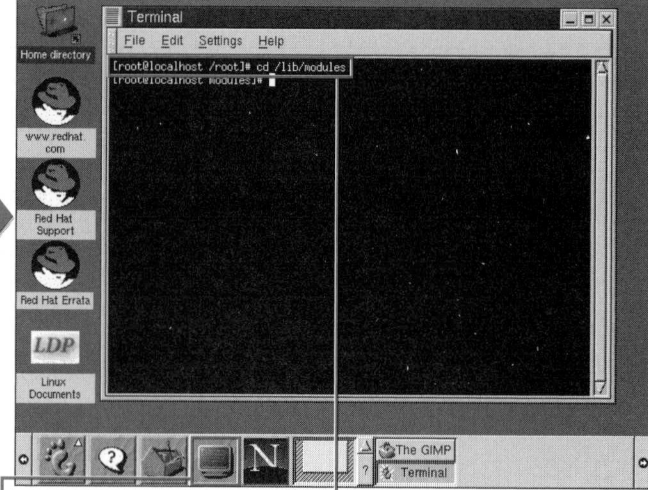

1 Insert a diskette into the floppy drive and mount it from the Linux Terminal or by using the Disk Manager.

2 Click Mount by the file system `/mnt/floppy` to mount the floppy disk.

3 Click the Linux Terminal icon to open the Terminal screen.

4 Change the directory by typing **cd /lib/modules** at the command prompt.

5 Press Enter.

When should I make a boot disk?

- ASAP, if not sooner. In fact, when you installed Linux, you should have been asked to create a boot disk during the installation process. If you get the chance, always choose Yes at this prompt.

I have a boot disk from a different brand of Linux. Can I use it to boot my machine?

- You can try to use it. In some cases, it might work, so long as the two brands of Linux are not too dissimilar. However, by no means should you rely on this method to back up your machine.

I have a boot disk from a UNIX installation. Can I use it to boot my machine?

- UNIX, while a close relative to Linux, usually has more differences in its boot processes and kernel configurations than most flavors of Linux. Most likely you won't be able to boot from a disk of this sort.

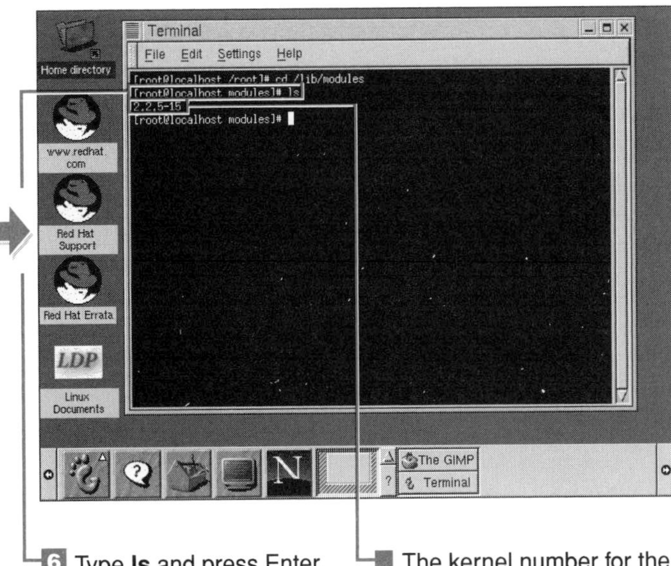

6 Type **ls** and press Enter.

■ The kernel number for the version of Linux you're running appears. You need this number for the command that creates the boot disk.

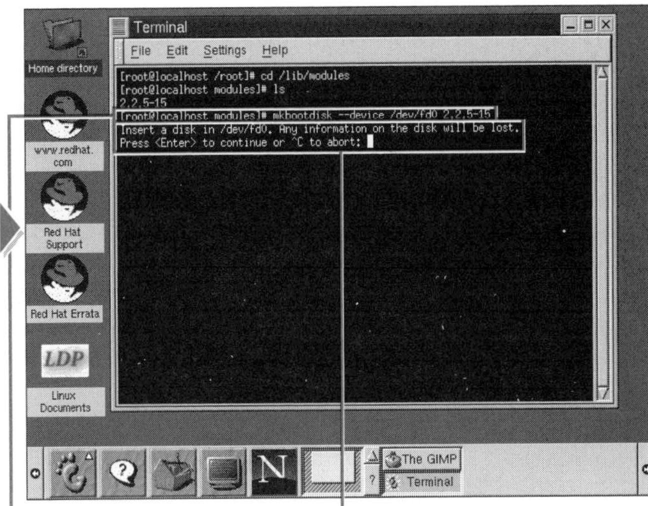

7 At the prompt, type **mkbootdisk --device /dev/fd0 2.2.5-15**.

8 Press Enter.

9 Press Enter to confirm if you're sure.

■ After the copying completed, the command prompt returns.

■ Don't forget to label your disk Emergency Boot Disk or something similar.

CREATE A LINUX RECOVERY DISK

You can create a Recovery disk to restore your system in the event of a system crash. As long as your crashed or malfunctioning system is still bootable, you can use a *Recovery disk* to boot up. Sometimes you may be unable to get to the root of the problem from the GUI or even the Terminal side of things. In such a case, you need to boot the machine with a Recovery disk, which can scan and repair entire file systems and disks on a machine with comparative ease.

A Recovery disk has stored on it procedures and system diagnostic tools copied over from the CD-ROM. When you actually activate and use the tools on the disk, it completes the tasks automatically or at most with a little prompting from you in a user menu. You should always have a Recovery disk, like you would a boot disk, somewhere in your lab or equipment room.

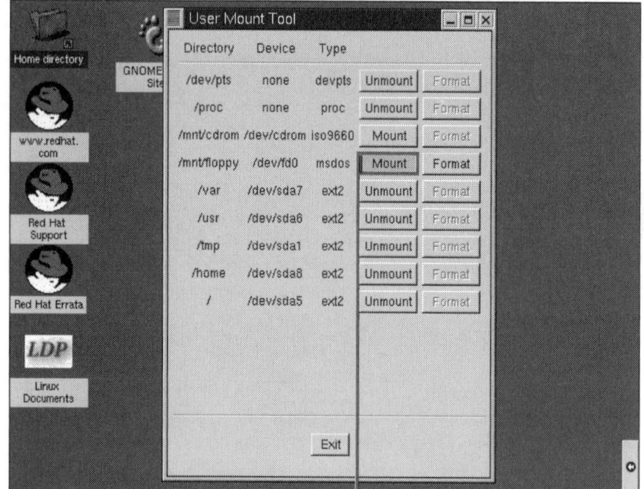

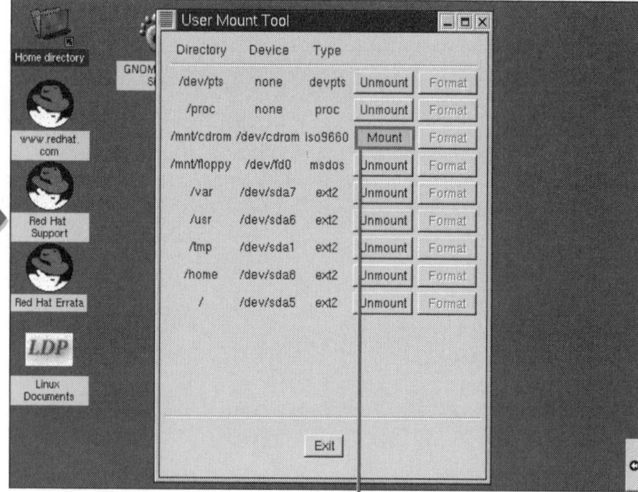

1 Insert a diskette into the floppy drive and mount it either from the Linux Terminal or by using the Disk Manager.

2 Click Mount by the `/mnt/floppy` file system to mount the disk.

3 Insert a CD in the CD-ROM drive and mount it from the Linux Terminal or by using the Disk Manager.

4 Click Mount by the `/mnt/cdrom` file system to mount the CD-ROM.

When should I make a Recovery disk?

- As soon as you are able. Unlike when you create a boot disk, when you install Linux, you don't get a prompt encouraging you to make a Recovery disk. However, this is an extremely important utility so if you get the chance, always make a Recovery disk to keep around for emergency maintenance.

I have a Recovery disk from a UNIX installation. Can I use it to boot my machine?

- Very doubtful. UNIX is closely related to Linux but usually has more differences in its boot processes and applications than most flavors of Linux. If you try to use the recovery mechanisms to boot the system, you probably won't succeed, but you won't make the damage worse by trying.

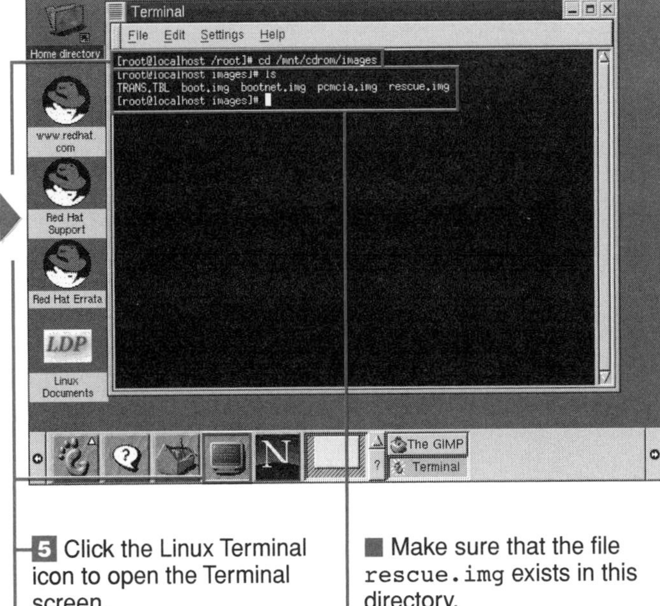

5 Click the Linux Terminal icon to open the Terminal screen.

6 Change directories by typing **cd /mnt/cdrom/images** at the prompt.

■ Make sure that the file `rescue.img` exists in this directory.

7 Type **ls** to list the directory's contents.

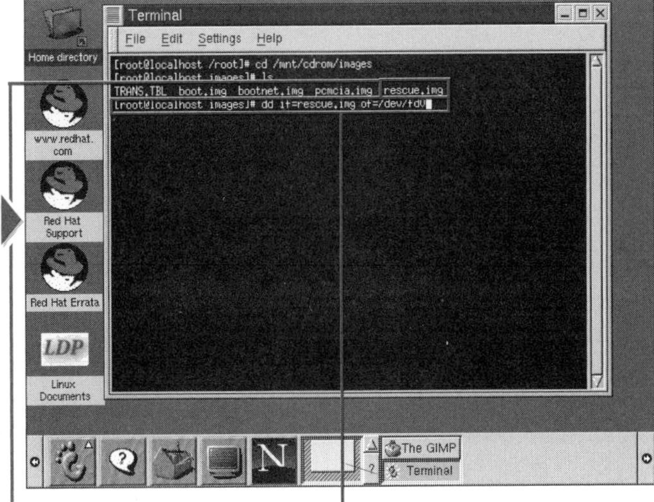

8 If the file appears, type the following after the command prompt:

dd if=rescue.img of=/dev/fd0

9 Press Enter.

■ This copies the rescue file to the floppy disk for your future use.

BACK UP FILES WITH TAR

The `tar` utility backs up and restores files on your system either after a system crash or as a regular part of your system maintenance. `tar` is a very reliable and effective way to compress and store many large files into an area of finite space, such as a magnetic tape unit.

`tar` is actually an acronym for *tape archive resource*. It was originally designed to store files directly to a tape unit. However, `tar` has since then expanded its role, and you can use it to compress text files, programs, executables, sound files, and even picture graphics like bitmaps and JPEGs. Although some of the variables that work with `tar` seem obscure at first, they're actually pretty handy and easy to work with because they're consistent.

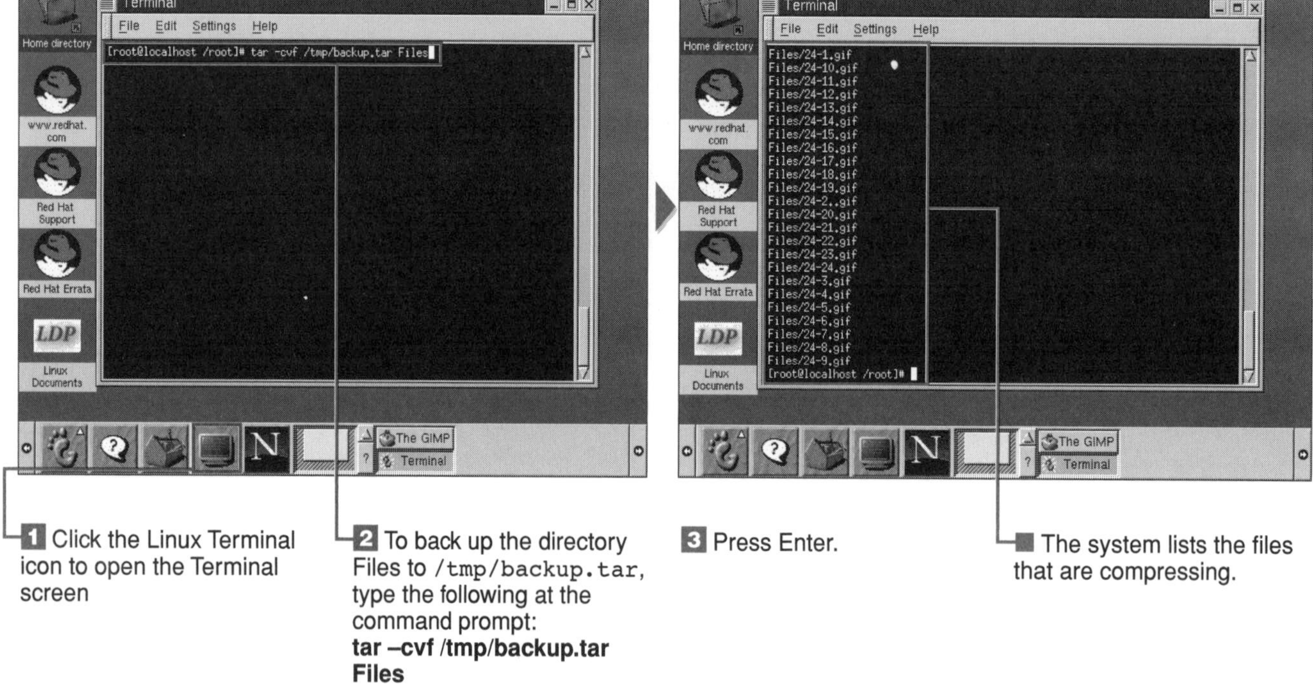

1 Click the Linux Terminal icon to open the Terminal screen

2 To back up the directory Files to `/tmp/backup.tar`, type the following at the command prompt: **tar –cvf /tmp/backup.tar Files**

3 Press Enter.

■ The system lists the files that are compressing.

TIPS

What does the cvf command option used with the tar command stand for?

- The `cvf` command option is actually three command options used together: `c`, for compress; `v` for verbose; and `f` for file name.

What does it mean if the tar command is set to use the verbose command option?

- In `tar`, or any command in the Linux operating system, verbose means that if the command runs into a problem or an error, it returns an error message instead of just exiting without telling you what's wrong.

What's the most common error that tar encounters, and how can I prevent it from happening?

- The most common error that `tar` encounters is running out of disk space when it's backing up a file in a directory. To avoid this problem, back up your files in to the `/tmp` directory, which is usually empty.

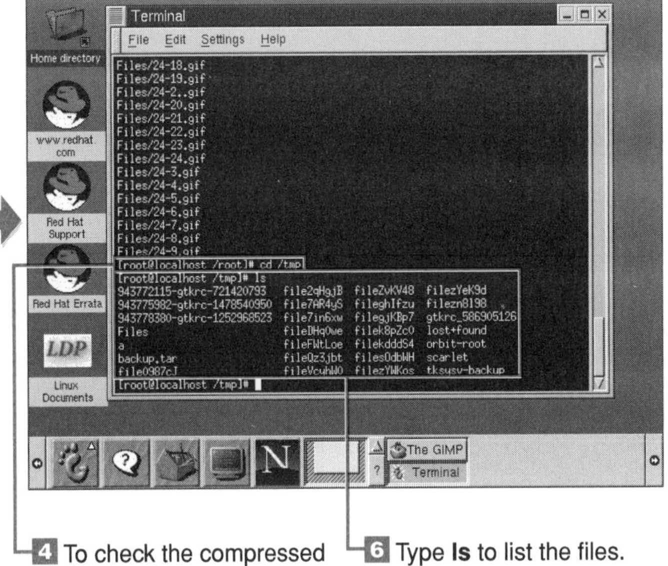

4 To check the compressed files, change directories to the location of the file and **type cd /tmp**.

5 Press Enter.

6 Type **ls** to list the files.

■ This creates the `backup.tar` file.

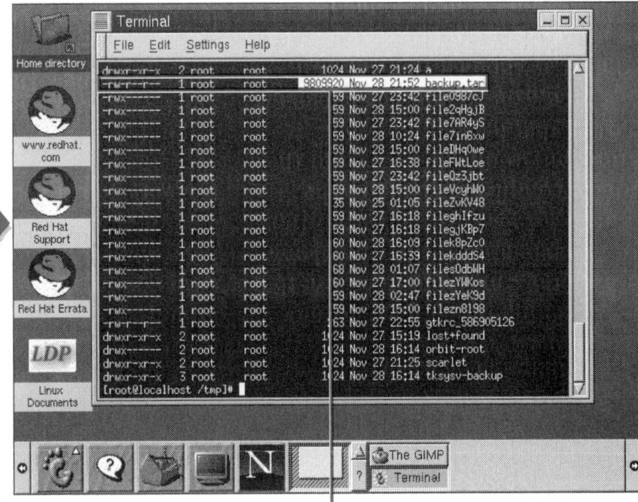

7 Type **ls –l** and press Enter.

■ Notice that `backup.tar` that you just created is fairly large.

RESTORE FILES WITH TAR

You can restore files that you've backed up with the tape archive utility (`tar`) with the same command and different command options. The key difference is that when you want to use the restoration process, you use the `x` command option, which stands for extract.

The most important task you should complete before you begin restoring a compressed file with `tar` is to make sure that you have enough space on your hard drive to accommodate the restored file. When you restore a file with the `tar` command, you're also returning the file to its full size. A compressed `tar` file can expand up to 50 percent larger when you restore it. You can check the amount of disk space you have available with the System Information utility, which is discussed in detail in Chapter 12.

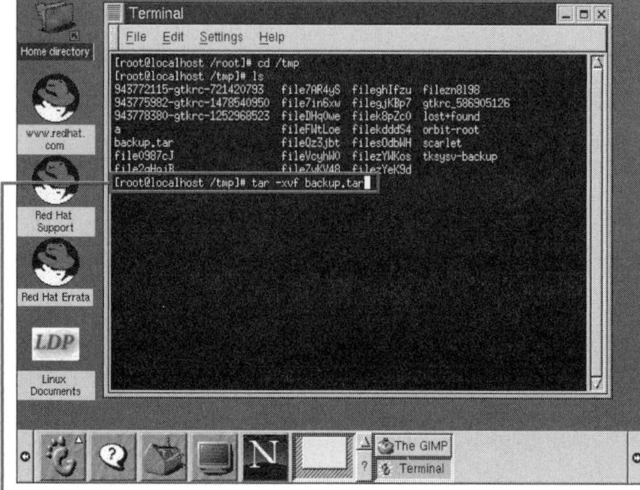

1 To restore a file compressed with tar, type the following at the command prompt: **tar –xvf backup.tar**

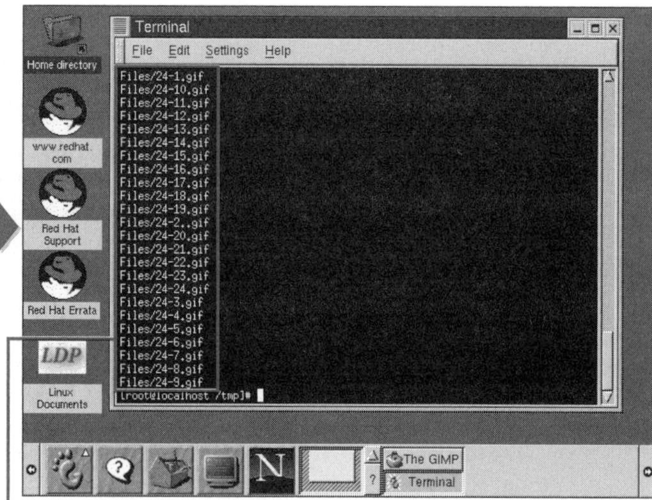

■ When you press Enter, the entire contents display as they decompress.

How can I install a tape drive on my system?

- There are several methods, some more complex than others depending on how sophisticated your equipment is. However, if you have a standard external tape drive, you should be able to hook it into the back of your local machine to back up files, so long as you have a tape inside of it. Any store-bought tape backup device comes with standard instructions on how to set up the machine.

How often should I back up my system?

- That depends on two factors: (1) How much you have to spend in time and money? (2) How important is the data? How will a loss of, say, a day's worth of data affect people versus a week's worth of data loss? When you've determined those factors, you can set up a backup schedule.

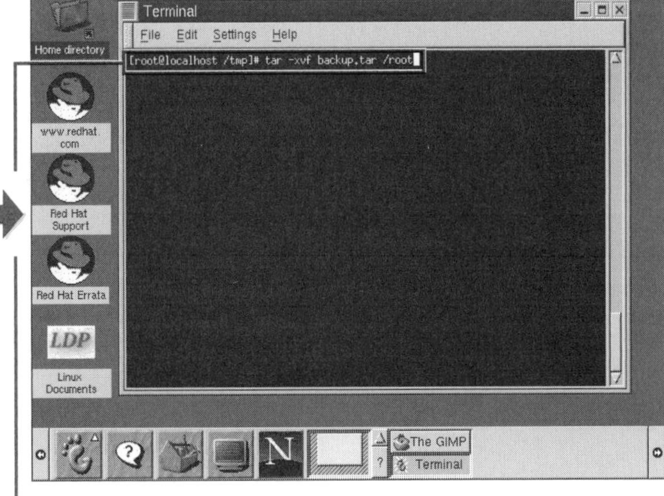

2 To un-`tar` a file to a different location, such as `/root`, type the following at the prompt:
tar –xvf backup.tar /root

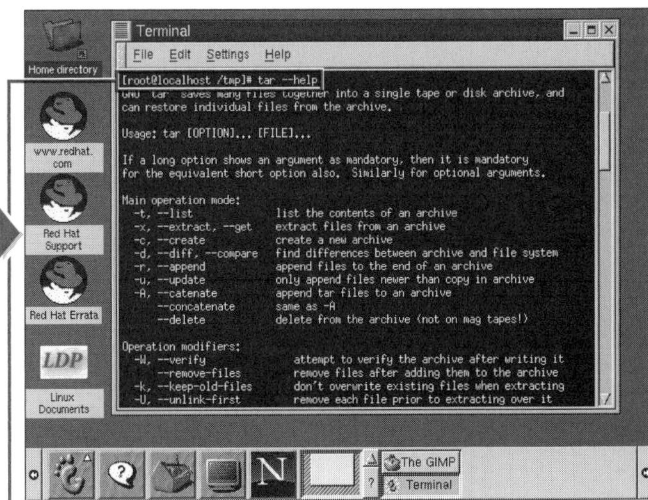

3 For more help in `tar`, type **tar --help** at the command prompt and press Enter.

COMPRESS FILES WITH GZIP

You can use the `gzip` utility as an alternative to `tar`. `gzip` is usually faster and compresses more space out of text files on average than the `tar` process. However, in the larger picture, `gzip` is not as efficient a compression process as is `tar`, so it's not as suited for backing up large files, or an entire system.

What's more, `gzip` isn't designed to work as closely with tape storage as `tar`. Your best use of `gzip` is as a storage utility to place large amounts of text (say from stored e-mails) into a directory set aside for compressed files.

`gzip` stands for Gnu-zip, and it can be used in conjunction with `tar`. In fact, if you are short on space but not on time, you can actually take a file, `tar` it, and then gzip the `tar` file. In cases like this, the resulting file has two suffixes, such as `file.tar.gz`.

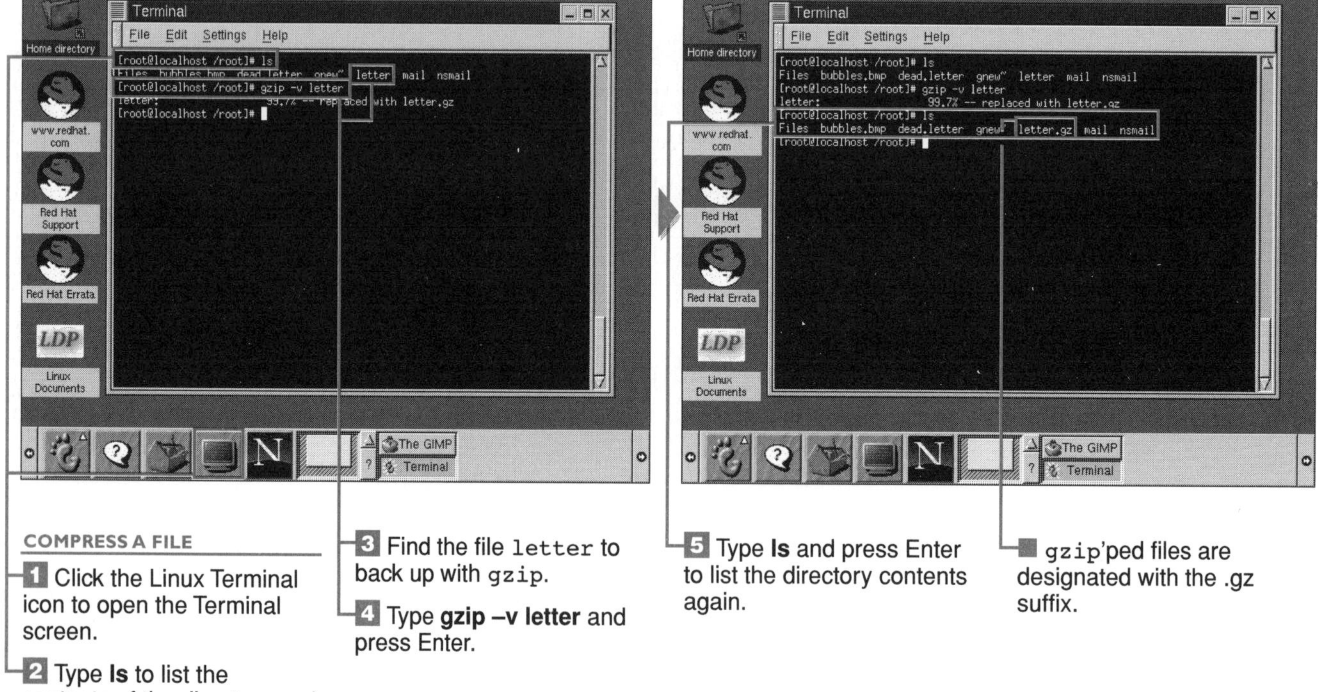

COMPRESS A FILE

1 Click the Linux Terminal icon to open the Terminal screen.

2 Type **ls** to list the contents of the directory and press Enter.

3 Find the file `letter` to back up with `gzip`.

4 Type **gzip –v letter** and press Enter.

5 Type **ls** and press Enter to list the directory contents again.

■ `gzip`'ped files are designated with the .gz suffix.

Why use the v option?

- The `v` is optional; it stands for "verbose" and enables you to see, among other things, how much space you're saving by compressing a file.

You've talked about saving a file with both tar and gzip. How do you restore a file like file.tar.gz?

- You always work from the outside in. In other words, the outermost suffix of the file is .gz, so you must first unzip the file before you un `tar` it. After you unzip it, the file looks like this: `file.tar`. Finally, you need to remove the final suffix from the file by un-`tar`'ing it back into a normal, decompressed file on your system.

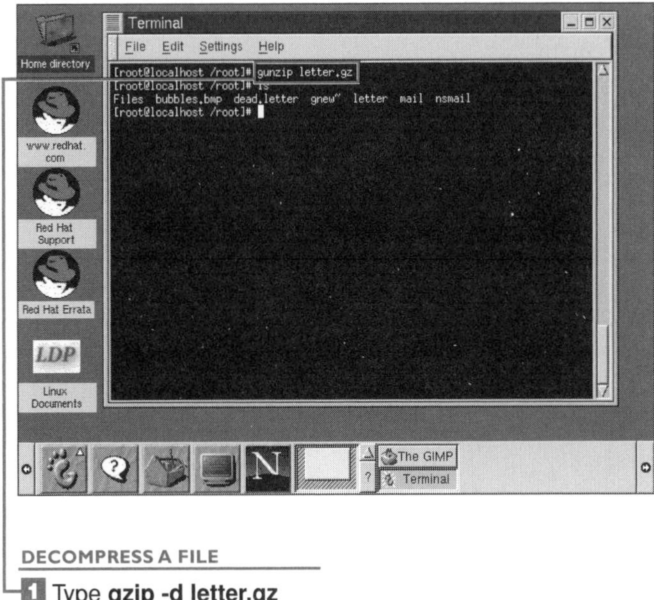

DECOMPRESS A FILE

1 Type **gzip -d letter.gz** and press Enter.

Note: -d stands for decompress.

2 Type **gzip --help** or **gzip -h** at the command prompt if you need help working with `gzip`.

3 Press Enter.

- The system displays a list of help commands.

CHANGE THE SYSTEM DATE

You can change the system date on your computer with either the GNOME Control Panel or the Linux Terminal. You can use this utility to verify that the Y2038K bug will not affect your application. This bug is similar to the bygone Y2K bug in that some of your software may not run at the start of the year 2038.

If you don't think that you'll be administering the system in 30-odd years, you don't have much to worry about. However, if you want to be thorough and you have nothing else pressing on your administration duties, you can test your current applications.

You can set your system date to right before midnight of the 2038 New Year. Sit back, watch for any fireworks that might appear, and correct any problems that you see. If none, then congratulations! You have job security for the next 30+ years.

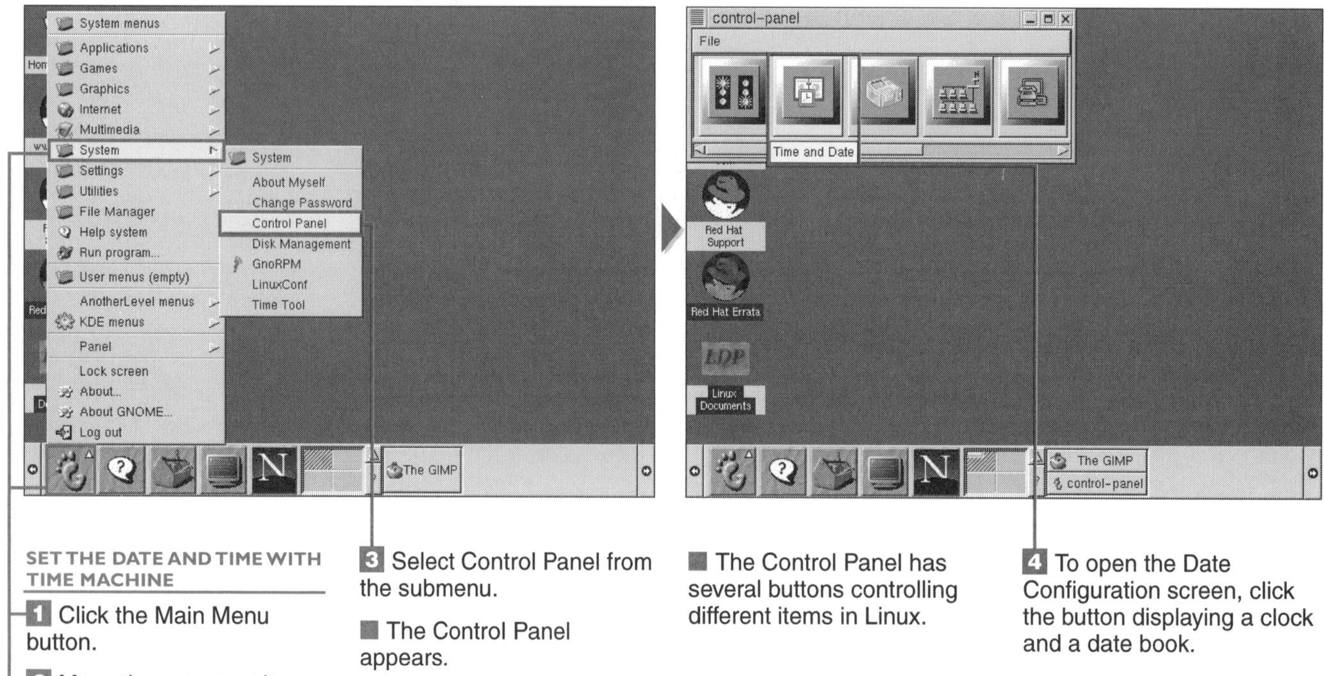

SET THE DATE AND TIME WITH TIME MACHINE

1 Click the Main Menu button.

2 Move the mouse pointer to System.

3 Select Control Panel from the submenu.

■ The Control Panel appears.

■ The Control Panel has several buttons controlling different items in Linux.

4 To open the Date Configuration screen, click the button displaying a clock and a date book.

TIPS

When I change the system date, should I log out, halt, or reboot the system?

- To change the system date, halt or reboot the system, do not log out. For the date change to take effect, the system must shut down completely. Logging out does not shut down the system at the level required.

Will I cause any problems for my Linux machine if I set the system date a few hours ahead or behind the real time in my time zone?

- Adjusting the time will not cause any problems. However, any e-mail you send out reflects your system time, which may confuse the recipients, who may wonder why you're working such odd hours.

What does the 24 Hour Time setting in the Time Machine utility do?

- This setting switches the displayed time to military time, which runs by a 24-hour clock. For example, 11 p.m. is 2300 hours in military time.

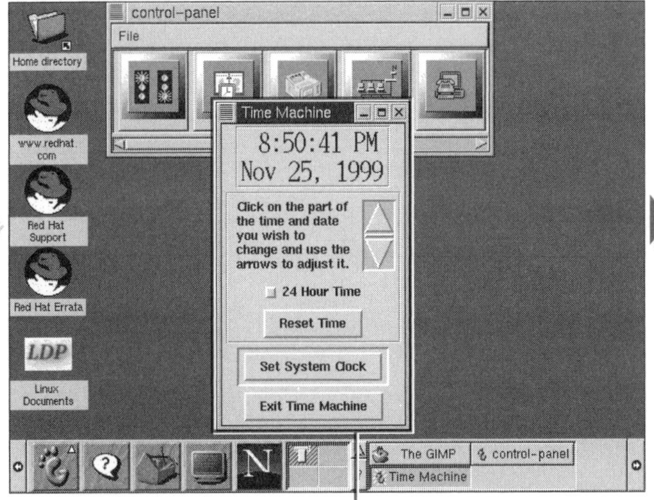

■ The `Time Machine` utility starts up.

5 Click in the window to activate the tool.

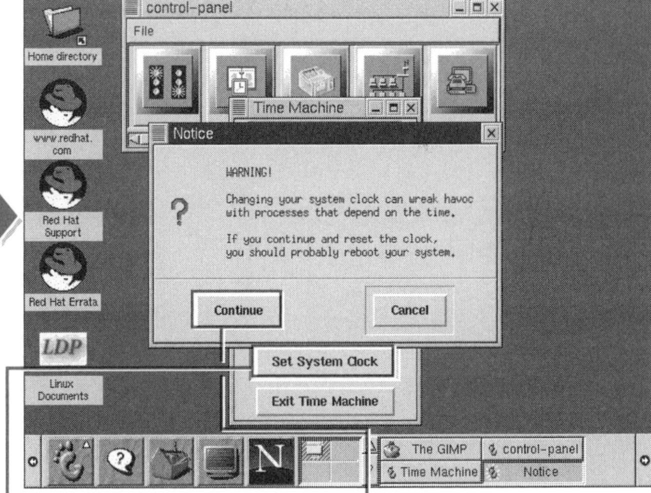

6 Click Set System Clock.

■ You're reminded that you should reboot the system after resetting the system clock.

7 Click Continue if you want to complete the task.

CONTINUED

CHANGE THE SYSTEM DATE CONTINUED

You can also change the system date from the Linux Terminal with the `date` command. While the `date` command is not as intuitive to work with as the `Time Machine` utility on the GNOME desktop, people who don't like clicking multiple times on arrow buttons to set a new date and time will prefer to work with this command instead.

The `date` command can be confusing to the new Linux user, because the date is written numerically in one long string of text. The date is set out with pairs of numbers in the following order: month, day, year, hour, minute. For example, January 1, 2000 at 11:15 p.m. would be written as: 0101002315. If you need more information or want to make sure that you're entering a date properly, you can type **date — help** to view the command's help file.

8 Click the portion of the clock that you want to change.

■ For example, if you wanted to change the minutes portion of the time, click the 51 in 8:51.

■ Your selection highlights, enabling you to make changes with the arrow buttons on the right.

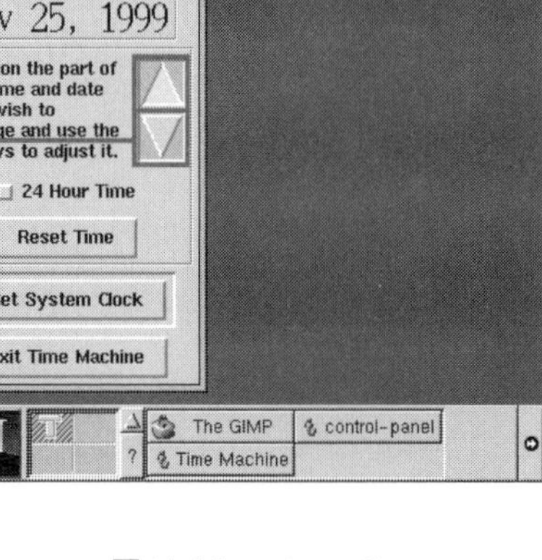

9 Click the up arrow to increase the value of the highlighted digit.

10 Click the down arrow to decrease the value of the highlighted digit.

■ Holding down the arrow button enables you to scroll through the values more quickly.

Why does GNOME's Time Machine warn me that changing the system time could cause problems?

- On rare occasions, playing with the system date and not restarting the server can lead to programs such as `cron` to crash. This happens because these programs are time and date dependent. If they run into an internal contradiction anywhere, they don't handle it well and shut down of their own accord.

What other things can I do with the date command?

- Use `date` is to calculate the exact time a project will conclude, or simply to display your system time in a different format. For full information on all the options that you have available with `date`, check the man pages. To access these, simply type **man date** at the Linux Terminal command line.

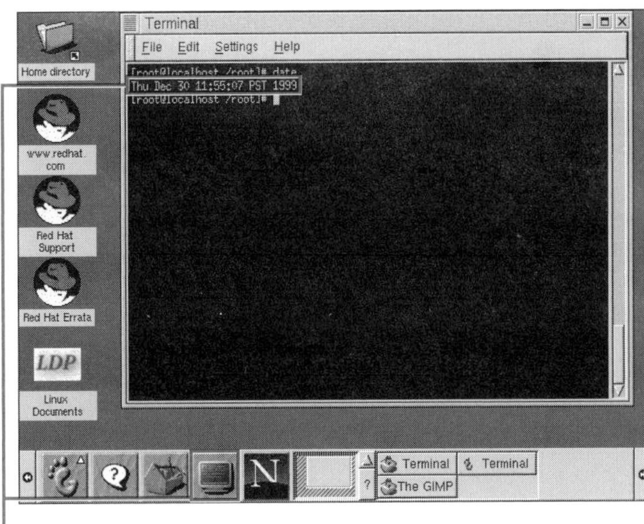

SET THE DATE AND TIME IN A LINUX TERMINAL

1 Open a Linux Terminal.

2 Type **date** at the system prompt.

3 Press Enter.

■ The system displays the current system date.

4 To reset the date (for Y2K testing, for example), type the following to change the date to just before the critical time, say to December 31, 1999 at 11:55 p.m.: `date -s 1231115599`

5 Press Enter to accept the date.

6 Allow the time to pass the critical date. Check your system logs for any errors.

TEST AND VERIFY WITH GNOMERPM

You can detect errors and compliance problems in your Linux application with the GNOME Red Hat Package Manager. As more packaged programs become available for installing on your Linux machine, this aspect of GnomeRPM will become even more valuable.

The *verification* process can detect any flaws or bugs in a package after installation. Should further damage occur during a Y2K or Y2038K date change, verification can notify you of it, if not repair the flaw.

The *query* process is more valuable from a preventative point of view.

When a package is queried, it reveals all of the information that the company producing it feels is relevant. Compliance with date-centric problems is always considered relevant, so if the data exists, it shows up during a query.

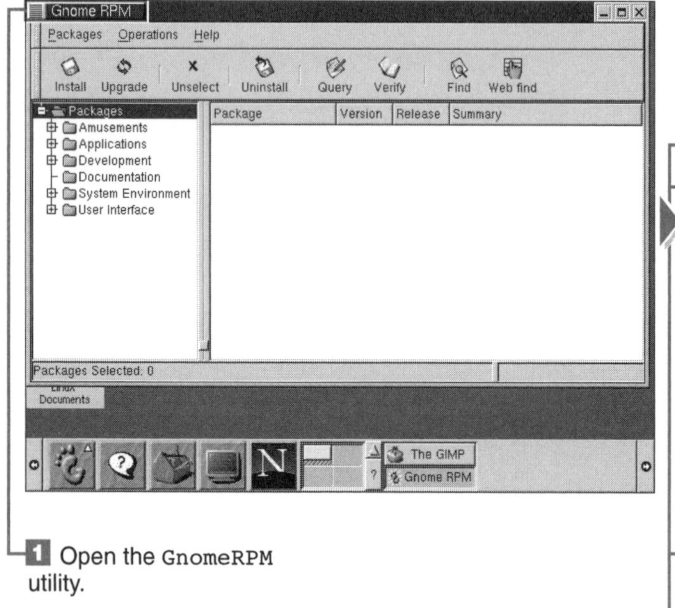

1 Open the GnomeRPM utility.

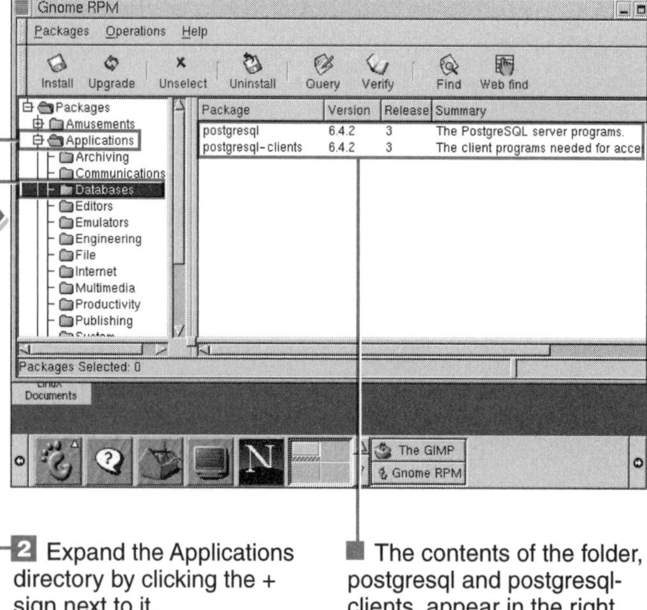

2 Expand the Applications directory by clicking the + sign next to it.

3 Select Databases from the submenu by clicking it.

■ The contents of the folder, postgresql and postgresql-clients, appear in the right pane.

TIPS

Why does the verify process take longer with some packages than others?

- Verify examines each component of a package before it completes its task. If you use the `Verify` utility on a large package or a series of packages, the verification process takes a little longer.

If I'm verifying a large package or a series of packages, how can I speed up the process?

- Although you can't speed up the verification process, you can ensure that the system is running as fast as it can when you run it. Perform your verification tasks after hours when the fewest people are using your Linux system.

If I find a problem with a package, what action should I take?

- If you find a problem with a package, delete it and then reinstall the package from whichever of the two Red Hat Linux CD-ROMs it came from.

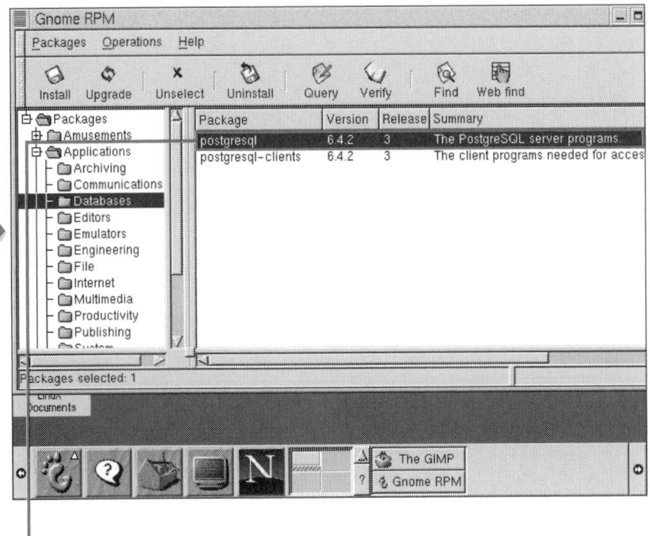

4 Select postgresql by clicking it.

■ It appears as highlighted.

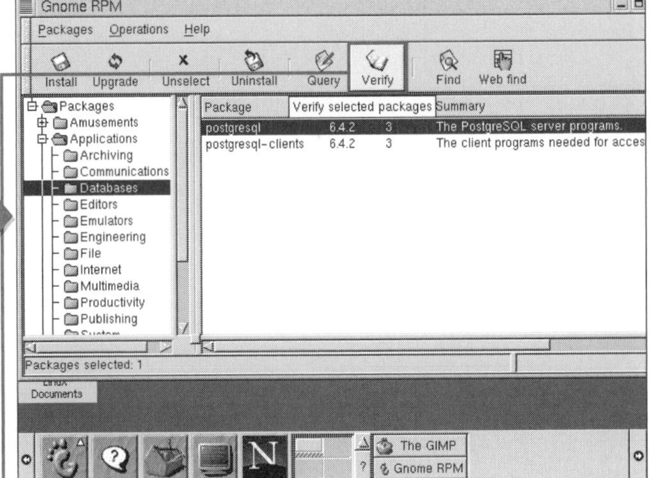

5 After the date change has run its course, verify the package by clicking the Verify button on the toolbar.

CONTINUED

TEST AND VERIFY WITH GNOMERPM
CONTINUED

You can gather detailed information about the software packages on your Linux system by using the `Query` utility in the GNOME Red Hat Package Manager. Where the `Verify` utility can identify bugs, errors, and improper installations in software packages, the `Query` utility displays all the information on the package's problems that are already known.

For example, if a software company releases a product that they know crashes under certain conditions, they add it to the package information. This information is conveniently displayed in the Package Info screen in GnomeRPM.

`Query` is also useful if you're trying to determine if you have the latest version of a product. While a binary file in the Linux Terminal won't tell you much about itself, the `Query` utility displays the package's version number and even the date you installed the package on your hard drive.

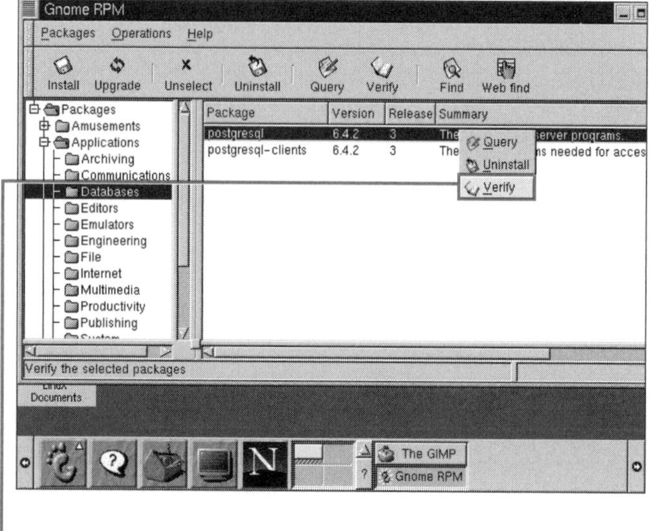

6 Right-click the highlighted entry and select Verify from the pop-up menu.

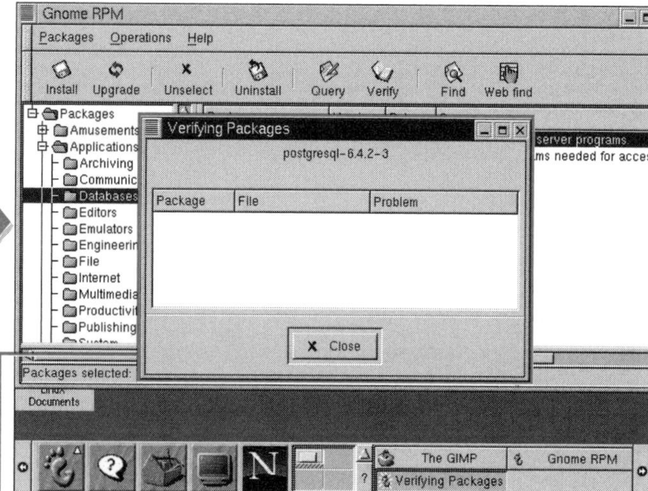

■ The Verifying Packages screen shows any new abnormalities caused by the date changeover. Otherwise, the screen is blank, as it is shown here.

What kind of problems can a noncompliant program cause?

- Most noncompliant programs run into problems when they handle data or calculations that involve dates and times. For example, a noncompliant spreadsheet can give inaccurate numbers. The worst case scenario is that the program refuses to run at all, freezing the system until you reboot.

What's the quickest way to get compliance information if it's not listed in the Query?

- Use your mouse to click the company's Web site as listed by the query. The Web site is listed as a hypertext link; therefore, if you've installed and configured your modem connections and your Web browser, you are taken directly to that Web page on the Internet. There, you can find the latest information on the product release.

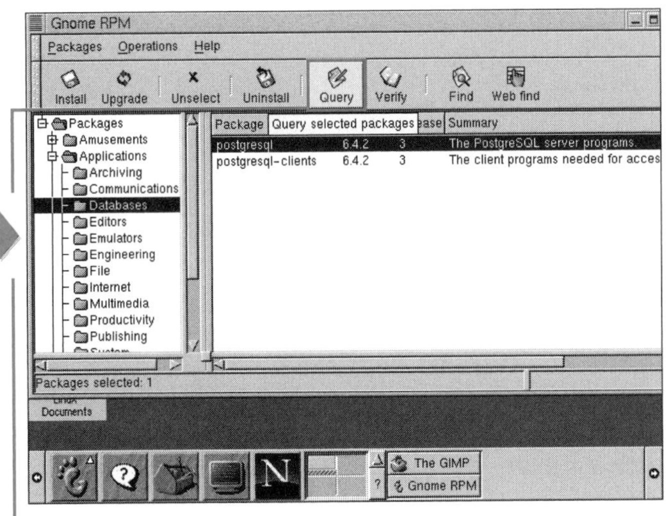

■ If you're still preparing for Y2K or Y2038K, you can also run Query.

■ The information in the package tells you that it is already compliant, or it tells you the package's origin so you may search for information on a company Web site.

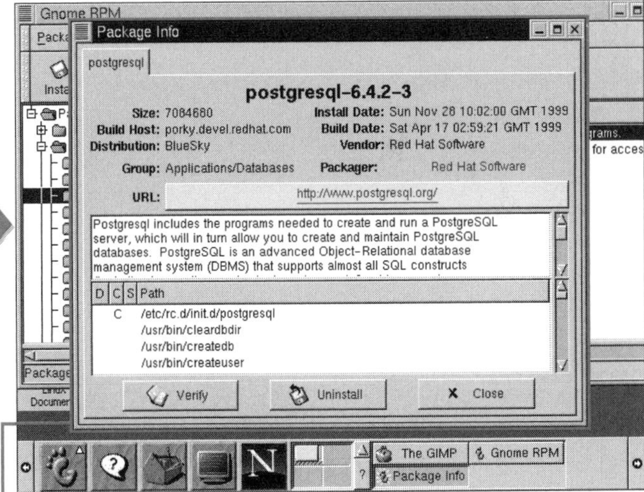

■ The Package Info window tells you either about the product's compliance, or, as here, the company's Web site.

REASSIGN A FORGOTTEN ROOT PASSWORD

When administering the system, forgetting the root password is the worst mistake you can make and is also one of the most embarrassing. It creates a security hazard and an administrative nightmare should something go wrong while you are without your password. Fixing this problem is inconvenient because in the worst case scenario, you may have to reinstall the operating system to fix it because it's during the installation process that you select the root account password.

To prevent mishaps of this sort, consider writing down the administrative password (or passwords) and placing the paper somewhere secure. If you have a locked file cabinet, wall safe, or lab room with a locking door, you can place the file there. If not, consider keeping the paper somewhere other than your workstation, such as in your car or at home.

This won't be as inconvenient as you might think because on a busy system, you won't be able to reboot the machine until everyone else goes home at the end of the day, anyway.

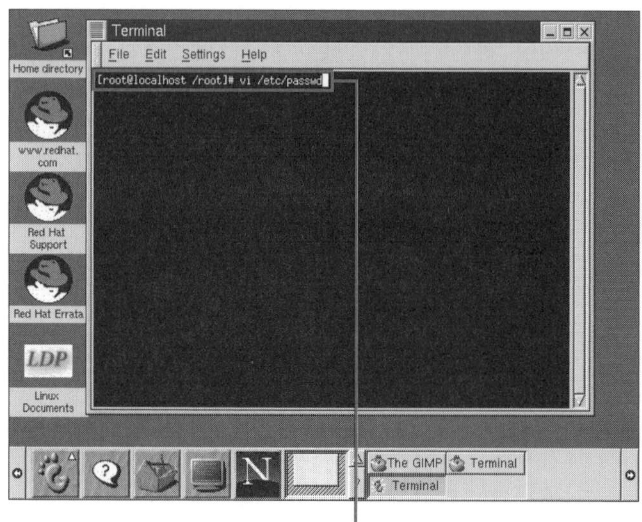

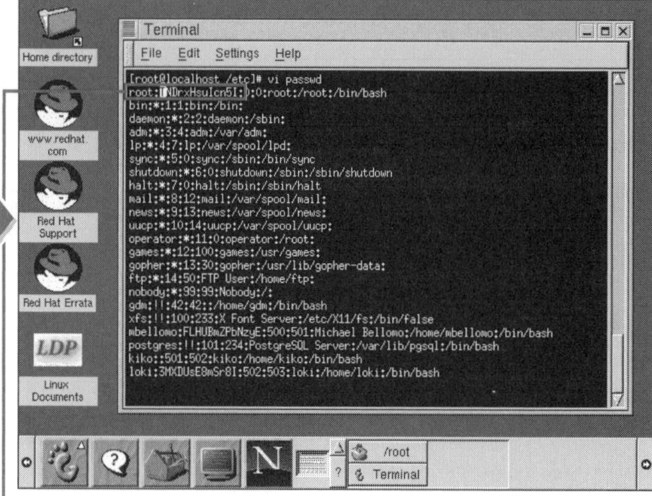

1 Shut the computer down.

2 Reboot the system with your Linux boot disk.

3 To edit the `/etc/passwd` file in the `vi` editor, type **vi /etc/passwd** and press Enter to edit the `passwd` file.

■ The `/etc/passwd` file always lists the root account information in the top line. The encrypted password is a string of what looks like nonsense letters to the right of root and the field delimiter (a colon).

4 Move your cursor to the start of the encrypted password field to delete the existing encrypted password.

TIPS

Because I have to add a password again anyway, should I add a new root password while I'm at it?

- Doing so won't hurt, particularly if it's been a while since you last changed the password. As a general rule, you should change passwords every three months. Of course, if you're on a low-security system, you may not need to do this at all — but on a high-security system, consider changing the password every month to prevent unscrupulous users or crackers from hacking into your system.

What if I forget the root password on a system that isn't my main server?

- This is still a problem, but it's not as large a problem. Unless there's a major issue on that machine, simply wait until the end of the day for people to go home before you work on it. You might even be able to log into it remotely and, if your server's root account has root permissions, fix the problem remotely.

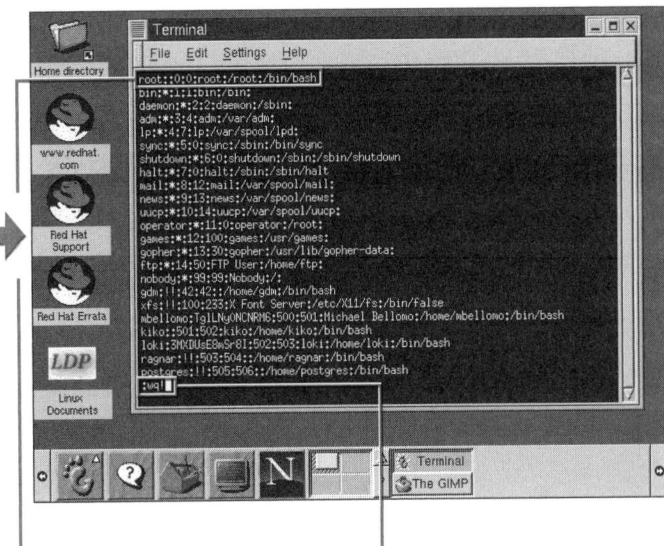

5 Delete the encrypted password in this field until the two colons, marking the end of the field, are next to each other.

6 Press Esc and type **:wq!** to save your changes.

■ This action also quits the `vi` editor and returns you to the Linux command prompt.

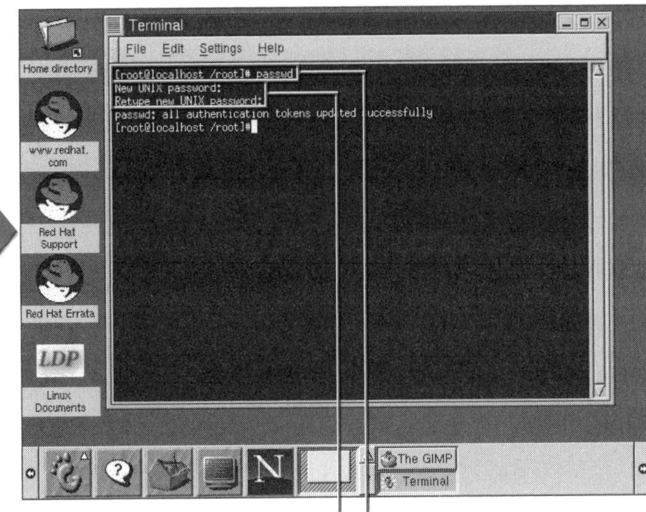

7 At the Linux Terminal command prompt, change the root password with the `passwd` command immediately to close this security gap.

8 Type **passwd** as the root account and press Enter.

9 Follow the prompts to add the new password.

DIAGNOSE DEVICE PROBLEMS ON REBOOT

You can run into severe difficulties if the devices on your system either refuse to be written to or mounted for use. If you have problems when you shut down, your machine is probably not unmounting all the disks. By contrast, if your system complains on bootup that it can't read a given device, you may have to review the device listings in the `/etc/fstab` file.

Device problems are a serious malfunction of your Linux system and could mean that you have either a physical problem or a software problem.

A software problem could mean that you have corrupted files or sectors on the disk drive. You'll normally get this if you've had a power outage or if you haven't been shutting the machine down properly. A hardware failure could be a scratched disk drive, an aging disk head, or even a speck of dust that has demagnetized a portion of the disk. In either case, you need to fix the problem. Here are some variations on the problem and some solutions.

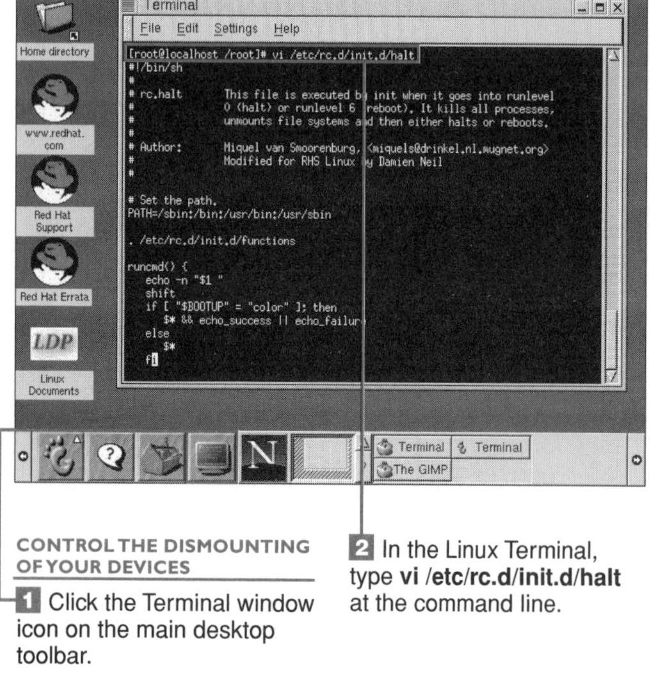

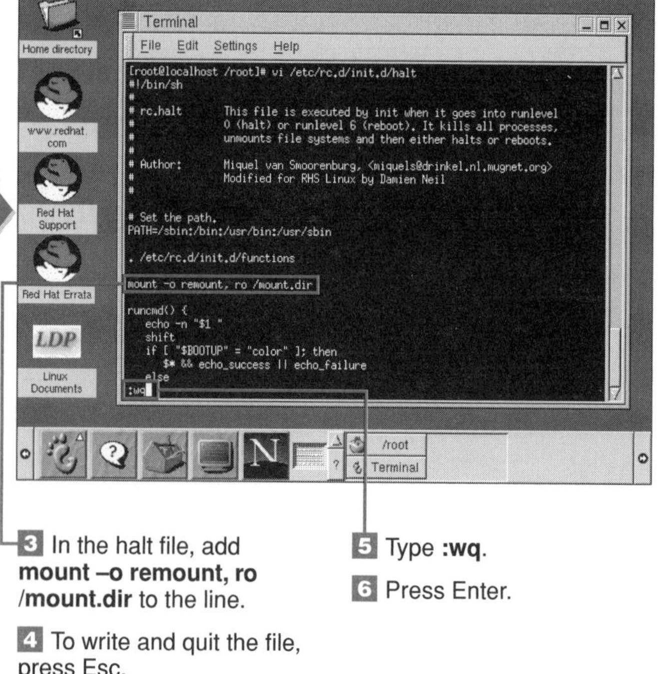

CONTROL THE DISMOUNTING OF YOUR DEVICES

1 Click the Terminal window icon on the main desktop toolbar.

■ A Linux Terminal window appears on the desktop.

2 In the Linux Terminal, type **vi /etc/rc.d/init.d/halt** at the command line.

3 In the halt file, add **mount –o remount, ro /mount.dir** to the line.

4 To write and quit the file, press Esc.

5 Type **:wq**.

6 Press Enter.

What is fsck?

- `fsck` is a disk and device repair utility. It's an old utility imported from the original UNIX systems to find and correct abnormalities on the disk drives. `fsck` in its current form is both accurate and fast, so much so that you should accept its recommendations without hesitation, even though there is a small chance that you may lose some user data when you perform a repair.

Why might I lose data in a repair?

- The data might be corrupt, causing the problem. Often, the only way to correct the data is to remove it so the disk, as a whole, can function.

What if I want to accept all of fsck's repair suggestions by default?

- Type **fsck –y <device name>** and press Enter. The `-y` option answers Yes to all of the repair questions.

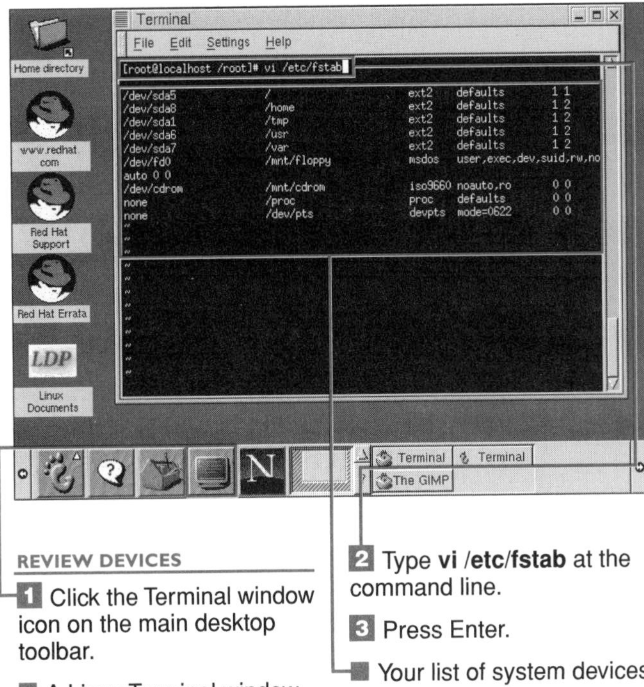

Terminal
File Edit Settings Help
[root@localhost /root]# fsck /dev/sda5

REVIEW DEVICES

1. Click the Terminal window icon on the main desktop toolbar.

■ A Linux Terminal window appears on the desktop.

2. Type **vi /etc/fstab** at the command line.
3. Press Enter.

■ Your list of system devices appears.

4. Press Ctrl+D to enter the preboot administrative mode.
5. Type the bad device number, like **fsck/dev/sda5**, at the command prompt.
6. Follow the instructions to fix the device.

■ The boot process continues until you're at the login screen.

FIND DISK AND CPU HOGS

You can find users or processes that are taking up more than their fair share of computer resources in Linux. Although you have certain tools in the LinuxConf configuration utility, the Control Panels, and the Administration Tools submenu to tell you the state and space left on your hard drive, going through the Terminal is still helpful. With the `du` (disk usage) command and the `sort` command, you can actually locate the exact files that are taking up too much space on your system.

Similarly, you can use the `sort` command with additional parameters to locate who's running a process that is slowing down the system. At times, a person's `find` or `list` command can be done at too high a directory level, causing the computer to work extra hard at completing the task, essentially depriving other users of needed system resources. These commands can help you track down the cause.

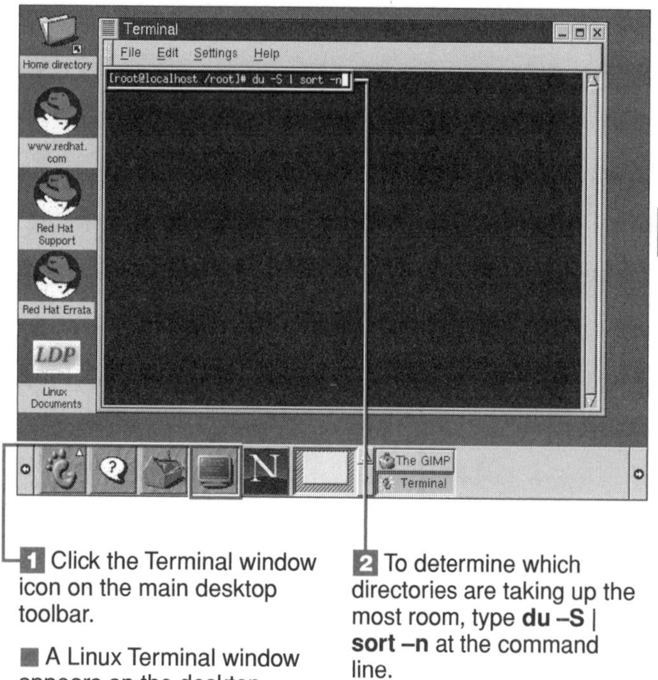

1 Click the Terminal window icon on the main desktop toolbar.

■ A Linux Terminal window appears on the desktop.

2 To determine which directories are taking up the most room, type **du –S | sort –n** at the command line.

3 Press Enter.

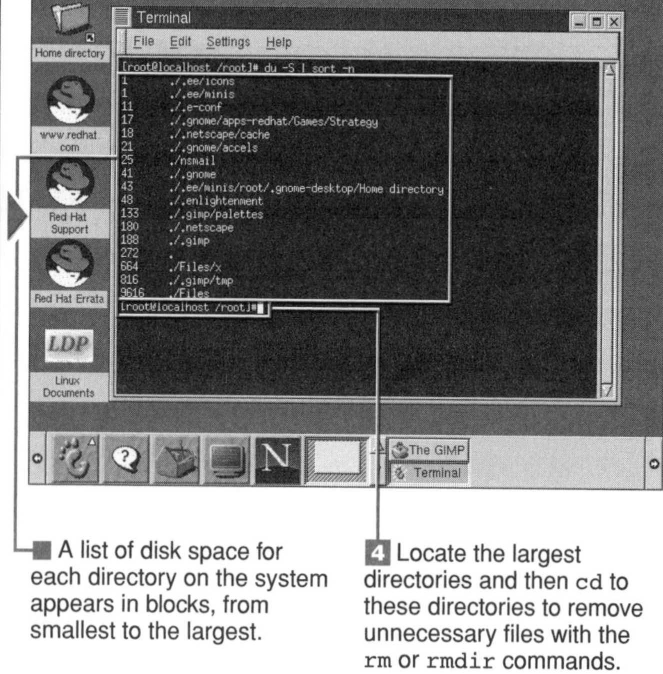

■ A list of disk space for each directory on the system appears in blocks, from smallest to the largest.

4 Locate the largest directories and then `cd` to these directories to remove unnecessary files with the `rm` or `rmdir` commands.

Why does running a command like find take up a large amount of CPU cycles?

- `find` takes up CPU cycles in direct proportion to the scope of its search. If you search `/root` and there's only two subdirectories under it, that's a small scope. On the other hand, if you search from the `/` directory, you could have dozens — even hundreds — of subdirectories, which is a very large scope indeed.

I ran the CPU hog command and found that someone running a telnet session was the cause. How did this happen? People run telnet all the time without hogging the system!

- Sometimes, the hogging of CPU cycles for a given process is not the user's fault. A utility like `telnet` can go out of control every now and again, growing and absorbing resources until it is stopped or it crashes the system. It's best to detect these early and `kill` them as quickly as possible.

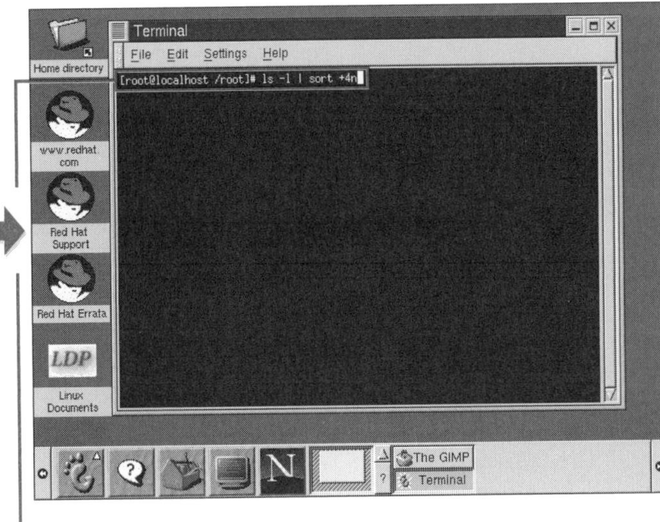

5 To start finding CPU hogs, type **ls –l | sort +4n** at the command prompt.

6 Press Enter.

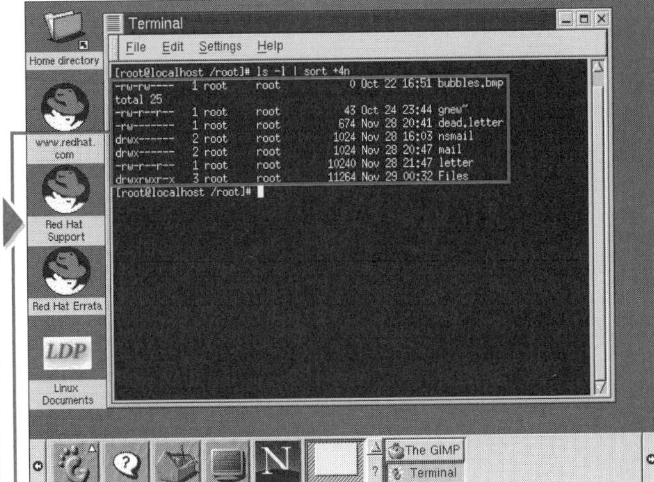

■ The `sort` command lists usage in bytes, from smallest to largest. Once you've located the largest usage, check to see if you want to stop these processes or not.

STOP HUNG OR SPAWNED PROCESSES

You need to stop running Linux processes in three instances: if they are growing to the point where they crash a system; if they hang and cause the system to stop working; or if they start spawning uncontrollably, eventually causing a system failure. To stop a process in Linux, you need to use the `kill` command. (See Chapter 5 for more information on the `kill` command.)

Spawning is the Linux/UNIX terminology that has come to mean when a process creates a new copy of itself. Some processes, like the print daemon (`lpd`), do this routinely, spinning off a new copy of themselves each time a new print job comes along.

However, finding a few dozen `telnet` or other processes running amok on your system means you have to use the `kill` command and put it to use before the `telnet` processes begin to act as a drag on how fast your system can run.

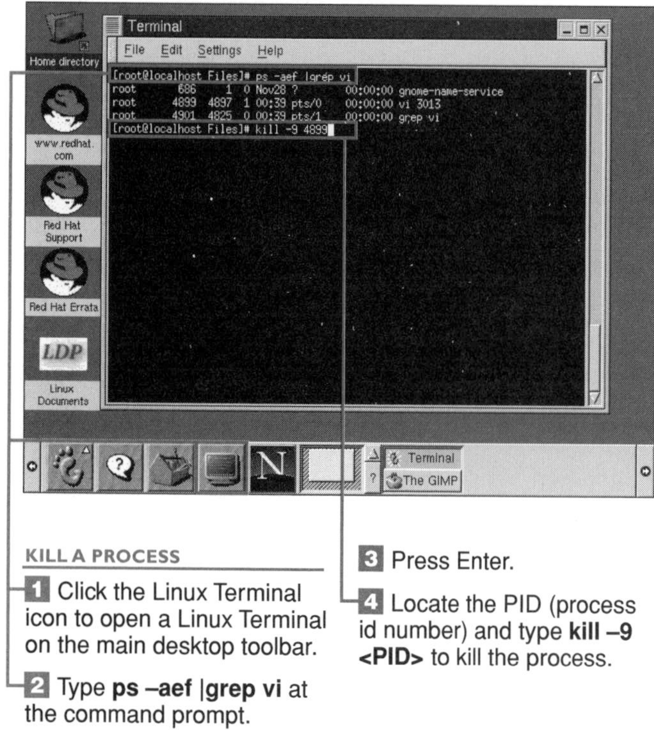

KILL A PROCESS

1. Click the Linux Terminal icon to open a Linux Terminal on the main desktop toolbar.
2. Type **ps –aef |grep vi** at the command prompt.
3. Press Enter.
4. Locate the PID (process id number) and type **kill –9 <PID>** to kill the process.

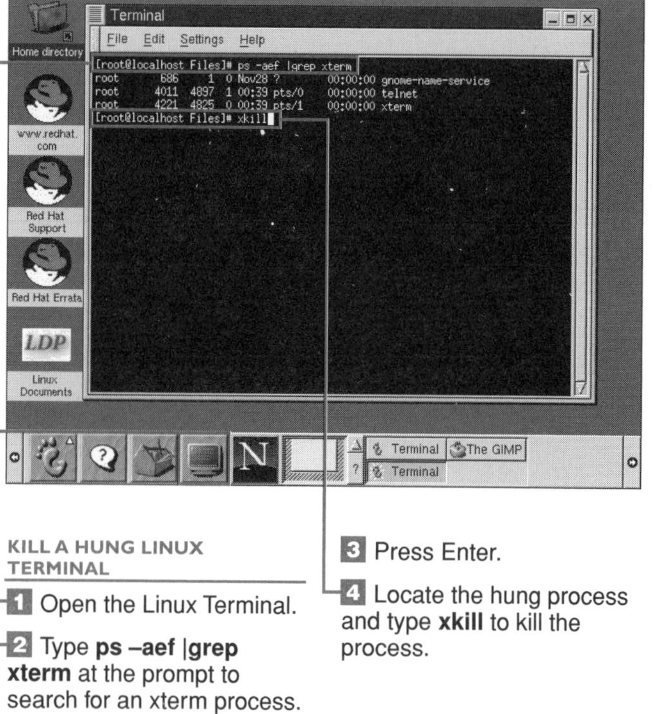

KILL A HUNG LINUX TERMINAL

1. Open the Linux Terminal.
2. Type **ps –aef |grep xterm** at the prompt to search for an xterm process.
3. Press Enter.
4. Locate the hung process and type **xkill** to kill the process.

Why is the -9 kill option more powerful than the regular kill command?

- `kill` essentially sends an electronic signal to a given process. It tells it to "hang up," or gently shut down. The `-9` option is the equivalent of a "force quit" in Windows. The process will shut down, but it won't go through its polite shutdown procedures. It might core dump, or otherwise leave its work unfinished when you use `kill -9`, so you should always use `kill -9` sparingly.

Are there other kill options like –6 or –8?

- Believe it or not, there are. They each perform different functions, but they're a little more esoteric than the most common ones. As a general rule, the higher the number, the more powerful (and problematic) the shutdown signal becomes.

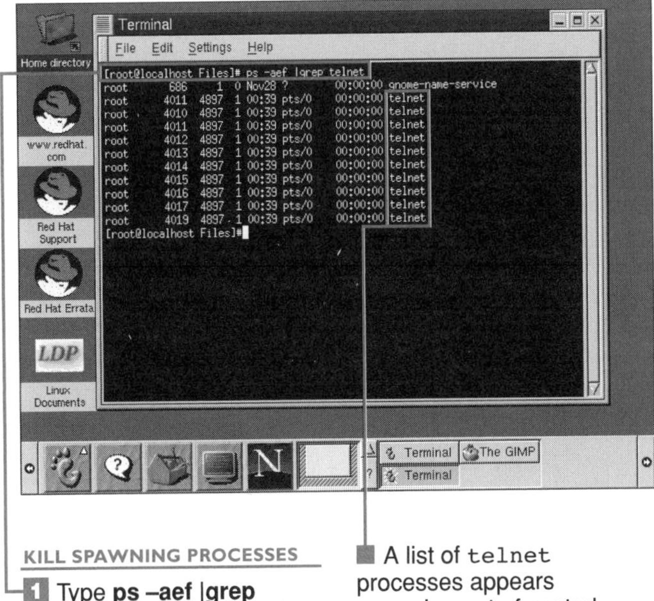

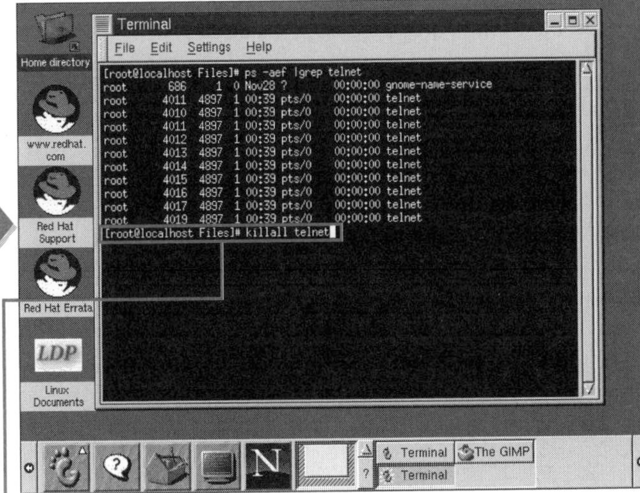

KILL SPAWNING PROCESSES

1. Type **ps –aef |grep telnet** at the command prompt.
2. Press Enter.

■ A list of `telnet` processes appears spawning out of control.

3. To kill all processes with the same name, type **killall telnet**.
4. Press Enter.

TROUBLESHOOT IN THE GUI

You can locate tips to help troubleshoot problems in the GUI. The majority of the troubleshooting techniques take place in the Linux Terminal. This is because the Terminal is a whole layer closer to the actual programs that run your Linux operating system, without an additional layer of graphics to make things look pretty.

However, a few tools in the GUI can do things that are much more tedious in the Terminal. In fact, the GNOME GUI system has some good toolkits and utilities designed specifically for kernels and printers that are more difficult to do from the Linux Terminal.

In addition, the GUI also contains menus with Help information. If you're stuck on a given problem, you may be able to find the solution in there. Compared with the GUI, only a few command utilities, such as `tar` and `gzip`, have good help files available to you.

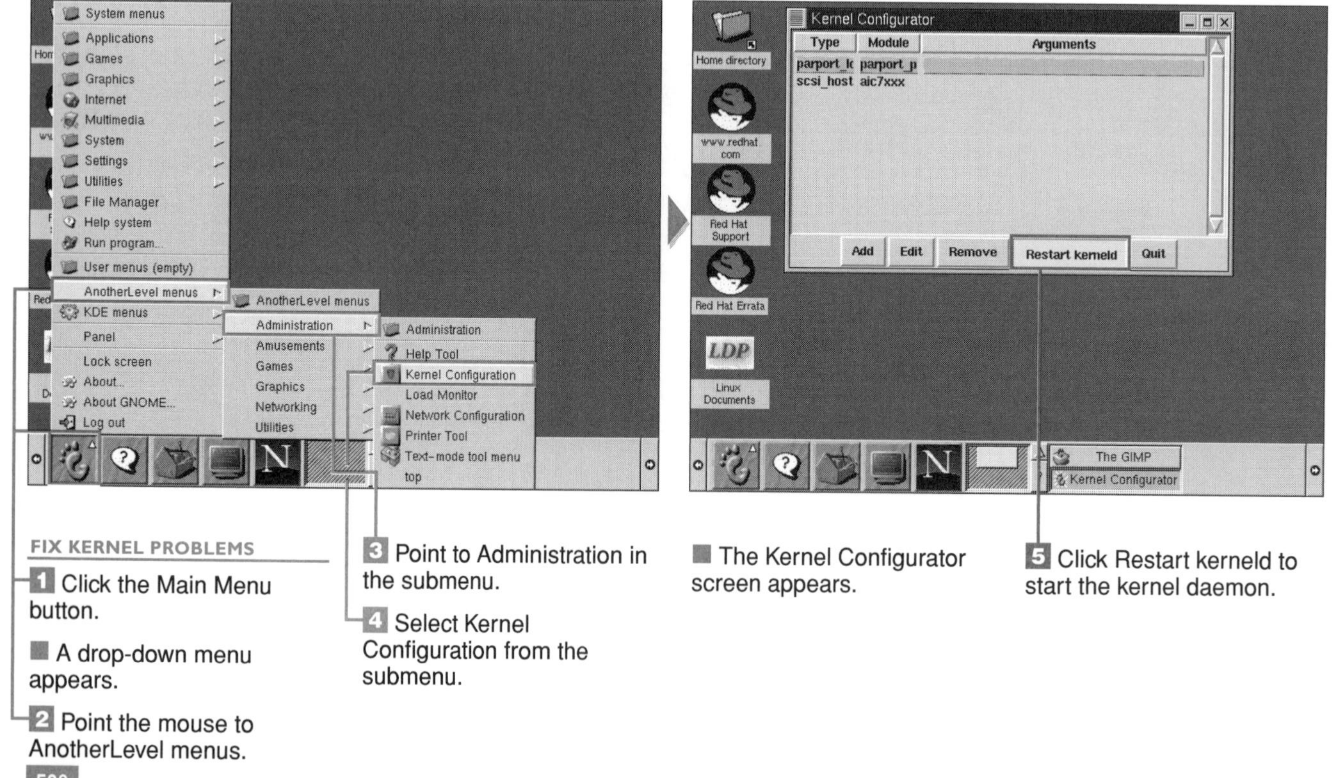

FIX KERNEL PROBLEMS

1 Click the Main Menu button.

■ A drop-down menu appears.

2 Point the mouse to AnotherLevel menus.

3 Point to Administration in the submenu.

4 Select Kernel Configuration from the submenu.

■ The Kernel Configurator screen appears.

5 Click Restart kerneld to start the kernel daemon.

TIPS

How do I know when the kernel daemon dies?

- Because the kernel is what the shell and all the other utilities that run on Linux depend on, system errors alert you when the kernel daemon dies. Even if you aren't told by the error messages up front that this is your problem, it's always good to run a process search to verify that all the system daemons like `kerneld` are still in good working order.

How else can I open the Kernel Configuration screen?

- If you go through Control Panel, you see a button that's marked with what looks like an unpopped popcorn kernel. Click this button to be taken directly to the main Kernel Configurator screen.

How can I search through the Help text in the Troubleshooting selection from the Printer Configuration screen?

- Unfortunately, there's no Troubleshooting search function. The text that appears when you select Troubleshooting from the Help drop-down menu in the Print System Manager window is only a brief listing of several of the common problems you run into when printing in Linux.

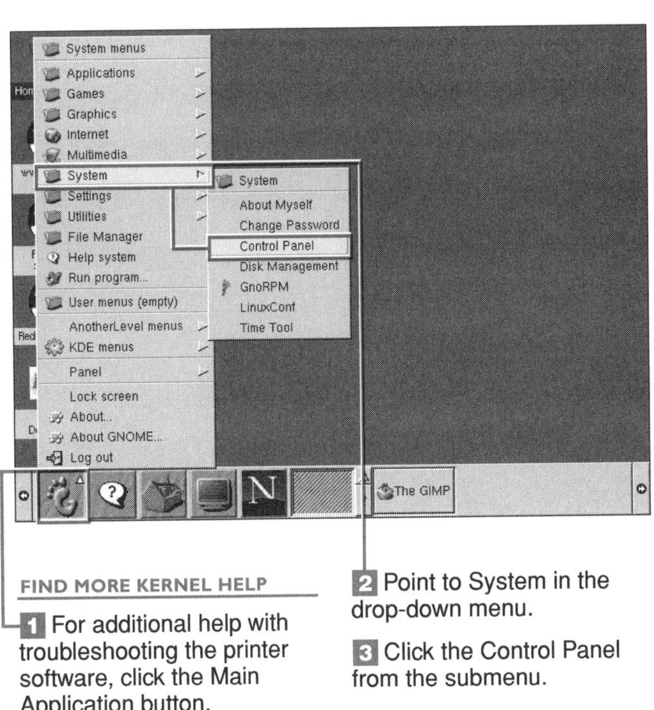

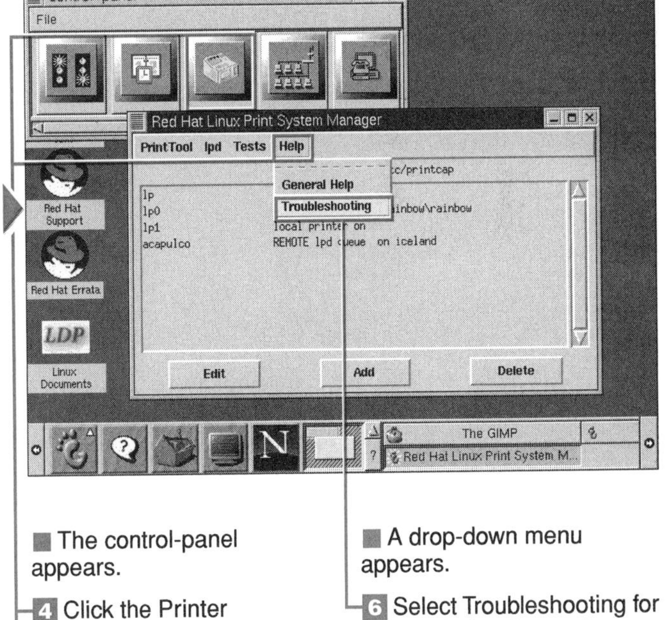

FIND MORE KERNEL HELP

1 For additional help with troubleshooting the printer software, click the Main Application button.

2 Point to System in the drop-down menu.

3 Click the Control Panel from the submenu.

■ The control-panel appears.

4 Click the Printer Configuration button.

5 Select Help from the menu.

■ A drop-down menu appears.

6 Select Troubleshooting for some printing tips and solutions to the most common printing problems.

SECTION IX

APPENDIX A: INSTALLING LINUX

Start the Linux Installation Process 512
Set Up Disk Partitions 516
Set Up Linux Components 518
Set Up Monitor Parameters 520
Set the base Parameteres................................524
Set Printers and Root Password 526

APPENDIX B: BEWARE OF LINUX APPLICATIONS

Use the GNOME CD Player 528
Paint with XPaint 530
Organize with GNOMECARD 532

APPENDIX C: VI EDITOR COMMANDS

APPENDIX D: LINUX COMMANDS

APPENDIXES

START THE LINUX INSTALLATION PROCESS

You can install Red Hat Linux directly from the CD-ROM onto a computer exclusively devoted to Linux. Or you can install Linux on a computer where you are running another operating system, like NetWare or Microsoft Windows, creating a dual-boot machine. When you start up a dual-boot machine, you get to choose the operating system of your choice.

Before you start the installation process, always check your system and CD-ROM's documentation to make sure that you have enough space for the installation. Then start the install process by inserting your Linux CD-ROM into your CD-ROM drive.

During the installation process, use the arrow keys to move your highlighted selection bar up or down, the Tab key to move between fields, and the space bar or the Enter key to make your selection. You don't need the mouse at all for this task.

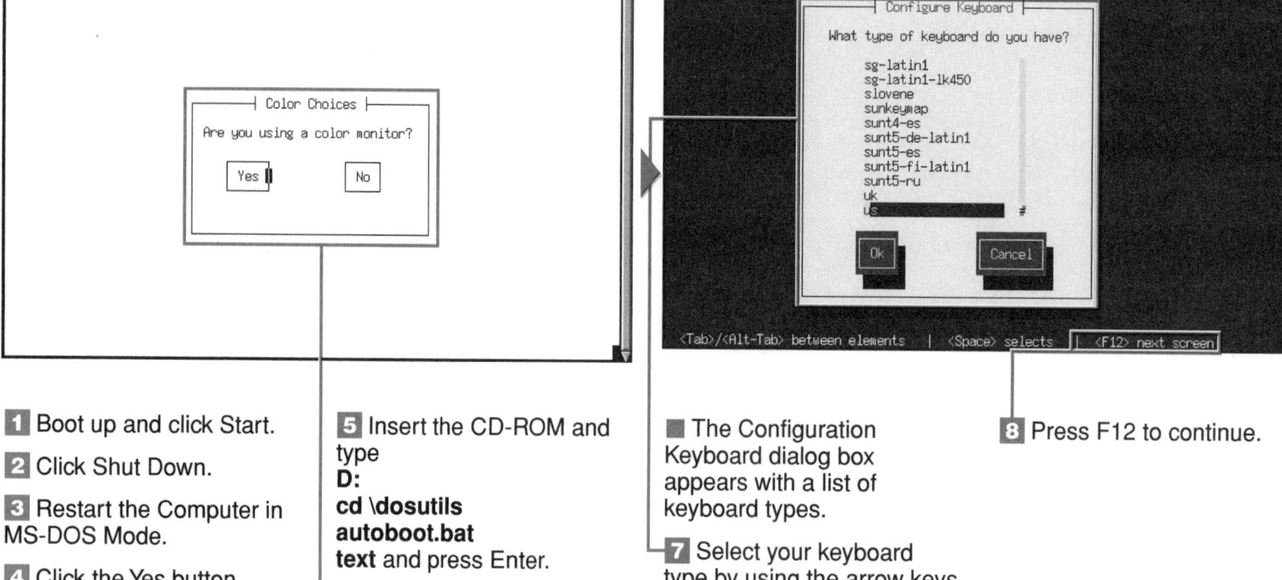

1 Boot up and click Start.

2 Click Shut Down.

3 Restart the Computer in MS-DOS Mode.

4 Click the Yes button.

5 Insert the CD-ROM and type
D:
cd \dosutils
autoboot.bat
text and press Enter.

6 Tab to Yes or No and press Enter to continue.

■ The Configuration Keyboard dialog box appears with a list of keyboard types.

7 Select your keyboard type by using the arrow keys to highlight your choice and then press the spacebar.

8 Press F12 to continue.

How can I tell which SCSI driver I have?

- Note that if you're not sure whether you have a SCSI device or which driver you should use, check the system information for your computer. See your documentation or the System information (for a Windows machine).

Can I open a DOS window on my Windows desktop so I don't have to shut down my machine?

- This isn't a recommended way of starting the Linux installation process. Installing a new operating system on top of another one as it is running almost guarantees a system crash.

What if my machine won't read my CD-ROM?

- Try starting your machine with the CD-ROM in the drive. By default, the machine will look into the CD-ROM to start booting, kicking off the installation program.

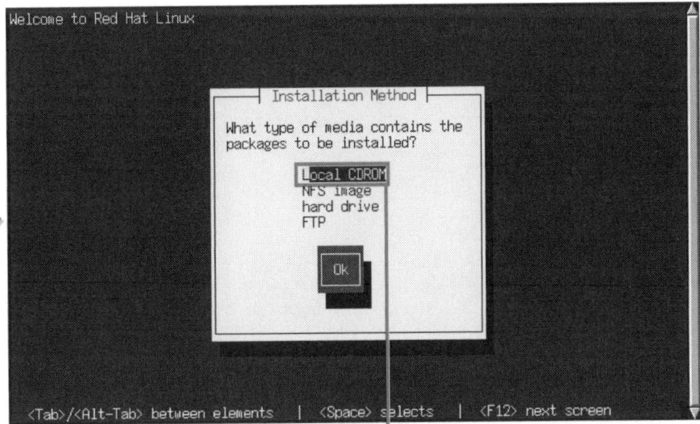

■ The Installation Method dialog box appears. By default, Local CDROM appears highlighted.

9 Because you are installing Red Hat Linux from the CD-ROM, press Enter to select Local CDROM.

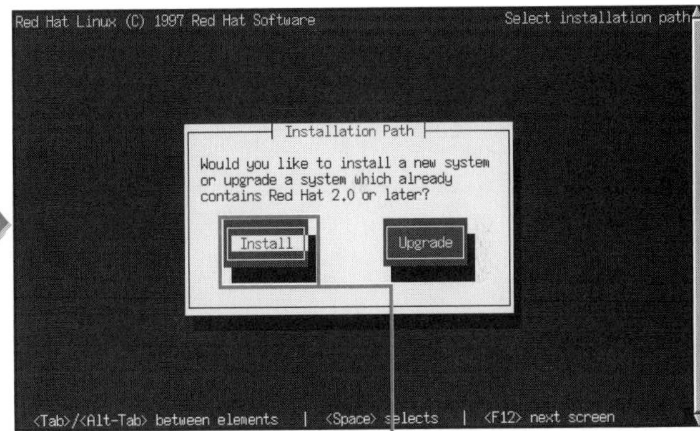

■ The Installation Path dialog box appears.

10 Tab to highlight Install and press Enter if this is your first time installing Red Hat Linux.

CONTINUED

START THE LINUX INSTALLATION PROCESS CONTINUED

You can ensure that Linux will install properly on your hard drive by selecting the correct SCSI adapter. The SCSI (Small Computer System Interface) is a type of drive that most computer system use. An adapter is a piece of software that enables your SCSI device to interact with your operating system.

As a rule, you can find the adapter type by checking the manual that came with your system, or by looking on the container box. Your adapter choice depends on the device's manufacturer. You can't change the setting as it is embedded into the hardware itself.

After selecting the adapter, pick one of two utilities to work with the partitions of your hard drive. A partition is a slice of your hard drive that the operating system uses to divide the binaries and files it needs to run.

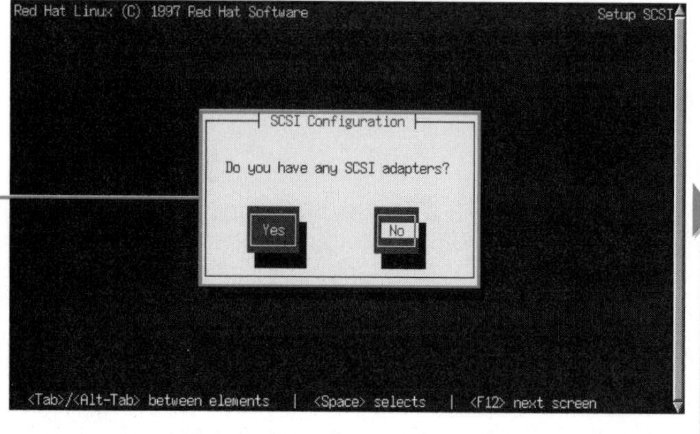

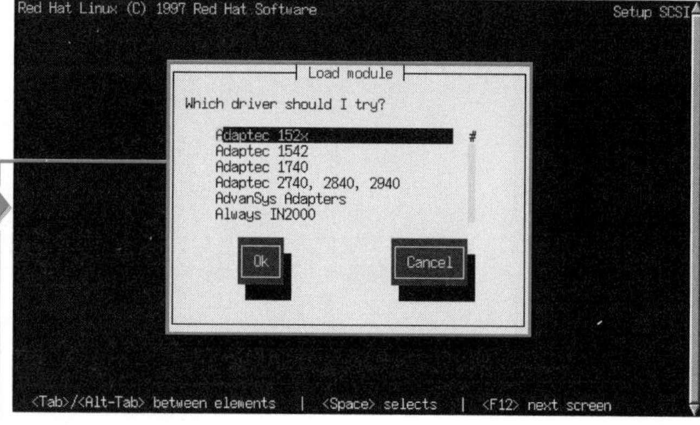

■ The SCSI Configuration dialog box appears, asking if you have any SCSI adapters on your PC.

11 Tab to highlight Yes or No and press Enter.

■ If you chose Yes, then you must select the appropriate driver for your SCSI device from the Load module dialog box.

12 Use your arrow keys to highlight your driver and press Enter.

Why should I use Disk Druid?

- If you are new to Linux, Disk Druid is slightly easier to use. Disk Druid has the rudiments of a graphic interface, much like MS-DOS, and is preferred more than other utilities.

Should I delete any existing partitions?

- You can if you want to, but this will delete all information in that partition. If you want to continue running MS-DOS on your machine, for example, don't delete or edit that partition.

How can I tell which partition has my current operating system running on it?

- The Linux installation process automatically detects all existing partitions. If you have MS-DOS, NetWare, or Windows on your machine, it shows up as it own partition. If you don't want to delete it, create new partitions as described in the following task.

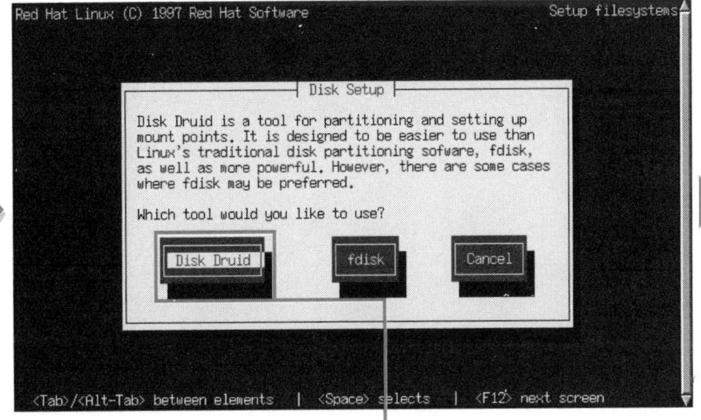

■ The Disk Setup dialog box appears, asking which disk partitioning utility you want to use.

13 Unless you're experienced with Linux or Unix, select the `Disk Druid` utility and press Enter.

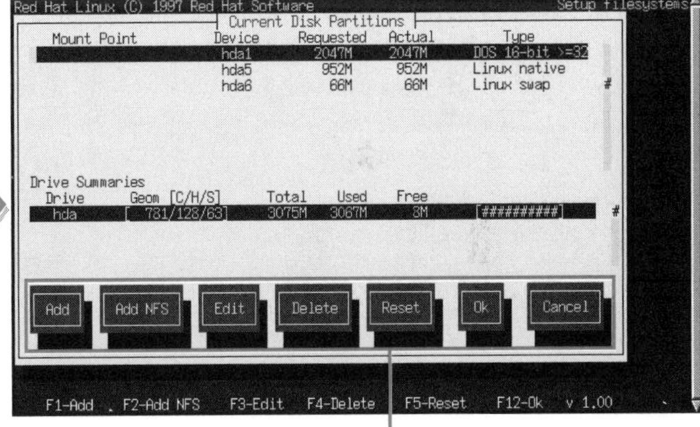

■ The main `Disk Druid` screen appears.

14 Press the Tab key to highlight the Add, Edit, or Delete disk partition option and then press Enter to select.

SET UP DISK PARTITIONS

You can set up the disk partitions that Linux needs to run properly on your computer with a disk partition utility. For this example, you use Disk Druid.

You need a minimum of five partitions to run Linux. These include the `/root` partition (/hr), the `/var` and `/etc` partitions (which hold binaries and mail folders), and the `/tmp` partition, which you use for storing any files that you don't plan on keeping permanently. Also, add a *swap partition*, which is space Linux uses when it needs extra computing power.

Follow any defaults or documentation you may have to set up your partitions. If you're inheriting a Linux or UNIX network, compare how other similarly sized drives are set up by `vi`'ing the `/etc/fstab` file.

Say that you have a 8GB hard drive. You could divide your drive up as follows:

Dividing Up a Hard Drive

File Type	Use	Space
/	Root partition	4 GB
/etc	Binaries and programs	1GB
/usr	Binaries and programs	1GB
/var	Mail and more binaries	1GB
/tmp	Temporary Storage	500MB

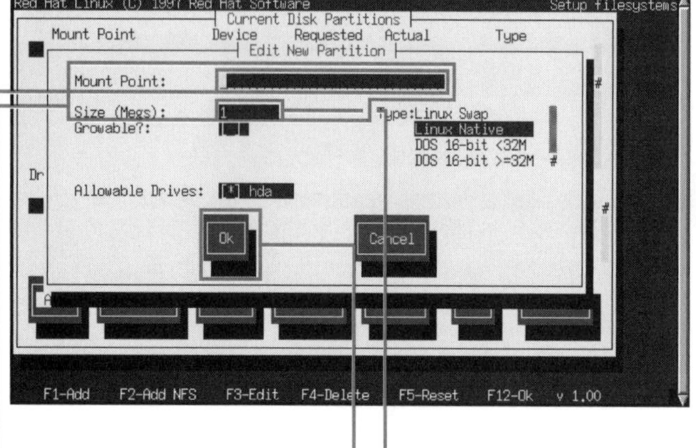

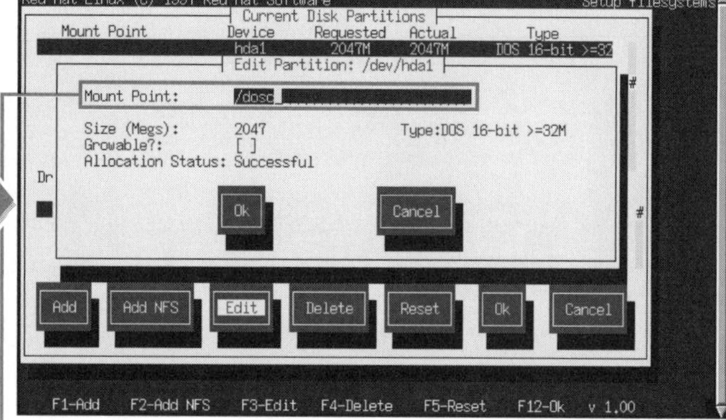

CREATE PARTITIONS IN DISK DRUID

1. Press F1.

- The Edit New Partition dialog box appears.

2. Type / in the Mount Point field.

3. Tab to the Size field and type a number.

4. Tab to the Ok button and press Enter.

- Repeat this process for creating the / other partitions.

5. Click Ok in the main Disk Druid Screen.

6. Type in a new name for the partition.

7. After you complete your changes, Tab to the Ok button and press Enter.

Note: If you are installing Linux from scratch, you do not have to edit your partitions after creating them.

What is swap space?

- *Swap* is space Linux uses as a kind of 'virtual memory'. When the machine becomes so busy that it runs out of computing power on its RAM (random access memory) it "grabs" some of the allocated disk space and performs computations or graphics processing and does it there.

Why does swap need a separate partition and formatting process?

- If the Linux operating system were to just grab whatever hard drive space that was available, it could possibly take the space that a program was saving a file to or otherwise interfere with another process. This would cause the entire machine to freeze up or crash.

What happens if I configure a partition with too little disk space?

- If you don't give a partition enough disk space to install of its information, the Linux installation process will complain, and allow you to edit the partition to expand it.

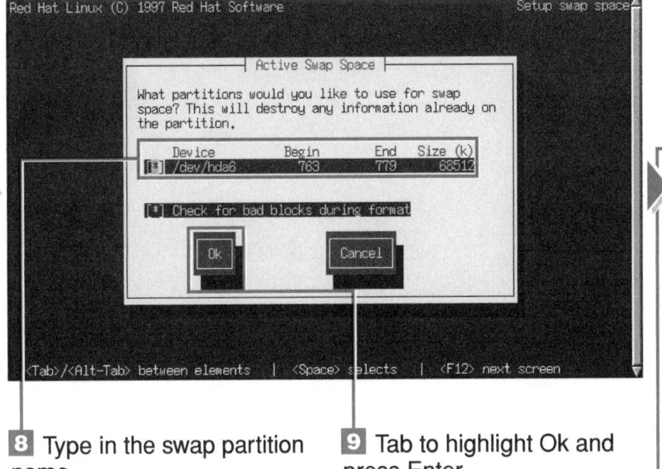

8 Type in the swap partition name.

9 Tab to highlight Ok and press Enter.

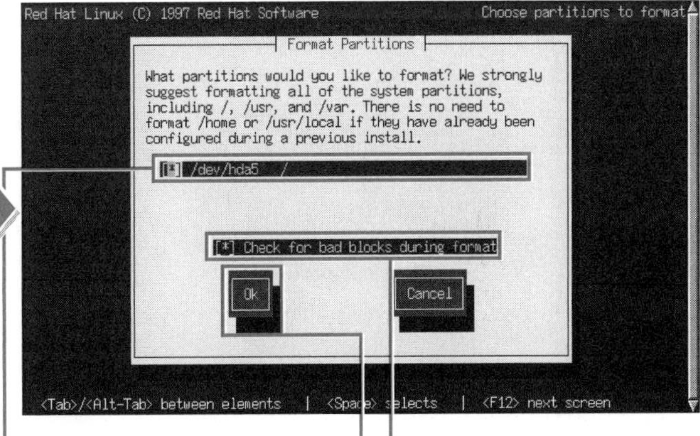

■ The Format Partitions dialog box appears.

10 Press Tab to highlight the partition's name and then press the spacebar to format.

11 Now press Tab to highlight Check for bad blocks during format and press the spacebar.

12 Press Tab to highlight Ok and then press Enter to continue.

SET UP LINUX COMPONENTS

You can next set up which *components* you want to work with in your Linux environment. Components can be software, such as games or other applications. Components can also be types of hardware, such as keyboards or mouse devices.

Unfortunately, the Linux installation process doesn't set up all software or hardware components first. Instead, it sets them up in no particular sequence, asking you to pick software components to install, and then asking whether you want to work with a certain kind of mouse or monitor. However, each procedure itself is simple and straightforward.

When you select your software components, don't be too choosy about which to take and which to leave behind. If you have enough space, go ahead and install each package. Unless you know the specific needs of your user community for the next ten years, it never hurts to have as many tools as possible.

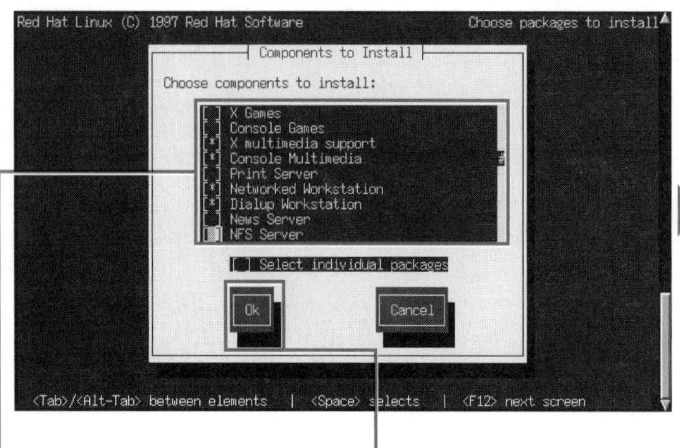

■ The Components to Install dialog box appears.

1 Use your arrow keys to scroll up and down the Components to Install list. Press the spacebar to select and deselect components.

2 Tab to choose Ok and press Enter to continue after selecting all your components.

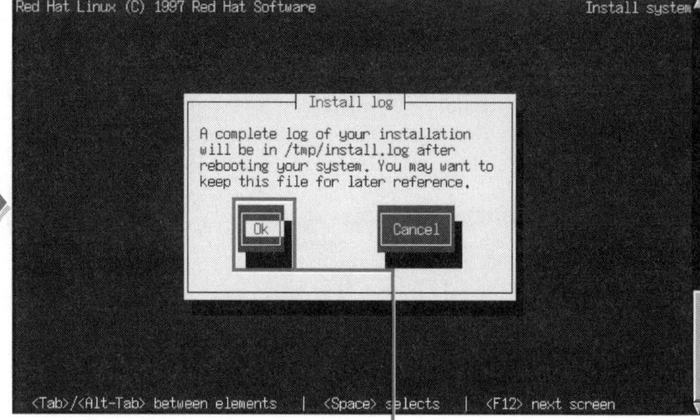

■ The Install log reminder appears. Check it out after the installation.

3 Tab to choose Ok and press Enter to continue.

What if I already have a three-button mouse and don't need emulation?

- If you have a three-button mouse, the system detects it and doesn't display this screen.

Which software components can I skip if I'm not planning to connect to a network, and I'm short on disk space?

- If you don't plan to connect to a Linux network, it doesn't mean that you should leave out all of the networking components. For example, even if you don't plan to network your machine, you may want to use a modem to connect to the Internet. If you want to leave a network component out in this situation, deselect the NFS Server package.

Which software components can I leave out if I don't support any software developers, and if I'm short on disk space?

- If you don't have developers and you don't ever plan on writing software code yourself, you can leave out C Development and Development Libraries.

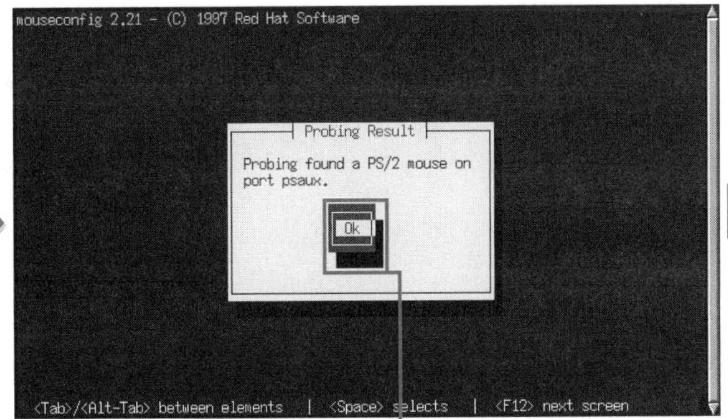

■ The Probing Result appears after it locates your mouse.

4 Tab to highlight Ok and press Enter to continue.

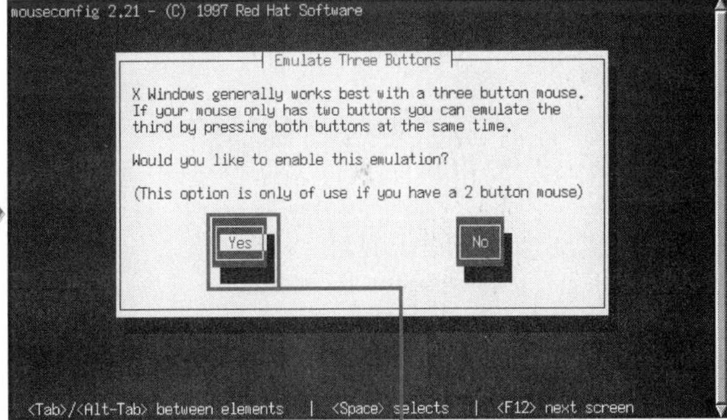

■ The Emulate Three Button dialog box appears. If you have a two-button mouse, you'll be asked if you want three-button emulation.

5 Tab to choose Yes and press Enter to continue.

■ The Welcome screen for the X Window System Component appears.

SET UP MONITOR PARAMETERS

You can complete the setup of the last hardware component when you configure your monitor settings. Because Linux is so new to the graphics-intensive world of desktops and icons, the installation program takes pains to be very specific about the technical aspects of monitor setup.

To start, you are presented with welcome and information screens to tell you what aspects you'll have to be setting up a little farther on in the install process. You also have to select the type of monitor that you're using. As with the other hardware devices that you've set up by now, each monitor's manufacturer has slight differences between their product and another's. You may also have to take into account a specialized graphics or video card on your machine, if you've installed one already.

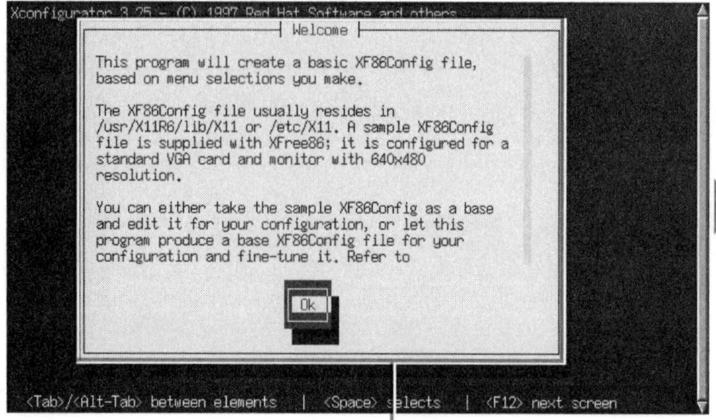

■ The Welcome dialog box from the `Xconfigurator` program appears.

1 Press Enter to continue after reading the Welcome screen.

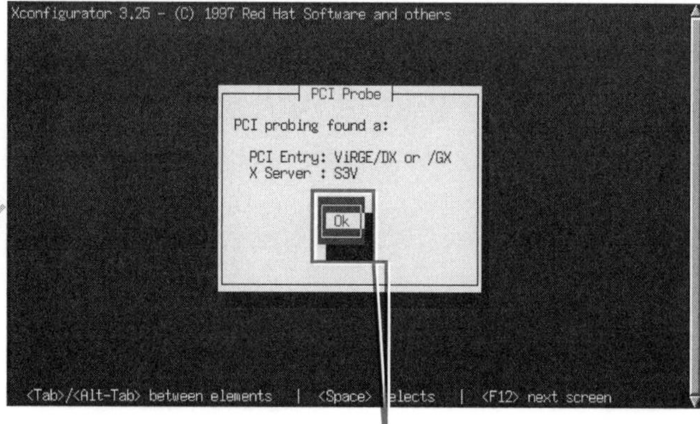

■ The PCI Probe dialog box appears after locating your computer's video card.

2 Tab to highlight Ok and press Enter to continue.

What if my monitor's brand shows up on the Monitor Setup screen, but not my particular model?

- This could mean that your model was discontinued, mislabeled, was out too long ago — or too recently — to make the list. Select the closest model to yours on the Setup screen. Similar models from the same manufacturer rarely use completely different settings.

What if I have a monitor that doesn't appear on list of monitors in the Monitor Setup screen?

- If you have a rare or out of date monitor, you must select Custom from the Monitor Setup menu when it appears. The Custom setting runs your monitor with default settings that are compatible with more than 90 percent of all monitors.

What is Xconfiguration?

- Xconfiguration is the configuration program for the X Window System, the software that Linux uses to display graphic backgrounds. Because the X Window software is so crucial to display options, just about any Linux file that starts with X is graphics related.

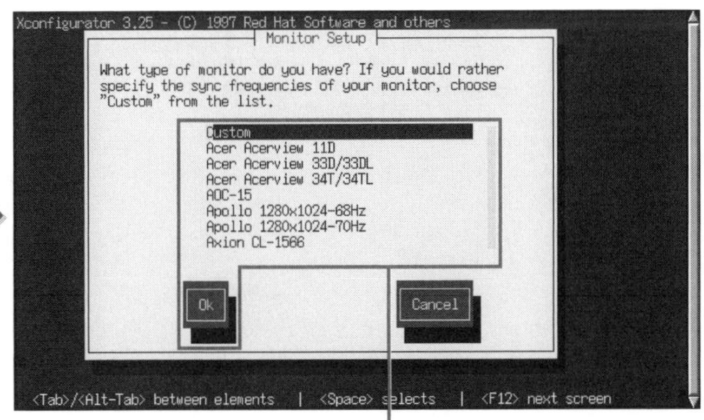

■ The Monitor Setup dialog box appears.

3 Use the arrow keys to highlight your monitor and then press Enter to move on.

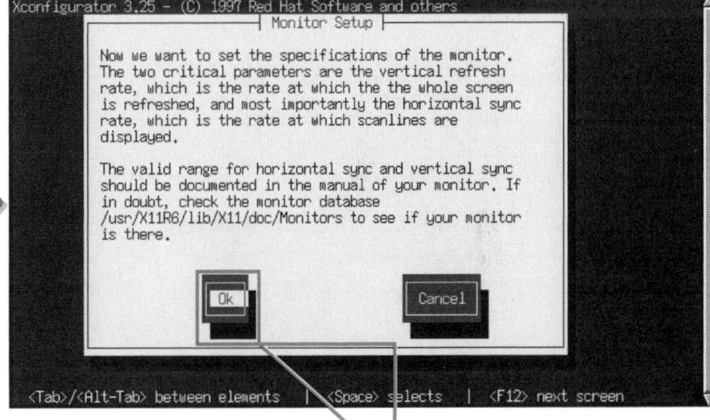

■ A screen appears that describes the parameters you're going to set.

4 Tab to highlight Yes and press Enter.

CONTINUED

SET UP MONITOR PARAMETERS

CONTINUED

You need to complete the monitor setup by setting the parameters that control your screen's refresh rate and overall clarity. Because Linux is new to the graphics world, this portion of the installation presents you with many more choices than if you installed Windows 95, 98, NT 4.0, or Windows 2000.

Keep in mind that you are not bound by the settings you select in the installation process here. If you misconfigured your settings so that your screen looks out of focus or too big for the small space, you can use the Enlightenment Window Manager on the GNOME desktop environment to recalibrate the size or settings of the screen.

Linux can help you configure how clearly you can see images, but it cannot help you increase or decrease screen brightness. To do that, use the manual control buttons or knobs on your monitor.

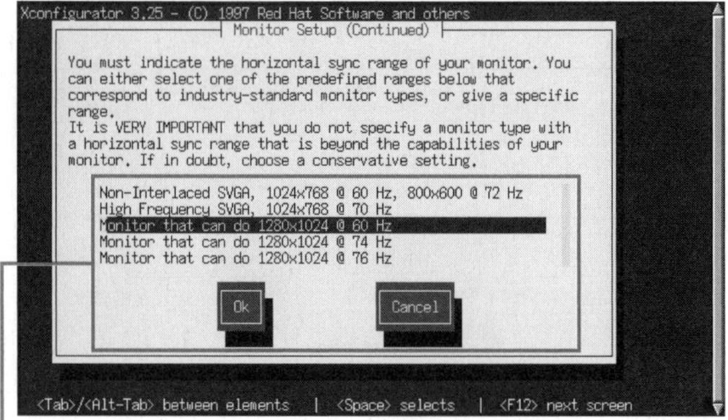

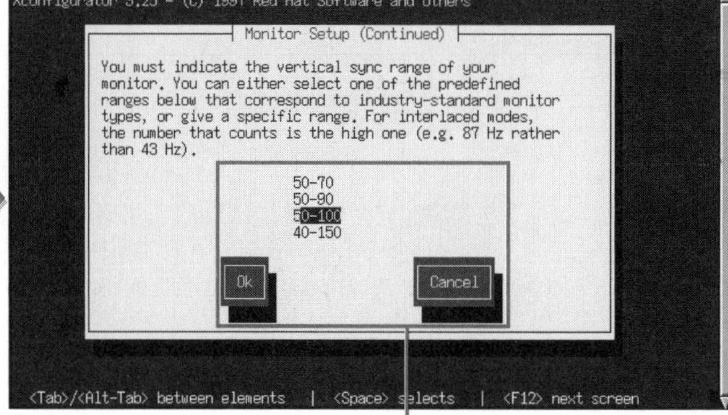

■ The Linux installation process always offers the default setting of 1280 x 1024 @ 60 Hz.

■ Because this setting affects your screen clarity, take the default selection by pressing Enter.

■ The vertical sync range of your monitor appears. This determines the level of detail that your monitor is capable of displaying.

5 The Linux installation process always offer you the default setting 50–100. Take the default by pressing Enter.

What is *horizontal sync?*

- Essentially, this is the setting that affects the horizontal synchronization of the light beam projection that makes up your screen images. It affects your screen resolution and hence its clarity. It's easier to set the defaults and then adjust your monitor later when you're in GNOME.

What is *vertical sync?*

- This setting affects the vertical synchronization of the light beam projection of your screen images. This setting works with the horizontal sync to give you the best screen clarity.

What is the probing that Linux is doing?

- Whenever any operating system is installed, it inspects and tests any video components on your system to see how to best send images to the hardware. A video component could be the standard video card that comes with your computer, or a sophisticated graphics card you've installed for 3-D games.

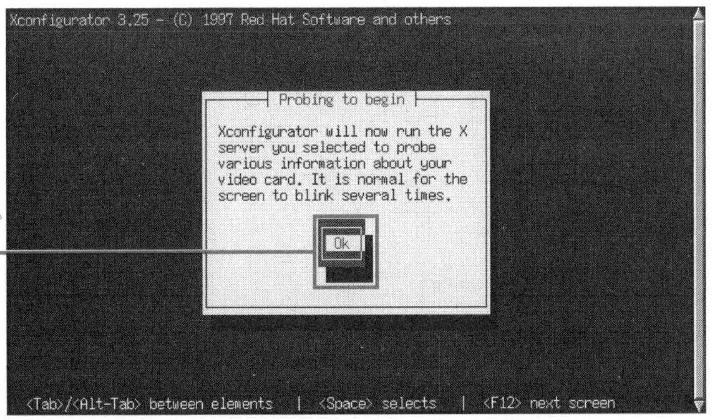

■ Linux notifies you that it will complete the monitor tests. The Probing to Begin dialog box appears.

6 Press Enter after reading.

■ The Network Configuration dialog box appears, asking if you want to start your network configuration.

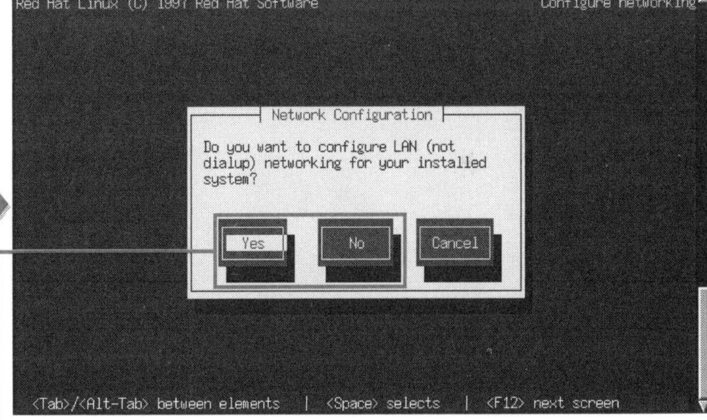

7 Tab to choose No if you on a standalone machine, otherwise, choose Yes and press Enter.

■ The Configure TCP/IP dialog appears, where you configure your network.

SET THE BASE PARAMETERS

Setting the base parameters of your network is the final big step in completing the installation process. If you're on a stand-alone machine, some of these steps may not be displayed. If you're hooked up to a network and you're installing Linux on a new machine, be sure to check your administration documents to make sure that you select an Internet address that isn't already in use on your network.

Your final step is to select a root password. Ideally, you should assign a password that you can remember, but that others cannot guess easily. You should choose a mix of numbers and letters, and perhaps a special character such as the plus sign and asterisk. For example, *cool dude* is too easy for a password-cracking program to figure because it's made of words found in the dictionary or everyday speech. A better one would be "c001*dude," which is almost impossible to break, but just about as easy to remember.

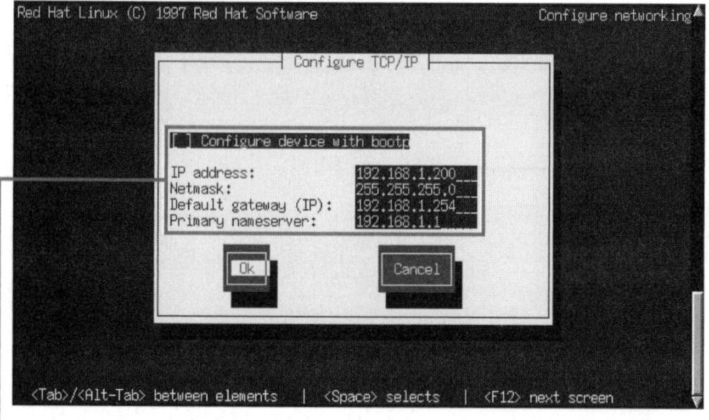

1 Type your IP addresses in the Configure TCP/IP dialog box and press Enter.

■ The Configure Network dialog box appears.

■ If you're adding this system to an established network, fill in this network screen.

■ Check your administration documents for the name of your domain and name servers.

2 Type the information into the Configure Network dialog box and press Enter.

Why is selecting all of the services available a desirable action?

- In Linux, if a service starts up and it is not used, it runs quietly in the background or is shut down. However, if you need to start using a service that hasn't been installed, you'll either have to start it up manually, which is a chore, or reinstall the whole operating system to get it installed properly.

How old can my machine be and still handle all of the services I am selecting?

- Linux's biggest strength is that it is considered a "lightweight" operating system. In other words, it takes very little computing power to run it, even when it is configured with all available services. If you have a x386 computer or better, this will not cause you problems.

Why is selecting the time zone important?

- Although a Linux machine can run properly in any time zone, it's best to set the parameter to match the zone of your actual geographic location. If you ever set Linux to perform tasks automatically, it's easier to set the machine to do tasks in the early morning hours when no one is using the machine and competing for resources.

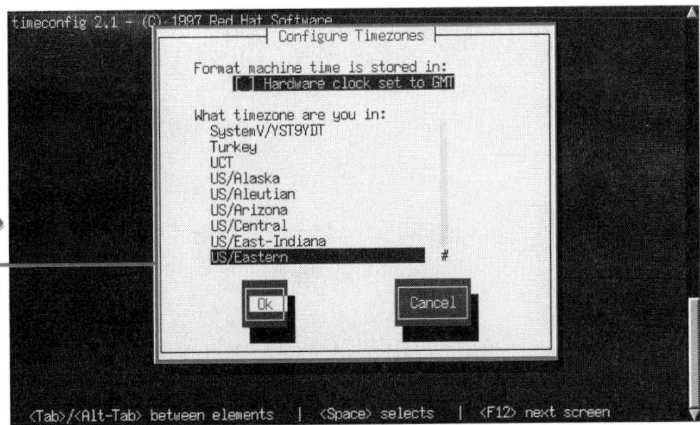

■ The Configure Timezones dialog box appears.

3 Use the arrow keys to highlight your timezone and press Enter.

■ The Services dialog box appears, requesting the type of service you want to start your Linux system. Select all services available.

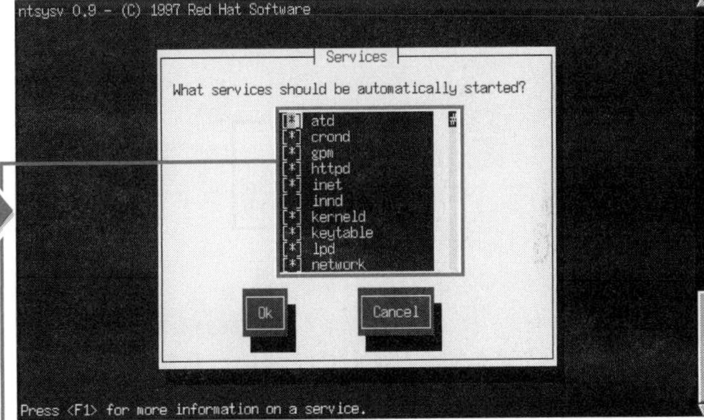

4 Use the arrow keys to highlight each service and press the spacebar to select. Then press Enter when all services are selected.

SET PRINTERS AND ROOT PASSWORD

You can set up your printers and the Linux system password in the installation process. If you don't have a printer ready to go, or can't come up with a good Linux password, there's no need to worry. Utilities in the GNOME desktop enable you to reset your password and add printers at any time.

Printers, like SCSI devices, come with different *drivers*, depending on the manufacturer. A driver is a piece of software that allows a device to talk to the operating system. Red Hat Linux comes with all the drivers used by the major companies, plus a generic driver that's compatible with all printers.

After setting your system password, keep the password written down somewhere in case you forget it. However, keep the written password somewhere private, such as a locked drawer or wall safe and refer to it only in an emergency. Luckily, you don't have to worry about typos when entering in your password, as Linux asks you to enter the password twice to confirm it.

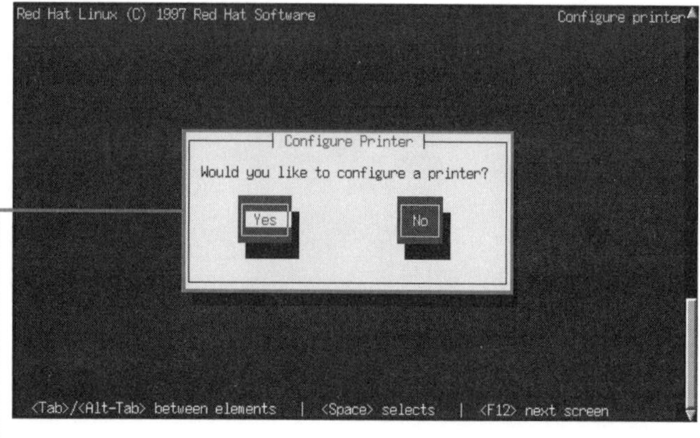

1 Tab to highlight Yes or No and press Enter.

■ The Select Printer Connection dialog box appears.

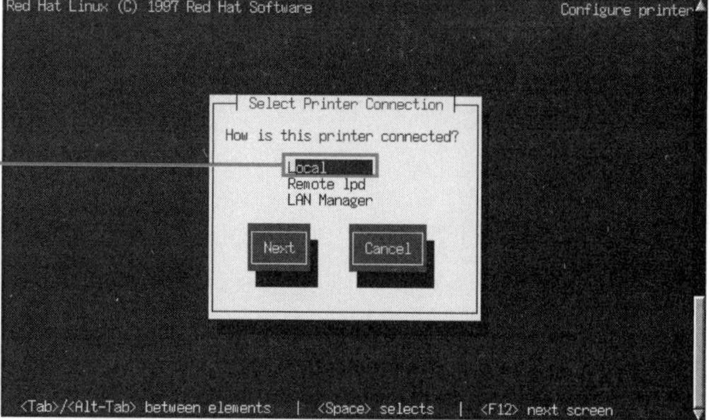

2 Tab to select Local (if the printer is physically hooked up to your machine) or Remote (if it is on the network) and then press Enter.

■ The Standard Printer Options dialog box appears.

TIPS

What if I don't have a blank floppy disk available for creating a boot disk?

- You can create a boot disk manually from the GNOME desktop if need be. However, you should do this as soon as possible or you may forget, leading to a disaster down the road.

Does the blank floppy disk that I use have to be preformatted?

- You must make sure that the disk you're using is formatted to work with a PC or a Macintosh computer. Although you can format disks in Linux, the Linux installation program doesn't know how to do this. If you need to format the floppy disk, do that on a different Linux, Windows, or Macintosh machine.

My printer doesn't show up on the list of printer configurations, what should I do?

- Select the Generic printer from the list. Linux uses a generic print driver that works reasonably well for most off-brand or older printer models.

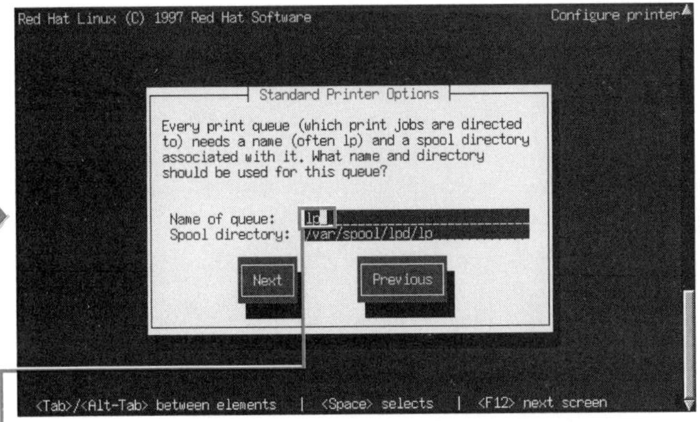

3 Type **lp** in the Name Of queue field and press Enter.

4 Use the arrow keys to highlight your printer port and press Enter.

■ If you are prompted, select the paper orientation.

■ The Root Password dialog box appears.

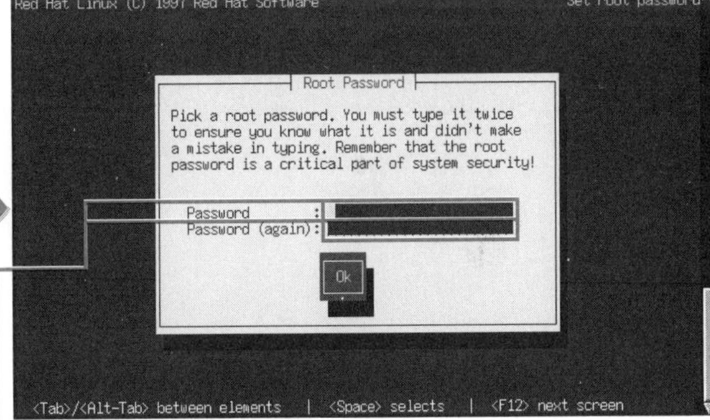

5 Type your password and tab to the next field.

6 Type your password again and press Enter.

■ If you are prompt to create a boot disk, highlight Yes and press Enter.

■ You're prompt to restart your machine.

7 Remove the Red Hat Linux CD-ROM from your CD-ROM drive.

8 Restart your machine.

USE THE GNOME CD PLAYER

You can use the GNOME CD player utility to play music CDs on any computer running Red Hat Linux. Although you can't administer files, users, groups, or discs with it, the GNOME CD player is fun for those who want to catch some tunes while working on their system.

Note that this program can only play musical CD-ROMs. The CD player cannot help you read or install software packages. Some installation media, particularly for advanced graphics or computer-aided design (CAD) programs, will come with both music and software packages on the same disc.

In such a case, the GNOME CD player will be able to access the music portions of the disc, while GNOME RPM can handle the technical component of the disc. For more information on how to use the GNOME Red Hat Package Manager program, see Chapter 12.

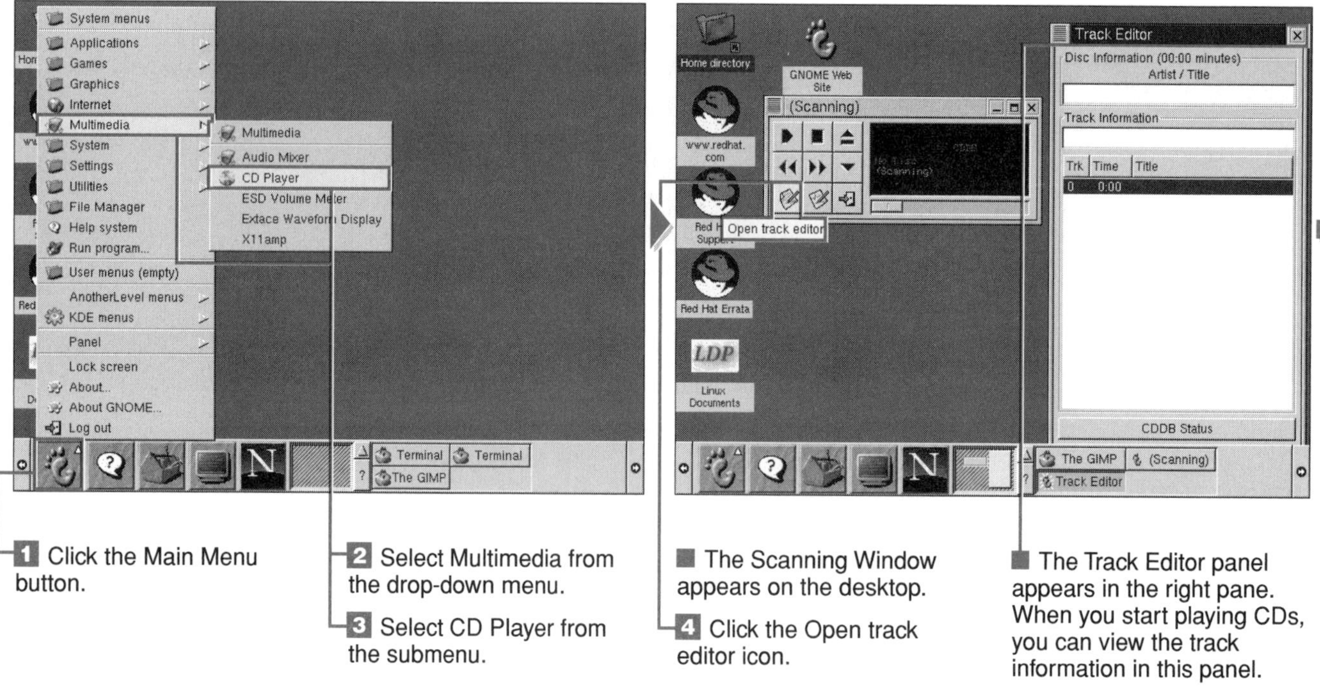

1 Click the Main Menu button.

2 Select Multimedia from the drop-down menu.

3 Select CD Player from the submenu.

■ The Scanning Window appears on the desktop.

4 Click the Open track editor icon.

■ The Track Editor panel appears in the right pane. When you start playing CDs, you can view the track information in this panel.

I've set this program up properly, and it seems to be working. Why don't I hear anything?

- If you're running a standard Linux or UNIX server, most of these machines will not come with speakers. This is because few UNIX or Linux workstations had programs to play more than beeps or pings when performing network tasks. Be sure to find a pair of external speakers and plug them in.

I have the speakers plugged in, and I still can't hear anything.

- You must have a sound card (or a sound board, which is really the same thing) installed on your computer. Some of the most rudimentary sound cards refuse to work with CDs because they're designed to make ping or beep sounds on startup, not provide stereophonic sound. If this is your problem, buy a sound card that is compatible with your computer and install it. Installation instructions are normally available in the packaging of whatever sound card you buy.

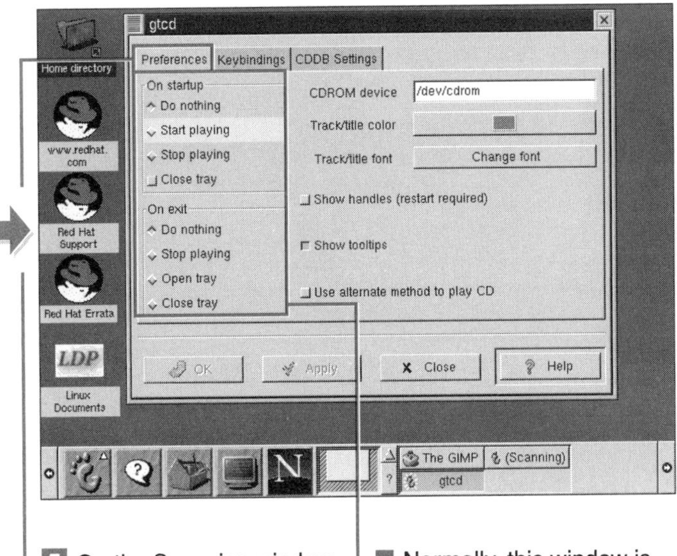

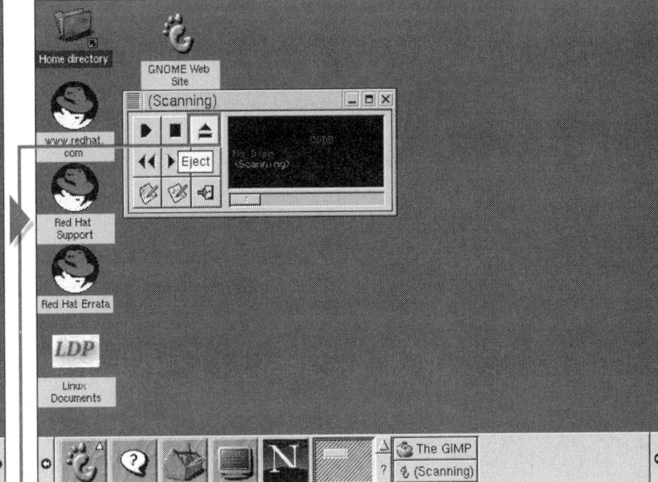

5 On the Scanning window, click the Preferences tab.

■ The gtcd window that controls the CD preferences appears.

■ Normally, this window is so large that it hides the Scanning window.

■ You can specify the startup and exiting setting for the CD Player in the gtcd window.

6 When you finish selecting your preferences, click the OK or Apply button to exit the gtcd window.

■ If you had a CD in the drive while working with the CD Player application, you can remove the CD from the drive by pressing the Eject button on the Scanning window.

APPENDIX B

PAINT WITH XPAINT

To release the artist in you and let the creative juices start to flow, you can use the XPaint program. XPaint is a full-option, complex painting tool to complete picture quality graphics. It's called XPaint because it was one of the first to adapt this technology to the X Windowing system used by Red Hat Linux and other variations of both the Linux and UNIX operating system.

XPaint allows you to use a full graphics palette, much like Microsoft's Paint program. You'll be able to select brush sizes, shapes, grab pieces of your work to move around and manipulate, and you'll be able to create geometric shapes and fill in colors with the click of a mouse. The full explanation of how to use every one of XPaint's capabilities is beyond the scope of this book, so take your time and explore what each tool will do for your painting technique.

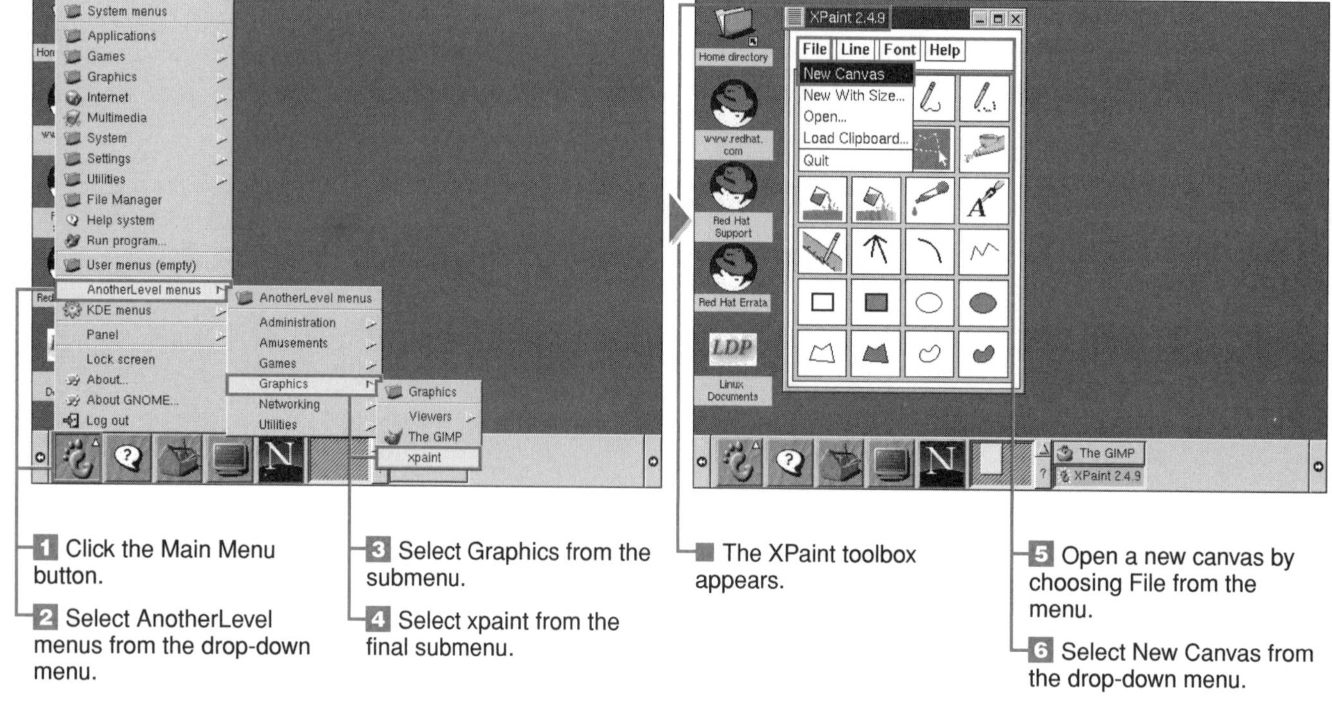

1 Click the Main Menu button.

2 Select AnotherLevel menus from the drop-down menu.

3 Select Graphics from the submenu.

4 Select xpaint from the final submenu.

■ The XPaint toolbox appears.

5 Open a new canvas by choosing File from the menu.

6 Select New Canvas from the drop-down menu.

What if I want to paint a graphic in XPaint, but I want to import it into the Microsoft Paint program?

- With XPaint, you can save paintings you've created in several formats, including .bmp and .jpeg, which you can import into other drawing programs. Keep in mind, however, that sometimes an imported file can come out with mismatched colors and a slightly grainy look.

If I want to create a picture in XPaint, how many colors are available?

- XPaint can handle up to 16 million colors. However, your choices will be limited by how well your monitor can display that number of colors.

Where can I find more information about a given tool in XPaint?

- XPaint comes with a fairly good Help Index. To access this index, open XPaint and select Help from the tools window. Select Help in the pulldown menu and you'll find lots of explanatory documentation.

■ The new Untitled canvas appears.

7 To paint on this canvas, click a tool from the left panel to paint.

■ These tool buttons are labeled with pictures of their various shaped brushes.

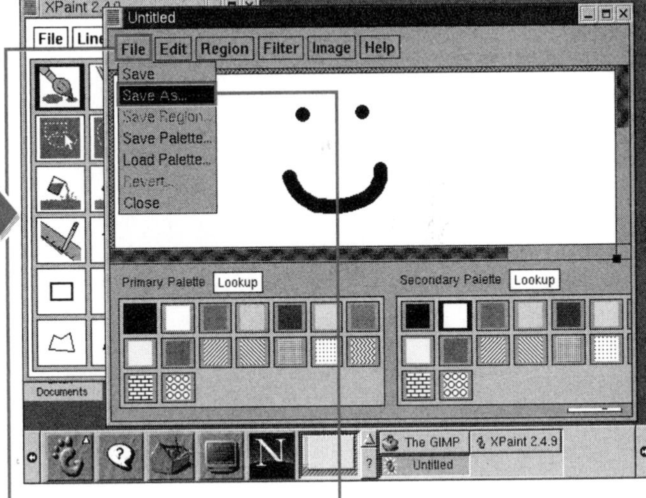

8 To save your painting, choose File from the menu.

9 Select Save As.

ORGANIZE WITH GNOMECARD

You can use GnomeCard as a virtual Rolodex if you have users or company personnel to keep straight. GnomeCard works much like several of the more expensive business planning applications, which allow you to organize contact lists and names of the people in your organization. If you're administering a large number of users, you may find this helpful in remembering who is in which department.

You'll be able to use the GnomeCard program successfully whether you're an administrator or a salesperson. In fact, if your organization or company has certain individuals, such as administrative assistants who need the services of a program like GnomeCard, be sure that the machines they work on have this program available. If it's not available over the network, you can use the GNOME Red Hat Package Manager to install it on local machines when necessary.

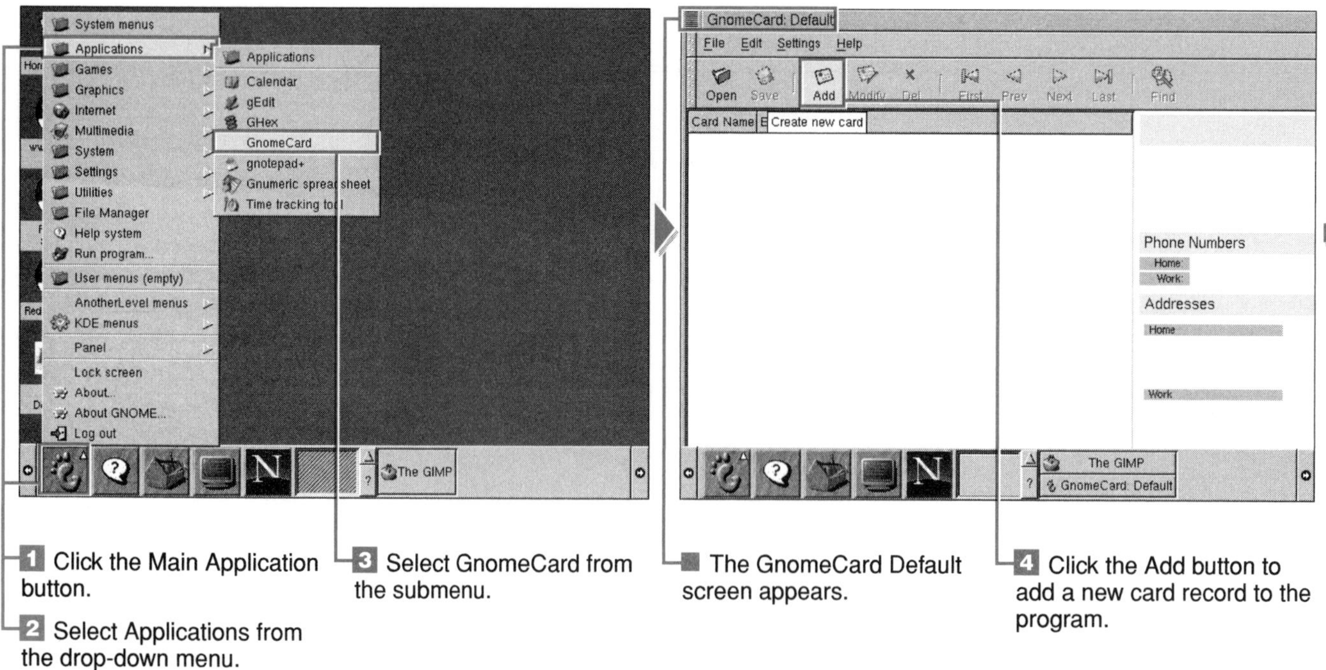

1 Click the Main Application button.

2 Select Applications from the drop-down menu.

3 Select GnomeCard from the submenu.

■ The GnomeCard Default screen appears.

4 Click the Add button to add a new card record to the program.

How many cards can I store in this virtual Rolodex program?

- In theory, no limit. However, depending on the limitations of your system, you may find the program slowing down if you have several hundred people stored on a GnomeCard list.

Under the Security tab, what does PGP stand for?

- PGP stands for Pretty Good Privacy. When you and another person use PGP, you create encryption keys, which you use to lock or unlock encoded files. You can store PGP key information in the open field of this tab.

Where can I learn more about GnomeCard's capabilities?

- In the Default screen of GnomeCard, you can select GNOME Address Book User's Guide from the Help drop-down menu. You'll find a very detailed guide on how you can get the most use out of the GnomeCard program.

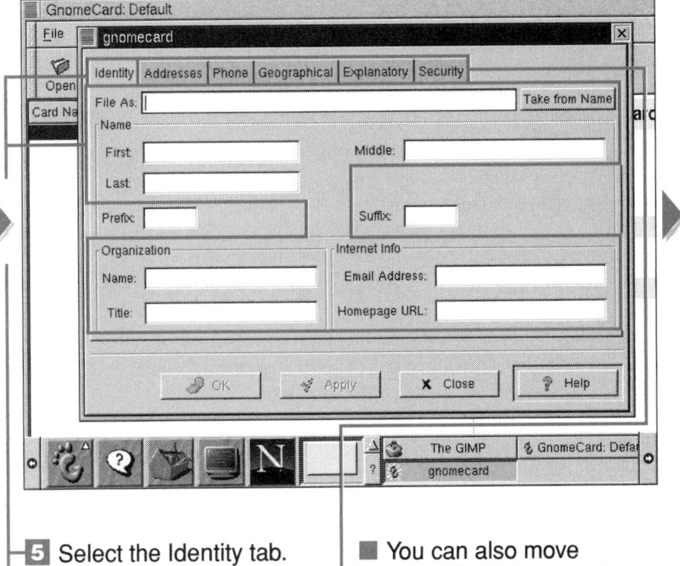

5 Select the Identity tab.

6 Click in each field and type the identity of the person you want to add to your card file.

■ You can also move between fields by pressing the Tab key.

7 Click the other tabs to add more relevant information.

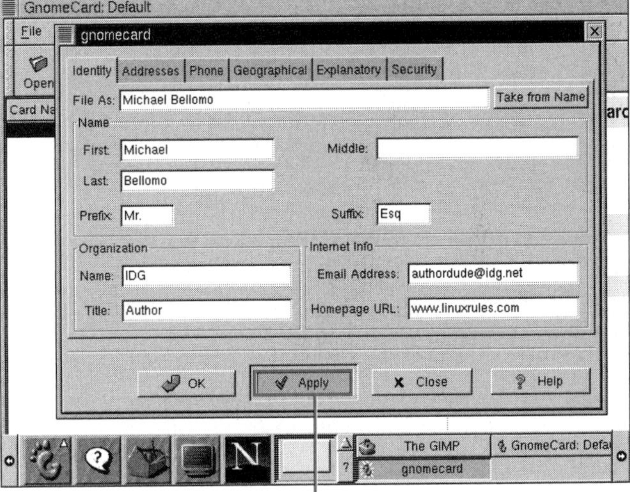

8 Click Apply to add the card to your virtual Rolodex when done.

APPENDIX C

EDIT COMMANDS IN VI

You can use the vi editor to work with your files and documents in Linux most efficiently by learning the commands to edit your text. The commands to edit text in vi come in several categories, including moving around in the editor, appending text, or undoing a change made to the document. The more commands you have at your fingertips, the easier it is to get the vi editor to do what you want.

The vi editor in Linux is very complex. In fact, to do it justice requires an entire book. However, for your basic administration needs, you'll rarely have to go beyond the command sets in this appendix.

In the description of each command is two notations, such as the <char> notation, which stands for character.

Appending Commands

Command Option	What It Does
a	Append text after the cursor.
A	Append text at the end of line.
i	Insert text before the cursor.
o	Open a new line below the current one.
O	Open a new line above the current one.

Deleting Commands

Command Option	What It Does
x	Delete chars under and after the cursor.
X	Delete chars before the cursor.
dd	Delete an entire line.
D	Delete the rest of the line after the cursor.
:[x,y]d	Delete lines x through y.

VI Move Commands

Command Option	What It Does
h	Moves the cursor 1 character to the left.
j	Moves the cursor 1 line downward.
l	Moves the cursor 1 character to the right.
k	Moves the cursor 1 line upward.
$	Moves the cursor to the end of the current line.
^	Moves the cursor to the first char of the line.
F<number>	Moves the cursor the number of spaces to the left specified in <number>.
w	Moves the cursor words forward.
b	Moves the cursor words backward.
e	Moves the cursor forward to the end of the next word.
M	Moves the cursor to the middle line of the screen.
}	Moves the cursor a paragraph forward.
{	Moves the cursor a paragraph backward.
n	Repeat last action.

Text Change Commands

Command Option	What It Does
r<char>	Replace one character with another.
R	Overwrite the rest of the line.
s	Substitute a character.
S	Substitute one line with new text.
c<move>	Change from begin to endpoint of < >.

Copy Text Commands

Command Option	What It Does
y<move>	Yank—Linux-speak for copy from begin to endpoint of < >.
yy	Yank< > lines.
m<a-z>	Mark the cursor position with a letter.

Undo Commands

Command Option	What It Does
u	Undo the latest change.
U	Undo all changes on a line.
:u	Undo the last substitution on the line.
:q!	Quit vi without writing (Linux-speak for saving).
:e!	Re-edit file. Useful if you've accidentally added or deleted lines from a file.

Writing & Editing Commands

Command Option	What It Does
:q	Quit vi.
:q!	Quit vi without writing.
:w	Write to the file.
:w <name>	Write to the file with a different file name.
:w >> <name>	Append your changes to the file <name>.
:w! <name>	Overwrite the file <name>.
:x,y w <name>	Write lines x through y to the file <name>.
:wq	Write the file and quit vi.

APPENDIX D

SUMMARY OF LINUX COMMANDS

You use commands on your Linux machine to perform a variety of tasks, such as listing files, changing directories, saving text changes, and many other system tasks. Commands allow you to administer the Linux system quickly and efficiently. A *command* is a text string or word, such as `ls`, `cd`, or `tar` that the Linux operating system recognizes as a signal to perform a given action. You type a command in a Linux Terminal window, next to the command prompt. Linux takes action when you execute the command by pressing the Enter key.

Most of the Linux commands you see here are ones you will encounter throughout your use of Linux. For more information these commands, see the chapters where they are covered. Some of the commands in this appendix are not covered in this book because they are rarely used, although you may find yourself using them from time to time.

Basic Operational Commands

Command Option	What It Does
`ls`	List the content of the current directory.
`cd <directory>`	Change directory. Using `cd` without the directory name will take you to your home directory.
`cp <source> <destination>`	Copy files.
`mv <source> <destination>`	Move or rename files.
`ln -s source destination`	Create a symbolic link.
`rm –rf <dir>`	Remove files or directories.
`mkdir <directory _name>`	Make a new directory.
`rmdir <directory>`	Remove a directory.
`rm –r`	Remove a directory with files.
`tar -xvf filename`	Untar a tarball file.
`tar - cvf filename`	Create a tarball file.
`find / -name "filename"` root	Find the file "filename" on your filesystem starting from the directory.
`pine`	A good text-mode mail reader. Another good and standard one is `elm`.
`talk <username>`	Talk to another user currently logged on your host.
`telnet <machine_ name>`	Connect to another machine using the telnet protocol.
`rlogin <machine_ name>`	Connect to another machine
`rsh <machine_ name>`	Yet another way to connect to another machine
`ftp <machine _name>`	Ftp another machine `.startx` Start an XWindows server and the default windows manager.
`xterm`	Run a simple X Windows terminal. Typing **exit** will close it.
`netscape`	Run Netscape (requires a separate Netscape installation if you're not using Red Hat Linux).
`netscape -display host:0.0`	Run netscape on the current machine and direct the output to machine named `"host"display 0screen 0`. (An X Windowscommand only.)
`shutdown -r now`	Shut down the system to a halt. Must be root.
`halt`	Halt the machine, but without shutting running processes down. Not recommended unless the machine is completely frozen.
`Reboot`	Shut the machine down and then re-start it.

Common Linux Commands

Command Option	What It Does
pwd	Display the name of the current directory on the screen.
hostname	Display the name of the machine on which you are working.
date	Displays the date your machine thinks it is.
who	Display the users currently logged on the machine.
finger <user _name>	Information about a selected user account.
last	Show listing of users last logged-in on your system.
uptime	Amount of time since last reboot.
ps	List all processes.
uname –a	Display all info on your host.
cat /etc/printcap	Show the setup of printers.
echo $PATH	Show the content of the environment variable PATH.

Process Control Commands

Command Option	What It Does
ps	Displays the list of currently running processes with their process IDs (PID) numbers.
kill PID	Force a process shutdown.
killall <program_name>	Kill program(s) by name.

Basic Administration Commands

Command Option	What It Does
adduser <user _name>	Create a new account.
useradd <user _name>	This is the same as adduser.
userdel <user _name>	Remove an account (you must be a root).
groupadd <group_name>	Create a new group
.passwd	Change the password on your current account. If you are root,you can change the passwordfor any user using: passwd <user_name>
chmod <perm> <filename>	Change the file access permission for the files you own. As root, you can change any file.
su	Become root
touch <filename>	Create an empty file if the file does not exist.
mkfs -c -t ext2	Perform low-level formatting of a floppy.
mount -t auto /dev/fd0 /mnt/ floppy	Mount the floppy. You must create the directory /mnt/floppy, but not be in it.
mount -t auto /dev/cdrom /mnt/ cdrom	Mount the CD-ROM. You must create the directory /dev/cdrom,but not be in it.
umount <directory>	Unmount the mounted directory.

INDEX

A

accidental deletions, 169
administration commands, 537
aliases, adding, 192–193
Apache software, 447
Apache Web server
- Administrator e-mail address, 445
- CD-ROM, latest version on, 441
- configuring, 444–447
- domain name, choosing, 447
- error log, 444–445
- etc/httpd directory, components located in, 442–443
- GNOME file system used to check components of, 442–443
- http daemon, 443
- installing, 440–443
- LinuxConf, 442, 444, 446
- logo, use of, 443
- Netscape Navigator used to check components of, 442–443
- server log, 445
- site building, 447
- success of installation, checking, 442–443
- virtual host setup, 446

append command, 154–165
applications
- adding icons, 81
- arrow keys, re-directing output with, 146–149
- closing, 82–83
- executing, 151
- exiting, 82
- icons, removing, 83
- improper shutdowns, 83
- launching, 80–81
- re-directing output, 146–149
- refusal to shutdown, 83
- running multiple, 81
- scripts compared, 81
- symbolic links, 84–85

arrow keys, re-directing output with, 146–149
automation of system tasks, 206–207

B

background color, 40–41
background wallpaper. *See* wallpaper
backup files. *See* file backups
backward search, 175
bang, 182–183
.bashrc files, 64, 186–187
boot disk, creating, 482–483, 527
bridges, 326
broadband connection, 420–423
burn-in, preventing, 44, 45

C

Caps Lock key and, 163
case sensitivity, 137, 163, 175
CD player
- described, 528
- musical CDs, ability to only play, 528
- starting, 528–529
- troubleshooting, 529

CD-ROM drive
- click and drag used to copy files, 282
- configuring, 272–275
- copy process, speed of, 283
- copying files, 280–283
- ejecting, 284–285
- etc/fstab file, accidentally editing, 279
- ISO9600, system other than, 279
- Linux terminal, mounting from, 278–279
- Macintosh CD-ROM, 273
- mounting, 276–277, 278–279
- problems with, 279
- reading files, 280–281
- refusal to mount, 275
- right clicking used to copy files, 282–283
- settings, 273
- unmounting, 275, 284–285
- User Mount Tool, 277

center of screen, moving to, 173
chgrp command, 154–155
chmod command, 150–151
chown command, 152–153
closing. *See also* exiting
- applications, 82–83
- gnotepad+, 299
- tear-off menus, 319

color
- background color, 40–41
- color wheel, 96–97
- Custom Colors, 430–431
- desktop theme, 48–49
- editing, 430–431
- Linux Terminal, 96–97
- machine specificity of color changes, 97
- screen colors, choosing, 97
- settings, 97

Command mode, 160–161, 163, 166, 172, 178
configuration logs, checking, 478
Control Panel
- described, 408
- functions on, finding, 409
- LinuxConf compared, 408–409

network configuration, opening, 408–409
Network Configurator, 422
opening, 408
system date, changing, 492–494
copying
CD-ROM drive, copying files, 280–283
directories, 70–73
accidentally copying directory over itself, 115
copying, 114–115
floppy disk, copying to, 115
home directory, copying remotely to, 115
remote location, copying to, 115
subdirectories and files, not copying, 115
files, 70–73
accidentally copying file over itself, 113
copying, 112–113
multiple files, copying, 113
remote location, copying file to, 113
FTP
copying files, 344–345
multiple files, copying, 348–349
gnotepad+, copying text with, 306–307
multiple files, 74–75
rcp
directories, copying recursively, 342–343
files, copying, 342–343
recursive copying, 70–73
symbolic links, 85, 133
text, 176
to floppy disks, 266–269
uucp, copying file to directory, 340–341
copying text, 176
core files, 144–145
crackers, 472–473
cron, 206–207
.cshrc files, 64, 65, 186–187
cutting text, 176–177, 179
cvf command, 487

D

databases
Access, 396–397, 399
Informix, 396–397, 399
Oracle, 396–397, 399
PostgreSQL. *See* PostgreSQL
Sybase, 396–397
date command, 494–495
date, setting, 492–495
decompressing files with gzip, 491
default editor, 53
default gateways, 326–327, 423
deleting
cleaning out file without deleting, 148
directories, 78–79, 118–121
e-mail, 452
exported file systems, 373
files, 78–79, 118–121
folders, 455
GNOME file manager, deleting files and directories, 78–79
gnotepad+
deleting text from document, 304–305
line of text, deleting, 305
text in single document, deleting all, 305
hidden files, not deleting, 119
line of text, 168
multiple files, 79, 121
printers, 362–363
remote file systems, 378
remotely located files, 121
root account, deleting files as, 121
safeguards to, 120
safeguards to deleting directories, 120
symbolic links, 85, 133
text, 166–169, 177
undeleting messages, 455
user accounts, 222–223, 230
user groups, 235, 238–239, 243, 245, 246–247
users from user groups, 237
vi editor
deleting commands, 534
deleting text, 166–169, 177
line of text, deleting, 168
deleting text, 166–169, 177
desktop theme
changing, 48
checking, 48
color, 48–49
described, 48
fonts, 48–49
importing, 49
device problems, diagnosing, 502–503
direct connection
activating network interface, 421
configuring, 420–423
deactivating network interface, 421
described, 420
directories
changing, 60–61
copying, 70–73
accidentally copying directory over itself, 115
copying, 114–115
floppy disk, copying to, 115

home directory, copying remotely to, 115
remote location, copying to, 115
subdirectories and files, not copying, 115
creating, 68–69
deleting, 78–79, 118–121
..directory, 61
editing file in another directory, 159
executable, marked, 151
executable directories, making, 249
folders compared, 69
GNOME File Manager
copying directories, 70–73
deleting files and directories, 78–79
directories, changing, 60–61
directories, creating, 68–69
directory view, 54
moving directories, 70–71
recursive copying of files and directories, 70–73
renaming files and directories, 76–77
group ownership, changing, 154–155
Home Directory, 59
Location text box, 61
moving, 70–71
naming, 69
ownership, changing, 152–153
recursive copying, 70–73
renaming, 76–77
root directory, 58
tmp directory, 267
viewing style, switching, 61
directory icon, 60
Disk Free utility, 288–289
disk space
Disk Free utility, 288–289
filling up rapidly, cause for, 287
monitoring available, 288
saving system information, 288–289
sending system information, 289
shortage of, 287
System Info used to check, 286–287
verifying available, 286–289
DNS information, 412–413
drag bars, creating, 28–29
drop-down menus, 14
du command, 504–505
dynamic routing, 328

E

e-mail
attachments, 439
described, 434–435
disk space for, 437
Get Mail button, 438
ISPs and, 435
mail server, 434
Messenger, 438–439
pine mail. *See* pine mail
POP server, 434
receiving, 436–437, 438–439
return receipts for, 435
sending, 438–439
storing, 436–437
echo command, 184–185, 187
edit properties, 53
emacs editor, 53
Enlightenment Window Manager, 32–33
Environment Variables
aliases, adding, 192–193
.bashrc files, 186–187
changing paths, 190
changing variables, 185, 186–187
.cshrc files, 186–187
described, 184
determining preset, 184
echo command, 184–185, 187
.login files, 186
$PATH variable, 188–189
searches, 190
setenv command, 186
setting, 185
source changes, 190–191
viewing values for, 184
Ethernet connection, 420–421
executable files, making, 150–151, 249
executable permissions, 86–87
exiting. *See also* closing
applications, 82
FTP, 351
LinuxConf, 211
pine mail, 456–457
vi editor, 180–183
external hard drives, mounting, 261

F

file access, granting, 202–205
file backups, 64
boot disk, creating, 482–483
decompressing files with gzip, 491
gzip used to compress files, 490–491
Recovery disk, creating, 484–485
restoring files with tar, 488–489
schedule for, 489

tape drives, installing, 489
with tar, 486–487
file extensions
changing, 77
GNOME desktop, 52
Linux Terminal, 117
file permissions. *See* permissions
file systems. *See also* files
access to files, 59
CD-ROM drive
click and drag used to copy files, 282
configuring, 272–275
copy process, speed of, 283
copying files, 280–283
ejecting, 284–285
etc/fstab file, accidentally editing, 279
ISO9600, system other than, 279
Linux terminal, mounting from, 278–279
Macintosh CD-ROM, 273
mounting, 276–277, 278–279
problems with, 279
reading files, 280–281
refusal to mount, 275
right clicking used to copy files, 282–283
settings, 273
unmounting, 275, 284–285
User Mount Tool, 277
described, 248
external hard drives, mounting, 261
floppy disks
copying files to, 266–269
destination for files, 268–269
displaying information on, 265
documents, saving, 269
ejecting, 284–285
formatting, 270–271
locating files from, 265
low-level format, 271
reading, 264–265
storing files from, 267
tmp directory, 267
unmounting, 284–285
floppy drives
configuring, 256–257
creating, 256–259
dos floppy drive, 260–261
formatting, 256–257
Linux terminal, mounting from, 262–263
Linux-only disks, 257, 259
LinuxConf, 258
mount command, 262–263
mounting, 259
reconfiguring, 257
unmounting, 263
user mountable option, 259
GNOME file manager. *See* GNOME file manager
Home Directory, 59
LinuxConf, 250–251
listing, 250–251
Microsoft Word files, 269
mount command, 251
root directory, 58
saving files, 59
swap space, 252–255
transferring documents to PC, 269
tree structure, 58
WordPerfect files, 269
Zip drives, adding, 263
File Transfer Protocol. *See* FTP
filenames, 76–77, 157
files. *See also* file systems
access, restricting, 155
alternate files, placing text in, 149
appending contents, 148
cleaning out file without deleting, 148
click-and-drag method used to copy, 71
copying, 70–73
creating, 66–67
deleting, 78–79
executable files, making, 150–151, 249
execute privileges, limiting, 151
filtering, 62
floppy disk, moving files to, 71
group ownership, 88–89, 154–155
hiding, 65
Menu method used to copy or move, 72
moving, 70–72
multiple files, copying and moving, 74–75
non-executable, marked, 151
ownership, 88–89, 152–153
permissions. *See* permissions
re-directing output to, 146–149
recursive copying, 70–73
renaming, 76–77
restoring temp's ownership, 153
saving, 67
scripts, creating, 249
sharing, 248–249
user accounts, 88–89
user groups, 88–89
Filtered view, 63
filtering files, 62
find command, 126–129
finger command, 471

floppy disks
- copying files to, 115, 266–269
- destination for files, 268–269
- displaying information on, 265
- documents, saving, 269
- ejecting, 284–285
- fitting files on, 99
- formatting, 270–271
- locating files from, 265
- low-level format, 271
- reading, 264–265
- storing files from, 267
- tmp directory, 267
- unmounting, 284–285

floppy drives
- configuring, 256–257
- creating, 256–259
- dos floppy drive, 260–261
- formatting, 256–257
- Linux terminal, mounting from, 262–263
- Linux-only disks, 257, 259
- LinuxConf, 258
- mount command, 262–263
- mounting, 259
- reconfiguring, 257
- unmounting, 263
- user mountable option, 259

folders
- administration of, 454–455
- deleting, 455
- directories compared, 69
- navigating between, 454–455

fonts
- desktop theme, 48–49
- gnotepad+
  - fonts, changing, 316–317
  - recommended font type and size, 317
- importing, 49
- Linux Terminal
  - font settings, 95
  - font size, choosing, 95
  - font style, choosing, 95
  - fonts, changing, 94–95
- vi editor, 49, 165

forward search, 174–175

fsck utility, 503

FTP
- binary files, 347
- cd command, 350–351
- connecting to server, 344, 346
- copying files, 344–345
- directories, changing, 350–351
- exiting, 351
- get command, 345
- hash command, 346–347
- hash signs, 346–347
- lcd command, 350–351
- limitations of, 346
- logging in to secure FTP server, 345
- mget command, 346, 348–349
- mput command, 346, 348–349
- multiple files, copying, 348–349
- options, 346–349
- put command, 345
- statistics, file transfer, 351
- wildcards, 348–349
- write permissions needed to copy files, 345

G

gated daemon, 329

gateways, 326–327, 423

GNOME Control Panel. *See* Control Panel

GNOME desktop
- background, customizing, 40–41
- color, changing, 40–41
- customization of, 40–53
- default editor, 53
- described, 8
- directory icon, 60
- edit properties, 53
- emacs editor, 53
- file extensions, 52
- keyboard bell, setting, 50
- keyboard properties, 43
- launching applications from, 80
- Mime properties, 52
- mouse properties, 43
- multimedia properties, 50–51
- peripheral properties, 50–51
- screen saver customization, 44–47
- sound, 50–51
- theme, 48–49
- vi editor, 53
- wallpaper, 41, 42
- windows
  - copying files between, 30–31
  - moving files between, 30–31
  - opening, 20–21

GNOME File Manager
- automatic scroll bar placement, 57
- browsing, 58–59
- copying
  - directories, 70–73
  - files, 70–73

core files, 57
deleting files and directories, 78–79
described, 54
directories
changing, 60–61
creating, 68–69
directory view, 54
displaying file properties, 55
displaying files, 56–57
File Properties window, 55
Filtered view, 63
filtering files, 62
hidden files, displaying, 64–65
icons, displaying files as, 56
Last Access On field, 55
listing files, 62
Menu method used to copy or move files, 72
moving
directories, 70–71
files, 70–72
multiple files, copying and moving, 74–75
opening, 54
Preferences command, 64
recursive copying of files and directories, 70–73
renaming files and directories, 76–77
searches, 62, 63
Show Backup Files option, 65
sort order, changing, 57
system-wide searches, 63
text format, displaying files in, 56
tree view, 54
viewing file details, 56–57
GNOME Help Index, 34–39
GNOME Red Hat Package Manager. *See* GnoRPM
GnomeCard, 532–533
GnoRPM
CD-ROM, preparing, 290
downloading new module or utility, 291
file corruption, 293
file incompleteness, 293
installing software packages, 294–295
leftover files, checking for, 297
missing files on CD-ROM, 295
query process, 496–499
removing software packages, 296–297
starting, 290–291
temporarily removing software packages, 297
uninstall command, 297
UNIX packages, installing, 294–295
upgrades, software, 294–295
verifying software packages, 292–293, 496–498
gnotepad+, 66–67
Autosave setting, 315
clipboard, text on, 307
closing, 299
copying text, 306–307
creating new documents, 300–301
deleting text from document, 304–305
described, 298
fast method to open documents, 303
Find command, 310
fonts, changing, 316–317
graphic, inability to bring document up as, 313
inserting text into document, 304–305
Landscape mode, printing in, 313
line of text, deleting, 305
moving text, 306–307
Open window, document not in, 303
opening documents, 302–303
preferences for, 314–317
printing documents, 312–313
Recent Documents list, 315
recommended font type and size, 317
Redo All Command, 308–309
redo changes, 308–309
replacing text, 310–311
saving documents, 299, 301
searching for text, 310–311
selection of word with mouse, 305
settings, 314–317
starting, 298
tear-off menus
closing, 319
described, 318
losing, 319
removing, 319
text in single document, deleting all, 305
text patterns
making multiple copies of, 307
searching for, 311
toolbar, reducing size of, 317
transferring documents
to another machine, 299
to another program, 301
Undo All command, 308–309
undo changes, 308–309
wrapping txt, 305
grep command
case sensitivity, 137
pattern count, 137
specific text phrase, search for, 136–137
text phrases in home directory, search for, 136
gzip used to compress files, 490–491

H

hacking, 220, 460
hard drive
  external hard drives, mounting, 261
  partitions
    root partition, 516
    setting up, 516–517
    swap partition, 516–517
hard links, 130
hash mark, 183
help index, 34–39
hidden files, displaying, 64–65
Home Directory, 59
host information, retrieving, 322–323
host name
  changing, 323
  ping via, 324–325

I

icons
  adding, 81
  creating, 28–29
  desktop icons used as Internet icons, 425
  directory icon, 60
  displaying files as, 56
  removing, 83
importing
  desktop theme, 49
  fonts, 49
  screen savers, 47
  sound, 51
INSERT mode, 160–161, 162, 170–171
installation
  Apache Web server, 442–443
  base parameters, setting, 524–525
  boot disk, creating, 527
  CD-ROM, 512–513
  components, setting up, 518–519
  computing power needed for, 525
  creating partitions in Disk Druid, 516–517
  Disk Druid, 515–517
  disk space shortage, components to skip with, 519
  DOS window used for, 513
  dual-boot machine, creating, 512
  horizontal sync setting, 523
  monitor parameters, setting up, 520–523
  partitions and, 515–517
  printers, setting up, 526–527
  probing during, 523
  root password, selecting, 524, 526–527
  SCSI devices, 513–514
  services available, selecting all, 525
  setting up disk partitions, 516–517
  starting, 512–515
  swap partition, 516–517
  time zone selection, 525
  vertical sync setting, 523
  Xconfiguration, 521
Interface types, 423
IP address, 412
  NFS, 375
  ping via, 325
  rlogin, 330–331
  rsh, 335
  telnet, 336–337

K

keyboard bell, setting, 50
keyboard properties, 43
keyboard shortcuts, 536
kill -9 command, 144–145
kill command, 82, 142–143, 144–145, 506–507

L

launching
  applications, 80–81
  Netscape Web browser, 424–425
line by line, moving, 173
line of text, deleting, 168
link command, 130
Linux
  commands. *See also* specific commands
    administration commands, 537
    common commands, 536
    keyboard shortcuts, 536
    list of, 536–537
    networking commands, 538
    operational commands, 536–537
    process control commands, 537
  customizing, 5
  drop-down menus, 14
  e-mail, 7
  installation
    base parameters, setting, 524–525
    boot disk, creating, 527
    CD-ROM, 512–513
    components, setting up, 518–519
    computing power needed for, 525
    creating partitions in Disk Druid, 516–517
    Disk Druid, 515–517
    disk space shortage, components to skip with, 519
    DOS window used for, 513

dual-boot machine, creating, 512
horizontal sync setting, 523
monitor parameters, setting up, 520–523
partitions and, 515–517
printers, setting up, 526–527
probing during, 523
root password, selecting, 524, 526–527
SCSI devices, 513–514
services available, selecting all, 525
setting up disk partitions, 516–517
starting, 512–515
swap partition, 516–517
time zone selection, 525
vertical sync setting, 523
Xconfiguration, 521
logging out, 15
login to, 12–13
menu buttons, 14
networking, 6
overview, 4–7
resource sharing, 6–7
security, 7
shut down, 16–19
starting, 10–11
user and group management, 6
Web access, 7
Windows compared, 4–5
Linux Administration For Dummies (Bellomo), 381
Linux Configuration. *See* LinuxConf
Linux Print System Manager
ASCII test page, 367
Auto-Detection Information screen, 357
broken printers, print jobs stacked up on, 363
Configure Filter screen, 366
Control Panel, 355
deleting printers, 362–363
documentation, 367
editing printer configuration, 364–367
engineering plotters, running, 361
information screen flaw, 361
local printer, adding, 356–357
naming scheme for printers, 359
NCP printers, 367
Netware printers, adding, 360–361
nonexistent printers, print jobs stacked up on, 363
opening, 354–355
port, printing directly to, 367
Postscript test page, 367
print spool, location for, 365
print spool, size of, 365
remote UNIX printer, adding, 358–359
SMB printers, 367
Suppress Headers option, 359
testing printers, 364–367
Windows printers, adding, 360–361
Linux Terminal
CD-ROM drive mounted from, 278–279
color settings, 97
color wheel, 96–97
color, changing, 96–97
creating new files, 108–109
defaults, user accounts, 227
desktop, opening from, 92
directories
accidentally copying directory over itself, 115
advantages of using Linux Terminal with, 107
cd command, 104–107
changing, 104–107
copying, 114–115
cp command, 114–115
creating, 110–111
deleting, 118–121
execute permissions, 105
File exists message, 111
floppy disk, copying to, 115
home directory, copying remotely to, 115
home directory, returning to, 105, 107
mkdir command, 110–111
moving to different, 105
multiple directories, moving with one command, 106
mv command, 116–117
name restrictions, 111
naming, 117
permissions for, 105
pwd command, 106
-R option, 114–115
read permissions, 105
recursive option, 114–115
remote creation of, 111
remote directories, renaming, 117
remote location, copying to, 115
renaming, 116–117
rm command, 118–121
rmdir command, 119
safeguards to deleting, 120
subdirectories, 107, 115
write permissions, 105
files
accidentally copying file over itself, 113
copying, 112–113
cp command, 112–113
deleting, 118–121
extensions, changing, 117
hidden files, not deleting, 119

listing. *See* subhead: files, listing
moving and renaming, 117
multiple files, copying, 113
multiple files, deleting, 121
mv command, 116–117
naming, 117
remote files, renaming, 117
remote location, copying file to, 113
remotely located files, deleting, 121
renaming, 116–117
rm command, 118–121
root account, deleting files as, 121
safeguards to deleting, 120
files, listing
-1 option, 98
-l option, 100
-r option, 102
-s option, 99
-S option, 99
and size, 99
by size, 99
by time, 101
by time edited in reverse order, 102
command options, 98, 103
complete information on all files, 101
described, 98
detailed information, 100
floppy disk, fitting files on, 99
hidden files, 100–101
in columns, 98–99
in directories outside your current directory, 102
in rows, 98–99
ls command, 98–103
remote listing of files, 102–103
security issues, 103
stacking options, 102–103
floppy drives mounted from, 262–263
font settings, 95
font size, choosing, 95
font style, choosing, 95
fonts, changing, 94–95
gray window, reason for, 93
information on, 93
machine specificity of color changes, 97
Main Menu, opening from, 93
multiple windows, creating, 93
networking
host information, retrieving, 323
host name, ping via, 324–325
IP address, ping via, 325
ping used to check network connectivity, 324–325
new password, entering immediately, 231
online help, 93
opening, 20–21, 92–93
passwd file
editing, 228–229
opening, 230
rcp
described, 342
directories, copying recursively, 342–343
files, copying, 342–343
passwords, lack of, 343
rcp refused message, 343
write permissions, 343
remote creation of new files, 109
screen colors, choosing, 97
system date, changing, 495
testing creation of user accounts, 227
touch command, 108–109
user accounts
adding, 226–227
creating, 226–227
defaults, 227
deleting, 230
disabling, 230–231
editing, 228–229
user groups
adding, 240–241
backups, 247
chgrp command, 241
default placement in new, 241
deleting, 243, 245, 246–247
disabling, 247
editing, 242–245
files, owning, 241
groupadd command, 240
merging, 243
multiple users, 244–245
testing creation of, 241
uucp
-n option, 341
-R option, 341
checking all subdirectories were copied, 341
command options, list of, 341
copying file to directory, 340–341
described, 340
notification when done with copy job, 341
recursive command, 341
speed of, 341
vi editor, 228–229
window, 9
LinuxConf, 250–251
Account Enabled button, 215
account names, 219

Apache Web server, 442, 444, 446
Archive option, 223
basics of, 208–209
command interpreter, 215
Control Panel compared, 408–409
date & time, editing, 209–210
Delete option, 223
described, 208
enabling users to perform changes, 221
exiting, 211
features to edit, list of, 209
field size, increasing, 213
file systems, 250–251
floppy drives, 258
group, selecting, 217
Leave in Place option, 223
login name, changing, 219
mail alias, creating, 219
multiple panels, 210–211
Name field, user not listed under, 213
name, listing users by, 213
networking
    bridges, 326
    default gateways, 326–327
    dynamic routing, 328
    gated daemon, 329
    host information, retrieving, 322–323
    host name, changing, 323
    Routed daemon, 328–329
    routers, 326
    routing table, 328
    static routing, 328–329
new users
    adding, 214–217
    adding to a group, 218
NIS. *See* NIS
opt listing, 217
panels, 210–211
passwords
    adding user, 216–217
    changing user, 220–221
shell, 215
UID, listing users by, 213
user accounts
    adding, 214–217
    deleting, 222–223
    disabling, 224–225
    editing, 218–221
    listing, 212–213
    user changes to, 225
user groups
    accidental deletion of, 239
    adding, 234–235
    adding users to, 237
    adm accounts, 233
    daemon accounts, 233
    deleting, 235, 238–239
    deleting users from, 237
    disabling, 239
    dummy accounts, 233
    editing, 236–237
    emptying, 239
    enabling users to make changes to, 237
    listing, 232–233
    lp accounts, 233
    naming, 233
    root account, 235
    root, adding, 237
    selecting, 235
username, changing, 219
listing files, 62
ln command, 130
Location text box, 61
log files, 64
logging in, 196
.login files, 65, 186
ls command, re-directing output of, 146

M

Main menu
    launching applications from, 80
    Linux Terminal opening from, 93
man pages, 200–201
Menu method
    files, copying or moving, 72
    multiple files, copying and moving, 75
Mime properties, 52
modems
    configuring, 410–411
    described, 410
    external, 417
    internal, 417
    port selection, 411
    telephone lines, use of, 411
.motd file, 472–473
mount command, 251
mouse properties, 43
moving
    directories, 70–71
    directories, moving to different, 105
    files, 70–72
    files, moving and renaming, 117
    floppy disk, moving files to, 71

multiple directories, moving with one command, 106
multiple files, 74–75
multiple files, copying and moving, 74–75
symbolic links, 132
text, 306–307
to center of screen, 173
vi editor
center of screen, moving to, 173
line by line, moving, 173
moving around in documents, 172–173
paragraph, moving to next, 173
screen by screen, moving, 173
word by word, moving, 172
moving around in documents, 172–173
MP3 files, 51
multimedia properties, 50–51
multiple processes, killing, 143
multiple use of su command, 198–199

N

naming files, 159
Netscape Web browser
advanced settings, configuring, 432–433
Back button, 426–427
bookmarking a site, 426–427
cache, 426–427
cache settings, 432–433
color, editing, 430–431
configuring, 428–429
cookies, 432
Custom Colors, 430–431
described, 426
desktop icons used as Internet icons, 425
downloaded files, location for, 429
e-mail
attachments, 439
described, 434–435
disk space for, 437
Get Mail button, 438
ISPs and, 435
mail server, 434
Messenger, 438–439
POP server, 434
receiving, 436–437, 438–439
return receipts for, 435
sending, 438–439
storing, 436–437
editing features, 428–429
Forward button, 426
FTP servers, 431
home page selection, 429
HTTP servers, 431
hyperlinks, 430
Java, 432
launching, 424–425
Linux terminal window, launching from, 425
Main Application button, launching from, 424
Netscape button, launching from, 424
news servers, 437
pre-loaded sites, 427
proxy servers, 433
publishing location, 431
Reload button, 427
revisiting sites, 427
templates, 430–431
Web page settings, configuring, 430–431
network connectivity
broadband connection, 420–423
Control Panel
described, 408
functions on, finding, 409
LinuxConf compared, 408–409
network configuration, opening, 408–409
Network Configurator, 422
opening, 408
default gateway, 423
direct connection
activating network interface, 421
configuring, 420–423
deactivating network interface, 421
described, 420
DNS information, 412–413
Ethernet connection, 420–421
gateways, 423
Interface types, 423
IP address, 412
modems
configuring, 410–411
described, 410
external, 417
internal, 417
port selection, 411
telephone lines, use of, 411
PPP interface
Activate button, 419
adding, 414–418
area codes and, 415
Clone button, 419
configuring, 416–417
Deactivate button, 419
described, 414, 415
hanging, preventing, 418
line speed, 416–417

timeout procedure, 418
routers, 423
tuplets, 412–413
URLs, 412
Network File System. *See* NFS
Network Information System. *See* NIS
network printers
Linux Print System Manager
ASCII test page, 367
Auto-Detection Information screen, 357
broken printers, print jobs stacked up on, 363
Configure Filter screen, 366
Control Panel, 355
deleting printers, 362–363
documentation, 367
editing printer configuration, 364–367
engineering plotters, running, 361
information screen flaw, 361
local printer, adding, 356–357
naming scheme for printers, 359
NCP printers, 367
Netware printers, adding, 360–361
nonexistent printers, print jobs stacked up on, 363
opening, 354–355
port, printing directly to, 367
Postscript test page, 367
print spool, 365
remote UNIX printer, adding, 358–359
SMB printers, 367
Suppress Headers option, 359
testing printers, 364–367
Windows printers, adding, 360–361
networking
bridges, 326
default gateways, 326–327
dynamic routing, 328
gated daemon, 329
host information, retrieving, 322–323
host name, changing, 323
host name, ping via, 324–325
IP address, ping via, 325
ping used to check network connectivity, 324–325
Routed daemon, 328–329
routers, 326
routing table, 328
static routing, 328–329
networking commands, 538
Networking For Dummies (Lowe), 388–393
new document, creating, 156
NFS
accepting options, 379
access, blocking, 373
adding remote file systems, 374–377
administration of, 381
availability of, checking for, 369
Background mount option, 383
Comment field, entering text in, 371
deleting
exported file systems, 373
remote file systems, 378
described, 368
disadvantage of, 370
editing in LinuxConf, viewing location for, 368–369
Exported File Systems setting, installing, 369
exporting file systems, 370–372
information on, 383
IP address connections, 375
Linux terminal used to verify mounting/unmounting file systems, 379
man pages, 383
Mount setting, 379
mounting remote file systems, 375–379, 380–381
multiple systems, mounting, 381
NFS daemon, checking for, 369
Nolock mount option, 383
options, selecting, 382–383
permissions, granting, 372
recursive exporting, automatic, 372
Secure port setting, 371
server machine, computer not recognizing, 375
server name, not knowing, 379
special devices and setuid prgrams, preventing use of, 381
translate symbolic links option, 371
unmounting remote file systems, 379
verifying mounting of remote file systems, 378
write privileges, granting, 373
NFS and NIS Networking, 385
NIS
configuring, 384–387
described, 384
domains, 385
information on, 385
yp directory, 386–387
ypbind, 386–387
No Screensaver option, 47

O

opening files, 158–159
operational commands, 536–537

P

paragraph, moving to next, 173
passwords, 199

adding user, 216–217
changing, 460–463
Changing Password screen, 461
changing user, 220–221
dictionary terms as passwords, 463
-l password, 333
LinuxConf
password length, setting, 466
password policies, setting, 466–467
Password/Account setting policies, 466
used to change passwords, 461–462
new password, entering immediately, 231
rcp passwords, lack of, 343
root password
changing, 476
reassigning forgotten, 500–501
selecting, 524, 526–527
root user account, 199
screen savers, 46
system utility used to change passwords, 460–461
user account password, changing, 460–463
users changing passwords, 461
pasting text, 176–179
$PATH variable, 188–189
PCs not recognizing Linux disk, 271
permissions
asterisk symbol, 477
changing, 86–87, 248–249, 475–476
checking, 474–477
described, 86
directories, 105
executable permissions, 86–87
execute permissions, 86–87, 105
file systems permissions, checking, 474
locking account, 476–477
read permissions, 86–87, 105
root password, changing, 476
setting, 469
user's permissions, editing, 475, 477
write permissions, 86–87, 105, 343
write permissions needed to copy files, 345
PIDs, 142–143
pine mail
advantages of, 448
composing, 449
deleting
e-mail, 452
folders, 455
described, 448
exiting, 456–457
folders, administration of, 454–455
inbox, changing order of messages in, 451
menu options, 451
navigating between folders, 454–455
opening, 448
receiving e-mail, 450–451
saving e-mail, 453
storing messages, 457
undeleting messages, 455
ping used to check network connectivity, 324–325
pipe utility, 134–135, 136, 149
PostgreSQL
advantages of, 398
automatic startup, 405
DCL, 403
DDL, 403
described, 396
DML, 403
downloading, 397
home directory, selecting, 401
information on, 405
initializing server, 404–405
installing, 396–399
new user account, adding, 400–401
PGLIB, 403
postgres user account, 402
postmaster, 404–405
SQL, 403
superuser, 402
variables, adding, 402–403
Power Management, setting, 46
PPP interface
Activate button, 419
adding, 414–418
area codes and, 415
Clone button, 419
configuring, 416–417
Deactivate button, 419
described, 414, 415
hanging, preventing, 418
line speed, 416–417
timeout procedure, 418
Print System Manager. *See* Linux Print System Manager
printers. *See also* Linux Print System Manager
deleting, 362–363
installation, 526–527
printing. *See also* Linux Print System Manager
gnotepad+
Landscape mode, printing in, 313
printing documents, 312–313
in telnet, 339
port, printing directly to, 367
process control commands, 537

programs. *See* applications
ps command, 149

R

rcp
  described, 342
  directories, copying recursively, 342–343
  files, copying, 342–343
  passwords, lack of, 343
  rcp refused message, 343
  write permissions, 343
re-direction command, 146–149
read permissions, 86–87, 89
Recovery disk, creating, 484–485
Red Hat Linux Secrets (Barkakati), 381
Red Hat Package Manager. *See* GnoRPM
remote locations, re-directing output to, 147
remote login
  described, 338
  inability to log into remote machine, 339
  Linux commands, remote machine ignoring, 339
  rlogin, 330
    administrative tasks, performing, 333
    described, 330
    freezing, 333
    hanging, solution for, 331
    IP address, log in using, 330–331
    Kerberos authentication, 331
    kill command, 331
    -l option, 332–333
    -l password, 333
    multiple rlogins, 339
    refusal of, 333
    root, logging in as, 332–333
    rsh compared, 335
    su command, 333
    superuser account, 333
  rsh
    described, 334
    IP address, using, 335
    -l option, 335
    logging in, 334
    rlogin compared, 335
    username, specifying different, 335
    vi editor, inability to use, 335
  telnet
    -a option, 337
    described, 336
    host, not specifying, 337
    Hyperterminal compared, 337
    IP address, 336–337
    logging in with, 338
    printing files, 339
  transparent interface, 338
renaming
  directories, 76–77
  files, 76–77
  remote directories, 117
  remote files, 117
  symbolic links, 85
repeating previous action, 166
replacing words, 169
restricting file access, 202–205
rlogin
  administrative tasks, performing, 333
  described, 330
  freezing, 333
  hanging, solution for, 331
  IP address, log in using, 330–331
  Kerberos authentication, 331
  kill command, 331
  -l option, 332–333
  -l password, 333
  multiple rlogins, 339
  refusal of, 333
  root, logging in as, 332–333
  rsh compared, 335
  su command, 333
  superuser account, 333
root directory
  access to, 59
  described, 58
root password
  changing, 476
  reassigning forgotten, 500–501
  selecting, 524, 526–527
root user account
  /etc/password file, 204
  access, restricting, 155
  automation of system tasks, 206–207
  changing group ownership, 202
  cron, 206–207
  described, 196
  file privileges, restoring, 152
  granting file access, 202–205
  logging in, 196
  making file widely available, 203
  man pages, 200–201
  multiple use of su command, 198–199
  passwords, 199
  restricting file access, 202–205
  safeguarding files, 203–205

- su command, 196–197, 198–199
- verifying file ownership, 202

Routed daemon, 328–329
routers, 326, 423
routing table, 328
rsh
- described, 334
- IP address, using, 335
- -l option, 335
- logging in, 334
- rlogin compared, 335
- username, specifying different, 335
- vi editor, inability to use, 335

S

safeguarding files, 203–205
Samba
- configuring, 388–393
- connecting your machine as Samba client, 394–395
- described, 388
- Disk Share console, 390
- exporting files, 392
- information on, 395
- naming convention for, 395
- parameters, configuring, 395
- setting up Samba server, 388–393
- Share Setup console, 390–391
- starting server, 392–393
- Synchronize Linux and SMB passwords button, 389

Samba For Dummies (Haberberger), 395
saving
- changes to document, 180–181
- documents, 180–182, 269, 299, 301
- e-mail, 453
- files, 59, 67
- quitting and, 182
- quitting without saving, 183
- system information, 288–289

scheduling backups, 489
screen savers
- availability of, 45
- burn-in, preventing, 44
- changing, 44–45
- creators of, 45
- customization, 44–47
- default screen saver, 44
- described, 44
- importing, 47
- No Screensaver option, 47
- passwords, setting, 46
- Power Management, setting, 46
- purpose of, 44
- Shutdown Monitor, 46, 47
- testing changes, 47

scripts
- applications compared, 81
- creating, 249

searches, 62, 63, 174–175, 190
- asterisk (*) symbol used in, 127
- case sensitivity, 137
- files that don't belong, 129
- find command, 126–129
- grep command, 140–141
  - case sensitivity, 137
  - pattern count, 137
  - specific text phrase, search for, 136–137
  - text phrases in home directory, search for, 136
- home directory, 126
- limitations, 129
- methods for, 127
- options, 138
- other users, processes used by, 140
- pattern count, 137
- pipe utility, 140–141
- process search command, 138–141
- ps command, 138–141
- remote directory, 126
- remote machines, 129
- remote use of process search command, 141
- root account, 128
- root account-owned processes, 139
- running processes
  - grep command, 140–141
  - options, 138
  - other users, processes used by, 140
  - pipe utility, 140–141
  - process search command, 138–141
  - ps command, 138–141
  - root account-owned processes, 139
- specific text phrase, search for, 136–137
- text phrases in home directory, search for, 136
- uid option, 128
- user's ID number, 129
- wildcard, 127

security, 182
- breach of, repairing damage after, 474–479
- Changing Password screen, 461
- closing applications, 82–83
- configuration logs, checking, 478
- crackers, 460
- deleting files, 79
- dictionary terms as passwords, 463

- file permissions, setting
  - GNOME desktop, 468
  - Linux Terminal, 469
- hacking, 220, 460
- hidden files, displaying, 64–65
- Linux Terminal, setting file permissions, 469
- LinuxConf
  - changing passwords, 461–462
  - file policies, setting, 466–467
  - password length, setting, 466
  - password policies, setting, 466–467
  - Password/Account setting policies, 466
- passwords, 199
  - adding user, 216–217
  - changing, 460–463
  - Changing Password screen, 461
  - changing user, 220–221
  - dictionary terms as passwords, 463
  - -l password, 333
  - LinuxConf, 461–462, 466–467
  - new password, entering immediately, 231
  - rcp passwords, lack of, 343
  - root password, changing, 476
  - root password, reassigning forgotten, 500–501
  - root password, selecting, 524, 526–527
  - root user account, 199
  - screen savers, 46
  - system utility used to change passwords, 460–461
  - user account password, changing, 460–463
  - users changing passwords, 461
- passwords, adding user, 216–217
- passwords, changing, 460–463
- restricting file access, 202–205
- screen savers, 464–465
- system daemons, shutting down, 479
- system permissions, checking, 474–477
- system utility used to change passwords, 460–461
- tracking users
  - crackers, 472–473
  - determining user activity, 472–473
  - finger command, 471
  - .motd file, 472–473
  - retrieving user information, 471
  - w command, 472–473
  - who utility, 470
- user account password, changing, 460–463
- users changing passwords, 461

setenv command, 186
Shutdown Monitor, 46, 47
SMB, 388, 394–395
soft links. *See* symbolic links
sort command, 504–505
sound
- configuring specific, 51
- importing, 51
- MP3 files, 51
- setting, 50

sound cards, 51
sound event, changing, 51
source changes, 190–191
SQL For Dummies (Taylor), 405
static routing, 328–329
su command, 196–197, 198–199
substitute user account. *See* root user account
substituting text, 170–171
substitution commands, 170–171
swap space
- active use of, 253
- allocating, 253
- described, 252
- determining, 252–253
- free command, 254–255
- installing by default, 255
- on UNIX machine, 255
- size of, increasing, 255

symbolic links, 84–85
- copying, 133
- creating, 130–131
- deleting, 133
- listing, 133
- moving, 132
- naming, 131
- renaming, 132
- testing, 131
- to directories, 131
- use of, 131

system daemons, shutting down, 479
system date, changing, 492–495
system password. *See* root password
system-wide searches, 63

T

tape archive resource, 486–489
tape drives, installing, 489
tar
- file backups, 486–487
- restoring files with, 488–489

tear-off menus
- closing, 319
- described, 318
- losing, 319
- removing, 319

telnet
- -a option, 337
- described, 336
- host, not specifying, 337
- Hyperterminal compared, 337
- IP address, 336–337
- logging in with, 338
- printing files, 339

text
- adding, 162–165
- buffer, 176
- copying, 176
- cutting, 176–177, 179
- deleting text from document, 304–305
- gnotepad+, 176
  - clipboard, text on, 307
  - copying text, 306–307
  - deleting text from document, 304–305
  - inserting text into document, 304–305
  - line of text, deleting, 305
  - moving text, 306–307
  - replacing text, 310–311
  - searching for text, 310–311
  - text in single document, deleting all, 305
  - text patterns, 307, 311
- line of text, deleting, 305
- phrases in home directory, search for, 136
- single document, deleting all text, 305
- specific text phrase, search for, 136–137
- substituting text, 170–171
- vi editor
  - deleting text, 166–169, 177
  - line of text, deleting, 168

text patterns
- making multiple copies of, 307
- searching for, 311

time, setting, 492–495

toolbars, lack of, 159

Torvalds, Linus, 4

tracking users
- crackers, 472–473
- determining user activity, 472–473
- finger command, 471
- .motd file, 472–473
- retrieving user information, 471
- w command, 472–473
- who utility, 470

transparent interface, 338

troubleshooting
- CD player, 529
- device problems, 502–503
- hung processes, 506–507
- in GUI, 508–509
- resource drains, 504–505
- root password, reassigning forgotten, 500–501
- spawned processes, 506–507

tuplets, 412–413

U

undo command, 171

undoing last command, 169

URLs, 412

user account identity
- determining, 122–123
- displaying user's account name, 123
- id utility, 122
- logged in, determining who else is, 124–125
- multiple logins, 125
- remote use of w command, 125
- remote use of who command, 125
- root privileges, 123
- w command, 124–125
- who command, 124–125
- whoami command, 122

user groups
- adding, 240–241
- backups, 247
- chgrp command, 241
- default placement in new, 241
- deleting, 243, 245, 246–247
- disabling, 247
- editing, 242–245
- files, owning, 241
- groupadd command, 240
- merging, 243
- multiple users, 244–245
- testing creation of, 241

user information, retrieving, 471

uucp
- checking all subdirectories were copied, 341
- command options, list of, 341
- copying file to directory, 340–341
- described, 340
- -n option, 341
- notification when done with copy job, 341
- -R option, 341
- recursive command, 341
- speed of, 341

V

verifying file ownership, 202

vi editor, 53
- accidental deletions, 169

append command, 154–165
appending commands, 534
backward search, 175
bang, 182–183
Caps Lock key and, 163
case sensitivity, 175
case-sensitivity, 163
center of screen, moving to, 173
changes to document, saving, 180–181
Command mode, 160–161, 163, 166, 172, 178
commands, list of, 534–535
copy text commands, 535
copying text, 176
cutting text, 176–177, 179
deleting commands, 534
deleting text, 166–169, 177
described, 156
directory, editing file in another, 159
editing commands, 535
exiting, 180–183
filename, starting with existing, 157
font, changing, 165
forcing a save, 182
forward search, 174–175
hash mark, 183
INSERT mode, 160–161, 162, 170–171
line by line, moving, 173
line of text, deleting, 168
move commands, 534
moving around in documents, 172–173
naming files, 159
new document, creating, 156
opening files, 158–159
paragraph, moving to next, 173
pasting text, 176–179
quitting, 180–183
quitting without saving, 183
repeating previous action, 166
replacing words, 169
saving and quitting simultaneously, 182
saving documents, 180–182
screen by screen, moving, 173
searches, 174–175
security, 182
substituting text, 170–171
substitution commands, 170–171
text buffer, 176
text change commands, 535
text, adding, 162–165
toolbars, lack of, 159
undo command, 171
undo commands, 535
undoing last command, 169
word by word, moving, 172
writing commands, 535
yank command, 178
vi process, killing, 142

W

w command, 472–473
wallpaper
customizing, 41
Internet graphics as, 41
lack of, 41
selecting, 42
Web browsers. *See* Netscape Web browser
Web servers
Apache Web server
Administrator e-mail address, 445
CD-ROM, latest version on, 441
configuring, 444–447
domain name, choosing, 447
error log, 444–445
etc/httpd directory, components located in, 442–443
GNOME file system used to check components of, 442–443
http daemon, 443
installing, 440–443
LinuxConf, 442, 444, 446
logo, use of, 443
Netscape Navigator used to check components of, 442–443
server log, 445
site building, 447
success of installation, checking, 442–443
virtual host setup, 446
described, 440
who utility, 470
windows
closing, 24–25
drag bars, creating, 28–29
icons, creating, 28–29
maximizing, 24–25
minimizing, 24–25
moving, 26–27
opening, 20–21
resizing, 22–23
word processing. *See* gnotepad+
write permissions, 86–87

X

XPaint, 530–531

Y

Y2038K bug, 492–495
yank command, 178
Yellow Pages. *See* NIS

GNU LICENSE AGREEMENT

Preamble

The licenses for most software are designed to take away your freedom to share and change it. By contrast, the GNU General Public License is intended to guarantee your freedom to share and change free software—to make sure the software is free for all its users. This General Public License applies to most of the Free Software Foundation's software and to any other program whose authors commit to using it. (Some other Free Software Foundation software is covered by the GNU Library General Public License instead.) You can apply it to your programs, too.

When we speak of free software, we are referring to freedom, not price. Our General Public Licenses are designed to make sure that you have the freedom to distribute copies of free software (and charge for this service if you wish), that you receive source code or can get it if you want it, that you can change the software or use pieces of it in new free programs; and that you know you can do these things.

To protect your rights, we need to make restrictions that forbid anyone to deny you these rights or to ask you to surrender the rights. These restrictions translate to certain responsibilities for you if you distribute copies of the software, or if you modify it.

For example, if you distribute copies of such a program, whether gratis or for a fee, you must give the recipients all the rights that you have. You must make sure that they, too, receive or can get the source code. And you must show them these terms so they know their rights.

We protect your rights with two steps: (1) copyright the software, and (2) offer you this license which gives you legal permission to copy, distribute and/or modify the software.

Also, for each author's protection and ours, we want to make certain that everyone understands that there is no warranty for this free software. If the software is modified by someone else and passed on, we want its recipients to know that what they have is not the original, so that any problems introduced by others will not reflect on the original authors' reputations.

Finally, any free program is threatened constantly by software patents. We wish to avoid the danger that redistributors of a free program will individually obtain patent licenses, in effect making the program proprietary. To prevent this, we have made it clear that any patent must be licensed for everyone's free use or not licensed at all.

The precise terms and conditions for copying, distribution and modification follow.

TERMS AND CONDITIONS FOR COPYING, DISTRIBUTION AND MODIFICATION

This License applies to any program or other work which contains a notice placed by the copyright holder saying it may be distributed under the terms of this General Public License. The "Program", below, refers to any such program or work, and a "work based on the Program" means either the Program or any derivative work under copyright law: that is to say, a work containing the Program or a portion of it, either verbatim or with modifications and/or translated into another language. (Hereinafter, translation is included without limitation in the term "modification".) Each licensee is addressed as "you".

Activities other than copying, distribution and modification are not covered by this License; they are outside its scope. The act of running the Program is not restricted, and the output from the Program is covered only if its contents constitute a work based on the Program (independent of having been made by running the Program). Whether that is true depends on what the Program does.

1. You may copy and distribute verbatim copies of the Program's source code as you receive it, in any medium, provided that you conspicuously and appropriately publish on each copy an appropriate copyright notice and disclaimer of warranty; keep intact all the notices that refer to

this License and to the absence of any warranty; and give any other recipients of the Program a copy of this License along with the Program.

You may charge a fee for the physical act of transferring a copy, and you may at your option offer warranty protection in exchange for a fee.

2. You may modify your copy or copies of the Program or any portion of it, thus forming a work based on the Program, and copy and distribute such modifications or work under the terms of Section 1 above, provided that you also meet all of these conditions:

(a) You must cause the modified files to carry prominent notices stating that you changed the files and the date of any change.

(b) You must cause any work that you distribute or publish, that in whole or in part contains or is derived from the Program or any part thereof, to be licensed as a whole at no charge to all third parties under the terms of this License.

(c) If the modified program normally reads commands interactively when run, you must cause it, when started running for such interactive use in the most ordinary way, to print or display an announcement including an appropriate copyright notice and a notice that there is no warranty (or else, saying that you provide a warranty) and that users may redistribute the program under these conditions, and telling the user how to view a copy of this License. (Exception: if the Program itself is interactive but does not normally print such an announcement, your work based on the Program is not required to print an announcement.)

These requirements apply to the modified work as a whole. If identifiable sections of that work are not derived from the Program, and can be reasonably considered independent and separate works in themselves, then this License, and its terms, do not apply to those sections when you distribute them as separate works. But when you distribute the same sections as part of a whole which is a work based on the Program, the distribution of the whole must be on the terms of this License, whose permissions for other licensees extend to the entire whole, and thus to each and every part regardless of who wrote it.

Thus, it is not the intent of this section to claim rights or contest your rights to work written entirely by you; rather, the intent is to exercise the right to control the distribution of derivative or collective works based on the Program. In addition, mere aggregation of another work not based on the Program with the Program (or with a work based on the Program) on a volume of a storage or distribution medium does not bring the other work under the scope of this License.

3. You may copy and distribute the Program (or a work based on it, under Section 2) in object code or executable form under the terms of Sections 1 and 2 above provided that you also do one of the following:

(a) Accompany it with the complete corresponding machine-readable source code, which must be distributed under the terms of Sections 1 and 2 above on a medium customarily used for software interchange; or,

(b) Accompany it with a written offer, valid for at least three years, to give any third party, for a charge no more than your cost of physically performing source distribution, a complete machine-readable copy of the corresponding source code, to be distributed under the terms of Sections 1 and 2 above on a medium customarily used for software interchange; or,

(c) Accompany it with the information you received as to the offer to distribute corresponding source code. (This alternative is allowed only for noncommercial distribution and only if you received the program in object code or executable form with such an offer, in accord with Subsection b above.)

The source code for a work means the preferred form of the work for making modifications to it. For an executable work, complete source code means all the source code for all modules it contains, plus any associated interface definition files, plus the scripts used to control compilation and installation of the executable. However, as a special exception, the source code distributed need not include anything that is normally distributed (in either source or binary form) with the major components (compiler, kernel, and so on) of the operating system on which the executable runs, unless that component itself accompanies the executable.

If distribution of executable or object code is made by offering access to copy from a designated place, then offering equivalent access to copy the source code from the same place counts as distribution of the source code, even though third parties are not compelled to copy the source along with the object code.

4. You may not copy, modify, sublicense, or distribute the Program except as expressly provided under this License. Any attempt otherwise to copy, modify, sublicense or distribute the Program is void, and will automatically terminate your rights under this License. However, parties who have received copies, or rights, from you under this License will not have their licenses terminated so long as such parties remain in full compliance.

5. You are not required to accept this License, since you have not signed it. However, nothing else grants you permission to modify or distribute the Program or its derivative works. These actions are prohibited by law if you do not accept this License. Therefore, by modifying or distributing the Program (or any work based on the Program), you indicate your acceptance of this License to do so, and all its terms and conditions for copying, distributing or modifying the Program or works based on it.

6. Each time you redistribute the Program (or any work based on the Program), the recipient automatically receives a license from the original licensor to copy, distribute or modify the Program subject to these terms and conditions. You may not impose any further restrictions on the recipients' exercise of the rights granted herein. You are not responsible for enforcing compliance by third parties to this License.

7. If, as a consequence of a court judgment or allegation of patent infringement or for any other reason (not limited to patent issues), conditions are imposed on you (whether by court order, agreement or otherwise) that contradict the conditions of this License, they do not excuse you from the conditions of this License. If you cannot distribute so as to satisfy simultaneously your obligations under this License and any other pertinent obligations, then as a consequence you may not distribute the Program at all. For example, if a patent license would not permit royalty-free redistribution of the Program by all those who receive copies directly or indirectly through you, then the only way you could satisfy both it and this License would be to refrain entirely from distribution of the Program.

If any portion of this section is held invalid or unenforceable under any particular circumstance, the balance of the section is intended to apply and the section as a whole is intended to apply in other circumstances.

It is not the purpose of this section to induce you to infringe any patents or other property right claims or to contest validity of any such claims; this section has the sole purpose of protecting the integrity of the free software distribution system, which is implemented by public license practices. Many people have made generous contributions to the wide range of software distributed through that system in reliance on consistent application of that system; it is up to the author/donor to decide if he or she is willing to distribute software through any other system and a licensee cannot impose that choice.

This section is intended to make thoroughly clear what is believed to be a consequence of the rest of this License.

8. If the distribution and/or use of the Program is restricted in certain countries either by patents or by copyrighted interfaces, the original copyright holder who places the Program under this License may add an explicit geographical distribution limitation excluding those countries, so that distribution is permitted only in or among countries not thus excluded. In such case, this License incorporates the limitation as if written in the body of this License.

9. The Free Software Foundation may publish revised and/or new versions of the General Public License from time to time. Such new versions will be similar in spirit to the present version, but may differ in detail to address new problems or concerns.

   Each version is given a distinguishing version number. If the Program specifies a version number of this License which applies to it and "any later version", you have the option of following the terms and conditions either of that version or of any later version published by the Free Software Foundation. If the Program does not specify a version number of this License, you may choose any version ever published by the Free Software Foundation.

10. If you wish to incorporate parts of the Program into other free programs whose distribution conditions are different, write to the author to ask for permission. For software which is copyrighted by the Free Software Foundation, write to the Free Software Foundation; we sometimes make exceptions for this. Our decision will be guided by the two goals of preserving the free status of all derivatives of our free software and of promoting the sharing and reuse of software generally.

NO WARRANTY

11. BECAUSE THE PROGRAM IS LICENSED FREE OF CHARGE, THERE IS NO WARRANTY FOR THE PROGRAM, TO THE EXTENT PERMITTED BY APPLICABLE LAW. EXCEPT WHEN OTHERWISE STATED IN WRITING THE COPYRIGHT HOLDERS AND/OR OTHER PARTIES PROVIDE THE PROGRAM "AS IS" WITHOUT WARRANTY OF ANY KIND, EITHER EXPRESSED OR IMPLIED, INCLUDING, BUT NOT LIMITED TO, THE IMPLIED WARRANTIES OF MERCHANTABILITY AND FITNESS FOR A PARTICULAR PURPOSE. THE ENTIRE RISK AS TO THE QUALITY AND PERFORMANCE OF THE PROGRAM IS WITH YOU. SHOULD THE PROGRAM PROVE DEFECTIVE, YOU ASSUME THE COST OF ALL NECESSARY SERVICING, REPAIR OR CORRECTION.

12. IN NO EVENT UNLESS REQUIRED BY APPLICABLE LAW OR AGREED TO IN WRITING WILL ANY COPYRIGHT HOLDER, OR ANY OTHER PARTY WHO MAY MODIFY AND/OR REDISTRIBUTE THE PROGRAM AS PERMITTED ABOVE, BE LIABLE TO YOU FOR DAMAGES, INCLUDING ANY GENERAL, SPECIAL, INCIDENTAL OR CONSEQUENTIAL DAMAGES ARISING OUT OF THE USE OR INABILITY TO USE THE PROGRAM (INCLUDING BUT NOT LIMITED TO LOSS OF DATA OR DATA BEING RENDERED INACCURATE OR LOSSES SUSTAINED BY YOU OR THIRD PARTIES OR A FAILURE OF THE PROGRAM TO OPERATE WITH ANY OTHER PROGRAMS), EVEN IF SUCH HOLDER OR OTHER PARTY HAS BEEN ADVISED OF THE POSSIBILITY OF SUCH DAMAGES.

END OF TERMS AND CONDITIONS

OTHER 3-D Visual SERIES

SIMPLIFIED SERIES

Windows 98 Simplified
ISBN 0-7645-6030-1
$24.99 USA/£23.99 UK

MORE Windows 98 Simplified
ISBN 0-7645-6037-9
$24.99 USA/£23.99 UK

Windows 95 Simplified
ISBN 1-56884-662-2
$19.99 USA/£18.99 UK

MORE Windows 95 Simplified
ISBN 1-56884-689-4
$19.99 USA/£18.99 UK

Excel 5 For Windows Simplified
ISBN 1-56884-664-9
$19.99 USA/£18.99 UK

Office 97 Simplified
ISBN 0-7645-6009-3
$29.99 USA/£28.99 UK

Microsoft Office 4.2 For Windows Simplified
ISBN 1-56884-673-8
$27.99 USA/£26.99 UK

Creating Web Pages Simplified
ISBN 0-7645-6007-7
$24.99 USA/£23.99 UK

World Wide Web Color Yellow Pages Simplified
ISBN 0-7645-6005-0
$29.99 USA/£28.99 UK

Internet and World Wide Web Simplified, 2nd Edition
ISBN 0-7645-6029-8
$24.99 USA/£23.99 UK

POCKETGUIDES

The Proven 3-D Visual Approach To Learning Computers In A Handy Pocket Size.

Windows 98 Visual PocketGuide
ISBN 0-7645-6035-2
$16.99 USA/£15.99 UK

Windows 95 Visual PocketGuide
ISBN 1-56884-661-4
$14.99 USA/£13.99 UK

Word 6 For Windows Visual PocketGuide
ISBN 1-56884-666-5
$14.99 USA/£13.99 UK

SATISFIED USERS!

MASTER VISUALLY SERIES

Teach Yourself Microsoft Excel 97 VISUALLY

ISBN 0-7645-6063-8
$29.99 USA/£28.99 UK

Teach Yourself Computers and the Internet VISUALLY, 2nd Edition

ISBN 0-7645-6041-7
$29.99 USA/£28.99 UK

Master Windows 98 VISUALLY

ISBN 0-7645-6034-4
$39.99 USA/£36.99 UK

Master Windows 95 VISUALLY

ISBN 0-7645-6024-7
$39.99 USA/£36.99 UK

Teach Yourself the Internet and World Wide Web VISUALLY

ISBN 0-7645-6020-4
$29.99 USA/£28.99 UK

Master Office 97 VISUALLY

ISBN 0-7645-6036-0
$39.99 USA/£36.99 UK

Visit our Web site at www.maran.com

FOR CORPORATE ORDERS, PLEASE CALL: **800-469-6616**